the PROCESS of GROUP
PSYCHOTHERAPY

Edited by Ariadne P. Beck and Carol M. Lewis

the
PROCESS
of
GROUP
PSYCHOTHERAPY

SYSTEMS
FOR
ANALYZING
CHANGE

American Psychological Association
Washington, DC

Published by
American Psychological Association
750 First Street, NE
Washington, DC 20002

Copies may be ordered from
APA Order Department
P.O. Box 92984
Washington, DC 20090-2984

In the U.K., Europe, Africa, and the Middle East, copies may be ordered from
American Psychological Association
3 Henrietta Street
Covent Garden, London
WC2E 8LU England

Typeset in Goudy by EPS Group Inc., Easton, MD

Printer: Port City Press, Inc., Baltimore, MD
Cover Designer: Watermark Design Office, Alexandria, VA
Technical/Production Editor: Jennifer Powers

The opinions and statements published are the responsibility of the authors, and such opinions and statements do not necessarily represent the policies of the APA.

Library of Congress Cataloging-in-Publication Data
The process of group psychotherapy : systems for analyzing change / edited by Ariadne P. Beck and Carol M. Lewis.
    p. ; cm.
    Includes bibliographical references and index.
    ISBN 1-55798-658-4 (alk. paper)
    1. Group psychotherapy.   I. Beck, Ariadne P.   II. Lewis, Carol M.
    [DNLM: 1. Psychotherapy, Group.   2. Group Processes. WM 430 P963 2000]
    RC488.P75 2000
    616.89'156—dc21

                                                            99-052724

British Library Cataloguing-in-Publication Data
A CIP record is available from the British Library.

Printed in the United States of America
First Edition

To our parents
George and Panagiota,
and Harry and Caroline,
and to Robert.

CONTENTS

Contributors xi

Foreword xiii
   Leslie S. Greenberg

Preface xvii
   Ariadne P. Beck and Carol M. Lewis

Chapter 1.   Introduction 3
             Ariadne P. Beck and Carol M. Lewis

I. The Study of Process Analysis of Groups 21

Chapter 2.   Process Analysis of Group Interaction in
             Therapeutic Groups 23
             Les R. Greene

Chapter 3.   Interaction Process Analysis in Task-Performing
             Groups 49
             Janice R. Kelly

Chapter 4.   Observational Coding of Family Therapy Processes:
             State of the Art 67
             Myrna L. Friedlander

II. The Case Example 85

Chapter 5.   Group A: The First Five Sessions 87
             Ariadne P. Beck and Carol M. Lewis

III. Well Established Systems for Group Process Analysis 111

    Chapter 6.   The Group Emotionality Rating System 113
                     Sigmund W. Karterud

    Chapter 7.   The Hill Interaction Matrix: Therapy Through
                     Dialogue 135
                     Addie Fuhriman and Gary M. Burlingame

    Chapter 8.   The Member–Leader Scoring System 175
                     Solomon Cytrynbaum

IV. Newer Systems for Group Process Analysis 219

    Chapter 9.   The Group Development Process Analysis
                     Measures 221
                     Carol M. Lewis, Ariadne P. Beck, James M. Dugo,
                     and Albert M. Eng

    Chapter 10.   The Psychodynamic Work and Object Rating
                     System 263
                     William E. Piper and Mary McCallum

    Chapter 11.   The Individual Group Member Interpersonal
                     Process Scale 283
                     Michael Sean Davis, Simon H. Budman, and
                     Stephen Soldz

V. Systems Developed for Other Contexts and Now Being Applied
    to Group Psychotherapy 309

    Chapter 12.   Three Complementary Systems for Coding the
                     Process of Therapeutic Dialogue 311
                     Adrienne S. Chambon, A. Ka Tat Tsang, and
                     Elsa Marziali

    Chapter 13.   The System for Analyzing Verbal Interaction 357
                     Anita Simon and Yvonne Agazarian

    Chapter 14.   Use of Structural Analysis of Social Behavior for
                     Interpersonal Diagnosis and Treatment in Group
                     Therapy 381
                     Lorna Smith Benjamin

VI. An Overview of the Systems 413

Chapter 15. Comparison of the Systems of Analysis: Concepts
and Theory 415
Ariadne P. Beck and Carol M. Lewis

Chapter 16. A Summary of the Application of the Systems of
Analysis to Group A, Session 3 443
Carol M. Lewis and Ariadne P. Beck

Author Index 469

Subject Index 479

About the Editors 493

CONTRIBUTORS

Yvonne Agazarian, Systems-Centered Training Center and Friends' Hospital, Philadelphia, PA

Ariadne P. Beck, private practice, Oak Brook, IL

Lorna Smith Benjamin, Department of Psychology, University of Utah, Salt Lake City

Simon H. Budman, Innovative Training Systems, Newton, MA

Gary M. Burlingame, Department of Psychology, Brigham Young University, Salt Lake City, UT

Adrienne S. Chambon, Faculty of Social Work, University of Toronto, Toronto, Ontario, Canada

Solomon Cytrynbaum, School of Education and Social Policy, and Department of Psychiatry and Behavioral Sciences, Northwestern University, Evanston, IL

Michael Sean Davis, Innovative Training Systems, Newton, MA

James M. Dugo, Illinois School of Professional Psychology, Rolling Meadows

Albert M. Eng, Community Mental Health Services, Department of Public Health, San Francisco, CA

Myrna L. Friedlander, Department of Educational and Counseling Psychology, State University of New York at Albany

Addie Fuhriman, assistant to the president for Planning and Assessment and Department of Psychology, Brigham Young University, Salt Lake City, UT

Leslie S. Greenberg, Department of Psychology, York University, Toronto, Ontario, Canada

Les R. Greene, Department of Psychology, Department of Veterans Affairs Medical Center, West Haven, CT

Sigmund W. Karterud, Department of Psychiatry, Ulleval University Hospital, Oslo, Norway

Janice R. Kelly, Department of Psychological Sciences, Purdue University, West Lafayette, IN

Carol M. Lewis, Mental Health Center, Mercy Hospital and Medical Center, Chicago, IL

Elsa Marziali, Faculty of Social Work, University of Toronto, Toronto, Ontario, Canada

Mary McCallum, Department of Psychiatry, University of Alberta, Edmonton, Alberta, Canada

William E. Piper, Department of Psychiatry, University of British Columbia, Vancouver, British Columbia, Canada

Anita Simon, SAVI Communications and Friends' Hospital, Philadelphia, PA

Stephen Soldz, Health and Addictions Research, Boston, and Harvard Medical School, Cambridge, MA

A. Ka Tat Tsang, Faculty of Social Work, University of Toronto, Toronto, Ontario, Canada

FOREWORD

LESLIE S. GREENBERG

Ever since the statement of Xeno's Paradox many centuries ago, in which it was noted that if an object repeatedly travels half the distance of its remaining journey, it will never reach the end, understanding the process of change has remained a vexing problem. In studying change the majority of psychotherapy researchers have tended to focus on the easier question "Has change occurred?" and have left the much more difficult question "How does change occur?" to those of heartier souls. Not so the courageous investigators in this book! They have tackled, head on, the difficult problem of measuring processes, not only in individuals but also of individuals in interaction in groups and of groups as a whole. The authors of this book are dedicated system developers who all show that special fascination with and keen interest in observing and measuring what actually occurs. Theirs is a highly laudable effort that will promote further study of the process of change in groups.

A useful view of science is that it proceeds by observation, measurement, explanation, and prediction. Limited attention in psychotherapy research, however, has been paid to the initial steps of observation of the process of treatment and its measurement. In fact, intensive rigorous observation of how change takes place in groups has probably been the most sorely neglected. Investigators need to *observe* the process of change to provide practitioners with the kind of *explanation* of how change takes place, an explanation that goes beyond prediction and involves a new understanding of what actually occurs. This book, by placing a special emphasis on the use of process measures to clarify theoretical constructs, moves in this direction.

One of the major difficulties inherent in the current use of clinical trials or comparative outcome studies in psychotherapy research is the assumption of direct and linear cause–effect relations between the independent variable (treatment) and dependent variables (outcomes) without taking into account the complex performances (processes) that occur in between treatment delivery and outcome effects. Rather than treating therapy as a black box, looking only at input and output variables, investigators need to study and track the complex performance patterns and interaction sequences that constitute the treatment. It is possible to find order in the complexity of psychotherapeutic process by rigorously observing actual performance, and to my knowledge, this book is the first compendium of measures for helping find order in group process.

Clearly, the study of group psychotherapy, like the study of individual psychotherapy, will never be a deterministic science, one in which specific processes or, for that matter, specific outcomes can be predicted for a particular person or group, any more than will meteorology be an exact science, where the flap of a butterfly's wings in South America affects the weather in China. The interactions in groups clearly are complex and sensitive to many initial and subsequent conditions, but there is order in the complexity of psychotherapeutic process in groups, and it is waiting to be observed and described. With better description and understanding of group process, investigators' ability to promote change will improve vastly and their ability to predict will improve. Investigators do not need to rely only on complex analytical or statistical methodologies that track one or two variables over time, to tease out imperceptible trends or complex patterns. What they do need to do to find patterns is to observe closely actual behavior in sessions, rigorously measure a variety of features of the performance, and capture observable changing configurations over time. This will help establish key phases and episodes in group process. The instruments in this book will help investigators rigorously code actual group interactions and processes, look at emerging configurations, and see how these change over time, as have Beck and Lewis in their chapter on group development.

The editors of this book, Beck and Lewis, have performed a labor of love over many years both in stimulating and promoting group psychotherapy process research at meetings of the American Group Psychotherapy Association and the Society for Psychotherapy Research and in bringing this book to fruition. By looking back at the history of process research books, it appears that it takes about 13 years to produce a new book of process research. The *Psychotherapeutic Process* by Greenberg and Pinsof (1986) followed Kiesler's (1973) seminal work, *The Process of Psychotherapy*, by 13 years, and now about 13 years later, this book, *The Process of Group Psychotherapy: Systems for Analyzing Change*, appears. This interval between books speaks to the labor-intensive aspect of developing and applying process instruments.

A unique contribution of this book, over and above providing a rich source of state-of-the-art process research instruments and methods in group therapy, is its emphasis on the use of process research to aid in the clarification and further development of theoretical concepts such as that of group cohesiveness. Another distinguishing feature of this book is its emphasis on the need to apply multiple process systems to group process to more fully describe what is occurring. The book in fact is organized around this theme. It actually presents a description of five sessions of a group process and then has a chapter in which the systems of analysis covered in the book are applied to a session of group therapy. This chapter demonstrates how the combination of multiple measures provides a more complex and detailed description of group process than any one measure could provide. This opportunity alone, to see multiple systems at work on the same material, makes this book an invaluable resource.

Group psychotherapy is a field ripe for discovery-oriented investigation because, although a vast domain of practice exists, little is known empirically about how change actually occurs in groups. This book will help to mobilize and capture the curiosity and wonder that motivates many practitioners and students of group therapy and will help them study how change actually occurs in groups. Rather than deaden their investigative urges within the restricting methodological straitjacket of clinical trials and outcome research, this book provides a vision of other research possibilities. The contributions to this book give the reader the tools to follow the complexity of group process and to begin to understand how to better facilitate the process of change in groups.

It will be interesting to look back 13 years from now to see where process research in the field in general and in group more specifically has taken us. I am sure we will see advances based on the instruments in this book and the development of new instruments that this book will surely stimulate. I encourage young investigators to take on the baton and move forward in spite of the complexity of process research. The difficult path is often the most satisfying.

REFERENCES

Greenberg, L. S., & Pinsof, W. M. (Eds.). (1986). *The psychotherapeutic process: A research handbook.* New York: Guilford Press.

Kiesler, D. J. (1973). *The Process of Psychotherapy: Empirical foundations and systems of analysis.* Chicago: Aldine.

PREFACE

Our goal in creating this book is to provide a summary of the current state of process research on group psychotherapy to stimulate new research work and a new level of integration in our understanding of group process. We hope that the readers of this book who either enter or continue in this field will surprise all of us with their own creative insights and integrations. We also hope that the research efforts summarized in this book will facilitate the process of uncovering understandings of why and how such a complex enterprise as a therapy group is able to make a truly profound impact on individual lives. The authors in this book look at nine systems of analysis that have been designed to study therapy groups. These systems of measurement investigate specific theories of group psychotherapy, but they also draw on influences from more general theories of group process and social interaction and from individual dynamics and therapies.

We believe that the systems of measurement that now exist, and the process research that has been facilitated by the use of these instruments, form a body of work that enables further integration of efforts among researchers. If researchers consider the use of other available instruments as well as their own in continuing their investigations, a body of work may emerge in which the basic theoretical concepts are better informed by objective measurement and their relation to one another is clarified. Current theories of psychotherapy, group process, and individual development will continue to contribute to the understanding of research results. However, we believe that the formulation of an overall conceptual framework is needed to make use of the rich potential in the current theories of group therapy.

OUR COMMITMENT TO PROCESS RESEARCH

The coeditors of this book have worked collaboratively on process research for many years. During that time we have worked with a team that has at various times included Jo Ann Brusa, James M. Dugo, Albert M. Eng, Lana Peters, Mark Stone, and Paul Sullivan. Our research work has focused on the study of developmental processes in group psychotherapy, in the cotherapy relationship, and in the study of emergent leadership roles in small groups. This work has required the development and adaptation of measures suitable to facilitate the investigations based on a theory of group development.

The complexity and power of groups presents a continual intellectual challenge. We have understood from the start that this complexity is such that our efforts will contribute only a small step to the evolution of understanding this subject. Our interest in process research in group psychotherapy comes not only from theoretical questions and interests but also from the manner in which the insights we have gained from the study of groups have always led to useful ideas and practices in our work as clinicians, teachers, group leaders, consultants, and administrators. Although the various tasks involved in process research require great amounts of work, performing them generates the reward of encounter with the real substance of ideas, which are fruitful in everyday practice.

One of the immeasurable benefits of performing research work has been the privilege of knowing and working with other researchers, including some who have been pioneers in individual and group psychotherapy and in process research, and whose work has influenced and informed our own. The benefits of learning from others in the field, and our relationships to one another within our team and to our extended network of colleagues, sustains us in our ongoing involvement with groups, process analysis, and learning in general. All of these experiences in collaboration have been enriching.

THE HISTORY OF THIS BOOK

An eminent group of psychotherapy researchers contributed the systems of analysis presented in this book. They have written chapters on systems that they have developed themselves or that were developed by others but that they applied to group psychotherapy. Some of them have been active participants in the American Group Psychotherapy Association (AGPA) and its research committee. It was in the meetings of the research committee, during Ariadne Beck's tenure as chairperson, that the decision was made to collaborate on the creation of this book. Several other researchers and the specialists in family and work group process research were then also invited to participate. The editors wish to thank all the contributing authors for their excellent work and for their perseverance through the many stages of this project.

One of the researchers in this field who has worked with Bale's Symlog system and with the Gottschalk–Gleser system of analysis was invited to contribute chapters on those methods but was unfortunately unable to participate at that time.

This book and its editors owe an even earlier debt to the informal group of process researchers that annually convened at the meeting of the International Society for Psychotherapy Research. That group collaborated to create *The Psychotherapeutic Process: A Research Handbook*, edited by Leslie S. Greenberg and William M. Pinsof (1986). These researchers sustained process research in psychotherapy during a period when it was not in vogue, and we are grateful to all those colleagues for their ongoing support. In particular, we are grateful to Les Greenberg for his ongoing support of our interests in this project and his graciousness in providing the foreword.

The origin of the editors' interest in process research has to be credited to the work done in the University of Chicago's Counseling and Psychotherapy Research Center and, in particular, to the influence of Eugene Gendlin, Laura N. Rice, and Carl Rogers, who led the way and inspired others to follow on the path of process research on psychotherapy. All three have been teachers and friends whose wisdom we have treasured. The early work on developing measures to track our theory of group development was facilitated by David Wiley (when he was at the University of Chicago), whose methodological skills with modeling were invaluable.

We also owe a debt of gratitude to our colleagues at AGPA who participated in the systems theory committee, which was led by Helen Durkin. Her passion to understand and make use of this emerging formulation gave all of us the opportunity to exchange ideas among ourselves and with workers in other specialties such as J. G. Miller, H. von Foerster, and H. A. Goolishian. With James Durkin's direction and editorial assistance, this committee produced a book, *Living Groups: Group Psychotherapy and General System Theory* (1981), that is filled with creative applications of systems theory to the theory of group psychotherapy. Our own theoretical work was influenced by general system theory in the 1950s and 1960s, but it was Walter Gruen who connected us to this committee at AGPA in 1978, and we remember him with affection for that.

ACKNOWLEDGMENTS

Like process research itself, the preparation of a book of this complexity requires the collaborative efforts of many individuals. We want to first thank the reviewers who, through their reading and comments on individual chapters, contributed to the clarity and completeness of the work. We are deeply indebted to them for their generous contributions of time and wisdom. They are, in alphabetic order, James F. Alexander, John Bair, Richard Lee Bednar, Hylene Dublin, Les Greene, John J. Hartman, Priscilla Hill, William F. Hill, Leonard Horowitz, Adam O. Horvath, E. Michael Kahn, Nick Kanas, Roy MacKenzie, Richard Lee Moreland, Fred Newman, Peter Schlachet, William B. Stiles, Walter Stone, and Dorothy S. Whitaker. The entire book was reviewed by two colleagues chosen by APA Books, and we thank them for their time, effort, and guidance. From the inception of this project, one colleague has offered ongoing active support and occasional mentoring. We are indebted to Les Greene for his personal and professional attention to us and to this book. The competent typing of several chapters, and of correspondence with authors and reviewers, was handled by our typists, Dale Malinowski and Dorothy Vodicka. The preparation of mailings was handled by our administrative assistants, Margaret Clutter and Marge Pokin. Our own copy editor, Clare La Plante, contributed clarity and succinctness by reviewing all the chapters. All five of these women have been very supportive to our efforts to complete this book.

Our editor from APA Books, Margaret Schlegel, has guided the book and the editors through complex and difficult terrain with grace, insight, generosity, and support. We thank her for all those qualities. Linda McCarter, Development Editor, has helped shape the final product with her suggestions for revisions. Chris Davis as Supervisor of Technical Editing and Design and Jennifer Powers as Technical/Production Editor have skillfully brought this book to completion. The thoughtful attention to both substance and detail by each of these editors is greatly appreciated by all the authors.

These acknowledgments would not be complete unless we thanked the many clients who generously gave their time and their stories to be participants in all of our projects. We are especially indebted to the members of Group A.

On a personal level, we wish to acknowledge the continuous support, intellectual stimulation, challenge, and blessings of Ariadne's husband, Robert N. Beck, and the support of our parents, Caroline and Harry Lewis and Panagiota B. Plumis.

REFERENCES

Durkin, J. (Ed.). (1981). *Living groups: Group psychotherapy and general system theory.* New York: Brunner/Mazel.

Greenberg, L. S., & Pinsof, W. M. (Eds.). (1986). *The psychotherapeutic process: A research handbook.* New York: Guilford Press.

the PROCESS of GROUP PSYCHOTHERAPY

1

INTRODUCTION

ARIADNE P. BECK AND CAROL M. LEWIS

OVERVIEW OF THE BOOK

This book presents the current work on applying systems of process analysis of interaction to group psychotherapy to facilitate research in the fields of group psychotherapy and group dynamics. Because group process is so complex, the task of comprehensively understanding the influences that determine any particular act or development is a difficult one. It is a challenge to study individual change within the group context and to try to understand the dynamic flow of individual, dyadic, subgroup, and group-as-a-whole phenomena. Yet, as any seasoned group therapist knows, group therapy is a powerful medium for change whether or not all its dimensions and processes are understood.

The therapeutic group is a natural laboratory for process analysis studies. In this book nine systems of process analysis are presented for the study of psychotherapy groups. These include three systems that were developed in the 1950s to 1960s and that have had fairly wide application to psychotherapy and to other kinds of groups: the Group Emotionality Rating System, the Hill Interaction Matrix, and the Member–Leader Scoring System. These are followed by three systems that began in the 1970s and 1980s and, although still being developed, they have been applied to studies of group psychotherapy process: the Group Development Process Analysis Measures, the Psychodynamic Work and Object Rating System, and the Individual Group Member Interpersonal Process Scale. The final three systems have been applied to other kinds of groups or to family or individual therapy but are now being applied to therapy groups: Three Complementary Systems for Coding the Process of Dialogue, the System for Analyzing Verbal Interaction, and the Structural Analysis of Social Behavior.

These nine systems have bases in theories from a number of fields: psychoanalysis, interpersonal and humanistic psychotherapies, social psychology, developmental psychology, linguistics, and information and systems theories. Each of the systems of analysis offers a different set of lenses for viewing the process of a therapy group. They each contribute an understanding of some aspects of the many layers of activity that exist in a group. To compare the systems, the authors were asked to rate the transcript, audio recording, or both of the third session of one time-limited therapy group provided by the editors (Beck, 1970). To give the reader a context (both before and after the third session), we have provided a description of the first five sessions of the group. One later chapter compares the results of the application of the systems to the third session, and another chapter compares the theories and concepts used in the systems. The entire project has been placed into a broader context by presenting three chapters that summarize recent work with process research on family, task, and therapy groups. Finally, this introduction will provide a conceptual framework within which the rest of the book may fit. It will give a road map to the contents of the chapters.

This book was conceived as a "state-of-the-art" document to allow researchers, theorists, and clinicians to view current work on therapy group process. For the most part, the researchers featured in this book have spent a lifetime studying the complex structure and process of the therapy group. They have done the hard work of establishing this special field. They built directly on a previous generation who founded process research on task and training groups or on individual psychotherapy. Everyone who has contributed to this book believes that researchers are at an important time in the evolution of this field and that it is time to pause, take stock, and get a clear picture of where they are now. Our goal in this book is to help to provide such a perspective on process research on group psychotherapy. We hope that our students and their students after them will generate far more complex and better integrated systems of analysis with more sophisticated methodologies. We also hope they continue to uncover the processes that make group therapy so effective in facilitating individual change and the processes that make small groups so meaningful in every aspect of human life.

There are a number of factors converging today that create an opportunity for development in this field. They are briefly outlined below.

Renewed Interest in the Study of Groups

A renewed interest in the formal study of small groups, their processes, and their dynamics has emerged in recent years. The community at large has recognized that groups that work well together can have a great deal of influence and are capable of exceptional productivity in all walks of life.

This new work comes from the business and organizational worlds and from social psychology, all of which are contributing a great deal to the current interest in studying groups and leadership. There is, however, a great deal that is not yet understood about the dynamics of group process. How groups evolve, how leadership emerges and affects a group, how decisions are made, and what determines task success or failure are among the questions still under investigation in these settings.

Technological Changes

Until recently, the technical problems involved in studying natural groups of any kind at the level of moment-to-moment process were enormous. Many participants in natural groups objected to being recorded and observed in detail. The task of transcribing group interaction was lengthy and difficult. The tasks of coding and analyzing large volumes of data were labor intensive and tedious. Although some problems in each of these areas still exist, the introduction of less obtrusive recording devices, voice recognition software that can convert voice to readable text, more powerful computers, and more relevant applications for computer analyses have improved the chances that a study can be done in a reasonable period of time. In addition, the use of video allows analyses of nonverbal and verbal communication. Innovations in facial analysis based on digital images raise the opportunity for detailed side-by-side visualization of speaker/spoken-to pairs and more detailed analyses of interpersonal processes in the entire group.

The State of Research on Group Psychotherapy

The psychotherapy group process is complex and has as its primary task positive individual change. Recent researchers have made progress in this area with outcome studies establishing the efficacy of group therapy as a comparable treatment mode (as far as outcome is concerned) to individual therapy (Burlingame, Fuhriman, & Anderson, 1995; Smith, Glass, & Miller, 1980). In chapter 2 in this book, this topic is developed further.

However, the efficacy of individual therapy was established much earlier. As a result, the field of research on individual psychotherapy has moved well beyond simple outcome studies to address the relationship of outcome to a variety of processes or therapy styles. It has moved beyond that to the study of specific microprocesses of change that are especially important to the achievement of therapeutic goals. This is a large literature in its own right, but some examples include studies by Crits-Christoph et al. (1999); Hardy et al. (1999); and Greenberg, Ford, Alden, and Johnson (1993). It is possible for the study of the therapeutic group to make comparable shifts to process–outcome studies, studies of specific microprocesses during treatment and of critical change events, and studies of leader interventions that facilitate positive change processes.

The Need for a Conceptual Framework

During the 20th century many ideas, theories, practices, and empirical studies have been generated in a number of disciplines to explain the power, impact, and potential of small groups and their leaders. These efforts have generated a rich and stimulating body of material that is in need of a theoretical framework to facilitate the integration of the many strands that have been produced.

Fuhriman and Barlow (1994) made a strong plea for the "conceptualization of an organizing structure" to model the therapy group. They concluded that the therapy group's basic components have not yet all been identified, but they suggested some directions for research. They proposed combining the use of measures from different research efforts. The concepts and measures in this book are potential candidates for this type of work.

The need for a fundamental organizing conceptual structure has been recognized for a number of years. Durkin (1981), in referring to her own response during the 1970s to the emergence of many new ideas and methods about group therapy, stated that "it seemed to me that what was needed at this point was a more comprehensive framework—a conceptual umbrella which could encompass the major current approaches and could logically incorporate the best of the new techniques" (p. 7). Although her focus in this statement was on the practice of group psychotherapy, she was primarily interested in theory that could inform and guide practice. For her, the organizing framework that seemed potentially most useful for bringing an integrated perspective to this field was general systems theory as defined by von Bertalanffy (1950, 1968) and by Miller (1978).

The human group is only one of many systems in the world that can be described as spontaneously self-organizing, multidimensional, complex, adaptive, and "in balance at the edge of chaos." These systems range from the biochemical level, such as the behavior of DNA, to the human population level, as in large-scale political and economic processes. There is the theory that the Earth itself is such a system (Lovelock, 1988). In his book on complexity, Waldrop (1992) summed up the characteristics common to such systems as follows: "In every case, groups of agents seeking mutual accommodation and self-consistency somehow manage to transcend themselves, acquiring collective properties such as life, thought, and purpose that they might never have possessed individually" (p. 11). Somehow the phenomenon of "group" accomplishes its purpose of psychotherapy through just such a transcendent process, generating a momentum for change in the individual member. The relatively new fields of chaos and complexity theories are attempts to bring mathematical rigor to the patterns of complex systems (Bak & Chen, 1991; Kauffman, 1992; Nicolis & Prigogine, 1989). These theories are building on the work done earlier in systems theory by specialists in biology and cybernetics. This new work is coming primarily from physics and mathematics.

It is not possible to bring the new mathematical work together with the systems of analysis in this book. That is a step ahead in the evolution of this work. However, the measures presented in this book do generate data at a number of levels of organization within the psychotherapy group that may be amenable to mathematical modeling and that may uncover important patterns in this complex system.

For now, it is clear that living systems are basically in process at all times. Therefore, process analysis of data over time is one useful methodology for understanding specific levels of interaction and change in a therapy group. The therapy group also offers opportunities for the study of multiple layers of interaction and their relationships to each other. Systems theory provides the basic conceptual framework for addressing the complexity of the group. Methodologies are now emerging for analyzing such systems and the interrelations among their parts.

Process Research

This book was in large part inspired by two books that preceded it: Kiesler's (1973) *The Process of Psychotherapy* and Greenberg and Pinsof's (1986) *The Psychotherapeutic Process: A Research Handbook*. Both books have affected process research on individual psychotherapy. In the years since the publication of these books, a rich variety of research efforts have produced new understandings of the change process in several different theoretical approaches to individual psychotherapy. We hope that this book will provide some impetus to the extension and evolution of process analysis research on group psychotherapy.

Kiesler (1973) defined process research as "any research investigation that, totally or in part, contains as its data some direct or indirect measurement of patient, therapist or dyadic (patient–therapist interaction) behavior in the therapy interview" (p. 2). Kiesler also argued that too strict a distinction between process and outcome in psychotherapy research causes problems in the design of research studies. He observed that the process–outcome distinction has led to continued use of pre- and post-treatment designs that have overlooked the study of how change takes place.

Bergin and Lambert (1978), working from the perspective of outcome research, also emphasized that to develop a scientific knowledge of psychotherapy, it was necessary to determine both what works in psychotherapy and how it works. The essential characteristics of a treatment must be identified for its usefulness to be evaluated.

Greenberg and Pinsof (1986) noted that during the years after Kiesler's (1973) book, research became increasingly focused on the study of how the process in psychotherapy leads to change. This focus on change, and on the description, explanation, and prediction of change, linked process research to outcome and reduced the dichotomy in conceptualizing process and outcome. Process research had become the study of the mechanisms of change.

For their book, Greenberg and Pinsof (1986) formulated the following definition of process research:

> Process research is the study of the interaction between the patient and therapist systems. The goal of process research is to identify the change processes in the interaction between these systems. Process research covers all of the behaviors and experiences of these systems, within and outside of the treatment sessions, which pertain to the process of change. (p. 18)

The study of the group processes involved in facilitating change is more complex than in individual therapy because of the number of simultaneous relationships that operate in a group and the fact that both clients and therapists participate in the interactions with any particular client.

Here we offer the following definition of process research for group psychotherapy: Process research on group psychotherapy is the study of the group-as-a-whole system and changes in its development, the interactions within the patient and therapist subsystems, the patient and patient (dyadic or subgroup) subsystems, the therapist and therapist subsystem if there are coleaders, and the way each of the subsystems interacts with and is influenced by the group as a whole. The goal of process research is to identify the change processes in the interactions within and between these systems. Process research covers all of the levels of behaviors and experiences of these systems, within and outside of the treatment sessions, that pertain to the process of therapeutic change.

Although many important theoretical concepts and dimesions of rateable categories have been formulated in group psychotherapy, there is still a long way to go to identify the critical characteristics of therapy in a group context. For one thing, simultaneous influential events can be occurring at the individual, dyadic, subgroup, and group-as-a-whole levels. Some information exists now about many levels of process, but it is not complete. In addition, researchers do not thoroughly understand how the levels interact with each other, with the group's immediate context at the organization or community levels, or with the contexts in which the individual members live between group sessions.

ORGANIZATION OF THE BOOK

To set the context for the process analysis systems chapters, the book contains three preliminary chapters on the following topics: (a) a summary of work on the study of group psychotherapy process, (b) a summary of recent process analysis studies in task-performing groups, and (c) a summary of studies in the field of family therapy processes. These three chapters together provide an overview of the state of the art of process analysis studies of small face-to-face groups of several kinds.

Chapter 2: Process Analysis of Group Interaction in Therapeutic Groups

Greene provides an overview and critique of process versus outcome studies and concludes that group psychotherapy is effective, but the task is now to clarify how that happens. An in-depth summary of two classic studies by Powdermaker and Frank (1953) and Lieberman, Yalom, and Miles (1973) is followed by an overview of recent reviews of the literature in this field. Then, an in-depth review of the most recent quantitative literature is followed by a thoughtful assessment of the current state of group psychotherapy research.

Chapter 3: Interaction Process Analysis in Task-Performing Groups

Kelly reviews the systems of process analysis currently in use to study task-performing groups. Using a framework that organizes the systems into process-focused, setting-focused, and activity-focused categories, Kelly provides an overview of the progress in this area since the creation of the Bales Interaction Process Analysis system in 1950. The strengths and limitations of the three kinds of systems are discussed, and proposals for supplementing their limitations are offered. The challenge of relating the findings of broadly applicable process measures to group productivity or outcome is also discussed.

Chapter 4: Observational Coding of Family Therapy Processes: State of the Art

Friedlander reviews the most frequently used coding systems for family therapy analysis. Also included is a synopsis of emerging measures. Family therapy research has focused on dominance and submission, resistance and cooperation, and conflicts and coalitions. Research is summarized regarding the characteristics of effective family therapy and the way power and conflict are handled in family sessions. Newer systems focusing on both family and couple sessions are described and assessed.

Before discussing each of the nine systems of process analysis that form the core of this book, we present a summary of the first five sessions of the therapy group from which Session 3 was chosen.

Chapter 5: Group A: The First Five Sessions

An important aspect of the book is the application of each system to the same clinical material, namely the transcription, audio recording, or both of the third session from an outpatient psychotherapy group, referred to as *Group A* (Beck, 1970; Beck et al., 1986). This application will make it possible for readers to see the specific and unique contributions of each system as well as the ways in which they overlap. Beck and Lewis present a description and sections of transcripts from the first five sessions of Group A. The authors wanted to give readers context before and after Session 3 as well as a running description of the issues and topics that engaged the group members' attention.

The next three chapters present well-established systems for group process analysis that have been applied to a wide range of therapeutic and task groups and that have been found to be useful in understanding group interaction in both contexts: the Group Emotionality Rating System, the Hill Interaction Matrix, and the Member–Leader Scoring System.

Chapter 6: The Group Emotionality Rating System

The Group Emotionality Rating System (GERS) was developed in its current use by Karterud but is based on the early work of Stock and Thelan. GERS measures the presence of effects in the group that are related to Bion's concept of "basic assumption emotionality" and to his theory of how defenses are expressed at the group-as-a-whole level with fight or flight, pairing, or dependency. Although Bion contrasted basic assumption emotionality with work in groups, the GERS does not directly rate work statements. Karterud's focus has been on the study of basic assumption emotionality in therapeutic groups and milieus in inpatient settings. He also addresses the interaction of individual personality and diagnostic factors with the expression of basic assumption emotionality in group interaction.

The qualitative analysis of measurements made with the GERS is conducted in this chapter from the perspective of group focal conflict analysis, although other perspectives may also be applied to the interpretation of data.

Chapter 7: The Hill Interaction Matrix: Therapy Through Dialogue

As a student of Herbert Thelan, William Fawcett Hill began his work on the Hill Interaction Matrix (HIM) early in the history of research in group psychotherapy process. Hill was interested in understanding the effect of group dynamics in clinical treatment and in discovering what qualities of group interaction facilitate therapeutic conditions and change. He was influenced by the work of Bion and the theories of Lewin, but his goal was to construct a measure of therapeutic processes in groups that would not depend on a particular theory or therapeutic method. Rather, his goal was to construct a measure that would enable the development of a data-based theory of therapeutic processes in groups. This approach led to the current version of the HIM, which is based on research conducted over a long period of time. Hill first identified several aspects of group interaction that hold therapeutic value: member centeredness, interpersonal threat, and patient–therapist role taking. These values helped guide the organization and weighting of the categories in the current version of the HIM. The system has categories grouped by content areas, including topic, group, personal and relationship, and by work styles, including conventional, assertive (which is defined as aggressive), speculative, and confrontive. As an instrument designed specifically to investigate process in therapeutic groups, the HIM has facilitated the empirical study of groups in many settings.

Chapter 8: The Member–Leader Scoring System

The Member–Leader Scoring System (MLSS), introduced by Mann and further developed by Mann, Gibbard, and Hartman, investigates the relationship of the members to the designated leader. The MLSS postulates that group members' effects are determined by authority issues, stimulated by the group situation, and experienced in relationship to the formal designated leader. The MLSS investigates how aspects of individual psychodynamic development affect the members' feelings and behavior in the group situation. Theoretically linked to psychodynamic theories of ego psychology and the clinical theory of Melanie Klein, this system is designed to study processes in many types of small groups. The category system rates impulse (hostility and affection), power relations, and ego states (anxiety, depression, guilt, and self-esteem). The system assumes that unconscious psychological processes affect behavior. This assumption has led to the development of a method to identify degrees of inference required in the rating process.

The next three chapters discuss several newer systems for group process analysis. These have had limited applications but appear promising for the study of the therapeutic group: the Group Development Process Analysis Measures, the Psychodynamic Work and Object Rating System, and the Individual Group Member Interpersonal Process Scale.

Chapter 9: The Group Development Process Analysis Measures

The Group Development Process Analysis Measures (GDM) were developed to investigate the process of change in the structure of the psychotherapy group. The theory on which it is based draws heavily on concepts from systems theory and developmental theory perspectives. The GDM includes five measures. Three measures have been used in tandem to identify the boundaries of phases in the early stages of group development and to describe within-phases processes: the Hostility Support Scale, the Experiencing Scales (adapted for the study of group interaction), and the Normative Organizational/Personal Exploration Scale. Two additional measures have been designed to assess leadership behavior among all members of a group: the Speech Behavior Measures and the Sociometric Test of Leadership Emergence. Although these measures are designed to observe processes at the group-as-a-whole level, they are also useful in the study of change at the individual level. Research work with these measures has provided an understanding of how tasks inherent in the development of a group affect the psychotherapy process for individual members.

Chapter 10: The Psychodynamic Work and Object Rating System

The Psychodynamic Work and Object Rating System, developed by Piper and McCallum, investigates the traditional concept of psychodynamic work, including the expression of components of psychodynamic conflict. Measures for therapists include participation, self-based work, and object focus; measures for patients include participation, self- and group-based work, and object focus. This process-analysis system is just one segment of a growing body of carefully conducted research projects.

Chapter 11: The Individual Group Member Interpersonal Process Scale

The Individual Group Member Interpersonal Process Scale (IGIPS), developed by Davis, Budman, and Soldz, is designed to investigate assumptions underlying an interpersonal and interaction-oriented approach to group therapy, most commonly known from the work of Yalom and Budman. The IGIPS investigates factors that facilitate the therapeutic potential of a group, such as cohesiveness. It has several scales that can be combined to produce a particular set of measures. They are also capable of being recombined to address a variety of questions by use of a flexible method of analysis. The measure described in this chapter resulted from several other measures that preceded it and presents an unusually adaptive system for analyzing group process. The IGIPS emerged from a broader research program in which personality characteristics are related to behavior in group and to outcome. The relationships among cohesion, alliance, and outcome have been of special interest to this group of researchers. The IGIPS shows promise for identifying other group process dimensions in addition to cohesion.

The final three systems have been used primarily in one-on-one interactions, family interactions, or nontherapy groups and are now being applied to group therapy interaction: the Three Complementary Systems for Coding the Process of Therapeutic Dialogue, the System for Analyzing Verbal Interaction, and the Structural Analysis of Social Behavior.

Chapter 12: Three Complementary Systems for Coding the Process of Therapeutic Dialogue

The three complementary systems for coding therapeutic dialogue are Strategies of Talking and Telling (STT), Negotiation of Therapy Agenda (NOTA), and the Psychological Space Coding System (PSCS). This set of measures addresses the heart of the therapeutic process: Does the meaning a client attributes to experience change, and how is this change formulated? Does a client perceive, tolerate, and grow from the complexity and tentativeness of his or her own experience? Does the client perceive a broader range of possibilities in the interpretation of life? The three methods complement each other in a multimethod, multilevel system of analyses. Combining different processes of microanalysis of communication in a group, this team brings together in one study both quantitative analyses of coded data and qualitative discourse analysis of narratives. The NOTA measures collaboration of group members by assessing continuities and discontinuities in speaking patterns. The PSCS also addresses collaboration and therapeutic alliance. It tracks the influence of therapists on clients regarding the "openness of space" and the ability to experience alternative meanings and options. The STT is a discourse analysis that tracks the way a group member represents his or her experience and how and when that experience changes in interaction with therapists and other members.

Chapter 13: The System for Analyzing Verbal Interaction

The System for Analyzing Verbal Interaction is designed to assess the degree of effective communication and potential for problem solving within a group. Simon and Agazarian use a foundation of principles from Lewin's field theory and Howard and Scott's theory of stress. The categories of the instrument allow the assessment of approach versus avoidance of problems (Howard and Scott) as well as the identification of driving and restraining forces (Lewin). Von Bertalanffy's general systems theory, which states that a system has several isomorphic levels, implying here that an individual member's behavior is partly determined by group-as-a-whole interactions, also influenced the system's design. Based on these concepts, Agazarian develop a theory of the hierarchy of isomorphic levels in small-group processes and therapeutic methods to address dysfunctional aspects of interaction.

Chapter 14: Use of Structural Analysis of Social Behavior for Interpersonal Diagnosis and Treatment in Group Therapy

The Structural Analysis of Social Behavior (SASB), developed by Benjamin, is based on an interpersonal perspective on psychoanalytic theory, including the work of Sullivan, Murray, and Bowlby. The SASB is a method to define an individual's patterns of perceptions and expectations about interpersonal issues. It is also useful in the formulation of psychodynamics and of therapeutic goals. Most clinicians can easily relate to this framework because it focuses on the here-and-now interactions of a client and on the influence of the there-and-then of a client's relationship to parents (or others of significance). The SASB builds on earlier circumplex models, with the primary axes being emancipate/control and attack/active love. All positions on the circle have three possible levels of code and interpretation. This method has had wide application in the individual and family therapy contexts and is only now being applied to group therapy.

Outline for Each Chapter

To allow the use of this book as a resource guide to measures relevant to the study of psychotherapy groups, we asked the authors to follow an outline in preparing their chapters. To the extent possible for each system, the chapters have the following sections:

HISTORY AND THEORY OF THE SYSTEM

CORRESPONDENCE BETWEEN THE THEORY AND THE SYSTEM

Challenges in Constructing Operational Definitions; Indexes of Group Process, Development or Change; Further Developments

DESCRIPTION OF THE SYSTEM

Rating; Categories; Limitations and Strengths; Reliability; Validity; Norms; Learning the Rating Method

METHODOLOGY FOR ANALYSIS

PREVIOUS RESEARCH WITH THE SYSTEM

Studies by Name

APPLICATION OF THE SYSTEM OF ANALYSIS TO GROUP A, SESSION 3

CLINICAL INTERPRETATION

RELATIONSHIP BETWEEN THE RESEARCH AND THE THEORY

ASSESSMENT AND FUTURE DIRECTIONS

REFERENCES

Naturally, this model does not fit every system perfectly. It does, however, allow readers the opportunity to compare the systems on the particular issues addressed by each one.

Finally, the closing chapters, prepared by the editors, compare the nine systems in terms of theory and concepts studied and on the results of their analyses of Group A.

Chapter 15: Comparison of the Systems of Analysis: Concepts and Theory

The systems of analysis have developed along with the fundamental theoretical work in group psychotherapy, and they are tools for investigating and refining the understanding of group interaction and of the process of change and growth in psychotherapy. This chapter summarizes the psychodynamic, group dynamic, and psychotherapeutic theories and concepts that the systems are constructed to study. Each system of analysis is described relative to its theoretical base, the concepts for which it provides measures, and the level of the group system that is addressed. The set of concepts and aspects of process that the systems taken together have addressed is then summarized. Dimensions of process are identified and future directions considered.

Chapter 16: A Summary of the Application of the Systems of Analysis to Group A, Session 3

The data from the application of each of the systems to the example of Session 3 of Group A (Beck, 1970; Beck et al., 1986) is summarized. The sample session was chosen because part of the session takes place in Phase II of group development and part takes place in Phase III. The dimensions of change identified by Beck (1983) are used to organize the findings from the systems' analyses of the session. The ways the systems of measurement assess the processes of interaction at the group-as-a-whole level and provide information about the individual's work and psychodynamics are summarized.

AUDIENCE FOR THE BOOK

The audience for this book is broad. Group leaders, clinicians, researchers, teachers, and students should find material from which they can benefit.

Theory Building

There is not a great deal of theory available that is specifically concerned with the therapeutic group. Furthermore, existing theories have not been adequately validated, a process that could lead to their refinement and evolution. The editors and contributors of this book hold that empirical research has as one of its major purposes the development and clarification of concepts. In this way and through the generation of research results, the theory underlying the work becomes further elaborated and revised. The systematic empirical analysis of interaction processes is an especially fruitful endeavor for theory building about group therapy. We hope that theorists in the field will make use of the work of these researchers to amplify and develop their own respective theoretical work. Even more pressing is for future efforts to begin to bring some order to the existing data within an integrated framework that will define the multi-levels of process in group interaction.

Research

The field of therapeutic group work has only recently entered a period in which the systematic study of process and outcome is becoming possible and practical. The current trend in psychotherapy research in general is to determine the aspects of process that relate to outcome and to identify the critical factors and precise strategies underlying change. There are many aspects of process that can be examined as well as a variety of theories that point to crucial dimensions of process from their own frameworks. This book provides easy access to useful measures for the analysis of interaction in groups for researchers, teachers, and students. The book has been deliberately organized to facilitate easy searches for potentially useful measures. The chapters are arranged in a systematic but flexible manner to allow a researcher or teacher of research to compare systems on specific issues.

Teaching and Training

The systems of analysis described in this book were developed to conduct research. However, the authors also discovered how useful these measures were for training clinicians and other researchers. Each system illuminates certain aspects of group interaction. As such, it is also a method for training the observer to attend to those aspects of interaction. We anticipated that the comparative analysis of the rating of Group A will contribute to training in both clinical and research contexts. The book is also a resource for research courses and dissertation planning.

Clinical Implications

Several of the systems of analysis presented in this book are being developed or applied by scientist-clinicians who also conduct groups or teach or supervise group work for therapeutic or leadership development purposes. It is this multiplicity in their roles that brings depth and richness to the material presented.

The examples of how various theoretical concepts and clinical processes are operationally defined and observed can assist clinicians in the ongoing process of assessment and hypothesis generation within their clinical practices. Research brings more systematic, articulate, and rigorous thinking to the clinical process. Familiarity with the systems of analysis for groups will enhance clinicians' understanding of their own current work. It will help them to apply theoretical concepts to treatment procedures, to enrich the conceptual framework they use in daily practice, and to develop a more scientific attitude in observing clinical phenomena. Contributing to this process, each chapter includes observations on clinical implications drawn from the work with that system.

REFERENCES

Bak, P., & Chen, K. (1991). Self-organized criticality. *Scientific American, 1,* 46–53.

Bales, R. F. (1950). *Intraction process analysis: A method for the study of small groups.* Cambridge, MA: Addison-Wesley.

Beck, A. P. (1970). *Transcript of fifteen sessions of Group A.* Unpublished manuscript: Chicago.

Beck, A. P. (1983). A process analysis of group development. *Group, 7,* 19–26.

Beck, A. P., Dugo, J. M., Eng, A. M., & Lewis, C. M. (1986). The search for phases in group development: Designing process analysis measures of group interaction. In L. S. Greenberg & W. M. Pinsof (Eds.), *The psychotherapeutic process: A research handbook* (pp. 615–705). New York: Guilford.

Bergin, A. E., & Lambert, M. J. (1978). The evaluation of therapeutic outcomes. In S. L. Garfield & A. E. Bergin (Eds.), *Handbook of psychotherapy and behavior change* (pp. 139–189). New York: Wiley.

Burlingame, G. M., Fuhriman, A., & Anderson, E. (1995, August). *Group psychotherapy efficacy: A meta-analytic perspective.* Paper presented at the 103rd Annual Convention of the American Psychological Association, New York.

Crits-Christoph, P., Connolly, M. B., Shappell, S., Elkin, I., Krupnick, J., & Sotsky, S. (1999). Interpersonal narratives in cognitive and interpersonal psychotherapies. *Psychotherapy Research, 9,* 22–35.

Durkin, H. (1981). The group therapies and general system theory as an integrative structure. In J. Durkin (Ed.), *Living groups: Group psychotherapy and general system theory* (pp. 5–23). New York: Brunner/Mazel.

Fuhriman, A., & Barlow, S. H. (1994). Interaction analysis: Instrumentation and issues. In A. Fuhriman & G. M. Burlingame (Eds.), *Handbook of group psychotherapy: An empirical and clinical synthesis* (pp. 191–222). New York: Wiley.

Greenberg, L. S., Ford, C. L., Alden, L., & Johnson, S. M. (1993). In-session change in emotionally focused therapy. *Journal of Consulting and Clinical Psychology, 61,* 78–84.

Greenberg, L. S., & Pinsof, W. M. (Eds.) (1986). *The psychotherapeutic process: A research handbook.* New York: Guilford Press.

Hardy, G. E., Aldridge, J., Davidson, C., Rowe, C., Reilly, S., & Shapiro, D. A. (1999). Therapist responsiveness to client attachment styles and issues observed in client-identified significant events in psychodynamic-interpersonal psychotherapy. *Psychotherapy Research, 9*(1), 36–53.

Kauffman, S. A. (1992). *Origins of order: Self-organization and selection in evolution.* Oxford, England: Oxford University Press.

Kiesler, D. J. (1973). *The process of psychotherapy: Empirical foundations and systems of analysis.* Chicago: Aldine.

Lieberman, M. A., Yalom, I. D., & Miles, M. B. (1973). *Encounter groups: First facts.* New York: Basic Books.

Lovelock, J. (1988). *The ages of Gaia: A biography of our living earth.* New York: Norton.

Miller, J. G. (1978). *Living systems.* New York: McGraw-Hill.

Nicolis, G., & Prigogine, I. (1989). *Exploring complexity.* New York: Freeman.

Powdermaker, F. B., & Frank, J. D. (1953). *Group psychotherapy: Studies in methodology of research and therapy.* Cambridge, MA: Harvard University Press.

Smith, M. L., Glass, G. V., & Miller, T. I. (1980). *The benefits of psychotherapy.* Baltimore: Johns Hopkins University Press.

von Bertalanffy, L. (1950). The theory of open systems in physics and biology. *Science, 3,* 23–29.

von Bertalanffy, L. (1968). *General system theory: Foundations, development, applications.* New York: Braziller.

Waldrop, M. M. (1992). *Complexity: The emerging science at the edge of order and chaos.* New York: Simon & Schuster.

I

THE STUDY OF PROCESS
ANALYSIS OF GROUPS

2

PROCESS ANALYSIS OF GROUP INTERACTION IN THERAPEUTIC GROUPS

LES R. GREENE

GROUP PROCESS VERSUS GROUP OUTCOME

Group psychotherapy works! Armed with a growing number of meta-analytic studies, beginning with the classic work of Smith, Glass, and Miller (1980) and complemented by a recent influential national survey of consumers (Seligman, 1995), reviewers of the group psychotherapy research literature can now state with a reasonable degree of confidence that group psychotherapy yields beneficial effects when compared with no treatment and equivalent results when compared with more costly individual psychotherapy. The prototypical laboratory study in these meta-analytic reviews convincingly demonstrates that treating a small group of individuals who manifest a discrete, circumscribed, and homogeneous set of symptoms, such as those who have social phobia, trauma, or depression, in a time-limited, cognitive–behavioral format is ameliorative. Although questions have been raised about the representativeness and relevance of these studies to the way group therapy is actually practiced in the field, the experimental findings per se are uncontested.

Depending on one's perspective of the aims of psychotherapy research, this conclusion is either good news or bad news. To be sure, the demonstration of positive outcomes is necessary for the very viability of any psychotherapeutic intervention in the context of the current revolution in health care delivery. Accountability, in the form of efficacy studies that yield findings of statistical and clinical significance and that result in so-called "empirically validated treatments," is now a requisite for third-party reimbursement. In this regard, the amassing of positive outcome findings is good news.

However, as critics of psychotherapy research point out, outcomes-focused research narrowly limits the kinds of conclusions that can be drawn. Experimental outcome research is designed only to offer predictions, a set of causal inferences that link a tightly scripted, complex set of therapeutic techniques with a battery of standardized, reliable, and validated measures of clinical improvement. An understanding of how and why therapeutic improvement takes place is left out of the equation. As Bednar and Kaul (1978, 1994; Kaul & Bednar, 1986) have repeatedly suggested, the greater the focus on methodological rigor in outcomes research, the less the relevance of the findings for theory building and hypothesis generation about the inner workings of the therapeutic enterprise. Without an understanding of the specific inner processes of psychotherapy, a range of problems ensue. Most prominent is the question of the generalizability or external validity of findings from laboratory-based efficacy studies to treatment as naturally practiced in the field (cf. Speer & Newman, 1996). An assessment and elucidation of the therapeutic processes that make a difference would help link laboratory and field and bridge the distinction between efficacy and effectiveness studies. Failure to identify mediating variables can also lead to causal misattribution. Whether the effects of group cognitive–behavioral therapy, for example, are due to specific therapist techniques, as typically concluded, or to pantheoretical dynamic processes occurring at the interpersonal or group level is an open but empirically addressable question. Finally, the typical outcome experiment that ignores process variables yields findings of the lowest common denominator; pre- to postmean change scores from experimental and control groups fail to illuminate those dynamic aspects of the situation and person that could enhance or maximize therapeutic gain as well as those processes that impede clinical progress.

Two observations from the meta-analytic reviews of group psychotherapy serve to highlight the consequent problems of an exclusive focus on outcome. As stated earlier, most laboratory-based group outcome studies use cognitive–behavioral theory to guide therapeutic interventions. It is ironic that the most empirically studied group therapy modality ignores the group qua group as a potential therapeutic agent. Only recently have practitioners and researchers alike been urged to examine group process within cognitive–behavioral group treatment to enhance therapeutic gain (Ettin, 1992; Satterfield, 1994). A second illustration is from probably the most comprehensive meta-analytic review of group therapy outcome to date (Burlingame, Fuhriman, & Anderson, 1995). In their effort to discern structural and dynamic factors that contribute to greater or lesser improvement over the aggregated studies, Burlingame et al. found attrition rate to be one of the most robust predictors. Overall clinical improvement in the group suffers as increasing numbers of patients prematurely or unilaterally terminate. This relationship seems all too obvious to the practitioner in the field, for whom attrition serves as a clear signal of a negative therapeutic group process. This finding underscores the need to understand, as well as therapeutically manage, these kinds of within-groups dynamics.

In their latest critique, Bednar and Kaul (1994) seemed to have gone as far as to suggest a moratorium on outcome research, viewing it as premature in terms of the developmental status of group psychotherapy research. Bednar and Kaul (1994) argued for the need for process studies: "The underlying reason we know little about the most central group process variables is that we devote so little time to clarifying their essential nature and meaning with astute observation and careful description" (p. 640). As exhaustively reviewed by Burlingame, Kircher, and Taylor (1994), this call for a focus on clinical processes within group therapy has been the most frequently raised critique over the past 50 years. Of interest, and perhaps of some solace, is the observation that the very same critical analysis has been raised recently with individual psychotherapy research (Greenberg, 1986, 1994). Greenberg dubbed the focus on outcome studies as prescientific because it is devoid of essential observation, description, and explanation of the fundamental processes and relationships—the inner workings of the therapeutic enterprise—by which outcome becomes outcome. Some might view these criticisms as being overreactive, arguing that process and outcome research endeavors can be complementary. The vast majority of studies over the years, however, have been either outcome or process, suggesting that the integration of these two enterprises is not easily achievable.

Of course, exactly how best to study process within the psychotherapy situation is subject to considerable debate. Within individual psychotherapy process research (cf. Garfield, 1990; Greenberg & Newman, 1996; Marmar, 1990; Shoham-Salomon, 1990), a range of controversies abound, both conceptual ones, such as the role of theory for explicitly guiding research (Hill, 1990; Luborsky, Barber, & Crits-Christoph, 1990) and methodological issues in data aggregation and analysis (cf. Elliot & Anderson, 1994). Such issues are present but expressed in more muted tones in the study of group psychotherapy process because the field is less developed, due partly to its inherently greater complexity (Fuhriman & Burlingame, 1990).

Having provided a rationale for the study of group process, in the rest of this chapter I orient the reader to the nature of this work. What follows is a review of early efforts in the field, a summary of recent overviews, and a description and critique of the latest attempts to examine the process of therapeutic groups.

TWO CLASSICS ON PROCESS–OUTCOME

This very complexity of the process of group psychotherapy has been captured in two classic projects: Powdermaker and Frank's (1953) early study of psychodynamically oriented inpatient and outpatient groups and Lieberman, Yalom, and Miles's (1973) largest-scale study of experiential and personal growth groups. The first of these was conducted in the Veterans Administration after World War II, when group psychotherapy was experiencing its first of three peaks of popularity as a treatment modality. Powdermaker and Frank's aim was to discover those internal processes that underlie clinical change. Faced with a wide array of questions regarding methodological approaches to the work, they decided not to adopt the standardized observational methods available at that time. They argued that segmenting the flow of data into discrete categories would not facilitate the understanding of dynamic interaction. Theirs was a qualitative approach informed primarily by psychodynamic theory.

Powdermaker and Frank (1953) coined the term *situation analysis*. This concept refers to a highly inferential process in which segments from the detailed written narrative of each session are extracted because they are judged to contain implicit cause-and-effect elements of therapeutic significance. The causal inferences are then made explicit. Thus, any behavior, such as a therapist intervention, that was followed by a noticeable change in tension, behavior, or attitude within the group was subject to this analytical method, an approach not unlike the one proposed by Greenberg (1986, 1994). Monologues by individual patients, conflict between group participants, and resistant behaviors such as silence and withdrawal were the types of clinical phenomena intensively studied by Powdermaker and Frank. By comparing those situations with similar precipitating elements but differing consequences, they could then make inferences about qualifying contextual or additional process elements that were needed for positive therapeutic change. These comparative analyses between situations led to the development of an increasingly complex set of dynamic formulations. For example, they extracted nine situations involving the expression of anger by one of the patients toward the therapist. In six of these situations, the heightened tension within the group ultimately resolved, accompanied by the patient's increased awareness of underlying feelings and thoughts that had been defensively concealed by the blaming orientation. In the remaining situations, the hostile patient was either attacked or isolated by other group members, and neither the patient nor the other group members gained new insights about the meaning of the angry stance. Through inference and abstraction from the raw clinical data, the researchers concluded that the capacity of the group therapist to tolerate the attack without insecurity or defensive reactivity was the key factor in distinguishing the therapeutically successful from the unsuccessful episodes. They also identified what is now called a *moderator variable*: cohesiveness or interpersonal support. That is, they proposed that the adverse effects of the therapist's failure to contain a hostile attack were lessened when others in the group provided encouragement and support for the hostile patient.

Aside from the lack of methodological rigor as judged by today's standards, a major disappointment of Powdermaker and Frank's (1953) study is that only a few of the 63 situations were subjected to this kind of comparative analysis. Consequently, the number of inferences drawn and hypotheses generated were few relative to the amount of work spent in identifying the clinical situations. Nevertheless, the study highlights the potential for discovery of general principles of therapeutic action by means of an approach that stays close to the clinical phenomena.

The study by Lieberman et al. (1973) was developed during the 1960s, the second major ascendance of group work in the country. At this time, encounter groups reflected and epitomized the norms and values of the prevailing culture. In contrast to Powdermaker and Frank's (1953) study, Lieberman et al. attempted to quantitatively measure all aspects of the clinical situation that could influence outcome, defined broadly as changes in cognitive–affective experiences of self and others. Lieberman et al. began by constructing a schema of the personality and group-level variables that were thought to mediate task accomplishment. They included personality constructs such as coping style and self-esteem; dimensions of leadership such as theoretical orientation and style; structural and dynamic features of the group as a whole such as its norms and emotional climate; members' in-group experiences such as their attraction to the group and their level of activity; and, multiple aspects of the learning experience. Then, primarily by adapting existing questionnaires and developing their own ad hoc measures, they set out to assess all of these variables.

Unfortunately, in their analysis of the data, Lieberman et al. (1973) tended to ignore the interactive complexity depicted in their initial schema of the overall group process. Their work instead consisted of an examination of bivariate, linear relationships between each of their structural or process variables and outcome. Although they did find a sizable number of provocative associations, their statistical procedures would likely be criticized today as overly simplistic. Notwithstanding the methodological shortcomings of this and Powdermaker and Frank's (1953) study, these two ambitious projects taken together offer considerable illumination of the complex, multilayered, and dynamic interplay of variables implicated in group therapeutic processes and make understandable why progress in the field is slow.

RECENT REVIEWS OF THE LITERATURE

Fuhriman and Barlow (1994) and Crouch, Bloch, and Wanlass (1994) offered comprehensive assessments of this progress up to the recent past. Fuhriman and Barlow's review focuses on studies in which methodologies designed to identify moment-by-moment behavioral segments of the overall social interaction were used. These individual segments were categorized according to theoretically or empirically derived classification schema. Their associations to outcome were then examined, usually in terms of simple frequency counts or, more rarely, in terms of complex patterns (e.g., Beck, Dugo, Eng, & Lewis, 1986; Hartman & Gibbard, 1974). Their review documents that most of the classification systems for analyzing group interaction, such as Bales's (1950) well-known Interaction Process Analysis and the System for the Multiple Level Observation of Groups (SYMLOG; Bales, Cohen, & Williams, 1979), were developed for and have been applied almost exclusively to nonclinical task groups. Echoing the concerns of Powdermaker and Frank (1953), Fuhriman and Barlow asked whether such systems can capture the clinically relevant processes of psychotherapeutic groups. As I discuss below, some early empirical returns pertinent to this question are now available. In general, the reviewers paint a pessimistic picture. They cite a the lack of systematic, cumulative, and replicated works and a dearth of studies that have examined convergent and discriminant validity of these measurement systems. One promising note suggested by these reviewers is the recent development of ad hoc clinically guided systems of group interaction (e.g., Beck et al., 1986; Karterud & Foss, 1989).

The review by Crouch et al. (1994) evaluated studies in which more global clinical processes subsumed by the term *therapeutic factors* were measured. This is an ambiguously defined concept that seems to represent the crystallization or condensation (or "function," as described by Bloch & Crouch, 1985) of the ongoing flow of behaviors within the group that purportedly contribute to therapeutic gain. In these studies, group process is typically assessed in a more abstract, less microanalytical manner than the studies reviewed by Fuhriman and Barlow (1994). Typically, group participants or observers retrospectively rated their overall impressions of dimensions such as cohesion or interpersonal feedback. Fuhriman, Drescher, and Burlingame (1984) have termed this type of group process data *group phenomena*, in contrast to the behaviorally based, circumscribed observations that they called *group interaction*. It may be more helpful to define these two approaches to the study of group process as investigations of *implicit* versus *explicit* interaction because the clinical phenomena that were studied as therapeutic factors presumably arose from the verbal and nonverbal interchanges of the group members. Crouch et al. (1994) stated that the cumulative findings to date from this methodological approach are sparse and generally disappointing. As with the studies of systems of analysis, many of the investigations subsumed under this rubric used analogue conditions and nonclinical groups, making the generalizability of the findings to the clinical situation questionable.

AN IN-DEPTH REVIEW OF THE MOST RECENT QUANTITATIVE LITERATURE

Because a number of process studies do not fall squarely within the purview of the two preceding reviews and because the most recent studies are not included, I conducted an independent appraisal of the current state of the group psychotherapy process literature to further clarify the conceptual and methodological problems plaguing the research. Specifically, I conducted an intensive search of the literature from 1990 through 1995 using the PsycINFO data retrieval system. *Group psychotherapy, group therapy,* and *group counseling* were the key words used to retrieve the pertinent articles. Although these broad terms resulted in a listing of nearly 2,000 references, I thought it better to err on the side of overinclusiveness than to overlook any process studies that might escape a narrower net. The titles and abstracts of articles were scanned for their bearing on quantitative investigations of group therapy. Certain exclusionary criteria were then applied; articles not written in English and groups whose aims were not specifically psychotherapeutic, such as personal growth groups or psychoeducative groups, were chief among these criteria. A total of 78 studies resulted from this search. What follows is a critical evaluation of this collection that is organized by critical issues and dimensions raised in previous reviews of the group process literature.

New Clinical Applications of Early Systems of Analysis of Task Group Process

The first observation has to do with the use of those formally devised systems of analysis outlined in Fuhriman's (Fuhriman & Barlow, 1994; Fuhriman & Packard, 1986) previous reviews. Fuhriman observed that the majority of such systems have not been applied to clinical groups. This conclusion was supported by the current analysis with one significant exception: the most recent series of interrelated studies by Tschuschke and colleagues (Catina & Tschuschke, 1993; MacKenzie & Tschuschke, 1993; Tschuschke & Dies, 1994; Tschuschke, MacKenzie, Haaser, & Janke, 1996). In an intensive investigation of two long-term, psychodynamically oriented inpatient groups, Tschuschke applied the SYMLOG (Bales et al., 1979) in a clinically creative manner. Although the work needs construct validation, Tschuschke operationally defined three core therapeutic processes of self-disclosure, feedback, and interpersonal learning by means of specific reconfigurations of standard SYMLOG categories. Self-disclosure consisted of overt references to self in relation to others either inside or outside the group. Feedback received by a group participant was calculated in a straightforward manner as the sum of all verbal and nonverbal acts directed at that individual. Interpersonal learning was constructed in a more complex manner; for each patient, a set of factors representing an individual-specific empirical clustering of interpersonal behaviors was derived via factor analysis. Such creative adaptations of the SYMLOG categories seem to address some of the concerns raised by Powdermaker and Frank (1953) about the lack of clinical relevance of these kinds of scoring systems. Beyond this unique application of SYMLOG, the studies also demonstrated other important methodological strengths. Correlations among these three process variables and their associations to a self-report cohesion construct, assessed at different points in the course of the treatment, facilitated the development of a preliminary model of the complex interrelationship among these core process variables. In addition, all of the process variables were related to a methodologically sophisticated assessment of outcome. This furthered the generation of hypotheses about the ways and means of effecting psychological change in groups. It remains to be seen whether the important addition to the literature represented by this series of studies reflects a new trend given the labor-intensive nature of the work and the limited funding for such efforts. Nevertheless, there are some corroborating signs that suggest that the psychometrically sound SYMLOG system may be increasingly regarded as a clinically relevant process tool (cf. Lion & Gruenfeld, 1993). In any case, the Tschuschke studies make a substantial contribution in their own right in furthering the understanding of therapeutic processes in groups.

New Systems of Analysis

Regarding another of the observations by Fuhriman and Barlow (1994), there are clearer signs in the current sampling of the literature that new systems of analysis specifically geared for the study of processes in clinical groups are being developed: the Individual Group Member Interpersonal Process Scale (IGIPS; Budman, Soldz, Demby, Davis, & Merry, 1993; Soldz, Budman, Davis, & Demby, 1993), the Group Sessions Rating Scale (GSRS; Getter, Litt, Kadden, & Cooney, 1992), and the Matrix Representation Grid (MRG; Ahlin, Sandahl, Herlitz, & Brimberg, 1996). These articles represent preliminary reports of scale development by researchers with considerable clinical expertise. These articles are accompanied by promising initial estimates of reliability and validity, as generated from tape-recorded segments of multiple groups led by experienced clinicians. The first of these, the IGIPS, has undergone significant revision since this initial publication and is discussed in detail in chapter 11 in this book.

The GSRS was developed as part of a larger outcome study on the group treatment of alcoholism; its seven observational categories were specifically designed to identify and differentiate the core components of two contrasting types of group therapy: namely cognitive–behavioral and interactional approaches. The initial findings confirm the differences in the process of these two group modalities. Moreover, the process categories were found to be related to outcome measures of alcohol abuse, thus providing some promising predictive validity for this instrument.

Coincidentally, the initial psychometric assessment of the MRG also derives from a comparison of behavioral and dynamic approaches to the group-based treatment of alcoholism. Unlike the GSRS, however, in which behavioral process categories were selected on the basis of empirical and pragmatic considerations, the eight variables of the MRG are rooted in Foulkes's (1964) depth theory of group process. Despite this difference in system construction, the comparative analysis of the behaviorally oriented and analytically oriented groups using the MRG also reveals significant contrasts in process across the two kinds of groups. Although the authors did not report associations of their process variables with outcome measures, they did examine the relationship of the MRG to another group-as-a-whole rating system: the System for Analysis of Verbal Interaction developed by Agazarian (1989), described in detail in chapter 13 in this book. Their comparison suggested a modest degree of empirical overlap, thus providing some convergent validation. Taken together, these three new systems, although clearly needing further conceptual development and methodological refinement, are promising examples of clinically relevant tools for identifying salient processes in therapy groups and for shedding light on how those processes effect change. Moreover, it is important to note the direct applicability of all three systems to psychodynamically oriented or interactive group psychotherapy. This is an important development given the underrepresentation of quantitative investigations of psychodynamic groups in the literature, especially compared with studies of cognitive–behavioral group approaches. These new systems may serve to redress this imbalance by stirring interest in process–outcome investigations of psychodynamic group work.

Development and Refinement of Individual Variables of Group Interaction

Many of the studies in the current sampling have focused on isolated process variables chosen on the basis of their relevance to some (usually implicit and generic) model of group therapy. Historically, group cohesion has been the most frequently investigated of these individual dimensions.

Its study is well represented in the current literature (Braaten, 1990; Isbell, Thorne, & Lawler, 1992; Slavin, 1993; Stockton, Rohde, & Haughey, 1992). Group cohesion is usually viewed as the analogue of the therapeutic alliance in dyadic psychotherapy, which also receives the greatest amount of empirical attention in process studies. As critics point out (Bednar & Kaul, 1994; Drescher, Burlingame, & Fuhriman, 1985), the conceptual integration of the amassed research findings has been hampered by the proliferation of meanings and measures of this construct. The good news here is the current efforts, both conceptual and empirical, to refine this theoretically and clinically important group dimension. Braaten (1991) offered an exhaustive review of this concept in research and attempted a creative synthesis of the findings, developing a five-factor model. Of greater relevance for the present book are the two studies in which relationships were examined between cohesion, measured as a global rating (or what one would call a measure of implicit interaction), and in-group behaviors. In the more methodologically rigorous of these two studies, Budman et al. (1993) reported a number of theoretically meaningful associations between observer impressions of cohesion and specific moment-to-moment behaviors such as emotional tone and verbalizations about other group members. Budman et al. also discovered that these behavioral correlates of cohesion depended on the stage of group development, underscoring the importance of a temporal dimension in process research. In the study by Braaten (1990), the level of group cohesion was also related to specific behavioral events in the group session that were deemed important by the participants. In addition to their lending construct validation for the specific measures of cohesion used in these studies, the findings offered empirical evidence that global impressions of therapeutic factors are determined by measurable, interactive behaviors in the group.

The dimension that captured the greatest empirical attention in the latest process studies was that of leader behavior. Researchers have examined what the leader says (Flowers & Booraem, 1990a, 1990b; Kapur, 1993; Kennard, Roberts, & Winter, 1990; Nehls, 1992; Page, Campbell, & Wilder, 1994; Stinchfield & Burlingame, 1991; Voigt & Weininger, 1992), thinks about (Hines, Stockton, & Morran, 1995; Kivlighan & Quigley, 1991), and values (Hamblin, Beutler, Scogin, & Corbishley, 1993). Although methodological sophistication varied widely across these studies, they all seem committed to identifying specific in-group leader behaviors, both overt and covert, that make a difference either in terms of patient responses that immediately follow the therapist intervention (known as small "o") or ultimate outcome (i.e., big "O"). It may be that this focused attention reflects the increasingly acknowledged need toward greater specification and detailed observation in process research as well as the understanding that the therapist dimension has been relatively neglected in psychotherapy research (cf. Bergin, 1997; Beutler, 1997; Garfield, 1997).

With respect to leader behavior, earlier means of classification in terms of schools of therapy or theoretical orientations have simply not proved robust enough to capture significant variance in process or outcome research (cf. Lieberman et al., 1973). Of note, several of the current studies reflect efforts to improve earlier classification schemes either by greater elaboration, as in Stinchfield and Burlingame's (1991), efforts to differentiate subtypes of directive interventions made by group therapists, or by reconfiguration, as in Voigt and Weininger's (1992) examination of activating and stabilizing behaviors. These technical refinements in instrumentation, although too few, signify progressive development in a focused field of study.

Other variables that have captured the interest of process researchers include activity level (Isohanni & Niemiren, 1992; Soldz, Budman, & Demby, 1992), affect and arousal (Burgoon, 1993; Flowers, 1991; Tschuschke, Hettinger, Enke, & Lolas, 1990), self-disclosure (Robison, Stockton, & Morran, 1990; Schectman, Vurembrand, & Malajak, 1993), and the therapeutic relationship (Blaauw, 1994). These have also been implicated as important components in generic models of psychotherapy. Unfortunately, to my knowledge, none of these dimensions is being investigated in an ongoing, systematic way that could provide the empirical feedback needed for theory building and hypothesis generation. The one exception may be the construct of work developed by Piper and his colleagues (McCallum & Piper, 1990; Piper, Joyce, Rosie, & Azim, 1994) and discussed in detail in chapter 10 in this book. Given its specification in terms of components of psychological conflict, it adds to the recent, and long overdue, developments in the quantitative study of psychodynamically oriented groups. Because of its centrality in most models of therapeutic change, this new operationalization, as well as its antithesis as represented by a unique measure of resistance (Wheeler & Kivlighan, 1995), is the type of variable useful in the reciprocally related processes of data collecting and theory development.

New Methodologies

Although much of the work discussed in the preceding paragraphs represents thoughtful, arduous, and creative effort, there is a degree of methodological oversimplification. The statistical handling of the data primarily comprises simple frequency counts followed by the calculation of linear, bivariate associations, a methodology disparagingly dubbed the "drug metaphor" within individual psychotherapy process research (cf. Elliot & Anderson, 1994). Although group psychotherapy process research has thus far been spared this criticism, there are preemptive signs in the recent literature of new, more sophisticated approaches toward the study of the complex change processes that occur within the psychotherapy group.

One of the more innovative approaches is the social relations analysis model borrowed from social psychology and recently introduced into the group psychotherapy research literature by Marcus (Marcus & Holahan, 1994; Marcus & Kashy, 1995). Marcus provided a compelling rationale regarding its methodological and conceptual advantages for the study of group process. The model is, in essence, a means for assessing group participants' interpersonal behaviors (as well as interpersonal perceptions) and their determinants. It is a data-analytical procedure that conforms to the actual interactive structure of small-group life in which each participant can respond to the others in the group and serve as the target of the others' behaviors in a so-called "round-robin" fashion. Unlike other methods in small-group research that typically violate core statistical assumptions, particularly the assumption of independence of data across group participants, the social relations model takes the likely nonindependence of data points into account. The variance of the data can be partitioned into separate components: the group effect (which determines how much of the behavior under investigation is unique to a particular group), the actor effect (which assesses the degree to which an individual behaves similarly to other group participants), the target effect (which measures the degree to which an individual is responded to similarly by all other participants), and the relationship effect (which assesses the degree to which specific dyadic interactions uniquely contribute to the behavior). Marcus applied this procedure to several types of group therapy data to illustrate its clinical relevance and theoretical meaningfulness.

Marcus and colleagues (Marcus & Holahan, 1994; Marcus & Kashy, 1995) demonstrated, for example, how a process variable such as interpersonal feedback can be systematically investigated to capture its multidirectional and interpersonally reciprocal nature. By incorporating outcome variables into the procedure, they showed how a range of clinically relevant questions can be empirically addressed: Is there a direct relationship between receiving positive feedback and outcome? Is there an inverse association between giving negative feedback and outcome? In addition, they demonstrated how personality variables, a temporal dimension, and multiple groups are readily accommodated by the procedure. In summary, the social relations model seems to be a significant new tool for group therapy process research that helps generate substantive clinical hypotheses.

Sexton (1993), who used time series analysis to explore relationships between process and outcome, provided a second illustration of a sophisticated data-analytical procedure applied to group therapy. As in the social relations model, this statistical procedure uses the dependencies among observations to determine temporal patterns and regularities among variables. Using a generic model of the psychotherapy process, Sexton constructed a set of process variables that represented the abstractions of moment-to-moment interactions within the group, such as a sense of positive alliance, negative experience, emotional intensity, and insight. These same statistical procedures could be applied directly to behavioral data.

By referring to these variables as immediate outcomes (i.e., assessed at the end of each session), intermediate outcomes (i.e., assessed at the beginning of each subsequent session), and overall outcomes (i.e., assessed at the end of therapy), Sexton (1993) illustrated the artificial distinction between process and outcome and highlighted the utility of conceptualizing the therapeutic process as a complex but identifiable series of intermediary changes. He demonstrated, for example, how changes in the patients' experiences immediately after one session can lead to changes in clinical status at the beginning of the next session. This in turn is associated with overall change assessed at the end of the treatment. Because these techniques take a temporal dimension into account, they are capable of capturing more of the inherent relational complexity of the therapeutic process than can be revealed by simple bivariate linear associations. Like the social relations model, these could prove useful for building and testing models of the change process.

The recent quantitative literature suggests a burgeoning interest in assessing social perceptions and cognitions within the therapy group as a means of exploring the nature of and changes in patients' interpersonal relationships. A variety of methodological and statistical procedures are being used to examine the perceptions of the current social environment. Although they are not strictly new methodologies, there does seem to be a growing appreciation of their utility for group process research. These methods include multidimensional scaling (MDS; Gazda & Mobley, 1994), the repertory grid technique (Winter, 1992), the semantic differential (Greene, 1990, 1993), and sociometric techniques (Brusa, Stone, Beck, Dugo, & Peters, 1994). Developed from diverse theoretical traditions, these data-analytical methods share the assumption that differences in personal traits (or behaviors) ascribed to different individuals in the social field have psychological meaning. That is, inferences can be drawn about the nature of the interpersonal ties within the group on the basis of the specific qualities attributed to the participants and the degree to which these attributes differ across participants. As such, the social–perceptual and cognitive data analyzed by these means can be considered implicit reflects of group interaction.

The essence of the MDS procedure is the construction of a mapping of the social field in two-dimensional space or greater. Group participants can be located on the map by an algorithm that equates perceived similarity with physical proximity; the more the targets share the same perceived attributes, the closer they are placed in the derived geometric configuration. Kivlighan (Kivlighan, Mullison, Flohr, Proudman, & Francis, 1992; Kivlighan & Quigley, 1991) offered examples of the evocative power of this procedure. In one of these studies, Kivlighan and colleagues found that experienced group therapists used a three-dimensional model to think about group process, compared with beginning-level therapists who used only two-dimensional space, suggesting that greater complexity in conceptualizing group interaction accrues with increased clinical experience. These three dimensions overlapped considerably with the three dimensional space of SYMLOG, again supporting the clinical applicability of this formal scoring system. In the second study, the mappings of group sessions suggested that participants' positive experience of a group session is associated with flexibility of the leaders' behaviors. In general, the mapping of group participants, with the attending implications of relational dynamics, facilitates the generation of more complex associations than the simplistic bivariate correlations typically assessed in process research.

The repertory grid and semantic differential methodologies do not afford the same kind of visualization of interpersonal relations as in MDS. These data-generating and data-analytical techniques do, however, invite the development of sophisticated hypotheses about the nature of and changes in interpersonal dynamics within the group. Winter (1992) conducted a comprehensive review of applications of the grid to group therapy that reveals its flexibility for assessing a range of clinical phenomena and processes. Of importance is the convergent validation recently provided by Catina and Tschuschke (1993) and Greene (1993), who found significant associations between social cognitions used by these procedures and interpersonal behaviors, thus reinforcing the argument that these data can mirror actual group interaction.

The best example of renewed interest in sociometric applications is the theory-driven study by Brusa et al. (1994), who attempted to develop a questionnaire to identify the four types of leadership roles theorized to emerge in groups. This study is one of an integrated series of works, described in chapter 9 in this book, guided by Beck's (1974, 1981) theory of group development. This large-scale study, spanning 273 patients in 31 psychotherapy groups, provides preliminary validation of the sociometric instrument under construction as well as empirical support for the underlying theory of differentiated role relations.

Finally, the literature shows the preliminary development of applying chaos theory to the study of group interaction. Although too embryonic to describe in significant detail, the articles underscore an appreciation of the complexity of the interactive process. The search for order, structure, and regularity, a set of rules that governs the content, style, and flow of the group communication, might not be realized through linear logic (cf. Lichtenberg & Knox, 1991) but may require the application of nonlinear dynamic models of assessment (cf. Fuhriman & Burlingame, 1994).

Intensive Study of Process Over Time

A few of the current investigations reflect a back-to-basics quality in terms of the intensive analysis of group process over sessions (Isbell et al.,

1992; Kanas, Schoenfeld, Marmar, Weiss, & Koller, 1994; Kanas & Smith, 1990). They essentially are qualitative studies that applied descriptive-level statistics to frequency counts of behavioral categories across the entirety of the course of therapy groups. In a sense, they are discovery-oriented works whose value, unfortunately only partially realized, is in the articulation of hypotheses about group process and development. These types of works also provide potentially useful databases for comparative purposes by other studies using similar groups and clinical populations.

Contributions to the Process–Outcome Literature

Of the studies that have examined process variables relative to outcome, the four interrelated works by Tschuschke and colleagues (Catina & Tschuschke, 1993; MacKenzie & Tschuschke, 1993; Tschuschke & Dies, 1994; Tschuschke et al., 1996) are the most ambitious to date. The studies focused on two intermediate-term, analytically oriented inpatient groups for patients with neuroses and character disorders. The data yielded associations among a well-conceived measure of clinical outcome and (a) the individual's relatedness to the group; (b) the amount of self-disclosure; (c) the amount of feedback (regardless of specific content) received; and (d) changes in representations or schemata of self and others, such as the psychological distance between the actual and ideal self. Although limited in their value for theory building because of the unnecessarily simplified data-analytical procedures, these findings affirm basic clinical wisdom about isolated elements important for therapeutic change.

AN ASSESSMENT OF THE CURRENT LITERATURE

The current intensive sampling did not permit an assessment of future trends; sampling from earlier time periods would be required to estimate the directions in which the field is going. Nevertheless, the studies taken together can be evaluated in light of recent critiques and controversies about group psychotherapy process research and by comparison to the state of individual psychotherapy process research. What follows is a critical analysis of the current literature. I have included suggestions for furthering the study of interaction and process in group therapy.

Productivity

The first impression of the current database concerns the sheer quantity of studies published over the past 6 years. The output is small compared with the outcome research. Besides the methodological shortcomings that plague the studies, their limited number makes conceptual synthesis and generalization of the accrued findings difficult. It is clear that Bednar and Kaul's (1978, 1994; Kaul & Bednar, 1986) repeated calls for more group process research have been unheeded. Given the press for the demonstrability of treatment efficacy, economics alone would seem to forecast the continuing of this imbalance between outcome and process studies. Other factors also seem to contribute, however. For one, process studies are inherently more difficult to design and execute than outcome studies. The latter are guided by a straightforward, explicit formula involving randomization; adequate control groups; and standardized, multicomponent instrumentation. A similar gold standard for what constitutes rigorous and meaningful process studies has not been consensually agreed on. Without such explicit guidelines, the researcher must rely on clinical observation, hypothesis and, above all, theory. Compared with the individual psychotherapy literature, models about the pathways and dynamics by which psychological change is effected in the small group are less well articulated. As a consequence, the process researcher must also act as a theorist, developing at least partial theories about essential relationships among variables. There is also the question of payoff. Process studies, particularly those collecting moment-to-moment interaction data, tend to be more labor intensive. Although hardly an exhaustive comparative analysis, these differences can account for much of the imbalance in quantity between process and outcome studies.

A second observation concerns the researchers doing the work. Most of the studies in the current sampling were conducted by well-established researchers who were also seasoned clinicians. Their works, such as those by Piper and McCallum (Chapter 10, this volume), tend to be ongoing and systematic. The programmatic nature of the work facilitates the integration of accumulated findings and the accounting for inconsistencies across studies by means of higher level interactions. Studies by experienced researchers show significantly fewer incidences of one-shot demonstrations that yield only isolated facts. In this regard, the current sampling is encouraging for the development of empirically grounded models of group therapy process.

Data Collection

As described earlier, few process measures have garnered significant degrees of convergent and discriminant validity. Measures purportedly assessing the same construct, such as those designed to assess cohesion, tend to yield inconsistent findings across studies. Given the lack of psychometric grounding, it is difficult to deduce the degree to which such inconsistencies are attributable to differences in measurement tools. The current literature seems to lend credence to critics who argue that insufficient attention is paid to the preliminary scientific steps of observation and measurement.

Before examining cause-and-effect relationships, one needs to ascertain the psychometric soundness of instrumentation. Such an endeavor needs to include estimations of reliability and considerations of unit of observation and unit of analysis. The issue here is not only methodological, however. Lack of articulation in conceptualization compounds the problems. Measures of cohesion, for example, vary considerably in how data are collected and analyzed. Cohesion assessed at the level of the individual (as in self-ratings of attraction to the group) is a construct different from the same term measured retrospectively by observers as a global, group-level clinical state. Both of these variables in turn can be conceptually distinguished from a measure that explicitly examines group-level variance (rather than or in addition to the mean) of participants' ratings of attraction. This kind of operationalization may be well suited to take into account bipolar dynamic splits within the group, such as between two subgroups or between the group and one deviant member. A variation of the last type of measure is an assessment of each participant's departure from the rest of the group on rating scales of cohesion. These last two types of measures include possible group dynamic processes as part of the assessment procedure, a theoretically informed advantage often ignored in current operationalizations.

Beyond these psychometric considerations, the construct validity of the measures of group process and interaction is also relatively unsupported. Too often, there is vagueness or ambiguity about the theoretical concepts that the instrument is purportedly assessing and the expected theoretically derived relations that would provide positive construct validation of the measure under investigation. Multitrait–multimethod procedures would be useful in clarifying what process measures are actually measuring. The good news is that a few of the studies have attempted assessments of convergence, such as the Budman et al. (1993) investigation of cohesion and Catina and Tschuschke's (1993) study of associations between the repertory grid technique and SYMLOG. I hope that the focus of the current book, precisely this kind of comparison among many systems of analysis all applied to the same clinical data, will stimulate additional psychometric work on convergence and discrimination.

Data Analysis

The research in the current sample reflects the simplifying, empiricist, and mechanistic assumptions about the aggregation and analysis of data that are frequently criticized by reviewers of individual psychotherapy research (Elliot & Anderson, 1994; Stiles, Shapiro, & Harper, 1994). In essence, most of the current studies are correlational and have attendant assumptions about linearity, unidirectionality, and causality. These works imply that an isolated ingredient, such as the therapist's degree of support, is directly associated with subsequent change and outcome; the more of the "antecedent" variable, the more of the "consequent" variable. Also inherent in this view is that so-called "process variables" always temporally precede so-called "outcome variables," a view that blinds researchers to the possibility that changes in clinical status might facilitate the development of subsequent therapeutic processes. One can hope that as researchers become familiar with more sophisticated data-analytical techniques and adopt the pioneering approaches undertaken by researchers of individual psychotherapy, the findings obtained from process studies will have greater theoretical relevance to the complexities of the therapy group.

Additional Thoughts

The state of group psychotherapy research has not evolved to the level of maturity attained by its individual psychotherapy counterpart (Orlinsky & Russell, 1994) for several of the reasons previously enumerated: the inherently greater complexity of the clinical phenomena, the lack of guiding and explicit models of group therapy, and the less well psychometrically established measures. To a small degree, however, all of these factors have been addressed in the current sampling of studies. It does seem that a degree of progress is genuinely being made in the field.

What would further help the state of the research? One problem is the lack of research-friendly theoretical models analogous to Orlinsky and Howard's (1987) generic model of individual psychotherapy. Such explicit mappings of relationships among well-operationalized constructs, as in a path analysis, would move the field beyond the examination of simplistic, bivariate, and linear associations. All of the prevailing theoretical frameworks for group psychotherapy could benefit from further precision in defining constructs and further articulation of the group-level, interpersonal, and intrapsychic processes that induce a change in the individual patient's behaviors, attitudes, feelings, and cognitions. Articulating a series of probabilistic statements of conditions and sequences that create therapeutic change might help to focus attention and the limited resources on core, rather than peripheral, issues, as is increasingly reflected in individual psychotherapy research (e.g., Kolden, 1996).

In complementary fashion, it would be useful for researchers and editors to be more critical of "outcomelike" process studies, investigations that yield only isolated facts, unconnected to an embedding theoretical context. Given the state of the scientifically grounded knowledge base, it seems better to err on the side of overgeneralizing, in the service of model building, than to present only fragmentary empirical findings. The numerous process studies of Yalom's (1985) so-called "therapeutic factors" is a case in point. In these descriptive studies, group members are merely asked to rank order a predefined list of therapeutic factors for their salience and influence. The lack of guiding theory and the methodological naiveté of this approach has resulted in a sizable database of inconsistent findings about the perceived helpfulness of therapeutic processes across varying groups, a database that is intractable to synthesis. Moreover, as Piper (1993) critiqued, asking group participants what was helpful is not the same as discovering actual therapeutic processes in the group. Not only may participants consciously manipulate their responses but they may also be genuinely unaware of the group forces that induce change. Simply put, the Yalom-type questionnaire, with its attending methodological weaknesses and absence of theoretical context, offers minimal insight into the interactive processes that lead to psychological change in groups. In this regard, critics of both the group and individual psychotherapy process research are correct: A theoretical framework and sound measurements are both needed.

Despite these criticisms, the current sampling of studies provides reason for optimism about the future of group psychotherapy process research. The repeated calls for greater measurement precision and conceptual clarification are at least being heeded, at least to a degree by some of the current process researchers. This book is aimed at furthering these developments. Its application of both well-established and innovative systems of process analysis to a common set of clinical data, essentially a multitrait–multimethod procedure, should provide further momentum to the sharpening of terms and clarifying of relationships among key constructs that critics agree is the necessary, albeit painstaking, work to advance the field.

REFERENCES

Agazarian, Y. (1989). Group-as-a-whole systems theory and practice. *Group, 13,* 131–154.

Ahlin, G., Sandahl, C., Herlitz, K., & Brimberg, I. (1996). Developing the Matrix Representation Grid (MRG): A method for observing group processes—Findings from time-limited group psychotherapy for alcohol-dependent patients. *Group, 20,* 145–173.

Bales, R. (1950). *Interaction Process Analysis: A method for the study of small groups.* Cambridge, MA: Addison-Wesley.

Bales, R., Cohen, S., & Williams, S. (1979). *SYMLOG: A system for the multiple level observation of groups.* New York: Free Press.

Beck, A. P. (1974). Phases in the development of structure in therapy and encounter groups. In D. Wexler & L. N. Rice (Eds.), *Innovations in client-centered therapy* (pp. 421–463). New York: Wiley Interscience.

Beck, A. P. (1981). A study of group phase development and emergent leadership. *Group, 5,* 48–54.

Beck, A. P., Dugo, J. M., Eng, A. M., & Lewis, C. M. (1986). The search for phases in group development: Designing process analysis measures of group interaction. In L. S. Greenberg & W. M. Pinsof (Eds.), *The psychotherapeutic process: A research handbook* (pp. 615–705). New York: Guilford Press.

Bednar, R. L., & Kaul, T. J. (1978). Experiential group research: Current perspectives. In S. L. Garfield & A. E. Bergin (Eds.), *Handbook of psychotherapy and behavior change: An empirical analysis* (2nd ed., pp. 769–815). New York: Wiley.

Bednar, R. L., & Kaul, T. J. (1994). Experiential group research: Can the canon fire? In S. L. Garfield & A. E. Bergin (Eds.), *Handbook of psychotherapy and behavior change: An empirical analysis* (4th ed., pp. 631–663). New York: Wiley.

Bergin, A. (1997). Neglect of the therapist and the human dimensions of change: A commentary. *Clinical Psychology: Science and Practice, 4,* 83–89.

Beutler, L. (1997). The psychotherapist as a neglected variable in psychotherapy: An illustration by reference to the role of therapist experience and training. *Clinical Psychology: Science and Practice, 4,* 44–52.

Blaauw, E. (1994). The therapeutic relationship: A study on the value of the Therapist–Client Rating Scale. *Behavioural and Cognitive Psychotherapy, 22,* 25–35.

Bloch, S., & Crouch, E. C. (1985). *Therapeutic factors in group psychotherapy.* Oxford, England: Oxford University Press.

Braaten, L. (1990). The different patterns of group climate critical incidents in high and low cohesion sessions of group psychotherapy. *International Journal of Group Psychotherapy, 40,* 477–493.

Braaten, L. (1991). Group cohesion: A new multidimensional model. *Group, 15,* 39–55.

Brusa, J. A., Stone, M., Beck, A., Dugo, J., & Peters, L. (1994). A sociometric test to identify emergent leader and member roles: Phase I. *International Journal of Group Psychotherapy, 44,* 79–100.

Budman, S., Soldz, S., Demby, A., Davis, M., & Merry, J. (1993). What is cohesiveness? An empirical examination. *Small Group Research, 24,* 199–216.

Burgoon, J. (1993). Nonverbal indices of arousal in group psychotherapy. *Psychotherapy, 30,* 635–645.

Burlingame, G. M., Fuhriman, A., & Anderson, E. (1995, August). *Group psychotherapy efficacy: A meta-analytic perspective.* Paper presented at the 103rd Annual Convention of the American Psychological Association, New York.

Burlingame, G. M., Kircher, J. C., & Taylor, S. (1994). Methodological considerations in group psychotherapy research: Past, present, and future practices. In A. Fuhriman & G. M. Burlingame (Eds.), *Handbook of group psychotherapy: An empirical and clinical synthesis* (pp. 41–80). New York: Wiley.

Catina, A., & Tschuschke, V. (1993). A summary of empirical data from the investigation of two psychoanalytic groups by means of repertory grid technique. *Group Analysis, 26,* 433–447.

Crouch, E. C., Bloch, S., & Wanlass, J. (1994). Therapeutic factors: Interpersonal and intrapersonal mechanisms. In A. Fuhriman & G. M. Burlingame (Eds.),

Handbook of group psychotherapy: An empirical and clinical synthesis (pp. 269–315). New York: Wiley.

Drescher, S., Burlingame, G., & Fuhriman, A. (1985). Cohesion: An odyssey in empirical understanding. *Small Group Behavior, 16,* 3–30.

Elliot, R., & Anderson, C. (1994). Simplicity and complexity in psychotherapy research. In R. L. Russell (Ed.), *Reassessing psychotherapy research* (pp. 65–113). New York: Guilford Press.

Ettin, M. (1992). *Foundations and applications of group psychotherapy: A sphere of influence.* Boston: Allyn & Bacon.

Flowers, J. (1991). Focusing on emotion in group therapy: What clients, what problems, and what for. *Psychological Reports, 69,* 369–370.

Flowers, J., & Booraem, C. (1990a). The effects of different types of interpretation on outcome in group psychotherapy. *Group, 14,* 81–88.

Flowers, J., & Booraem, C. (1990b). The frequency and effect on outcome of different types of interpretation in psychodynamic and cognitive–behavioural group psychotherapy. *International Journal of Group Psychotherapy, 40,* 203–214.

Foulkes, S. H. (1964). *Therapeutic group analysis.* London: Allen & Unwin.

Fuhriman, A., & Barlow, S. H. (1994). Interaction analysis: Instrumentation and issues. In A. Fuhriman & G. M. Burlingame (Eds.), *Handbook of group psychotherapy: An empirical and clinical synthesis* (pp. 191–222). New York: Wiley.

Fuhriman, A., & Burlingame, G. (1990). Consistency of matter: A comparative analysis of individual and group process variables. *Counseling Psychologist, 18,* 6–63.

Fuhriman, A., & Burlingame, G. (1994). Measuring small group process: A methodological application of chaos theory. *Small Group Research, 25,* 502–519.

Fuhriman, A., Drescher, S., & Burlingame, G. (1984). Conceptualizing small group process. *Small Group Behavior, 15,* 427–440.

Fuhriman, A., & Packard, T. (1986). Group process instruments: Therapeutic themes and issues. *International Journal of Group Psychotherapy, 36,* 399–425.

Garfield, S. (1990). Issues and methods in psychotherapy process research. *Journal of Consulting and Clinical Psychology, 58,* 273–280.

Garfield, S. (1997). The therapist as a neglected variable in psychotherapy research. *Clinical Psychology: Science and Practice, 4,* 40–43.

Gazda, G., & Mobley, J. (1994). Multidimensional scaling: High-tech sociometry for the 21st century. *Journal of Group Psychotherapy, Psychodrama & Sociometry, 47,* 77–96.

Getter, H., Litt, M., Kadden, R., & Cooney, N. (1992). Measuring treatment process in coping skills and interactional group therapies for alcoholism. *International Journal of Group Psychotherapy, 42,* 419–430.

Greenberg, L. S. (1986). Research strategies. In L. S. Greenberg & W. M. Pinsof (Eds.), *The psychotherapeutic process: A research handbook* (pp. 707–734). New York: Guilford Press.

Greenberg, L. S. (1994). The investigation of change: Its measurement and explanation. In R. L. Russell (Ed.), *Reassessing psychotherapy research* (pp. 114–143). New York: Guilford Press.

Greenberg, L., & Newman, F. (1996). An approach to psychotherapy change process research: Introduction to the special section. *Journal of Consulting and Clinical Psychology, 64,* 435–438.

Greene, L. R. (1990). Relationships among semantic differential change measures of splitting, self fragmentation and object relations in borderline psychopathology. *British Journal of Medical Psychology, 63,* 21–32.

Greene, L. R. (1993). Primitive defenses and the borderline patient's perceptions of the psychiatric treatment team. *Psychoanalytic Psychology, 10,* 533–549.

Hamblin, D., Beutler, L., Scogin, F., & Corbishley, A. (1993). Patient responsiveness to therapist values and outcome in group cognitive therapy. *Psychotherapy Research, 3,* 36–46.

Hartman, J. J., & Gibbard, G. S. (1974). Anxiety, boundary formation, and social change. In G. S. Gibbard, J. J. Hartman, & R. D. Mann (Eds.), *Analysis of groups* (pp. 154–176). San Francisco: Jossey-Bass.

Hill, C. (1990). Exploratory in-session process research in individual psychotherapy: A review. *Journal of Consulting and Clinical Psychology, 58,* 288–294.

Hines, P., Stockton, R., & Morran, K. (1995). Self-talk of group therapists. *Journal of Counseling Psychology, 42,* 242–248.

Isbell, S., Thorne, A., & Lawler, M. (1992). An exploratory study of videotapes of long-term group psychotherapy of outpatients with major and chronic mental illness. *Group, 16,* 101–111.

Isohanni, M., & Niemiren, P. (1992). Participation in group psychotherapy in a therapeutic community for acute patients. *Acta Psychiatrica Scandinavica, 86,* 495–501.

Kanas, N., Schoenfeld, F., Marmar, C., Weiss, D., & Koller, P. (1994). Process and content in a long-term PTSD therapy group for Vietnam veterans. *Group, 18,* 78–88.

Kanas, N., & Smith, A. (1990). Schizophrenic group process: A comparison and replication using the HIM–G. *Group, 14,* 246–252.

Kapur, R. (1993). Measuring the effects of group interpretations with the severely mentally ill. *Group Analysis, 26,* 411–432.

Karterud, S., & Foss, T. (1989). The group emotionality rating system: A modification of Thelen's method of assessing emotionality in groups. *Small Group Behavior, 20,* 131–150.

Kaul, T. J., & Bednar, R. L. (1986). Experiential group research: Results, questions, and suggestions. In S. L. Garfield & A. E. Bergin (Eds.), *Handbook of psychotherapy and behavior change: An empirical analysis* (3rd ed., pp. 671–714). New York: Wiley.

Kennard, D., Roberts, J., & Winter, D. (1990). What do group analysts say in their groups? Some results from an IGA/GAS questionnaire. *Group Analysis, 23,* 173–190.

Kivlighan, D., Mullison, D., Flohr, D., Proudman, S., & Francis, A. (1992). The interpersonal structure of "good" and "bad" group counseling sessions: A multiple-case study. *Psychotherapy, 29,* 500–508.

Kivlighan, D., & Quigley, S. (1991). Dimensions used by experienced and novice group therapists to conceptualize group process. *Journal of Counseling Psychology, 38,* 415–423.

Kolden, G. (1996). Change in early sessions of dynamic therapy: Universal processes and the generic model. *Journal of Counseling and Clinical Psychology, 64,* 489–496.

Lichtenberg, J., & Knox, P. (1991). Order out of chaos: A structural analysis of group therapy. *Journal of Counseling Psychology, 38,* 279–288.

Lieberman, M. A., Yalom, I. D., & Miles, M. B. (1973). *Encounter groups: First facts.* New York: Basic Books.

Lion, C., & Gruenfeld, L. (1993). The behavior and personality of work group and basic assumption group members. *Small Group Research, 24,* 236–257.

Luborsky, L., Barber, J., & Crits-Christoph, P. (1990). Theory based research for understanding the process of dynamic psychotherapy. *Journal of Consulting and Clinical Psychology, 58,* 281–287.

MacKenzie, K. R., & Tschuschke, V. (1993). Relatedness, group work, and outcome in long-term inpatient psychotherapy groups. *Journal of Psychotherapy Practice and Research, 2,* 147–156.

Marcus, D., & Holahan, W. (1994). Interpersonal perception in group therapy: A social relations analysis. *Journal of Consulting and Clinical Psychology, 62,* 776–782.

Marcus, D., & Kashy, D. (1995). The social relations model: A tool for group psychotherapy research. *Journal of Counseling Psychology, 42,* 383–389.

Marmar, C. (1990). Psychotherapy process research: Progress, dilemmas, and future directions. *Journal of Consulting and Clinical Psychology, 58,* 265–272.

McCallum, M., & Piper, W. (1990). The Psychological Mindedness Assessment Procedure. *Psychological Assessment, 2,* 412–418.

Nehls, N. (1992). Group therapy for people with borderline personality disorder: Interventions associated with positive outcomes. *Issues in Mental Health Nursing, 13,* 255–269.

Orlinsky, D., & Howard, K. (1987). A generic model of psychotherapy. *Journal of Integrative and Eclectic Psychotherapy, 6,* 6–27.

Orlinsky, D., & Russell, R. (1994). Tradition and change in psychotherapy research: Notes on the fourth generation. In R. L. Russell (Ed.), *Reassessing psychotherapy research* (pp. 185–214). New York: Guilford Press.

Page, R., Campbell, L., & Wilder, D. (1994). Role of the leader in therapy groups conducted with illicit drug abusers: How directive does the leader have to be? *Journal of Addictions and Offender Counseling, 14,* 57–66.

Piper, W. (1993). Group psychotherapy research. In H. Kaplan & B. Sadock (Eds.), *Comprehensive group psychotherapy* (3rd ed., pp. 673–682). Baltimore: Williams & Wilkins.

Piper, W., Joyce, A., Rosie, J., & Azim, H. (1994). Psychological mindedness, work, and outcome in day treatment. *International Journal of Group Psychotherapy, 44,* 291–312.

Powdermaker, F. B., & Frank, J. D. (1953). *Group psychotherapy: Studies in methodology of research and therapy.* Cambridge, MA: Harvard University Press.

Robison, F., Stockton, R., & Morran, D. (1990). Anticipated consequences of self-disclosure during early therapeutic group development. *Journal of Group Psychotherapy, Psychodrama and Sociometry, 43,* 3–18.

Satterfield, J. (1994). Integrating group dynamics and cognitive–behavioral groups: A hybrid model. *Clinical Psychology: Science and Practice, 1,* 185–196.

Schectman, Z., Vurembrand, N., & Malajak, N. (1993). Development of self-disclosure in a counseling and therapy group for children. *Journal of Specialists in Group Work, 18,* 189–199.

Seligman, M. (1995). The effectiveness of psychotherapy: The *Consumer Reports* Study. *American Psychologist, 50,* 965–974.

Sexton, H. (1993). Exploring a psychotherapeutic change sequence: Relating process to intersessional and posttreatment outcome. *Journal of Consulting and Clinical Psychology, 61,* 128–136.

Shoham-Salomon, V. (1990). Interrelating research processes of process research. *Journal of Consulting and Clinical Psychology, 58,* 295–303.

Slavin, R. (1993). The significance of here-and-now disclosure in promoting cohesion in group psychotherapy. *Group, 17,* 143–150.

Smith, M. L., Glass, G. V., & Miller, T. I. (1980). *The benefits of psychotherapy.* Baltimore: Johns Hopkins University Press.

Soldz, S., Budman, S., Davis, M., & Demby, A. (1993). Beyond the interpersonal circumplex in group psychotherapy: The structure and relationship to outcome of the Individual Group Member Interpersonal Process Scale. *Journal of Clinical Psychology, 49,* 551–563.

Soldz, S., Budman, S., & Demby, A. (1992). The relationship between main actor behaviors and treatment outcome in group psychotherapy. *Psychotherapy Research, 2,* 52–62.

Speer, D. C., & Newman, F. L. (1996). Mental health services outcome evaluation. *Clinical Psychology: Science and Practice, 3,* 105–129.

Stiles, W., Shapiro, D., & Harper, H. (1994). Finding the way from process to outcome: Blind alleys and unmarked trails. In R. L. Russell (Ed.), *Reassessing psychotherapy research* (pp. 36–64). New York: Guilford Press.

Stinchfield, R., & Burlingame, G. (1991). Development and use of the directives rating system in group therapy. *Journal of Counseling Psychology, 38,* 251–257.

Stockton, R., Rohde, R., & Haughey, J. (1992). The effects of structured group exercises on cohesion, engagement, avoidance, and conflict. *Small Group Research, 23,* 155–168.

Tschuschke, V., & Dies, R. (1994). Intensive analysis of therapeutic factors and outcome in long-term inpatient groups. *International Journal of Group Psychotherapy, 44,* 185–208.

Tschuschke, V., Hettinger, R., Enke, H., & Lolas, F. (1990). Verbal affective expression during group and individual psychotherapy: Towards a description of therapist- and setting-related variables. *Psychotherapy and Psychosomatics, 54*, 44–49.

Tschuschke, V., MacKenzie, K. R., Haaser, B., & Janke, G. (1996). Self-disclosure, feedback, and outcome in long-term inpatient psychotherapy groups. *Journal of Psychotherapy Practice and Research, 5*, 35–44.

Voigt, H., & Weininger, R. (1992). Intervention style and client progress in time-limited group psychotherapy for adults sexually abused as children. *Psychotherapy, 29*, 580–585.

Wheeler, J., & Kivlighan, D. (1995). Things unsaid in group counseling: An empirical taxonomy. *Journal of Counseling and Development, 73*, 586–591.

Winter, D. (1992). Repertory grid technique as a group psychotherapy research instrument. *Group Analysis, 25*, 449–462.

Yalom, I. (1985). *Theory and practice of group psychotherapy* (3rd ed.). New York: Basic Books.

3

INTERACTION PROCESS ANALYSIS IN TASK-PERFORMING GROUPS

JANICE R. KELLY

Research on group process analysis, as a method for systematically observing group interaction, reached its peak of popularity in social psychology in the 1950s with Bales's development of the Interaction Process Analysis (IPA) system (Bales, 1950, 1953; Bales & Slater, 1955). However, by the 1970s, research on interaction process as it applies to the functioning of task-performing groups, and research on small groups in general, was on the decline. Although research on group interaction process has not yet regained its popularity, there is evidence that research on small groups in general is increasing (Moreland, Hogg, & Haines, 1994). Furthermore, process-oriented research can be found in applied fields that are related to social psychology, such as communications and industrial/organizational psychology.

Several factors have contributed to the decline in interaction process research. First, interaction process research proceeded independently from other more outcome-oriented research on groups. That is, group process researchers were interested in the flow of communication within groups as an end in itself, whereas other group researchers were interested in conditions that affected the quality and quantity of group output. Although

49

several researchers proposed that an input–process–output model of group behavior was potentially the most productive way of conceptualizing groups (Hackman & Morris, 1975; McGrath, 1964), most researchers failed to explore the process–output relationship. This different emphasis and lack of connection between the bodies of research contributed to an overall reduction in attention paid to the social psychology of groups in general.

Second, and partly in response to the lack of attention given to group outcomes, some researchers began to develop idiosyncratic observation systems to fit a particular empirical need. The lack of systematic connection between these different observation systems resulted in a failure to develop strong theoretical underpinnings for predicting process–performance relationships. The difficulty in comparing across different systems was pointed out by Trujillo (1987), who identified six dimensions on which interaction analysis systems may vary: (a) a philosophical perspective with respect to the meaning of the categories; (b) types and numbers of theoretical and operational categories proposed by the systems; (c) the degree of observer inference entailed; (d) aspects of methodological design, such as mutual exclusivity and exhaustiveness of categories contained in the system; (e) the unit of analysis for both observation and aggregation purposes; and (f) the type of recording device. Such differences make it extremely difficult to draw strong conclusions across studies using different systems.

Finally, interaction process analysis is difficult. It is extremely time and labor intensive. Some systems can involve high setup costs as well. The pressure on researchers to "publish or perish" prohibits many from investing in such high-cost research. It has been suggested, however, that improvements in the quality and availability of technology related to observational systems may increase interest in this area.

Despite these limitations, some interest in and research on interaction analysis in task-performing groups has continued. In this chapter I review a number of systems currently in use in social psychology and fields that conduct research related to task-performing groups. The review is organized according to a framework proposed by Futoran, Kelly, and McGrath (1989), who identified three approaches to interaction process analysis in the literature: process focused, setting focused, and activity focused. *Process-focused systems* are perhaps the most well-known and code the process meaning, rather than the literal content, of verbal utterances. *Setting-focused systems* may use either process or content coding, but they are distinguished by having an application only to a specific group-task situation. Finally, *activity-focused systems* code only for the presence or absence of activity. In this chapter I examine some of the historical and current research that is being conducted within each of these three approaches and discuss their advantages and disadvantages. I also concentrate on systems as they have been applied to group-task performance.

A PROCESS-FOCUSED APPROACH

As stated earlier, process-focused systems, and especially the IPA system (Bales, 1950, 1970), are perhaps the best known of group observation systems. Process-focused systems are distinguished by attempts to categorize verbal utterances in terms of their process meaning for the interaction (e.g., a compliment would be coded more abstractly as a "positive socioemotional" act) rather than in terms of literal content. The avoidance of literal content makes these systems flexible over many types of groups and many types of tasks, except when such group or task features vary too greatly from the theoretical categories proposed by the system. However, it is sometimes difficult to test hypotheses that differ from the theoretical underpinnings of the system. Finally, exploration of the input–process–output relationship is difficult to do with these systems because it is rare that the process meanings of the categories fall in line with the requirements for an effective task outcome (Hackman & Morris, 1975). For example, Littlepage, Schmidt, Whisler, and Frost (1995) found that the quality of group performance was related to, among other things, the degree to which group members were able to recognize experts within their group. It would be difficult to argue that a process category, such as active task behavior or positive socioemotional behavior, would have a direct relationship to recognition of expertise.

The IPA System

The process-focused approach is perhaps most strongly identified with the pioneering research of Bales and associates (Bales, 1950, 1953, 1970). The IPA system provided a systematic framework for making observations important to Bales's theoretical ideas on group problem solving. Bales's equilibrium hypothesis proposed that task-oriented activity necessarily created interpersonal tension, which must then be reduced for work on the task to progress. Thus, process acts in these problem-solving groups were observed to alternate between task-oriented and expressive activity. Bales also proposed that as a group moves from the beginning to the completion of a task, the group moves through a particular sequence of problem solving phases: (a) orientation (i.e., gathering information and clarifying the task); (b) evaluation (i.e., assessing that information); and (c) control (i.e., deciding what to do). A corresponding set of expressive phases were also identified: (a) decisions (i.e., statements of agreement and disagreement); (b) tension management (i.e., expressions of tension buildup and release); and (c) group identification (i.e., statements of solidarity or antagonism). Specific categories were developed to chart those phases. The result was a

12-category system that could be collapsed across categories to examine particular theoretical principles about groups.

The actual implementation of the IPA system shares many characteristics with other process-focused systems. Coders classify each act into 1 of 12 categories (e.g., gives suggestion, shows tension release). The system defines an *act* as the smallest segment of behavior that is meaningful in terms of the categories of the system. This is usually a sentence, but it can also be a single unit such as a laugh or a distinct portion of a sentence. The categories are presumed to be mutually exclusive and exhaustive (i.e., no act will fall into more than one category and every act will fall into one category). The coder is required to code the act in terms of what impact the act would have on the group (e.g., an "opinion" might have the impact of a "disagreement" on the group, so it would be coded as a disagreement). Finally, it is possible, but difficult, to code a group "on-line" as the interaction occurs. More typically, the interaction is taped and transcribed to written form, or is videotaped.

Role Differentiation and Leadership Behavior

Bales was interested in process itself, especially in how it related to group structure and the differentiation of various roles within the group. In his observations of initially leaderless groups, Bales concluded that two distinct roles, task and social leader, emerged during group interaction (Bales & Slater, 1955; Slater, 1955). These leadership roles are defined by their associations with particular classes of behavior. That is, task leaders are oriented primarily to task achievement and engage in behaviors such as directing, summarizing, and providing ideas to other group members. Because of the tension produced by these task behaviors, the socioemotional leader emerges. In a second leadership role, the socioemotional leader helps reduce this tension and hostility and is therefore oriented primarily to the expressive, interpersonal affairs of the group. He or she engages in behaviors such as alleviating frustrations, resolving tensions, and mediating conflicts.

Other researchers have associated the task leader with behaviors that are specifically directed at the procedural functioning of the group (Hirokawa, 1980; Putnam, 1982; J. T. Wood, 1977). Here the task leader engages in behaviors that inform the group about how to do the task, such as proposing group strategies, controlling the use of time, and encouraging member participation. This procedural role is distinct from an "analytical" role (J. T. Wood, 1977), which involves behaviors such as giving opinions and clarifying ideas. Research suggests that the analytical role is less likely to correspond to the task leader but is instead associated with influence within the group (Ketrow, 1991).

Other Applications

Bales also attempted to generalize the task versus social leader structure to women and men, with women adopting the social role and men adopting the task role (Bales, 1953; Parsons, 1955; Parsons & Bales, 1955; Zelditch, 1955). Although support for this role specialization in families is weak (Leik, 1963), the gender-typed distinction has been found consistently in the interaction patterns of laboratory task groups (Aries, 1976; Strodtbeck & Mann, 1956). Meta-analyses by Carli (1982) and Anderson and Blanchard (1982) showed that women in group settings engaged in relatively more positive socioemotional activity than men and that men in group settings engaged in relatively more active task activity than women. This differential emphasis by women and men on these two functions of the interacting group contributes to the recurring theme in this line of research that women are the "socioemotional specialists" and men are the "task specialists." However, many researchers have noted objections to this implied orthogonality of task and socioemotional dimensions (W. Wood & Rhodes, 1992).

Other researchers have used process-focused systems to explore aspects of the input–process or the process–outcome relationship. For example, Morris (1966) used a 16-category system that focused exclusively on task-oriented acts to explore the effects of different types of tasks on group interaction. Katzell, Miller, Rotter, and Venet (1970) used the IPA system to examine the relationship between leader directiveness and member compatibility on solution effectiveness. Kelly and McGrath (1985) used an adaptation of Bales's IPA system to explore the relationships among time limits and task types, interaction process, and solution quality. Unfortunately, many of the attempts to relate process variables to outcome variables in meaningful ways have not been successful (Hackman & Morris, 1975).

Newer Process-Focused Systems

The IPA system and its various adaptations dominated the research on interaction process analysis in the 1950s and 1960s (Bales & Slater, 1955; Bales & Strodtbeck, 1951; Borgatta, 1962; Landesberger, 1955; Morris, 1966). Bales's revision of the IPA system in 1970 stimulated some additional research (Butler & Jaffee, 1974; Hare, 1978; Norton, 1976), including some applications to medical settings (Advani, 1973). However, the same features that led to the success of the system (e.g., the system is generic, it uses contentless and mutually exclusive categories, and it has a group perspective) were also its limitations (McGrath, 1984). Although its focus on the process meaning of the interaction made the system applicable to a wide range of types of groups engaged in a wide range of activities, that same focus made the data difficult to tie to indexes of the group's performance, such as the quality of the solution.

Some researchers have suggested that a system that codes the literal content of utterances may have a more direct relationship to outcomes variables (Futoran et al., 1989; Hackman & Morris, 1975). One system, designed by Futoran et al., attempts to combine the important aspects of a process-focused system with the ability to code literal content. This system, called TEMPO (Time by Event by Member Patterned Observation), codes verbal utterances into a series of hierarchically arranged process categories such as "proposing content" or "evaluating process (i.e., solution strategies)," processes found to be important in McGrath's (1991) theory of group process. The system also allows coders to identify specific types of acts (e.g., propose new content) for further coding of the literal content of those acts. Karau and Kelly (1992) used this technique to explore the relationship between the quality of solution of proposals produced during a problem-solving group's interaction and the overall quality of the group's final solution. The use of such content coding may improve the understanding of how interaction variables relate to group outcome.

Bales also offered a more recent interaction coding system designed to match theoretically and empirically identified dimensions of social interaction. Bales, Cohen, and Williamson's (1979) System for the Multiple Level Observation of Groups (SYMLOG) allows for the quantification and graphical representation of observation data. SYMLOG proposes a three-dimensional conceptual space comprised of Dominant (U) versus Submissive (D), Friendly (P) versus Unfriendly (N), and Task-Oriented (F) versus Emotional (B) dimensions. Definitions are provided for each of 26 different singly named (e.g., U), doubly named (e.g., UP), or triply named (e.g., UPF) items, but these 26 categories are reorganized into the original three dimensions. SYMLOG can be used for act-by-act coding of verbal content, although this application is rare. More generally, researchers use the Adjective Checklist. The Checklist is a standardized set of 26 scale items corresponding to the 26 categories just described. Untrained coders or members of some interacting group can retrospectively rate, on 3-point scales, each group member on each of the 26 scale items. The scores are then tallied and arranged to produce a location for each coder's perception of each group member in the three-dimensional space, thereby producing a graphical representation of interpersonal relations and group dynamics.

Researchers have offered critiques and revisions of SYMLOG (Hare, 1985; Polley, 1987, 1991; Wish, Deutsch, & Kaplan, 1976). Many of these critiques focus on the task versus emotion dimension and are similar in kind to critiques of the Bales IPA system. Polley (1987), for example, derived a third dimension of conventional versus unconventional behavior. He argued that the emotional dimension is subsumed by the friendly–unfriendly dimension and thus avoids the disputed task-oriented versus emotional dichotomy. Polley, Hare, and Stone (1988) also developed a practitioner's handbook with examples of applications of SYMLOG to management, educational, and therapy settings. Although more heavily used in Europe than in the United States, this manual may be a useful tool for stimulating further research.

THE SETTING-FOCUSED APPROACH

Setting-focused systems are designed for a specific group-task-setting situation. Examples include a system designed to study interaction among the cockpit crew of an aircraft (Foushee, 1984) and a system designed to code the deliberation of a mock jury (Kaplan & Miller, 1987). Many of these systems involve some sort of process coding, but they may also involve the coding of specific content. For example, Kaplan and Miller were interested in the general categories of "informational influence" and "normative influence" as forms of social influence within groups, but they also coded the specific testimony recalled by their deliberating juries as instances of forms of influence. These setting-focused systems are valuable for analyzing interaction in specific groups in specific situations, but they cannot be used with any other type of group or even with the same group in any other performance context because categories are often idiosyncratically defined.

Examples

Hirokawa (1980, 1988) developed a coding system called the Function-Oriented Interaction Coding System that examined the relationship between group discussion and decision quality in decision-making groups. The system is based on Hirokawa's functional theory of decision-making groups, which posits that specific decision-making functions, such as the assessment of the requirements for an acceptable choice and assessment of positive qualities of alternative choices, must be satisfied for groups to make quality decisions. Therefore, verbal units are coded into subcategories within each of the four decision functions. Although the specific content of the discussion is not examined, Hirokawa discovered strong relationships between the amount of group discussion spent on these decision functions and the quality of the group decision. Note, however, that this system is not applicable to any type of group task other than decision making.

Foushee, Lauber, Baetge, and Acomb (1986) developed a system for coding statements made by airplane cockpit crew members and air traffic controllers during flight. Their 18-category system contained both process-oriented categories (e.g., tension release, task-oriented agreements) and specific content categories (e.g., preflight checklist). In one application of the system, Kanki and Foushee (1989) examined the effect of recent flight experience on communication and flight performance for crews in a flight simulator. Crews who had flown together recently used more total communication, whereas crews who had not engaged in more nontask and tension-release statements. Furthermore, crews who had not flown together recently made more errors and more serious errors.

As another example, Kaplan and Miller (1987) developed a multi-level system for coding the content of mock jury deliberations. Participants read a case in which a verdict had been reached in favor of the plaintiff. They were then divided into groups to deliberate on a damage award for the plaintiff. These group interactions were coded into content specific categories, such as "testimony" and "verdict preferences" as well as other more general categories. Statements in these categories were later aggregated into two hierarchical categories representing normative and informational influence attempts. Input variables, such as the type of question (i.e., intellective or judgmental) being deliberated and the decision rule (i.e., unanimity or majority) imposed on the mock deliberations, were found to affect the amount of communication within these two categories, although specific process–outcome relationships were not examined.

Other interaction systems have been designed to test specific hypotheses about the relation of a group process feature to specific input characteristics (e.g., instructions, group composition, etc.). For example, Liang, Moreland, and Argote (1995) provided group members with previous group or individual experience working on a task. They then had trained coders identify instances of memory differentiation (i.e., the tendency for group members to specialize in remembering particular categories of information), a phenomenon that is thought to increase with group experience, from a videotape of a subsequent group interaction. For systems like these, the categories are often specific to the particular experimental conditions and to the particular levels of the conditions that are being studied. These, too, are useful for their specific purposes, but they cannot be applied to other groups or in other contexts.

Conclusions

Setting-focused systems tend to be more successful than other approaches at identifying relationships between process and performance, presumably because interaction categories can be identified that have direct relationships to important solution qualities. However, the extensive use of these systems has furthered the lack of integration of knowledge about group process. The use of unique systems in different settings prevents the accumulation of knowledge centering around particular independent or dependent variables.

THE ACTIVITY-FOCUSED APPROACH

Activity-focused research concentrates on the single dimension of vocalization and silence. These systems do not take into account the literal content of a vocalization but merely record content-free features of the vocalizations such as tone of voice, turn taking, interruptions, and so forth. Many of these systems are particularly sensitive to the temporal patterning of activity over time. The obvious benefits of such systems are the ease and reliability with which such observations can be made and the flexibility of the system in terms of applicability to many group-task-setting situations. An obvious drawback is the sometimes lack of conceptual clarity of the meaning of sound–silence patterns. However, there has been a resurgence of interest in activity-focused interaction analysis stemming from the advancement of technological support.

Examples

Much of this approach is based on the pioneering work of Chapple (1942, 1970). Chapple's observation system, the Interaction Chronograph, recorded the frequency and duration of interactants' "actions" and "inactions." Chapple believed that the timing and sequencing of acts of individuals in interaction could be an objective way of measuring personality. Matarazzo and Wiens (1972), using a human recorder, felt that the patterns of sound and silence would reveal the interactants' motivational, emotional, and attitudinal states.

Jaffe and Feldstein (1970), using the Automatic Vocal Transaction Analyzer (Cassotta, Jaffe, Feldstein, & Moses, 1964), examined patterns of sound and silence in monologues and dialogues. In this system, microphones attached to interacting group members are connected to a computer. The computer scans the microphones continuously and can digitize the on–off states of each person's vocalization. The research demonstrated how these patterns can be aggregated and defined in terms of psychologically meaningful parameters, such as turns and switching pauses. In particular, five parameters were defined (i.e., speaker switches, vocalizations, pauses, switching pauses, and simultaneous speech) with which interaction patterns could be defined.

Dabbs and colleagues (Dabbs & Ruback, 1987; Dabbs, Ruback, & Evans, 1987; Ruback, Dabbs, & Hopper, 1984) have in turn related some of these vocal parameters to the content of the group interaction and to outcomes in group task performance. For example, Ruback et al. related indexes of vocalizations, switching pauses, and interruptive simultaneous speech to outcome measures of group members' likability, leadership, and generation of ideas during a brainstorming interaction. They found that ratings of both leadership and likability were significantly related to amount of talking time and longer pauses before turn changes in the discussion. Leadership was also related to longer pauses before relinquishing one's conversational turn. Furthermore, the generation of ideas tended to follow periods of silence rather than periods of talk, but it was also strongly correlated with the sheer amount of talk.

Applications to Leadership and Other Psychological Variables

Numerous researchers have found a direct relationship between the perceptions of emergent leadership and the simple rate of participation or total talking time (Stein & Heller, 1979, 1983; Stogdill, 1974). As early as 1946, Chapple and Donald, using Chapple's interaction chronograph, demonstrated that participation rate was an element of leadership. Chapple and Donald measured the duration of talking and time between periods of talk on a continuously moving tape. They found that supervisors differed significantly from individuals in nonsupervisory positions on indexes such as activity rate, quickness of response, and speed of response when interrupted.

Other researchers have included "time-talking" measures as well as other, more elaborate measures of group interaction. For example, Kirscht, Lodahl, and Haire (1959) measured both the amount of time each participant in a three-person group spent talking and also scored their comments with a classification system similar to Bales'. Not only did the "time-talked" index significantly differentiate leaders from nonleaders, but this simple index also produced a slightly stronger correlation than did the more detailed coding of comments with an additional, discrete measure of leadership. Ruback et al. (1984) also found that simple talking time was highly related to perceptions of leadership and was more strongly related than other types of vocal parameters.

Some researchers have identified regular patterns for individuals in cycles of vocalization while in conversation (Cobb, 1973; Warner, 1979). Others have examined how these individual conversational patterns mesh when individuals are in interaction with one another. For example, Hayes and Cobb (1979) found that cohabitating couples had periods of high and low vocalization that were synchronized with one another, such that peak periods of vocal activity occurred at approximately the same times.

Warner (1984, 1988) argued that there are a host of interaction tempos that researchers can identify in daily life. For example, interaction partners must somehow adjust their own individual conversational rhythms to those of their partners. Warner argued that the degree to which individuals are able to coordinate such rhythms could be related to psychologically meaningful variables such as interpersonal attraction and dominance. Tickle-Degnen and Rosenthal (1987) in fact argued that interactional synchrony, including smooth and efficient turn taking among speakers and listeners, is an indication of a high degree of positive group rapport.

Conclusions

Although perhaps more limited in terms of substantive meaning, these general types of systems can inform group researchers about interaction parameters such as the amount and distribution of interactions or the sequencing of interactions among group members. In addition, these systems, being content free, are widely applicable. However, also because of the lack of content, these systems are difficult to relate to task performance variables.

CONCLUSIONS AND FUTURE DIRECTIONS

In this chapter I have reviewed some of the approaches to group process analysis that have been applied to group task performance. The research is drawn from a number of different fields, including social psychology, sociology, speech communication, and business. The three approaches presented each have particular strengths and weaknesses that make them more or less appropriate for the study of particular group phenomena. These strengths and weaknesses are summarized next.

Summary of Approaches

Both process-focused and activity-focused approaches, being content free, are widely applicable across a variety of groups and tasks. Many of the process-focused systems, however, were developed to test particular theories of group process. Although these systems may be useful for garnering support for their respective theories, they are less useful for testing novel hypotheses. Furthermore, it has been difficult to relate them to group task performance. Activity-focused approaches, on the other hand, suffer from a lack of strong theoretical explanations for the various parameters proposed and thus are used in a more exploratory manner.

Setting-focused systems have been perhaps the most successful at identifying aspects of the interaction process that can be related to specific group outcomes. Setting-focused systems thus have had an important place in the study of group task performance. Unlike the above two approaches, however, they are group-task-setting specific. Categories are often idiosyncratically defined and may be identified by specific verbal content that is not applicable in other settings. Perhaps the overuse of such systems has contributed to the lack of theory on how interaction process variables relate to group performance.

New Directions

Interaction process analysis has been more of a fringe than a mainstream research focus in the study of task-performing groups. There is some reason to believe, however, that interest in approaches to measuring group process is increasing. Recent technological and conceptual developments have prompted researchers to reexamine the benefits of process analysis.

First, several technical and statistical advances, mostly in the form of computers, video recorders, and statistical packages, are solving some of the problems of interaction process analysis. For example, the use of video recorders has improved the accuracy and reliability with which category observations can be made. Furthermore, PCs easily handle the sometimes large set of data that interaction observation can generate. These advances may make interaction analysis a more feasible enterprise for many investigators.

Second, there has been a continuing frustration for many small-group researchers on identifying the ways in which various aspects of group composition or structure affect group performance. Many researchers believe that it is only by examining the entire input–process–outcome sequence of group interaction that a true understanding of group behavior is possible (Hackman, 1987; Hackman & Morris, 1975; McGrath, 1984). An increase in attention given to group process analysis may come as people pay more attention to the important mediating role of process for the input–outcome relationship.

Third, there are some new and interesting research questions, prompted by recent technological creations, that may be most directly investigated through some sort of analysis of communication flow. In particular, the new forms of electronically mediated communication, such as E-mail and the Internet, have given rise to questions of how communication changes as the interaction itself becomes technologically mediated (Hollingshead, McGrath, & O'Conner, 1993; Kiesler & Sproull, 1992). For example, Kiesler and Sproull, in comparing computer-mediated with face-to-face decision-making groups, found that computer mediation led to some more negative forms of interaction, such as "flaming" (i.e., rude and impulsive remarks and criticism). McGrath and Hollingshead (1993) proposed a model that suggests that different forms of mediation vary in the richness of interaction information that they transmit and that performance on particular types of tasks may vary as this richness becomes more or less necessary for successful performance on the task. In a partial test of the model, Strauss and McGrath (1994) found that the advantage of face-to-face over computer-mediated groups increased as the degree of interdependence required by different tasks increased. The increase in the use of these forms of technologically mediated interaction may serve as an impetus for further research on group process in task-performing groups.

In summary, the next decade may be a critical period in the advancement of process research on task-performing groups. However, for this research to significantly advance the state of knowledge about performing groups, researchers need to pay more attention to the commonalities among system. It is only with an eye toward a degree of standardization that a critical mass of information about group process will accumulate to inform researchers about group dynamics.

REFERENCES

Advani, M. (1973). Observing doctor–patient interaction in a small community general hospital. *Manas, 20,* 9–19.

Anderson, L. R., & Blanchard, P. N. (1982). Sex differences in task and social-emotional behavior. *Basic and Applied Social Psychology, 3,* 109–139.

Aries, E. (1976). Interaction patterns and themes of male, female, and mixed groups. *Small Group Behavior, 7,* 7–18.

Bales, R. F. (1950). *Interaction Process Analysis: A method for the study of small groups.* Cambridge, MA: Addison-Wesley.

Bales, R. F. (1953). The equilibrium problem in small groups. In T. Parsons, R. F. Bales, & E. A. Shils (Eds.), *Working papers in the theory of action* (pp. 111–161). New York: Holt, Rinehart & Winston.

Bales, R. F. (1970). *Personality and interpersonal behavior.* New York: Holt, Rinehart & Winston.

Bales, R. F., Cohen, S. P., & Williamson, S. A. (1979). *SYMLOG: A system for the multiple level observation of groups.* New York: Free Press.

Bales, R. F., & Slater, P. E. (1955). Role differentiation in small decision-making groups. In T. Parsons & R. F. Bales (Eds.), *Family, socialization, and interaction process* (pp. 259–306). Glencoe, IL: Free Press.

Bales, R. F., & Strodtbeck, F. L. (1951). Phases in group problem solving. *Journal of Abnormal and Social Psychology, 46,* 485–495.

Borgatta, E. F. (1962). A systematic study of interaction process scores, peer and self-assessments, personality and other variables. *Genetic Psychology Monographs, 65,* 219–291.

Butler, R. R., & Jaffee, C. L. (1974). Effects of incentive, feedback, and manner of presenting the feedback on leader behavior. *Journal of Applied Psychology, 59,* 332–336.

Carli, L. L. (1982). *Are women more social and men more task oriented? A meta-analytic review of sex differences in group interaction, reward allocation, coalition formation, and cooperation in the Prisoner's Dilemma Game.* Unpublished manuscript, University of Massachusetts at Amherst.

Cassotta, L., Jaffe, J., Feldstein, S., & Moses, R. (1964). *Operating manual: Automatic Vocal Transaction Analyzer (Research Bulletin No. 1).* New York: Alanson White Institute.

Chapple, E. D. (1942). The measurement of interpersonal behavior. *Transactions of the New York Academy of Science, 4,* 222–233.

Chapple, E. D. (1970). *Culture and biological man: Explorations in behavioral anthropology.* New York: Holt, Rinehart & Winston.

Chapple, E. D., & Donald, G., Jr. (1946). A method of evaluating supervisory personnel. *Harvard Business Review, 24,* 197–214.

Cobb, L. (1973). *Time series analysis of the periodicities of casual conversations.* Unpublished doctoral dissertation, Cornell University, Ithaca, NY.

Dabbs, J. M., & Ruback, R. B. (1987). Dimensions of group process: Amount and structure of vocal interaction. *Advances in Experimental Social Psychology, 20,* 123–169.

Dabbs, J. M., Ruback, R. B., & Evans, M. S. (1987). Grouptalk: Patterns of sound and silence in group conversation. In A. W. Siegman & S. Feldstein (Eds.), *Nonverbal behavior and communication* (2nd ed., pp. 501–521). Hillsdale, NJ: Erlbaum.

Foushee, H. C. (1984). Dyads and triads at 35,000 feet. *American Psychologist, 39,* 885–893.

Foushee, H. C., Lauber, J. K., Baetge, M. M., & Acomb, D. B. (1986). *Crew factors in flight operations: III. The operational significance of exposure to short-haul air transport operations* (NASA Technical Memorandum 88322). Moffet Field, CA: NASA Ames Research Center.

Futoran, G. C., Kelly, J. R., & McGrath, J. E. (1989). TEMPO: A time-based system for analysis of group interaction process. *Basic and Applied Social Psychology, 10,* 211–232.

Hackman, J. R. (1987). The design of work teams. In J. W. Lorsch (Ed.), *Handbook of organization behavior* (pp. 315–342). Englewood Cliffs, NJ: Prentice Hall.

Hackman, J. R., & Morris, C. J. (1975). Group tasks, group interaction process, and group performance effectiveness: A review and proposed integration. *Advances in Experimental Social Psychology, 8,* 45–99.

Hare, A. P. (1978). A comparison of Bales' IPA and Parsons' AGIL category systems. *Journal of Social Psychology, 105,* 309–310.

Hare, A. P. (1985). The significance of SYMLOG in the study of group dynamics. *International Journal of Small Group Research, 1,* 38–50.

Hayes, D. P., & Cobb, L. (1979). Ultradian biorhythms in social interaction. In A. W. Siegman & S. Feldstein (Eds.), *Of speech and time: Temporal speech rhythms in interpersonal contexts* (pp. 57–80). Hillsdale, NJ: Erlbaum.

Hirokawa, R. Y. (1980). A comparative analysis of communication patterns within effective and ineffective decision-making groups. *Communication Monographs, 47,* 312–321.

Hirokawa, R. Y. (1988). Group communication and decision-making performance: A continued test of the functional perspective. *Human Communication Research, 14,* 487–515.

Hollingshead, A. B., McGrath, J. E., & O'Conner, K. M. (1993). Group task performance and communication technology: A longitudinal study of computer-mediated versus face-to-face work groups. *Small Group Research, 24,* 307–333.

Jaffe, J., & Feldstein, S. (1970). *Rhythms of dialogue.* New York: Academic Press.

Kanki, B. G., & Foushee, H. C. (1989). Communication indices of crew coordination. *Aviation, Space, and Environmental Medicine, 60,* 402–410.

Kaplan, M. F., & Miller, C. E. (1987). Group decision making and normative versus informational influence: Effects of type of issue and assigned decision rule. *Journal of Personality and Social Psychology, 53,* 306–313.

Karau, S. J., & Kelly, J. R. (1992). The effects of time scarcity and time abundance on group performance quality and interaction process. *Journal of Experimental Social Psychology, 28,* 542–571.

Katzell, R. A., Miller, C. E., Rotter, N. G., & Venet, T. G. (1970). Effects of leadership and other inputs on group processes and outputs. *Journal of Social Psychology, 80,* 157–169.

Kelly, J. R., & McGrath, J. E. (1985). Effects of time limits and task types on task performance and interaction of group-person groups. *Journal of Personality and Social Psychology, 49,* 395–407.

Ketrow, S. M. (1991). Communication role specializations and perceptions of leadership. *Small Group Research, 22,* 492–514.

Kiesler, S., & Sproull, L. (1992). Group decision making and communication technology. *Organizational Behavior and Human Decision Processes, 52,* 96–123.

Kirscht, J. P., Lodahl, T. M., & Haire, M. (1959). Some factors in the selection of leaders by members of small groups. *Journal of Abnormal and Social Psychology, 58,* 406–408.

Landesberger, H. A. (1955). Interaction process analysis of the mediation of labor-management disputes. *Journal of Abnormal and Social Psychology, 51,* 552–558.

Leik, R. K. (1963). Instrumentality and emotionality in family interaction. *Sociometry, 26,* 131–145.

Liang, D. W., Moreland, R. L., & Argote, L. (1995). Group versus individual training and group performance: The mediating role of transactive memory. *Personality and Social Psychology Bulletin, 21,* 384–393.

Littlepage, G. E., Schmidt, G. W., Whisler, E. W., & Frost, A. G. (1995). An input–output analysis of influence and performance in problem-solving groups. *Journal of Personality and Social Psychology, 69,* 877–889.

Matarazzo, J. D., & Wiens, A. N. (1972). *The interview: Research on its anatomy and structure.* Chicago: Aldine-Atherton.

McGrath, J. E. (1964). *Social psychology: A brief introduction.* New York: Holt, Rinehart & Winston.

McGrath, J. E. (1984). *Groups: Interaction and performance.* Englewood Cliffs, NJ: Prentice Hall.

McGrath, J. E. (1991). Time, interaction, and performance (TIP): A theory of groups. *Small Group Research, 22*, 147–174.

McGrath, J. E., & Hollingshead, A. B. (1993). Putting the "group" back in group support systems: Some theoretical issues about dynamic processes in groups with technological enhancements. In L. M. Jessup & J. S. Valacich (Eds.), *Group support systems: New perspective* (pp. 78–96). New York: Macmillan.

Moreland, R. L., Hogg, M. A., & Haines, S. C. (1994). Back to the future: Social psychological research on groups. *Journal of Experimental Social Psychology, 30*, 527–555.

Morris, C. G. (1966). Task effects on group interaction. *Journal of Personality and Social Psychology, 5*, 545–554.

Norton, R. (1976). Manifestations of ambiguity tolerance through verbal behavior in small groups. *Speech Monographs, 43*, 35–43.

Parsons, T. (1955). The American family: Its relations to personality and to the social structure. In T. Parsons & R. F. Bales (Eds.), *Family, socialization, and interaction process* (pp. 3–33). Glencoe, IL: Free Press.

Parsons, T., & Bales, R. F. (1955). *Family, socialization, and interaction process.* Glencoe, IL: Free Press.

Polley, R. B. (1987). The dimensions of interpersonal behavior: A method for improving rating scales. *Social Psychology Quarterly, 50*, 72–82.

Polley, R. B. (1991). Group process as diagnostic: An introduction. *Small Group Research, 22*, 92–98.

Polley, R. B., Hare, A. P., & Stone, P. J. (1988). *The SYMLOG practitioner: Applications of small group research.* New York: Praeger.

Putnam, L. L. (1982). Procedural messages and small group work climates: A lag sequential analysis. In M. Burgoon (Ed.), *Communication yearbook 5* (pp. 331–350). New Brunswick, NJ: Transaction.

Ruback, R. B., Dabbs, J. M., & Hopper, C. H. (1984). The process of brainstorming: An analysis with individual and group vocal parameters. *Journal of Personality and Social Psychology, 47*, 558–567.

Slater, P. E. (1955). Role differentiation in small groups. *American Sociological Review, 20*, 300–310.

Stein, R. T., & Heller, T. (1979). An empirical analysis of the correlations between leadership status and participation rates reported in the literature. *Journal of Personality and Social Psychology, 37*, 1993–2002.

Stein, R. T., & Heller, T. (1983). The relationship of participation rates to leadership status: A meta-analysis. In H. H. Blumberg, A. P. Hare, V. Kent, & M. Davies (Eds.), *Small groups and social interaction* (Vol. 1, pp. 401–406). New York: Free Press.

Stogdill, R. M. (1974). *Handbook of leadership.* New York: Free Press.

Strauss, S. G., & McGrath, J. E. (1994). Does the medium matter? The interaction of task type and technology on group performance and member reactions. *Journal of Applied Psychology, 79*, 87–97.

Strodtbeck, F. L., & Mann, R. D. (1956). Sex role differentiation in jury deliberation. *Sociometry, 19,* 3–11.

Tickle-Degnen, L., & Rosenthal, R. (1987). Group rapport and nonverbal behavior. In C. Hendrick (Ed.), *Group processes and intergroup relations* (Vol. 9, pp. 113–136). Newbury Park, CA: Sage.

Trujillo, N. (1987). Toward a taxonomy of small group interaction-coding systems. *Small Group Behavior, 17,* 371–394.

Warner, R. M. (1979). Periodic rhythms in conversational speech. *Language and Speech, 22,* 381–396.

Warner, R. M. (1984). *Rhythm as an organizing principle in social interactions: Evidence of cycles in behavior and physiology.* Unpublished manuscript.

Warner, R. M. (1988). Rhythm in social interaction. In J. E. McGrath (Ed.), *The social psychology of time: New perspectives* (pp. 63–88). Newbury Park, CA: Sage.

Wish, M., Deutsch, M., & Kaplan, S. (1976). Perceived dimensions of interpersonal relations. *Journal of Personality and Social Psychology, 33,* 409–420.

Wood, J. T. (1977). Leading in purposive discussions: A study of adaptive behavior. *Communication Monographs, 44,* 152–165.

Wood, W., & Rhodes, N. (1992). Sex differences in interaction style in task groups. In C. L. Ridgeway (Ed.), *Gender, interaction, and inequality* (pp. 97–121). New York: Springer-Verlag.

Zelditch, M., Jr. (1955). Role differentiation in the nuclear family: A comparative study. In T. Parsons & R. F. Bales (Eds.), *Family, socialization, and interaction process* (pp. 307–352). Glencoe, IL: Free Press.

4

OBSERVATIONAL CODING OF FAMILY THERAPY PROCESSES: STATE OF THE ART

MYRNA L. FRIEDLANDER

Despite the growing popularity of family therapy, there have been many fewer investigations of family therapy processes[1] than group therapy processes. In a recent literature review (Friedlander, Wildman, Heatherington, & Skowron, 1994), only 36 process studies of conjoint couples and family therapy were located. To extend the knowledge base, family process investigators have been developing new coding systems and devising creative methods for obtaining meaningful clinical data. In this chapter, the most frequently used coding systems are reviewed,[2] followed by a synopsis of emerging directions in family therapy process research.

Although the widely acknowledged "father of family therapy," Ackerman (1958), applied psychoanalytic constructs to couples and families,

---

[1]"Family therapy" is a class of theoretical approaches to treatment and is not synonymous with conjoint treatment. For purposes of this chapter, I review only conjoint treatment research. Studies of family therapy with one client (e.g., Beyebach & Escudero Carranza, 1997) are not included.

[2]Only instruments used in at least two published family therapy studies since 1980 are included in this review. Furthermore, studies are included only if the coding system was used to identify in-session behavior. See Pinsof (1981) for a comprehensive review of the earlier literature.

few contemporary therapists approach families from an analytic perspective. In the 1970s, several approaches uniquely designed for conjoint therapy began appearing in the literature. By the 1980s, the leading approaches were structural–strategic (e.g., Haley, 1976; Minuchin, 1974), multigenerational (Bowen, 1978), systemic (Selvini Palazzoli, Boscolo, Cecchin, & Prata, 1980), behavioral (e.g., Jacobson, 1981; Patterson, 1971), and experiential (Satir, 1964; Whitaker & Keith, 1981). In recent years, solution-focused (de Shazer, 1988) and narrative or constructivist (e.g., Goolishian & Anderson, 1987; Sluzki, 1992; White & Epston, 1990) approaches seem to have had the greatest appeal among family therapists.

Apart from a few process studies comparing different therapeutic orientations, the most well-researched approaches are the behavioral and structural–strategic treatments for families and emotion-focused therapy for couples (Greenberg & Johnson, 1988). The objectives of family therapy researchers differ notably from those of the group researchers whose work is featured elsewhere in this book. The substantive and methodological differences reflect important clinical differences in group and family therapy, as illustrated by the following fictitious case.

Consider Suzanne, a chronically unemployed 27-year-old woman who recently attempted suicide. Seeking professional help for the first time, Suzanne meekly suggested that living with her parents was related to her emotional difficulties. Not only did Suzanne feel like a failure in relation to her peers, but she also worried that she had profoundly disappointed her mother. Her guilt was punctuated by rage about the many ways she felt her father had annihilated her sense of self. On reflection, Suzanne lays much of the blame for her problems at his doorstep.

After considering Suzanne's strengths and areas of difficulty, her therapist considered the options. She could recommend individual therapy to help Suzanne find her voice within the context of a safe, nurturing relationship. In group therapy, Suzanne would have the opportunity to experience herself positively with peers and learn to take from and give to others meaningfully. Family therapy was also a reasonable option because Suzanne was not able to leave home—literally or emotionally.

The choice of treatment in a case like this depends on the clinical setting and availability of services; the therapist's expertise and comfort with different modalities; and, of course, the client's motivation, expectations, and preferences. For purposes of this discussion, let's say that Suzanne was choosing between group and family therapy. The therapist believed that either format could provide Suzanne with the momentum she needed to begin making changes. Using family sessions to learn to interact differently with her parents might free Suzanne to become more independent. On the other hand, receiving support from other young adults in a group might encourage Suzanne to risk experimenting socially and otherwise.

Because both pathways had the potential to reduce Suzanne's depression, generally improve her well-being, and help her gain important life skills, choosing between them required considering differences in the process of treatment—what Suzanne would actually experience as a group or family therapy participant. Considering group therapy, Suzanne had concerns about how best to describe her problems, how receptive others would be to her, and whether she would be able to express herself effectively. In other words, the important group processes for her—at least initially—were risk, inclusion, acceptance, and feedback. In family therapy, however, the salient group processes have to do with power, control, and conflict. Considering family therapy, Suzanne anticipated a nasty argument with her father, feared being vulnerable and exposed, and worried that the therapist would not support her. Indeed, the real-life consequences for a bad experience in family therapy can be enormous.

The point is that, although families are groups, there are some important distinctions between group and family therapy that are reflected in the therapeutic process. Differences in the process are in turn reflected in different research objectives. Three distinctions are particularly noteworthy. First, because families are natural rather than artificial groups and family members have patterns of interaction that tend to be fairly rigid, studies of group development are not particularly meaningful. Rather, researchers have sought to discover how rigidity is reduced in family treatment because, theoretically, inflexibility maintains symptomatic behavior and prevents the optimal growth of individuals (e.g., Minuchin, 1974). Second, whereas the emotional life of a therapy group revolves around issues of inclusion and affiliation, the emotional life of a family is reflected in its patterns of interpersonal control. For this reason, rather than being concerned with group atmosphere and cohesiveness, family therapy researchers have tended to focus on dominance and submission, resistance and cooperation, and conflicts and coalitions. A third distinction has to do with the therapeutic relationship. Whereas group researchers have long been interested in effective leadership qualities, family process researchers have focused on the degree to which effective therapists relate differently to family members on the basis of their gender or family role (e.g., child, parent, spouse).

In the next sections I address two substantive questions that have guided the empirical efforts to date: What are the characteristics of effective family therapy? How are power and conflict handled in family sessions?

WHAT ARE THE CHARACTERISTICS OF EFFECTIVE FAMILY THERAPY?

In the early 1960s, marital and family therapy began as a psychological experiment. Gradually, theories began to inform the work of family therapists. Thus, it is not surprising that the earliest process studies had the modest goal of identifying what actually goes on in family therapy sessions (see Pinsof, 1981, for a review). In the past 20 years, researchers have sought to determine (a) which therapist behaviors and strategies are common to family therapy; (b) the degree to which therapist behaviors differ by theoretical approach; (c) if and how gender plays a role in family therapy transactions; and (d) how successful therapists and families behave in therapy.

To address these questions, researchers have used a variety of observational systems in which the speech act is the coding unit. The most frequently used coding systems are the Family Therapist Coding System (FTCS; Pinsof, 1979, 1981, 1986), the Therapeutic Interaction Coding System (TICS; Shields, Sprenkle, & Constantine, 1991), the Defensive and Supportive Communication Interaction Coding System (DSC; Alexander, 1973a, 1973b; Alexander, Barton, Schiavo, & Parsons, 1976; Waldron, Turner, Alexander, & Barton, 1993), and the Structural Analysis of Social Behavior (SASB; Benjamin, 1974; Benjamin, Foster, Roberto, & Estroff, 1986). A brief description of each instrument and of the salient research findings are presented below.

The Family Therapist Coding System

This complex measure of therapist behavior, evolved from a 19-category instrument, the Family Therapist Behavior Scale (Pinsof, 1979, 1986), to the FTCS (Pinsof, 1980, 1986), an observational system with nine categorical dimensions. Pinsof's aim in creating the FTCS was to provide a means of identifying clinically meaningful features of behavior that are unique to family therapists of all theoretical orientations. The nine dimensions include the following: topic, intervention, temporal orientation, interpersonal structure, system membership, route, to whom, grammatical form, and event relationship. Within each dimension are a number of categories. In the temporal orientation dimension, for example, the codes are present, past, future, now, and atemporal.

In developing and refining this system, Pinsof (1986) used five criteria: specificity, reconstructivity, universality, exhaustiveness, and novice–expert discrimination. The last criterion, novice–expert discrimination, was the basis for assessing not only the validity of the FTCS but also the characteristics of effective family therapists. In a study conducted at McMaster University, data were analyzed from family interviews conducted by eight trainees and their supervisors. After observing the trainee's session for 20 minutes from behind a one-way mirror, the supervisor conducted the remainder of the interview with the trainee present but silent. Using log-linear statistics to discriminate the frequencies of each FTCS code by interviewer status, Pinsof (1986) demonstrated many significant and clinically meaningful novice–expert differences. In particular, the supervisors intervened in a more interpersonal fashion than did the trainees (Interpersonal Structure scale), focusing on sequences of family behavior and patterns of relational communication. Their technical repertoire was greater as well; they used more explicit and here-and-now interventions (temporal orientation) and more open questions (grammatical form), and they were generally more process oriented and interpretative (intervention) than the trainees. Furthermore, the supervisors addressed the parents more often (to whom) and focused more on negative behavior (topic), on communication dynamics (intervention), and on events in time (event relationship).

In a pre- to postdesign examining changes in therapeutic skills from the beginning to the end of the first year of graduate training, Tucker and Pinsof (1984) used the FTCS to code family therapy interviews with a simulated family (professional actors). Results indicated increases in trainees' activity level and in their range of interventions, including a greater focus on negative emotion.

In two subsequent comparisons of expert therapists representing different theoretical approaches, Friedlander and colleagues (Friedlander, Ellis, Raymond, Siegel, & Milford, 1987; Friedlander, Highlen, & Lassiter, 1985) observed remarkable similarities across approaches—and across families—on several FTCS dimensions. In both studies, for example, the therapists tended to use indirectly routed interventions (e.g., "Why doesn't your mother trust you?") and focused on the parental subsystem. On the other hand, the FTCS differences that did emerge were consistent with differences in theoretical orientation. The psychodynamic and insight-oriented family therapists, for example, concentrated more on individuals, on the past, and on family-of-origin experiences than did the more experiential and strategic therapists. The experiential therapist used more self-disclosure and here-and-now messages, and the strategic therapist emphasized dyadic and triadic relations more so than did the other therapists.

The FTCS research was important because it clearly demonstrated that experienced family therapists, even those with different orientations, behave in similar ways and that an active, interpersonal focus is a significant characteristic of family therapy. On the other hand, the exclusive focus on therapist behavior ignores the systemic aspects of the treatment process that are, after all, the sine qua non of family therapy. A more systemic perspective requires studying reciprocity (i.e., behavior Y is viewed simultaneously as an antecedent to X and a consequent of Z). In the sections that follow, I describe interaction-based coding systems.

The Therapeutic Interaction Coding System

The recently developed TICS (Shields & McDaniel, 1992; Shields et al., 1991) was derived from other family therapy coding systems, including those of Pinsof (1980) and Ericson and Rogers (1973). Like the FTCS (Pinsof, 1980), the TICS is a complex system. Unlike the FTCS, however, the TICS has family codes (i.e., social information, problem information, solution/goal information, agreement, disagreement, structuring, support) and therapist codes (i.e., exploring, structuring, directing, agreement, disagreement, support, problem explanation, solution explanation, and self-disclosure), allowing reciprocity to be observed using conditional probabilities.

In two analyses of 63 initial interviews of structural–strategic therapy, the authors reported that therapist interventions, particularly executive behaviors, were predictive of outcome, defined as treatment continuance (Shields et al., 1991), and varied systematically by therapist gender (Shields & McDaniel, 1992). More important, perhaps, are the data about intragroup collaboration and conflict. Families who completed treatment had the most frequent occurrence of family interaction about problems, family member structuring toward the therapist, and therapist structuring in response to family disagreements and the least frequent occurrence of within-family disagreement (Shields et al., 1991). Male and female therapists responded differently to family member structuring and disagreement, and family members responded differently to male and female therapists (Shields & McDaniel, 1992). Specifically, male therapists, who were on the whole more active and directive, tended to engage in a competitive struggle with families. When the therapist was a woman, family members tended to disagree more among themselves.

The Defensive and Supportive Communication Interaction Coding System

Recognizing the importance of cooperation in family therapy, Alexander (cited in Waldron et al., 1993) developed the DSC to distinguish between supportive and defensive messages. The measure, based on family systems theories and Gibb's (1961) model of defensive communication, evolved from an ordinal rating of defensiveness and supportiveness (ranging from *never occurring* [1] to *almost always occurring* [4]; Alexander, 1973a; Alexander et al., 1976) to an observational coding system. In Newberry, Alexander, and Turner (1991), supportive, structuring, pejorative, and non–therapy-related speech acts were coded; in Waldron et al. (1993), there were four defensive (judgmental-dogmatism, control, indifference, and superiority) and four supportive (genuine information, spontaneous problem-solving, empathy, and equality) codes. The criterion validity of the instrument was supported by the reliability of experts who judged examples of each category in the coding manual (Newberry et al., 1991). Its construct validity was supported by the ability of the DSC to discriminate between normal and delinquent families and between parents and adolescents (Waldron et al., 1993).

In Alexander et al. (1976), 15-minute excerpts from the initial and next-to-last family sessions were rated. Because only family members' behaviors were observed, Alexander et al. sequential analyses could not be performed. Results indicated main effects for outcome and session and an Outcome × Session interaction, indicating that improved families used more supportive messages over time. This result is consistent with the notion that movement toward functional family behavior is reflected in increased support for individuals.

Newberry et al. (1991) observed reciprocity. Therapist–client interactions during the early stage of therapy were transcribed, and each thought unit was categorized as either supportive, structuring, pejorative, or non-therapy related. Results of a contingency analysis showed that male and female therapists responded differently to family members' supportive behaviors but not to their pejorative (i.e., defensive) behaviors. Family members behaved differently with male and female therapists. In particular, female therapists were responded to more supportively than male therapists, and fathers responded more favorably than did mothers to therapist structuring. Interestingly, no differences were observed in therapist behavior based on gender.

Using a modification of the Alexander et al. (1976) coding system, Cline, Mejia, Coles, Klein, and Cline (1984) conceptualized therapist interventions as either behavioral (i.e., directiveness, reflectiveness, relationship orientation, problem orientation, and affect and behavior integration) or global (i.e., relationship skills and structuring skills). The outcome (and maintenance) of therapy was compared for middle- and lower-income couples. Results indicated a number of differences based on gender and socioeconomic status (SES). Among middle-SES couples, for example, therapist directiveness was inversely related to outcome; the opposite pattern was observed among low-SES couples, at least from the wives' perspective.

Taken together, these research findings underscore the point that effective therapists need to consider individual differences and contextual factors and to be aware that, even if they do not respond in gender-typical ways, such behavior may be expected of them by family members. As Newberry et al. (1991) pointed out, female therapists may be "punished" by the family for using too many task-oriented and structuring behaviors.

The Structural Analysis of Social Behavior

Recognizing the importance of how positive and negative messages are expressed between family members, several researchers have used the SASB (Benjamin, 1974; Benjamin et al., 1986) to study therapist–family member interactions and the interaction patterns of couples who are successful in family therapy. The pantheoretical SASB model, described in detail in chapter 14 in this book, has been used far more extensively in research on individual psychotherapy than family therapy. However, focusing as it does on social behavior, the SASB has particular relevance for understanding the family system.

Based on a circumplex model of interpersonal behavior, the SASB is derived from the theoretical work of Murray (1938), Sullivan (1953), and Leary (1957). Its validity has been widely tested using factor analysis, dimensional ratings, and autocorrelation (Benjamin et al., 1986). The enduring clinical importance of this coding system is underscored by a special section in an issue (December 1996) of the *Journal of Consulting and Clinical Psychology*. In that issue, Ratti, Humphrey, and Lyons's (1996) work comparing family interactions with adolescents who were polydrug dependent, bulimic, or nonsymptomatic highlights the relevance of the SASB for understanding family systems.

In brief, the SASB model consists of three surfaces: focus on self, focus on other, and introjected focus on other. On each diamond-shaped surface are two axes representing affiliation and interdependence, and 36 behaviors at and between the four poles represent varying degrees of these dimensions. On the focus on other surface, for example, the code "annihilating attack" is the extreme of negative affiliation and contrasts with "tender sexuality," the positive extreme on that axis. Interpersonal transactions can be identified as complementary or noncomplementary depending on their circumplex positions on the focus surface and the affiliation and interdependence axes. Theoretically, complementary interactions are mutually rewarding, whereas noncomplementarity reflects stress in the interpersonal relationship.

To date, four family therapy studies have been conducted using the SASB. In Laird and Van de Kemp (1987), a case study of successful structural family therapy with Salvador Minuchin, family members' responses to the therapist and his behavior toward them were observed over time. Results supported the authors' predictions that greater complementarity would be observed in the early and late phases of treatment than in the middle phase and that noncomplementarity in the middle phase would be predictive of change in family members' behaviors.

In three studies of emotion-focused therapy (Greenberg, Ford, Alden, & Johnson, 1993; Johnson & Greenberg, 1988; Plysiuk, cited in Greenberg, Heatherington, & Friedlander, 1996), SASB codes for successful couples supported the theoretical tenets of emotion-focused therapy that (a) "soft-ening" (a shift from blaming toward affiliative, autonomous responding) distinguishes successful cases; (b) over time, successful couples engage in more supportive, affirming, and understanding interactions; and (c) best sessions (as rated by couples) and important change events (as rated by couples and therapists) are characterized by movement toward greater af-filiation, openness, and experiencing.

The SASB studies support the theoretical tenets of emotion-focused therapy, suggesting that effective therapists reduce blame by moving clients away from power tactics toward an experience of shared intimacy. To do this, therapists need to be comfortable with conflict and be aware of resis-tance and the dynamics of interpersonal control. These constructs were the focus of the investigations described in the next section.

HOW ARE POWER AND CONFLICT HANDLED IN FAMILY SESSIONS?

In the pragmatic view of human communication (Watzlawick, Beavin, & Jackson, 1967), people use language not only to deliver messages but also to develop and maintain social relationships. From this perspec-tive, a social relationship is defined less by the content of messages and more by how the messages are exchanged. Because family therapists often need to intervene in ways that support one individual or subgroup and challenge another, researchers have sought to identify sequences of thera-pist–client behavior that reduce defensiveness and resistance and increase cooperation. Additionally, because family members' relationships are re-vealed in communication patterns that reflect important structural prop-erties (e.g., hierarchy, alliances, subsystems) and interpersonal dynamics (e.g., resistance, conflict, disengagement), researchers have sought to iden-tify relational patterns of communication that occur naturally in family therapy sessions. The two coding systems that have most often been used to accomplish these goals are the Therapy Process Coding System (TPCS; Chamberlain et al., 1985; Patterson & Chamberlain, 1988) and the Family Relational Control Communication Coding System (FRCCCS; Friedlan-der & Heatherington, 1989; Heatherington & Friedlander, 1987).

The Therapy Process Coding System

Developed and refined at the Oregon Social Learning Center, the TPCS (Chamberlain et al., cited in Patterson & Chamberlain, 1988) has been used to observe resistance and cooperation in behaviorally oriented outcome research with antisocial children. Of particular interest is the "within-session struggle" (Patterson & Chamberlain, 1988, p. 193), an event that occurs when the therapist's attempt to teach parents specific social learning procedures is met by resistance or noncooperation. The TPCS, a revision of the Client Noncompliance Code and the Therapist Behavior Code (Patterson & Forgatch, 1985), includes nine categories of client messages (i.e., confront/challenge, hopeless/blame, defend self/other, sidetrack/own agenda, answer for, not answering, disqualify previous statement, interfamily conflict, and nonresistant) and eight categories of therapist messages (i.e., support, teach, question, structure, disagree, interpret/reframe, talk, and facilitate). The validity of the TPCS is supported by findings indicating significant relationships between within-session struggles, marital conflict, and children's aversive behavior (Patterson & Chamberlain, 1988).

Chamberlain, Patterson, Reid, Kavanagh, and Forgatch (1984) combined various categories of the Client Noncompliance Code to create two supercategories: resistance and cooperation. In a process–outcome study with 27 families, Chamberlain et al. found that resistance scores varied as a function of referral source and predicted treatment completion and outcome. Early resistance predicted mid- but not late-treatment resistance (Chamberlain et al., 1984). In a study of six families (Patterson & Forgatch, 1985), conditional probabilities were compared with base-rate frequencies. Results indicated that the therapist's use of teach and confront messages was significantly followed by maternal noncompliance, whereas less noncompliance was observed following therapist support and facilitate.

In a more recent and extensive study of parent training for child conduct problems, Stoolmiller, Duncan, Bank, and Patterson (1993) found, in a latent growth curve analysis, that mothers ($N = 68$) who were more resistant in therapy scored the highest on measures of inept discipline and antisocial behavior. Furthermore, the failure to "struggle and work through resistance" (Stoolmiller et al., 1993, p. 927) in therapy was significantly related to the mother's pretreatment depressed mood and to the number of child arrests in the 2 years after treatment.

In the TPCS studies, resistance, one form of interpersonal conflict between therapist and parent, was observed. The research described next was focused on other aspects of power and control, namely dominance and submission.

The Family Relational Control Communication Coding System

Drawing on Bateson's (1936/1958) work on schismogenesis in primitive societies, Mark (1971) and Sluzki and Beavin (1965/1977) proposed a method for observing dominance and submission in the exchange of verbal messages. Developing these concepts into an observational coding system, Rogers and colleagues (Ericson & Rogers, 1973; Rogers & Farace, 1975) conducted many studies of verbal interaction in dyads, particularly married couples (e.g., Escudero Carranza, Rogers, & Gutierrez, 1997; Rogers & Bagarozzi, 1983). Rogers's dyadic relational control system was first applied to therapist–client interaction in individual psychotherapy (e.g., Heatherington & Allen, 1984; Lichtenberg & Barke, 1981) and subsequently extended to the family therapy context (Friedlander & Heatherington, 1989; Heatherington & Friedlander, 1987).

In the FRCCCS (Heatherington & Friedlander, 1987), messages are coded on three dimensions: participants (speaker, direct and indirect targets), format (e.g., open and closed question, talk over, assertion), and response mode (e.g., topic shift, instruction, support). Next, control codes ($\uparrow$, $\downarrow$, $\rightarrow$) are assigned on the basis of the specific combination of format and response mode. An assertion topic shift, for example, is assigned a one-up ($\uparrow$) code, which represents an attempt to gain control, whereas an open question support is assigned a one-down ($\downarrow$) code, representing an attempt to relinquish control. Neutral control codes ($\rightarrow$) tend to be assertion extensions. Finally, reciprocal interactions (A speaks to B, who then responds to A) are identified in the stream of discourse. One-up messages followed by one-down messages (and vice versa; i.e., $\uparrow/\downarrow$ and $\downarrow/\uparrow$) are complementary, reflecting mutuality in the relationship, whereas $\uparrow/\uparrow$, $\downarrow/\downarrow$, and $\rightarrow/\rightarrow$ patterns are symmetrical. Competitive symmetry ($\uparrow/\uparrow$) occurs when one person's bid to take control is responded to by another's bid for control, as is the case when an order is not followed or when a topic shift is interrupted or disconfirmed.

In extending the original dyadic coding system to group contexts of three or more people, Heatherington and Friedlander (1987; Friedlander & Heatherington, 1989) took into account triadic situations, ones in which a person speaks directly to one person and indirectly to another. This can occur, for example, when A "intercepts" the dialogue of B and C, or when B avoids responding to A by turning instead to C, and so forth. A coalitionary move is identified when a speaker is simultaneously $\uparrow$ to one person and $\downarrow$ to another (Friedlander & Heatherington, 1989). Some gross motor movements can also be identified as $\uparrow$ and $\downarrow$ messages, such as head nods, shoulder shrugs, and so forth (Siegel, Friedlander, & Heatherington, 1992).

The validity of the verbal and nonverbal aspects of the FRCCCS was tested by asking experienced family therapists to rate the interpersonal control dynamics of messages in experimentally manipulated conversations (Gaul, Simon, Friedlander, Heatherington, & Cutler, 1991; Siegel et al., 1992). Results were generally supportive. The construct validity of the FRCCCS was further demonstrated in a comparative study of structural versus systemic family therapy (Friedlander, Heatherington, & Wildman, 1991). Whereas all of the therapists in the study, experts in each approach, tended to engage in predominantly complementary interactions with individual family members, theoretically predicted differences in the two approaches were reflected in the FRCCCS coding. Structural therapists, for example, engaged in significantly more competitive symmetry with family members, reflecting the authoritative role of the therapist and the unbalancing strategy of structural therapy. Systemic therapists, on the other hand, used significantly more complementarity and delivered more neutral, indirect messages, reflecting their emphasis on circular questioning and maintaining neutrality with all family members.

Other FRCCCS studies have also shown that therapists, in both couples and family sessions, tend to respond in complementary (therapist ↑/ client ↓) ways with family members (Heatherington & Friedlander, 1990b; Raymond, Friedlander, Heatherington, Ellis, & Sargent, 1993). In an unpublished study of the work of master therapists, Walsh (1993) found no gender-based differences in relational control. In case studies of structural family therapy (Heatherington & Friedlander, 1990a; Raymond et al., 1993), the therapists' patterns of interaction changed over time with the problem adolescents, and some evidence indicated clinically meaningful shifts in rigid control patterns between family members.

In large part, the FRCCCS research has supported the basic premise of family systems theory: that interpersonal power is reflected in the ways in which messages are delivered and responded to. Furthermore, FRCCCS findings are consistent with the major tenets of structural therapy: that the therapist needs to be in charge of the treatment process and that rigid interactional patterns need to be modified for growth to occur.

EMERGING DIRECTIONS

I return momentarily to the example of Suzanne. The available process research suggests that Suzanne's concerns about power, control, and conflict in family therapy were well founded. A positive experience would require her therapist to be active and dominant, to be aware of the potential for a "split" therapeutic alliance with family members (Heatherington & Friedlander, 1990c), to focus on interpersonal dynamics and patterns of communication, and to explore negative emotion in the family with the goal of moving family members toward greater openness, affiliation, and mutuality.

Unfortunately, these recommendations go only so far in informing family therapists how to proceed effectively. For this reason, many authors have called for the development of more contextually and systemically informed coding systems (Alexander, Newell, Robbins, & Turner, 1995; Heatherington, 1989; Pinsof, 1989) and the use of alternative methodologies to track the process of change (e.g., Greenberg et al., 1996; Heatherington & Friedlander, 1990a; Stoolmiller et al., 1993). In recent years researchers have been responsive to this call. Various new coding systems, such as Brown-Standridge and Piercy's (1988) Marital Therapy Interaction Scale, Robbins, Alexander, Newell, and Turner's (1996) therapist frames and reframes, Friedlander and Heatherington's (1998; Friedlander, Heatherington, & Marrs; in press) Cognitive Constructions Coding System, and a recent book on family therapy methodology (Sprenkle & Moon, 1996), exemplify their response.

One recommended approach—change event research—has the potential to elucidate the complex steps needed to modify rigid family systems (Greenberg et al., 1996; Heatherington & Friedlander, 1990a). As an example, the emotion-focused therapy studies by Greenberg and colleagues reviewed earlier provide guidelines for moving couples away from blame and toward intimacy. Other change process research, qualitative in nature, has identified sequences of interaction that can effectively shift family members' constructions of the presenting problem (Coulehan, Friedlander, & Heatherington, 1998), increase family engagement in problem solving (Friedlander, Heatherington, Johnson, & Skowron, 1994; Heatherington & Friedlander, 1990a), and break through interpersonal impasses between parents and adolescents (Diamond & Liddle, 1996).

The rich data produced by these investigations underscore the points made by Alexander et al. (1995)—that observation of the family therapy process in all its complexity requires coding at high as well as low levels of inference—and by Greenberg (1995)—that "moment-to-moment processes ... should be studied in the episodic context of the particular type of in-session problem in which they occur" (p. 367). The therapist interventions and family responses in blaming events, for example, are likely to differ greatly depending on the issue under discussion (e.g., consider children blaming their parents for abuse or neglect vs. for a too strict curfew) (Friedlander et al., in press).

Despite the thoughtful points made by reviewers and critics of the psychotherapy literature, clinicians delude themselves if they believe that they can observe all that is salient for clients in a therapy interview. This is particularly true for family treatment. Because families bring to their sessions a lifetime of interaction, emotionally charged memories, and idiosyncratic language with hidden meanings, the events that take place in a family interview can be powerful, and the effects of discussing family concerns with a therapist can be delayed and covert. For this reason, clinicians must recognize the limits of science in this area. Nonetheless, to advance knowledge clinicians must try to observe the changes that family members are able and willing to let clinicians see. Respectfully, clinicians can try to understand—and to help.

REFERENCES

Ackerman, N. (1958). *The psychodynamics of family life*. New York: Basic Books.

Alexander, J. F. (1973a). Defensive and supportive communications in normal and deviant families. *Journal of Consulting and Clinical Psychology, 40,* 223–231.

Alexander, J. F. (1973b). *Defensive and supportive communication interaction manual.* Unpublished manuscript, University of Utah, Salt Lake City.

Alexander, J. F., Barton, C., Schiavo, R. S., & Parsons, B. V. (1976). Systems-behavioral intervention with families of delinquents: Therapist characteristics, family behavior, and outcome. *Journal of Consulting and Clinical Psychology, 44,* 656–664.

Alexander, J. F., Newell, R. M., Robbins, M. S., & Turner, C. W. (1995). Observational coding in family therapy process research. *Journal of Family Psychology, 9,* 355–365.

Bateson, G. (1958). *Naven.* Stanford, CA: Stanford University Press. (Original work published 1936)

Benjamin, L. S. (1974). Structural Analysis of Social Behavior. *Psychological Review, 81,* 392–425.

Benjamin, L. S., Foster, S. W., Roberto, L. G., & Estroff, S. E. (1986). Breaking the family code: Analysis of videotapes of family interactions by Structural Analysis of Social Behavior (SASB). In L. S. Greenberg & W. M. Pinsof (Eds.), *The psychotherapeutic process: A research handbook* (pp. 391–438). New York: Guilford Press.

Beyebach, M., & Escudero Carranza, V. (1997). Therapeutic interaction and drop out: Measuring relational communication in solution-focused therapy. *Journal of Family Therapy, 19,* 173–212.

Bowen, M. B. (1978). *Family therapy in clinical practice.* Northvale, NJ: Jason Aronson.

Brown-Standridge, M. D., & Piercy, F. P. (1988). Reality creation versus reality confirmation: A process study in marital therapy. *American Journal of Family Therapy, 16,* 195–215.

Chamberlain, P., Davis, J. P., Forgatch, M. S., Frey, J., Patterson, G. R., Ray, J., Rothschild, A., & Trombley, J. (1985). The Therapy Process Code: A multidimensional system for observing therapist and client interactions (OSLC Tech. Rep. No. 1Rx). Eugene, OR: Oregon Social Learning Center.

Chamberlain, P., Patterson, G., Reid, J., Kavanagh, K., & Forgatch, M. (1984). Observation of client resistance. *Behavior Therapy, 15,* 144–155.

Cline, V. B., Mejia, J., Coles, J., Klein, N., & Cline, R. A. (1984). The relationship between therapist behaviors and outcome for middle- and lower-class couples in marital therapy. *Journal of Clinical Psychology, 40,* 691–704.

Coulehan, R., Friedlander, M. L., & Heatherington, L. (1998). Transforming narratives: A change event in constructivist family therapy. *Family Process, 37,* 465–481.

de Shazer, S. (1988). *Clues: Investigating solutions in brief therapy.* New York: Norton.

Diamond, G., & Liddle, H. A. (1996). Resolving a therapeutic impasse between parents and adolescents in multidimensional family therapy. *Journal of Consulting and Clinical Psychology, 64,* 481–488.

Ericson, P. M., & Rogers, L. E. (1973). New procedures for analyzing relational communication. *Family Process, 12*, 245–267.

Escudero Carranza, V., Rogers, E., & Gutierrez, E. (1997). Patterns of relational control and nonverbal affect in clinic and nonclinic couples. *Journal of Social and Personal Relationships, 14*, 7–29.

Friedlander, M. L., Ellis, M. V., Raymond, L., Siegel, S. M., & Milford, D. (1987). Convergence and divergence in the process of interviewing families. *Psychotherapy, 24*, 570–583.

Friedlander, M. L., & Heatherington, L. (1989). Analyzing relational control in family therapy interviews. *Journal of Counseling Psychology, 36*, 139–148.

Friedlander, M. L., & Heatherington, L. (1998). Assessing clients' constructions in family therapy discourse. *Journal of Marital and Family Therapy, 24*, 289–303.

Friedlander, M. L., Heatherington, L., Johnson, B., & Skowron, E. A. (1994). "Sustaining engagement": A change event in family therapy. *Journal of Counseling Psychology, 41*, 438–448.

Friedlander, M. L., Heatherington, L., & Marrs, A. (in press). Responding to blame in family therapy: A constructionist/narrative perspective. *American Journal of Family Therapy.*

Friedlander, M. L., Heatherington, L., & Wildman, J. (1991). Interpersonal control in structural and Milan systemic family therapy. *Journal of Marital and Family Therapy, 17*, 395–408.

Friedlander, M. L., Highlen, P. S., & Lassiter, W. L. (1985). Content analytic comparison of four expert counselors' approaches to family treatment: Ackerman, Bowen, Jackson, and Whitaker. *Journal of Counseling Psychology, 32*, 171–180.

Friedlander, M. L., Wildman, J., Heatherington, L., & Skowron, E. A. (1994). What we do and don't know about the process of family therapy. *Journal of Family Psychology, 8*, 390–416.

Gaul, R., Simon, L., Friedlander, M. L., Heatherington, L., & Cutler, C. (1991). Correspondence of family therapists' perceptions with the FRCCCS for triadic interactions. *Journal of Marital and Family Therapy, 17*, 379–394.

Gibb, J. R. (1961). Defensive communications. *Journal of Communications, 3*, 141–148.

Goolishian, H. A., & Anderson, H. (1987). Language systems and therapy: An evolving idea. *Psychotherapy, 224*, 529–538.

Greenberg, L. S. (1995). The use of observational coding in family therapy research: Comment on Alexander et al. (1995). *Journal of Family Psychology, 9*, 366–370.

Greenberg, L. S., Ford, C. L., Alden, L., & Johnson, S. M. (1993). In-session change in emotionally focused therapy. *Journal of Consulting and Clinical Psychology, 61*, 78–84.

Greenberg, L. S., Heatherington, L., & Friedlander, M. L. (1996). The event-based approach to couple and family therapy research. In D. Sprenkle &

S. Moon (Eds.), *Handbook of family therapy research methods* (pp. 411–428). New York: Guilford Press.

Greenberg, L. S., & Johnson, S. (1988). *Emotionally focused therapy for couples.* New York: Guilford Press.

Haley, J. (1976). *Problem solving therapy.* San Francisco: Harper Colophon.

Heatherington, L. (1989). Toward more meaningful clinical research: Taking context into account in coding psychotherapy interaction. *Psychotherapy, 26,* 436–447.

Heatherington, L., & Allen, G. (1984). Sex and relational communication patterns in counseling. *Journal of Counseling Psychology, 31,* 287–294.

Heatherington, L., & Friedlander, M. L. (1987). *The Family Communication Control Coding System: Coding manual.* (Available from L. Heatherington, Department of Psychology, Williams College, Williamstown, MA 01267)

Heatherington, L., & Friedlander, M. L. (1990a). Applying task analysis to structural family therapy. *Journal of Family Psychology, 4,* 36–48.

Heatherington, L., & Friedlander, M. L. (1990b). Complementarity and symmetry in family therapy communication. *Journal of Counseling Psychology, 37,* 261–268.

Heatherington, L., & Friedlander, M. L. (1990c). Couple and family therapy alliance scales: Empirical considerations. *Journal of Marital and Family Therapy, 16,* 299–306.

Jacobson, N. S. (1981). Behavioral marital therapy. In A. S. Gurman & D. P. Kniskern (Eds.), *Handbook of family therapy* (Vol. 1, pp. 556–591). New York: Brunner/Mazel.

Johnson, S. M., & Greenberg, L. S. (1988). Relating process to outcome in marital therapy. *Journal of Marital and Family Therapy, 14,* 175–183.

Laird, H., & Van de Kemp, H. (1987). Complementarity as a function of stage in therapy: An analysis of Minuchin's structural family therapy. *Journal of Martial and Family Therapy, 13,* 127–137.

Leary, T. (1957). *Interpersonal diagnosis of personality: A functional theory and methodology for personality evaluation.* New York: Ronald Press.

Lichtenberg, J. W., & Barke, K. H. (1981). Investigation of transactional communication relationship patterns in counseling. *Journal of Counseling Psychology, 28,* 471–480.

Mark, R. A. (1971). Coding communication at the relational level. *Journal of Communication, 21,* 221–232.

Minuchin, S. (1974). *Families and family therapy.* Cambridge, MA: Harvard University Press.

Murray, H. A. (1938). *Explorations in personality.* New York: Oxford University Press.

Newberry, A. M., Alexander, J. F., & Turner, C. W. (1991). Gender as a process variable in family therapy. *Journal of Family Psychology, 5,* 158–175.

Patterson, G. R. (1971). *Families: Application of social learning theory to family life*. Champaign, IL: Research Press.

Patterson, G. R., & Chamberlain, P. (1988). Treatment process: A problem at three levels. In L. C. Wynne (Ed.), *The state of the art in family therapy research: Controversies and recommendations* (pp. 189–223). New York: Family Process Press.

Patterson, G. R., & Forgatch, M. S. (1985). Therapist behavior as a determinant for client noncompliance: A paradox for the behavior modifier. *Journal of Consulting and Clinical Psychology, 53,* 846–851.

Pinsof, W. M. (1979). The Family Therapist Behavior Scale (FTBS): Development and evaluation of a coding system. *Family Process, 18,* 451–461.

Pinsof, W. M. (1980). *The Family Therapist Coding System (FTCS) manual*. Chicago: Family Institute of Chicago.

Pinsof, W. M. (1981). Family therapy process research. In A. S. Gurman & D. P. Kniskern (Eds.), *Handbook of family therapy* (Vol. 1, pp. 699–741). New York: Brunner/Mazel.

Pinsof, W. M. (1986). The process of family therapy: The development of the Family Therapist Coding System. In L. S. Greenberg & W. M. Pinsof (Eds.), *The psychotherapeutic process: A research handbook* (pp. 201–284). New York: Guilford Press.

Pinsof, W. M. (1989). A conceptual framework and methodological criteria for family therapy process research. *Journal of Consulting and Clinical Psychology, 57,* 53–59.

Ratti, L. A., Humphrey, L. L., & Lyons, J. S. (1996). Structural analysis of families with a polydrug-dependent, bulimic, or normal adolescent daughter. *Journal of Consulting and Clinical Psychology, 64,* 1255–1262.

Raymond, L., Friedlander, M. L., Heatherington, L., Ellis, M. V., & Sargent, J. (1993). Communication processes in structural family therapy: Case study of an anorexic family. *Journal of Family Psychology, 6,* 308–326.

Robbins, M. S., Alexander, J. F., Newell, R. M., & Turner, C. W. (1996). The immediate effect of reframing on client attitude in family therapy. *Journal of Family Psychology, 10,* 28–34.

Rogers, L. E., & Bagarozzi, D. A. (1983). An overview of relational communication and implications for therapy. In D. Bagarozzi, A. Jurich, & R. Jackson (Eds.), *Marital and family therapy* (pp. 48–78). New York: Human Sciences Library.

Rogers, L. E., & Farace, R. V. (1975). Analysis of relational communication in dyads: New measurement procedures. *Human Communications Research, 1,* 222–239.

Satir, V. (1964). *Conjoint family therapy*. Palo Alto, CA: Science and Behavior Books.

Selvini Palazzoli, M., Boscolo, L., Cecchin, G., & Prata, G. (1980). Hypothesizing-circularity-neutrality. *Family Process, 19,* 73–85.

Shields, C. G., & McDaniel, S. H. (1992). Process differences between male and female therapists in a first family interview. *Journal of Marital and Family Therapy, 18,* 143–151.

Shields, C. G., Sprenkle, D. H., & Constantine, J. A. (1991). Anatomy of an initial interview: The importance of joining and structuring skills. *American Journal of Family Therapy, 19,* 3–18.

Siegel, S. M., Friedlander, M. L., & Heatherington, L. (1992). Nonverbal relational control in family communication. *Journal of Nonverbal Behavior, 16,* 117–139.

Sluzki, C. E. (1992). Transformations: A blueprint for narrative changes in therapy. *Family Process, 31,* 217–230.

Sluzki, C. E., & Beavin, J. H. (1977). Symmetry and complementarity: An operational definition and a typology of dyads. In P. Watzlawick & J. H. Weakland (Eds. and Trans.), *The interactional view* (pp. 71–87). New York: Norton. (Original work published 1965)

Sprenkle, D. H., & Moon, S. M. (1996). *Research methods in family therapy.* New York: Guilford Press.

Stoolmiller, M., Duncan, T., Bank, L., & Patterson, G. R. (1993). Some problems and solutions in the study of change: Significant patterns in client resistance. *Journal of Consulting and Clinical Psychology, 61,* 920–928.

Sullivan, H. S. (1953). *The interpersonal theory of psychiatry.* New York: Norton.

Tucker, S. J., & Pinsof, W. (1984). The empirical evaluation of family therapy training. *Family Process, 23,* 437–456.

Waldron, H. B., Turner, C. W., Alexander, J. F., & Barton, C. (1993). Coding defensive and supportive communications: Discriminant validity and subcategory convergence. *Journal of Family Psychology, 7,* 197–203.

Walsh, K. G. (1993). *Politics of gender in family therapy: Do therapists reinforce traditional stereotypes?* Unpublished doctoral dissertation, University at Albany, State University of New York.

Watzlawick, P., Beavin, J. H., & Jackson, D. D. (1967). *Pragmatics of human communication.* New York: Norton.

Whitaker, C., & Keith, D. (1981). Symbolic-experiential family therapy. In A. Gurman & D. Kniskern (Eds.), *The handbook of family therapy* (Vol. 1, pp. 187–225). New York: Brunner/Mazel.

White, M., & Epston, D. (1990). *Narrative means to therapeutic ends.* New York: Norton.

II

THE CASE EXAMPLE

5

GROUP A: THE FIRST FIVE SESSIONS

ARIADNE P. BECK AND CAROL M. LEWIS

The focus of this book is the systems of process analysis used in the study of process in psychotherapy groups. To allow readers to better understand and compare the systems, we invited the authors of the chapters to apply their systems to one session of a short-term psychotherapy group that we provided. They graciously agreed. Each chapter therefore presents a system of process analysis, summarizes research that has been conducted with that system, and presents the results of applying the system to the third session of Group A.[1] Authors received a transcript of the audiotape recording of the entire session. In addition to the transcript, the audiotape recording of the session was used for the rating process of some systems. We also provided data from two measures used in our own research: a table showing who spoke to whom (Eng & Beck, 1982) and the unitizing of the session based on the Topic-Oriented, Group Focus Unitizing Procedure (Dugo & Beck, 1983). More information about these measures can be found in chapter 9 in this book.

Transcripts of the first and second sessions of Group A were available

---

[1] *Transcript of fifteen sessions of Group A* (Sessions 1–5) by A. P. Beck, 1970, Chicago, IL. Portions of the transcript of session 3 are from "The Search for Phases in Group Development," by A. P. Beck et al., 1986, in L. S. Greenberg and W. M. Pinsof (Eds.) *The Psychotherapeutic Process: A Handbook* (pp. 682–696). Coyright 1986 by Guilford Press. Reprinted with permission.

if any of the authors wanted to have access to the interaction that preceded the third session. Authors applied their system to the transcript of the sample session just as they would in other research. They unitized and rated or coded the data as they might normally do. In a later chapter, we present a comparison of the results produced by applying the nine systems to Session 3 of Group A. At the request of some authors, several segments were selected from an early, middle, and later section of the third session. Throughout the book these selections are referred to as Segments 1, 2, 3, or 4. Some authors present results about those segments, whereas others address the whole session. A few present results about both the segments and the whole session.

We selected Session 3 based on our own team's theory of group development and our analysis of Group A. We work with a system of analysis that is being designed to identify phase boundaries in group development (see chapter 8 in this book). Session 3 of Group A stood out because a phase shift occurred from the second to the third phase toward the middle of the session (Beck, Dugo, Eng, & Lewis, 1986). Phase II of group development is characterized by a considerable amount of anxiety and stress in response to the task of forming the group structure (i.e., identifying or modifying norms), selecting leaders for crucial roles, formulating long-term goals for the group, and beginning the formation of a group identity. It tends to be conducted in a competitive style of interaction. Phase III is the beginning of getting to know each member better as an individual, clarifying individual goals, and addressing personal histories, historical impasses, and parent–child relationships. This phase is characterized by the beginnings of cooperative behavior in a framework of clear dependency on the client–therapist relationship. We believe that the behavior of the group is sufficiently different in Phases II and III that it would give each system an opportunity to track a greater variety of statements than the study of only one phase would provide.

In this chapter we present a description of the content and action of the group during its first five sessions (Beck, 1970; see Footnote 1). This will give readers a context for the third session. The purpose is to allow readers to better understand the various authors' comments about the session. It will also give them a sense of how the group progressed before and after Session 3. To organize the material more coherently, we have identified content themes in all five sessions and indicated them in parentheses. The themes address the focus of attention of the group members on particular topics that are listed in Table 5.2. Later in the chapter the sequence and evolution of the topics are discussed (see Table 5.4). It is not necessary, however, for readers to attend to these thematic issues. In fact, it may facilitate the first reading to ignore the parentheses and just follow the flow of the story.

SESSION 1

Group A met for a prearranged 15 sessions in an outpatient university clinic. They met once a week for 90 minutes. All clients had been in prior therapy for at least 2 years. One client was self-referred for the group, but all the rest were referred by their therapists and interviewed by the group cotherapists before their acceptance into the group. At that time, they agreed to be audiotape recorded and to take pre- and posttests as well as some tests during the group experience. There were three male clients, Brad, Greg and Joe; three female clients, Diane, Martha, and Pat; and two female therapists, Alice and Helen. A fourth client, Dan, was scheduled to be in this group but did not arrive. The clients ranged in age from 24 to 52 (see Table 5.1). Alice was in her first year as a staff member of the clinic. She was leading her third group. Helen was an intern (predoctoral), coleading her first group. This was intended to be a training experience for her under Alice's supervision. The therapists also participated together in a peer group consultation with colleagues from several other organizations who represented several theoretical orientations. The coleaders of Group A were client-centered counselors. They had an individual therapy focus and were not experienced with group-as-a-whole or interpersonal interventions. Group A was collected during the 1960s.

TABLE 5.1
Participants of Group A

Group Members	Age	Marital Status	No. of Children	Work	Reason to Be in Group (as stated in Sesion 1)
Clients					
Brad	30	Married	2	Stockbroker	Stuck in individual therapy
Joe	52	Married	2	Maintenance worker	Adjusting to lifestyle and job change
Martha	29	Single	0	Administrative assistant	Adjusting to job change; working on separation issues
Greg	24	Single	0	Student; job hunting	Ending school and individual therapy; group a transition
Pat	35	Single	0	Hospital nurse	Feels isolated even around people she's close to
Diane	38	Married	1	Graduate student; intern	Has problems with people in groups
Therapists					
Alice	27	Married	0	Staff psychologist	
Helen	24	Single	0	Graduate student	

Because of the need of one client, the therapists set the meeting time for a later evening hour. The others agreed to this time, but some of them knew it would mean getting home at a late hour. This creates some distress on the first evening when all the clients show up except Dan, the person with the time constraint (Theme 1; see Table 5.2). He called to say that he could not make it because of a problem on his job. In addition, the first session starts later than planned because a couple of clients were a little late. Alice explains that the group will begin on time in the future. She addresses a number of issues about the clinic, the new group therapy

TABLE 5.2
Emerging Content Themes in Group A

Sessions 1 and 2
1. The missing client, Dan; discussion to continue without him.
2. The relative inexperience of the therapists and their interest in studying group therapy.
3. Problems in being closely connected to others make one want to flee; there is responsibility involved in closeness.
4. Job loss; need for toughness.
5. "Cheap counseling."
6. Arrangements: time; furniture; contact between individual and group therapists; dealing with crises; time limit of group.
7. Religious backgrounds (not everyone participated).
8. Criteria for participation in group (i.e., previous therapy).
9. Fear of talking in group; what's OK to talk about. Fear of hostility emerging. Honesty/hostility. Need to understand what goes on in angry interactions; in competition.
10. Is pain and suffering necessary? Does maturity mean being impervious to being hurt by others? Would it be better to have a shell?
11. Talking versus feeling. If you do too much of one, can you do the other?
12. Waiting for space (or invitation to talk) versus breaking in; listening and hearing versus tuning others out.

Session 3
13. Sharing painful experiences.
14. Talking with and about feelings.
15. Self-reflection and ownership of own psychological issues; ownership of one's interpersonal impacts on others or confrontation of other members regarding their issues.
16. Building on each other's themes and content.
17. Playing with competition.
18. Sharing family histories both painful and loving.
19. Is there love? What is love?

Sessions 4 and 5
20. Consequences of failures to meet the expectations of authority figures.
21. Resiliency as an overarching concept (especially in integrating the "dichotomy" between the shell and openness to pain dialogue).
22. The complexity and risk involved in giving feedback to others.
23. Commitment to the group in the face of life changes and crises.
24. Sharing "shameful" experiences and the isolation that comes with not sharing them.
25. Consequences of failure to meet one's own expectations or fulfill one's own potential.

program, confidentiality, and the research. She then introduces herself and addresses her interests in groups and in the problems involved in being closely connected to and helping each other (Themes 2 and 3; see Table 5.2). Brad introduces himself next. (The basic information that each client gave in these introductions is listed in Table 5.1.) Helen then tells the group that she is a beginner in group leadership and that she has experienced group therapy herself and found it helpful.

Joe introduces himself, talking a long time about his job loss and subsequent economic and emotional difficulties (Theme 4; see Table 5.2). The theme of Joe's job loss is picked up by each client sharing his or her experiences with strange jobs or job losses. In the midst of this process, Joe talks extensively about his experience, expressing considerable anxiety about it:

> I was on top of the world—and then it was a let down—you're in jail, all the noise and regimentation. My age has been against me in finding a selling job—I'm almost 50. Being locked up in a factory for 8 hours makes me panicky. I get heart palpitations.

Brad says he has also held such jobs during the summers. Joe responds that he also did as a young person, but now at his current age he resents it. Martha responds with empathy to Joe; she was fired the previous summer from a high-pressure job. She describes her intense reaction to this and subsequent return to work at a previous job. She also indicates a high level of dependency on her individual therapy and says that she is also currently involved in a discussion group because she feels the need to be around people. During these interactions with Joe there is a high level of disjunctive communication, including interruptions and laughter.

Greg enters the discussion by talking about his experience with difficulties finding a job the previous year, the employment agency he went through, and the factory piecework job he took temporarily. He then describes how he started in therapy with a psychiatrist when he was a senior in college but came to this university clinic because he heard that "there was counseling that was just as good, but cheap" (Themes 4 and 5; see Table 5.2). He feels it is time now to terminate individual therapy and he plans to do this midway through group. He sees group therapy as a good way to get reintegrated into a regular life routine.

Joe responds with "We should never give up. I mean, we all have a lot of weaknesses and troubles, but I think I was lucky. I had sort of a fighting spirit: I would never say die." Martha says supportively, "Oh, you sure did." The discussion continues about how hard the world and people in it are, how tough one has to be to survive (Theme 4; see Table 5.2).

Diane introduces herself. She says she is here because she has problems with people in groups: "I've always felt extremely uncomfortable if I was running it and extremely uncomfortable if I was withdrawn from it."

Later she says, "I would like to feel free in a group, but then other people change and I back off into a corner" (Theme 3; see Table 5.2). As the group lets this sink in they become anxious, and there is a good deal of laughter by everyone. Greg says, "Let's not get in deeper; I'm nervous already." Martha says, "Let's get to the top before we get to the bottom, huh?"

Through a series of questions, Martha clarifies that Diane is an intern in the counseling field and then concludes, "Gee, they've got almost the same troubles we do." (laughter throughout; Theme 2; see Table 5.2).

Brad confesses that he hears some of his own issues in everything the others are saying, and "it piles up"—it's too much for him at one time.

The focus shifts back to Joe and a conclusion is reached by Helen that "we still have time to prove ourselves, that there's a chance; that's why he's here, cuz he hasn't . . . lost faith [in humanity]."

Pat says she is bursting, waiting for her turn. She feels a great sense of isolation, even when she is around people she is close to. She is in group to learn to relate to people better (Theme 3; see Table 5.2).

Late in the session Helen reminds everyone that Dan did not come. A discussion about the meeting time clarifies that everyone present prefers an earlier time, but they agree to come at 8:00 p.m. next time unless Dan cannot come at all (Theme 6; see Table 5.2).

The session ends after a discussion involving Brad, Martha, and Greg about their parent's religious affiliations and the denominations in which they were raised. The other clients do not yet reveal their affiliations or feelings about religion (Theme 7; see Table 5.2).

SESSION 2

Martha is absent from the second session because of illness. The session begins with an awkward conversation. Greg asks if the group therapists will have contact with the individual therapists; he requests that they tell him anything they tell his counselor. The other clients present are comfortable with the therapists communicating with each other (Theme 6; see Table 5.2).

The members note that Dan is not there again (this time he did not call). Pat suggests that they should forget about him. Alice says it is tonight or never. Brad turns the chair facing out of the group (Theme 1; see Table 5.2). Joe plunges into a long presentation on the mental health services available in the community if one is in an emergency or an emotional crisis (this is in response to something Martha said during the previous session) (Theme 6; see Table 5.2). Pat expresses annoyance with Joe and raises the question, Should individual therapy be a prerequisite to participation in groups? Pat thinks that Joe "doesn't know the ropes." She also formulates a goal that she has. She would like to respond spontaneously in group and then be able to look back and learn something about how and why she feels the way she does (Themes 8 and 9; see Table 5.2).

Greg and Brad talk about their fears of talking too much and of the consequences of "taking the gloves off." Joe responds to these communications by encouraging everyone to bring all their issues out in the open (Theme 9; see Table 5.2). Greg then responds to the discussion of whether prior individual therapy is a requirement for group, thus blocking the creation of group prerequisites. He says, "I sort of thought I detected a note of 'we're further along.' I have an automatic reaction against anything being held up as a salvation" (i.e., counseling in this case; Theme 8; see Table 5.2).

Helen helps Joe to acknowledge his nervousness and impatience with any silence in the group (Theme 8; see Table 5.2).

Alice then focuses on Pat's generic issue, that she frequently rationalizes why she does not express her own views or feelings but then gets uncomfortable or even upset with the other person, to whom she has not said what is on her mind (Themes 9 and 15; see Table 5.2). Diane then enters this discussion, addressing her problems "when she is frank with people":

> I personally am here to find out if I am defensive in this area or if I am as honest as I think I am and, if so, then I want to look at what frankness does or what the reaction to it does to me.

Pat agrees it would be helpful to be able to express such feelings in the moment. Greg agrees and talks about what he sees as the "poker game in the group." They all acknowledge feeling competitive and that they have hostile feelings that they think are juvenile. Pat says, "I thought of it last week as, 'Can you top this'?" (Theme 9; see Table 5.2).

The group members enter into a lengthy discussion initiated by Joe about immaturity and maturity. He aspires to be a "mature person" who is not hurt by other people's hurtful behaviors. At this time, however, he gets tired of people after a few weeks and wants to move on. Brad and Greg think this is an impossible goal and "we're always going to feel pain." Brad continues, "in a way what we're here for is to learn to dissolve this shell, to be pervious or to be open." This issue is not really resolved with Joe (Theme 10; see Table 5.2).

Instead, Joe and Greg begin a type of parallel play sequence in which they seem to be competing for group attention. Greg reveals the difficulty he is experiencing regarding his girlfriend. The thought of getting close makes him feel ready to flee to the West Coast. Joe says he has had a lifelong problem with responsibility. With temporary relationships it is easier: "You don't have to live with them" (Theme 3; see Table 5.2).

Greg feels that closeness involves risk and danger. The group discusses

Greg's problem and options with him at some length. Pat says that the crucial issue is what the options mean to him and how he feels about them; in particular, he sees moving west as meaning running away from his girl-friend. Greg says, "I am afraid to really enter into a relationship where I can't go into a shell, afraid maybe that the counseling right now is getting to a point where it's gonna break down my shell, you see."

Joe draws an analogy between a problem of his own and Greg's. Joe wants to move to Florida, but his wife is afraid to take the chance of going there (Theme 9; see Table 5.2). Greg offers a story about his own parents. His dad kept pressuring his mom to move from North Dakota to Arizona or California. Finally, she got a job and they moved. His dad was more restless there than before. In 1 year he initiated the move back to North Dakota. These stories just reinforce Greg's suspicion that going west (in his own case) "is better cuz that's someplace else" (Theme 3; see Table 5.2). He refers again to his fantasy (when he lived on the West Coast) that the "cheap counseling" at the university here would be a great solution for him (Theme 5; see Table 5.2). After group laughter, Greg says that now when he says anything he looks back to see what he meant. "I'm a very frank person, but I usually find that there were barbs." Alice says, "Barbs in your frankness?" Greg says yes (Theme 9; see Table 5.2).

Joe responds to this by stating one of his generalizations: "Well, I mean everybody has problems, life is a continuous problem of solving your troubles." He then applies this to a movie star he read about. Pat goes after him again, attacking his generalizations. A verbally confusing set of inter-actions follows involving Joe, Pat, and Diane. Joe is visibly upset and does not seem to get the others' meanings. An intense discussion occurs around the fact that "social" conversation actually prevents people from talking about what they are really feeling. They also address Joe's need to fill every silence (Themes 9 and 11; see Table 5.2).

Alice and Helen repeatedly address the fact that people seem to be feeling pressed by the time limit in the group (Theme 12; see Table 5.2).

Alice tries to point out to Pat and Diane that they feel helpless to modify the direction of the discussion to meet their needs. "Joe just won't let them" is their view. Greg comments that everyone except Pat seems helpless in the face of Joe's style of communicating. Alice emphasizes that if Pat would just talk, Joe would stop talking (Themes 9, 11, and 12; see Table 5.2).

Joe then suggests that it would be better if everyone had a turn to talk. Pat dislikes this idea. The argument continues. Pat is resentful, and Joe is trying to be helpful but is perceived as missing the point. Pat finally acknowledges her need to feel connected to Joe and says that the group is "browbeating" him. Greg then suggests that instead of trying to get Joe to change that they should just break in. Pat says she does not have the ability to buck him. Alice says, "You get so busy reacting to Joe and then feel he doesn't leave space for you." Joe says, "It's sort of like at home. The wife always says she can't get through." Greg confronts Pat's issue about speaking up and she backs away. Alice says they are talking about three or four different people's problems as though they were all one problem. Pat notes that group time is over (Theme 6; see Table 5.2).

Some more confused interaction finally leads Greg to say to Joe, "In other words, don't treat the group like you treat your wife." The session ends as everyone says good night and agrees to meet at 7:00 p.m. next week (Theme 6; see Table 5.2).

SESSION 3

As mentioned earlier, the segments of interaction were selected within Session 3 to illustrate the behavior during parts of the session that are postulated to be in Phases II and III of the group's development. The transition from Phase II to Phase III occurs about halfway through Session 3. Segments 1 and 2 are examples of interaction that occur toward the end of Phase II. Segment 3 is a portion of the interaction during the phase shift, or transition, from Phase II to Phase III. Segment 4 is an example of the group's interaction after Phase III has begun. These segments were used by many of the authors in their application of their rating systems to Group A, Session 3. The description below notes the points at which those segments appear during the description of the group's interaction in session 3. The four segments selected from Session 3 are also listed in Table 5.3 along with their locations in the original transcript of the audiotape recording. Portions of transcript are included in the description to give readers a sample of the communication as it actually took place.

Session 3 begins with a long repartee regarding men and women and the idea that each believes he or she is in some ways superior. When everyone but Joe has arrived, Diane expresses concern about Joe returning to group. Greg informs Martha and Brad, "We gave Joe a hard time during the last part of the session [last week]" (Themes 9, 15, and 17; see Table 5.2).

TABLE 5.3
Group A, Session 3: Segments and Their Locations in the Original Transcript of the Audiotape

Segment No.	Unit No.	Location in the Transcript
1	64–66	p. 85, Item 14 to p. 88, Item 4a
2	69	p. 90, Item 4 to p. 97, Item 10
3	71–73	p. 98, Item 13 to p. 100, Item 18
4	82–84	p. 112, Item 1b to p. 115, Item 9

Beck, A. P. © 1970

Joe comes in and addresses his reaction to the last session: He was in turmoil and confused for a couple of days. He concludes the following:

> Each one of us is a different personality, we have different problems, we have different ways of presenting it, which may be confusing to the other person. But, I think if we at least present it, it's helpful to us. It gives us a lot of confidence, and if you can develop confidence you got the battle half licked. (Themes 13 and 14; see Table 5.2)

Joe then tells of his encounter with an African American supervisor in his job setting and the negative reaction of coworkers to the idea of being supervised by an African American. He, on the other hand, felt his supervisor was intelligent and diplomatic. Martha says, "Good for you," to Joe.

Alice and Helen interact with Joe about how he felt after last week and, as a result, his experience is restated several times (Theme 13; see Table 5.2).

Segment 1 begins here.

Martha finally asks if there was anything Joe wanted "to get across last week that [he] didn't get across." He said no. Brad then offers an interpretation to Joe: "You were looking for peace and, pow, you got a disturbance."

Pat:	Well, I'm really with you every inch of the way, uh, talking about this and, uh, and I feel like, uh, well first of all, Joe, when, uh, you were talkin' about your experience today I admired you for that—very much. I thought that showed a lot of, uh, character. And, uh, then I wished that, uh, you would talk more about how you felt last time and, uh, you said you were irritated. I kept thinking now I wonder, uh, who was irritating him, and it must've been me, and how, in what way were you irritated with me and, uh, so on. (Themes 9, 13, and 14; Table 5.2)
Alice:	You would really kind of like some feedback. . . .
Pat:	Yeah, but I don't wanna press him for this cuz I feel that this is—
Alice:	'Cause you feel that you were the one that affected him.
Pat:	Uh, hard for him and, uh (Mm hm), I'm not saying that he doesn't wanna (Mm hm).
Joe:	It's nothing person—personally, I mean it's just like I say it's a matter of, it's a matter of personality. I mean we're—we're all different and uh—
Pat:	Sure.

Joe: We have a different personality, a different—

Alice: But I think Pat was trying to say that. . . .

And, a little later in Segment 1:

Alice: Well, but may—maybe she, she's suggesting that for her it would be profitable to explore the difference and try to understand it, if you feel like you want to, was that right?

Pat: Yeah, that's right.

Joe: You mean exploring the, the personality or, uh—

Pat: Well, uh, uh, the thing I was, the specific question I had in mind was, Were you irritated with me? (Themes 14 and 15; see Table 5.2)

Joe: Well, yes.

Pat: Mm hm. Well, and then the next question was, I wanna know in what way, how do you feel or, if you feel like tellin' me to go to hell or what.

Joe: No, it was just a matter, I thought, uh, you were holding something back, or there was something was irritating you and, uh, I figured, well, you were a little self-conscious or a little timid or, you were afraid to bring, uh, something out that was bothering you, and I thought maybe I was talkin' too much, and I was irritating you because I was spillin' everything that was on my mind and, you may have been a little timid at saying something—

Alice: Like, like, she had something to say but you were taking up too much room (Joe: That's—) and not giving her a chance (Joe: That's right.) to get it said, uh huh, uh huh.

Pat: Well, maybe in a way that was the way I felt because, uh, I was feeling like, uh, I kept being distracted by the things you were wanting to talk about, and they weren't things that concerned us—I didn't think, and uh, so, I guess I was, uh, I didn't wanna go ahead and blurt out what I had to say because, well I couldn't, um, because my mind was full of the things you were saying (mild laugh). (Themes 9 and 12; see Table 5.2)

Joe: Well, it's something that, uh, I mean I get bitter on because I, I mean I been burnt a lot, er, I got a lot of troubles in my life, you know, with people, uh, I try to be nice to them, and then they would take advantage of me er put me in the middle, and I mean it, uh, sorta gets me, uh, riled up where I start talkin,' er I don't wanna stop talkin' on all the things that, uh, happened that, uh, in the same—in the same predicament, so I—

Alice: You mean you feel like there's been lots of times when you've been used?

Joe: Yeah.

Pat acknowledges that she did have something she needed to talk about but felt she had to listen to Joe. Joe in turn acknowledges that he sometimes feels so pressed by all the problems in his life that he cannot stop talking once he starts (Themes 9, 12, and 15; see Table 5.2).

Segment 1 ends here.

Joe continues with the subject, that when he is nice to people, they often take advantage of him. As an example, he tells a lengthy story about how a friend played a dirty trick on him, giving Joe's name, address, and telephone number to girls he met at a nightclub. Joe later dropped this person after a 20-year friendship (Themes 10 and 13; see Table 5.2). Alice, Helen, and Martha interact with him to clarify his feelings that people are unpredictable, that they can even be mean, and that people have to learn to "take it."

Diane sums up that Joe has needs and expectations in this group just as everyone else does and that he wants to be accepted for who he is and how he feels he must behave (Theme 8; see Table 5.2).

Joe says, "That's right. I wanna be one of the group, too. I understand and sympathize with everybody else, and I'm just as anxious to hear everybody else's problems as I am to talk about my own."

Segment 2 begins here.

Diane goes on, however, to say that this feels unfinished. She says it is as though she and Pat are on one level and Joe is on another. They do not connect with each other.

Brad questions whether Joe is finished with his feelings in reaction to last week. Alice says she thinks it is Diane who is not finished.

Diane agrees. She hears Joe saying, "Now if you can't know me on these terms, then you can't know me." She's not sure she can know him on those terms. "There's something about what he said, that closed the door for me—and somehow I can't come in. To me it felt like, 'You can only know me with my door closed.'" Martha then says, "Oh, then you can't know me" (Theme 8; see Table 5.2).

Helen questions the meaning of this sentence and then contradicts Diane's interpretation.

Helen: And he was saying, I thought, exactly the opposite thing. I think he was saying, I'm telling you some of the most important things about myself, some of the (*Diane:* Mm) inner things about myself, that this is the way I, I can tell them to you. Now this is my way, and I think also he was saying, "I get disturbed about your way too, as you get disturbed by my way." (Theme 15; see Table 5.2).

Diane: Mm hm, mm hm. Yeah, and I guess there is an element of judgment in here or evaluation on my part, in that what the things that Joe was telling last week for me were not, were not his internals, they were his externals (laugh).

Diane: This is a matter of judgment on my part. . . . (Beck et al., 1986)

A little later:

Diane: But I think it is more frustration. It's more like, "Gee I'll spend 15 weeks with you and never really know, you. I'll know all about what you think of racial prejudice and Marilyn Monroe and the, and the UN [United Nations] and that sort of thing, but I'll never really know what is clickin' around inside you!" (laugh).

Joe: I don't know myself (laugh). (Theme 15; see Table 5.2). (Beck et al., 1986)

A little later:

Diane: I think (Greg, then Brad, start, then stop), I think Helen really hit it right on the head when she said to me, I mean, that, it can, as you started to talk again, it hit me what you said (laugh).

Martha: Um, well, what?

Diane: You're absolutely right, I'm not willing to accept him on his terms (Martha: Uh huh) cause that's who he is.

Martha: That's right. (Theme 15; see Table 5.2). (Beck et al., 1986)

Segment two ends here.

Between Segments 2 and 3, an important interaction takes place in which the group members begin to reflect on their own behavior during the recent period in the group's life. Part of the dialogue follows:

Brad: I'm just a little curious—does, um, despite what you do when you tell jokes, I suppose that measured in minutes Joe has, mostly because we kept after him, has probably talked the most and said the most, uh, revealed I think the most—

Alice: And expressed—

Helen: Yes.

Brad: In both sessions, all three sessions now, why are we after him—

Greg: Every generation needs its scapegoat.

Martha: Ah, you're crazy. (Beck et al., 1986)

At this point in the session, Greg, Brad, and Martha all acknowledge their own concerns about revealing their issues and therefore themselves. They admit that it has been easier to keep focusing on Joe (Themes 9, 15, and 16; see Table 5.2).

Segment 3 begins here.

Diane contributes to the discussion at this point by saying there are "a lot of things" she would like to tell the group about herself, but she does not have the nerve to do it. She thinks that she has been envious of Joe, who has spoken so freely. Joe responds, "Well, speak, get your money's worth." Everyone laughs (Beck et al., 1986). Martha goes on to ask Diane if she feels she has gotten the same reaction from this group that she usually gets from other groups. She says that she has not yet because she has not "pushed forward; hasn't taken a chance yet" (Themes 9 and 15; see Table 5.2).

Martha then shares a story that she imagines is similar to Diane's concern about group reactions. She "burst out laughing" at a lecture, in response to the speaker's humor. However, everyone else was quiet, which felt like a rebuke to Martha (Themes 9 and 15; see Table 5.2).

Brad observes that Diane may have been angry with Joe because he was so "Byronic, so peaceful," and she wanted to keep the waters "rough and rumpled." Greg thinks "she was ready for a fight." And, as a matter of fact, he is, too, he says, and has been all week. Martha challenges him, "Who's gonna start it?" Greg says, "I just went back in [my shell]"; (Themes 9 and 17; see Table 5.2). (Beck et al., 1986).

Segment 3 ends here.

Martha addresses Diane in a serious manner and asks her to bring up the things she was thinking about. Joe says he, too, was wondering what the details were of Diane's problem in groups. Diane says that when she speaks spontaneously, out of a deeply held value, she is often rebuked. Everybody in the group jumps into interviewing Diane.

With some persistence on Joe's part, Diane begins to describe her family and childhood experiences, the small town she lived in, and how her family was perceived. There is a theme of isolation from the social domain and violent behavior on the part of her father. She talks about the pressures to perform and do well in order to have an identity (Themes 13, 14, and 18; see Table 5.2).

Eventually, Greg comes in with a story about his family. He discusses his mother's dominance. Diane draws analogies between her family and Greg's. Both say that their mothers were dominant, running the households and managing the children, and that they kept the fathers at bay (Themes 16 and 18; see Table 5.2).

Segment 4 begins here.

Martha enters this discussion with her negative feelings toward her parents.

Alice: There were, it sounds like you're saying, there were so many bonds that were so strong (*Martha:* Yeah), and it was so hard to disconnect yourself from their views—

Martha: Oh yeah, I was completely dependent on them.

Alice: —that to be able to say that they were a loss, uh, and to not feel lost yourself, in saying it is really a very big thing.

Martha: My sister went ahead of me and was in counseling and just changed the course of her life completely. I resisted all the things that she said and that she found out. It upset me terribly, but I resisted them as long as I could and finally last summer I—I just finally broke down. So it's hard for me to answer your question (Mm hm) exactly but I—I think, because I was floored to realize how deeply I love my parents. I thought love had something to do with the object of your love. You love a person because they're wonderful you know. . . .
I think the toughest thing for me was to separate myself emotionally and not in any day-to-day relationship because I (*Alice:* Mm hm) have no relationship with them, to—to um, say uh, they were wrong, their way of life is wrong, and the way I've been living is wrong, and I choose to go my different direction, and I am right in doing this, and um, I can make my own kind of life. I am not bound to being the kind of person I've been . . . to have the confidence to say that I—I maybe this is the toughest thing for me—I, Martha am an individual that is completely unlike anybody in the world—this is the terrifying thing for me. Not like my parents, not like my sister, and I declare for myself, um, independence: I am going to find now who I am and what kind of way of life I want to live, and I'm gonna do this on my own (laugh). (Themes 13–16; see Table 5.2).

Martha, Diane, and Greg go on to develop a theme together that addresses the ways their mothers "left them free" yet seemed to powerfully control them (Themes 16 and 18; Table 5.2).

Greg: Us kids were always free, too. It was much stronger than, it was a much stronger bond she had over us than to—to have to force us to do something.

Martha: Yeah, that's what I was gonna say. She never ever told me anything that I had to do. It was progressive education. It was never any constriction, that is, spoken, that you had to do or that she was trying to get you to do. But that's why it was so tough with me.

Diane: We didn't have to get—the thing that we had to do was to compete and be best. (*Martha:* Uh huh) Which we did— all of us. The only time we ever got attention was if we were outstanding and we were outstanding all the time, all the time. . . .

Segment 4 ends here.

Joe enters with a description of his family. His father was a bully, mean, and beat his kids. However, all the neighbors thought he was a great guy, a wonderful father (Themes 14 and 18; see Table 5.2).

Joe: I mean he was always that way, he'd, uh, as I look back, I mean he'd, uh, he would give you an inferiority complex, he was just, uh, mean, you know, and high strung. If my brothers were out playin' ball, and one of 'em got hurt, uh, they'd come in the house cryin' er bleeding, and he'd come in and he, then he'd beat me up, uh, and say well, I shoulda been out there watchin' 'em so they'd—

Helen: . . . You couldn't win . . . .

Joe: So, after a while, you know, you—I, Joe—you built up a hatred and, uh, I mean he was knockin' me down. What tickled me is if I'd go outside the house to neighbors—hey were all by—all the neighbors would say, "What a wonderful father you have"—

Martha: Oh, yes.

Joe: —"Oh, he's so nice and considerate" (Martha laughs), and anyplace you'd go, everybody was, you know, praised him. I'd say, "Gee" (slight laugh)—

Alice: What's wrong?

Joe: —what's wrong? (laughter, especially Greg). It really confused me.

Joe talks about his own parenting behavior with his son. Joe says he tries to be good to his son, so he has become cocky and smart. He says, "I suppose a parent should strike a happy medium."

Diane says, "Just love." And, this triggers an intense response from Greg. They enter into a dialogue to define love in nonperfectionist–human terms. Greg wants to believe there is such a thing, but he is afraid that it "seems sort of over the rainbow" (Theme 19; see Table 5.2).

Pat and Brad, who have been quiet during the sharing about parents, enter the discussion. Brad offers, "Love is something you do." Joe says, "Everyone wants to be wanted, needs someone they can go to, and that there are probably a dozen kinds of love." Helen says, "(Sigh) Well, I am disturbed because I think that this has a lot of significance for all of us, but everybody thinks their own thoughts and are impressed by them (Mm hm) (slight laughter)" (Theme 19; see Table 5.2).

Diane asks Pat where she has been.

Pat: . . . I went along about two years hating both my parents, and a couple more years feeling that, uh, there was no such thing as love and, uh, now I've come to feel that maybe there is and, when you start to define it I kinda sneer in a way, because I . . . I think that it's pretty hard to define and . . . .

Greg: Yeah.

Pat: I was controlled by so-called love and I. . . . I resisted it too, even though I want it. (Themes 15, 16, 18, and 19; see Table 5.2)

Alice pushes for a summary in order to end the session:

Alice: Well, and I also kinda felt like we were saying, the word at least stands for to each of us something we want, but there are a lot of ways that it—(Greg: Mm hm)—it can come that we don't want it. (Themes 3 and 10; see Table 5.2)

Diane: It can have so many strings.

Alice: There are lots of—

Alice: Yes. (Martha laughs.) There are lots of—there are lots of strings that could come with it that we don't want.

Joe: So many ways you can get burnt by it, too. (Theme 10; see Table 5.2)

Alice confirms that the new time works for everyone, and the session ends (Theme 6; see Table 5.2).

SESSION 4

In the sections to follow, we continue the format of presenting description and quotations from the transcript so that readers see how the discussion progressed through Sessions 4 and 5 of Group A. In Session 4, after initial interaction with greetings, it is Joe who turns the group's focus to the task. He recalls the discussion about parents in the previous session and shares information about his own parents, making associations to the difficulties other members had presented about separating from their parents' influence. Pat in turn makes disclosures about her childhood family environment and difficulties dealing with school mates. Both she and Joe felt like outsiders when they were growing up. During this time other group members facilitate the process by asking pertinent questions, contributing ideas about similarities they perceive among the experiences shared or joining in self-exploration with associations to their own family experiences (Themes 16 and 18; see Table 5.2). Pat again addresses the theme of love:

> Pat: Why, uh, I always had the feeling that, uh, now that I, uh, look back on it that my mother controlled me with love (*Martha*: Mm hm) with uh, if I uh, if I didn't do things that, that a good girl does, then I didn't love her, and uh—

> Martha: Oh! Not that she would draw her love from you.

> Pat: Well (sigh), I think um, I think to me it meant that because if I didn't love her then she wouldn't love me (*Alice*: Mm hm).

> Martha: Oh brother, you really had to pay your way.

> Pat: And, I, I think that's one of the reasons why I'm so suspicious of love or, or any, um, loving (*Martha*: Yeah) act or anything. And, and the slightest rejections are very hard for me to take (*Martha*: Mm hm, yeah) (*Greg*: Mm).

> Martha: The people that I do care about, whose opinion I value, I can hardly deviate you know, further away from the way they believe. I—I, if they say anything that sounds like different from what I'm doing I think it's a censure.

> Alice: Is that the kind of thing you meant too? I—I wasn't sure.

> Martha: Well, that's probably not what you meant, but it's how I act on that same principle. (*Alice*: Yeah, Mm hm).

This is followed by Pat and Martha discussing difficulties and frustrations in their personal change processes. Pat talks about a break in her individual therapy relationship, her disappointment in her therapist, and her therapist's disappointment in her. This issue generates anxiety in the group members. Martha in particular is activated to interact with Pat to clarify what happened. Others get into the discussion, which includes a focus on failure to meet the expectations of authorities in contexts outside of the relationship with parents and on vulnerability to hurtful and rejecting experiences. Joe returns to the example of the trauma of loss in the context of losing his job. He emphasizes the communality of aspects of that experience with the difficulties Pat and Martha discuss about meeting the expectations of authorities (Themes 10, 19, and 20; see Table 5.2).

Joe brings up the need to defend oneself against hurt, and a discussion follows about the concept of a shell to protect oneself. The group tries to understand what he means and whether he has the right idea. Joe, Greg, and Brad all express thoughts about reacting to and coping with hurtful experiences, continuing the theme that began in Session 2 (Themes 10 and 16; see Table 5.2). An intense discussion follows when Diane is perceived as criticizing Joe once again. Concerns are expressed that an unfair process of blame or criticism should not be resumed. Diane is put on the spot during that interlude, and in fact she sees Joe's responses as limiting the depth of Pat's work rather than as a helpful form of mutual participation. Joe comes to her rescue by taking up the part of what she says about him that he recognizes as accurate and giving a pertinent example about himself from outside the group. In listening to it, Diane sees a way that Joe can cope with hurt and conflict in some situations more easily than she can, and she acknowledges that: "I can't do that, I guess I've just gotta suffer." Diane feels that Joe really understands her remarks better than the others do (Themes 9 and 10; see Table 5.2).

During this discussion the topics of "having a shell" or "being open to hurt" are placed into the context of a new perspective, in which the concept of resiliency is introduced. They conclude that when being resilient, there are times when one may temporarily use a shell in order to regroup and that that does not make one less courageous (Themes 10 and 21; see Table 5.2). In this context Joe's previous experience with therapy emerges again as an issue, and the group members finally hear that he has previously been in therapy (Theme 8; see Table 5.2).

The group focuses on Diane, and she tries to use the experience to work on her problem of "what happens to me in a group and why others react the way they do to me." The group members discuss the difficulties of giving feedback and the potential that exists for misunderstanding and hurting one another. Strong feelings are generated in the group members, and some confused interactions take place in relation to Diane (Themes 3, 9, and 15; see Table 5.2).

Martha brings up the importance of speaking from one's own experience and how hard it is to get an understanding of what another person says. This leads to the question of whether she is suggesting that they should avoid giving feedback about their perceptions of one another (Themes 3 and 22; see Table 5.2).

The group session ends with a return to Pat's situation. Joe seeks affirmation, from Pat, of her continued involvement in the group (Themes 13 and 23; see Table 5.2). In the process of this session the group members have plunged into a more intense and spontaneous group process.

SESSION 5

As session 5 begins, both Joe and Greg are absent. The therapist tells the group that Joe will not be coming and is uncertain whether Greg will attend. Greg arrives shortly after the session begins, but until he does, Brad is the only male group member present. The women all sit together opposite him. Brad feels conspicuous and aware that he has been a nondisclosing participant in the group so far. He also notes that Joe usually gets the group started. In that regard they all feel a little on the spot without him (Theme 9; see Table 5.2).

As Greg comes in, Martha tells Brad about her wish that he would talk. She wonders what he thinks and feels. Greg draws an analogy to poker, when a player may hold back until others have placed their bets and he knows where they stand. Martha feels as though she may have put Brad on the spot. Pat observes that Brad has been silent about himself but responsive about things going on within the group. Martha anxiously clarifies that she feels it would be wrong for her to press Brad to talk about himself more; however, she also discloses that she has some anxiety because she feels as if Brad is an observer. Greg articulates a similar feeling. Brad responds, acknowledging that he has been holding back and describing himself as wanting to find out a bit more of what others were thinking and why they are here, sort of "trying to get a commitment before I commit" (Themes 9 and 15; see Table 5.2). He explains that he has been feeling isolated from others and that he is different from them, because he feels there are "shameful elements" in the problem he has had. Although he feels embarrassed, he is able to tell the group about his problem in general terms. The themes of difficulty in sharing certain personal matters and the feelings of isolation that come from not doing so continue to be discussed by Greg, Martha, and Brad (Themes 16 and 24; see Table 5.2).

However, Greg interrupts this discussion to announce this may be his last time in the group, and he may be moving to another state to begin a job. Greg feels ambivalent, as if he is trying to run away and yet trying to "get out and fight something a little bit." So the theme of conflict between avoidance and encountering problems continues (Themes 3 and 15; see Table 5.2).

The focus of the discussion turns to the specifics of Greg's situation, his fear about a commitment to his girlfriend, and his sense that at times he has been so anxious about being on his own and has such uncertainties about himself, that he has "jumped" at a chance for some certainty or structure, only to have to undo it later. There is a sense of awareness in both Greg and the other group members of frustration and even anguish. They want to feel equal to the challenges within themselves but share an anxiety about whether they are able to do so (Themes 16 and 25; see Table 5.2). Brad proposes that although Greg seems to fear going for the new job, it could be the same sort of grasping at structure that he has done before. However, it may also be that Greg is building a platform from which he can go on. Greg then returns to the topic of love, wondering if there is such a thing (Theme 19; see Table 5.2). Then he states the internal conflict this uncertainty causes:

> Greg: Th—there's a real tension in me right now between just sort of wanting to stand back and say, "All right I understand, the world and me, we're made to fight, so let's fight," and other half of me, "Aw, that's ridiculous, that's paranoid, uh—go out and search for relationships you know." And that gets all mixed up with being afraid of being dependent, too, I suppose. (pause). (Themes 14 and 23; see Table 5.2)
>
> Pat: Afraid of being dependent. Well, aren't you dependent, though?
>
> Greg: Yeah, but, but and, uh, and I don't exactly know where I am in this group either. I—I'll say something that I think is gonna help make friends, and then I'll put some clever remark on it at the end designed to sort of push myself back out a little bit and say, "Watch out, I've still got arrows you know."

And later:

> Martha: What did you mean by that remark, "Watch out, I've still got arrows?"
>
> Greg: No, what I, (sigh) yeah, that is, don't get too close to me because you might wanna, you might wanna kill me or something so I'm gonna stand back and I'm ready to fight, you see. Even as—even as I conceive of myself as sort of opening up a little bit. (Themes 3 and 9; see Table 5.2)
>
> Alice: You might wanna kill me, was that your feeling?
>
> Greg: You might wanna kill me, yeah.
>
> Martha: Don't get too close to me, yeah.
>
> Helen: I guess the moment you may say to somebody, "I love you," or something like this, or show this to somebody, therefore—
>
> Greg: Yeah, well, I hear a big echo chamber, "sucker, sucker, sucker —"(laughter, especially Martha).

Greg says that his ideas about love and commitment almost spoiled his relationship with his girlfriend. They both began trying to measure up to their own preconceptions about love, and these preconceptions caused some difficulties as they tried to get to know each other better (Themes 19 and 25; see Table 5.2).

A rather confused discussion takes place regarding some comments Brad made in an earlier session about love being "something you do."

In fact, the group has thus far avoided addressing the fact that Greg is planning to leave town and the group.

As the session approaches closing, Alice asks Diane, who has been silent during the session, "did you sign out for the day?" Diane assures the group that she is "taking it all in" but has had to "retrench" because she had gotten battered outside of the group. She asks them "please don't make me bring it up." The members make comments about the revelations that have occurred during this session and their thoughts about going further next time. Greg suggests a task for next time in which each member would write down his or her most shameful secret and would read each other's aloud (Themes 17 and 24; see Table 5.2). Alice suggests that this is his curiosity about everyone and that by leaving he will miss hearing their stories and secrets. It is only then clarified that Greg will be at group next time but probably not after that (Themes 6 and 23; see Table 5.2). The session ends.

Content Themes

The identification of content themes in Table 5.2 was introduced to help readers see the development of the issues that preceded the behavior and dynamics in Session 3. We did this in an ad hoc manner, seeking to identify in simple language the content on which the group members were focused. The list is not exhaustive, because the goal was to identify the major themes that engaged group members' energies and time.

We found this so helpful in Sessions 1–3 that we repeated the process for Sessions 4 and 5 as well. According to the Group Development Measures (Beck et al., 1986), these five sessions constitute the first three phases in this group's process. The results show the generation of new themes across the five sessions as well as a process of doubling back in later sessions to pick up themes introduced in earlier sessions. Table 5.2 shows the themes that were identified. Some themes contain more than one topic, but we listed them together because the group members tended to talk about them together or in sequence with each other regularly. Twelve of the 25 themes were introduced during the first two sessions of the group. Table 5.4 shows the frequencies of the appearance of each theme during each of the five sessions. In the discussion below the themes are identified by name and number.

Looking first at the content themes (see Table 5.2), one notices a sequence that takes place from Session 1 through Session 2. This sequence includes concerns about the structure and rules of the group (1, 2, 6, and 8); fear of talking in the group relating to fear of hostility and anger (9); expressions of loss, pain, and suffering and the best ways to cope with these

TABLE 5.4

Frequencies of the Appearance of Themes in Sessions 1–5, Group A

Theme	Session 1	Session 2	Session 3	Session 4	Session 5
1	1	1			
2	2				
3	3	2	1	2	2
4	3				
5	1	1			
6	1	4	1		1
7	1				
8		3	2	1	
9		8	8	2	3
10		1	3	4	
11		2	3		
12		2	2		
13			6	1	
14			6		1
15		1	11	1	2
16			5	2	2
17			2		1
18			5	1	
19			3	2	2
20				2	
21				1	
22				1	
23				1	2
24					2
25					2

experiences (10); struggles with sharing time and space in the group and with being attentive to others' issues versus addressing one's own issues (12); and the responsibilities involved in closeness to others (3).

In the first half of Session 3 the members continue to focus on some of their concerns from Sessions 1 and 2. They discuss fear of talking in the group as this relates to hostility and anger (9), and they talk about suffering by sharing some painful experiences (10 and 13). They add the theme of the importance of talking with and about feelings (14). In the second half of the session they emphasize self-reflection and ownership of their own histories and issues, combined with questioning other members regarding their issues (15). They build on each other's work by sharing family histories and by discussing the concept and reality of love (16, 18, and 19).

Session 4's themes build on those in Sessions 2 and 3, including intimacy issues and how to deal with pain and suffering (3 and 10). New themes are introduced as well, including the consequences of failure to meet the expectations of authority figures (20); the introduction of resiliency as an overarching concept (21); the complexity and risk involved in giving feedback to others (22); and the question of commitment to the group at times of personal crisis or major personal changes (23).

Session 5 continues this discussion and adds two more themes: whether to share "shameful" experiences and the isolation that comes with not sharing them (24) as well as the consequences of failure to meet one's own expectations or fulfill one's own potential (25). Of special interest in Sessions 4 and 5 is the connecting of existing themes with new themes. Some examples follow (see Table 5.2 and the descriptions of Sessions 4 and 5 for the context of these examples):

- connecting Theme 10 (the ongoing discussion about how to handle and/or protect oneself from pain and suffering) with Themes 16 (building on each other's themes and content), 19 (is there love?), 20 (the consequences of failure to meet the expectations of authority figures), and 21 (resiliency, the concept used to integrate the dichotomy between openness to pain vs. having a shell)
- connecting Themes 3 (problems in being closely connected to others) with 9 (fear of talking in group), 15 (owning one's own issues), and 22 (the complexity and risk involved in giving feedback to others)
- connecting Theme 19 (is there love?) with Theme 25 (the consequences of failure to meet one's own expectations).

Group A established patterns of interaction and content themes during these five sessions that continued to evolve over the next 10 sessions. The limited experience of the leaders and the members with group process created a variety of sometimes awkward and sometimes dramatic developments. However, the clients showed a high level of responsiveness, coping skills, and persistence. In the process, they achieved some important changes and understanding as individuals and as a group.

REFERENCES

Beck, A. P. (1970). *Transcript of fifteen sessions of Group* A. Unpublished manuscript: Chicago.

Beck, A. P., Dugo, J. M., Eng, A. M., & Lewis, C. M. (1986). The search for phases in group development: Designing process analysis measures of group interaction. In L. S. Greenberg & W. M. Pinsof (Eds.), *The psychotherapeutic process: A research handbook* (pp. 615–705). New York: Guilford Press.

Dugo, J. M., & Beck, A. P. (1983). Tracking a group's focus on normative–organizational or personal–exploration issues. *Group, 7*, 17–26.

Eng, A. M., & Beck, A. P. (1982). Speech behavior measures of group psychotherapy process. *Group, 6*, 37–48.

III

WELL ESTABLISHED
SYSTEMS FOR GROUP
PROCESS ANALYSIS

6

THE GROUP EMOTIONALITY
RATING SYSTEM

SIGMUND W. KARTERUD

The Group Emotionality Rating System (GERS) is a rating system for group basic assumption functioning according to the theory of W. R. Bion (1961). The system explores the basic assumption theory itself and compares groups, therapists, and group members in terms of levels and patterns of emotional interaction. Bion's 1961 book, *Experiences in Groups*, was a landmark in the history of the psychoanalytic theory of groups, bridging Freud's (1921/1955) contribution, "Group Psychology and the Analysis of the Ego," with Melanie Klein's (1946) new psychoanalytic concepts and Bion's own clinical experiences based on conducting groups according to psychoanalytic principles.

HISTORY AND THEORY OF THE SYSTEM

Bion's (1961) therapeutic experiences with groups were short-lived. They lasted for a few postwar years at the Tavistock Clinic in London. His writings were originally presented as a series of articles (1948–1952) in the journal *Human Relations* and were later collected in the book *Experiences in Groups* (Bion, 1961). Bion left the group scene in the early 1950s and devoted himself to individual psychoanalysis and the utmost boundaries of psychoanalytic theory (e.g., philosophy and psychosis).

Regression to primitive behavior in groups had been a topic of interest (Freud, 1921/1955) for a long time. Bion's fundamental contributions were his systematic descriptions and a new theoretical organization of group observations. His theory can be divided into a group dynamic part, a phenomenological part that described the so-called "basic assumption groups," and a metapsychological part that explains the group dynamics in Kleinian psychoanalytic terms.

Bion's (1961) main thesis was that the task activities of any group are threatened by collective regressive forces from within the group. His theory states that these forces are not random but are unconsciously organized in certain configurations that he labeled *fight–flight*, *dependency*, and *pairing*. When regressed, groups act "as if." They would either act as if their main purpose was to attack or fly from an enemy, to be fed from an omnipotent object, or to indulge in messianic hopes for future salvation. These regressive aspects of groups were called "basic assumptions (BA) groups" and were conceived of as being opposed to the "work group" aspect that carried rationality and the reality principle.

The main points of Bion's (1961) theory, that there exist total group phenomena, that the rationality of a group is threatened by collective unconscious forces, and that these forces have a certain configuration but do not necessarily exclude other unconscious forces, today are uncontroversial and accepted by most group psychotherapists and psychoanalytically oriented group theorists.

The role of projective identification (Klein, 1946) is also widely accepted as a significant mechanism of the fundamental group dynamic. This is most convincingly demonstrated in the fight–flight group, in which hated aspects of self are aggregated among group members and collectively projected onto a conjoint object. Bion (1961) argued that this capacity for unconscious "cooperation" need not be learned. It is a manifestation of a primitive protomental layer in humans. He labeled the readiness to join fellow group members in BA activity *valence*. He postulated individual differences in this respect. People might have high or low valences for any of the basic assumptions.

More controversial are Bion's (1961) metapsychological explanations. He regarded BAs as collective defense mechanisms against psychotic anxiety aroused in the group. This anxiety is aroused, he said, because "the group approximates too closely, in the minds of the individuals composing it, the very primitive fantasies about the contents of the mother's body" and thereby fantasies of "an extremely early primal scene" (Bion, 1961, p. 162). Bion thus resorted to an intrapsychic discourse and neglected the dialectics between the intrapsychic and the interpersonal (e.g., the significance of self objects for maintaining higher levels of psychic functioning). The critics of Bion would paraphrase him and say that he himself, in his activity as group conductor, approximated too closely, in the minds of the individuals composing the group, primitive nonresponsive and rejecting internal objects and thus activated fantasies of isolation, inhumanness, and death.

In defense of Bion (1961), one might say that his *Experiences in Groups* never was intended to be a textbook for group psychotherapy. In some passages he even warned against his own style, which, he said, was adapted for "scientific purposes." What is assumed to be his style has survived at Tavistock conferences, where learning about group regression and how to cope with it is a principal task. Bion's approach to group psychotherapy is outdated, especially since the follow-up study by Malan, Balfour, Hood, and Shooter (1976), which found poor results of group psychotherapy conducted according to the principles of Bion (1961) and Ezriel (1950). In Europe, group analysis according to Foulkesian principles (Pines, 1983) has gained an unquestionable hegemonic position.

In contrast to Foulkes (1973), no school of group psychotherapy has been built on the work of Bion (1961). However, his contribution has been integrated into a variety of group psychotherapy approaches. In particular, these include approaches grounded in object relations theory (Ganzarain, 1989), dealing with group-as-a-whole phenomena (Horwitz, 1977), group-as-a-whole interpretations, collective transferences toward the conductor, borderline patients in groups (Greene, Rosenkrantz, & Muth, 1985), small- and large-group processes at psychiatric wards (Kernberg, 1976; Kibel, 1978), and therapeutic communities (Hinshelwood & Manning, 1979; Karterud, 1989d). He has also stimulated research in the areas of how to avoid malignant BA group phenomena through careful selection and preparation of group members, monitoring boundary issues, and adjusting the conductor style according to the prevailing group developmental phase.

According to Bion (1961), there is a certain contradiction between the work aspect of the group and one of the BAs. At a particular time the work aspect may be dominating and the BA subordinated or vice versa. Along a time axis the operant BA may subside, and another will take its place and enter into the dialectic interplay with work. Bion did not offer any reason for these changes. Neither did he include a theory of development that would imply that certain group configurations were more mature than others, except for the general statement that work should dominate BA. From a group developmental point of view, his theory has been described as a recurring-cycle model (Gibbard, Hartman, & Mann, 1974). Concerning change processes in the individual, he held the Kleinian view that the capacity of the group conductor and the group as a whole to contain and interpret envy, greed, and hatred would ultimately pave the way for the depressive position that implies a higher level of integration, symbol formation, and capacity for love and gratitude.

Bion's (1961) theories contained a set of statements about groups that lent themselves readily to empirical investigations. Herbert Thelen and his colleagues at the University of Chicago capitalized on the momentum. In describing the inception of his work, Stock and Thelen (1957) wrote the following:

> It was decided to take off from the concepts of W. R. Bion, then at Tavistock Institute in London. His notions of the dynamic relation-ships between work and emotionality, his identification of categories of emotionality, his conception of valence and of group culture,—all seemed to provide the basis for a parsimonious theoretical system of concepts for studying the group as an organism.

The research was carried out mainly with training groups at the Na-tional Training Laboratory in Group Development (now called the NTL Institute) in Bethel, Maine. The team developed a battery of research methods (Thelen et al., 1954). Of special importance were a sentence completion test (the Reaction to Group Situation Test), a Q-sort test for group members and observers, and the Behavioral Rating System (BRS). The research team published a vast amount of material in the years 1951–1958 (Stock & Thelen, 1957). The Hill Interaction Matrix was developed based on experiences with the BRS of Thelen et al. (1954) and is mainly a development of the work section of BRS, leaving the BAs aside. The following generation of clinical researchers who explored the relationship of BAs and group developmental stages resorted to global interpretations or indirect means of assessing BA functioning (Armelius & Armelius, 1985; Babad & Amir, 1978).

My own interest in Thelen's work began with a research project that investigated the BA functioning of groups in therapeutic communities. I wanted to compare different groups with different diagnostic compositions and different boundary conditions with respect to the occurrence of BA. This required a valid and reliable method useful for ratings on location independent of laboratories, one-way screens, and complicated electronic devices. Working with Thelen's original manual, it soon became apparent that there were several unresolved methodological difficulties. These were obviously the reasons why the BRS was abandoned by small-group re-searchers in the late 1950s. Based on a series of trials with measurements of reliability and examining the construct and face validity, we (Karterud & Foss, 1989) revised the system. The most fundamental revision, required because of low reliability, was a total omission of the work categories. The rating system was reduced to a seemingly simple procedure (the GERS) for rating some types of verbal emotionality in groups.

CORRESPONDENCE BETWEEN THE THEORY
AND THE SYSTEM

The GERS deviates from the BA theory in several respects. First, the behavioral unit assessed for emotionality is not a natural sequence of BAs, which may last for larger parts or whole group sessions, but singular verbal statements. Second, the BA fight–flight is split into the two categories of fight and flight. Finally, except for pairing, the categories are defined according to common sense, not to the theory of projective identification. My colleague and I (Karterud & Foss, 1989) have constructed a positivist rating system based on theoretical formulations derived from hermeneutical investigations. Understanding the nature and scope of this difference is of fundamental importance for scoring procedures, reliability and validity assessings, and relevant research strategies.

Challenges in Constructing Operational Definitions

Are these behavioral units valid as microbits of BAs, which was the original aspiration of Thelen? The phenomenal units that Bion called "basic assumptions" are not isolated verbal statements, but instead are long sequences of total group phenomena that can last for whole sessions, a series of group sessions, or both. In our rating system the microunits (verbal statements) are not regarded as small bits of BAs. However, the emotionally loaded statements should approximate such bits. The theoretical possibility exists that the sum of a certain amount of such bits will transcend the fragments and become identifiable as a BA. This question is open for empirical investigation.

The extent to which the microbits approximate BA elements depends largely on the definitions of the categories. Only pairing is defined according to Bion, whereas fight, flight, and dependency have commonsense definitions. Therefore, what one would define as "sound angry assertiveness" in a group would be scored as a manifestation of fight. This would obviously not in itself be a microbit of a fight–flight phenomenon. Another manifestation of fight would certainly be such a microbit, such as when it is an individual contribution to a collective mechanism of projective identification. Should one then reserve the category of fight for those manifestations of aggressiveness that belong to the class of projective identification? Should do the same with the other categories? There are also many types of dependency. A healthy dependency in the orientation stage (Lacoursiere, 1980) will urge the participant to ask for rules and norms. Such behavior can be distinguished from manifestations of oral needs, clinging behavior, and resorting to projections of omnipotent fantasies on the group leader.

Thelen et al. (1954) decided to stick to commonsense definitions for the emotional categories. With one exception, I agree with this. Commonsense definitions provide high face validity and usually better reliability. The level of reliability is related to the degree of inference that the raters must perform.

Within the empirical method of emotional content should be derived from the statement itself. Examples include: "I am angry with you" and "This is too difficult for me. Somebody else must take the decision." Or should it be derived from the immediate relational context? This is of special importance for the category of flight. One can easily imagine groups, from a strict primary task (Rice, 1963) point of view, properly characterized as fleeing through an entire session. Such a context would be too broad and would put the flight category in a different position from the others.

Concerning projective identification, an experienced research and group therapist will realize a full-blown BA when it is there. But what about its precursors and initial phases? When does it start or become manifest? The scoring process is difficult. With an in vivo scoring technique, there are seldom opportunities to reflect on earlier doubts and go back in the registration scheme and rescore. A definition based on projective identification would imply, as a matter of necessity, that the scorings were checked at least by an audiotape. A rescoring according to projective identification leads to the microbits being scrutinized in the light of whole sequences. It would be possible to say that, yes, this sequence seems to start here, and here one starts the ratings. The elements will derive their meaning from the totality, and the totality will take on new significance from new elements that are added to the whole. However, then one has entered the hermeneutic circle and moved far beyond the ideals of logical empiricism.

The category of pairing is in a special position. This concept is a psychoanalytic construct with no commonsense counterpart. Thelen et al. (1954) also gave this concept a commonsense definition and declared that "pairing statements express warmth, intimacy, and supportiveness." (p. 24). This definition has low face validity. Few experts would define warmth and supportiveness themselves as pairing. Because of the psychoanalytic nature of this construct, we (Karterud & Foss, 1989) found it necessary to stick to Bion's (1961) original definition. This implies that statements that are candidates for a pairing notation, more than the other categories, should be scrutinized according to their immediate contextual relationships. The intimacy should have a messianic flavor of hope and optimism. The researcher's countertransference reactions should also be taken into consideration. This category is difficult for students and untrained observers to grasp. For trained observers, there is high reliability.

This rating system splits the fight–flight reaction into fight and flight. This does not imply that flight is regarded as a separate BA. The main argument for this separation is that it refines the categories. This is especially important in the fight category. Many research and clinical problems involve general human aggression. It is preferable not to confound this category with flight behavior. When one is dealing with problems related to fight–flight phenomena, the separated data can simply be added.

Limitations and Strengths

The great advantage of a positivist method is that it provides access to statistics and modern computer technology. However, the positivist simplification may seem grotesque and could invalidate the findings. The rating categories treat the verbal statements as identical bits, regardless of the duration of the statements or whether they are meaningless grunts or long interpretations of paramount importance to the group. They also treat the emotionally charged elements as if they are equal. A slightly critical statement is equal to insulting hostility. Significant pauses, absences, and all types of nothingness loaded with significance are ignored. Would this create a distorted picture of reality? The argument against these objections is that if the variations of the elements are normally distributed, it will not matter for practical purposes. If Group A and Group B both contain short and long statements and different types of emotional subcategories, the deviations will balance each other and disappear in the mean.

However, these objections need to be taken seriously when interpreting the data from rating systems such as the GERS. The positivist position in the science of humans is strongly criticized (Sartre, 1968). Opponents declare hermeneutics to be the scientific paradigm for the social sciences (Skjervheim, 1959). My own point of view is that the science of humans should use methods belonging to both the positivist and the hermeneutic schools of science. Diverse methods used on the same object give the researcher a binocular view. This approach also provides ample opportunities for construct validation, which is regarded as the ultimate goal of science (Kerlinger, 1981).

In my view, the GERS yields limited information when used alone. However, combined with a qualitative analysis, such as the one I have used in research reported here, the Group Focal Conflict Analysis (GFCA) of Whitaker and Lieberman (1962), it is powerful. To maximize the binocular view, one should keep the methods as separate as possible.

DESCRIPTION OF THE SYSTEM

Rating

Five categories of emotionality are rated with the GERS: fight, flight, dependency, pairing, and neutral. The behavioral unit for rating is defined as the total speech, or verbal statement, by one person bounded on either side by speeches by other people or by a pause.

Rating Categories and Rules

The researcher, as a nonparticipant group observer, records the time every minute and rates every verbal statement from the group members according to the following categories and rules:

Category 1: Fight (f). A commonsense definition, this category includes all verbal expressions of aggression, ranging from boredom and devaluation to open hostility. Examples include "Can't we proceed? This topic bores me," "I hate that creeping attitude of yours," and "It's time to proceed. We have wasted enough time."

Category 2: Flight (fl). A commonsense definition, this category includes statements that express avoidance of the problem or withdrawal from participation. The flight constellation may include humor, intellectualization, statements out of context, inappropriateness, tension-releasing laughter, trivia, or off-the-point comments. Examples include "I will be absent next week. It belongs under the item Positive News." Therapist: "What were you going to ask Dr. X about? Perhaps we have the answer here." Patient: "It was something quite private."

Category 3: Dependency (d). A commonsense definition, this category includes statements that express reliance on some person or thing external to the membership in the group; appeals for support, direction, approval, or undue attention from the leader; statements that express reliance on outside authorities; statements that express reliance on structure, procedure, or tradition; and expressions of weakness, helplessness, and fear of initiative and trying things out are included. Examples include "I feel very confused. Couldn't you (Therapist X) sort this out?" "Do these things usually happen in other groups too?" and "My pain is almost unbearable, I need more medication."

Category 4: Pairing (p). A "Bionian" definition, this category includes statements that are inviting and appealing and while also conveying intimacy, friendliness, and unusual interest and responsiveness. The content has an idyllic flavor and the immediate context is light and cheerful. There is expressed hope for the future. The statements are often ambiguous and the metaphors or loaded symbols may stimulate sexual fantasies in the observer. Examples include "I think it would be much better if we got a swimming pool at this hospital," "It's so nice to have you in the group, Nancy," and "Why don't we meet at the cafe after the group meeting?"

Category 5: Neutral (n). This category contains no emotionality or is below the threshold of sensory experience. Examples include "How does this fit with your situation at home?" and "Let's compare our expectations with what actually happens."

Mixed emotionality. All emotionality contained in a statement should be registered. In ambivalence there will be a double emotionality; this should be noted. Most common is the combination of fight and dependency, as in angry demandingness (fd). There is seldom a need for three notations.

For statistical purposes, there is a great advantage of the Principle 1 statement: one emotional rating. This implies that the notations of mixed emotionality have to be split. This should be done at random to escape the bias of consistently splitting off one type of emotionality. For convenience, I add all split-off emotionality ratings and treat the sum as a separate variable on the group level. Detailed principles have been identified for rating collective reactions from the group, short statements, long statements, psychotic statements, the relationship of the statement to its immediate versus group-as-a-whole context, reliability testing, and so on (Karterud, 1990b).

Reliability

The reliability for the GERS has been tested on the transcripts and audiotapes of 12 inpatient group sessions 45 min long, drawn at random from a pool of 65 group sessions (Karterud & Foss, 1989). Two independent raters performed an act-by-act assessment of the 4,343 verbal statements contained in these 12 sessions. According to Table 6.1, Rater A rated 1,493 as emotionally charged, whereas Rater B rated 1,484 statements as emotionally charged. Overall agreement was .77, whereas specific agreement ranged from .57 (dependency) to .85 (neutral statements). Kappas ranged from .54 (dependency) to .64 (fight).

A detailed act-by-act scrutiny showed that the emotional categories

TABLE 6.1
Interrater Agreement and Reliability of the GERS

Category	Rater A	Rater B	M	Total agreement	Specific agreement	κ	r
E	1,493	1,485	1,488.5	929	.62	—	.80
n	2,850	2,859	2,854.5	2,427	.85	.56	—
d	362	295	328.5	188	.57	.54	.58
f	436	373	404.5	269	.67	.64	.87
fl	606	705	655.5	409	.62	.55	.82
p	89	111	100.0	63	.63	.62	.93

Note. GERS = Group Emotionality Rating System; E = total number of emotionally charged statements; n = neutral; d = dependency; f = fight, fl = flight; p = pairing.

were seldom confounded. For example, there was a probability of .002 that a statement rated as fight by one would be rated as pairing by the other. This is an argument for construct validity. It indicates that the categories correspond to well-delimited phenomena. The main disagreement was on the question of threshold, that is, how "much" emotionality is necessary for a statement to qualify for an emotional rating. In approximately 30% of the cases, when one rater rated an emotional category, the other rater rated neutral.

The general level of reliability was found to be satisfactory. In fact, it was higher than the most thoroughly tested system in small-group research: the Interaction Process Analysis (IPA) system of Bales (1950). The only study of the IPA system that I know of based on act-by-act agreement was reported by Waxler and Mishler (1966). Analyzing 10,910 units of interaction, they found an overall agreement of .62. Waxler and Mishler (1966) concluded that "we have found in our experience with the category system that it is impossible to raise the act-by-act reliability level through training much beyond 60%" (p. 39). Based on these and my own studies, I would recommend the following standards for an authorized rater: Compared with expert opinion, the correlation coefficient should be greater than .75, the overall agreement greater than .65, the specific agreement greater than .55, and the kappa greater than .50.

Learning the Rating Method

The rating method was tested on eight hospital psychiatrists who had some group therapy practice and "average" knowledge of Bion's (1961) theories. I prepared a standard protocol ("expert opinion") of two subsequent group sessions that contained certain amounts of all types of emotionality. The psychiatrists received 2 hours of theoretical instruction on the method and the manual. They then listened to one group session, during which they could compare their judgments with the expert opinion to get a feel for the method. They rated the subsequent group session, which I compared with the standard protocol.

I found that the beginners had the most difficulty with flight and pairing. Flight is the category with the most detailed prescriptions in the manual, and pairing presupposes a higher level of abstraction than do the others. The best single results from the training test were close to what I would prescribe as minimum skills for an authorized rater (overall agreement = .66). I estimate that another testing and discussion of ratings of approximately three to four tapes would be necessary before adequate skills would be obtained in the group as a whole. With instructions and practical training work, this would come to approximately 20 hours of work.

METHODOLOGY FOR ANALYSIS

Quantitative Analysis

Data from the GERS are appropriate for most types of statistical analyses (see the section on previous research with the system for examples).

Qualitative Analysis

In the work reported here, I used the GFCA of Whitaker and Lieberman (1962) as the method of qualitative analysis to accompany the quantitative analysis of the GERS. The method contains adequate conceptual tools for the dialectics among the intrapsychic, the interpersonal, and the group as a whole. It accounts for development (i.e., enabling group solutions) and developmental arrest (i.e., restrictive group solutions). It has been thoroughly discussed in light of hermeneutics (Karterud, 1989b) and tested for reliability (Karterud, 1988a). The hermeneutic structure of the method provides an opening for the dialectics between the parts and the totality of the material under study.

Generally speaking, the theory views the individual group member as being motivated by certain drives, wishes, and needs conceptualized as disturbing motives that will become activated to different degrees in the group. These motives will, by necessity, be frustrated. They will activate anger and reactive fears such as fear of retaliation, fear of loss of wished for object, fear of being castrated, fear of disintegration, and so on. To survive as a group, members are forced to negotiate compromise solutions. These will eventually give the group matrix (Foulkes, 1973), a certain structure according to agreed-on norms, rules, values, modes of communication, hierarchy, taboo areas, emotional freedom, among others. "Agreed on" must be understood at all levels: unconsciously, preconsciously, and consciously. The same is true for the term *negotiating*. According to Whitaker and Lieberman (1962), certain group solutions are enabling in the sense that they open up the possibilities for further exploration of anxiety-laden material. On the other hand, restrictive group solutions have mainly defensive purposes (e.g., the ultimate purpose of survival of the group as an entity). They may represent a blockage toward further self-exploration. Reactive fears and disturbing motives are also influenced by reality factors, such as past events, acting in, boundary problems, and existential facts (e.g., the date for termination). The question of reliability of a hermeneutic method such as the GFCA is a complex matter. It is possible to obtain adequate reliability with the GFCA. However, such reliability cannot be expressed by ordinary statistical means; instead, it has to be demonstrated and proved by hermeneutical explanatory procedures (Karterud, 1988a).

PREVIOUS RESEARCH WITH THE SYSTEM

The examples of research that are presented here are from the project titled "Group Processes in Therapeutic Communities" (Karterud, 1989d). The material for this study consisted of 75 inpatient group therapy sessions 45 minutes long and involved 91 patients and 53 staff members. A total number of 28,950 verbal statements from these 144 individuals were classified and analyzed.

Group Differences With Respect to BA Functioning

Based on GFCA (Karterud 1989a; Whitaker & Lieberman, 1962), I defined 10 sessions as being dominated by BA dependency and 41 sessions as being dominated by BA fight–flight. This categorization was arrived at by consensus between two researchers based on the nature of the disturbing motives (irritation, anger, hatred, revenge, etc.), the reactive motives (fear of expressing anger, fear of retaliation, fear of disintegration), and the solutions (the therapist deserves hard critics, it is wise to be careful and cooperate, etc.). Table 6.2 shows the differences in quantitative ratings according to the GERS classification. The fight–flight groups had a higher total interaction, a lower level of dependency, a higher level of fight and flight, a higher pairing level, and higher total emotionality. All differences were statistically significant at the .01 level. These results demonstrate the system's power to discriminate between groups dominated by different BAs.

Differences Between Therapists

Three different therapeutic communities (TCs) were investigated in this research project. One major finding was that TC-1 was suffering from a collective burnout syndrome with a preponderance for fight–flight reactions, whereas TC-2 was functioning fairly well and was dominated by BA dependency. Table 6.3 shows the ratings of the staff group behavior in these communities (Karterud, 1988c). Therapists in the fight–flight com-

TABLE 6.2
Differences (Mean per Session) Between Dependency Groups and Fight–Flight Groups

Type of Groups	I-tot	d	%	f	%	fl	%	p	%	E-tot	%
Dependency	330	40.9	11.9	7.1	2.1	34.5	10.7	2.5	0.9	85.0	25.6
Fight–flight	408	28.8	7.3	43.5	10.5	56.4	13.5	9.5	2.3	138.2	33.6

Note. I-total = total number of statements per session; d = dependency; f = fight; fl = flight; E-tot = total number of emotionally charged statements; % = percent of each type of BA statement. From "A Comparative Study of Six Different Inpatient Groups With Respect to Their Basic Assumption Functioning," by S. Karterud, 1989, *International Journal of Group Psychotherapy, 39* (3), p. 363. Copyright 1989 by Guilford Press. Reprinted with permission.

TABLE 6.3
Therapists' Group Behavior in Two Therapeutic Communities

Therapists in	d%	f%	fl%	f–fl%	p%	E-tot%
TC-1 (*n* = 31)	1.1	3.2	7.7	10.9	1.9	13.7
TC-2 (*n* = 8)	0.8	1.3	3.2	4.5	0.4	7.4

Note. TC-1 = Therapeutic Community 1; TC-2 = Therapeutic Community 2; d = dependency; f = fight; fl = flight; f–fl = fight–flight; E-tot = total number of emotionally charged statements.

munity (TC-1) differed from the other therapists by being more emotionally involved (E-tot), particularly regarding fight–flight and pairing. These differences were significant at the .01 level. These quantitative ratings confirmed the clinical impression that the therapists in TC-1 acted with the rest of the group and had trouble containing their countertransference reactions.

The Valence Theory

"The individual's readiness to enter into combination with the group in acting on the basic assumptions" was labeled *valence* by Bion (1961, p. 116). To explore individual differences, 87 of the patients in the study were divided into nine diagnostic categories from the third edition of the *Diagnostic Statistical Manual of Mental Disorders* (American Psychiatric Association, 1980). The personality disorders were classified into "rejective" (schizotypal, antisocial, and narcissistic), borderline, and Cluster C personality disorders. The 87 patients participated in a mean of 6.6 group sessions, which means that the study was based on 570 individual-in-session observations. The valence was defined as the percentage of total behavior that was emotional BA behavior. The valence pattern was calculated for each diagnostic category. For example, 18% of the verbal statements of rejective personality disorders contained fight, whereas only 7% of the statements of patients with Cluster C personality disorders ($p < .05$) were rated in the fight category. On the basis of these calculations, it was possible to construct tables demonstrating the valence hierarchy for different personalities. Table 6.4 demonstrates the fight-to-dependency ratio. The table can be interpreted as the most likely way for these diagnostic entities to react when frustrated in groups. Although rejective personality disorders have a high tendency to react with fight–flight, the major depressions have an equally strong tendency to react with dependency. The border position of borderline personality disorder is neatly demonstrated. Borderline is midway between the paranoid-schizoid position and the depressive position.

The validity of the valence theory was confirmed by a study of the explained variance by the variables diagnoses, gender, and age. Together, gender and age explained, on average, only 2% of the differences in BA behavior, whereas diagnoses explained 7%–20%. The diagnostic categories

TABLE 6.4
The Fight-to-Dependency Ratio for Nine Diagnostic Categories

Category	Ratio	Valence
"Rejective" personality disorders	3.3	Major valence
Major affective disorder, manic	1.4	for fight–flight
Schizophrenic disorder	1.4	↑
Alcohol dependency	1.0	
Borderline personality disorder	0.9	
Cluster C personality disorder	0.7	
Neuroses	0.7	↓
Schizophreniform disorder	0.6	Major valence
Major depression	0.3	for dependency
Total mean	0.9	

differed mostly on fight valence. The variance explained by diagnoses concerning fight behavior was 20%, whereas gender and age explained only 0.1% and 0.8%, respectively. In short, aggression in groups does not relate to gender or age but to personality characteristics. These results (Karterud, 1988b) confirm Bion's (1961) observations, which had not yet been verified so clearly by strict behavioral ratings.

Group Process Studies: The Relationship Between the Different BAs

Can BAs be detected by quantitative measures alone? Based on a comparison between groups and a study of frequency distributions, I have suggested the following guidelines: There is a strong likelihood of a manifest BA fight–flight when there are more than 40 fight statements during a 90-minute session; BA dependency when the fight-to-dependency ratio is below .50; BA pairing when there are more than 30–40 pairing statements per 90 minutes. Group sessions with emotionality ratings beyond these levels may be regarded as "true" BA groups (Karterud, 1989c).

APPLICATION OF THE SYSTEM OF ANALYSIS TO GROUP A, SESSION 3

The GERS was used to rate Session 3 of Group A. Most of this report was on Session 3 summaries. Session 3 contained 859 verbal statements (see Table 6.5); 590 were rated neutral and 269 were rated with emotionality (E% = 31%). Flight was the dominant emotionality (fl = 172, 20%), followed by fight (f = 45, 5%), pairing (p = 36, 4%), and dependency (d = 16, 2%). It contained 35 mixed statements.

These results clearly indicate that the session was dominated by BA fight–flight. A total interaction of 859 verbal statements per 90 minutes is in itself an indicator of a fight–flight group. A dependency group is

TABLE 6.5
GERS Rating of Group A in Session 3 and the Individual Members

Member	Neutral	Dependency	Fight	Flight	Pairing	E%	I-total
Greg	65	3	3	25	4	35	100
Alice[a]	143	1	7	33	5	24	189
Helen[a]	63	2	0	5	1	11	71
Diane	124	3	10	40	10	34	187
Brad	20	2	1	2	3	29	28
Martha	106	4	13	30	8	34	161
Pat	17	0	1	0	1	11	19
Joe	49	1	9	34	4	49	97
Group	3	0	1	3	0		7
Total	590	16	45	172	36	31	859

Note. GERS = Group Emotionality Rating System; E% = percentage of emotionality charged statements; I-total = total number of statements per session.
[a]Therapist.

slower and more careful. In fact, in Session 3 there were long periods with much noise. People were laughing, talking simultaneously, and competing for the speech, and it was difficult to get in. The level of BA emotionality (E% = 31) was slightly below the mean E% for inpatient groups (E% = 32.4). The flight category is a poor indicator of a particular BA; it is the combination with fight and the absence of dependency that counts. As previously noted, a level of more than 40 fight statements per 90 minutes is indicative of a BA fight–flight. The relationship between fight and dependency provides further evidence. The f-to-d ratio for Session 3 was 2.8. This is on the same level as the other fight–flight groups that I have recorded. A dependency group should have an f-to-d ratio below 0.5.

According to Table 6.5, the individuals who contributed most to this particular group atmosphere were Alice, Diane, Martha, Joe, and Greg. Helen was more neutral and Pat and Brad more withdrawn. Joe had the highest proportion of statements rated BA emotionality (E% = 49), and Pat had the lowest proportion (E% = 11). Diane, Martha, Alice, and Joe were the dominant fight–flight pairing protagonists, with high scores on these BAs. Table 6.5 also shows the unusual behavior of the main therapist, Alice. In fact, she was the most active person in the group (I-total = 189), and this activity was loaded with an emotional investment (E% = 24). This hardly differentiated her from the other members. The subordinate therapist, Helen, displayed an activity (I-total = 71) and an emotional involvement (E% = 11) more in accordance with general recommendations for group therapists.

Figure 6.1 shows how the emotionality was distributed throughout the third session. It indicates three BA phases: one initial phase, one middle fight–flight phase, and one terminating pairing phase.

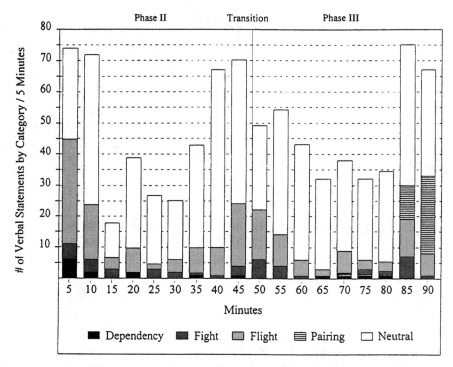

Figure 6.1. Summary of group emotionality ratings, Session 3, Group A. The total column represents the sum of all verbal statements per 5 minutes. The different interaction types (depending, fight, etc.) are added on each other.

The boundary between Phases II and III that was identified by Beck, Dugo, Eng, and Lewis (1986) is indicated by a vertical line near the 50 minute column in Figure 6.1. The Phase II sample segment occurred during Minutes 17–32, the transition segment during Minutes 44–48, and the Phase III sample segment during Minutes 72–77. The Phase II segment preceded the middle fight–flight phase, the transition marked the peak and beginning decline of the middle fight–flight phase, and the Phase III segment preceded the terminating pairing phase. The analysis presented here is based on ratings of the whole of Session 3, and these smaller sample segments are identified here to facilitate the reader's comparison of the GERS with other systems.

Based on the GERS data, one may make the following observations about Session 3: It seems to be a group with a high level of BA emotionality, comparable to inpatient groups; the high level of BA fight–flight is likely to trigger fear of disintegration, particularly at this early time in the group; the group seems to contain an outsider, Joe, who displays considerably more regressed behavior (E% = 49) than the other group members; the therapist, Alice, is unusually active; and the terminating BA pairing period is probably reactive to a fear of disintegration.

CLINICAL INTERPRETATION

The following events from the first two sessions constitute reality factors of dynamic significance for Session 3. Group A is a group of 6 people with two female cotherapists who declared that they do not know much about groups. This inexperience is reflected in several ways. They seem to harbor grandiose fantasies about their therapeutic project; they neglect setting firm and reliable boundaries for the group; and they demonstrate active and involved individualized styles. In this context, the monopolizer Joe kept going until it got to be too much for three other group members. They began to attack Joe in a scapegoating manner.

In Session 3, Martha, who was absent in Session 2, initiates a confusing discussion (the first BA/fight–flight period) about which gender is the most superior, until the central issue of the previous session comes up (Minute 6). At this point Greg says, "We gave Joe a hard time during the last part of the hour."

Joe tells how confused he was after that session. He says that he tried to telephone the therapists but that he eventually "straightened out things" for himself, coming to the conclusion that because "we all are different personalities," "we are bound to irritate each other." He provides evidence for belief with a long story about his job situation. Pat then tries to repair the relationship with Joe. The members then, mainly with reference to Joe, engage in a struggle to find a common platform, a place to meet, an opening for a true encounter. The group is working with its own frustration. In this second BA/fight–flight period (40–55 minutes), there is intense activity replete with laughter, interruptions, and fighting to speak.

This period is resolved by Brad's comment on the group's preoccupation with Joe. Brad makes a group intervention by pointing out that Joe was the only person who had tried to open up (Minute 44). Greg adds, "Well, the very fact that he's external makes it easier to jump on than it is to jump on something that might hurt."

Diane and Martha go on to say that when they are spontaneous and acting out of "deep-seated values," they are rebuked by others. Diane, Greg, Martha, and Joe then start to talk about their families of origin. One is then presented with a set of parental caretakers who are, as Martha states, "exceptionally negative." The problems of the parents include alcohol abuse, inappropriate aggressive behavior, rigid authoritarianism, and guilt-inducing control backed by religious injunctions.

At 83 minutes, when Joe says that parenting is not that easy, with reference to his own son, Diane introduces love as the missing remedy. An eager, increasingly hopeful discussion ensues. Diane says, "It's a very special kind of love that I speak of really . . . which I think does exist somewhere . . . and I don't mean God's love, I mean man's love." Diane encourages the rest of the group to express a mutual declaration and belief in love.

Even Joe, who in the previous sessions had said that it is better to be lonesome and aloof in this cruel world, now exclaims, "Everybody wants to be wanted, to be loved; they don't wanna be out in the world alone." Finally, they include Pat in a cheerful, optimistic group united by love.

In a qualitative analysis, the session was analyzed with the GFCA, which is summarized in Figure 6.2. The reality factors act through frustration of self object needs, which activate anger toward the monopolizer and therapists. This anger provokes reactive fears connected to guilt feelings and fear of disintegration of the group. The main part of the manifest behavior of the group is negotiating an acceptable solution to alleviate the

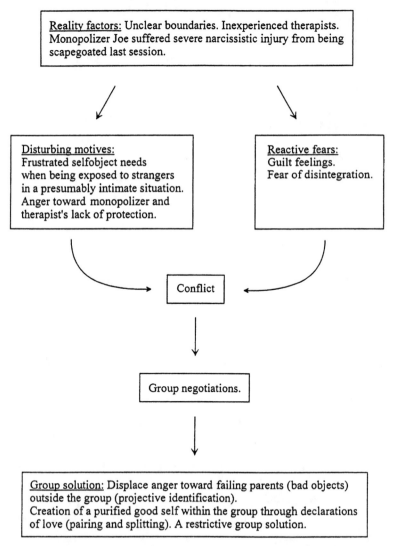

Figure 6.2. Group focal conflict analysis of Sesion 3, Group A.

fears and rescue the group. The decisive turning point is in Minute 44, when Brad rescues Joe. The next move is to find a container outside the group for the activated rage. The group solution is considered restrictive because its dominating purpose is survival of the group at the cost of self-understanding. The solution embodies the defense mechanisms of projective identification and splitting. It is a well-known solution in early group developmental stages and in groups fixated at early stages due to unfavorable boundary conditions, such as psychiatric wards (Karterud, 1989a).

ASSESSMENT AND FUTURE DIRECTIONS

Research with the GERS has confirmed the existence of BA phenomena and the valence theory. It has also added empirical details to the broad conceptualizations that Bion (1961) presented in his pioneering contributions to the science of group dynamics. However, Bion's metapsychological explanations, that BA are collective phenomena reactive to "an extremely early primal scene" (p. 164), could not be confirmed. Bion derived such explanations from his general Kleinian theoretical outlook.

In my research, my colleagues and I gradually arrived at a position of separating the phenomenology of BA from its Kleinian theoretical framework. Such a position allows for different theoretical explanations of these powerful group dynamic phenomena. Based on research evidence of the relationship between BA fight–flight and BA pairing, I have outlined an alternative explanation grounded in the theory of self psychology (Karterud, 1990a; Kohut, 1976).

The GERS is a theory-derived rating system with high reliability and validity. It does not presuppose complicated technology devices and is easy to learn. It measures the occurrence of BA phenomena, their quality and intensity, and the interactional style of the individual members. The GERS also allows comparisons of group sessions, groups, and individuals. By itself, the GERS is not useful for a detailed process analysis of one particular session. However, combined with other methods, particularly hermeneutical methods, it is a powerful tool. The combined quantitative and qualitative analysis of Session 3, Group A, contains substantial evidence for the existence of a fight–flight group in combination with a pairing group as well as an account with high explanatory power for the dynamics behind these phenomena.

REFERENCES

American Psychiatric Association. (1980). *Diagnostic and statistical manual of mental disorders* (3rd ed.). Washington, DC: Author.

Armelius, K., & Armelius, B. A. (1985). Group personality, task and group culture. In M. Pines (Ed.), *Bion and group psychotherapy* (pp. 255–273). London: Routledge & Kegan Paul.

Babad, E. Y., & Amir, L. (1978). Bennis and Shepard's theory of group development: An empirical examination. *Small Group Behavior, 4,* 77–93.

Bales, R. F. (1950). *Interaction process analysis.* Chicago: University of Chicago Press.

Beck, A. P., Dugo, J. M., Eng, A. M., & Lewis, C. M. (1986). The search for phases in group development: Designing process analysis measures of group interaction. In L. S. Greenberg & W. P. Pinsof (Eds.), *The psychotherapeutic process: A research handbook* (pp. 615–705). New York: Guilford Press.

Bion, W. R. (1961). *Experiences in groups.* London: Tavistock.

Ezriel, H. (1950). A psychoanalytic approach to group treatment. *British Journal of Medical Psychology, 23,* 59–74.

Foulkes, S. H. (1973). The group as matrix of the individual's mental life. In L. R. Wolberg & E. K. Schwartz (Eds.), *Group therapy* (pp. 211–220). New York: Intercontinental Medical Book Corporation.

Freud, S. (1955). Group psychology and the analysis of the ego. In J. Strachey (Ed. and Trans.), *The standard edition of the complete psychological works of Sigmund Freud* (Vol. 18, pp. 69–143). London: Hogarth Press. (Original work published 1921)

Ganzarain, R. (1989). *Object relations group psychotherapy.* Madison, CT: International Universities Press.

Gibbard, G. S., Hartman, J. J., & Mann, R. D. (1974). Group process and development. In G. S. Gibbard, J. J. Hartman, & R. D. Mann (Eds.), *Analysis of groups* (pp. 83–93). San Fransisco: Jossey-Bass.

Greene, L. R., Rosenkrantz, J., & Muth, D. Y. (1985). Splitting dynamics, self-representations and boundary phenomena in the group psychotherapy of borderline personality disorders. *Psychiatry, 48,* 234–245.

Hinshelwood, R. D., & Manning, N. (1979). *Therapeutic communities: Reflections and progress.* London: Routledge & Kegan Paul.

Horwitz, L. (1977). A group-centered approach to group psychotherapy. *International Journal of Group Psychotherapy, 27,* 423–439.

Karterud, S. (1988a). A reliability study of a hermeneutic method: Group Focal Conflict Analysis. *Group Analysis, 4,* 333–346.

Karterud, S. (1988b). The valence theory of Bion and the significance of (*DSM-III*) diagnoses for inpatient group behavior. *Acta Psychiatrica Scandinavica, 78,* 462–470.

Karterud, S. (1988c). The influence of task definition, leadership and therapeutic style on inpatient group culture. *International Journal of Therapeutic Communities, 4,* 231–247.

Karterud, S. (1989a). A comparative study of six different inpatient groups with respect to their basic assumption functioning. *International Journal of Group Psychotherapy, 3,* 355–376.

Karterud, S. (1989b). On methods and principles of hermeneutics: With reference to psychoanalytic study of small groups. *Free Association, 18,* 73–89.

Karterud, S. (1989c). A study of Bion's basic assumption groups. *Human Relations, 4,* 315–335.

Karterud, S. (1989d). *Group processes in therapeutic communities.* London: Artesian Press.

Karterud, S. (1990a). Bion or Kohut: Two paradigms of group dynamics. In B. E. Roth, W. N. Stone, & H. D. Kibel (Eds.), *The difficult patient in group: Group psychotherapy with borderline and narcissistic disorders* (pp. 45–66). Madison, CT: International Universities Press.

Karterud, S. (1990b). *Group Emotionality Rating System manual.* Oslo, Norway: Ulleval University Hospital.

Karterud, S., & Foss, T. (1989). Group Emotionality Rating System: A modification of Thelen's method of assessing emotionality in groups. *Small Group Behavior, 2,* 131–150.

Kerlinger, F. N. (1981). *Foundations of behavioral research.* New York: Holt, Rinehart & Winston.

Kernberg, O. (1976). Toward an integrative theory of hospital treatment. In O. Kernberg (Ed.), *Object relation theory and clinical psychoanalysis* (pp. 241–275). Northvale, NJ: Jason Aronson.

Kibel, H. D. (1978). The rationale for the use of group psychotherapy for borderline patients on a short term unit. *International Journal of Group Psychotherapy, 28,* 339–358.

Klein, M. (1946). Notes on some schizoid mechanisms. In M. M. R. Khan (Ed.), *Envy and gratitude and other works 1946–1963* (pp. 1–24). London: Hogarth Press.

Kohut, H. (1976). Creativeness, charisma, group psychology. In P. H. Ornstein (Ed.), *The search for the self: Vol. 2. Selected writings of Heinz Kohut 1950–78* (pp. 793–843). Madison, CT: International Universities Press.

Lacoursiere, R. (1980). *The life cycle of groups.* New York: Human Sciences Press.

Malan, D. H., Balfour, F. H. G., Hood, V. G., & Shooter, A. M. (1976). Group psychotherapy: Long term follow-up study. *Archives of General Psychiatry, 33,* 1303–1315.

Pines, M. (1983). The contribution of S. H. Foulkes to group therapy. In M. Pines (Ed.), *The evolution of group analysis* (pp. 265–285). London: Routledge & Kegan Paul.

Rice, K. (1963). *The enterprise and its environment.* London: Tavistock.

Sartre, J. P. (1968). *Being and nothingness.* New York: Washington Square Press.

Skjervheim, H. (1959). *Objectivism and the study of man.* Oslo, Norway: University Press.

Stock, D., & Thelen, H. (1957). *Emotional dynamics and group culture.* Washington, DC: National Training Laboratories.

Thelen, H., Stock, D., Ben-Zeev, S., Gradolph, J., & Hill, W. (1954). *Methods for *studying work and emotionality in group operations.* Chicago: University of Chicago.

Waxler, N. E., & Mishler, E. C. (1966). Scoring and reliability problems in interactional analysis: A methodological note. *Sociometry, 29,* 28–40.

Whitaker, D. S., & Lieberman, M. A. (1962). Methodological issues in the assessment of total-group phenomena in group therapy. *International Journal of Group Psychotherapy, 12,* 312–325.

7

THE HILL INTERACTION MATRIX: THERAPY THROUGH DIALOGUE

ADDIE FUHRIMAN AND GARY M. BURLINGAME

The Hill Interaction Matrix (HIM) is a behavioral rating system that measures the therapeutic quality of group participant interactions. Accordingly, the HIM articulates an explicit value system for what is deemed "therapeutic" in group member interactions. This value system emerged from a rich theoretical heritage of group dynamics, which is summarized first. In the next section we briefly describe the most recent version of the HIM and how the value system was used to develop the two dimensions of member behavior (i.e., content and work style) rated by the Hill Interaction Matrix–Statement by Statement (HIM–SS). We then focus on the correspondence between the theory and measure, examining the psychometric strengths and limitations of the HIM–SS as well as findings from previous research. After applying the HIM–SS to a common transcript, we close with a discussion on the unique contribution made by HIM to both the group literature and the training of neophyte group therapists.

The development of the HIM extended over two decades (1950s–

We acknowledge the contribution of William Fawcett Hill, who furnished historical and contextual background, and Priscilla S. Hill, who provided consultation on the history, development, and recent use of the Hill Interaction Matrix.

135

1960s), fostered primarily by the efforts of William Fawcett Hill. It has become one of the most widely used measures of group interaction in the small-group literature. In its first decade of existence in its final form, it spawned nearly 150 studies that explored group development, leadership style, and group composition questions (W. F. Hill, 1977). A more recent tabulation of empirical work using the HIM indicates that it continues to be used, but less frequently.

The HIM is a family of four process measures—HIM–SS, HIM–A, HIM–B, and HIM–G—rather than a single instrument. These different measures range from rating systems that classify member and leader statements to more global paper-and-pencil instruments measuring group behavior intent. Nevertheless, all four HIM variations are based on the same conceptual framework.

Before describing the conceptual framework of the current HIM, we provide a brief genealogy of W. F. Hill's intellectual heritage because these theories of group process and therapy clearly influenced the development of his system. An equally important consideration in understanding the final infrastructure of the system is the methodology W. F. Hill used. W. F. Hill was influenced by the theoretical literature, but, more important, he grounded his measure on observations of ongoing therapy groups. His scrutiny of these groups is remarkable because it spanned a decade and involved groups drawn from three clinical settings. These empirical observations spawned three preliminary versions and, ultimately, the final versions of the HIM.

HISTORY AND THEORY OF THE SYSTEM

The theoretical heritage of the HIM is difficult to determine if one relies solely on the sources cited in the monograph (W. F. Hill, 1965a). A careful examination of W. F. Hill's intellectual lineage and training environment reveals an ambience rich in small-group dynamics. The chair of W. F. Hill's committee at the University of Chicago was Herbert Thelen, who familiarized him with the group dynamics literature of the day, including concepts such as the group as a whole. Thelen's focus on group dynamics was predictable because his mentor was Kurt Lewin (1951), who, along with several of his students, elevated group dynamics to an identifiable field of study in the United States. Indeed, the experimental work of Thelen and his students (i.e., William Hill, Morton Lieberman, Carl Whitaker, and Dorothy Stock Whitaker) is considered to be one of the major bridges between group dynamics investigations in social psychology and the clinical applications of small groups (E. M. Pattison, 1969).

One example of this experimental work is W. F. Hill's dissertation (1955), which inspired aspects of the current HIM (P. S. Hill, personal communication, April 30, 1994). He used Bethel T-group data and Bion's (W. F. Hill, personal communication, November, 1996) emotionality model to investigate subgrouping. W. F. Hill (personal communication, August 1994, 1965a), in part, attributed features (e.g., the work style dimension) of the HIM to this early experimental work, Bion's influential writings, and the interdisciplinary climate of the Committee on Human Development, the academic unit at the University of Chicago where he obtained his degree.

Unmistakable evidence of the influence of the extant small-group dynamics literature on the development of the HIM include W. F. Hill's focus on rating member interpersonal interactions, the belief that psychotherapy groups could be differentiated by different work styles, the importance of interpersonal risk as an essential therapeutic component, and the elevation of the member to a status that was equivalent to the therapist in effecting change in the operation of the group (group as a whole).

Although the influence of small-group dynamics theory is more easily traced, there is only subtle evidence of the impact of more traditional therapeutic theories on the HIM. This influence is most manifest in the therapeutic value system of the HIM (see the section on the description of the system). For instance, the influence of nondirective group therapy (Gorlow, Hoch, & Telschow, 1952) is apparent in the value for "patient–therapist role taking." The group-analytical emphasis on the here and now (Foulkes, 1948) as a technique to facilitate the corrective emotional experience (Frank & Ascher, 1951) can be implicitly seen in both the "interpersonal threat" and "member-centered" values where the relationship category is awarded the highest rank. Acknowledgment of psychodynamic theory to "substantiate the significance" (W. F. Hill, 1965a, p. 5) of the HIM categories is also found in the manual, but no traditional psychodynamic terminology appears.

Note that W. F. Hill seemed to perceive these theoretical influences as the background to a larger goal, that is, the construction of a measure that would assist in the development of a theory of group process for therapy groups (cf. Castore, Hill, & Lake, 1959). Thus, a unique characteristic of the HIM is the absence of an identifiable theory of group process or psychotherapy to guide the selection of key elements in the rating system. Unlike most therapy rating systems that rely on a key theory to target important constructs to operationalize, W. F. Hill used an empirical, inductive approach based on emerging clinical data. This endeavor was supported primarily by National Institute of Mental Health funding. In fact, his reliance on grounded theory resulted in three versions of the rating system during the 1950s and 1960s, until the therapy groups being observed were adequately described by the last version published in 1965 (see Table 7.1).

W. F. Hill's (1965a) intention was to build a pantheoretical scale that

TABLE 7.1
Summary of Instruments that Preceded the HIM–SS–1965

Instrument	Purpose	Description	General Observations
Blackfoot scale and HIM–1954 (Castore, Hill, & Lake, 1959)	Track the complexity of interpersonal interaction in state hospital psychotherapy groups.	Five-level system for member interaction: 1. No social recognition of others. 2. Social recognition but no discrimination of interpersonal cues. 3. Social recognition and isolated discrimination of interpersonal cues. 4. Response to interpersonal cues and limited awareness of relationship with others. 5. Discrimination of subtle interpersonal cues and multiple relationship options.	Recognition of the coarseness of scale led to the development of a scoring guide that significantly improved agreement.
HHIM, 1957 (I. S. Hill & Hill, 1957)	Track (a) the development level of psychotherapy groups composed of a wide variety of patients (severely regressed to functioning outpatients) guided by different theoretical orientations and (b) the content and style of verbal interactions.	Four levels of work: 1. Simple verbalization 2. Social conversation 3. Preparatory work 4. Problem-oriented work Four levels of content and style of interaction: 1. Nonpersonal 2. Personal 3. Interpersonal 4. Group	Separate ratings made for therapist and patient ratings. A 55-page manual was developed to guide ratings. A preliminary version of this scale was developed subsequent to the Blackfoot scale but was too unwieldly (108 cells) to use.
HIM-SS (1962)	Track interpersonal interactions of diverse psychotherapy groups.	Four levels of content: 1. Nonpersonal 2. Group 3. Personal 4. Relationship Five levels of work styles 1. Responsive 2. Conventional 3. Assertive 4. Speculative 5. Confrontive	Content styles are reordered to reflect a different value system. Two risk rating work styles added. No separate ratings for therapist and patient.

Note. HIM–SS = Hill Interaction Matrix–Statement by Statement; HHIM = Hill and Hill Interaction Matrix.

"would not depend on knowledge of any particular personality theory" (p. 5) to successfully rate the verbal interactions in psychotherapy groups. He wanted to measure all types of groups irrespective of the therapeutic orientation of the leader. He knew that he had to base his system on the observation of diverse patients (diagnosis) and therapists (theoretical orientations) using both inpatient and outpatient psychotherapy groups. Given these goals, the empirical evolution of W. F. Hill's categories is especially instructive as he moved from a controlled group dynamics academic environment into two state hospitals. What follows is a brief synopsis of the evolution of the measures (B/HIM–1954, HHIM–1957, HIM–SS–1962) that led to the HIM–SS–1965, all of which are driven primarily by empirical observations (see Table 7.1).

Blackfoot Scale and the HIM–1954

The Blackfoot scale was developed in the early 1950s when W. F. Hill was a staff psychologist at the state hospital in Blackfoot, Idaho (W. F. Hill, personal communication, August 14, 1994). It was seen as the first step in "the development of a theory of group process, specifically relating to the therapeutic value of interpersonal interaction as expressed in verbal communication" (Castore et al., 1959, p. 1). The need for such a theory (and scale) appears to be related to interviews that W. F. Hill conducted during the same time period with 19 group therapists, including both psychologists and psychiatrists, practicing at state and Veterans Affairs hospitals in Idaho and Utah (W. F. Hill, 1957). These therapists reported virtually no academic training in group therapy, were unable to articulate a clear theoretical rationale for group treatment, and described the therapist role as being primarily passive and nondirective. This conceptual void was in stark contrast to W. F. Hill's substantive theoretical grounding in group process and dynamics.

The Blackfoot scale was W. F. Hill's response to the disparity between his training and the state hospital context. In short, it reflected his expectation that the regularities of the group processes he observed in the controlled laboratory settings at Chicago had a parallel in less controlled clinical settings (i.e., state hospital groups). This B scale was developed to empirically ascertain whether verbal behavior in group therapy behaved in a lawful manner across a diversity of patient diagnoses and therapeutic orientations. The patient groups studied ranged from chronically regressed inpatients (schizophrenic patients) to outpatients (high-functioning neurotic patients). Therapists leading these groups endorsed a variety of theoretical orientations. The degree of complexity of interpersonal interaction between group members (including the leader) was targeted as the primary variable to rate in the Blackfoot scale using a five-level scale (see Table 7.1). The lowest level of interactional complexity reflected members who exhibited no recognition of others' presence and no ability to discriminate interpersonal cues. At the highest level, members could not only discriminate relevant interpersonal cues but they could also conceive of alternative relationship possibilities for themselves and others.

Although the Blackfoot scale demonstrated adequate interrater reliability, the primary conclusion (Castore et al., 1959) was that its discrimination was too coarse to tap into the richness of interaction complexity. The HIM–1954 emerged from W. F. Hill and Ida Stewart Hill's observation of the salient and differentiating characteristics of the Blackfoot therapy groups. I. S. Hill suggested an empirical approach identifying the prominent characteristics of the groups. The conversion of these emergent categories into 108 separate ratings was considered too unwieldy and refined. The next rendition of the HIM, the HHIM–1957, appears to be a compromise between these two systems.

HHIM–1957

The Hill and Hill Interaction Matrix (I. S. Hill & Hill, 1957) was a collaborative effort between William and Ida Hill and was based on their collective clinical experience with groups in two state hospitals (Utah and Idaho). The HHIM–1957's infrastructure set the tone for later revisions and is dramatically different from the simple 5-level system used in the Blackfoot scale and the complexity of the 108-level HIM–1954. The realization that psychotherapy groups could successfully function at different developmental levels was introduced as a key concept by the HHIM–1957, a concept not surprising given the patient groups observed (e.g., chronic inpatients to high-functioning outpatients).

The developmental stage of a group was captured in the level of work inherent in member interactions using a 4-point work scale that is similar to the Blackfoot scale (see Table 7.1). For instance, a member at the lowest level of work in the HHIM–1957 can react only to therapist questions and is unable to initiate or maintain interaction with peers, which is akin to the second level in the Blackfoot scale. Problem-oriented work is the highest level of functioning for a psychotherapy group in the HHIM–1957 (Level 4) and resembles the 5th level of the Blackfoot scale. The sequential conditions for the occurrence of problem-oriented work in the HHIM–1957 were that a patient be able to talk, talk to peers, grasp the significance of psychological concepts, and talk with peers about applying these psychological concepts to his or her problems.

The perceived goal of therapists in the HHIM–1957, irrespective of their therapeutic orientation, was to facilitate movement from the lower to the higher levels of work. Thus, their verbalizations were rated separately from group members because the members' response is the primary indicator of the developmental level of the group.

The HHIM–1957 system recognized that the topics discussed in a group have greater or lesser therapeutic potential; thus, it introduced a separate rating for the content contained in each member verbalization. It became important not only to rate *how* the group was interacting (work style) but also to rate *what* they were talking about. Four levels were used to capture the content of interaction. Content with the lowest therapeutic potential consisted of nonpersonal topics (e.g., weather) that revealed little about personal problems. Interaction that focused on group topics (e.g., group as a whole) were seen as having the most therapeutic potential. In these interactions, the group was viewed as a potent force for change. By crossing these four *how* and *what* dimensions, a 4 × 4 matrix was generated.

HIM–SS–1962

Three major changes occurred in this last major revision of the HIM. First, the importance of the content styles introduced in the HHIM–1957 (nonpersonal, personal, interpersonal, and group) were rearranged in a new order in the HIM (nonpersonal, group, personal, and relationship). This reordering reflected differences between interactions in the small groups W. F. Hill initially studied (e.g., T-group and small-group dynamics) and member interactions observed in inpatient and outpatient groups conducted in the state hospitals (P. S. Hill, personal communication, April 30, 1994). Although this reordering moved away from the group-as-a-whole emphasis found in the earlier version, it accommodated the perceived therapeutic potential of the groups under observation.

The second major change in the HIM was the addition of two work styles (i.e., speculative and confrontive) instead of the single work style of the HHIM–1957 (i.e., problem-oriented work). The "therapeutic" work style of the HHIM–1957 was viewed as being more cognitively referenced. The addition of these two work styles added an emotionality not found in the earlier version. As will become evident in the system description, both of these changes reflect a greater emphasis on the importance of interpersonal risk exhibited by members of therapeutic groups.

The final change in the HIM was the elimination of separate analyses of therapist and members' ratings. W. F. Hill realized that members often played the role of the therapist in their interaction with other members (P. S. Hill, personal communication, April 30, 1994). This decision was implicitly supported by Corsini and Rosenberg's (1955) classic article on "curative factors" (e.g., patients helping each other, or altruism) cited in the HIM manual. Dropping separate ratings essentially empowered the role of the member and attenuated role differences between the therapist and members found in the HHIM.

DESCRIPTION OF THE SYSTEM

HIM–SS–1965

The two-dimensional framework that emerged in 1962 (content and work styles) was not revised in the last version of the HIM–1965 (see Figure 7.1). Rather, changes in the manual included an updated validity profile of the HIM using "classical schools of group psychotherapy" (W. F. Hill, 1965a, p. 9), normative data for 50 diverse psychotherapy groups (including additional research), and the introduction of the HIM–B (i.e., a self-report measure for classifying group members modeled after the Fundamental Interpersonal Relations Orientation–Behavior [FIRO–B]).

A better understanding of the content and style dimensions of the HIM lie in the definition of the three major therapeutic values held by W. F. Hill: member centeredness, interpersonal threat, and patient–therapist role taking. These values established the higher order conceptual framework that weights the individual dimensional ratings. Moreover, they also revealed the underlying theoretical inclinations of W. F. Hill in organizing his empirically based rating scale.

In articulating the value of member centeredness, W. F. Hill asserted that the individual member's treatment should take precedence over concern for group processes:

> The goal of Group Psychotherapy is not to have a strong, cohesive, well-developed group nor to have insightful discussions about emotional problems ... [but rather] the recovery, rehabilitation and improvement of the individual members through the achievement of self-understanding, by individual members. (W. F. Hill, 1965a, p. 17)

In short, he argued that although group development, awareness of group processes, and the management of critical group incidents are important issues for the group therapist, they should always be considered in the service of the individual member's treatment. Hence, interpersonal interaction involving a "topic person" is viewed as being having the most therapeutic value.

The second therapeutic value guiding the HIM system revolves around the notion of *interpersonal threat*. W. F. Hill (1965a) assumed that all humans have a common fear of interacting with other humans: "Being in group situations mobilizes the free-floating anxiety connected with this fear" (p. 18). He maintained that when members are open about their insecurities and human irrationalities—engaging in interpersonally risky behavior—they will invariably move beyond intellectual insight to a more therapeutic level of interaction. Interaction judged to be more interpersonally risky is given a higher rating in the HIM.

In the therapeutic value of *patient–therapist role taking*, W. F. Hill spe-

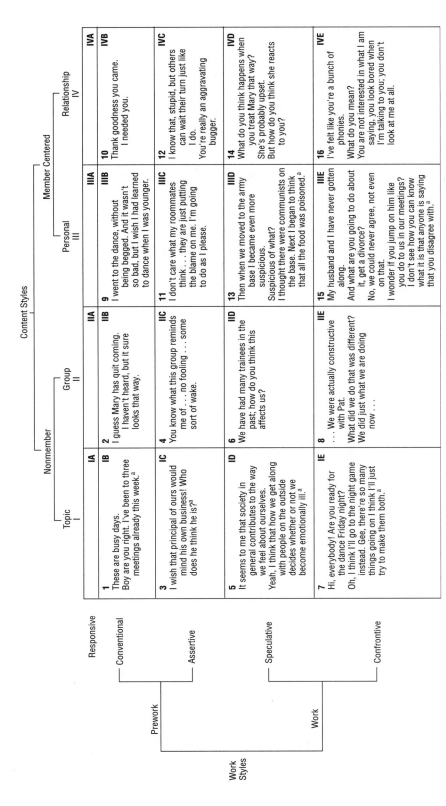

Figure 7.1. The Hill Interaction Matrix. Regarding the cell weights, the higher the number, the more therapeutic. Adapted from W. F. Hill, 1965b. [a]Statements taken from the Hill Interaction Matrix (HIM–SS) practice decks.

cifically postulated that for therapy to occur, the group must not only have a topic person but also that the topic person must be willing to be treated as a patient by other members or by the therapist. This proposal parallels Corsini and Rosenberg's (1955) construct of altruism as a therapeutic factor unique to group psychotherapy in that members help themselves by helping others in the group (i.e., playing the therapist role). In summary, W. F. Hill (1965a) stated that "without someone in both the therapist and patient role the unique potential of group psychotherapy cannot be fully realized and a group cannot be considered as working on members' problems" (p. 19). Group interaction in which both patient and therapist roles are evident is rated as having a higher therapeutic potential than interaction in which neither or only one role is evidenced.

These three values essentially guide the weighting of the HIM system, as group activity is classified on two dimensions or styles: content and work. The content and work style dimensions are fully crossed, thus creating a matrix of 20 cells (see Figure 7.1). However, in practice, the first work style (responsive: topic, IA; group, IIA; personal, IIIA; relationship, IVA) is typically dropped, yielding a 16-cell matrix (W. F. Hill, 1965b, pp. 1–8). The organizational principle underlying this matrix is an application of the three therapeutic values. More specifically, W. F. Hill proposed a weighted scoring system to rank, in an ordinal manner, the therapeutic value of various types of interaction as they are plotted on the two dimensions.

The weighting system results in the ordinal placement of categories and cells within the matrix. Table 7.2 illustrates the manner in which the three therapeutic values are emphasized across the two dimensions. For instance, although the interpersonal threat value contributes to both dimensions, the other two therapeutic values (i.e., member centeredness and patient–therapist role taking) are located exclusively in separate dimensions. The member-centeredness value is not only found exclusively in the content dimension but also contributes the most to the weighted score from this dimension. The patient–therapist role value dominates scoring in the work style dimension and is used to divide the work dimension into a prework and work dichotomy. Armed with the therapeutic values, category rankings in each dimension are better understood.

Content Style Dimension

The content dimension classifies *what* the group is talking about and consists of four categories: topic (I), group (II), personal (III), and relationship (IV). A brief definition of these four content categories can be found in Table 7.3. The topic category codes talk that is exclusively external to the group proper (e.g., weather, sports, politics). Talk external to the group can occur in other content categories but takes on a different meaning. Table 7.2 demonstrates how these categories are rank ordered in

TABLE 7.2
Derivation of Indexes of Therapeutic Potential for Each Cell from the Weighted Scores Assigned by Interpersonal Threat, Member Centeredness, and Work

	Content Style						Work Style				
	Interpersonal Threat				Member Centered		Interpersonal Threat		Patient–Therapist Role		Sum Weighted Scores (Index)
Category	I	II	III	IV	I II	III IV	B D	C E	B C	D E	
Weight Scale	1	2	3	4	0	6	0	2	0	4	
IB	1				0		0		0		1
IIB		2			0		0		0		2
IC	1				0			2	0		3
IIC		2			0			2	0		4
ID	1				0		0			4	5
IID		2			0		0			4	6
IE	1				0			2		4	7
IIE		2			0			2		4	8
IIIB			3			6	0		0		9
IVB				4		6	0		0		10
IIIC			3			6		2	0		11
IVC				4		6		2	0		12
IIID			3			6	0			4	13
IVD				4		6	0			4	14
IIIE			3			6		2		4	15
IVE				4		6		2		4	16

(The letters C E L L S appear vertically at the left of the IB–IVE rows.)

Note. Content: I = Topic; II = Group; III = Personal; IV = Relationship. Work: A = Responsive; B = Conventional; C = Assertive; D = Speculative; E = Confrontive.

the weighted scoring system on two therapeutic values: interpersonal threat and member centeredness. Group interaction is ordered from low to high (scores range from 1 to 4) on the interpersonal threat value when members are discussing topics external to the group (e.g., current events, social amenities); content about the group (e.g., group business, impressions about the group); personal problems of a member (e.g., both current and historical); or here-and-now relationships and reactions of members to each other within the group proper (e.g., interpersonal conflict with another member).

TABLE 7.3
Definitions of Content and Work Style Categories

Style	Definition
Content	
Topic (I)	Any one of an infinite number of topics of general interest that are exclusive of the group or its members (extra-group content).
Group (II)	Speaker identifies the group as an entity, and reactions to the group are relayed, probed for, or given in response to probes.
Personal (III)	Always involves a group member as the primary topic and is usually about a member's actions, problems, or personality.
Relationship (IV)	Interaction demonstrates, alludes to, or discusses a relationship between members or between a member and the group.
Work	
Responsive (A)	A probe, sponsoring interaction to invite a member to interact, or the minimal response of a member who is unaccustomed to reacting interpersonally (typical of highly regressed institutional inpatients; this style is seldom used because of its limited applicability).
Convention (B)	Statements or questions typical of an informal social gathering used to update someone or exchange greetings, pleasantries, and amenities.
Assertive (C)	Statements or questions presented in an argumentative or hostile fashion or that suggest that the speaker cannot be influenced on the topic; reveals biases, prejudices, cherished beliefs (delusions), or sounding off.
Speculative (D)	Exchange of opinion and information to gain knowledge or clarify thinking. Discussion is cooperative and task oriented as topic is explored or introduced in an intellectual, controlled manner. Topic is related to mental health in that it informs members about why people behave as they do.
Confrontive (E)	Exchange that penetrates and forces the members to come to terms with the essence of an idea experientially so that they can test it against their own experience. These comments usually integrate or synthesize in an insightful, affective manner.

Note. Adapted from the Hill Interaction matrix scoring manual (W. F. Hill, 1965b).

In addition, these topical categories are given different therapeutic weights with respect to whether they are member centered (6) or not (0). For instance, the personal and relationship categories involve a focus person and are seen as having the greatest therapeutic potential in the entire weighting system. W. F. Hill's (1965a) justification for this weighting is the following: "The establishment of relationships and the analysis of these relationships has had a prominent place in psychotherapy for a long time especially if one thinks of them in transference and countertransference terms" (p. 21). He continued by incorporating a broader understanding of relationship in the system by encompassing the works of Taft, Sullivan, Rogers, and Bach (cf. W. F. Hill, 1965a), in which the therapeutic significance of interpersonal relationships is consensually underscored. The relationship category receives the highest overall value in the system because of its higher interpersonal threat rating. Personal content is still accorded a high therapeutic index because this activity parallels the importance of intrapersonal insight in psychotherapy.

Although the group and topic categories are seen as having less therapeutic potential with respect to the member-centeredness value, they are viewed as "not only desirable but necessary for group development" (W. F. Hill, 1965a, p. 23). These categories are thought to represent the type of content discussed by group members in the early stages of group development, providing the foundation for later group interactions that involve higher levels of interpersonal risk. The primary rationale for the therapeutic value of group content lies in "the significance for patients in being concerned with and making identification with the group [which] is often stressed by those who see much of our illness stemming from the breakdown of primary group ties and from anomie" (W. F. Hill, 1965a, p. 23). General-interest content topics are valued in that they do the following: (a) provide a needed flight when the group becomes too traumatic, (b) generate material that leads members into more interpersonally risky categories, and (c) impart information that may enhance the development of self-understanding. Note that W. F. Hill continued to give a rating of zero to both of these categories on the member-centeredness value.

Work Style Dimension

The work style dimension focuses on the *how* of the dialogue and categorizes all interaction into five styles: responsive (A), conventional (B), assertive (C), speculative (D), and confrontive (E) (see Table 7.3). Some of these terms are dated, however. For instance, assertiveness in today's vernacular denotes an appropriate interpersonal stance. In the HIM, it reflects an argumentative, aggressive, or more hostile posture. The dominant feature of the work style dimension in Table 7.3 is the concept of prework versus work. A requisite for a group interacting in the work mode involves someone in the group assuming the patient role and actively seeking self-understanding. Only two types of group interactional styles are considered to be work: speculative and confrontive.

The confrontive work style penetrates problems that the group (or an individual) is avoiding. W. F. Hill (1965a) described it as "pinning a member to the mat with material and behavior of his own contrivance and from which he cannot escape or deny convincingly" (p. 26). He contended that confrontive interactions have value for both the person confronting and the member being confronted given that he or she has accepted the patient role. For the confronting person, the probability of future effectual human contact is increased through the act of engaging his or her own person in honest feedback (i.e., there is no anonymous confrontation). The person being confronted is helped through the process of reality testing in the service of self-understanding (cf. Fuhriman & Burlingame, 1990).

The speculative work style also involves a group member adopting the patient role. However, this role is limited because other members (or the therapist) are allowed to ask questions or speculate only about the person or problems rather than confronting or describing them directly. The person in the patient role operates from a more secure position, maintaining interpersonal threat at a relatively low level. Although significant insights and reformulations of problems often result from this style, such interactions typically do not make the affective penetration on the patient that confrontive interactions involve. This category is given the same score as confrontive interactions in that there is an identified member in the patient role.

Responsive, conventional, and assertive are considered prework styles. In this prework mode, it is conceivable and likely for someone to be the focus person of a group interaction without that person necessarily taking on the role of patient. For instance, the assertive work style always describes a central person who talks a lot about himself or herself, problems, and how he or she feels about various matters. In contrast to the work categories, this person is essentially unwilling to assume the patient role and to seek help for problems; rather, he or she dominates or challenges the group to "just try and help me." There is often a feeling of testing the limits in that the member wants the group to accept personal convictions rather than respond to them. This category of interaction requires a higher degree of therapist management because it can result in "gripe sessions" or counteraggressive responses from other group members. Its value lies in the fact that a large measure of catharsis and self-disclosure is typically associated with assertive interactions. These lay the foundation for later, more therapeutic interactions (e.g., speculative or confrontive).

The remaining two styles, conventional and responsive, are given the lowest therapeutic value rating (see Table 7.2) of any category in the work style dimension (i.e., zero). Conventional styles can be recognized as interactions that are so socially oriented that they are devoid of any meaning other than participating in social pleasantries. Although there is no direct therapeutic value assigned to this type of interaction, W. F. Hill considered it to be important in that it often serves as the vehicle for the development of important relationships within the group. The final style, responsive, characterizes typical interactions drawn from groups of highly regressed patients in which the goal is for patients to respond to therapist inquiries. In groups of individuals with chronic schizophrenia, the goal might be to move members from responding to a question to engaging in a more formal, conventional social interaction.

The interpersonal threat value further categorizes these five work styles by posing the dichotomy of protected versus vulnerable modes. Vulnerable modes are those interactions that are considered to have higher levels of interpersonal threat for the members. The assertive and confrontive styles are considered to be vulnerable modes and are given the highest therapeutic value in the prework and work subdivisions. The work dimension describes the extent to which the group is actively dealing with a member in a patient role (work vs. prework) and the degree of interpersonal threat inherent in the prework or work interactions.

The matrix generated by fully crossing the two dimensions creates a rating system that simultaneously classifies a statement on its focus (content) and style (work). Examples of statements that simultaneously reflect different content and work style are found in Figure 7.1. Evidence for the effect of the three therapeutic values is manifest in the differences between the illustrative statements.

CORRESPONDENCE BETWEEN THE THEORY AND THE SYSTEM

It is important to note a distinction between the conceptual framework of the HIM (therapeutic values) from which the weighted scoring system is derived (see Table 7.2), and the descriptive aspects of group interaction that are being captured by the rating system proper. The core elements of the rating system (i.e., categories of the work and content dimensions) were derived from careful observations of ongoing psychotherapy groups. Beyond W. F. Hill's aforementioned theoretical predilections, no single theory, including the therapeutic values, seems to have guided the creation of the substantive aspects of the HIM.

There is a considerable theoretical preference revealed in the therapeutic values and how they are used to "weight" the observationally based categories of group interaction. For instance, in an earlier version (the HHIM–1957), interaction reflecting group and interpersonal dynamics was given the highest therapeutic value, undoubtedly reflecting W. F. Hill's earlier training in group dynamics. W. F. Hill also applied group dynamics concepts when writing on the developmental stages of psychotherapy groups (W. F. Hill & Gruner, 1973; Martin & Hill, 1957). However, his theoretical predilection was overridden by the pragmatics of mental health practice because individual member progress took precedence over group dynamics in the final weighting system. W. F. Hill suggested group dynamics as a secondary component in achieving meaningful member change by the proposed weighting system. However, the value of group dynamics is clearly evident in the importance given to the interpersonal context in which member change takes place.

Further Developments

W. F. Hill (1965a) did not take a dogmatic stance on the weighting system: "It is possible to accept the set of categories comprising the HIM rating system without accepting the value system by which the cells and categories are ordered" (p. 56). As shown in later use of the HIM, some researchers have followed this advice and used other weighting systems in exploring group process and outcome. This practice was encouraged by W. F. Hill (1965a) because he saw "the task of the HIM to be both a conceptual framework and an instrument for research" (p. 57). Thus, perhaps the largest piece of work left for the HIM is to explore alternative weighting systems. Unfortunately, there is a paucity of such work in the literature.

Reliability, Validity, and Normative Data

HIM–SS

W. F. Hill (1977) described the HIM–SS as having "extensive reliability, validity and normative" data (p. 254) and referred interested readers to the 1965 monograph as the primary source for said data. When this assertion is carefully examined with respect to the data found in both the monograph and the literature, two equal observations arise. First, the HIM–SS, when compared with other group psychotherapy process measures, is in fact one of the few instruments for which a systematic attempt has been made to gather reliability, validity, and normative data. However, the data currently available on the HIM–SS do not support the manner in which this instrument is often used in group psychotherapy research.

In the original monograph, W. F. Hill (1965a) examined the degree of interrater reliability among three judges who rated three different groups. He reported that the average percentage of agreement across the 16 cells was 70%. Additionally, the reliability of his weighted scoring system was examined with measures of association used for both interval- and ordinal-level scales. The average Pearson product–moment correlation for the three raters was .76, with the ordinal measure of association (Spearman's rho) yielding a much higher average of .90. Subsequent researchers using the HIM–SS (e.g., Barlow, Hansen, Fuhriman, & Finley, 1982) have typically reported interrater reliability coefficients within these ranges (.72–.92), suggesting that the HIM–SS can be used with a moderate-to-high degree of reliability. This satisfactory reliability data are undoubtedly attributable to the conceptual clarity, intuitive appeal, and apparent breadth of the HIM–SS. However, as we show, it is these very points that create problems for validity studies.

Because the HIM–SS was originally developed as a method for describing the verbal process of psychotherapy groups, it was imperative for W. F. Hill to demonstrate that the measure could systematically discriminate between groups guided by various theoretical orientations. Hence, the primary thrust in the validation process was determining the ability of the HIM–SS to discriminate between qualitatively distinct groups. W. F. Hill carefully examined seven theoretically distinct groups (i.e., group-analytic, neopsychoanalytic, pure psychoanalytic, nondirective, didactic, rational, and guided group interaction) and found that they appeared to have different content and work style patterns when rated by the HIM–SS.

The guided group interaction experience produced the highest frequencies in the relationship content style and the assertive (aggressive) and confrontive work style, which matched the goals of this group's orientation. The nondirective group produced the highest frequencies in the topic-centered content style and conventional work style categories. After carefully presenting comparative data for all seven groups, W. F. Hill (1965a) concluded that the HIM–SS yields "meaningful and significant description of total group operation so that groups can be systematically compared" (p. 57).

To further assist the group researcher in describing and comparing the verbal process of different psychotherapy groups, Priscilla Hill conducted an ambitious normative study in collaboration with W. F. Hill (1965a, 1969). The goal was to establish cell and quadrant norms for the HIM–SS to interpret the verbalization patterns of a particular group against a known sample. The normative study was based on 50 different psychotherapy group transcripts solicited from members of the American Group Psychotherapy Association ($n = 35$) and transcripts from W. F. Hill's previous work ($n = 15$). Fifty different group therapists were used (i.e., no therapist duplication) in the sample, with gender, age, and discipline (psychiatry, psychology, and social work) tabulated for readers. Every statement in each group was rated, resulting in 21,000 ratings that formed the basis for the norm tables. Percentile norm tables were created from this sample for both individual cells and loadings by category.

The norm tables reflect an amalgam of data from groups that vary on many important characteristics, including therapist theoretical orientation, developmental stage of group, and composition. These variations pose some obvious problems for straightforward interpretations of the percentiles found in the norm table. W. F. Hill (1965a) asserted and provided more recent supporting data (W. F. Hill & Gruner, 1973) that change in group verbalization depends on the group's developmental stage. The expectation then would be that norms should be organized across a developmental stage stratagem rather than a compilation of sessions drawn at random from different group time periods. Similar limitations exist in the norm tables regarding other important characteristics of the group (therapist orientation, composition, etc.). Nevertheless, the mere existence of a norm table for a group process measure was, and is, a rare accomplishment for a group psychotherapy process measure.

If the use of the HIM–SS in the literature was restricted to comparative differences in verbal patterns between qualitatively distinct groups, the aforementioned validity and normative studies would represent an adequate beginning for a sound psychometric foundation. Unfortunately, this is not the case. In many instances, researchers go beyond the descriptive properties of the HIM–SS in their studies and wholeheartedly adopt the theoretical ordinality of the categories proposed by W. F. Hill. Some researchers use the weighted scoring system directly by treating the cell weights as if they were drawn from an interval-level scale. In this instance, data are analyzed with analysis of variance procedures using weighted scores compiled from HIM–SS ratings, with conclusions that reflect the therapeutic potential of groups under investigation.

The more typical scenario is an indirect use of the weighted scoring system in which group talk is tabulated by quadrants (instead of cells). Conclusions on therapeutic quality are drawn based on whether a group interaction occurs more frequently (typically determined by chi-square procedures) in the therapeutic quadrants (i.e., Quadrants III and IV). The degree to which these quadrants are deemed more therapeutic is directly related to the validity of the weighted scoring system proposed, which, as pointed out earlier, has received little empirical attention. In one of the few empirical studies that sheds light on the validity of the weighting system, Lambert and DeJulio (1977) reported findings that are partially supportive. Therapeutic interaction was shown to be positively related to ratings of therapist empathy and specificity ratings (i.e., groups with more therapeutic interaction on the HIM also had higher therapist empathy and specificity ratings); ratings of therapist genuineness and respect had no relationship with HIM ratings.

One of the primary problems associated with testing the validity of the weighted scoring system is variability in group goals, which in turn may alter the emphasis given to the underlying values of the original weighting system. W. F. Hill (1965a) initially cautioned that the weighted scoring system was purely theoretical in origin and that groups having different goals would predictably have higher percentages of talk in particular cells. In a later elaboration, W. F. Hill (1973) stated that

> it should be borne in mind and needs repeating several times that the HIM can be used as a nominal scale rather than an ordinal scale; that is, one could subscribe to the validity of the categories without subscribing to the notion that one category is superior to another in terms

of therapeutic effectiveness or growth potential. Also it would be possible to rearrange the value system. In fact, at one time the arrangement was different than is now reported. (p. 163)

This fact underlies the findings of the few studies in which the HIM–SS was unsuccessfully related to other measures of therapeutic potential or change. Barlow et al. (1982) found no relationship between variation in quadrant talk and improvement in a group member's self-concept. DeJulio, Bentley, and Cockayne's (1979) study produced similar results when they compared variation in quadrant talk with changes in therapeutic growth and self-esteem. Therefore, the most prudent psychometric conclusion about the HIM–SS is that it can be reliably used to discriminate variations in group process. Further research is needed to test its ability, either by quadrant or by cell, to measure how these varying processes are related to therapeutic growth in groups having different goals.

The HIM–G, HIM–A and HIM–B

Derived from the HIM conceptual framework are three additional measurement scales that vary in format: HIM–G, HIM–B, and HIM–A. A Q-sort was also developed at this time that contained four typical interactions in each of the 16 HIM categories (64 items). The HIM–G is a 72-item rating scale, completed by a judge, observer, or group member *after* viewing a session, listening to an audiotape, or reading a group transcript. After the rater completes the 72 items, the statement scores are summed into a single score that reflects the therapeutic level of group interaction. The instrument has been widely used to categorize group composition, leadership style, and the status of the group's interaction (W. F. Hill, 1971). It also provides systematic feedback about the group's structure and progress to the therapist or the members. The method appears to be hampered by problems of internal consistency and attendant problems with the interpretability of the scores (Powell, 1977). W. F. Hill (personal communication, November, 1996) has suggested that the HIM–G be used for a cursory examination of group interaction because the psychometric properties of the HIM–SS are far superior to those of the HIM–G.

The HIM–A and HIM–B are identical to one another structurally and differ only in a simpler language version in the HIM–A. The HIM–B is a 64-item test requiring members to rate their reactions to particular group situations on a 6-point continuum. This instrument was designed to measure the group member's level of acceptances for operating in the various cells and quadrants of the HIM. The test (W. H. Hill, 1965b) was designed primarily for selecting members for group, categorizing group therapists, and diagnosing problems stemming from conflicts in group composition. A scintilla of studies exist that have formally explored the psychometric properties (reliability and validity) of these two instruments. W. F.

Hill's (1965a) original monograph reported a test–retest reliability coefficient of .82 for the HIM–B, and no reports were found that examined the internal consistency of either scale. Validity data are primarily garnered from normative studies in which different populations are compared (e.g., chronic inpatients, college students) and found to vary on the HIM–B (cf. W. F. Hill, 1965a). More recent evidence (Muro & Drummond, 1974) empirically supported W. F. Hill's contention that the HIM–B is an effective predictor of an individual's behavior in a group, although the psychometric properties of the HIM–A and B, for the most part, remain uncertain.

PREVIOUS RESEARCH WITH THE SYSTEM

The HIM, in all forms, has been used extensively since its publication. There are approximately 90 published articles and papers, 145 dissertations, and a number of master's theses, for an average of more than 8 studies a year using some form of the HIM. The instrument has captured the attention of most therapeutic disciplines, including psychology, psychiatry, nursing, and social work; it also has been applied in educational ventures.

Although formulated from a state hospital population, the HIM has been applied to research a diverse set of populations and aspects of group process. Chronic patients, inpatients, outpatients, undergraduate and graduate students, adolescents, married couples, children, therapists, high school counselors, parents, and teachers have all come under the purview of researchers using the HIM. Although personal growth, encounter, and therapy groups are dominant in the studies, other structures have also been examined to discover the quality of interaction. Most notably, client–therapist dyads, marriage enrichment and interpersonal workshops, supervision dyads, and analog settings represent the variation from traditional group therapy modalities.

The length of time spent in the therapeutic situation also varies a great deal in the HIM studies, although the vast majority of the studies are short term. Excluding the analog studies (ranging from 30 minutes to 2 hours), the groups meet for 3–16 weeks with one or two meetings a week, each of a couple hours' duration. The encounter groups are more likely to have group sessions of extended length. Research focuses on comparisons of therapist–client talk, leader style, amount of structure, timing of structure, supervision and counseling, models of intervention, therapist style and client personality, and initial group with later (2 years) group experience. Attention has been given to discovering the correlation of the HIM with other measurement systems (e.g., the Bonney, Truax, and Carkhuff scales).

The HIM–B and HIM–G Research Findings

HIM–B studies are few in number and, in most cases, have been used as a pre- to postmeasure to identify the change that individuals experience as a result of a therapy or encounter group. Some studies note change in participants' understanding of self and others (Hardcastle, 1972), in attitudes toward interaction (Landy, 1970), and in the preference by happily married couples for a nonpersonal style of interaction about topics and events outside the relationship (McIntire, Drummond, & Carter, 1977). Other studies show less success or no change in the use of videotape feedback (Anderson, Hummel, & Gibson, 1970), human relations training (Dye, 1974), or individual or group orientation (Anderson et al., 1970) on outcome.

The HIM–G has been used almost exclusively with short-term therapy groups, albeit with various populations and therapists. Some studies have shown leader-led groups to be more therapeutic and stable than self-directed ones (Conyne & Rapin, 1977a, 1977b) and therapist-led sessions in an inpatient group to be higher in therapeutic quality than those of leaderless sessions (Seligman & Sterne, 1969). These latter results were later supported (Sterne & Seligman, 1971), describing therapist-led sessions as being more task-oriented, speculative, and confrontive.

Different approaches to therapy have been tested using the HIM–G, with some success noted for feedback techniques (Leith & Uhlemann, 1972); self-viewing and discussion (Robinson, 1970); individualized behavior goal setting (Uhlemann & Weigel, 1977); therapist activity (Kanas, Barr, & Dossick, 1985; Kanas & Smith, 1990); experiential leader style (Lewis & Mider, 1973); and short-term models of therapy with marital couples, adults, and adolescents (Silbergeld, Manderscheid, & Koenig, 1977). In comparing the HIM–G with other measures, Roe and Edwards (1978) found that the HIM–G and the Truax and Carkhuff scales complemented each other, whereas Sisson, Sisson, and Gazda (1977) determined that the Bonney scale and HIM–G were not independent, discovering a linear relationship between the two rating systems.

HIM–SS Therapy Research Findings

Although published studies on the HIM–SS are fewer in number than the HIM–G, the use of the measure has remained fairly constant over the past few decades. As with the other formats, researchers and clinicians have focused on various group structures and processes: using analog designs (Bednar & Battersby, 1976; Boyd, 1970); examining interactions in dyad counseling (Dowd & Blocher, 1974; Kaul, Kaul, & Bednar, 1973), supervision (Lambert, 1974), interpersonal courses (Silbergeld & Manderscheid, 1976), and training models (Zarle & Boyd, 1977); cohesion (Stava & Bednar, 1979); and risk-taking theory (Lee & Bednar, 1977). Nevertheless, therapy and personal growth groups have been the focus for the majority of HIM–SS studies. Various populations of clientele are involved, and in most cases short-term treatment groups are the main focus (see Table 7.4). One of the strengths of this body of research is that the studies have been conducted in actual, viable groups, thus reducing generalization problems.

The effect of leader communication on group member talk has been demonstrated by three studies (Barlow, 1988; Barlow et al., 1982; Hammonds & Worthington, 1985) in three types of groups (i.e., short-term therapy, personal growth, and marriage enrichment groups). Member interaction mirrored that of the leader, although in some cases the content and style of the interaction mirrored the follower statement. Toseland, Rossiter, Peak, and Hill's (1990) recent study of caregiver groups showed that peer-led groups produced more topical statements, whereas professionally led groups produced more personal, group, and relationship statements.

Comparative studies have shown that reality-oriented groups exhibited more therapeutic interaction than client-centered groups (Bigelow & Thorne, 1969) and that T-groups demonstrated more group-centered interaction than therapy groups, with the latter being more member centered (Fisher & Werbel, 1979). In both studies, the therapy and the T-groups functioned at a high personal and relationship level (80%) throughout the group sessions.

A handful of HIM–SS studies have assessed the impact of structure on group interaction. Crews and Melnick (1976) found little difference in interaction that occurred in initially imposed, delayed, or no-structure groups. Personal speculative and confrontive talk (defined as self-disclosure) was more prominent in the initial structure group, but only at the first data collection point; nevertheless, talk in these cells increased over time in the delayed and no-structure groups. Group speculative and confrontive talk decreased over time; overall, all groups increased their "work-level" talk from the beginning to the 8th session. In comparing pregroup norm setting with no norm setting, DeJulio et al. (1979) found that groups that had pregroup structuring moved more quickly into therapeutic interaction but that they grew less productive as the group developed. Yalom, Houts, Newell, and Rand (1967) were also interested in the effect of pregroup structuring, more specifically a 25-minute lecture on group therapy. Overall, the preoriented groups had a greater proportion of directly oriented statements than nonoriented; there was also more here-and-now interpersonal interaction in the preoriented groups. The authors concluded that the prestructure members engaged more readily in the therapeutic task.

In related structure studies, the inclusion of a fish-bowl experience in a group was not as effective in producing work statements as was a non–fish-bowl group (White, 1974). Sklar, Yalom, Zim, and Newell (1970) did not find any differences in the rate of group development in groups com-

TABLE 7.4
HIM–SS Studies

Author	Type of Group	Duration	Population
Barlow (1988)	Therapy	15 weeks, 90 min/week	Outpatient
Barlow, Hansen, Fuhriman, & Finley (1982)	Personal growth	30 hr	University students
Bigelow & Thorne (1969)	Personal growth	6 sessions	Children aged 9–11 years
Conyne & Rapin (1977b)	Personal growth	5 weeks, 120–150 min/week	Graduate students
Crews & Melnick (1976)	Encounter	8 3-hr sessions	Undergraduates
DeJulio, Bentley, & Cockayne (1979)	Encounter	30 hr, 6 sessions	University students
Fisher & Werbel (1979)	Therapy and encounter	NA	Graduate students and residents
Gilstein, Wright, & Stone (1977)	Encounter	6 weeks, 90 min/week	Undergraduates
Hammonds & Worthington (1985)	Marriage enrichment	3 weeks, 150 min/week	Undergraduates and spouses
Hartson & Kunce (1973)	Personal growth	6 sessions	Undergraduate students and clients
Houts & Wittner (1968)	Therapeutic community meetings	2 sessions/week 45-min sessions	Inpatients
Lindberg, Morrill, & Kilstrom (1974)	Therapy	NA	Chronic mental patients
Peterson & Pollio (1982)	Therapy	17 sessions 90 min/week	Outpatient, young adults
Silbergeld, Thune, & Manderscheid (1980)	Therapy	15 sessions	Married couples
Sklar, Yalom, Zim, & Newell (1970)	Therapy	16 sessions	Outpatient
Toseland, Rossiter, Peak, & Hill (1990)	Therapy and support	8 weeks, 2 hr/week	Caregivers of frail older people
White (1974)	Encounter	24 hr over 7 weekly sessions	University students
Yalom, Houts, Newell, & Rand (1967)	Therapy	First 12 meetings	Outpatient

Note. HIM–SS = Hill Interaction Matrix–Statement by Statement. NA = not apparent.

paring the effect of extended time in session (6-hour session at first meeting, 6-hour session at 11th meeting). Intermember involvement did increase immediately after the extended session held during the 11th session. Using Kagan, Krathwohl, and Miller's (1963) Interpersonal Process Recall, Hartson and Kunce (1973) discovered the presence of more therapeutic interaction in the Interpersonal Process Recall group. They a priori determined that the speculative–relationship cell was the most therapeutic, followed by speculative–personal; all remaining cells were rated the least therapeutic. Examining humor and its relationship to therapeutic effectiveness, Peterson and Pollio (1982) found that humorous remarks directed at other group members followed or occurred during times of therapeutic effectiveness, whereas those directed at generalized others occurred during less therapeutic periods. Self-targeted humor produced inconsistent effects.

Lindberg, Morrill, and Kilstrom (1974) studied the effect of reinforcement of appropriate feedback on leaderless groups and found an increase of 37% in therapeutic talk, concluding that such reinforcement affects group interaction. Focusing on leader-directed and self-directed personal growth groups, Conyne and Rapin (1977b) found more therapeutic interaction in the leader-directed group. A nondirective leadership style resulted in more group interaction and more member-centered work than did a directive style. Also, members whose personality was defined as liberal exhibited a more work-oriented interaction (Gilstein, Wright, & Stone, 1977). Houts and Wittner (1968), interested in what was remembered by participants from an inpatient group therapy experience, concluded that talk centering on the business of the ward was the most relevant (recognized content later), followed by relationship–speculative interaction; thus, topics that focused on the patients' shared experiences were remembered the most. Silbergeld, Thune, and Manderscheid (1980) examined a 15-session therapy group with married couples. After a 2-year recess, the group was reconvened for another 15-session group. During both groups, the therapeutic quality of interaction improved over time. Additionally, spouse-to-spouse interaction was somewhat greater in the follow-up group. Spouses became more congruent in their use of conventional talk and less congruent in confrontive talk.

Collectively, these findings suggest that the HIM has been used as a dependent variable to track the process of group treatment, to describe differences between groups, and to plot the impact of structural manipulations on a group's verbal interactions. Although these types of studies are informative and useful, they miss the mark initially established by W. F. Hill for the HIM. W. F. Hill was interested in creating a scale that would link process (verbal interaction measured by the HIM) to outcome (client improvement) that would suggest a theory of group psychotherapy based on member interaction. Indeed, the importance of client improvement is embodied in the member-centeredness value of the weighting system. The fact that most empirical effort misses this focus is disappointing. Clearly, more attention needs to paid to linking HIM ratings to the individual and collective outcome of group members.

APPLICATION OF THE SYSTEM OF ANALYSIS TO GROUP A, SESSION 3

The HIM–SS was used to analyze the entire third session of Group A. In the HIM–SS, W. F. Hill intended that therapist and client members serve similar roles in similar styles. Given the recent interest in and evidence of therapist influence on the group's interaction, the current analysis separates therapist and client talk. Also, given the illustrative purpose of the analysis and the limited amount of dialogue, we use only the global percentages of client and therapist talk in the interpretation of the therapeutic interaction. To demonstrate the utility of various aspects of W. F. Hill's underlying theory, we describe and interpret the percentages of client and therapist talk in the four quadrants, the columns (content style), and the rows (work style) alongside the cell percentages.

All uttered statements were rated and classified into one of the HIM cells. If the content changed within the utterances, in the case of some lengthy or complex statements, then the cell assignment changed. In all, 647 rateable statements were identified: 452 made by the clients in the group and 195 by the two therapists. The therapists, in combination, accounted for 31% of the total talk in the group, with the primary therapist contributing 22%. Given the size of the group and expectation of equal contribution among all members, an individual would be expected to contribute approximately 12% of the total talk. In this group, the primary therapist dominated the therapist-contributed talk and also spoke more often than would be expected from an individual participant.

The total group talk was first examined by percentage of talk in each cell as contributed separately by the clients and the therapists (see Figure 7.2). Analyzed by quadrant, 47% of the talk was in Quadrant IV (most therapeutic) and 21% in Quadrant II. Defined by content style, 47% of talk fell in personal, followed by 23% in topic, whereas by work style, 53% was in speculative, followed by 23% in conventional.

It is important to recall that the *combination* of content and work provides the basis for the therapeutic valuing. Thus, more revealing as to therapeutic value is an examination of the talk by individual cells, demonstrating the dominance of one cell (personal–speculative, 27%) to the overall percentage in the fourth quadrant. Moreover, in this session, talk in this cell clearly eclipsed all talk when compared with any other cell in the matrix. Thus, the greatest percentage of talk occurred in the personal–speculative (27%) and topic–speculative (14%) cells.

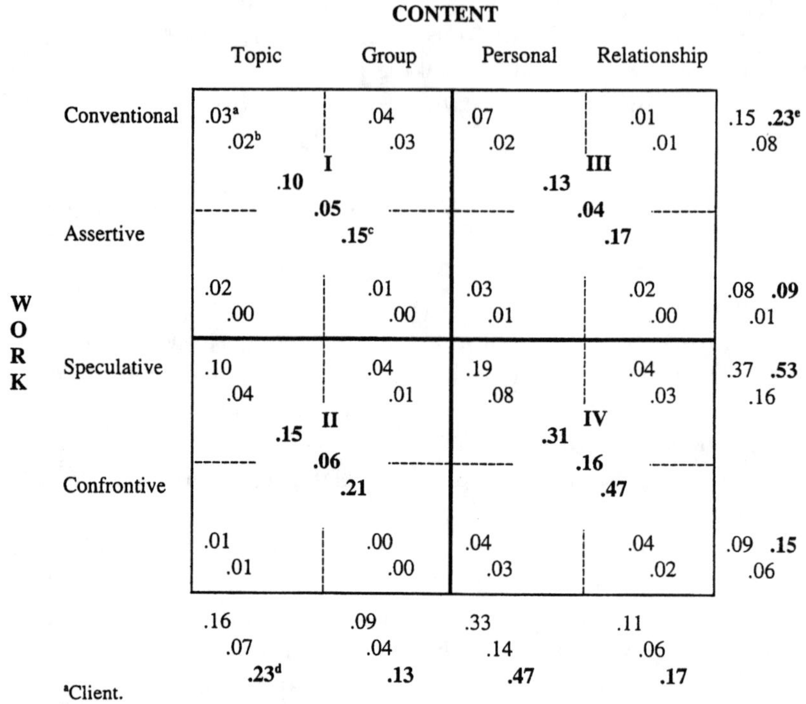
CONTENT
Topic
Group
Personal
Relationship
WORK
Conventional
Assertive
Speculative
Confrontive
.03a .02b
.04 .03
.07 .02
.01 .01
.15 .23e .08
I
III
.10
.13
.05
.04
.15c
.17
.02 .00
.01 .00
.03 .01
.02 .00
.08 .09 .01
.10 .04
.04 .01
.19 .08
.04 .03
.37 .53 .16
II
IV
.15
.31
.06
.16
.21
.47
.01 .01
.00 .00
.04 .03
.04 .02
.09 .15 .06
.16 .07 .23d
.09 .04 .13
.33 .14 .47
.11 .06 .17

[a]Client.
[b]Therapist.
[c]Total quadrant
[d]Total column.
[e]Total row.

Figure 7.2. Percentage of total group talk examined by client and therapist talk per cell and quadrant.

Examining by total session dialogue, this therapy group was functioning close to 50% of the time in the most therapeutic quadrant of the HIM, albeit the least therapeutic cell within the quadrant. The remaining percentage of talk was distributed across the other three quadrants. Group members contributed 69% of the total conversation, whereas the leaders contributed 31%, yet leaders made up only 25% of the membership.

Inspecting the total group interaction by the content and style in the fourth quadrant reveals information about the nature of this group. Almost half of the content falls in the personal category, and more than half of the work style is in speculative. Thus, dialogue is individually focused, is tentative, and is reflective in style. Both clients and leaders spend the most time communicating by interaction that is characterized as being member centered and cognitively oriented. Such dialogue is less threatening *interpersonally* and, given the cognitive orientation, is to some degree less emotionally penetrating. The cognitive focus is on the individual and his or her problem. We would expect the therapeutic factor of insight to be present more than factors associated with interpersonal interaction and responsiveness or factors threaded with more affect (e.g., cohesion, feedback, and catharsis).

It is interesting to compare the talk in this group session with the original normative data cited by W. F. Hill (1965a). In the percentage loadings of talk in the four quadrants, this group falls in the 50th percentile of the normative sample in speaking in Quadrant I, the 75th percentile in Quadrant II, the 25th percentile in Quadrant III, and the 65th percentile in Quadrant IV. Clearly, this group deviated from the normative sample in that it spent a significant amount of time in less therapeutic talk (e.g., Quadrant II). Caution should be exercised in interpreting this comparison, however, as the original normative data did not attend to the existence of a particular phase or developmental stage and was not based on limited segments of therapy sessions. Considering the content style categories, the group falls in the 60th percentile in topic, group, and personal categories and the 50th percentile in relationship dialogue. More variation is noted across the work style categories, with the group talk at the 35th percentile in conventional, 50th percentile in assertive, 60th percentile in speculative, and 90th percentile in confrontive styles. The percentage of therapist talk is at the 85th percentile, indicating that the 30% of group talk by the therapists is not only more than an individual's proportion of talk but is far more than the average therapist talk in the normative group sample. Comparing this group with the groups in the normative sample, it is more similar in its interaction to the group-analytical, guided group interaction, and rational groups than the nondirective, didactic, or neo- or pure psychoanalytic groups.

Although the total group interaction provides a global perspective, the analysis of specific phases gives a better understanding of the underlying dynamics. For the analyses in this section, we used 56% of the total session interaction, omitting 168 rateable units at the beginning and 108 rateable units at the session end. (This section includes the segments that were identified by the editors for microanalysis and the portions of transcript in between those segments as well.) This analysis also includes a section of interaction from Phase II, the transition between Phases II and III, and a section of interaction from Phase III of Group A.

The section of Phase II has 138 rateable HIM units, making up 21% of total session talk. Forty-one percent of the dialogue falls in Quadrant IV, followed by 25% in I, 21% in II, and 16% in III (see Figure 7.3). Talk is evenly distributed across the content categories (approximately 25%), but talk in work style, on the other hand, is more uneven, predominantly in speculative (47%) and conventional (31%) manners, resulting in less than optimal penetrating interaction. Again, the group appears to be uncertain about how therapeutic it wants or is able to be. The personal–speculative cell (17%) still has the largest percentage of talk, followed by relationship–confrontive (13%) and topic–speculative (12%).

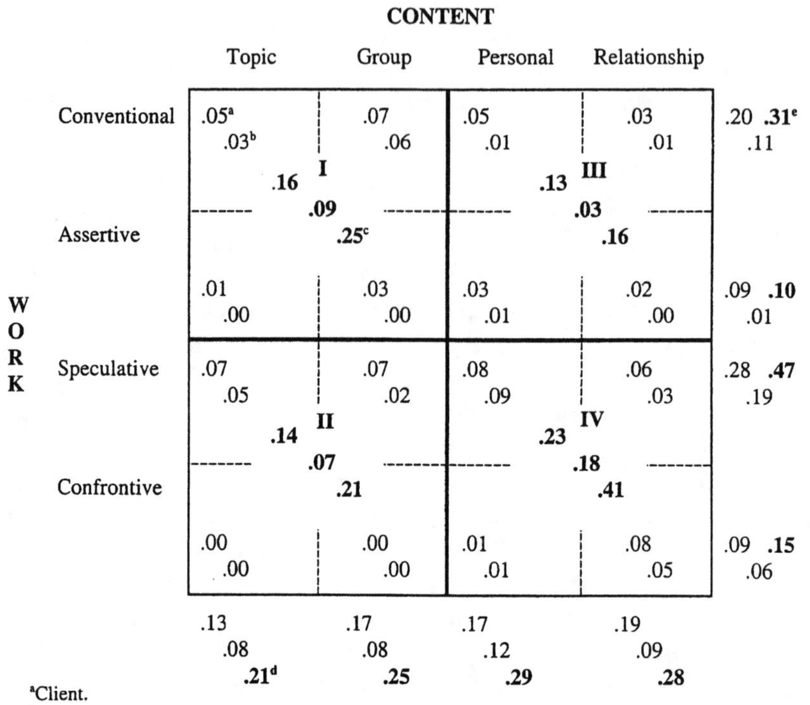

CONTENT

	Topic	Group	Personal	Relationship	
Conventional	.05[a]	.07	.05	.03	.20 .31[e]
	.03[b]	.06	.01	.01	.11
	.16 I		.13 III		
	.09		.03		
Assertive	.25[c]		.16		
	.01	.03	.03	.02	.09 .10
	.00	.00	.01	.00	.01
Speculative	.07	.07	.08	.06	.28 .47
	.05	.02	.09	.03	.19
	.14 II		.23 IV		
	.07		.18		
Confrontive	.21		.41		
	.00	.00	.01	.08	.09 .15
	.00	.00	.01	.05	.06
	.13	.17	.17	.19	
	.08	.08	.12	.09	
	.21[d]	.25	.29	.28	

(WORK — vertical label along left side)

[a]Client.
[b]Therapist.
[c]Total quadrant
[d]Total column.
[e]Total row.

Figure 7.3. Percentage of Phase II talk examined by client and therapist talk per cell and quadrant.

It is clear that the interaction in the Phase II section does not have much focus, particularly in the subject matter, with divided attention given to topic, group, personal, or relationship content styles. The group as a whole seems to be experiencing some ambiguity about who and what is going to be the center of attention. There is minimal distinction to any single content focus, although the client members focus more on group and relationship subjects than do the therapists. It may well be that the members are exploring interests, anxieties, and perhaps the motives of the therapists.

At this point, we have the beginning of a 15-session group. This is a time in group development when the members are becoming accustomed to individual styles and roles, experiencing the leaders' influence, developing norms, and establishing how the group is going to function. This group's interaction is revealing. For some reason, the group does not focus on any particular content for a substantial amount of time. This lack of focus, if adopted as normative, eventually will negatively affect the intensity and, in W. F. Hill's conceptualization, the therapeutic quality of the interaction. In the Phase II section, the underlying feature of such uniformity across content appears to rest on the difference in what the clients and the therapists talk about, with more talk about the group and relationships by the clients than the therapists. Are the differences problematic? If so, how will they be resolved? Given the therapists' greater proportion of talking in the group, will the way they talked win out, or will the clients persist in addressing the group, its relationships, and interpersonal influence, thus moving the group into discussing its process and eventually realizing the potential use of its social structure or ecosystem?

Additionally, the lower risk (*intra*personal vs. *inter*personal) evident in the interaction indicates a hesitancy for members to get involved with one another in an open, responsive manner. The members are functioning in an environment of low interpersonal threat and, at the same time, the leaders are fostering, through their dialogue, an interpersonally safe environment. In essence, the leaders' metamessage is the following: "Safety in group is talking about personal issues (self) in a probing, cognitive manner, and we are going to reinforce safe behavior." Given the evidence underscoring the influence of therapist talk on group members' style of interaction and this group's struggle in establishing group norms, the therapists' verbal pacing is reducing the potential of the group to be therapeutically effective, as per W. F. Hill's theory. In a short-term group, this is particularly problematic because it is important that effective norms arise quickly, thus providing an interactive seedbed that will nourish future group functioning.

The segment of Session 3 identified as a transition contains only 33 rateable HIM units, or 5% of the total session talk. The interactional pattern is strikingly different from the previous dialogue and indicates a marked shift on the HIM by both clients and therapists (see Figure 7.4). The interaction resides only in Quadrants III (85%) and IV (83%), with the vast majority of the interaction in the speculative work style, with an almost equal division between personal and relationship content. Additionally, almost 75% of the interaction resides in the relationship–speculative and personal–speculative cells. In this segment, the group continues in an inquiring, tentative style of speaking but shifts dramatically from what it was talking about in Phase II (topic and group) to more personal and relationship themes. All talk is in only six of the HIM cells. This period demonstrates a transition in the communication—a pivotal period in facilitating the interpersonal dynamics and supporting the ecosystem of the therapy group. It is the only time in this session when the dialogue in relationship content equals that in personal and when one would expect more therapeutic benefit from feedback, cohesion, and interpersonal learning among the members, three of the distinctive therapeutic features of a group therapy format, two theoretically underscored by W. F. Hill himself. The group continues to reflect the following: "We are going to discuss

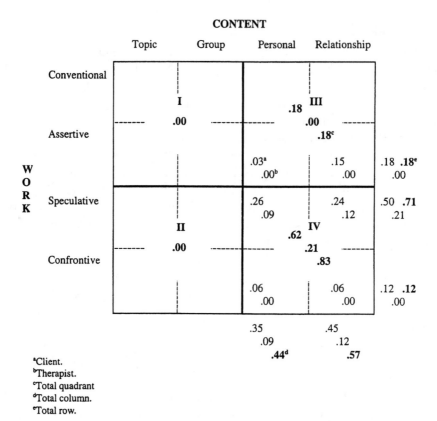

CONTENT

Figure content:

	Topic	Group	Personal	Relationship
Conventional				
	I .00		.18 III .00	.18ᶜ
Assertive			.03ᵃ .00ᵇ	.15 .00	.18 .18ᵉ .00
Speculative			.26 .09	.24 .12	.50 .71 .21
	II .00		.62 IV .21	.83
Confrontive			.06 .00	.06 .00	.12 .12 .00
			.35 .09 .44ᵈ	.45 .12 .57	

(Left axis label: **W O R K**)

ᵃClient.
ᵇTherapist.
ᶜTotal quadrant
ᵈTotal column.
ᵉTotal row.

Figure 7.4. Percentage of transition segment talk examined by client and therapist talk per cell and quadrant.

things in a tentative, speculative manner," but now adds "We are going to talk about *ourselves* and our effect on *one another.*" The leaders' communication is of special note during this transition because they do not exhibit any dialogue in either of the two work styles of highest risk.

Furthermore, the leaders' level of relationship talk is at the same level as in Phase II, but it is now concentrated in the safe, speculative style. In other words, except for the modest venture into relationship talk, the leaders continue on in the same fashion as they had up to this point. It may be that they are not sensitive to the transitional shift into relationship issues or are hesitant or unwilling to model or reinforce a more open, penetrating, and responsive style of interaction. This is unfortunate on two counts: the therapeutic component of a group format as the interpersonal nature of the group and the potential for feedback (certainly espoused by W. F. Hill) and the leader's modeling influence on the verbal context of the group.

The potential for this group to use its interpersonal nature is not realized in Phase III, and the possibility for change into a more interpersonally risky environment is left wanting. The section of Phase III consti-

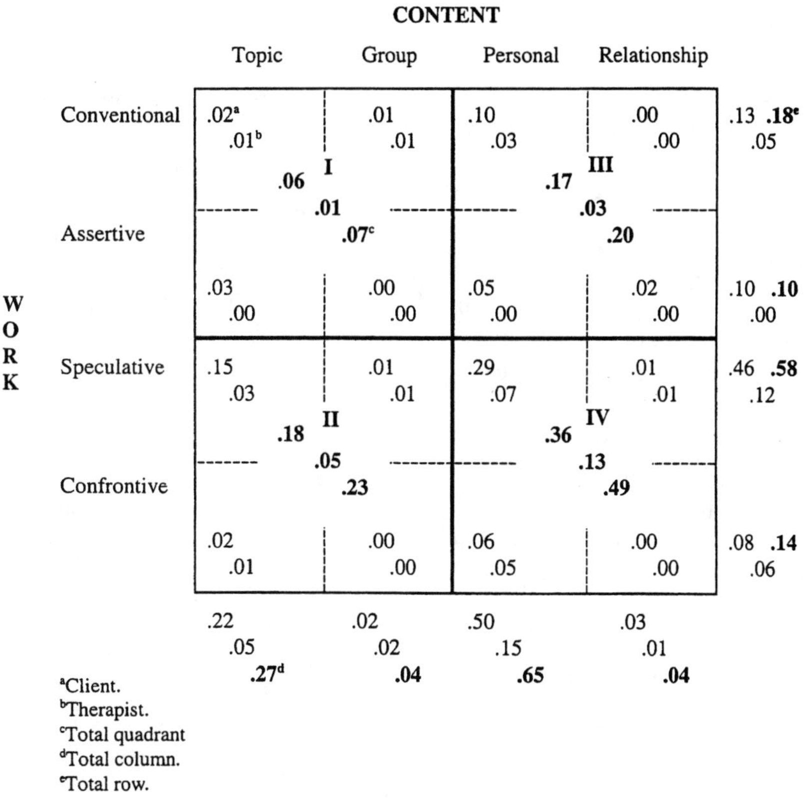

	Topic	Group	Personal	Relationship	
Conventional	.02ᵃ / .01ᵇ	.01 / .01	.10 / .03	.00 / .00	.13 .18ᵉ / .05
	I .06		**III** .17		
		.01		.03	
Assertive		**.07ᶜ**		**.20**	
	.03 / .00	.00 / .00	.05 / .00	.02 / .00	.10 .10 / .00
Speculative	.15 / .03	.01 / .01	.29 / .07	.01 / .01	.46 .58 / .12
	II .18		**IV** .36		
		.05		.13	
Confrontive		**.23**		**.49**	
	.02 / .01	.00 / .00	.06 / .05	.00 / .00	.08 .14 / .06
	.22 / .05	.02 / .02	.50 / .15	.03 / .01	
	.27ᵈ	**.04**	**.65**	**.04**	

(Left margin label: **W O R K**)

ᵃClient.
ᵇTherapist.
ᶜTotal quadrant
ᵈTotal column.
ᵉTotal row.

Figure 7.5. Percentage of Phase III talk examined by client and therapist talk per cell and quadrant.

tutes 190 rateable HIM units, or 29% of the entire talk within this session; half of all that interaction falls into Quadrant IV (similar to the percentage in total session talk), followed by 23% in II, 20% in III, and 7% in I (see Figure 7.5). Sixty-five percent of the content falls in personal, whereas 58% of work talk is in speculative. This personal focused talk dominates the content of the Phase III section. Now the members are its chief contributors. Although almost 30% of the communication in the entire session is in this section of Phase III, it has the lowest percentage in relationship interaction. The group continues to concentrate on a personal focus and returns to more "topic" talk than that found in the section of Phase II just before the transition period. Examination by cells reveals 36% of the talk occurring in the personal–speculative cell, followed by 18% in topic–speculative.

Although the therapists venture into confrontive work, their verbal dialogue in personal–speculative remains constant. The predominant dialogue in the Phase III section is once again focused on personal content spoken in an inquiring, low-risk fashion. The group has settled into "working," and the norm governing how the group is to work seems to be established: "We talk (work) about ourselves in a safe, speculative manner." The norm reflects a high value for safety, and the way to obtain safety is through individual, therapist-directed interaction. The momentary influence of the members in the transition phase is not realized, and the stylistic influence (personal–speculative) of the therapists appears persuasive. Although it is not obvious from the percentage analysis, a review of the transcript indicates that client talk in the personal category contains long, uninterrupted monologues in which the client is describing self and the circumstances surrounding his or her problem. Reinforcement of this focus increases the likelihood that the *what* of the group is, and will be, topic (the least therapeutic of all the "whats") and personal. This process, combined with the norm of safety, is more indicative of an *individual* counseling mode, one marked by a cognitive, insight-oriented style. Group and relationship talk is almost totally nonexistent, negating, in part, a core therapeutic component of group therapy and the chief rationale for using a group format. It appears that the group does not take advantage of the critical moments of change within the group.

Nested within the Phase III section is the segment of interaction described as higher experiencing. It consists of 52 rateable HIM units, or 8% of the total session interaction. Qualitatively, it can be described as "experiencing," with Quadrant IV dominating this period with 85% of the talk (see Figure 7.6). Again, personal content (95%) and speculative work (58%) rule the style categories. Thus, it is not surprising that the highest percentage of talk falls in personal–speculative (58%). Personal–confrontive talk (27%) shows an increase in confrontive style, indicating higher risk and expanded feedback. Clearly, these two cells demonstrate higher experiencing of self *with* self. The HIM analysis is supportive of the description of this phase as being one of higher experiencing of self, as 95% of the content falls in the personal category. The highest percentage of confrontive dialogue is during this brief period, adding a more emotional and here-and-now dimension to the personal nature of the interaction—creating an intensity of presence. Higher experiencing of the self is also operating; it is an experiencing of self in the presence of others. The experiencing of self is likely occurring only with the client on whom the group is focused. Because of the lack of dialogue in the relationship style, it appears that an experience of self emerges from self-disclosure and feedback about self from others (e.g., insight) rather than feedback about self's effect on another (e.g., interpersonal learning).

RELATIONSHIP BETWEEN THE RESEARCH AND THE THEORY

The extensive application of the HIM to the empirical study of group process attests to its perceived utility. The HIM has been repeatedly found,

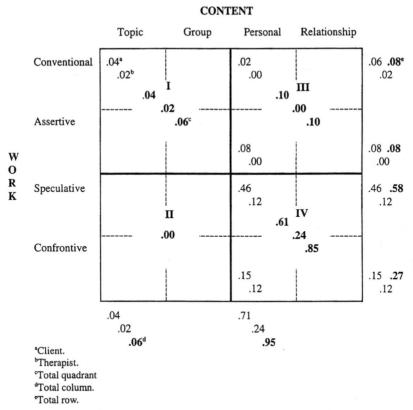

Figure 7.6. Percentage of higher experiencing segment talk examined by client and therapist talk per cell and quadrant.

across various kinds of groups, to be useful as a descriptive tool for the measurement of verbal interaction (Fuhriman & Barlow, 1994). Originally designed and developed out of a therapy group context, the HIM is in marked contrast to many other process measures whose conceptual bases emerged from dyadic therapy or encounter and task groups. The bases for the HIM are reasonably clear, given its three general therapeutic values of member centeredness, interpersonal threat, and patient–therapist role taking. It is for these reasons that the authors have incorporated the HIM as both a training tool for neophyte group therapists as well as a research tool to understand the therapeutic process operating within a group. Our collected experiences over the years drives the following observations.

Psychotherapy is often criticized because of the lack of a metaparadigm. The HIM is an example of one paradigmatic effort to conceptualize and define "what is therapeutic." As such, the measure has tremendous heuristic utility in understanding the dynamics of verbal interaction. Furthermore, the fact that the HIM is multidimensional *and* specific in its measurement of the different dimensions places it among a handful of group therapy instruments capable of analyzing the complex process of human interaction.

The HIM has all the problems associated with behavioral systems. A significant amount of training is involved in learning to rate group interaction on the HIM–SS for research application. It takes approximately 20–25 hours to understand the specifics of the scoring system so that established statements can be rated accurately. Additional practice is needed to rate transcripts or audiotaped records of group dialogue. Transcription is laborious and costly, but, in the long run, it is advantageous to rating from an audiotape (e.g., the written transcript increases the possible application of various statistical strategies such as sequential analysis).

The clinical implications for the HIM–SS are nested in its ability to track dialogue over time and, most importantly, to describe the therapist and group influence. It is apparent that clients mirror therapist dialogue in what they say and how they say it (Barlow, 1988). Therapist modeling is accomplished in a subtle but natural fashion. That therapists can be trained not only to understand the therapeutic meaning of the dialogue but also to speak in specific therapeutic styles becomes an important consideration.

Recent illustrations of what can be learned from the HIM–SS emerge by examining the group's process (i.e., verbal interaction) moment-by-moment over time to see the contribution of interaction to the ever-developing ecosystem of the group. Interactional patterns do exist and seem to develop in the life of the group; understanding those patterns and what they represent therapeutically is an important next step. Preliminary data indicate that the interactional patterns show greater variability in the early sessions of the group's life together (Burlingame, Fuhriman, & Barnum, 1995). As time goes on, the group settles into a "way of speaking" or interacting. Put another way, the norm-governing dialogue has been established in the group. Clinicians must be able to understand the group's involvement in creating and maintaining norms and to assist the group in the establishment of therapeutic norms. The window of opportunity to do such appears to open and close early in the group.

More than any other form of psychotherapy treatment, the gist of group therapy is interpersonal in nature, both in theory and in practice. Not only does interpersonal learning influence the functioning and health of the individual but it also influences the therapeutic functioning and health of the group—highlighting the two prongs of therapist focus: the well-being of the individual and the therapeutic quality of the group. The HIM provides a means of describing the interpersonal nature of group therapy by way of an embedded value system and in fact stands as one of the few that attend to and specifically value the interpersonal functioning of clients.

Although a substantial investment is required in learning the HIM–SS, once it is learned it has both clinical and research utility. The HIM–

SS provides a means not only of describing what is going on in therapy but also of conceptualizing the significance of such action (i.e., what is therapeutic?). Thus, the group therapist can use the system to guide therapy and, given the initial evidence, model dialogue deemed to be therapeutic. The conceptual framework further facilitates the therapist's understanding of the individual client's contributions to the overall process and, to some degree, integrates client diagnoses and behaviors in a "present," natural context.

ASSESSMENT AND FUTURE DIRECTIONS

Regarding research application, the HIM–SS addresses the problems of complexity and specificity that are nested within a human interactive system. The individual parts of the group (clients, therapist) can be examined separately to determine their contribution to the therapeutic quality of the group, their influence and relationship to one another, and their role in the process of the group. Contextually, both the momentary and cumulative impact of the individual members can be analyzed. The ability of the HIM–SS to measure the "moment-to-moment" bases of the group has recently been facilitated by the application of sequential analysis (Barlow, 1988).

Although it is understandable, it is unfortunate that the HIM–SS attends only to the verbal component of interaction. It is obvious, particularly from rating both transcribed and audiotaped interaction, that meaning is conveyed and understood through verbal and nonverbal aspects of talk. The motive, or intention of the talk, is often conveyed nonverbally and could affect how the interaction is rated. The word "style" infers some nonverbal influence. However, the classification defines style only in verbal terms and thus has no way to reflect such meaning.

Notwithstanding the substantial research using the HIM, there is still a need for continued research on the measure. The weighting system is tied to a specific value system and may be less applicable to some groups (e.g., career planning, cognitive–behavioral) with different goals or values (e.g., information giving or advice giving). This fact does not negate the utility of the HIM, but it serves to underscore the importance of a therapist having a conceptual framework for "what is therapeutic."

The HIM, specifically the HIM–SS, is a means of unraveling the complexity of group process by defining the space and time of the group through a description of its verbal interaction. The act of careful, reliable description enables the researcher not only to plot the how, what, and when of group interaction but also the degree to which the interaction may be associated with therapeutic benefit. Clearly, the latter is of fundamental concern for an empirically based practice of group psychotherapy.

The descriptive precision of the HIM is laudatory; the remaining challenge to future research centers on the HIM as an evaluative tool of therapeutic interaction.

REFERENCES

Anderson, A. R., Hummel, T. J., & Gibson, D. L. (1970). An experimental assessment of videotape feedback and two pregroup orientation procedures in a human relations training laboratory. *Comparative Group Studies, 1,* 156–176.

Barlow, S. H. (1988, August). *Interaction analysis of leader/member communication styles in time-limited group psychotherapy.* Paper presented at the 96th Annual Convention of the American Psychological Association, Atlanta, Georgia.

Barlow, S. H., Hansen, W. D., Fuhriman, A., & Finley, R. (1982). Leader communication style: Effects on members of small groups. *Small Group Behavior, 13,* 518–531.

Bednar, R. L., & Battersby, C. P. (1976). The effects of specific cognitive structure on early group development. *Journal of Applied Behavioral Science, 12,* 513–522.

Bigelow, G. S., & Thorne, J. W. (1969). Reality versus client-centered models in group counseling. *The School Counselor, 16,* 191–194.

Boyd, R. E. (1970). Whitehorn-Betz A-B score as an effector of client–counselor interaction. *Journal of Counseling Psychology, 17,* 279–283.

Burlingame, G. M., Fuhriman, A., & Barnum, K. R. (1995). Group therapy as a nonlinear dynamical system: Analysis of therapeutic communication for chaotic patterns. In F. D. Abraham & A. R. Gilgen (Eds.), *Chaos theory in psychology* (pp. 87–105). West Point, CT: Praeger.

Castore, G. F., Hill, W. F., & Lake, R. A. (1959). Measurement of a therapeutic group by a scale of communication complexity in interpersonal interactions: A study of interjudge reliability. *Provo Papers, 3,* 1–20.

Conyne, R. K., & Rapin, L. S. (1977a). A HIM-G interaction process analysis study of facilitator- and self-directed groups. *Small Group Behavior, 8,* 333–340.

Conyne, R. K., & Rapin, L. S. (1977b). Facilitator- and self-directed groups: A statement-by-statement interaction study. *Small Group Behavior, 8,* 341–350.

Corsini, R., & Rosenberg, B. (1955). Mechanisms of group psychotherapy: Processes and dynamics. *Journal of Abnormal and Social Psychology, 51,* 406–411.

Crews, C. Y., & Melnick, J. (1976). Use of initial and delayed structure in facilitating group development. *Journal of Counseling Psychology, 23,* 92–98.

DeJulio, S., Bentley, J., & Cockayne, T. (1979). Pregroup norm setting: Effects on encounter group interaction. *Small Group Behavior, 10,* 368–388.

Dowd, E. T., & Blocher, D. H. (1974). Effects of immediate reinforcement and awareness of response on beginning counselor behavior. *Counselor Education and Supervision, 13,* 190–197.

Dye, C. A. (1974). Self-concept, anxiety, and group participation as affected by human relations training. *Nursing Research, 23*, 301–306.

Fisher, B. A., & Werbel, W. S. (1979). T-group and therapy group communication: An interaction analysis of the group process. *Small Group Behavior, 10*, 475–500.

Foulkes, S. H. (1948). *Introduction to group-analytic psychotherapy*. London: Heinemann.

Frank, J. D., & Ascher, E. (1951). Corrective emotional experience in group therapy. *American Journal of Psychiatry, 108*, 126–131.

Fuhriman, A., & Barlow, S. H. (1994). Interaction analysis: Instrumentation and issues. In A. Fuhriman & G. M. Burlingame (Eds.), *Handbook of group psychotherapy: An empirical and clinical synthesis* (pp. 191–222). New York: Wiley.

Fuhriman, A., & Burlingame, G. M. (1990). Consistency of matter: A comparative analysis of individual and group process variables. *The Counseling Psychologist, 18*, 6–63.

Gilstein, K. W., Wright, E. W., & Stone, D. R. (1977). The effects of leadership style on group interactions in differing socio-political subcultures. *Small Group Behavior, 8*, 313–331.

Gorlow, L., Hoch, E. L., & Telschow, E. F. (1952). *The nature of nondirective group psychotherapy*. New York: Columbia University Press.

Hammonds, T. M., & Worthington, E. L. (1985). The effect of facilitator utterances on participant responses in a brief ACME-type marriage enrichment group. *American Journal of Family Therapy, 13*(2), 39–49.

Hardcastle, D. R. (1972). Measuring effectiveness in group marital counseling. *The Family Coordinator, 21*, 213–218.

Hartson, D. J., & Kunce, J. T. (1973). Videotape replay and recall in group work. *Journal of Counseling Psychology, 20*, 437–441.

Hill, I. S., & Hill, W. F. (1957). *Interaction matrix for group psychotherapy: A method for studying the quality of interaction in psychotherapy groups* [Monograph]. Provo, UT: Utah State Hospital.

Hill, P. S. (1963). *A heterogeneous sample of psychotherapy groups rated with a verbal interaction rating scale*. Unpublished master's thesis, University of Utah, Salt Lake City.

Hill, W. F. (1955). *The influence of subgroups on participation in human relations training groups*. Unpublished doctoral dissertation, University of Chicago, Chicago.

Hill, W. F. (1957). Analysis of interviews of group therapists practicing in the Rocky Mountain area. *Provo Papers, 1*, 25–39.

Hill, W. F. (1965a). *Hill Interaction Matrix*. Unpublished manuscript, University of Southern California, Los Angeles.

Hill, W. F. (1965b). *Hill Interaction Matrix Scoring manual*. Unpublished manuscript, University of Southern California, Los Angeles.

Hill, W. F. (1969). *Learning thru discussion*. Beverly Hills, CA: Sage.

Hill, W. F. (1971). The Hill Interaction Matrix. *Personnel and Guidance Journal,* *49,* 619–623.

Hill, W. F. (1973). *Hill Interaction Matrix (HIM): Conceptual framework for understanding groups.* New York: University Associates.

Hill, W. F. (1977). Hill Interaction Matrix (HIM): The conceptual framework, derived rating scales, and an updated bibliography. *Small Group Behavior, 8,* 251–268.

Hill, W. F., & Gruner, L. (1973). A study of development in open and closed groups. *Small Group Behavior, 4,* 355–381.

Houts, P. S., & Wittner, W. K. (1968). Patients' recognition memory for statements made in ward community meetings. *Journal of Consulting and Clinical Psychology, 32,* 130–133.

Kagan, N., Krathwohl, D. R., & Miller, R. (1963). Stimulated recall in therapy using videotape. *Journal of Counseling Psychology, 10,* 237–243.

Kanas, N., Barr, M. A., & Dossick, S. (1985). The homogeneous schizophrenic inpatient group: An evaluation using the Hill Interaction Matrix. *Small Group Behavior, 16,* 397–409.

Kanas, N., & Smith, A. J. (1990). Schizophrenic group process: A comparison and replication using the HIM-G. *Group, 14,* 246–252.

Kaul, T. J., Kaul, M. A., & Bednar, R. L. (1973). Counselor confrontation and client depth of self-exploration. *Journal of Counseling Psychology, 20,* 132–136.

Lambert, M. J. (1974). Supevisory and counseling process: A comparative study. *Counselor Education and Supervision, 14,* 54–60.

Lambert, M. J., & DeJulio, S. S. (1977). Toward a validation of diverse measures of human interaction and counseling process. *Small Group Behavior, 8,* 393–395.

Landy, E. E. (1970). Attitude and attitude change toward interaction as a function of participation versus observation. *Comparative Group Studies, 1,* 128–155.

Lee, F., & Bednar, R. L. (1977). Effects of group structure and risk-taking disposition on group behavior, attitudes, and atmosphere. *Journal of Counseling Psychology, 24,* 191–199.

Leith, W. R., & Uhlemann, M. R. (1972). The shaping group approach to stuttering: A pilot study. *Comparative Group Studies, 3,* 175–199.

Lewin, K. (1951). *Field theory in social psychology.* New York: Harper.

Lewis, J., & Mider, P. A. (1973). Effects of leadership style on content and work styles of short-term therapy groups. *Journal of Counseling Psychology, 20,* 137–141.

Lindberg, F. H., Morrill, R. S., & Kilstrom, D. R. (1974). Group therapy with hospitalized patients: Increasing therapeutic interaction using a feedback-escape technique. *Small Group Behavior, 5,* 486–494.

Martin, E. A., & Hill, W. F. (1957). Toward a theory of group development: Six phases of therapy group development. *International Journal of Group Psychotherapy, 7,* 20–30.

McIntire, W. G., Drummond, R. J., & Carter, C. E. (1977). The HIM-B as a family interaction assessment technique. *Small Group Behavior, 8,* 361–368.

Muro, J. J., & Drummond, R. J. (1974). A note on college level norms for the HIM-B. *Small Group Behavior, 5,* 145–156.

Pattison, E. M. (1969). *A brief history of the American Group Psychotherapy Association* [Monograph]. New York: American Group Psychotherapy Association.

Pattison, P. R., Rardin, M. W., & Lindberg, F. H. (1977). Effects of immediate feedback on the therapeutic content of group leaders' statements. *Small Group Behavior, 8,* 303–311.

Peterson, J. P., & Pollio, H. R. (1982). Therapeutic effectiveness of differentially targeted humorous remarks in group psychotherapy. *Group, 6,* 39–50.

Powell, E. R. (1977). HIM correlational study. *Small Group Behavior, 8,* 369–380.

Robinson, M. B. (1970). A study of the effects of focused videotape feedback in group counseling. *Comparative Group Studies, 1,* 47–75.

Roe, J. E., & Edwards, K. J. (1978). Relationship of two process measurement systems for group therapy. *Journal of Consulting and Clinical Psychology, 46,* 1545–1546.

Seligman, M., & Sterne, D. M. (1969). Verbal behavior in therapist-led, leaderless, and alternating group psychotherapy sessions. *Journal of Counseling Psychology, 16,* 325–328.

Silbergeld, S., & Manderscheid, R. W. (1976). Comparative asessment of a coping model for school adolescents. *Journal of School Psychology, 14,* 261–274.

Silbergeld, S., Manderscheid, R. W., & Koenig, G. R. (1977). Evaluation of brief intervention models by the Hill Interaction Matrix. *Small Group Behavior, 8,* 281–302.

Silbergeld, S., Thune, E. S., & Manderscheid, R. W. (1980). Marital role dynamics during brief group psychotherapy: Assessment of verbal interactions. *Journal of Clinical Psychology, 36,* 480–492.

Sisson, C. J., Sisson, P. J., & Gazda, G. M. (1977). Extended group counseling with psychiatry residents: HIM and the Bonney Scale compared. *Small Group Behavior, 8,* 351–360.

Sklar, A. D., Yalom, I. D., Zim, A., & Newell, G. L. (1970). Time-extended group therapy: A controlled study. *Comparative Group Studies, 1,* 373–386.

Stava, L. J., & Bednar, R. L. (1979). Process and outcome in encounter groups: The effect of group composition. *Small Group Behavior, 10,* 200–213.

Sterne, D. M., & Seligman, M. (1971). Further comparisons of verbal behavior in therapist-led, leaderless, and alternating group psychotherapy sessions. *Journal of Counseling Psychology, 18,* 472–477.

Toseland, R. W., Rossiter, C. M., Peak, T., & Hill, P. (1990). Therapeutic process in peer led and professionally led support groups for caregivers. *International Journal of Group Psychotherapy, 40,* 279–303.

Uhlemann, M. R., & Weigel, R. G. (1977). Behavior change outcomes of marathon group treatment. *Small Group Behavior, 8,* 269–280.

White, K. R. (1974). T-groups revisited: Self-concept change and the "fish-bowling" technique. *Small Group Behavior, 5,* 473–485.

Yalom, I. D., Houts, P. S., Newell, G., & Rand, K. H. (1967). Preparation of patients for group therapy: A controlled study. *Archives of General Psychiatry, 17,* 416–427.

Zarle, T. H., & Boyd, R. C. (1977). An evaluation of modeling and experiential procedures for self-disclosure training. *Journal of Counseling Psychology, 24,* 118–124.

8

THE MEMBER–LEADER
SCORING SYSTEM

SOLOMON CYTRYNBAUM

In this chapter I describe Mann's Member–Leader Scoring System, illustrate its utility by reviewing previous research in different group settings, and apply the system to Group A, Session 3.

HISTORY AND THEORY OF THE SYSTEM

Although Mann's scoring system is not derived from any particular theory of group process, model of group therapy, or therapeutic change in groups, it is firmly rooted in the conceptual frameworks embedded in literary, ego-psychological, and Kleinian clinical theories as well as other similar analyses of group process. Mann's early studies and applications of the scoring system have produced provocative findings and theorizing about the complex determinants and functions of different member role performances in groups and group development, as well as a conceptualization of developmental changes over time in groups.

I am indebted to Victoria Curran, PhD, for her contribution to scoring Session 3.

The Member–Leader Scoring System was first introduced by Mann, Gibbard, and Hartman in 1967 and was revised in 1970. It was repeatedly used in studies of small, self-analytic groups, Tavistock small study groups, and the college classroom as a small work group. In these contexts, Mann's system has been particularly useful in studying such aspects of group life as (a) group development (Cytrynbaum & Conran, 1979a; Gibbard, Hartman, & Mann, 1974; Hartman, 1969); (b) member performance and role specialization (Mann et al., 1967, 1970; Gibbard, Hartman, & Mann, 1974; Ringwald, 1973); (c) silent members (Rosenwein, 1970); (d) interracial authority relations (Cytrynbaum & Conran, 1979b); (e) gender and authority (Cytrynbaum & Curran, 1993; Cytrynbaum & Hallberg, 1993, 1995; Hallberg, 1995); (f) member–member relations (Gibbard, 1969; Hartman & Gibbard, 1974); and (g) the impact of leadership style on the member–leader relationship (Granda, 1992). Some efforts to apply the system to the patient–therapist relationship in psychotherapy have been reported but not published.

In Mann's Member–Leader Scoring System, the relationship to authority or the member–leader relationship is considered the central aspect of group life and that which affects process and development the most. The system focuses on what group members mean when they communicate with each other or with the leader. Observation and inference are simultaneously used in the scoring process. The system rests on three primary assumptions: First, a member may express feelings symbolically as well as directly. Second, the feelings expressed by a member must be understood and appreciated within the particular experiential framework of the listener. Third, in the process of expressing feelings, a member may establish internal symbolic equivalents or displacements for himself or herself and for the target of those feelings, usually involving the leader.

The Mann system considers both the manifest verbal content and the latent feelings that the member who is speaking may have or may be expressing toward the leader. The system requires a scorer to continually decide on the *level* of an act as well as the category or categories into which the act falls. The level of an act refers to both the manifest and latent level of the expression being scored and specifies via displacement which symbols represent the member, the leader, or other speaking members. The levels are described more fully later. The categories in the system provide a language with which the scorer records inferences about the feelings being expressed directly or via displacement and symbolization by the member, particularly the member's feelings toward the leader. Although it is assumed that the member–leader relationship is always influencing a member's expressed feelings and behavior to some extent, feelings about the leader never completely determine the member's manifest behavior at any given moment. Members may directly express their feelings about the leader or temporarily displace their feelings onto a symbolic equivalent for the leader, such as another group member or some external equivalent (e.g., a family member or the president).

EARLY RESEARCH AND APPLICATIONS

The Mann et al. (1967) original study of four self-analytic groups, derived from a course at Harvard titled Social Relations 120, illustrates how the Member–Leader Scoring System may be used to identify member roles, group development, and the complex determinants of the member–leader relationship. Six factors and 12 factor patterns were derived from a factor analysis of all member–leader category scores for all small-group sessions. These factor patterns were interpreted clinically by reviewing transcripts of the group's verbal interaction.

Statistically similar profiles in member factor patterns were used to identify individual member performances, labeled *nonrational roles*, which were then interpreted clinically. Individual member performances are thus conceptualized as nonrational role specialists who represent, express, and perform important unconscious group functions at different stages of the group's development. Dunphy (1964), in a conceptualization similar to Mann's, described the group function served by different member roles:

> The non-rational role specialists who emerge in groups ... [facilitate] ... projective identification by playing roles which represent important elements in the internal fantasies of group members. This externalization of internal fantasies through their acting out in the group results in the development of a generalized group fantasy, or "mythology," which exercises a controlling influence on the behavior of group members and on the evolution of the group (p. 55).
>
> Group integration occurs through the "matching" of similar internalized objects with externalized objects so that a de-limited range of modes of relating is established, i.e., the group arrives at a consensus about the class of internal objects to which links will be brought into play (p. 57).
>
> The group roles represent the externalization and dramatization of conflicts centering around the handling of primary processes in the relative absence of external restraints and the breakdown of traditional normative expectations. Thus the role specialists become symbols of the major alternatives which the group faces in the evolution of its culture and through the interaction of the specialists in the context of group response, patterns of action which resolve these basic dilemmas. (p. 67)

Illustrative member roles, individual predispositions, and the group functions served, identified by Dunphy (1964, 1968) and Mann et al. (1967), are summarized in Table 8.1.

TABLE 8.1
Nonrational Roles in Self-Analytic Groups

Role	Individual Predisposition	Group Function
Heroes	Rebellious men	Serve to weaken defenses against intimacy and impulse expression; challenge the leader and lead the "revolt"; press for impulse expression and honesty even at the expense of "sensitivity"; counterdependent and counterphobic suppression of anxiety, depression, and dependency.
Moralistic and paranoid resisters	Moralistic and suspicious men	Resist the hero; speak in support of tact and sensitivity; oppose harmful candor and analysis; challenge task norms of self-evaluation, impulse expression, and attending to the "here-and-now."
Independent enactors	Working men and women	Serve to resolve "intimacy–expressivity" versus "sensitivity" conflict in direction of work; mediate between hero's demand for complete self-exposure and the resister's defensiveness in the face of the hero's seemingly callous demands; conflict is over whether to expose group phenomena regardless of feelings versus a defensive reliance on sensitivity, tact, and compassion, which inhibits group analysis and work.
Sexual scapegoats	Inhibited or silent men	Represent the split-off and projected inadequacies of others or unacceptable aspects of member personality; usually involves concerns about sexual and personal adequacy.
Sociocenters	Loyal women	Supportive of the leader and accepts his or her authority; attempt to resolve interpersonal difficulties, often by appealing to the leader as a moral authority.
Aggressors	Rigid men	Strive to maintain control and impersonality in response to member expressions of personal feelings and ideas; have a difficult time with ambiguity; turn to and are seen as dependent on leader; are often attacked as other members repudiate their own anxiety and depression by projecting them onto these members as scapegoats.
Ombudsmen	Male or female oldest sibling	Serve as spokesman for distressed and silent members; remind others that a great deal is going on even for those who say little.
Sexual idols	Attractive women	Representation of incestuous sexuality; principal object of projected oedipal fantasies involving leader and male members.

Mann et al. (1967) also statistically identified five phases of group development by computing the moving averages of each factor pattern and determined significant differences among six blocks of sessions characterized by nonsignificant differences between sessions within each block. A careful review and clinical interpretation of the transcripts of all sessions within each of the five statistically different session blocks produced a conceptualization of the different tasks, themes, conflicts, and dominant member struggles associated with each of the five blocks of sessions or phases. The resulting five phases of development were labeled as follows: Initial Complaining, Premature Enactment, Confrontation, Internalization, and Separation and Terminal Review.

Group development or movement from one phase to the next in the terms of Mann et al. (1967) is propelled by the shifting nature, influence, and competition between member subgroups or their nonrational role representatives as the members struggle with connecting or resisting aspects of the leader's definition of work. Work includes enactment, independence, involvement, and expression components. Thus, for each of the phases in Table 8.2, it is resolution of the conflict between the dominant and deviant subgroups and their nonrational role representatives that propels group movement.

Finally, Mann et al. (1967) conceptualized the complexity of member–leader relationship by identifying the major contributing parameters. According to Mann et al., the determinants of the member–leader relationship include: (a) individual differences in member predisposition and capacity to work; (b) the nature of the real and fantasized situation; (c) the nature of members' self-presentation; (d) the nature and formation of subgroup cliques in different phases of group development; (e) the unfolding and constitution of the group's history; (f) the nature and outcome of the inevitable confrontation with the leader; (g) group adaptation and normative formation; (h) individual member adaptation to the shifts in the group after the confrontation; and (i) the members' management of termination.

The first application of the Mann Member–Leader/Leader–Member System beyond self-analytic groups involved two early studies of the college classroom conceptualized as a small work group. The first study involved four 40-session introductory psychology classes taught by White men for 127 students at the University of Michigan (Cytrynbaum & Conran, 1979a; Mann et al., 1970). The second was a study of interracial teacher–student relationships in four Black classes with White and Black teachers at the Tuskegee Institute (Cytrynbaum & Conran, 1979b).

The Michigan study focused on individual student affective and interpersonal styles, teacher task strategies, group development, and processes that contribute to disrupting or facilitating student work or learning. Classroom interaction was audiotaped and then scored with a slightly modified

TABLE 8.2
Member Subgroup Characteristic by Phase

	Phase			
Initial Complaining	Premature Enactment	Confrontation	Internalization	Separation and Terminal Review
Dominant subgroups				
Dependent complaining	"The sensitive ones"	Rebellion and complaining (including "the spokespersons")	Enactment and work	Depression and maniac denial
Lloyd compliance Counterdependent heroics	Withdrawal and denial "The accepting enactors"	Independence Anxiety and withdrawal		Personal involvement Complaining and abdication of responsibility
Self-sufficiency	"The heroic enactors"			
Deviant subgroup				
Enactment in the service of autonomy	Disappointment and resentment	"The heroes"	"The scapegoats"	

Note. From *Interpersonal Styles and Group Development: An Analysis of the Member–Leader Relationship* (p. 187), by Mann, R. D., Gibbard, G. S., and Hartman, J., 1967, New York: Wiley. Copyright 1967 by John Wiley & Sons, Inc. Reprinted with permission.

version of the Mann Member–Leader system and a parallel system developed to categorize the multiple functions of the teacher called the Teacher-As Typology (see Table 8.3).

Using factor analytic and cluster analytic techniques, the researchers (Cytrynbaum & Conran, 1979b; Mann et al., 1970) statistically classified individual differences in student performances into eight "clusters," or types of interpersonal styles or performances. A clinical description of each of these student clusters was constructed from the individual factor data, classroom observations, and an in-depth interview with each of the students. These eight clusters are described in Table 8.4.

Multivariate analyses were then used to create a statistically significant skeleton of member performances over time and of group development. Six statistically distinct phases of development of the four classes were determined: Opening Phase; Dissatisfaction and Discouragement Phase; Early Enactment, or Early Work Phase; Teacher-Controlling Dominance; Late Enactment, or Late Work Phase; and Separation, or Differentiated Work Phase. A careful listening to audiotapes of key segments and issues was then used to clinically flesh out this statistical skeleton of group life. The development of the classroom as a group is summarized in Table 8.5.

Synthesizing the member cluster and group development data, Cytrynbaum and Conran (1979a) described in some detail how each of the different student clusters related to each of the teacher's task strategies at different phases of the group's development. These analyses serve as the basis for a conceptualization of student work and antiwork strategies as well as a discussion of effective teaching.

In the Tuskegee study, Cytrynbaum and Conran (1979b) attempted to identify patterns of work and antiwork for Black students that were associated with the exercise of the six different task strategies and their combinations by Black and White teachers. In this study, the audiotapes of the four classes, two taught by White teachers and two by Black teachers, were scored with the Mann Member–Leader System and the Teacher-As Typology coding system for capturing teacher-to-student and student-to-teacher task strategies. The Mann member-to-leader affective scores and the Teacher-As Typology task strategy scores were factored together, and a number of facilitative and disruptive patterns by race of teacher were identified statistically. These were than analyzed clinically. These different patterns are summarized in Table 8.6. Some selected clinical interpretations of these patterns, taken from Cytrynbaum and Conran (1979b), are included after Table 8.6 so that readers can appreciate the interplay between statistically significant results and clinical interpretation that characterizes the Mann tradition of making sense of the complexity of group life.

The analyses of student responses to both Black and White teacher functioning produced factors that described student acceptance and dissat-

TABLE 8.3
Summary of the Teacher-As Typology

The Teacher As	Major Task Goals	Characteristic Behaviors
Expert (X)	To transmit relevant findings, fundamental concepts, and analytical perspectives of the field, and to ensure that students have mastered them.	Lecturing, scholarly organization, and preparation of materials; asking and answering questions, discussion questions, and terms; connecting students with other experts and resources.
Formal Authority (FA)	To set goals and clarify the procedures for achieving them; to ensure that students are doing what is expected of them and that they are in compliance with the rules of the institution; to provide students with clear indications of the progress in the course based on uniform standards; to control one's class and maintain quality control and the values of the school's currency.	Defining the course structure; setting deadlines and assignments; establishing the ground rules for discussion and decorum; curbing deviancy; establishing standards of excellence; preparing and grading exams; other uniform procedures for evaluating student performance.
Socializing Agent (SA)	To recruit the neophyte into the teacher's culture; to clarify goals and future career paths by introducing the student to the concerns and activities of those already working in the field and by clarifying the training and occupational possibilities.	Discussing one's own career, exploring the paths of entry into the inner circle, and sharing one's underlying values and assumptions; clarifying the demands, rewards, and obstacles of the major field and the academic work; clarifying career paths, future careers, and other opportunities; modeling a competent, knowledgeable professional.

Facilitator (F)	To foster intellectual and creative growth and learning in the direction of students' own interests and strengths; helping them to move beyond whatever is blocking their future potential; and assisting them in reaching their own goals more effectively on their own terms.	Bringing students out and assisting growth; sharpening self-awareness of strengths, interest and skills; using innovative learning and teaching experiences to help students reach personal goals; focusing on blocks to learning and modifying classroom structures to reduce reality-based affective responses that interfere with the learning task.
Ego Ideal (EI)	To convey to the students via the teacher's own enthusiasm, commitment, and involvement in the course material, the excitement, challenge, and value that he or she finds in his or her work and in a given field of study.	Demonstrating the worth of personal commitment to one's field and educational goals; modeling competence, enthusiasm; being alive and excited; using amusing stories or jokes, gripping illustrations, cases, and examples.
Person (P)	To engage the student in a satisfying relationship in which both student and teacher feel free to share their ideas and personal reactions; to convey the full range of human needs and skills relevant to and sustained by one's intellectual activity; to be validated as a human being and to validate the student's identity.	Being self-disclosing and self-revealing in ways that clarify one totality beyond the task at hand; expressing personal needs and tensions; revealing out-of-role aspects of oneself or role–person tension and incongruities.

Note. From Cytrynbaum and Conran, 1979a, p. 53.

TABLE 8.4
Student Clusters

Cluster No.	Cluster	Description
I	Compliant students (5 men and 7 women)	Traditional "good" students: very conventional, contented, trusting of authority, willing to go along, task oriented, focused on understanding content; not critical, with little capacity for independent thought; they prefer the teacher functioning as Expert and Formal Authority. They listen, take notes, do exactly as they are told, and do not really change over the course of the year.
II	Anxious-dependent students (12 men and 16 women)	Very concerned and dependent on what authorities think and expect; have low self-esteem and doubt their own self-worth and intellectual competence; extremely anxious about exams and grades; hesitant and tentative with their comments; they require a great deal of Expert and Formal Authority functioning because they need to know exactly what is going on, what the ground rules are, and where the teacher "is coming from." They experience some changes over the course of the year and become more able to accept independence-fostering facilitation on the teacher's part.
III	Discouraged workers (3 men and 1 woman)	Bright, try very hard, and are intellectually involved. They are also chronically depressed, very concerned about their own destructive impulses, and somewhat self-deprecating.
IV	Independents (9 men and 3 women)	Confident, interested, involved, and intelligent. They identify with the teacher as a colleague, have a firm sense of themselves and their identify, and understand that a certain amount of Formal Authority and Expert are useful and necessary; however, they are much more interested in and comfortable with the Teacher-As Facilitator and Person task strategies.

V	Heroes (10 men)	Very bright, creative, and involved. One part of them resents authority. They want to challenge and attack the teacher, but they need to be certain the teacher is solid and competent because they want to use the teacher as a model for identification. Teachers are very important and significant to them, and the teachers must pass the test before the students allow their more intimate longings for a closer relationship to emerge. If the teacher fails the test, the student will turn off to the teacher and withdraw psychologically or even physically.
VI	Snipers (7 men and 3 women)	As rebellious as Cluster V but more defensive, less creative, and with much lower self-esteem; afraid of and incapable of serious introspection; appear to be uninvolved and emotionally indifferent to the teacher; cannot take responsibility for the learning enterprise. They withdraw and wait the term out. They try to prove the teacher wrong, inadequate, and unworthy, and try to wipe the teacher out in a disguised but hostile manner.
VII	Attention seekers (5 men and 6 women)	Have a social orientation; are exhibitionists and center-stagers; want to please, to be liked, and to get good grades. Typically, men tell jokes and show off. Women tend to be flirtatious and are other-directed. Many have self-esteem and impulse-control problems, and all rely heavily on denial.
VIII	Silent students (8 men and 12 women)	Very vulnerable and feel an overwhelming sense of helplessness. These low- or nonpartici-pating students speak only when they are sure the teacher will approve. They often suffer much internal psychological pain and are often very distressed. They long for, but never really achieve, a special relationship with the teacher.

Note. From Cytrynbaum and Conran, 1979a, p. 57.

TABLE 8.5
Phases of Development of the Class as a Work Group

Phase No.	Phase	Description
1	Opening (first 9 sessions in a 40-session group)	Teacher and students struggle to get acquainted. The teacher is apprehensive about his or her role, and both teacher and students are defensive. The teacher functions as Formal Authority, but students begin to manifest a desire to have some control over the class. There is growing contention and challenge. The teacher manifests warmth in an attempt to gain support and to get things off to a good start. Students score high in exhibition. In general, the teacher experiences much role dissatisfaction, and this will motivate change.
2	Dissatisfaction and Discouragement (Sessions 9 to 11 in a 40-session group)	Both teacher and students experience dissatisfaction and discouragement. The teacher makes premeditated changes, introducing innovations designed to reduce disruptive affect interfering with learning. The teacher realizes the inability to connect with every student because of lack of skills and resources. The teacher feels that students have been too egocentric to begin work. The teacher falls back on Ego Ideal and Formal Authority functioning as a way of coping, becoming somewhat punitive and alienating certain students. Students begin to withdraw and to demonstrate much anxious dependence. Student and teacher discomfort present a growing pressure for change.
3	Early Enactment, or Early Work Phase (Sessions 12 to 17 in a 40-session group)	Effective learning, or work, takes place as affective and cognitive tasks are effectively integrated. Teacher arrives at a combination of strategies and styles that leads to increased student independence and identification. In some cases, exams have made it necessary for students to acquire more information and also have given them a sense of confidence. Teacher dissatisfaction begins to wane, but student discouragement persists because some teachers remain punitive. The teacher shifts to increased Facilitator functioning. Student discouragement eventually causes the teacher to take charge.

SOLOMON CYTRYNBAUM

4	Teacher-Controlling Dominance (Sessions 18 to 22 in a 40-session group)	The teacher realizes he or she cannot meet all the needs of all the different clusters of students, and classroom life is very oppressive. The teacher experiences role dissatisfaction and takes charge by falling back on lecturing. In some instances, this is normative for the remaining sessions. Teachers grow impatient with students' progress, lean toward formality, moving away from facilitation and toward more distant lecturing. The teacher may also manifest much Ego Ideal functioning as a survival tactic. Students become less discouraged or contentious and more supportive.
5	Late Enactment, or Late Work Phase (Sessions 23 to 29 in a 40-session group)	When the teacher is able to move beyond Phase 4, groups have experienced a major or minor series of rebellions. The teacher has been challenged, students and teachers have begun to express dissatisfaction with what is happening, and both have begun to explore why things are not working well. The teacher moves toward a more realistic collegial pattern and experiences more role satisfaction, and students become less discouraged.
6	Separation, or Differentiated Work (Session 30 to the end in a 40-session group)	There is the realization that the course is drawing to a close. Different students share a common need to retain a collegiate style and to cover much emotion and feeling. Teacher becomes role dissatisfied and students become withdrawn. Both students and teachers manifest warmth, and, in a final burst, students display what they have learned. Termination concerns become apparent.

Note.   From Cytrynbaum and Conran, 1979a, p. 59.

TABLE 8.6
Summary: Student Patterns of Work and Antiwork

Student Task Parameter	Relevant Factor Pattern by Race of Teacher	
	Student Relation to Black Teacher	Student Relation to White Teacher
Acceptance of the teacher as		
Expert (+X)	I+: Heroic Enactment	II+: Dependent Compliance IV−: Contention
Formal Authority (+FA)	I−: Dependent Complaining	II+: Dependent Compliance IV+: Acceptance
Socializing Agent (+SA)	I+: Heroic Enactment III+: Self-Blaming Colleague	II+: Dependent Compliance V+: Ambivalent Engagement
Facilitator (+F)		
Ego Ideal (EI)	II−: Distressful Distancing	II−: Superficial Placating
Person (+P)	IV+: High Involvement	III+: Veiled Support
Dissatisfaction with the teacher as		
Expert (−X)	II+: Loyal Compliance IV+: High Involvement V+: Attacking	I−: Resistant Complaining
Formal Authority (−FA)	I−: Dependent Complaining	I−: Resistant Complaining
Socializing Agent (−SA)	I+: Heroic Enactment	I−: Resistant Complaining
Facilitator (−F)	V+: Attacking	V+: Ambivalent Engagement
Ego Ideal (−EI)		II−: Superficial Placating
Person (−P)	IV+: High Involvement	I−: Resistance Complaining

Note. Taken from Cytrynbaum and Conran, 1979b, p. 476.

SOLOMON CYTRYNBAUM

isfaction in attempting to come to grips with the teacher's task demands and the more personal aspects of the teacher's task functioning. By graphically plotting selected factors against each other, it was possible to identify different student styles of responding to (a) Black and White teacher meritocratic and person-centered task functioning; (b) conflict, frustration, and hostility in the interracial stuent–teacher relationship; (c) the teacher's functioning as a model for emulation; and (d) the more authentic and personal aspects of the teacher–student relationship (Cytrynbaum & Conran, 1979b, p. 474).

Acceptance of the Black teacher as Expert and Socializing Agent was related to student Heroic Enactment, whereas similar acceptance of Black Formal Authority functioning was associated with Dependent Complaining, suggesting significant student conflict and strain in adopting a dependent or compliant orientation. The presence of depressive feelings, the counterdependent resisting component of Heroic Enactment, and the moralist blaming aspect of Dependent Complaining imply considerable ambivalence in responding to the Black teachers' meritocratic task functioning.

The situation with respect to student acceptance of the White teachers' meritocratic task leadership was much different and less complex. Acceptance of the White teacher as Expert, Formal Authority, and Socializing Agent was associated with unconflicted compliance evident in the Dependent Compliance factor pole. A second pattern, Contention, was also associated with the White teacher's functioning as Expert. This disruptive pattern captured the students' challenge to the White teacher's expertise, authority, and legitimacy.

Rejection of the Black teacher as Expert was related to Loyal Compliance, High Involvement, and Attacking. Students' rejection of the White teacher's meritocratic task leadership was much simpler. Rejection of the White teacher as Expert, Formal Authority, and Socializing Agent was clearly associated with Resistant Complaining (Cytrynbaum & Conran, 1979b, pp. 474–475).

DESCRIPTION OF THE SYSTEM

As discussed earlier, the Member–Leader (Leader–Member) Scoring System (Mann et al., 1967), revised by Mann et al. (1970), is used to code the act-to-act verbal interactions of members and leaders in small groups and has been used to study member-to-leader and leader-to-member relations in self-analytic, training, therapy, and classroom groups. Primary emphasis is on how members relate to authority.

The Mann system reflects ego-psychological and Kleinian object relations traditions. It is based on the assumption that the member–leader relationship is a central aspect of group life and contributes to the overall effectiveness or disruption of the group's task accomplishment. It assumes two commonplace clinical insights: "A person must be 'understood' or recognized within the particular conceptual framework of the listener" (Mann et al., 1967, p. 35) and within the context of other acts occurring simultaneously or in the immediate past. As such, members' performances are assumed to be complex and overdetermined; it is also assumed that the members are in part constantly expressing themselves in terms of the member–leader relationship, although expression may be symbolic or indirect. Thus, the meaning of a member's statement or action must be understood in the group's context. A related but separate system, the Process Analysis Scoring System for coding member-to-member relations, was developed later by Hartman and Gibbard (1974). This system builds on the Mann system, uses the same categories and assumptions, but has been used infrequently. Therefore, I do not discuss it further.

Rating

Definition of an Act

The Mann system focuses on the relationship between the members of a group and its leader by scoring not a sentence but an "act." Mann et al. (1967) defined an *act* as "a single speech or burst of sentences within which the experience of feelings are uniform" (p. 61). The length of an act can vary from a single word or sigh to a long monologue. The Mann scorer uses whatever data are already known about the speaker and the context of the act to interpret a given act. The scorer also reviews other instances in which this member has spoken, recalls the member's history in the group up to that point, and thinks back over the way in which the member has previously expressed his or her feelings. An act is not scored until both the symbolic equivalents for leader and member and the direct or symbolically displaced feelings being expressed are determined. Before an act can be scored, both the symbolic equivalents and direct expressions must make sense. The scorer must take into account the particular member and his or her history, the function served by the member at that point in the group's development, the work-related task pressures from the leader, and the group's struggles in the here and now.

The Mann scorer makes inferences about expressed statements tempered by the member's tone of voice, accompanying laughter or tears, nonverbal cues, and so on. The Mann scorer also attempts to capture the complexity of member expressions by painting an inferred, moment-to-moment portrait of thoughts and feelings by selecting the appropriate mix of categories.

For the Mann scorer, an act is considered to be complete at the point at which the scorer begins to turn to new categories to accurately capture the next set of feelings expressed. A sentence in a transcript is usually the effective unit of analysis, although in some studies a single act may be as long as one or two paragraphs. Furthermore, when a member is interrupted, his or her next statement is considered to be the start of a new act, even if the scoring has not changed. The number of acts generated in a 90-minute small study group session using this system typically ranges from 300 to 500.

Scoring Rationale

Before describing the categories, it may be helpful to have some idea of the orientation that a scorer brings to the task of using the system. Perhaps the most pertinent model is that of the clinician, faced with making decisions about the importance of statements made by a patient in therapy. For example, if a patient suddenly begins to complain that people in his or her environment, friends or coworkers, are ignoring, rejecting, or simply unresponsive to him or her, then the therapist, given his or her past history with the patient and the current nature of their relationship, may infer that the patient is in fact talking about him or her and, that the comment expresses a feeling of reproachfulness or accusation that the therapist interprets as a demand or pressure to take certain actions or to change his or her own behavior in certain ways.

Consider another example from one of the classes studied by Mann et al. (1970). A group of students was engaged in an animated conversation about the overthrow of a repressive government in a Southeast Asian country. This conversation occurred at a moment in the group's history when the teacher had just handed back a test that some students felt was not graded fairly. The Mann scorer would infer that the "repressive government" is a symbolic equivalent of the teacher and that the feelings expressed may represent displaced or indirect feelings toward him or her. This is not to say that such symbolic expression is consciously intended; there may be some conscious screening of remarks by indiviuals, or it may be something of which most people are well aware, or the feelings may be unconsciously displaced from their original object and directed at substitutes. In the scoring system, a primary convention is that, although the content of a remark (on the part of a student) may not make any direct reference to the teacher, the scorer listens carefully for any and all displaced or symbolic implications of these remarks about the teacher and uses the scoring categories accordingly. That is, the scorer assumes that at some level, there are indirect or unconscious implications in a student's remarks for feelings about the teacher.

Context

Returning to the second central proposition that a scorer brings to his or her task, one must now explain what is meant by the notion that the scorer makes inferences about acts in a context of simultaneous and previous acts that he or she has observed. As the scorer listens to group interactions, he or she begins to build a picture of their pattern or structure. For instance, the scorer may note that one member consistently makes disparaging remarks about the efforts of other members to find solutions to group problems. Remembering the other instances in which the member has spoken, listening carefully to the linguistic structure of the sentences, and paying attention to tone of voice and other extralinguistic cues, the scorer may conclude that the other members are not only serving as substitutes for the leader but also that the member is in a subtle way expressing his and her own sense of inadequacy, powerlessness, and dependency relative to the leader. Of course, as the member speaks further, the scorer may find that the equivalence between the leader and other members is not all that precise and may be forced to reconsider the scoring.

The context is similarly monitored by the scorer when it is necessary to decide whether a symbolic referent is equivalent to the leader or is perceived by the member to be the leader's antithesis. To use an example from Mann et al. (1967), when a group member says, "Freud would never have badgered a patient with his interpretations; he would have waited until it made sense to the patient himself" (p. 41), it may be clear from the context that Freud is a symbolic equivalent of the leader. However, is the member also indirectly attacking the leader for being too aggressive, intrusive, or manipulative with his or her interpretations, or is the member indirectly supporting the leader's passive, nondirective style by equating him with the Great Man himself? Again, the scorer's knowledge of the member's past history in the group, his or her feeling for what is going on at the moment, and a careful assessment of linguistic and extralinguistic cues can aid the scorer. In this system, scoring is a complicated task.

Levels

The term *level* is used to designate the degree of displacement and symbolization of the speaker's feelings. The dimensions of displacement that seem most relevant are (a) the extent to which either or both the subject and object are symbolized or displaced and (b) whether the displacement is toward objects within or outside of the group. For instance, in the classroom example presented earlier, the object (repressive government) is outside the group, but the subject (i.e., the student expressing the feeling) is clearly not. One could, however, imagine a conversation in which the students voice their feelings more directly, vehemently discussing how unfair, repressive, or arbitrary the teacher has been and how they should band together to force him or her to change. Or, again, one could imagine a conversation in which one student reports to another an interesting conversation he or she overheard in which a professor was expressing happiness at the overthrow of a totalitarian regime. In this case, both subject and object would be outside the group.

In the Mann system, the scorer is asked to distinguish from among four levels of inference about member feelings directed at the leader (see Table 8.7). Levels 3 and 4 are scored infrequently enough so that in most research studies they are collapsed into Level 2.

In summary, the notion of levels reflects the assumption that in any group, the leader, while his or her centrality for members waxes and wanes, is always contained somewhere either consciously or unconsciously via displacement, symbolization, or both in the member's psychological field. The four levels of inference used by Mann scorers, as summarized by Hallberg (1995), are presented in Table 8.7.

Categories

The 18 member–leader (leader–member) scoring categories are summarized in Table 8.8 and briefly defined in Table 8.9. The member–leader categories are divided into three main areas: impulse, power relations, and ego state. The impulse area is divided into two subareas—hostility and affection—and is intended to capture feelings members may have toward the leader. There are four categories in the hostility subarea and four in the affection subarea. The power relations area captures member feelings mobilized by the leader's authority and is characterized by three possible components (i.e., dependency, counterdependency, and independence) for coding member-to-leader expressions and two distinct categories for leader-to-member verbalizations (i.e., counterdominance and dominance). The third ego state area consists of seven categories and is designed to measure member feelings about themselves relative to the leader. Four of the seven

TABLE 8.7
Member–Leader Scoring System: Levels of Inference

Level	Description
1	Both member and leader referred to directly. Member makes direct reference to the leader and expresses his or her feelings as his or her own.
2	Member referred to directly but leader is symbolized by equivalent inside group. Member refers to objects inside the group and expresses his or her feelings as his or her own.
3	Member referred to directly but leader is symbolized by equivalent outside group. Member refers to objects outside the group and expresses his or her feelings as his or her own.
4	Member symbolized by equivalent inside or outside group; leader is referred to either directly or symbolically. Member refers to the leader either directly or indirectly, within or outside the group, but attributes those feelings to some other agent.

Note. From Hallberg, 1995, p. 127.

TABLE 8.8
Mann's Member–Leader (Leader–Member) Scoring System Categories

Area	Subarea	Category	Code
Impulse	Hostility	1. Moving Against	MA
		2. Resisting	RS
		3. Withdrawing	WI
		4. Guilt Inducing	GI
	Affection	5. Making Reparation	RP
		6. Identifying	ID
		7. Accepting	AC
		8. Moving Toward	MT
Power Relations		9. Members: Showing Dependency	DN
		Leader: Showing Counter-dominance	CD
		10. Showing Independence	IN
		11. Members: Showing Counter-dependency	CD
		Leader: Showing Dominance	DM
Ego State	Anxiety	12. Expressing Anxiety	AE
		13. Denying Anxiety	AD
	Depression	14. Expressing Depression	DE
		15. Denying Depression	DD
	Guilt[a]	16. Expressing Guilt	GE
		17. Denying Guilt	GD
	Self-Esteem	18. Expressing Self-Esteem	SE

[a]Added by Hartman and Gibbard (1974).

categories focus on members' direct expressions of feeling and the other three assess their denial of these specific feelings.

The partitioning of the categories into five subareas arises from an important convention regarding the scoring of single acts. Acts may be scored once in each of the subareas (except for expressing self-esteem, which is not scored when any of the anxiety, guilt, or depression categories are scored), but the scorer is prohibited from scoring an act within a single area more than once. This forces the scorer to choose between the types of hostility, affection, power relations, or ego states being expressed.

Reliability

The Member–Leader Scoring System is complex, and training and scoring are time-consuming. In several independent studies (e.g., Cytrynbaum & Conran, 1979a, 1979b; Cytrynbaum & Curran, 1993; Hallberg, 1995; Mann et al., 1970, 1967), the degree of interscorer reliability has ranged from satisfactory to high.

In the early studies, Mann et al. (1970, 1967) ran four interjudge

TABLE 8.9
Member–Leader Categories

Impulse Area
  Hostility subarea

1. Moving Against: expressing dislike, mistrust, or anger; attacking; rejecting; ridiculing; insulting. The focus in this category is on the expression of hostile feelings against the leader as a person rather than against his or her role-related contributions or overt behavior. The target of hostility tends to be the leader's personal motives, personality, or general competence.

2. Resisting: disagreeing, arguing, blocking, or parrying the leader's suggestions or interpretations. The hostility in this category is responsive or reactive, either to an actual initiation by the leader or to the implicit pressures of the whole-group situation. The target of this relatively impersonal hostility tends to be the role performance of the leader.

3. Withdrawing: ignoring the leader, leaving the room, or engaging in "out-of-field" behavior; expressing boredom, lack of involvement, or indifference. The hostility expressed through withdrawing is more passive and indirect than in the other three hostility categories. This category covers the various ways in which the member–leader relationship is broken or its importance denied.

4. Guilt Inducing: blaming; complaining; accusing; feeling misunderstood, abused, or ashamed. The crucial element that differentiates this category from the preceding three is the addition of a moral context for the hostility. By invoking a presumably shared value and comparing the leader's behavior unfavorably to it, the member expresses a type of moral indignation through which he or she allies with a set of superordinate values against the leader.

  Affection subarea

5. Making Reparation: giving, apologizing, denying hostility, blaming self rather than leader, "making up" for prior hostility of self or others. This category attempts to capture the expressions of affection that depend on their proximity to hostility for their full meaning. Making reparation may precede a hostile remark, as if to neutralize the hostility before the fact, or it may follow hostility of any kind, as if to undo, repair, and atone for the fantasized damage.

6. Identifying: playing the leader's role in relation to another group member, copying the leader, incorporating the leader's ideas as one's own, expressing a wish to be like the leader. A member's positive feelings toward the leader, or the degree to which he or she accepts what the leader has said, may be expressed through the member's interaction with other group members. The inference made from the manifest content of such acts is that the member is attempting to differentiate himself or herself from some other group member who appears to be not sufficiently identified with, or accepting of, the leader.

7. Accepting: agreeing, yielding, conforming, expressing satisfaction with the leader's role performance. The relatively impersonal affection recorded in this category is responsive or reactive to the leader's role performance.

8. Moving Toward: expressing liking, trust, or warmth, caring, admiring, and praising. This category focuses on the expression of affection in personal terms, with a clear implication that the relationship is personally important and meaningful to the member.

Table continues

TABLE 8.9 *Continued*

Power-Relations Area

9. Showing Dependency: members expressing a need for approval, direction, structure, or control; attempting to please the leader. The expression of dependency needs in the member–leader relationship tends to imply that (a) the member feels less sure of what to do, less able to carry out what he or she wishes to do, or less confident that what he or she is doing or has done is satisfactory and (b) the member expects or hopes that the leader can provide the necessary direction, assistance, or approval. Such manifestations on the leader's part are called Showing Counterdominance and imply that he or she is denying or disowning the real or perceived power or authority inherent in the relationship, a form of pseudoequality.

10. Showing Independence: relating to the leader as a peer, stating one's standards, or judging one's own behavior by them, emphasizing the mutuality of giving and receiving in the member–leader relationship, deciding on action on one's own grounds. In the act-by-act analysis of feelings, such a conception is mirrored best by evidence that the member feels able to accept or reject the leader and his or her contributions without reference to an implicit power structure that must be created, maintained, or destroyed. In addition, acts of independence express a member's capacity to act and reflect on his or her own behavior using his or her own standards without making sure that they are the same as, or different from, the leader's standards.

11. Showing Counterdependence: members who avoid direction, assistance, or support from the leader; opposing leader's power or authority, rebelling against rules or norms; or opposition to the leader appears to be based on an assumption that the leader is, or intends to be, more powerful than the group members. It represents a response from within an authority structure and can be best understood as an aversion to being in a weak, needy, dependent, or constricted position. A leader Showing Dominance captures the variety of ways in which the leader takes over the group, including calling on people, initiating discussions, making interpretations, and the like.

Ego-State Area

Anxiety Subarea

12. Expressing Anxiety: showing embarrassment, tension, or uncertainty; feeling criticized, judge, vulnerable, or threatened; fearing angry or a punitive response from leader. The member's anxious feelings may be expressed by an attempt to assess and describe either (a) in what way the leader seems threatening or (b) the inner consequences of the threat for him or her.

13. Denying Anxiety: denying feeling tense, worried, or concerned about the leader, joking about what others see as threatening in the leader's behavior or status, covering up tension with giddy or silly behavior, reassuring self or others regarding the leader's intentions or evaluations. It is assumed that an important component in the act is an attempt at self-reassurance through disparaging the potential danger, insisting that one is calm and not upset, or professing invulnerability in the face of apparent or fantasized danger.

Depression Subarea

14. Expressing Depression: feeling weak, sad, helpless, powerless; expressing a sense of being worthless or a sense of "sliding downhill." Acts scored in this category reflect the member's state of lowered self-esteem and lowered sense of potency in the context of the member–leader relationship.

Table continues

TABLE 8.9 *Continued*

15. Denying Depression: resisting an implied criticism, bragging and asserting one's own potency, showing elation after another member's expression of sadness, refusing to see any power differentiation between members and the leader, blaming the leader rather than self, showing manic denial of implied guilt or responsibility for having harmed others. Not all excitement or exhilaration is scored as Denying Depression. The fundamental question involves the antecedents and context of the act. This category focuses on the attempt to restore self-esteem and decrease feelings as helplessness through denial, suppression, and reaction formation.

Guilt Subarea

16. Expressing Guilt: expressions of worthlessness or helplessness in relation to inner impulses felt to be "bad" or unacceptable; acceptance of responsibility for real or fantasized destructive consequences, self-criticism, or apologies accompanied by heavy self-rebuke.

17. Denying Guilt: disavowing one's own guilt, externalization of blame and denial of responsibility disassociating oneself from the guilt of others.

Self-Esteem Subarea

18. Expressing Self-Esteem: feeling satisfied with oneself, capable of openness and honesty, proud, at ease, and "headed in the right direction." Many of the acts scored in this category could, in other contexts, be seen as denials of either anxiety or depression. The crucial differentiating features are that acts of self-esteem are not primarily reactions to increasing uncomfortable ego states but primarily expressive of what has been called "the secure and self-assured ego."

reliability trials. In three trials two scorers worked on the same tapes at the same time, and in the fourth one researcher scored the same session for a second time 3 years after the initital scoring. Interscorer agreement exceeded 90% on whether an act was relevant to the member–leader relationship and on the level of inference coded. The rate of agreement on content categories averaged 73% and ranged from 67% to 81%. Similar levels of interscorer agreement were reported by Cytrynbaum and Conran (1979b) and Cytrynbaum and Curran (1993).

Hallberg's (1995) study of small groups in several Tavistock Group Relations Conferences is typical of the way in which reliability is approached. In that study, four scorers were initially trained following Mann's guidelines. Scorers studied a procedure manual and were initially trained in the definition of an act and the scoring system categories. Random segments of tapes were scored, focusing on the criteria for scores and the scorer's decision-making process. Scorers practiced coding excerpts from previously taped group sessions for 9 months. Segments of taped group sessions were scored independently, and interscorer percentage of agreement ratings were repeatedly calculated until an acceptable percentage of agreement was achieved. A formal interscorer reliability test was conducted in a 75-minute small-group session. A Friedman multiple comparison procedure was used to assess the differences among scorers. No significant differences were found. Correlations were then computed on pairwise associations between scores on the combined Impulse, Power Relations, and Ego State categories. Correlations ranged from .86 to .99, all significant, with the majority being significant at the .001 level.

Finally, Kendall's coefficient of concordance (W) was used to assess the extent of scorer agreement on their overall rankings of member-to-leader scores. As is evident in Table 8.10, there is some variation, but on the whole the level of interscorer agreement ranged from acceptable to reasonably high. Experience indicates that it is possible to achieve a high degree of interjudge reliability when scorers are carefully chosen, intensively trained, introspective, self-critical, psychologically minded, and intuitive as well as when they have previous experience with groups. The utility of the Mann system as a training experience should also be noted. Well-trained and carefully selected scorers have the oportunity to learn a great deal more generally about authority, transference phenomena, and group process.

METHODOLOGY FOR ANALYSIS

In studying small groups using the Mann system, identifying acts and scoring categories for each act is only the first step. Scoring several small groups that have met for a large number of sessions results in an over-

TABLE 8.10
Interscorer Agreement for Affective Categories

Category	Kendall's W
Moving against	.68**
Resisting	.75**
Withdrawing	.63**
Guilt Inducing	.75**
Make Reparation	.66**
Identifying	.55**
Accepting	.52**
Moving Toward	#
Showing Dependency	.82**
Showing Independence	#
Showing Counterdependency	.78**
Expressing Anxiety	.84**
Denying Anxiety	.87**
Expressing Depression	.46**
Denying Depression	.53**
Expressing Guilt	.41*
Denying Guilt	.44*
Expressing Self-Esteem	#

Note. # Insufficient data to determine an association.
*$p < .05$. **$p < .01$.
*From Hallberg, 1995.

whelming amount of raw act data. For this data to be manageable and useful, it needs to be quantified and reduced. Quantification is usually accomplished by using mean scores for each act of each member or by converting each coded act for each member and session (or some other appropriate unit) to proportions, which are then standardized. These standard scores serve as the basis for determining patterns of group development (Mann et al., 1970, 1967; Hartman, 1969), for identifying individual member role performances (Mann et al., 1970, 1967; Ringwald, 1973; Rosenwein, 1970), and for comparing the impact on the member–leader relationship of different combinations of members and leaders by race and gender (Cytrynbaum & Curran, 1993; Cytrynbaum & Hallberg, 1995; Hallberg, 1995) via factor analysis, cluster analysis, analysis of variance, multiple regression, and other multivariate statistical procedures. The results of these quantitative analyses are then used as a basis for more indepth qualitative clinical analysis by listening to taped sessions, reviewing transcripts, or both. Findings are usually reported in terms of quantitative results whose meanings are clinically interpreted.

Hallberg's (1995) most recent study of five small groups in three different Tavistock Group Relations Conferences using the Mann system is useful in illustrating one version of the stepwise data-analytical procedures. First, the number of times a particular category was scored for each session in each conference was tallied. Then, summary statistics for each member, each category, and for each session were computed and used to test a series of null hypotheses. Hallberg (1995) described these steps as follows:

> An example of a summary statistic is the average number of times that moving against was scored by a person in the Conference held in 1990. Then the summary statistics were used in an ANOVA [(an analysis of variance)] which allowed for the testing of the hypotheses. In addition, the Duncan procedure, which is designed specifically for pairwise comparisons of means in an ANOVA, was used.
>
> The hypotheses were built around the idea that a group member's score on a particular category is a function of several things, including the year in which the member participated in the Conference (and this is directly related to the genders of the Director/Associate Director pairs that led the Conference in a particular year), the gender of the member, the gender of the small study group consultant, and, finally, an interaction effect brought about by combining the effect of the independent variable of conference year with the effect of the independent variable of gender. The main effects indicated where the significant differences were; they indicate that there is a difference, but not what the specific difference is. Therefore, the summary statistics were utilized to describe the quality of the difference. For example, when the member/leader gender interaction showed a significant difference, it was necessary to look at the summary statistics to find out what the differences were, e.g., female members with male leaders

showed more identification than female members with female leaders.

Within the ANOVA, the hypotheses, specifically a set of null hypotheses, were tested in an effort to disprove them. (pp. 136–137)

RECENT RESEARCH WITH THE SYSTEM

The most recent research using the Mann system has focused on member–leader gender effects or the impact of different gender combinations of member and leader in small groups in the context of the Tavistock Group Relations Conference. These conferences offer opportunities to study current collective gender-related processes in groups of different sizes.

Since 1986, faculty members and students in Northwestern University's counseling psychology program conducted research on gender and authority in Tavistock Group Relations Conferences in both small and large groups. These studies of conferences have generated empirical and clinical data and findings derived from several sources. These include rating, interview, audiotape, and process analysis scoring of member–consultant interaction as well as questionnaires drawn from members and consultants in group relations conferences in the Tavistock tradition held at Northwestern University from 1986 to 1995. These conferences included male and female members, large- and small-group consultants, and male and female directors and associate directors for gender comparison purposes. About 25 male-led and 25 female-led mixed-gender small groups, each with approximately 8–10 members for a total of more than 500 participants, were involved. In addition, conferences with different gender combinations of director and associate director, and all-female and all-male conferences, were similarly studied via audiotape and videotape.

For example, Cytrynbaum and Curran (1993) examined the data from small groups from the Northwestern Tavistock Group Relations Conferences held in 1986 and 1987 using data derived from the Mann et al. (1967) scoring system. They reported partial support for the expectation of gender differences in authority relationships. Although no clear and simple effect of member by consultant gender emerged, they did find that members experienced different effects for female compared with male consultants over time in terms of different factor patterns. Specifically, they found that female members did experience more distress, disengagement, and subtle feelings of anxiety with female consultants than with male consultants. Female members with male leaders expressed more direct anxiety. Male members with male consultants experienced greater anxiety and were more counterdependent. Male members with female consultants were more counterdependent than female members with male consultants. These findings led Cytrynbaum and Curran to conclude that the disruptive effect of the leader's gender during times of high anxiety or stress in the case of female consultants indicates that the group leader's gender makes a significant difference.

Most recently, Cytrynbaum and Hallberg (1995) and Hallberg (1995) explored whether and how the gender composition of conference directors and associate directors makes a difference for small-group members by gender and group process. Small groups in three weekend conferences, held at Northwestern University in 1988, 1989, and 1990, were studied. The 1988 conference had a female director and male associate director (i.e., the female–male conference). The same male director and same female associate directed the 1989 conference but they reversed roles (i.e., the male–female conference). The same male directed the 1990 conference with another male associate director (i.e., the male–male conference). In all, 61 men and 95 women, a total membership of 156, participated. All 80 small-group sessions of 16 groups, 8 with female and 8 with male consultants, were audiotaped and scored using the Member–Leader Scoring System.

Findings identified main effects for the conferences as a whole by gender of member and gender of consultant across and within the three conferences. For example, all small-group members experienced the most disruptive feelings (i.e., anxiety and depression) and dependency concerns in the 1990 male–male conference. Across all conferences, all small-group members expressed more withdrawal, dependency, counterdependency, anxiety expressed and denied, and guilt than female small-group consultants. All members scored significantly higher on 13 of 18 categories with male consultants in the 1990 male–male conference. Most interesting, male members with male consultants expressed significantly more moving against, identification, moving toward, and depression in the 1990 male–male conferences.

In general, these and related studies have suggested a complex, multidetermined, and inconsistent disruptive association between group leader and group member by gender reactions, especially during periods of stress, regression, or anxiety, implying the likelihood that powerful unconscious or covert conflicts are unleashed in response to women in authority.

APPLICATION OF THE SYSTEM OF ANALYSIS TO GROUP A, SESSION 3

With respect to the analysis of Session 3, it is important to reiterate that the Mann system is somewhat unique in (a) its emphasis on the centrality of member preoccupation with authority; (b) its usefulness in identifying member roles; (c) its appreciation of the overdetermined nature of member performances, especially the developmental context and group history; (d) its focus on the role of displacement and symbolization in understanding member expressions of feeling; and (e) its blending of quantitative and qualitative methods in understanding the dynamics of individual member roles and phases of group development.

The analysis of one session of Group A and the presence of cotherapists present the Mann scorer with several dilemmas and limitations because the Mann system relies on context, especially the group's history, to understand member performances. Scoring one session without the appreciation of the group's and members' previous history limits the Mann scorer. Lacking a historical, clinical sense of how the group related to the cotherapists, especially beyond Level 1 and Level 2 scores, makes it hard to decipher which of the cotherapists is the target of member displacement and symbolization. Finally, the Mann system relies on the generation of a large data set over the course of a group's life, which is then reduced to manageable proportions via complex multivariate statistical procedures. Clearly, this is impossible with respect to Session 3.

Given the limited amount of data generated by one session (or parts thereof) and the presence of coleaders, the usual multivariate analyses and search for clinical interpretation of these data were inappropriate. Therefore, I describe the data for Session 3 in raw and percentage form. The clinical interpretation of the session and the presumed shift is based on these data and careful clinical analyses of the tape and transcript. The raw data and percentages for individual members, all members, and the leaders based on analysis of the whole of Session 3 are reported in Table 8.11. Table 8.12 contains the raw scores and percentages comparing all of the editors' preselected segments from the prephase shift, the resolution of Phase II, and entry to Phase III. The analysis was complicated by the presence of coleaders and limited information about how they were being experienced.

The following data-based description of Group A, Session 3 is a useful illustration of how a Mann scorer functions and how the system coding categories and definitions facilitate the investigation of group processes but does not represent the kind of formal analysis recommended with the use of the Mann scoring system. More data would be required for that purpose.

The Leaders

Alice and Helen

Of the two coleaders, Alice was the more active. She was usually accurate in her reflections of members' overt or manifest struggles. For example, she was effective in refocusing Diane on her own affect and experience when Diane was leading the scapegoating of Joe. Both Alice and Helen produced a high percentage of acts that were scored as showing dominance, consistent with the role of any leader. There was some scatter into the pseudoequality and counterdominance categories, as might be ex-

TABLE 8.11
All Acts Members to Leaders and Leaders to Members: Frequencies and Percentages in Session 3

	Total No. of Acts	Hostility				Affection				Power Relations			Ego State							Total # Scores
		MA 1	RS 2	WI 3	GI 4	RP 5	ID 6	AG 7	MT 8	DN 9	IN 10	CD 11	AE 12	AD 13	DE 14	DD 15	GE 16	GD 17	SE 18	
Member to Leader																				
Diane	198																			
n		4	25	0	6	10	13	7	5	87	0	25	28	100	15	20	1	0	0	346
%		1.0	7.0	—	2.0	3.0	4.0	2.0	1.0	25.0	—	7.0	8.0	29.0	4.0	6.0	0.5	—	—	
Martha	169																			
n		1	17	0	3	3	10	3	3	58	1	13	35	78	14	16	1	1	0	257
%		0.3	3.0	—	1.0	1.0	2.0	1.0	1.0	23.0	0.3	5.0	14.0	30.0	5.0	5.0	0.3	0.3	—	
Joe	172																			
n		6	15	0	9	20	12	3	8	67	0	12	17	18	2	19	6	2	0	216
%		3.0	7.0	—	4.0	9.0	7.0	1.0	4.0	31.0	—	7.0	8.0	8.0	1.0	9.0	3.0	1.0	—	
Greg	96																			
n		1	6	0	6	3	5	5	0	34	0	6	17	59	3	2	2	0	0	149
%		0.7	4.0	—	4.0	2.0	4.0	4.0	—	23.0	—	4.0	11.0	40.0	2.0	1.0	1.0	—	—	
Brad	29																			
n		0	3	0	0	1	7	1	1	9	2	2	4	18	0	1	1	0	0	50
%		—	6.0	—	—	2.0	14.0	2.0	2.0	18.0	4.0	4.0	8.0	36.0	—	2.0	2.0	—	—	
Pat	17																			
n		0	2	0	0	0	0	1	1	10	0	0	4	8	0	0	2	0	0	28
%		—	7.0	—	—	—	—	4.0	4.0	36.0	—	—	14.0	29.0	—	—	7.0	—	—	
Group																				
n		12	68	0	24	37	47	20	18	265	3	58	105	281	34	58	13	3	0	1,046
%		1.0	7.0	0	2.0	3.0	5.0	2.0	2.0	25.0	0.5	6.0	10.0	27.0	3.0	6.0	1.0	0.5	0	

Table continues

TABLE 8.11 (Continued)

| | | Hostility | | | | Affection | | | | Power Relations | | | | | Ego State | | | | | |
	Total No. of Acts	MA 1	RS 2	WI 3	GI 4	RP 5	ID 6	AG 7	MT 8	DN 9	IN 10	CD 11	AE 12	AD 13	DE 14	DD 15	GE 16	GD 17	SE 18	Total # Scores
										CD		DM								
Leaders to Members																				
Alice																				
n		—	—	—	—	—	—	—	—	12	35	76	11	69	—	2	—	—	0	205
%										6.0	17.0	37.1	5.0	34.0	—	1.0	—	—	—	
Helen																				
n		—	—	—	—	—	—	—	1	0	7	29	7	25	1	1	—	—	0	71
%									1.0	0	10.0	41.0	10.0	35.0	1.0	1.0	—	—	—	

Note. In this Table, # = number of acts, % = percent of total acts, and the abbreviations represent the categories described in Tables 8.8 and 8.9: e.g., MA = Moving Against, RS = Resistance, WI = Withdrawing, GI = Guilt Inducing, etc.

TABLE 8.12

Comparison of Session 3 Prephase Shift (PRE), Resolution Phase 2 (RESOL) Early Phase III (III) by Members and Leaders: Frequencies and Percentages

Compare # and % of Pre, Resol, and III	Hostility				Affection				Power Relations					Ego State					Total # Scores
	MA 1	RS 2	WI 3	GI 4	RP 5	ID 6	AC 7	MT 8	DN 9	IN 10	CD 11	AE 12	AD 13	DE 14	DD 15	GE 16	GD 17	SE 18	
Member to Leader																			
Diane																			
Pre n	0	10	0	2	3	1	4	0	17	0	8	10	35	2	4	0	0	0	96
%	—	10.0	—	2.0	3.0	1.0	4.0	—	18.0	—	8.0	10.0	37.0	2.0	.04	—	—	—	
Resol n	0	0	0	0	1	2	0	0	3	0	1	4	7	1	0	0	0	0	19
%	—	0	0	—	5.0	11.0	—	—	16.0	—	5.0	21.0	37.0	5.0	—	—	—	—	
III n	0	2	0	1	0	1	0	2	13	0	5	2	5	5	13	0	0	0	49
%	—	4.0	—	2.0	—	2.0	—	4.0	27.0	—	10.0	4.0	10.0	10.0	.26	—	—	—	
Martha																			
Pre n	0	0	0	0	0	3	0	0	8	0	0	4	13	0	0	0	1	0	29
%	—	—	—	—	—	10.0	—	—	28.0	—	—	14.0	27.0	—	—	—	3.0	—	
Resol n	1	2	0	0	0	2	1	1	9	0	0	4	9	0	0	1	0	0	30
%	3.0	7.0	—	—	—	7.0	3.0	3.0	—	—	—	13.0	30.0	—	0	3.0	0	—	
III n	0	6	0	1	2	0	1	2	14	1	2	11	3	14	5	0	0	0	62
%	—	10.0	—	2.0	3.0	—	2.0	3.0	22.0	2.0	3.0	18.0	5.0	22.0	.08	—	—	—	

Table continues

TABLE 8.12 (Continued)

Compare # and % of Pre, Resol, and III	Hostility				Affection				Power Relations			Ego State							Total # Scores
	MA 1	RS 2	WI 3	GI 4	RP 5	ID 6	AC 7	MT 8	DN 9	IN 10	CD 11	AE 12	AD 13	DE 14	DD 15	GE 16	GD 17	SE 18	
Joe																			
Pre — n	0	4	0	3	8	1	0	0	13	0	5	6	16	0	6	2	0	0	64
%	—	6.0	—	5.0	13.0	2.0	—	—	20.0	—	8.0	9.0	25.0	—	.09	.03	—	—	
Resol — n	0	1	0	0	0	1	0	0	0	0	0	1	1	0	0	0	0	0	4
%	—	25.0	—	—	—	25.0	—	—	—	—	—	25.0	25.0	—	—	—	—	—	
III — n	1	0	0	0	0	1	0	0	2	0	0	0	0	0	1	0	0	0	5
%	20.0	—	—	—	—	20.0	—	—	40.0	—	—	—	—	—	2.0	—	—	—	
Greg																			
Pre	0	0	0	0	0	0	0	0	1	0	0	0	1	0	0	0	0	0	2
Resol	0	2	0	0	1	0	0	0	2	0	0	2	3	0	1	0	0	0	11
III	0	0	0	0	0	1	1	0	1	0	1	0	1	0	2	0	0	0	6
Brad																			
Pre	0	1	0	0	1	4	0	0	5	1	1	4	4	0	1	1	0	0	23
Resol	0	1	0	0	0	0	0	1	4	0	0	1	3	0	0	0	0	0	10
III	0	0	0	0	0	0	0	0	0	0	0	0	0	0	0	0	0	0	0
Pat																			
Pre	0	1	0	0	0	0	2	1	7	0	0	2	4	0	0	2	0	0	19
Resol	0	0	0	0	0	0	0	0	0	0	0	0	0	0	0	0	0	0	0
III	0	0	0	0	0	0	0	0	0	0	0	0	0	0	0	0	0	0	0

																			#
All Members to Leaders																			
Pre	n	0	16	0	5	12	9	6	1	61	1	14	26	73	2	11	5	1	0	238
	%	0	7.0	0	2.0	5.0	4.0	2.0	0.5	26.0	0.5	6.0	11.0	3.0	1.0	.06	2.0	0.5	0	
Resol		1	6	0	0	2	5	1	2	16	0	1	12	23	1	1	1	0	0	72
		1.0	8.0	0	2.0	2.0	5.0	1.0	2.0	22.0	0	1.0	16.0	31.0	1.0	1.0	1.0	0	0	
III		1	8	2	2	2	2	2	4	30	1	8	13	9	19	0	0	0	0	122
		1.0	7.0	2.0	2.0	2.0	2.0	2.0	3.0	25.0	1.0	7.0	11.0	10.0	16.0	0	0	0	0	
Leaders to Members										CD		DM								
Alice																				
Pre	n	0	0	1	0	0	0	0	0	0	15	16	2	20	0	0	0	0	0	55
	%	0	0	2.0	0	0	0	0	0	0	27.0	29.0	4.0	36.0	0	0	0	0	0	
Resol		0	0	0	0	0	0	0	0	0	5	0	0	1	5	0	0	0	0	11
		0	0	0	0	0	0	0	0	0	45.0	0	0	10.0	45.0	0	0	0	0	
III		0	0	0	0	0	0	1	0	1	2	8	1	2	0	1	0	0	0	16
		0	0	0	0	0	0	6.0	0	6.0	18.0	50.0	6.0	18.0	0	.06	0	0	0	
Helen																				
Pre	n	0	0	0	0	0	0	1	0	0	3	11	3	10	0	0	0	0	0	28
	%	0	0	0	0	0	0	4.0	0	0	11.0	39.0	11.0	36.0	0	0	0	0	0	
Resol		0	0	0	0	0	0	0	0	0	0	0	0	0	0	0	0	0	0	0
		0	0	0	0	0	0	0	0	0	0	0	0	0	0	0	0	0	0	
III		0	0	0	0	0	0	0	0	0	0	1	0	1	0	0	0	0	0	2
		0	0	0	0	0	0	0	0	0	0	50.0	0	50.0	0	0	0	0	0	

Note. In this table # = Numbers of acts, % = Percent of total acts, and the abbreviations represent the categories described in Tables 8.8 and 8.9, e.g., MA = Moving Against, RS = Resistance, WI = Withdrawing, GI = Guilt Inducing, etc.

pected given their presumed client-centered therapeutic orientation. Neither coleader at any time offered individual- or group-level transference interpretations. Both expressed a good deal of anxiety and some depression. Helen, who was much less active than Alice, kept a low profile throughout the session. She also seemed accurate and highly sensitive in reflecting members' conscious and manifest feelings. Lacking the prior and future group context, it is unclear whether the transference reactions explained below apply to either one or both coleaders.

The Members

An inspection of Table 8.11 reveals that the group was largely dependent and anxious. Member scores indicate a preponderance of dependency and anxiety, especially denied but also expressed. The individual members are presented next in order of their level of activity, from the most active to the least active in terms of categories used to capture their performances.

Table 8.11 reveals that Diane, Martha, and Joe were the principal players in this scenario. By contrast, Greg was moderately active and Brad and Pat were relatively silent and inactive. They produced so few acts that percentages were neither computed nor reported. However, the descriptions of the members and the processes associated with the phase shift can be useful in illustrating how one thinks about the group and its members from the viewpoint of the Mann system.

Diane

Diane was a slow starter who waited until about a third into the session before becoming more actively involved, especially in the scapegoating of Joe. When she did, she worked hard through an examination of affect, herself, and her relationship to her parents. Like Martha, she was actively wrestling with dependent and counterdependent feelings. She seemed able to express impulses and own them. She could be described as loyal and compliant, but her level of hostility was high relative to other members. Her depressed affect was notable; it was usually denied with occasional depression denial or manic overtones. Along with Martha, Diane seemed to have conflicting longings relative to one or both of the coleaders. On the one hand, she identified and longed for closeness to the leaders. On the other hand, Diane and Martha were involved in a hostile competitive struggle with each other and with the leaders. If there was a fight leader or "heroine" role in this session, it was played by Diane.

Martha

Martha missed the previous session. She sought information and shared thoughts about what may have happened. There were heroic features to her performance. She was active throughout the session, usually focused on promoting impulse expression. She was often defiant (or hostile when dependent) and ready for a fight. She was work oriented but was focused more on others than herself. It was when she was losing center stage that she was apt to either precipitate hostility in others or (late in the group) to become work-oriented and depressed. She blended productive yet indirect expressions of work with competitive strivings in relation to the leader or coleaders. Her peformance was distinguished by increased depression after the shift.

Joe

Joe was scapegoated at the end of the previous session and again in this session. He arrived late, an issue that was never discussed. He tended to either express affect, which he experienced fleetingly and with great difficulty, or to move quickly into a poorly organized and inarticulate intellectualization about individual differences that also showed a fledgling effort at differentiation. He oscillated between extremes of dependence, counterdependence, and withdrawal. His performance was usually colored with reparation or other affectionate expressions that had an ingratiating, self-blaming flavor. As can be seen in Table 8.12, Joe was very active during the preshift phase and then rapidly withdrew.

Greg

Greg was active mainly early in the session. He was virtually silent throughout the scapegoating and most of the subsequent efforts to work, except for occasional excellent work-oriented remarks. His involvement deepened and he was more active when the group was working. When he was active, he functioned as an effective work leader, literally making the transference interpretations neglected by the coleaders and supporting them with relevant evidence about himself. He was highly sensitive to and aware of the impulse life and current affective state of the group. His manner and stance suggested one of collegial identification with the analytical function of the coleaders, although the paucity of individual scores in this session makes this inference highly speculative.

Brad

Brad was relatively inactive and scattered his limited participation throughout the session. He was about one fifth as active as the first three members and a third as active as Greg. When he spoke, it was usually at a point of strong affect or impulse expression in the group. Yet, his statements were well grounded in data and impressive in their level of insight. He was strongly identified with the stance of the coleaders, rarely disclosed or discussed his own feelings or experience, and often seemed to be holding himself on the periphery of group life. He had not fully joined the group, and it was unclear what would happen if he did. He seemed to have the potential to move toward either an independent worker position or toward one of antiwork, probably organized around counterdependence, anxiety denial, and resistance.

Pat

Pat spoke only about 15–20 times. Her performance was centered on dependence and anxiety. Other than saying she was dependent and anxious, and had not yet joined the group, it was difficult to understand her struggle. The timing of her remarks suggested that she was frightened of any strong expression either of need or aggression. She could best be described as a relatively silent, vulnerable, and compliant member.

Analysis of the Phase Shift

As indicated, this group was composed of six members, 3 women and 3 men, plus 2 female coleaders who were fairly active and seemingly client-centered in their approach. Consequently, within the context of the Mann system, their scores included frequent counterdominant or pseudoequality statements and expressions of disruptive affect, particularly the expression and denial of anxiety. Alice was clearly the more active of the coleaders.

Early in the session, one of the leaders, Helen, told the group of an upcoming task. The members were to take a written test after the fourth session, a task they had agreed to earlier. In response to member inquiries, she refused to explain the testing procedure, preferring to wait until next week. Subsequent statements by the more active members, such as Martha, Diane, and Joe, involved highly emotional expressions of past experiences of parental manipulation and unpredictability, their sense of having no choices as children of parents acting out of self-interest as opposed to concern for their child's needs. Given the emphasis on the centrality of authority relations in the Mann system, the helpless, dependent, and anxious feelings expressed toward parents at this time would be seen as being displaced from one or both of the coleaders. In this discussion, members portray their mothers as quiet, seemingly empathic and caring, yet powerful manipulators of the family, responsible for fathers' drunkenness, violence, apathy, and stupidity. The Mann scorer would speculate about whether this is the way in which group members are symbolically handling their feelings about one or both coleaders who relate differently to the group. The coleaders, probably reflecting their client-centered orientation, never interpreted these feelings in terms of transferences to them but instead remained reflective of members' manifest statements and empathic to their conscious feelings. As the end of the session approaches, members again retreated from their more intense and disruptive emotionality into a more hypomanic and dependent stance, with smatterings of euphoric and counterdependent rebellious wishes focused on the theme of "down with parents."

Overall, the group in this session continued to struggle with dependent and counterdependent longings, hostile feelings, and a great deal of anxiety. The session opended with an intellectualized discussion of male–female differences and superiority that the Mann scorer would infer as reflecting their covert preoccupation with the female coleaders. The group selected a scapegoat (Joe) whom they apparently attacked vigorously at the end of the previous session for hiding his feelings "behind a closed door." The Mann scorer would see the scapegoating of Joe as a displacement of the underlying hostility toward one or both of the coleaders, who were experienced as distant and unavailable. In the prephase shift (Units 64, 65, and 66), the group, except for Diane, continued to attempt to resolve the dependency–hostility conflict and to repair their fantasized damage to Joe and, symbolically, to one or both of the coleaders. Joe attempted to break out of the scapegoat role and to differentiate on his terms but remained identified with the coleader Helen. The group continued its attack, again led by Diane (Units 68, 69, and 70). Joe, acting as a fight leader, responded with a meager attempt to differentiate through an intellectualized stance centered in a discussion of his belief in individual differences. The segment ended with Diane acknowledging that she would not accept Joe on his terms. The Mann scorer would understand Diane's performance as representing a partial displacement from the coleaders, who, despite their client-centered orientation, were demanding with respect to norms of what was acceptable.

This sequence was followed by a shift that corresponded to the resolution of Phase II segment (Units 71, 72, and 73). The shift was precipitated by Diane's resistance and Martha's involvement in an intense and subtle competition with Diane and the coleaders throughout this session. Diane emerged as a heroic work leader and led the group to greater involvement, enactment, and expression of affect generally. She poignantly described her painful relationship with her parents and her subsequent feelings of rage. This also signaled a burst of greater independence as the ongoing and displaced struggles between dependence and counterdependence in relation to the coleaders surfaced again. Before the last segment, some work took place. Greg and Diane struggled to differentiate their mothers and fathers. However, this was not characterized by true independence. It involved identification with the coleaders, particularly for Martha and Brad, secondarily for Diane and Greg. This was also evident in the last segment, entry into Phase III, described in Units 82, 83, and 84. This was followed by a return to the dependency and hostility issues described earlier. In this segment, Martha and Diane poignantly described their feelings of deprivation and hostility as well as and their longings for love, care, and approval from their inadequate or disturbed parents. Some further work on differentiating mothers and fathers took place. The Mann scorer would see this sequence again as a displaced but work-oriented expression of conflict, differentiation, and longing relative to a group leader or the coleaders. The segment ended with Joe joining the struggle. Some intense work had clearly taken place. The Mann scorer would assume that some of this work had to do with the members' struggle with aspects of authority in relation to the coleaders, insofar as this was worked-through displacement and symbolization with outside parental authority figures.

I again emphasize that the above inferential analysis is highly speculative and atypical of how a Mann scorer-researcher would analyze the complexity of a therapy group. Three major components of the Mann system's scoring and interpretation are missing: (a) the context of the member's role, (b) the history of the group, and (c) statistically significant results.

Once all member–leader interactions for all sessions of a group have been scored, as indicated previously, they are subjected to a series of multivariate (e.g., factor analysis, cluster analysis, analysis of variance, etc.) analyses to differentiate member performances over time and to identify blocks of sessions in the search for phases of development. Once statistically different clusters of member performances and blocks of sessions have been identified, then the clinical interpretative process begins in order to flesh out the significant findings. For example, consider a cluster of members who have been identified as scoring significantly higher on anxiety and dependency than any other cluster. The Mann researcher would then identify the most active member or members in this cluster and listen to these members' expressions across all sessions before offering an interpretation of the members' performance during the life of the group. Similarly, the Mann researcher would listen carefully to a block of sessions that had been identified as statistically, and significantly, different from the preceding and subsequent block of sessions to understand the major member tasks, issues, and themes that characterized that series of sessions or phase. Lacking these types of data for all sessions (not just Session 3) of the current group makes generating any further hypotheses about this group uncomfortably speculative.

CLINICAL INTERPRETATION

The above analysis of Session 3 was guided by several theoretical assumptions that characterize the Mann scoring system and theory of group process: (a) The central and ubiquitous presence of authority in the members' experience; (b) the notion that member performances at any point in the life of the group are multi- and overdetermined, involving individual predispositions, interpersonal pressures for peers, relations to authority as well as intergroup and subgroup tensions within the group and group-level defensive operations; and (c) the idea that group development is propelled by the resolution of internal group conflict and tension as represented in competing member nonrational specialists. As a group therapist, these assumptions and ideas unequally sensitize one to ask such questions as, What is this member indirectly telling me about his or her feelings about me? What does this member represent for a subgroup or the group as a whole at this moment? Who else is this member speaking for? Similarly, interpretations focus on surfacing feelings about the therapist or cotherapist (as was the case in Session 3), on exploring member roles and what they indicate about the group at the moment, and on supporting work group leaders.

RELATIONSHIP BETWEEN THE RESEARCH AND THE THEORY

It is important to keep separate the Mann Member–Leader Scoring System and Mann's theory of group process and development. The utility of the Mann scoring system is evident in its continued use, especially in the race and gender studies described earlier. Mann's theory of group functioning needs to be put into context. The original study (Mann et al., 1967) and related subsequent studies (e.g., Gibbard, 1969; Gibbard, Hartman, & Mann, 1974; Hartman, 1969) were conducted in the 1960s with groups led by White men. Authority struggles, rebellion, and conflict characterized the late 1960s. Mann's admiration for the male heroic role and the centrality of the resolution of conflict with authority in his theory of group development were certainly fueled by the climate of the 1960s. If the original studies were to be repeated today with leaders varying in race and gender, it is reasonable to expect to find a different array of member roles and perhaps even a modified phase sequence of group development.

ASSESSMENT AND FUTURE DIRECTIONS

The most recent program of research on gender and authority in Tavistock Group Relations Conferences (described earlier) has generated a series of questions with implications for group process research in general. Cytrynbaum (1995) and Cytrynbaum and Hallberg (1993) have attempted to reassess the confusing results of recent gender studies of small groups in these Tavistock conferences. Their results and conclusions may also have implications for the validity of process research in group therapy in general. Cytrynbaum and Hallberg identified 11 contextual and methodological parameters that need to be considered in unraveling these inconsistent results and complex main and interaction effects. They concluded that although gender effects exist, the assessment and interpretation of these effects depend on a variety of contextual, structural, and methodological contingencies.

These contextual and methodological contingencies were translated by Cytrynbaum (1995) into four working hypotheses, all of which were derived from the assumption that gender effects in small groups depend on such contextual and methological considerations.

1. *The results of gender and authority research in groups depend on the interpersonal and political nature of male–female relations in the external environment at the time of the study.* Cytrynbaum and Curran (1993), Patrick (1980), and Cytrynbaum and Brandt (1979) reported inconsistent findings using the same instrument (semantic differential ratings) and similar conference designs and populations. Cytrynbaum and Brandt's conference was held in 1971, Patrick's in 1978 and 1979, and Cytrynbaum and Curran's in 1986 and 1987. Although other factors may be operating, the changes in male–female relations in the external environment during this 16-year period must be considered because changes in the external environment will permeate any mental health service delivery organization and the groups included in it.

2. *The major parameter associated with disruptive affect and group process is gender rather than level of authority.* Tischler (1980) concluded that group process was less affected by the leader's gender relative to the level of authority within a co-consultant pair. Greene, Morrison, and Tischler (1981) concluded that members' attitudes about group coleaders were more influenced by gender than their authority status. Male co-consultants were described as being more patient, active, instrumental, and insightful regardless of degree of formal authority. Cytrynbaum and Hallberg's (1995) report on three conferences with different director–associate director gender pairs also suggests that gender has more impact than level of formal authority. Research designs are currently available that can address this question.

3. *The results of gender and authority research in small groups depend on the gender composition of the leadership of the institution in which the groups are embedded.* Hallberg's (1995) process analysis study of three conferences varying in director–associate director gender combinations clearly identified main effects by gender of conference leaders, members, and small-group consultants. More interesting for my purposes is finding that some small-group effects emerge only in a particular combination of small-group consultant (male) and small-group member (male) in the male–male directed conference. Gender of conference directorship or the head of the organization must be taken into account in any study of gender effects and small-group processes.

4. *The results of gender and authority research in groups depend on the*

data collection instruments, the level of data assessed, and the source of data. Researchers using different data collection methods, levels, and sources of data have found different results. Some researchers have used measures such as repeated ratings (e.g., Cytrynbaum & Brandt, 1979; Greene et al., 1981; Patrick, 1980) or questionnaires (e.g., Reed, 1979), which focus on more conscious and overt data. Other researchers have attempted to access more preconscious, unconscious, or covert attitudes using process analysis measures (e.g., Bair, 1993; Burton, 1983; Cytrynbaum & Curran, 1993; Cytrynbaum & Hallberg, 1995; Hallberg, 1995; Tischler, 1980). Others have used a variety of qualitative methods (e.g., Mayes, 1979; Taylor et al., 1979).

Cytrynbaum and Hallberg (1993) also noted two other questions concerning relatively unexamined areas: (a) the relationships among gender, group therapy process, and outcomes and (b) the impact of gender and race or ethnicity of cotherapy combinations on group therapy process and outcome. The extent to which the instruments selected influence the data, findings, and conclusions of small-group process research remains to be systematically investigated.

REFERENCES

Bair, J. (1993). The effect of member's ego styles on psychoanalytic work processes in small groups. In S. Cytrynbaum & S. A. Lee (Eds.), *Proceedings of the 10th Annual Scientific Meeting of the A. K. Rice Institute* (pp. 112–118). Washington, DC: A. K. Rice Institute.

Burton, M. (1983). Regression in Tavistock groups as a function of size of group, gender of consultant, and stage of group development (Doctoral dissertation, George Washington University, 1983). *Dissertation Abstracts International, 44*(01), 299B.

Cytrynbaum, S. (1995). Group relations research progress report: Contextual and methodological issues in the study of gender and authority in Tavistock group relations conferences, or "it depends." In K. L. West, C. Hayden, & R. M. Sharrin (Eds.), *Proceedings of the 11th Scientific Meeting of the A. K. Rice Institute* (pp. 47–56). Jupiter, FL: A. K. Rice Institute.

Cytrynbaum, S., & Brandt, L. (1979, September). *Women in authority: Dilemmas for male and female subordinates.* Paper presented at the 87th Annual Convention of the American Psychological Association, New York.

Cytrynbaum, S., & Conran, P. (1979a). Impediments to the process of learning. *Illinois School Research and Development, 15*(2), 49–65.

Cytrynbaum, S., & Conran, P. (1979b). Multiple task and boundary management in the interracial college classroom. *Journal of Negro Education, 48,* 457–478.

Cytrynbaum, S., & Curran, V. (1993). Gender and authority in group relations conferences. In T. W. Hugg, M. M. Carson, & R. L. Lipgar (Ed.), *Proceedings* of the Ninth Annual Scientific Meeting of the A. K. Rice Institute (pp. 86–121). Jupiter, FL: A. K. Rice Institute.

Cytrynbaum, S., & Hallberg, M. (1993). Gender and authority in group relations conferences: So what have we learned in fifteen years of research? In S. Cytrynbaum & S. A. Lee (Eds.), Proceedings of the 10th Scientific Meeting of the A. K. Rice Institute (pp. 63–73). Jupiter, FL: A. K. Rice Institute.

Cytrynbaum, S., & Hallberg, M. (1995, May). The effect of different gender combinations of group relations conference director and associate director on gender and authority in small groups. Paper presented at the 12th Annual Scientific Meeting of the A. K. Rice Institute, Washington, DC.

Dunphy, D. C. (1964). Social change in self-analytic groups (Doctoral dissertation, Harvard University, 1964). Dissertation Abstracts International, ADD, x1964.

Dunphy, D. C. (1968). Phases, roles and myths in self-analytic groups. Journal of Applied Behavioral Science, 4, 195–225.

Gibbard, G. S. (1969). The study of relationship patterns in psychoanalytic groups (Doctoral dissertation, University of Michigan, 1969). Dissertation Abstracts International, 31(05), 2983B.

Gibbard, G. S., Hartman, J., & Mann, R. D. (Eds.). (1974). Analysis of groups. San Francisco: Jossey-Bass.

Granda, K. L. (1992). Consultant personal and working framework and its impact on member-authority relations in small groups (consultants, group dynamics, leadership) (Doctoral dissertation, Northwestern University, 1992). Dissertation Abstracts International, 53(11), 6038B.

Greene, L., Morrison, T., & Tischler, N. (1981). Gender and authority: Effects on perceptions of small group co-leaders. Small Group Behavior, 12, 401–413.

Hallberg, M. (1995). The impact of gender and authority: Differential responses of males versus females in the context of three group relations conferences held in the Tavistock tradition (Doctoral dissertation, Northwestern University, 1995). Dissertation Abstracts International, 56(07), 4061B.

Hartman, J. (1969). The role of ego state distress in the development of self-analytic groups (Doctoral dissertation, University of Michigan, 1969). Dissertation Abstracts International, 31(05), 2986.

Hartman, J., & Gibbard, G. (1974). Anxiety, boundary evolution, and social change. In G. S. Gibbard, J. Hartman, & R. D. Mann (Eds.), Analysis of groups (pp. 154–176). San Francisco: Jossey-Bass.

Mann, R., Arnold, S., Binder, J., Cytrynbaum, S., Newman, B., Ringwald, B., Ringwald, J., & Rosenwein, R. (1970). The college classroom: Conflict, change and learning. New York: Wiley.

Mann, R., Gibbard, G., & Hartman, J. (1967). Interpersonal styles and group development: An analysis of the member–leader relationship. New York: Wiley.

Mayes, S. (1979). Women in positions of authority: A case study of changing gender roles. Signs, 4, 556–558.

Patrick, R. (1980). Gender and authority relationships: Member perceptions of males and females in authority positions in small groups (Doctoral dissertation, Northwestern University, 1980). *Dissertation Abstracts International, 41*(06), 2340B.

Reed, B. (1979). Differential reactions by male and female group members to a group experience in the presence of male and female authority figures (Doctoral dissertation, University of Cincinnati, 1969). *Dissertation Abstracts International, 40*(07), 3492B.

Ringwald, J. W. (1973). An investigation of group reaction to central group figures (Doctoral dissertation, University of Michigan, 1973). *Dissertation Abstracts International, 35*(01), 488B.

Rosenwein, R. E. (1970). Determinants of low verbal activity rates: A study of the silent person (Doctoral dissertation, University of Michigan, 1970). *Dissertation Abstracts International, 31*(12), 7578B.

Taylor, S., Bogdonoff, M., Brown, D., Hillman, L., Kurash, C., Spain, J., Thacher, B., & Weinstein, L. (1979). By women, for women: A group relations conference. In G. W. Lawrence (Ed.), *Exploring individual and organizational boundaries* (pp. 187–206). New York: Wiley.

Tischler, N. G. (1980). Effects of leader gender and authority position on work and defensive processes in small groups. *Dissertation Abstracts International, 41*(03), 1129. (University Microfilms No. 8018999)

IV

NEWER SYSTEMS FOR GROUP PROCESS ANALYSIS

9

THE GROUP DEVELOPMENT PROCESS ANALYSIS MEASURES

CAROL M. LEWIS, ARIADNE P. BECK, JAMES M. DUGO,
AND ALBERT M. ENG

HISTORY AND THEORY OF THE SYSTEM

The Group Development Process Analysis Measures were designed to facilitate the study of development in small groups. The measures include three scales for the process analysis of verbal content and style dimensions, a set of speech behavior codes, and a sociometric test for the identification of emergent leaders. The primary focus of this chapter is on the process analysis scales and the speech behavior measures. The process analysis scales are (a) the Hostility/Support Scale; (b) the Experiencing Scales (Klein, Mathieu-Coughlan, & Kiesler, 1986) adapted for use in the study of group psychotherapy; and (c) the Normative Organizational/Personal Exploration (NO/PE) Scale, which is used to rate units created by the Topic-Oriented Group Focus Unitizing Procedure. The Speech Behavior Coding System includes measures for length of statement, who is speaking, who is spoken to, and how frequently the group members refer to themselves as "we."

The process of development in small groups has been studied conceptually for about 50 years. The foundations of the theory of phases in this process of development include the work of Bales and Strodtbeck (1951), Bales (1953), Heinicke and Bales (1953), Bennis and Shepard (1956), Hill and Elmore (1957), Tuckman (1965), Tuckman and Jensen (1977), Mann (1967), Hare (1973), Beck (1974a), and Lacoursiere (1980). Although there are variations in some matters of detail across theorists, with some theoretical frameworks identifying more phases of development than others, there is considerable agreement across observers that there are phases of development and that they occur in a particular sequence. The Group Development Process Analysis Measures are being used to find evidence of the boundaries of phases in group process and to model and study aspects of the group process more thoroughly, including characteristic patterns of interaction or content and leader or member behavior that may be related to specific phases of development or to the developmental process across phases.

The term *process of development* refers to the growth of structure within the group during the course of interaction. The structure includes the development of norms for interaction, roles, and identity as the group members strive to become capable of doing the work for which they initially came together. The tasks of each phase of group development are encountered by the group members as they interact. Each must be addressed and solved for work to proceed.

During each phase the group participates in interactions that lead to the integration of diverse positions expressed among the members and to the formation and maintenance of a degree of cohesiveness among the members. The problem or issue of each phase is encountered experientially by each member in the group, producing a diverse and differentiated set of responses. These provide a base for the group to address the developmental issue at hand. The goal is to attain an aspect of structure that encompasses the various needs of the members and maintains a degree of relatedness or cohesion within the group. Bales (1953) described some aspects of this process in his work observing "laboratory" task-oriented groups. He developed the idea that the group moves back and forth between dealing with instrumental structural issues (at points when sufficient tension strains the integration of the group) and task issues when an adequate resolution occurs. Bales (1958) also introduced the idea that role differentiation among the members occurs as a part of this interaction process and increases the efficiency of the group. Group members in specific leadership roles emerge as critical participants in addressing phase-related issues as the group develops.

Most of the early theoretical work on the phases of development in small groups has been based on experimental encounter or task groups and classroom groups. The present research was guided by Beck's (1974a, 1981a, 1981b) theory of group development, which was originally based on observation of client-centered, time-limited, psychotherapy groups and a comparative review of the work from sociology and social psychology in observing phases. Another source of influence on the original conceptualization was Beck's training in developmental psychology and early exposure to systems theory at the University of Chicago. Beck was also strongly influenced by Rollo May and Eugene Gendlin to eventually develop a therapeutic leadership style that is existential and developmental in focus. The theory itself evolved further after the Group Development Research Team was formed. Lewis, Dugo, Eng, Peters, and Brusa were all trained in contexts that focused primarily on psychodynamic theory and therapy methods, and their perspectives have influenced many of the developments and applications of the theory. This theory identifies nine phases of development and four leadership roles in the group (Beck, 1974a, 1981a, 1981b).

The nine phases of group development as identified by Beck (1974a, 1981a, 1981b), and the major themes of each phase are briefly described as follows:

- *Phase I:* The members agree to become a group on the basis of an initial assessment by the members of one another and on an initial statement of goals among the members.
- *Phase II:* The group begins to form initial norms for how the members work together. These include management of anxiety, anger, and competitiveness. Initial processes for decision making and conflict resolution are achieved. Four leaders emerge: the Task Leader, the Emotional Leader, the Scapegoat Leader, and the Defiant Leader. These informal leadership roles are described in more detail later.
- *Phase III:* In this phase, the beginning of cooperative work takes place. Individual goals and personal histories are shared, and an initial work style is established. Early life experiences may be addressed and issues with authority figures explored.
- *Phase IV:* Stronger peer bonds are formed among the members, trust is deepened, and more creative work becomes possible. Issues of intimacy are addressed, and the relationship of the group to the Task Leader changes.
- *Phase V:* Mutuality is established in the context of the acknowledgment of limitations and defensiveness as they are experienced among members. A willingness to accept the realities of each member occurs, along with an increased commitment to work on personal goals.
- *Phase VI:* The group's structure is reorganized, allowing for greater sharing of leadership and fluidity of roles. Enough interpersonal encounter has taken place to allow members to take responsible ownership of the group and personal respon-

sibility for their own work. The Task Leader continues to be an expert resource person, but members assert leadership and management of the group.

- *Phase VII:* The members address their own work in the group more freely. They provide guidance to the group about how to help them best, and there is strong support from the group members to work through difficult aspects of individual therapeutic work. Creative work and individual initiative occur in an atmosphere of interdependence.

- *Phase VIII:* This phase includes a review of the accomplishments and learning that have occurred and the exploration of the transfer of what was learned in group to goals outside of the group.

- *Phase IX:* As the time for the end of the group and separation of the members draws near, the members acknowledge the significance of relationships in the group, addressing the meaning of the coming separation and termination and sharing feedback to each member.

All nine phases emerge only occasionally and only in groups with stable membership. When membership changes occur, the group usually begins again in Phase I. The length of time a group spends in any particular phase is related to the members' own developmental issues. Each phase facilitates the emergence of certain individual issues. A therapy group may productively spend a great deal of time in Phases III, IV, V, or VII if most members' issues are relevant to the skills needed to complete that phase. Groups composed of patients with chronic psychotic disorders may profitably spend time in Phase I. In our view, lengthy time spent in Phases II or VI is not generally productive.

Beck's (1974a, 1981a, 1981b) theory also identifies four leadership roles inherent in small-group interaction: the Task Leader, the Emotional Leader, the Scapegoat Leader, and the Defiant Leader. The four leadership roles emerge during the process of interaction and have important functions in the developmental process (Beck & Peters, 1981; Brusa, Stone, Beck, Dugo, & Peters, 1994; Peters & Beck, 1982).

- The *Task Leader* usually acts as the guide to the task of the group. This leader may have expertise relevant to the work or goals of the group and influences norm development, goal clarification, and style of communication from this vantage point. The Task Leader is responsible for any issues involving the group's relationship to the surrounding organization or environment.

- The *Emotional Leader* is generally the best liked person in the group and is an important support person to other members throughout the group's life. He or she is usually a group member who is highly motivated and well prepared to participate in the task of the group.

- The *Scapegoat Leader* helps to crystallize many group issues about norms. The Scapegoat Leader is often the object of open criticism or attack or of nonverbalized negative feelings from other group members during Phase II. This role is the vehicle for the clarification of many issues in the group.
- The *Defiant Leader* is usually a group member who openly expresses some ambivalence about participating in the group or in the group's task and models the struggle between dependence and independence for the group as a whole.

We believe that the process of group development is common to small groups of many kinds who meet with little imposed or formal structure to accomplish various types of work. Most psychotherapy groups meet this criterion. The manner in which the tasks of structural development are dealt with directly affects the working environment and potential of the group. For example, the difficult tasks of coping with conflict and anxiety in interpersonal dynamics is a crucial task in the structural development of the group and one that affects the therapeutic issues the group members will be able to work on in the group. The processes of development are important to the facilitation of work in psychotherapy groups of any particular theoretical modality and are useful for the therapist to understand and consider in implementing a particular type of group psychotherapy process.

A description of the first three phases of group development as these occur in a psychotherapy group illustrates how the task of therapy is affected by the developmental process (Beck, 1983b). In *Phase I*, the members must address the important task of agreeing to work together as a group. The members must make an initial assessment of one another and of their own abilities to cope with the others in the group. The interaction between group members includes the task of introducing themselves, usually with a degree of anxiety and tentativeness accentuated by the highly personal nature of the work lying ahead for them as a psychotherapy group. Questions from one member to another facilitate the disclosure of introductory information, but they may be few and expressed briefly. Members must find someone with whom they can form an initial bond, and members may leave if they feel too uncomfortable. The Task Leader plays an important role in setting the emotional tone, the pace, and the structure of the group. In the role of the Task Leader, the therapist functions as the expert on communication and self-exploration and influences many dimensions of the group's work. Usually by the end of Phase I another special leadership role is informally filled, that of the Emotional Leader, who is generally the most liked member of the group.

In *Phase II*, the group moves on the the actual testing of the assessments made in Phase I. Major group organizational issues are worked out, including the establishment of important norms, the identification of goals for the group and on a general level for the individual member, the management of negative emotions, the resolution of competitive needs, the emergence of leaders, and the definition of an initial group identity. Each of these must be dealt with in a manner that engages the entire group and enables the members to proceed cooperatively beyond this point.

During Phase II, interaction among members reflects the difficult task of sharing responses toward others as their individual characters and in particular their differences are encountered. The rate of self-disclosure will vary among members, with some members beginning to address the matters they wish to work on more directly than others do. A degree of confrontation is expected to occur as the group struggles with anxiety about becoming able to work together. Members must experience and recognize both anxiety and their initial defenses to establish a working therapeutic group. Members' sharing of responses to one another will reflect some recognition of their own anxiety and some critical and rejecting attitudes toward the behavior of others that arise partly from this anxiety.

This is a difficult phase in group development, and several leadership roles emerge and play an important part in addressing the issues of this phase. Phase II is usually characterized by a conflict with one person in particular, the Scapegoat Leader, who serves as a reference point against which the group defines itself. Some theories postulate that individual members' anxieties and defenses, including negative affect, are best understood as part of the transference toward the group therapist and that the occurrence of scapegoating toward another group member may indicate a deficiency in the therapist's attention and response to these transference issues. Our view is that coping with negative emotions responsibly is crucial to the achievement of a therapeutic structure within the group but that it is a developmental task common to groups with or without a formal leader and is part of a broader aspect of group dynamics, not soley a response to group therapist in the role of Task Leader. We see the role of the Scapegoat Leader as part of the emergent or distributed leadership structure of the small group. Responses to authority, or to its absence, are core aspects of group dynamics, and the need to cope with conflict in social groups is probably one of the determinants of the development of leadership or authoritarian structure in living groups. The therapist's skill and experience with both psychotherapeutic processes and the processes of group development affect the accomplishment of developmental tasks in this and other phases. Of course, the therapist's lack of skill in addressing any essential therapeutic task is bound to cause anxiety and negative emotion among the members and impede the development of the group. The Task Leader and the Emotional Leader participate in a manner that facilitates defining the group-level issues so that the members achieve the difficult tasks of this phase and the anxiety experienced by the members about the formative group process dissipates.

Phase III is the beginning of a cooperative process, during which the members become more personally disclosing This period introduces the therapeutic methods for dealing with personal change and growth in greater depth. Each member takes a turn to discuss the issues that brought him or her to the group and to clarify his or her goals. The members facilitate the process for one another by showing interest in issues already raised by others and asking specific questions that facilitate further disclosure of information. Members listen attentively with less anxiety and less competitive feeling as well as show recognition and understanding of the experiences and feelings expressed by others. The participation of each member in some degree of self-disclosure is important. In addition, members' self-disclosure shows an increased degree of association in this phase, with one member's work building on or linked to issues raised by another member.

During this phase, the Emotional Leader often plays a special role by beginning significant personal work and becoming a model of the change process to the group. The Defiant Leader begins to assume a therapistlike stance in relationship to others during Phase III while offering a minimal amount of self-disclosure. The Scapegoat Leader is reintegrated into the group, and the members acknowledge their role in the scapegoating process.

As the group continues to negotiate the developmental issues in later phases, work on the issues of individual members progresses. As the relationships among group members strengthen through experiences in interaction, the group members are able to address the personal work of therapy in more powerful ways. They take more responsibility for self-confrontation and build confidence in the commitment and support of other group members.

CORRESPONDENCE BETWEEN THE THEORY AND THE SYSTEM

The goals of the current research were to design a methodology for identifying phase boundaries, characteristic phase-relevant processes, and aspects of the four leaders' behaviors. The first goal was to find a set of variables that could describe the structural development of a therapy group. It was decided to select the second and third phases of development and the phase boundary between those two phases for our initial efforts at identifying a change process that might be similar across groups. The tasks addressed in Phases II and III are ones that engender significantly different characteristics of interpersonal process. During Phase II the members are competitively engaged as they consider and select the informal norms for working in their group. Phase III begins a cooperative process in which each member becomes more self-disclosing about personal issues and background relevant to therapeutic goals. These changes seemed to offer the possibility of objective measurement and description if appropriate measures could be found or developed. A long-term goal of this team is to empirically identify all nine phases and the shifts between them, and the differences between these two early phases seemed a logical place to start.

On the basis of a review of the literature on phases of group development, Beck (1974b) identified the characteristics of Phases II and III that had been generally agreed on among theorists. By comparing these, it was possible to identify the major changes that took place when the group moved from one phase to the other. These changes include the following:

1. Movement from a period of high tension, anger, criticism, or discomfort to a period of relatively positive feeling and mutual support.
2. Movement from relatively defensive behavior to more open mutually exploratory behavior.
3. Movement from concern, apprehension, and struggle related to organizational and norm development issues to a focus on individual members and their personal concerns.

To measure the three changes from Phase II to Phase III, we chose instruments that tap interpersonal, intrapersonal, and group-as-a-whole processes (Beck, Dugo, Eng, & Lewis, 1986). To measure the change in the emotional tone present in the group, we designed the Hostility/Support Scale. This scale taps the interpersonal dimension of process. To measure the second change, from defensive to exploratory behavior, we adapted the Experiencing Scale for use with group process. This instrument, designed to measure aspects of the process of exploration in psychotherapy, taps part of the intrapsychic or intrapersonal processes in the group members. For the third change, from struggle with organizational issues and norm development to a period of focus on the personal concerns of members, we designed the NO/PE Scale. This measure taps the group-as-a-whole process.

As much as possible, variables were chosen that are logical aspects of the interpersonal process envisioned by the theory. They are measures or signs of the operational definitions of aspects of the developmental process. The Hostility/Support Scale measures some dimensions of the overt emotions expressed in the group. The NO/PE Scale measures whether the group is focusing on normative issues or personal therapeutic issues. The Experiencing Scale measures the process of exploring and articulating experience as well as progress in working on personal self-understanding and understanding experiences within the group.

In addition to these three instruments, we designed the Speech Behavior Coding System to study various aspects of the interaction. The Speech Behavior Coding System measures relatively simple aspects of speech behavior among group members to investigate clearly defined theoretical questions. The measures include identification of who is speaking, who is spoken to, and the length of each statement. For the groups reported on here, the four emergent leaders were clinically identified through interviews with the therapists of each group and confirmed by an early version of the sociometric test used to identify emergent leaders in psychotherapy groups. The design of this test, which has just been completed, has been a parallel research project of this team (Brusa, Stone, Beck, Dugo, & Peters, 1994).

At this time, methods for modeling the first, second, and third phases of group development have been designed. The method and measures involved may not be adequate to describe all other phases in group development, but some of the measures are applicable to processes of interaction that occur consistently across phases. The Experiencing Scale and the NO/PE Scale are used together to identify some aspects of developmental process that recur in each phase. The Speech Behavior Coding System can be used to investigate changes in levels of participation, the focus of the group on particular members, and various aspects of pairing and subgrouping. With some modifications, the Hostility/Support Scale is expected to be useful for several other points in the developmental process. We expect to use a combination of measures for aspects of the developmental process that are consistent across phases and measures that are specific to each of the phases in further study of group development.

Several theoretical constructs are measured by the system:

1. Each phase involves a process of differentiation and integration among the members with regard to structural and normative issues. The integration represents a step in the formation of structure. The NO/PE Scale and the Experiencing Scale are used together to identify periods of integration in the group during which awareness, understanding, and articulation of experiences that have occurred are expressed. A high level of experiencing among the group as a whole, occurring along with a transition or shift from normative to personal issues, identifies an integrative process in the group. Variations in the level of experiencing and longer periods of consistent focus on normative issues accompany the process of differentiation.

2. The group will move back and forth in interaction from dealing with task matters directly to dealing with structural or normative issues when there is a need to do so. The NO/PE Scale tracks the focus of the group between these types of

focus of effort. The Experiencing Scale provides a qualitative measure of the work done on individual therapeutic goals or on addressing normative issues at the group level.

3. Early in the group's life many difficult structural issues, including the development of norms for coping with negative emotions such as anger, interpersonal tension and conflict, and competitiveness, must be addressed for group members to become a working group, able to address tasks more directly, and work in a cooperative, mutually supportive manner. The Hostility/Support Scale measures this change, focusing on the specific variable of the level of hostility and criticism directed by the group to the Scapegoat Leader to identify the transition from Phase II to Phase III.

4. Special role differentiation will occur among members of the group in the course of interaction and increase the efficiency of the group. Group members in specific leadership roles become critical participants in addressing phase-related issues as the group develops. The measures of speech behavior can help determine whether members in leadership roles are more active than other group members in aspects of the process.

DESCRIPTION OF THE SYSTEM

The measures described here—the Hostility/Support Scale, the Experiencing Scale, the NO/PE Scale, the Topic-Oriented Group Focus Unitizing Procedure, and the Speech Behavior Coding System—were originally designed to assess the shift from Phase II to Phase III in a pilot study that involved three groups (Beck et al., 1986). One of those groups was Group A, which is used as the basis for illustration and comparison of the systems in this book.

The Hostility/Support Scale

The Hostility/Support Scale is a three-category nominal scale designed to assess whether statements made in the course of interaction are supportive or negative toward the person being addressed (Beck, 1983a). The scale was developed as part of the current work of identifying the boundaries of phases of development in psychotherapy groups. It was devised to measure the change from a period characterized by tension, conflict, and criticism in Phase II of group development to a period of more mutual support in Phase III.

The statements of all group members can be rated with the scale, but for the focus on the shift from Phase II to Phase III, we used only the statements of the group members (not including the therapists) toward the Scapegoat Leader of the group. The behavior of the group members toward the Scapegoat Leader is hypothesized to change during the early phases of group development and may be one indication of phase change, especially for the shift from Phase II to Phase III. For the present study, the Scapegoat Leader was identified by clinical analysis and through the use of an early version of the sociometric test. The test was administered to all group members after the group ended.

The developmental theory postulates that early in the group's life, during Phase II, important normative issues are encountered, including the management of negative emotions, resolution of competitive needs, and the initial identification of group goals. As this process takes place, anxiety, discomfort, tension, and conflict are generated in the group. Furthermore, this often becomes expressed as negative reactions to one group member who is "scapegoated." As Phase II ends, these important normative issues are recognized and begin to be resolved, allowing the group to enter a period of more supportive and directly task-oriented interaction in Phase III. Focus on and criticism of the Scapegoat Leader is replaced by efforts at self-disclosure related to the tasks of therapy.

The following are the categories of the Hostility/Support Scale:

1. The statement expresses acceptance, agreement, or neutrality toward the person being addressed.

   Example:

   Martha: Excuse me. I was wondering if underneath or back of all this if you felt that there was anything you were trying to say last week that you didn't get across. I wasn't here, I was just wondering, I wanted to ask you whether there really was something that you were tryin' to get across that didn't get across? (Beck, 1970, pp. 85–86)

2. The statement expresses disagreement or mild negativity or criticism toward the person addressed.

   Example:

   Pat: Well, maybe in a way that was the way I felt because, uh, I was feeling like, uh, I kept being distracted by the things you were wanting to talk about, and they weren't things that concerned us I didn't think, and uh, so, I guess I was, uh, I didn't wanna go ahead and blurt out what I had to say because, well I couldn't, um, because my mind was full of the things you were saying. (Beck, 1970, p. 87)

3. The statement expresses openly negative, angry, or aggressive feelings toward the person addressed.

   Example:

Pat: Oftentimes when I'm, uh, with others and in this group, both last week and this week, I've felt like saying things but, uh, I always hold because I feel like I'm going to hurt somebody. Now for instance now I was getting real annoyed with you . . . (Beck, 1970, p. 39)

There are several ways in which the data from this scale can be summarized and displayed depending on which parts of the communication are rated. For example, if all of the statements made by everyone are rated, a table can be formed based on who spoke to whom (one of the speech behavior codes), filling in the number of statements of each rating (one, two, or three) made by each person to each other person. Such a table would show the patterns of dyadic intensity in the communication as well as the degree of support, criticism, or hostility being expressed by each member to each other member (Beck & Lewis, 1996).

For the analysis in the study of the phase shift from Phase II to Phase III, we identified all the statements made toward the Scapegoat Leader. Each statement was typed on a separate 3 × 5 card that was labeled with a random code number. Each statement's place in the sequence of interaction was identified with a page and item number code. A table of both codes was made to facilitate reordering the statement ratings for analysis. No indication of the speaker's identity or of the sequence of the statements in the group's interaction appeared on the card used for rating. The cards were arranged by the random codes, and each statement was rated out of context based only on a careful reading of the statement itself. This method focused the rating on the manifest verbal content of the statement, without influence from tone of voice or from the context of other statements.

After the statements were rated, we reordered the ratings according to the time sequence in which they occurred. The average rating on the Hostility/Support Scale of members' statements made to the Scapegoat Leader was calculated for each page of transcript.

The statements were rated by two raters. Reliability was assessed by calculating the percentage of item-by-item agreement for the rating of individual statements and by calculating the Pearson product–moment correlation for the average rating per page of transcript. The percentage of agreement for item-by-item ratings was 74.32 for Group A. The Pearson correlation for average ratings per page (127 pages of transcript of Group A) was .83. The reliability figures for the ratings of the other two groups in the pilot study were comparable (Beck et al., 1986).

The Experiencing Scale

The Experiencing Scales are constructed to measure both client and therapist statements. The Client Experiencing Scale (Klein, Mathieu-

Coughlan, & Kiesler, 1986) was developed to measure certain aspects of a client's engagement and involvement in the psychotherapy process. "The scale itself attempts to measure the way in which these theoretically important levels of experiencing appear, and are referred to in the client's speech during therapy sessions" (Klein et al., 1986, p. 21). The Therapist Experiencing Scale measures the degree to which a therapist's response is focused on the client's internal, personal perspective, immediate feelings or vivid reliving of past experiences or on emerging, directly sensed, and newly recognized or more fully realized feelings and experiences (Mathieu-Coughlan & Klein, 1984).

In our application of the Experiencing Scale to group therapy, we have used the Therapist Experiencing Scale to measure facilitative responses made by other group members and therapists. The behavior of all group members and therapists is rated using the statement as the unit for measuring. Each statement is first classified according to length (i.e., 1 = 1–5 lines of transcript, 2 = 6–10 lines of transcript, and 3 = 11+ lines of transcript). Each statement is then classified as either a "client" or a "therapist" statement (i.e., a self-exploratory or a facilitative type of statement). A statement classified as facilitative must show an effort by the speaker to present his or her understanding or perception of another group member's thoughts, feelings, or behavior, or the statement must show interest in finding out more about another member or encourage them to explore further. After the statement is classified as a self-exploratory (client) or facilitative (therapist) statement, it is rated on the appropriate Experiencing Scale (Lewis & Beck, 1983).

Brief definitions of the categories of the Experiencing Scale are presented here with examples for Stages 1–6.

Stage 1

Client scale: The client makes impersonal statements about events external to the process.

Therapist scale: The therapist makes a reference to events not including the patient or his or her response.

Example: *Alice*:   I guess I didn't get what you said, that men, that women aren't as bad as men or something?
Martha: Oh no, no, no. It's just the knowledge of being male is somehow superior you know?
Greg: You know I always hear that, but I always thought that women had an equally strong feeling that actually it's really the women who are domineering . . .
Martha: Oh they do, they do have that feeling, but still . . .

Alice: On the surface they act like they're submissive, but they're really not. (Beck, 1970, pp. 76–77)

Stage 2

Client scale: This is a description of events and ideas of importance to the client, or an intellectual self-description.

Therapist scale: This is a behavioral or intellectual elaboration of the patient's thoughts or actions or a description of events in which the patient is involved.

Example: *Joe:* Has this been true of your whole life, I mean since early childhood, er, as you were in grade school and high school and college and . . .
Diane: Yeah . . .
Joe: Your whole life?
Diane: It started there, except when I was young I didn't really understand what was happening. I guess I still don't, except now I know it's connected with my values.
Joe: I mean did you have a hard childhood? Were you an orphan er, shoved around from pillar to post?
Diane: Oh I think it was a tough childhood, I mean I was in a home with a mother and father and a family of children . . .
Joe: I mean, was it your own family?
Diane: I'm feeling now, "Well this will bore you so I don't want to say it."
Group: (Exclamation and laughter).
Joe: I mean was there always friction, or was there always trouble?
Diane: My father was an authoritarian and an alcoholic. He was a violent man to boot. I mean he, like, broke doors down. (Beck, 1970, p. 103)

Stage 3

Client scale: This is a narrative or self-description in which feelings are owned, but are rooted in external events.

Therapist scale: There is limited reference to the client's feelings or reactions to a specific event or situation.

Example: *Alice:* What do you mean, "toughen up"?
Joe: Well, they shouldn't think the world is coming to an end, uh.
Well, just like myself, uh, I mean I was with a company for 15 years and, I mean, it kinda bothered

me at first—well, I don't think it would ever bother me again, I mean, I think I've toughened up to the fact that I was let go and . . .

Alice: Are you saying something like before it happened you went along with the world, and the world had done nothing like this to you . . . ?

Joe: That's right. It was such a shock and a scare, I mean, I, like, when I was leaving the company and packin' my stuff, I mean, I was in tears. I could—you know it was like the company was just like a part of my home, and now I was goin' out in the cruel world.

Alice: It was shattering. (Beck, 1970, pp. 145–146)

Stage 4

Client scale: This is an account of feelings in which the inner experience is the subject rather than outer events.

Therapist scale: The therapist maintains the focus on the patient's inner experience and feelings.

Example: *Pat:* I'd like to go back to some of my feelings about, uh, I think I can understand, uh, some of what Martha is feeling because I feel that way myself, that I am very elusive to myself. Uh, and when I think I've got a hold of something, then I begin to doubt it and I can't really feel sure of it, and it just scares the life outta me to—to say now this is the way I am and by God I'm gonna stick to this, er, I'm gonna take the consequences. I'm gonna say to so-and-so that this is the way I feel, and if they get mad, to hell with them, or whatever . . . , I just feel like I'm a reed in the breeze, almost.

Helen: You can't vouch for your . . .

Pat: Yeah, and it's frightening to, uh, realize that you have some strong feelings that maybe, that you have something strong that is going to show, no matter what you do. (Beck, 1970, p. 257)

Stage 5

Client scale: A problem or hypothesis about the self is posed and explored explicitly in terms of inner feelings or experience.

Therapist scale: The therapist responds to or poses a problem on the basis of the client's feelings and personal experience and helps explore it.

Example: *Diane:* Because the way it feels for me is that when

I invest myself I'm projected way out there, you know? And then, that way out there, from back here is not safe, it's vulnerable, and then everybody pounces on it way out there, and I can't pull it back. It just stays out there and gets hurt, you know? Over and over.

Alice: What I'm hearing today, I want to catch it 'cause you've said it three or four times now, is that the way out there is a way of dealing with being way back here all by myself. That you've had experiences of being cut off and feeling, uh, unable to be in touch and then you have gone way out in an attempt to be in touch and this is not really any solution either. This has hurts and pains that may be different from the other ones but . . .

Diane: I think this is getting close to something maybe. I think, and this may not be true, I may have to say it to find out if it's true, um, I think that it's my most spontaneous self is the one that goes way out, and that If I'm acting spontaneously, I end up with this unprotected whatever it is, it really feels like sort of an unprotected projection that gets hurt, um, and I think that when I haven't been spontaneous then I experience what Pat describes. It isn't safe to project me, and so I don't and then . . . (Beck, 1970, p. 577)

Stage 6

Client scale: Clients show an awareness of a felt sense, an inner referent emerging and guiding the exploration of experience. Changes in self-awareness and self-understanding are integrated.

Therapist scale: The therapist focuses on the patient's directly sensed emerging feelings and on his or her articulation and integration.

Example: *Diane:* That's the whole thing that puzzles me, is, why does it take so much before . . .

Alice: That's an example of the same thing, isn't it.

Diane: Yeah, it's the same thing, why, why does it take that much before I do reveal where I am.

Martha: Well, you said literally, "One of these days you're gonna push me too far." And that was it, you have to be pushed.

Diane: Something, I think it was Alice said something about, some comment, my cup runneth over, or something like that.

Martha: Oh, that's right.

Diane: And this was a very interesting speculation for me to realize I have a cup, you know, and I thought, what the heck?

Martha: I've got a cup.

Diane: It—I can see it. There it is, you know, like a vat or something and it fills, and fills, and fills, and fills, and all of a sudden shshshsh, then I reveal myself, and up to that point, I go along. (Beck, 1970, p. 289)

Stage 7

Client scale: The statement shows a steady and expanding awareness with movement from one inner referent to another, linking and integrating these.

Therapist scale: The statement focuses on and facilitates the movement from one inner referent to another. The building, linking, and integrating functions are elaborated.

The categories of the Client and Therapist Experiencing Scales are parallel. Each level is rated according to a detailed definition found in the training manual (Klein, Mathieu, Gendlin, & Kiesler, 1969). The statements are rated on the basis of the manifest, verbally expressed thought processes of the speaker to minimize any inference in the rating process. Although some statements are more difficult to rate than others, the decision is assisted by detailed definitions and a set of examples rated by several expert raters, and these are used in the training process. For more complete descriptions of the scales and their use, see Klein et al. (1969, 1986).

Reliability for our application of the scales to Group A was established using cross-tabulation to compare item-by-item ratings across raters, yielding 67% complete agreement (Beck et al., 1986). Cohen's kappa was also calculated and equaled .57.

The Experiencing Scales have been found to be related to outcome and to be related primarily to the cognitive dimension of the psychotherapy process (Klein et al., 1986).

The theory from which the Experiencing Scale was derived indicates that experiencing level should correlate with successful therapy outcomes and with personality variables related to the ability for self-reflection or expression. Studies by many different investigators using the Experiencing Scale in a wide variety of studies have shown that although experiencing level varies within any individual and is responsive to various settings and therapeutic interventions, higher levels of experiencing, especially after the first few sessions of therapy, are related to better outcome. Studies indicate that experiencing is more closely related to introspection and cognitive complexity than with any particular affect or level of affective distress, suggesting that the Experiencing Scale is a measure of self-reflection or self-observational style (Klein et al., 1986). The process of self-reflection in verbal behavior that is represented by the Experiencing Scale is not always expected to be present or expressed in the same manner.

The Normative-Organizational/Personal Exploration (NO/PE) Scale and the Topic-Oriented Group Focus Unitizing Procedure

Normative-Organizational/Personal Exploration (NO/PE) Scale

The NO/PE Scale was designed to facilitate the observation and measurement of the focus of group's attention either to group-level issues of structural development or the exploration of the members' personal issues (Dugo & Beck, 1983). The rating is based on the manifest verbal behavior of all group members within the unit of interaction being rated. Our application of the scale has included the development and use of a special unitizing procedure, Topic-Oriented Group Focus Unitizing Procedure (Beck et al., 1986). This procedure, described in detail later in this section, defines a unit of interaction based on a topic being raised, focused on, and elaborated or sustained for varying lengths of time until a new topic emerges beginning a different unit. Once a transcript has been utilized, the NO/PE Scale is used to rate each unit. The NO/PE Scale rating is based on the entire unit. In our study two raters were used in the application of the NO/PE Scale. Reliability for the rating of the topic-oriented group focus units with the NO/PE Scale was computed with Pearson product–moment correlations, and the results ranged from .80 to .84 (Dugo & Beck, 1983).

The categories of the NO/PE scale are as follows:

1. *Mainly normative–organizational concerns:* This category is used when the focus within the unit being rated is on guidelines for how the group should operate or accomplish its task. This includes matters such as generating norms for behavior in the group, clarifying tolerance for differences, or creating pressure to conform.

   Example:

   Pat: Oftentimes when I'm, uh, with others and in this group, both last week and this week, I've felt like saying things but, uh, I always hold because I feel like I'm going to, uh, to hurt somebody. Now, for instance, now I was getting real annoyed with you . . .

   Joe: (Laugh).

   Pat: Because I don't think that's what we're here for. We don't wanna, er, at least my view, uh, I don't wanna talk about you know what's available, I wanna talk about things that maybe will help me. But anyway I . . .

Alice: Mm hm.

Pat: I think the thing I was trying to say was, uh, I'd like to feel free to do, to to respond and, uh, I feel like I'm—I'm asking permission in some way, or uh . . .

Helen: Mm.

Pat: . . . saying, "Well now don't." If I do something that hurts you I don't mean to er, well maybe I mean to, but (laughter) I don't want—I don't want to scare anybody and particularly you because I know that you haven't . . .

Joe: You can call me Joe (laughter).

Pat: That's fair. Uh, I know that you—that you haven't had much therapy or maybe, that's no criteria of anybody's courage particularly I guess but, um, I know you, uh, kinda don't know the ropes and, uh, so I feel like I have to be more patient with you but, uh, I don't feel it.

Alice: Are you saying someth-, yeah, are you saying something like in this particular case kind of stopping yourself from saying . . .

Pat: Yeah, and I'm always wound up inside, you know, cuz I—I, I'm feel like I'm controlling myself . . .

Alice: Mm hm.

Helen: And this is the kind of thing that you want to do, especially in this group.

Pat: Yeah, I—I'd like to be, uh, feel like I could react spontaneously and then try to see, well, what is it that's making me this way or makes me feel . . .

Alice: Yeah, you get so busy holding down the feeling that then you get all tied around it.

Pat: Yeah.

Alice: Uh huh, uh huh.

Greg: That's funny, I—I go—I—my feelings were somewhat the same. Uh, also sort of a fear of—of—of talking much too much and sort of—sort of—disrupting the group or fouling things up. Uh, all which makes me wonder if —if maybe we aren't a bunch of people sitting around feeling we're afraid to hurt somebody else and maybe partly —partly this is a fear of hurting ourselves, too. I mean, you know, I mean, this defensive attitude, it sorta works both ways, and you try to think, "Well I'm—I don't want to hurt Brad's feelings over there" and maybe (laugh), there's—there's some—something, uh . . . but you're actually—you're actually protecting him; this might be a rationalization partly, too.

Pat: Mm hm.

Brad: Oh I don't carry, uh, I have occasion sometimes to walk around the streets late at night. I have bought a walking stick which looks very fashionable if—if I were a hundred years old but, uh ... (laughter) ... or if I was living in the last century ... um, I could wang it on somebody's head, but I don't carry a knife or a gun, I wouldn't know what to do with it anyway. But, uh, if you pull a knife on somebody, and he has one too and he can use it better'n you can, why you're in trouble, real trouble. And I suppose ...

Helen: You're making an analogy to what he's saying.

Brad: I suppose. The same thing applies here that if you take the gloves off well um, it could be pretty damagin' for all, but I suppose that the whole point of the group process will gradually wear off the reserve and, you get mutual trust and, and uh, if not acceptance at least, uh, you know everybody ... you learn to take it or (laughter) ...

Alice: Mm hm, mm hm. I—I kinda feel to what, uh, Greg was saying was somehow more, uh, what can I say, I feel a little like you're saying, "Oh yeah of course it's like that, I mean, of course that's why you're afraid," uh, and I kinda felt like what Greg was saying wasn't really that obvious to him. Maybe I'm wrong, I mean I felt a little like you were saying, "Maybe when you're saying you're afraid to—to hurt someone or you're afraid to say something cuz you think it might hurt them what you're also saying is because if they get hurt they'll get mad and then they'll hurt you back, and you don't want to get hurt yourself."

Greg: Yeah, a—a—and this may be obvious on an intellectual level, I don't think it's always obvious, on an emotional level.

Alice: Yeah. (Beck, 1970, pp. 39–41)

2. *Equally normative–organizational and personal concerns:* This rating is used for a unit in which the group's focus appears to be equally addressing both the exploration of an individual members' personal issues and group-level normative issues.

Example:

Brad: But you've never broken down any doors yourself, I mean figurative ...

Diane: Not until late, not until the last ten years. But, uh, you mean figuratively? I mean literally. (laughter) I never broke a door, but I picked up the plates and threw them, which is just as good. But I couldn't do that until, uh, oh maybe as a teenager was the first time, but since then I've done it a few more times. I have this feeling everybody oughta have a room where they can throw things. (Ended with a laugh)

Alice: Oh.

Brad: Like for instance here.

Diane: You mean literally?

Martha: He's thinking of . . .

Brad: I mean more figuratively.

Alice: Here in this group you mean, is that what you mean?

Brad: Yeah, I mean listen I'm not being—

Diane: Yeah, I know, I—I guess what . . . what I hear you asking me is, yeah, do I wanta throw plates here? I don't think I do. I might be kidding myself, but I think what I wanta do here is find out, um . . .

Alice: May I come in? Cuz its gonna get lost . . . I couldn't help feeling . . . (Beck, 1970, p. 104)

3. *Mainly personal exploration issues:* This category is used to rate units in which the group's focus is primarily on helping a member explore his or her personal issues, whether to attain insight, clarify or define a problem, or work on change.

Example:

Alice: Your father, you never, you never knew how he would react to what you were feeling, maybe.

Diane: I knew only one reaction, if there was any re-action. It was just always one which was violent. Otherwise there was none.

Alice: Sounds like if he heard you which was (Diane laughs) to react, he reacted by batting, in essence.

Greg: For—for that very reason you—you maintained a sort of a mild, non-putting forth yourself toward him most of the time, I take it.

Diane: Toward him.

Greg: Yeah.

Diane: I wouldn't dare be anything else.

Helen: Are you suggesting that—that's a kind of pattern she . . .

Greg: Yeah.

Helen: She holds . . .

Greg: I—I—I—I—

Alice: Well, you never know when somebody's gonna bat

you because you know there's at least one person you know
who will really bat you one.
    Diane: (laughs) Yeah. (Beck, 1970, pp. 105–106)

The Topic-Oriented Group Focus Unitizing Procedure

Most unitizing methods currently used to study group process implement an arbitrary standard of time such as minutes or pages of transcript or are based on individual statements or bursts of speech. The Topic-Oriented Group Focus Unitizing Procedure was developed to allow unitizing based on the group-as-a-whole level of process. Our aim was to facilitate the exploration and testing of concepts of group development and other aspects of group process. This procedure defines units that are process oriented, group centered, determined by manifest verbal content, and have a semblance of wholeness of beginning and ending.

The task of the unitizer is to define units of interaction in the context of the group interaction. A new unit may begin when a new topic, or a new idea building on a previous topic, is raised. To meet the criteria for being a unit, another group member must then share in focusing on this topic and help sustain the focus with clarification or elaboration until the unit is ended by being brought to a close or by the interruption and diversion of the group's attention as a new topic is raised.

The unitizer notes the boundaries of the unit by identifying the beginning and ending statements and writes a brief statement of one sentence or less describing the manifest content of the unit. The unitizing decision is made in the context of the data, taking into account the two prior units and their boundaries as well as the material immediately following and beginning a new unit. Two raters undertake the unitizing procedure separately. A process of comparison then occurs, and a consensus is reached through discussion in regard to places where the unitizers identified different unit boundaries.

To assess the reliability of the unitizing procedure, one must compare each unitizer's separate decisions regarding units and boundaries with the final list arrived at after consensus is reached about differences. Two matters are assessed: (a) the boundaries of the units and (b) whether a rater first saw one unit or two compared with the final list. The percentage of agreement between each rater's identification of boundaries and the final list ranged from 98.2% to 99.9% (Dugo & Beck, 1983). The percentage of agreement regarding whether a unit was identified or not as compared with the final list ranged from 83% to 100%. Although the beginnings and endings of units are rated consistently, one rater may identify two units within the same boundaries that another rater has used to identify one larger unit.

Strengths and Limitations

When used together, the NO/PE Scale and the Topic-Oriented Group Focus Unitizing Procedure provide a unique system of observation and measurement. The units are defined in a manner determined by the process of interaction. A topic must be raised by one member and focused on or elaborated on by others, or with their assistance. The units are determined by the group's focus rather than by that of an individual member, and they are based on the manifest content of the verbal interaction. They are to be as free as possible from inferences about underlying motivation. The rating categories of the NO/PE Scale allow the group's process relative to normative or personal issues to be identified and for aspects of these processes to be compared. The NO/PE Scale provides a means to observe how the group copes with normative issues over time and finds a way of working that allows the task at hand, personal exploration and change, to be addressed.

The Speech Behavior Coding System

The Speech Behavior Coding System measures several aspects of behavior among group members in ways that are relatively simple to quantify. We sought to measure aspects of interaction that, although easily defined and measured, would together be useful methods for testing some hypotheses about group processes (Eng & Beck, 1982). The measures include the following:

1. *Length of statement:* the number of words, pauses, laughs, and other nonfluencies counted for each statement.
2. *Speaker:* an identification of the group member making each statement. This identification is made in this case by the transcriber of the audiotapes, who becomes familiar with each member's voice during the work of transcription.
3. *Spoken to:* an identification of the person spoken to for each statement. A statement can be rated as being addressed to the whole group or to an indiviudal group member or several members.
4. *We group:* the number of times the pronoun "we" is used to refer to the whole group or a subgroup within the group.

The behavior of all the group members is rated, but various subsets of data may be chosen as appropriate to explore various hypotheses. The statement is used as the basic unit of observation and rating, but data may be summed for units of various length as determined by the research questions. As with our other measures, the manifest aspects of verbal communication are used in making the ratings. Some degree of inference is involved in assessing the term *we group* and in making judgments about who is spoken to. A set of guidelines has been developed by the researchers to assist with rating these aspects of interaction. They are rated by more than one rater, sometimes an individual who has acquired an understanding of the interaction by working on the rating task of one of the other measurements (e.g., the Experiencing Scale or the NO/PE Scale).

These measures are strong in their objective and simple definitions, ease of measurement, and independence from the concepts that may be tested or explored with their use (Beck et al., 1986).

METHODOLOGY FOR ANALYSIS

For the rating process, the statement was used as the unit for measure in our applications of the Hostility/Support Scale, the Experiencing Scale, and the speech behavior measures. For our application of the NO/PE Scale, the unit for rating was defined by the Topic-Oriented Group Focus Unitizing Procedure.

In summarizing our ratings for analysis, we frequently use the page as our summarizing unit and make comparisons across measures based on the average rating per page for each scale. We have also used the session or phase as a summarizing unit, and we also plan to use the topic-oriented units as summarizing units.

To compare several of our measures across time with frequent points of measurement, we have used the page as the summarizing unit and applied a mathematical moving average to extract and demonstrate strong trends in the data (Beaton & Tukey, 1974). We have used regression analysis to study changes in experiencing level across time in the group (Lewis, Stone, & Beck, 1992) and z tests of proportions to compare measurements of data with the Experiencing Scale and the NO/PE Scale (Beck et al., 1986).

PREVIOUS RESEARCH WITH THE SYSTEM

In our study, to identify phase boundaries and phase-related developmental processes, we applied the measures described in this chapter to three outpatient psychotherapy groups conducted at the University of Chicago Counseling Center. The groups were time limited and met for 15–20 sessions each. Two of the groups were judged to have a satisfactory developmental process, and one was judged to have a problem in the developmental process. The study was exploratory in nature, having as a goal the development of a methodology for the study of developmental process. Through the study, we defined three criteria to identify the boundary between Phases II and III (Beck et al., 1986). The criteria were the following:

1. A change in the content of members' responses to the Scapegoat Leader clinically identified in each group, from mostly critical to mostly supportive.
2. A change in the focus of the group, from mostly normative issues to primarily exploration of personal issues.
3. A peak in the group-as-a-whole level of experiencing relative to the ongoing experiencing level of the group as a whole in these early phases.

It was possible to identify the phase boundary between Phase II and Phase III in two of the groups. In the third group, the criteria were not met (Beck et al., 1986). Figure 9.1 illustrates the shift from Phase II to Phase III in Group A during Session 3.

The first change, measured by the Hostility/Support Scale, was expected on the basis of the hypothesis of a change from a period of tension and discomfort coping with anger and negative feelings in Phase II to a period of more positive feeling and mutual support in Phase III. Because the Scapegoat Leader was hypothesized to be an object of focus in working out normative issues in Phase II, we chose the responses of other members to this one individual to examine this aspect of the process.

The change from a focus on normative–organizational issues to a focus on personal exploration was expected to be facilitated in Phase III based on the normative work done in Phase II. In Phase III the group achieved an initial basis to focus on task or work issues more freely; in a psychotherapy group, this means the exploration of personal issues.

The criteria for the peak in Experiencing Scale ratings for the group as a whole was defined in the course of the exploratory study. Initially, we expected a simple rise in the level of experiencing as the group proceeded to work on personal issues in Phase III. However, at this initial stage of the psychotherapy process, the level of the self-exploration process was still a modest one. The highest levels of experiencing involving the group as a whole, when measured with the moving average technique that eliminates or minimizes some of the variance, occurred when the group members were working together on aspects of process related to normative issues. One such peak occurred at the shift from Phase II to Phase III.

The resolution of normative issues in Phase II was expected to allow a focus on the tasks of self-disclosure and self-exploration in Phase III. The Experiencing Scale was able to identify a process within Phase III in which each group member in effect took a turn at an initial period of self-disclosure and individual work, with the support of other members. The ratings of each individual member on the Client Experiencing Scale were

HOSTILITY/SUPPORT SCALE: MEMBERS' STATEMENTS TO SCAPEGOAT LEADER

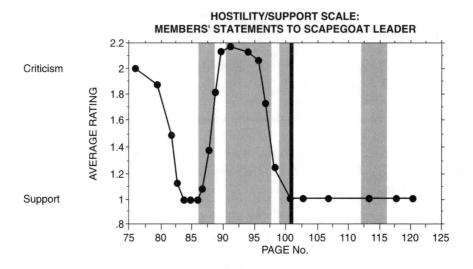

GROUP-AS-A-WHOLE EXPERIENCING SCALE

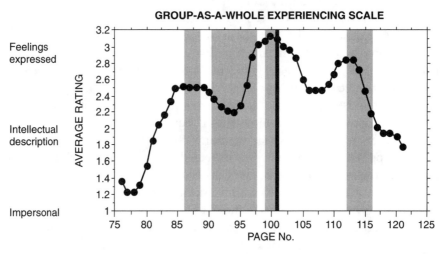

NORMATIVE–ORGANIZATIONAL/PERSONAL EXPLORATION SCALE

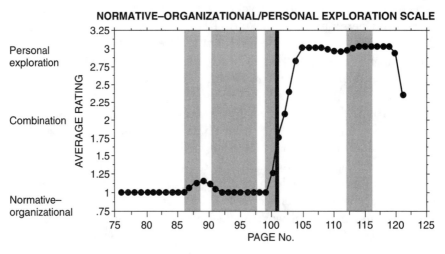

used to identify this pattern of process of individual work in Phase III (Lewis & Beck, 1983).

Using the ratings based on the Experiencing and the NO/PE scales, we further defined a dimension of the developmental process. An analysis was conducted to determine the frequency with which peaks in the experiencing level of the group as a whole would coincide with shifts in the group focus as measured by the NO/PE Scale. It was found that the z test for proportions was significant at or above the .01 level for each of the three groups studied (Beck et al., 1986). Figure 9.2 illustrates data from these two measures applied to the first five sessions of Group A. These two variables identify times in the group process when structural issues are articulated and linked to the process of work on personal issues. The two variables together identify periods when group members address interaction within the group in a highly personal manner and try to understand its meaning. These periods identify the integration of a shared understanding of an aspect of group process, which may facilitate further work (Lewis, 1985a).

The participation of individual group members during the periods defined as a peak in experiencing of the group as a whole or as a shift in group focus was examined in more detail. Members who were clinically judged to be filling one of the roles of distributed leadership as defined by Beck's (1974a, 1981a, 1981b) theory were found to be active participants in the periods defined more often than were nonleaders. However, incidents of peaks and shifts occurring together that were identified as phase shifts were characterized by the participation of most or all of the group members. This further defines the manner in which the developmental process is likely to proceed: Several group members are active in the initial work on developmental issues, but then there is a consensus involving the whole group about normative structure (Beck, Dugo, Eng, Lewis, & Peters, 1983; Lewis, Dugo, & Beck, 1981).

The speech behavior measures were used to further examine the par-

---

Figure 9.1. Hostility/Support Scale, Group-as-a-Whole Experiencing Scale, and Normative–Organizational/Personal Exploration Scale ratings are shown for Session 3 of Group A. The data are based on a moving average formula (Beaton & Tukey, 1974). During the first half of Session 3, the group is completing the work of Phase II. The phase shift occurs during segment 3 at page 100. The data illustrate changes that occur in the period of shift from Phase II to Phase III of group development. Criticism of the Scapegoat Leader ends, and the group's focus shifts to personal issues. The shift is accompanied by a peak in the level of experiencing, as an aspect of norms are integrated among the members, and a shared understanding of the group process is formed. The shaded bands on the graph show the location of each of the four segments of interaction within Session 3. The end of segment 3 marks the end of Phase II. Following segment 3, Phase III begins.

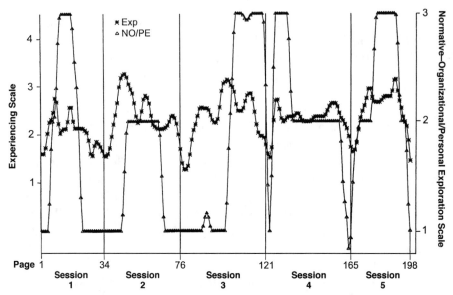

Figure 9.2. Group-as-a-Whole Experiencing Scale ratings and Normative–Organizational/Personal Exploration Scale ratings are shown for Sessions 1–5 of Group A. The data are based on a moving average formula (Beaton & Tukey, 1974). Changes or shifts in the focus of the group, from normative issues to personal exploration or vice versa, are often accompanied by peaks in the experiencing level of the interaction of the group as a whole. At these times an integrative process occurs among the members that facilitates further work.

ticipation of group members, with particular attention to the participation of those members filling leadership roles. An estimate of verbal participation, based on a count of the words spoken by each member, a measure of who speaks and who is spoken to, and a measure of how frequently the word *we* is used in reference to "the group" were used. In this exploratory study, the Scapegoat Leader was addressed more by other members in Phase II than in Phase III and spoke more in Phase II than in Phase III. The group members also used the word *we* in reference to the group more often in Phase II than in Phase III. These findings are consistent with expectations based on the role of the Scapegoat Leader in the early normative development of the group and the strong focus of the group on normative issues in Phase II (Beck et al., 1986).

The Sociometric Test of Emergent Leadership

Based on Beck's (1974a, 1981a, 1981b) theory of group development, a sociometric test was designed for identifying the four emergent leadership roles in psychotherapy groups (Beck & Peters, 1981; Brusa et al., 1994; Peters & Beck, 1982). The process of emerging leadership roles is similar from one group to another and addresses the creation and evolution of group structure. It is not determined by the specific personalities or therapeutic issues of the participants, although the manner in which these group-level issues is expressed is influenced by personality, by the substantive content that is discussed in the group, and by the level of problem-solving skills of all the participants, particularly the four leaders.

There is now a 10-question test available that identifies the leaders and the nonleader members with a high degree of reliability (Brusa & Beck, 1997).

All the steps in the design of this test involved factor analyses, with the results always showing two factors with most of the questions loading on Factor 1. A plot of all questions involved in the analysis on Factor 1 by Factor 2 showed a circumplex arrangement of the questions. All steps also involved stepwise discriminant analyses, which can be used to select a smaller number of questions based on using those questions that were most powerful in separating the five roles. For the final set of questions, 87% of the variance was accounted for by the first two of four functions. When these two functions are plotted, they show each of the four roles in a separate quadrant with the centroid for the nonleader member role falling close to the center.

APPLICATION OF THE SYSTEM OF ANALYSIS TO GROUP A, SESSION 3

To illustrate the measures, we have applied them to the sample segments of data within Session 3 of Group A. For segments of interaction have been chosen for this illustration. Tables 9.1–9.5 contain detailed information about the ratings of the data in these segments.

In the first segment, Units 64–66, the group members focused on Joe's experience of the last session. Martha began by asking if he got across what he wanted to say. Brad described what he imagined it was like for Joe and recognized Joe's effort to work things out only to have his attempt backfire. Pat asked Joe directly if he felt irritated with her, and Joe said he got the impression that it was he who was irritating Pat. After this exchange of views, Joe got into a monologue to try to explain his point of view of how people are different and how this can be troublesome. Pat and others interrupted to ask Joe again if he was irritated with Pat. Joe answered yes and wanted to hear more about Pat's feelings, too. Pat identified her own difficulty with what she called blurting things out, seemingly because of space Joe took up talking. All of the units in this segment were rated as having to do mostly with normative–organizational issues.

Joe was the most verbally active member in this segment. He spoke 32.7% of the total words. Joe was also the group member most frequently spoken to. About one third of the statements initiated in this segment were directed at Joe. Joe and Pat were the two group members who interacted with each other the most. Together, they accounted for 58% of the words spoken in these units. Most of the statements addressed to Joe were rated as neutral or supportive on the Hostility/Support Scale. Pat, however, expressed criticism to Joe in 2 statements.

Looking at the Experiencing Scale ratings for this segment, all the averages for each individual member and for the group as a whole were between 2.0 and 3.0. This indicates that group members were both describing their view of events and articulating some specific feelings and reactions to them. The averages of statements rated on the Client scale were close to 3.0. In this segment, the statements of Joe and Pat were rated on the Client scale because they were engaged in articulating the feelings that occurred in them toward one another while interacting in the group. Pat took the initiative in this regard by exploring and stating her own feelings. When she engaged Joe, she showed her interest in understanding him at a level comparable to herself. Other members addressed the issue in a supportive manner, showing concern and interest in Joe's feelings, but Pat was willing to address the specific point in interacting with Joe that evoked irritation in her and to look further into what that meant for her. We think that being able to interact with a Scapegoat Leader in this manner is one of the steps in resolving Phase II issues.

The second sample segment, Unit 69, began with Diane announcing that she had issues with Joe, stating that she and Joe were on different levels, and that she could not meet Joe on his. She saw his level as superficial and externally focused, and she experienced this as Joe "closing

TABLE 9.1
Summary of Data for Units 64–66

| | Experiencing Scale (Average Ratings) | | Speech Behavior Ratings | |
	Client scale	Therapist scale	Words Spoken (%)	Statements Received
Member				
Greg (EL)			0	0
Joe (SL)	2.88	3.0	32.7	13
Martha (DL)		2.0	5.9	1
Brad		3.0	11.4	1
Diane			0	0
Pat	3.0	3.0	25.9	7
Therapist				
Alice (TL)		2.57	21.6	8
Helen (cotherapist)		2.50	2.5	1
Group				2

Note. The units in this segment were rated as having to do with normative–organizational issues. Most statements made to the Scapegoat Leader were rated "supportive" on the Hostility/Support Scale. The average rating of all statements rated on the Experiencing Scale was 2.78. EL = Emotional Leader; SL = Scapegoat Leader; DL = Defiant Leader; TL = Task Leader.

TABLE 9.2
Summary of Data for Unit 69

	Experiencing Scale (Average Ratings)		Speech Behavior Ratings	
	Client scale	Therapist scale	Words Spoken (%)	Statements Received
Member				
Greg (EL)	2.0	3.0	0.5	1
Joe (SL)	2.25		10.6	10
Martha (DL)	2.0	2.2	6.5	9
Brad		3.75	10.9	2
Diane	2.41	2.0	44.6	49
Pat		3.0	0.7	1
Therapist				
Alice (TL)		2.48	17.7	19
Helen (cotherapist)		2.50	8.5	23
Group				10

Note. The unit in this segment was rated as having to do with normative–organizational issues. Most statements made to the Scapegoat Leader were rated as expressing criticism on the Hostility/Support Scale. The average rating of all statements rated on the Experiencing Scale was 2.46. EL = Emotional Leader; SL = Scapegoat Leader; DL = Defiant Leader; TL = Task Leader.

the door" on her. The therapists, and another member, Martha, tried to suggest that they thought Joe was trying to tell some important things about himself, but Diane continued to say that she got irritated. Joe tried to explain the problem by saying that he and Diane had different personalities. Diane remained adamant, however, that she could not accept Joe.

TABLE 9.3
Summary of Data for Units 71–73

	Experiencing Scale (Average Ratings)		Speech Behavior Ratings	
	Client scale	Therapist scale	Words Spoken (%)	Statements Received
Member				
Greg (EL)	3.4	2.5	7.6	2
Joe (SL)		2.0	1.5	0
Martha (DL)	3.6	3.2	38.0	8
Brad		3.0	16.2	0
Diane	3.14		27.8	11
Pat			0	0
Therapist				
Alice (TL)		3.0	8.9	5
Helen (cotherapist)			0	1
Group				7

Note. The units in this segment were rated as having to do with normative–organizational issues. The average rating of all statements rated on the Experiencing Scale was 3.14. EL = Emotional Leader; SL = Scapegoat Leader; DL = Defiant Leader; TL = Task Leader.

TABLE 9.4
Summary of Data for Units 82–84

	Experiencing Scale (Average Ratings)		Speech Behavior Ratings	
	Client scale	Therapist scale	Words Spoken (%)	Statements Received
Member				
Greg (EL)	2.0		3.3	3
Joe (SL)			0	0
Martha (DL)	3.29	2.33	53.2	31
Brad			0	0
Diane	3.07	4.0	30.3	28
Pat			0	0
Therapist				
Alice (TL)		2.43	10.6	10
Helen (cotherapist)		4.0	2.6	2
Group				3

Note. The units in this segment were rated as having to do with personal exploration. The Scapegoat Leader was not addressed in this segment. The average rating of all statements rated on the Experiencing Scale was 2.96. EL = Emotional Leader; SL = Scapegoat Leader; DL = Defiant Leader; TL = Task Leader.

This unit was rated as having to do mostly with normative–organizational issues.

In the second segment, Diane was the most verbally active member, speaking about 44.6% of the time. Although most of her statements were about Joe and her feelings of irritation toward him, Diane was primarily engaged in talking about this with other group members. Diane addressed the group leaders 31 times in this segment and addressed Martha 8 times,

TABLE 9.5
Hostility/Support Scale: Statements Made by Members to Scapegoat Leader Joe

	Segment 1, Units 64–66 Rating			Segment 2, Unit 69 Rating		
Group member	1	2	3	1	2	3
Greg						
Martha	1					
Brad	1				1	1
Diane				1	3	1
Pat	3	1	1			
Total	5	1	1	2	4	1

Note. Rating Category 1 = statement expresses acceptance, agreement, or neutrality. Rating Category 2 = statement expresses disagreement or mild negativity or criticism. Rating Category 3 = statement expresses openly negative, angry, or aggressive feelings. In Segment 1, most statements addressed to Joe were suportive. In Segment 2, most statements to Joe were critical. In Segments 3 and 4, no statements were addressed to Joe.

but she addressed Joe directly only 5 times. Diane was the person most frequently addressed, spoken to by other members 49 times.

Statements made to the Scapegoat Leader, Joe, by group members other than the therapists were rated on the Hostility/Support Scale (see Table 9.5). Brad and Diane addressed Joe. Five statements were rated as expressing criticism or negative comments, and 2 were rated as supportive.

The average ratings of statements rated on the Client Experiencing Scale in this segment remained near Level 2. The members were looking at events going on outside themselves and had limited comments on their feelings and reactions. The highest Experiencing Scale ratings in this segment occurred in statements made by group members but were rated on the Therapist Experiencing Scale, as they responded to Diane and tried to facilitate an understanding that reflected the feelings and reactions of all who were involved, particularly Joe. The efforts of the therapists to respond to Diane remained close to the Experiencing Scale level at which she herself was working. Other members, however, went beyond an intellectual manner of trying to influence Diane to one in which feelings were pinpointed.

This segment was another part of the resolution of scapegoating that was taking place. Members compared perspectives, challenging and attempting to influence one another. One member, Diane, was still insisting that the Scapegoat Leader, Joe, change his style of communicating, whereas other group members articulated a more empathic understanding of him.

The interpersonal struggles among Joe, Diane, and Pat were a vehicle for forming group norms about the contents to be addressed in the group, the proper style in which to work, the methods by which conflict could be addressed and coped with, and how problems could be worked with and resolved.

After this second sample segment, Unit 70 was initiated by Brad, who observed that Joe had probably revealed the most so far of any of them "partly because we keep after him," (Beck, 1970, p. 97) and confronted the group with the question "Why are we after him?" (Beck, 1970, p. 97). Other members joined in, acknowledging that they were "jumping on Joe," and Martha proposed that they were afraid to "jump in" (Beck, 1970, p. 98) with their own personal issues.

In the third sample segment, which included Units 71–73, the group members explored anxious feelings related to the anticipation of self-disclosure in the group and the risk of rejection that was involved. Diane reported thinking of things to tell the group as she wrote her journal but not having nerve enough to do so. She stated that she had not "taken a chance yet." Martha vividly described feelings she recalled of being rebuked by a different group. Brad remarked that some of the group members were wanting to pick a fight, and several members acknowledged this feeling. The units were all rated as normative–organizational.

In this segment, more statements were addressed to the whole group, 7 statements in all. In the first sample segment, 2 of 33 statements, or 6% of the statements, were judged to be spoken to the group as a whole rather than to any particular member. In the second segment, 10 of 124 statements were rated as being spoken to the whole group. In the third segment, 7 of 34 statements, or 20% of the statements, were rated as being spoken to the whole group. The group's attention was directed away from Joe.

Looking at the percentage of verbal participation of the Scapegoat Leader, Joe, across the sample segments, we observed a decline from 32.7% in the first sample segment to 10.6% in the second sample segment and 1.5% in the third segment. The group members had begun to focus on the members as a whole rather than on Joe and how they reacted to him.

In the third segment, Martha and Diane were the most active members, speaking more than 65% of the total words. They were relating personal experiences in support of the insight that they were afraid to begin self-disclosure because of the risk of rejection. The Experiencing Scale ratings for these units were the highest of the four samples we are comparing. The predominance of Level 3 ratings indicates that the group members maintained a level of awareness of specific feelings. Client Experiencing Scale average ratings of above 3.0 indicate that self-exploration moves beyond the description of feelings in the immediate situation to the group members linking the current experience to more general aspects of their inner life. They focus more intensely on their feelings so that the quality of their feelings or reactions are the main focus, with description of events playing a lesser role.

These units are an example of a shift from focusing on Joe as the problem to forming a contract to become more vulnerable with one another. In this segment, the group built an understanding together, associating to one another's thoughts and feelings rather than needing to contrast, correct, or differentiate their sense of self from one another.

In the fourth segment, Units 82–84, Martha was exploring her relationship with her parents, how it affected her ability to become independent, and how frightening independence was to her. Diane and Greg shared their own version of struggles with independence in their families. The therapists facilitated the articulation of these points of view.

Martha and Diane were the main speakers, together accounting for 80% of the total words spoken in the segment. They were also spoken to the most. Martha received 31 statements and Diane 28 statements. Martha and Diane addressed each other 25 times as they facilitated each other's participation. The therapists played a supportive role, but the frequency with which other group members addressed them remained low; 12 of the statements in this segment were addressed to the therapists. The group members continued to address one another more directly in a supportive and facilitative manner. Joe neither spoke nor was spoken to in this segment. The group members were able to interact and explore personal issues without using Joe as a vehicle for the process.

Martha, who was the main speaker, worked as a client at the average level of 3.29 on the Experiencing Scale. The average Experiencing Scale ratings were somewhat lower than those in the previous sample segment. This is a sample of group process in an early stage of self-exploration of the members. The members were sharing personal history that contributed a descriptive quality to their interaction. They described themselves from an inner stance in regard to their life outside the group. Once they had achieved an ability to show awareness and understanding of one another's feelings, this initial level of self-disclosure became possible. The focus at this time seemed to be information sharing about personal histories.

This segment contained units that were rated as focused on personal exploration issues. The focus of the group was on two members' issues and maintained the direction of self-exploration that was chosen by the main participants.

RELATIONSHIP BETWEEN THE RESEARCH AND THE THEORY

The application of the measures to the three groups in the pilot study provides information that facilitates the refinement of the theory of group development, adding detail to the understanding of the early phases, the phase shifts themselves, and how some aspects of structure are created during these processes. For example, based on the observation that there is input from all or almost all group members during critical periods of resolution of group-level issues such as phase shifts, we have an increased understanding of the role of involvement of each member and of the integration of perceptions about developmental processes in the group.

We also have more specific ideas regarding some of the course of events or typical processes within the early phases. For instance, we observed that in Phase III, an initial period of work on personal issues occurred in an atmosphere of careful listening, during which each member seemed to "take a turn." During this time members began to facilitate one another's work on individual issues and to build on one another's personal work. We observed that during Phase III in two groups in our pilot study there was a short period of return to work on normative issues, during which the conflict with the Scapegoat Leader was revisited. During this period of normative work the norms developed during Phase II, and the insights gained regarding the members' feelings and their roles, were tested. These kinds of observations allow for further empirical testing or investigation and provide information that can facilitate the therapist's task in assisting the group with its therapeutic work and developmental processes in clinical practice.

Clinical Insights

Our work has led us to think carefully about the ways in which the structural process of group development may affect the tasks of psychotherapy. From our analyses of the early phases of group development, we have learned several things that have contributed to our own leadership of and teaching about psychotherapy groups. One area in which the research has informed practice has to do with understanding the significance of phase-relevant tasks and the knowledge that some tasks are crucial to the progress of the group in developing an enabling environment for change (Beck, 1987). During Phase I, for example, it is important for each member of the group to identify at least one other person with whom they feel they share some similar issues. Those who do not frequently drop out. One intervention that a leader can make is to monitor that process during the initial session of the entry of a new member and to facilitate the articulation and acknowledgment of this kind of association. The task of forming a connection with another member of the group in Phase I is one aspect of forming a therapeutic alliance. This early task in psychotherapy treatment has significant therapeutic value in itself and facilitates future work. For patients with severe and chronic psychotic disorders, becoming part of a group, and forming an affiliation or attachment, is a valuable step that can begin to ameliorate isolation, experience of rejection, and self-doubt.

The tasks inherent in Phase II—managing conflict, allowing for differences, and coping with frustration and anxiety—are essential to enabling the group to work together productively, but they may also facilitate an individual's ability to begin to cope with these kinds of inner dynamics in a less limiting and confining way (Lewis, 1985b). Conflicts and difficult feelings begin to become something to understand and act on, not just react to. During Phase II it is an extremely important task for the group to resolve its competitive feelings and to let go of scapegoating as a defense mechanism. For this to happen efficiently, the leader can help identify the underlying anxiety that group members feel during this powerful structure-building phase. When this resolution occurs, the group is able to move on to a therapeutic work phase, Phase III, during which it is possible to address anger and resentment toward current and historical figures (especially authority figures) in a context of group support and expectation that these are feelings to be examined, not just acted out. One of the tasks of Phase III is to address the historical issues that have brought group members to their current situations. Traditional client–therapist formal and informal roles predominate in this phase, giving the leader the opportunity to introduce strong values regarding the therapeutic work.

In studying the development of facilitative behavior among members, using the Experiencing Scale, we have noted that some of the strengths of group psychotherapy are to afford an individual the opportunity to listen to the work of others, and to experience his or her ability to think about and respond to the dynamics of others, and that this allows an individual to form a clearer sense of what is important in the therapeutic process. In our case study, group members were active in the process of facilitation and showed an increasing ability to respond therapeutically during both initial and more advanced therapeutic processes (Lewis, Beck, & Stone, 1999).

Implications for Further Study

The perspectives that the group development theory and this set of measures contribute to the understanding of group process has implications for a number of issues that are of interest to the clinical community of group leaders. For example, coleadership is a topic that is being reexplored (Dugo & Beck, 1991; Roller & Nelson, 1991), and it would be of great interest to look at the ways in which coleaders complement, reinforce, or contradict each other during the conduct of a therapy group. The Group Development Process Analysis Measures could clarify whether one leader tends to guide the group into personal exploration or group-as-a-whole normative–organizational work more than the other leader.

As the case study in this book indicates, short-term groups are capable of progressing through a number of phases of group development, even through all nine phases described by this theory. However, we know from our clinical work that rapid progress through the phases is not necessarily a desirable goal for leaders or for clients. A group may be more successful in producing client change by spending a great deal of time in certain early phases such as Phase III or Phase IV than by trying to progress further. The Group Development Process Analysis Measures could contribute to the understanding of how groups help individuals to change if there were a study that looked intensively at the relationships among individual developmental issues, leadership behavior, and the quality of work done by groups in each of the phases of group development. The same framework could be used to study therapeutic process in groups of different client populations defined by diagnoses.

The measures may also be used to study other pertinent issues in group dynamics and group psychotherapy practice, either by themselves or in conjunction with other measures. For example, Whitaker's (1985) theoretical concepts of group focal conflicts and restrictive or enabling solutions to those conflicts are now assessed with a qualitative analysis. Qualitative analyses of several groups might be the basis for studying the difference between restrictive solutions (i.e., ones that result in norms that create a sort of safety at the cost of avoiding pertinent fears and anxieties) and enabling solutions (i.e., ones that facilitate work by addressing and acknowledging fears). The NO/PE Scale can assess whether the group is focused on the whole-group level or on individual issues, and the Experiencing Scale can assess the level of work at which the group explores group-level issues and the quality of personal work facilitated by the group members' efforts to address group-level issues. These instruments, together with others such as the Group Emotionality Rating System, might produce a more detailed understanding of critical aspects of group work and of how a therapist can intervene to facilitate the alleviation of reactive fears, so that restrictive norms can be discarded and enabling solutions formed. The actions of the therapist and the group members and their roles can be compared using qualitative analyses as a guide to successful and unsuccessful examples of process.

The Hostility/Support Scale has been used in our work on the developmental process to identify a change in the group's behavior toward the Scapegoat Leader early in the group. Another way to use the Hostility/Support Scale might be to study group interactions judged to be of high therapeutic value, such as by using the fourth quadrant of the Hill Interaction Matrix (Hill, 1965), which indicates personal risk and confrontation. Again, the level of work can be assessed with the Experiencing Scale, and the Hostility/Support Scale may be helpful in exploring the kind of feelings expressed in the course of facilitative confrontation. Again, qualitative analyses would be the basis for the selection of samples for further objective description and exploration.

CURRENT ASSESSMENT AND FUTURE DIRECTIONS

The Group Development Process Analysis Measures have shown an ability to facilitate investigation and further understanding of processes related to the structural development of therapeutic groups. The measures have potential usefulness for the investigation of issues from a wide range of theoretical concepts. For example, the Topic-Oriented Group Focus Unitizing Procedure may be useful in defining units appropriate to many theoretical concepts and may facilitate the process method of investigation with other measuring systems as well as this one. The other measures, too, have a potential for useful application to the study of a broad range of issues for therapy groups, as noted in the previous sections of this chapter.

Our goals continue to be found in the area of understanding how group process facilitates or hinders individual growth and constructive change. We are interested in what conditions facilitate members' growth and how the group therapist can intervene in ways that are most helpful to the group at various phases of group development.

REFERENCES

Bales, R. F. (1953). The equilibrium problem in small groups. In T. Parson, R. F. Bales, & E. A. Shils (Eds.), *Working papers in the theory of action* (pp. 111–161). New York: Free Press.

Bales, R. F. (1958). Task roles and social roles in problem solving groups. In E. E. Maccoby, T. M. Newcomb, & I. Hartley (Eds.), *Readings in social psychology* (pp. 437–447). New York: Holt, Rinehart & Winston.

Bales, R. F., & Strodtbeck, F. I. (1951). Phases in group problem solving. *Journal of Abnormal and Social Psychology, 46,* 485–495.

Beaton, A. E., & Tukey, J. W. (1974). The fitting of power series, meaning polynomials, illustrated on band spectroscopic data. *Technometrics, 16,* 147–192.

Beck, A. P. (1970). *Transcript of fifteen sessions of Group* A. Unpublished manuscript, Chicago.

Beck, A. P. (1974a). Phases in the development of structure in therapy and encounter groups. In D. Wexler & L. Rice (Eds.), *Innovations in client-centered therapy* (pp. 421–463). New York: Wiley Interscience.

Beck, A. P. (1974b). A review of the literature on phases of group development. Unpublished manuscript, Chicago.

Beck, A. P. (1981a). Developmental characteristics of the system forming process. In J. Durkin (Ed.), *Living groups: Group psychotherapy and general system theory* (pp. 316–332). New York: Brunner/Mazel.

Beck, A. P. (1981b). The study of group phase development and emergent leadership. *Group, 5*(4), 48–54.

Beck, A. P. (1983a). A process analysis of group development. *Group, 7*(1), 19–26.

Beck, A. P. (1983b). Group development: A case example of the first three phases. In L. R. Wolberg & M. D. Aronson (Eds.), *Group and family therapy 1983: An overview* (pp. 69–77). New York: Brunner/Mazel.

Beck, A. P. (1987, March). *Patterns in early sessions of group development.* Paper presented at the Illinois Group Psychotherapy Society, Chicago.

Beck, A. P., Dugo, J. M., Eng, A. M., & Lewis, C. M. (1986). The search for phases in group development: Designing process analysis measures of group interaction. In L. S. Greenberg & W. M. Pinsof (Eds.), *The psychotherapeutic process: A research handbook* (pp. 615–705). New York: Guilford Press.

Beck, A. P., Dugo, J. M., Eng, A. M., Lewis, C. M., & Peters, L. N. (1983). The participation of leaders in the structural development of therapy groups. In R. Dies & K. R. MacKenzie (Eds.), *Advances in group psychotherapy: Integrating research and practice* (pp. 137–158). Madison, CT: International Universities Press.

Beck, A. P., & Lewis, C. M. (1996, August). *Group process system: Group development process measures*. Paper presented at the 104th Annual Convention of the American Psychological Association, Toronto, Ontario, Canada.

Beck, A. P., & Peters, L. N. (1981). The research evidence for distributed leadership in therapy groups. *International Journal of Group Psychotherapy, 31*, 43–71.

Bennis, W. G., & Shepard, H. A. (1956). A theory of group development. *Human Relations, 9*, 415–438.

Brusa, J. A., & Beck, A. P. (1997, August). *A sociometric test of emerging leaders in group psychotherapy*. Paper presented at the 105th Annual Convention of the American Psychological Association, Chicago, IL.

Brusa, J. A., Stone, M. H., Beck, A. P., Dugo, J. M., & Peters, L. N. (1994). A sociometric test to identify emergent leader and member roles: Phase 1. *International Journal of Group Psychotherapy, 44*, 79–99.

Dugo, J. M., & Beck, A. P. (1983). Tracking a group's focus on normative-organizational or personal exploration issues. *Group, 7*(4), 17–26.

Dugo, J. M., & Beck, A. P. (1991). Phases of co-therapy team development. In B. Roller & V. Nelson (Eds.), *The art of co-therapy: How therapists work together* (pp. 155–188). New York: Guilford Press.

Eng, A. M., & Beck, A. P. (1982). Speech behavior measures of group psychotherapy process. *Group, 6*, 37–48.

Hare, A. P. (1973). Theories of group development and categories for interaction analysis. *Small Group Behavior, 4*(3), 259–304.

Heinicke, C., & Bales, R. F. (1953). Developmental trends in the structure of small groups. *Sociometry, 14*(23), 7–38.

Hill, W. F. (1965). *Hill Interaction Matrix*. Unpublished manuscript, University of Southern California, Los Angeles.

Hill, W. F., & Elmore, M. A. (1957). Toward a theory of group development: Six phases of therapy group development. *Journal of Group Psychotherapy, 7*, 20–30.

Klein, M. H., Mathieu, P. L., Gendlin, E. T., & Kiesler, D. J. (1969). *The Experiencing Scale: A research and training manual (Vols. 1 and 2)*. Madison: Wisconsin Psychiatric Institute.

Klein, M. H., Mathieu-Coughlan, P., & Kiesler, D. J. (1986). The Experiencing Scales. In L. S. Greenberg & W. M. Pinsof (Eds.), *The psychotherapeutic process: A research handbook* (pp. 21–71). New York: Guilford Press.

Lacoursiere, R. B. (1980). *The life cycle of groups: Group developmental stage theory*. New York: Human Sciences Press.

Lewis, C. M. (1985a). Symbolization of experience in the process of group development. *Group, 7*(2), 29–34.

Lewis, C. M. (1985b). The impact of tasks of group development on the psychotherapeutic treatment of depression in groups. *International Journal of Mental Health, 13*(3–4) 105–118.

Lewis, C. M., & Beck, A. P. (1983). Experiencing level in the process of group development. *Group, 7*(2), 18–26.

Lewis, C. M., Beck, A. P., & Stone, M. H. (1998). *The development of facilitative behavior among members*. Unpublished manuscript, Chicago.

Lewis, C. M., Dugo, J. M., & Beck, A. P. (1981, June). *The application of two process research variables to the analysis of structural development in small groups*. Paper presented at the meeting of the Society for Psychotherapy Research, Aspen, CO.

Lewis, C. M., Stone, M. H., & Beck, A. P. (1992, August). *Facilitative behavior among psychotherapy group members: A case study*. Paper presented at the 100th Annual Convention of the American Psychological Association, Washington, DC.

Mann, R. D. (1967). *Interpersonal styles and group development*. New York: Wiley.

Mathieu-Coughlan, P. L., & Klein, M. H. (1984). Experiential psychotherapy: Key events in client–therapist interaction. In L. N. Rice & L. S. Greenberg (Eds.), *Patterns of change: Intensive analysis of psychotherapy process* (pp. 213–248). New York: Guilford Press.

Peters, L. N., & Beck, A. P. (1982). Identifying emergent leaders in psychotherapy groups. *Group, 6*(1), 35–40.

Tuckman, B. W. (1965). Developmental sequence in small groups. *Psychological Bulletin, 63*, 384–399.

Tuckman, B. W., & Jensen, M. (1977). Stages of small group development revisited. *Group and Organizational Studies, 2*, 419–427.

Roller, B., & Nelson, V. (1991). *The art of co-therapy: How therapists work together*. New York: Guilford Press.

Whitaker, D. S. (1985). *Using groups to help people*. New York: Tavistock/Routledge.

10

THE PSYCHODYNAMIC WORK AND OBJECT RATING SYSTEM

WILLIAM E. PIPER AND MARY McCALLUM

The Psychodynamic Work and Object Rating System (PWORS) is a process analysis measure that is designed to assess two basic constructs in group psychotherapy. The first is the presence and complexity of psychodynamic work, and the second is reference to objects (one or more types of individuals). According to the system, psychodynamic work always includes a reference to objects, but the converse is not true. The theoretical framework of the system stems primarily from psychodynamic, object relations, and systems orientations.

In this chapter, we initially consider the origins of our interest in the construct of work and the interest of others. This includes theoretical interest in work and objects from the psychodynamic orientation. Correspondence between the theoretical formulations and the PWORS follows. We next describe the categories of the system and how they are rated. Some strengths and limitations regarding the scope of the system and the inference required for using the system are noted. Use of the system in a clinical trial involving 16 time-limited, short-term therapy groups is presented as a major application. Several significant findings are summarized. Next, the system is applied to Session 3 of Group A, the therapy group available for common analysis in the current book. Comparisons between the process of Group A and the process of the groups from the clinical trial are made. Finally, some summary comments and conclusions about future directions are offered.

HISTORY AND THEORY OF THE SYSTEM

We chose work as a basic construct for several reasons. We observed that the term *work* is commonly used to describe group activities in both clinical and nonclinical settings. In the case of group therapy, it describes the behavior of one or more patients (e.g., pair, subgroup), the therapist, or the group as a whole.

The people involved in work are believed to have performed some behavior that is instrumental to goal attainment. The goal may be an ultimate one (e.g., patient improvement) or a subgoal (e.g., self-disclosure) that is viewed as leading to an ultimate one. Somewhat similar to the field of physics, in which work is defined as the movement of mass, the mere expenditure of energy is not enough to qualify as work. Patients in a therapy group must do more than talk; they must achieve a subgoal or ultimate goal. We believe that there has been a natural tendency for mental health professionals to use the construct of work to refer to valued group phenomena.

Previous Attention to the Construct of Work

The term *work* has also been used in several important theories and assessment systems in the field of group therapy. One of the earliest references can be found in the writings of Bion (1959): "When patients meet for a group-therapy session it can always be seen that some mental activity is directed to the solution of the problems for which the individuals seek help" (p. 144). Bion called this particular mental activity the *work group*.

Bion's (1959) work group is characterized by rational processes, geared to a task and related to reality. However, the work group never exists in pure form; it is always infused with other types of mental activity that Bion called *basic assumption groups*. Because of their irrational, often unconscious, properties, the mental activities associated with basic assumption groups are typically confusing to the group therapist. Bion suggested that the mental activities can become more understandable if the therapist views the patients as sharing a basic assumption about pursuing a goal that is different from that of the work group. Such goals include attaining security from the therapist (i.e., the dependency group), attacking or avoiding an enemy (i.e., the fight–flight group), or joining someone to create something wonderful (i.e., the pairing group). We emphasize that Bion viewed group activity as a combination of both work and basic assumption groups.

Thelen, Stock, Hill, Ben-Zeev, and Heintz (1954) constructed a group process system to assess Bion's (1959) work and basic assumption groups. Four levels of work were presented, ranging from the individually oriented and routine to the group oriented and creative. The system was used to monitor phases of group development in nontherapy groups (Stock & Thelen, 1958).

One of Thelen's colleagues, William F. Hill, developed a process system specifically for group therapy. The Hill Interaction Matrix (Hill, 1965) consists of two major axes, one for work categories and one for content categories. Work is defined as the presence of someone who is taking the role of patient and actively seeking self-understanding. Two types of work are distinguished. Confrontive work, in comparison to speculative work, is characterized by the presence of greater responsibility taking and interpersonal threat.

Early findings concerning the reliability and validity of the matrix were promising, although by contemporary standards they must be regarded as modest. Evidence of predictive validity concerning therapy outcome has been minimal, including some of our studies (Piper, Debbane, Bienvenu, & Garant, 1982; Piper, Montvila, & McGihon, 1979) with the system. Part of the difficulty may lie in the general nature of the concepts being measured. In the case of the definition of work, taking the role of the patient and seeking self-understanding cover a wide range of behaviors. Only some of the behaviors may be directly and significantly related to outcome.

Work and Psychodynamic Therapy

A primary reason for our interest in the construct of work was the possibility that it might provide a useful way to conceptualize process events in dynamically oriented group therapy. However, a more specific definition based on psychoanalytic concepts and theory seemed to be required. The definition of work selected for the PWORS reflected the mainstream of psychoanalytic theory regarding the personality of the individual, its extension to the group situation, and adaptations of the theory by "group-dynamic" theorists such as Ezriel (1973) and Whitaker and Lieberman (1964). The different points of view of psychoanalytic theory have been delineated by Fenichel (1945). According to the structural point of view, the ego is the mediator among the id, superego, and external reality. Conflict takes place between the structural agents of the mind, within one of them, or between one of them and the external world. According to the dynamic point of view, wishes (the id) give rise to anxiety (the superego and external reality), which acts a signal to mobilize defenses (the ego). This depiction of psychoanalytic theory is oversimplified. However, it provides an indication of the primary theoretical components that previously have been used to operationalize the concept of interpretation in a process system that was constructed for individual therapy (Piper, Debbane, de Carufel, & Bienvenu, 1987). According to that system, an *interpretation* was defined as a statement that reveals one or more aspects of the dynamic sequence in the context of a conflictual situation. As such, interpretation was viewed as a central part of psychoanalytic work (Bienvenu, Piper, Debbane, & de Carufel, 1986).

Interpretations can be provided by both patients and therapists, which is particularly apparent in group psychotherapy. Our definition of work for the PWORS was a direct extension of the concept of interpretation (or therapist work) from our process system for individual therapy. However, the group situation is considerably more complex. Statements about conflictual dynamic components may refer not only to the intrapsychic events of individual members but also to interpersonal events (e.g., between individuals or between subgroups) and to events involving the group as a whole. Conflicts shared by all of the patients of a group are central features of group-dynamic theorists such as Ezriel (1973) and Whitaker and Lieberman (1964). They each provided their own terminology, adapted from psychoanalytic theory, to refer to the conflicts and dynamic events involving the entire group. To encompass group-as-a-whole conflicts, as well as the interpersonal and intrapsychic, the PWORS required a complete set of terms for the various objects involved.

Objects and Psychodynamic Therapy

Aside from our interest in taking into account the various objects involved in conflicts in the group situation, we think it important to note that there has been a considerable interest in object relations concepts in both past and contemporary formulations of psychoanalytic theory (Greenberg & Mitchell, 1983). We agree that an account of drives and their derivatives in the absence of a consideration of objects is incomplete. Previous research on the relationship between the object focus of interpretations and outcome has had heuristic importance (Malan, 1976a; Marziali & Sullivan, 1980; Piper, Debbane, Bienvenu, de Carufel, & Garant, 1986). In our current application of psychoanalytic theory to a definition of work for group psychotherapy, attention to objects reflects contemporary theoretical interest in object relations. It also allows a more precise statement of the nature of the conflicts being examined.

CORRESPONDENCE BETWEEN THE THEORY AND THE SYSTEM

The PWORS is used to rate each patient and therapist statement for the presence of work and reference to objects. *Work* is conceptually defined as an attempt by a group member to understand the problems of one or more members of the group, or the group as a whole, in terms of conflict among dynamic components.

Operationally, the "attempt . . . to understand" is implicit. The members' verbal productions are evaluated for their identifications of dynamic components. If a statement identifies dynamic components, it is considered work. If it does not include dynamic components, it is considered nonwork. Dynamic components are internal forces in the group that are part of a conflict. In other words, a dynamic component is assumed to be exerting an internal force on one or more members or on the group as a whole, and at some level the force is opposed. Excluded from the definition of work are the mere identification or description of resultant (end) states and consideration of dynamic factors that belong to people or situations external to the group. It is always challenging when operationalizing constructs to preserve the meaning of the theoretical concepts while maintaining high reliability of the ratings. By defining concepts that are familiar to psychoanalytic theory, the PWORS has preserved the meaning of theoretical concepts, such as defense or anxiety. By basing these operational definitions on behavioral referents (e.g., specific identification of an avoidance of feeling), the reliability of the PWORS has been preserved. Therefore, the PWORS promises to meet the challenge of operationalizing the complex construct of psychodynamic work.

There are five components in the system. Four are dynamic and one is nondynamic. The four dynamic components are wishes, reactive anxiety, defensive processes, and dynamic expressions. The nondynamic component is objects and is discussed below. The first three dynamic components—wishes, anxiety, and defenses—are familiar concepts of psychoanalytic theory. For example, Malan (1976b) referred to them as the *impulse-defense triad*. The fourth dynamic component—dynamic expressions—refers to the identification of an affective, behavioral, or cognitive expression that exerts a dynamic influence on the group. To be scored as a dynamic component, the expression must be presented as being in conflict with, causing, giving rise to, or having an impact on another expression of group. This second expression (resultant) must be stated, and the connection between the dynamic and resultant expressions must be clear in the rater's mind. For example, if a patient's guilt (affective expression) is identified as having a subsequent impact on his or her behavior, then this guilt is considered to be a dynamic expression. Conversely, if a patient's guilt is identified merely to describe his or her affect without cause or effect being identified, then that guilt is scored as a resultant expression (the end product).

Note that if a dynamic expression is also identified as a wish, reactive anxiety, or as a defense, then the component that is part of the impulse-defense triad takes priority over the dynamic expression. In practice, the dynamic expressions are often vague or ambiguous identifications of another dynamic component. In the previous example, if the speaker had pointed out that the behavior functioned to permit the avoidance of feelings of guilt then defense would have been rated.

The term *objects* refer to people internal or external to the group. Two aspects of objects are monitored: the object focus and whether there is object linking. The term *object focus* refers to whether the speaker is focusing on objects internal or external to the group. Internal objects include the speaker, another group member, a subgroup, or the group as a whole. These are called "Units of the group." External objects include a former or absent member of the group, family members, a specific person, another group or general classes of people. The term *object linking* refers to the identification of a shared interpersonal process between a unit of the group and two other objects. The linked objects may be internal to the group, external, or both. Object linking is included in the system because of the importance attributed to the process in the field of individual therapy (Malan, 1976a). The five components of the PWORS are used to differentiate four categories of nonwork and work, which correspond to progressively higher levels of analytical work.

DESCRIPTION OF THE SYSTEM

Categories

There are two nonwork categories. The first, Category 1, contains externalizing statements. These statements focus on topics that do not involve a unit of the group, that focus on objects external to the group, or both. They fail to indicate the process in which a unit of the group and the external object are engaging or the impact between the two. For example, the statement "Some people are so involved in the church that they ignore their own families" is nonwork. If a member of the group attempts to understand an external person's problems in terms of dynamic components, the statement is also considered nonwork. For example, the statement "My father has always denied his feelings" identifies a defensive process but, because the father is not a current member of the group, the statement is scored nonwork. That score is consistent with our conceptual definition of work. Because group members are the focus of treatment, the focus of therapeutic work should be on those same group members.

A similar example can be found from Session 3 of Group A, the therapy group available for common analysis with the systems of the current book. Referring to all women, Martha asked, "Isn't that contradictive, a contradiction in being submissive and still knowing that you're a superior being?" Martha's question identifies a defensive process in which either submissive behavior is atonement for feeling superior or feeling superior is compensatory for submissive behavior. Because the defense process is attributed to the general class—female—and not to any unit of the group, the question is scored as nonwork.

The second nonwork level, Category 2, contains descriptive statements. They provide or request information about a unit of the group (e.g., "You seem to be trying to help everyone, even us in the group"). An example from Group A is, "What about Brad? Weren't you worried about him?" The speaker is requesting information about the cognitive process (i.e., worry) of one member of the group about another member of the group (i.e., Brad). The question does not identify a wish, anxiety, or a defensive process. Similarly, it does not identify a dynamic expression because it does not identify a consequence or antecedent to the worry. Because no dynamics are identified, the question is considered both descriptive and nonwork. Because the worry belongs to a unit of the group, it is rated Category 2. If an external object is mentioned, its relationship to a unit of the group is also indicated in a Category 2 statement.

The first work level, Category 3, contains statements that identify a single dynamic component. For example, consider the statement "You [a unit of the group] ask everyone how they feel so that you don't have to talk about how you feel." In this example, the speaker is identifying a defensive process of a unit of the group. The statement conveys the essential quality of avoidance (i.e., the group member is avoiding talking about how he or she feels). Other qualities that can be associated with a defensive process are resistance, distortion, and reluctance. Another example of Category 3 is provided by Group A member Joe, who explains his tendency to monopolize the group by stating that "I mean I wanna be one o' the group too." This statement is rated as expressing a wish because it is presented as being causal.

The second work level, Category 4, contains statements that identify two or more dynamic components. For example, consider the statement "I think you [unit of the group] are afraid to feel vulnerable in here, and that's why you pretend to have all the answers." In this example, the speaker is identifying reactive anxiety and a defensive process of a unit of the group. "Afraid to feel vulnerable" was rated as expressing reactive anxiety because it was identified as a causal agent. Other qualities that can be associated with reactive anxiety include fears identified as counterdrives (i.e., in opposition to a wish or in reaction to an internal state). In the above example, the unit of the group's fear of feeling vulnerable gives rise to "[pretending] to have all the answers." The effect of the fear is rated as a defensive process because it conveys the quality of distortion (i.e., pretending). Thus, the two work levels differ only in complexity. The higher level usually indicates a greater appreciation of the conflictual nature of dynamic components. However, the fact that a conflictual process is underlying the dynamic components need not be explicitly communicated by the speaker. A similar example from Group A is provided by Joe: " . . . I thought you were holding something back. . . . You were a little self-conscious or a little timid, or you were afraid to bring something out that was bothering you." In this example, the speaker is again identifying reactive anxiety and a defensive process of a unit of the group. "You were afraid to bring something out" was rated as reactive anxiety because it was identified as a causal agent and was in reaction to an internal state (bothered). In this example, the unit of the group's fear of bringing something out gives rise to "holding something back." The effect of the fear is rated as a defensive process because it conveys the quality of reluctance or resistance. Hence, the statement is rated work with two conflictual dynamic components.

Note that this work may serve different functions. For example, a speaker may exhibit work (i.e., identify dynamic components) while supporting a unit of the group, confronting him or her or, ironically, avoiding his or her own issues. Just as someone can use work as a compulsive defense against emotional issues in everyday life, so, too, can the group member work to compulsively defend against emotional issues in the group. It is common in group therapy, for example, for one member to feel antagonistic toward a second member who shares similar issues. The first member may work hard at identifying the second member's issues. This identification is considered work because the second member may benefit from the astute observations of his or her dynamic conflicts. The PWORS rater does not, however, judge the intent of the work. It remains for the other group members, or therapist, to explore the intent of a member's tenacious observations. Perhaps they reflect the member's anger, fear, or concern and therefore represent confrontation, defensiveness, or supportiveness. Determining the intent of statements is highly subjective and demanding. The more that ratings depend on inference and subjective judgments, the greater the risk to reliability. A priority in developing the PWORS was to ensure high reliability. Hence, the PWORS does not rate the intent of work and nonwork ratings.

Rating

To use the PWORS, each patient and therapist statement from taped group therapy sessions is timed with a stopwatch. A *statement* is defined as a part of a sentence, a complete sentence, or several sentences spoken by a member of the group that is not interrupted by a statement by another member or by silence greater than 10 s. For each patient and therapist statement, the PWORS determines the category of work, the object focus, and whether or not there is object linking. Hence, the statement is the unit of measurement for each PWORS rating. The procedure for determining a PWORS rating of a statement is as follows. First, the object focus is determined; all objects mentioned by the speaker are noted. The presence of object linking is also noted. If there is an internal object focus noted, the rater proceeds to rate the level of work or nonwork. Toward this end, the rater determines whether the statement includes dynamic components that belong to a unit of the group. If there is one type of dynamic component scored, Category 3 is rated. If there are two or more types of dynamic components scored, Category 4 is rated. If there are no dynamic components scored, the rater decides the appropriate nonwork category. Toward that end, the rater determines whether the statement includes the resultant expressions. If there is at least one resultant expression, a rating of Category 2 is given. If there are no resultant expressions, Category 1 is given. Hence, if a unit of the group is identified as being the recipient of an external object's expression, the statement would be considered an externalization, Category 1.

Strengths and Limitations

The specific scope of the PWORS represents both a strength and a limitation. The system is consistent with psychoanalytic theory in that it gives primary emphasis to understanding the role of internal (intrapsychic or intragroup) conflictual components as they are related to patients' problems. The importance of the group context is also emphasized. Work includes one member's contribution to the therapy process of other members. The importance of the group context is also reflected in the system's ability to monitor conflicts involving the entire group, in addition to conflicts involving dyads, subgroups, or the other intrapsychic conflicts of individual members. Also, the object focus permits the distinction between work that addresses the speaker's dynamics and work that addresses another unit of the group's dynamics. The object focus and object linking parts of the system address the importance of patient–patient transference phenomena in addition to the more traditional patient–therapist transference phenomena. One use of object linking is to monitor the identification of maladaptive patterns of interaction being reenacted in the group situation.

The degree of inference required of a rater for the work–nonwork levels is greater than for objects, which are easily identified. In general, the greater the inference the more reliability is compromised. Nevertheless, by having raters make judgments solely about the presence of dynamic components, which then automatically determine the work level, inference is kept to a manageable limit. Several ratios can be calculated for each patient. Participation is the ratio of the patient's total statement duration over the total verbal production of the group. It is the individual's portion of speaking. Self-based work is the patient's work behavior (statements scoring Category 3 or 4) relative to his or her total participation. It is how much an individual works when he or she speaks. Group-based work is the patient's work behavior relative to the total work behavior of all the patients in the group.

Reliability

Reliability data for the PWORS is available from its use in a controlled outcome study of short-term psychodynamically oriented group psychotherapy (STGP) for psychiatric outpatients who experienced difficulties after losing someone important (McCallum & Piper, 1990a; Piper, McCallum, & Azim, 1992). The study investigated the effectiveness of treatment as well as the relationships among patient characteristics, psychodynamic work, and therapy outcome.

Four research assistants with undergraduate degrees in psychology or its equivalent were trained to use the PWORS. The training sessions involved approximately 7 hours/week over a 4-month period. The sessions involved familiarity with the detailed PWORS manual (Piper & McCallum, 1988) and practice ratings using previous group psychotherapy sessions. Subsequently, 7 of the 12 STGP sessions (i.e., 1, 2, 4, 6, 8, 10, and 12) from each of the first 12 groups of the study were analyzed with the system. The aim was to obtain a large database for all patients from each phase of therapy. The raters listened to the first 30 minutes of each session for context. They then rated the next 45-min segment.

Interrater reliability for the work and nonwork categories was determined by comparing pairs of independent ratings of 12 randomly chosen sessions, which provided 1,572 statements for categorization. The average percentages of perfect category agreement for Categories 1–4 were 87, 83, 67, and 66, respectively. The average kappa coefficient, which indicates the proportion of category agreement between two raters after removing the influence of chance-expected agreement, was .69. Most disagreements were between the two nonwork or the two work categories. The raters rarely disagreed about the work–nonwork distinction. The average percentages of perfect agreement for work and nonwork categories were 85 and 90. The mean kappa coefficient for the four raters over the 12 sessions on the work–nonwork distinction was .75. Thus, the data supported the reliability of the system for the work and nonwork categories.

PREVIOUS RESEARCH WITH THE SYSTEM

The recently completed STGP study was the first to make extensive use of the PWORS. It included 16 treated groups. In addition to providing an opportunity to test a number of hypotheses, the system served to validate the nature of the treatment being offered. Although training, using a manual, and monitoring sessions all enhance the likelihood of providing a standard form of therapy, the most convincing evidence comes from a thorough process analysis of the sessions. The theoretical orientation of the time-limited (12 once-weekly sessions) groups was psychoanalytical. The technical orientation required an active therapist role in which interpretation and clarification of conflicts were emphasized relative to support and direction. Focus on the group as a whole and the therapist as an object of transference was also emphasized. Personal disclosures by the therapist were not to be provided.

Because the PWORS provides information about both the frequency and duration of patient and therapist statements, several different indexes can be generated and used in statistical analyses. For questions concerning amount of work, either frequency or duration may be appropriate depending on the question. For references to objects, frequency indexes seem to be the most appropriate. It may also be useful to represent variables as percentages or proportions. Given that the system is relatively new, users should feel free to be innovative in their methods of representation and analyses.

The PWORS analysis of the groups indicated that the therapist spoke 14% of the time, whereas the average speaking time for patients was 17%. Thus, the therapist was nearly as active as the average patient. The average percentage of self-based work for patients was 54%. A higher percentage, 84%, of the therapist's speaking time was rated as self-based work. We define this as interpretive because it always involves reference to a dynamic component. The distribution of types of dynamic components within interpretations was wishes (22%), anxiety (20%), defenses (34%), and expressions (24%), which reflected a balanced emphasis. The distribution of internal objects within interpretation was patient (47%), subgroup (4%), group as a whole (39%), therapist as transference figure (10%), and therapist as person (0%). The analysis confirmed that the therapists were active and interpretive. It also placed a major focus on individual patients and the group as a whole. A lesser but definite focus was placed on the therapist as a transference figure. The therapists successfully avoided personal disclosures. The PWORS proved to be useful in verifying that the treatment in the study had been carried out as planned.

Because the STGP project and its findings are presented in detail in a recent book (Piper et al., 1992), here we provide only a summary of the findings that involved work. In addition to treatment per se, we investigated the patient personality characteristic known as *psychological mindedness* (PM) as a primary independent variable.

PM was assessed with an interview measure (McCallum & Piper, 1990b). The concept is defined as the ability to identify conflictual dynamic components and relate them to a person's difficulties. The patient being assessed watches a videotape of a sequence of patient–therapist interactions, which are portrayed by an actress and an actor. At the beginning the actress-patient describes a recent event in her life. The patient being assessed is asked an open question: "What seems to be troubling this woman?" The patient's responses are scored on a 9-point scale according to his or her ability to identify dynamic (intrapsychic) components such as wishes, anxiety, and defenses and to relate them to the actress-patient's difficulties (e.g., conflict leading to symptoms).

The statistical relationship between PM and several of the PWORS variables (e.g., participation, self-based work, group-based work) was investigated with Pearson product–moment correlations. The sample consisted of 58 patients who had experienced a loss through death and who had completed therapy in 1 of the first 12 groups. The correlation between PM and participation was not significant. In contrast, the correlation between PM and self-based work was significant, $r(51) = .43$, $p < .001$. When only the higher level (Category 4 of the PWORS) of self-based work was used, the correlation was somewhat larger, $r(51) = .48$, $p < .001$. As with participation, the correlations between PM and group-based work were not significant. Thus, although PM was not predictive of talkativeness in the group, it was predictive of the amount of self-based work (i.e., the proportion of time a patient worked when he or she talked). This finding has implications for the selection of patients for psychodynamically oriented group therapy. By choosing patients who are psychologically minded, a group could be primed for the facilitation of psychodynamic work.

Therapy outcome was assessed with a large set of measures that covered the areas of interpersonal functioning, psychiatric symptomatology, self-esteem, and personalized target objectives. Eighteen were measured both before and after therapy, and two were measured only after therapy. To investigate the relationship between the PWORS variables (i.e., participation, self-based work, group-based work) and outcome, we conducted a set of partial and Pearson product–moment correlations. The partial correlation, used with the 18 outcome variables measured both before and after therapy, removed the effect of the before-therapy score prior to determining the correlation between the PWORS variable and the after-therapy score. The correlation was used with the two measures that were assessed after therapy ended.

In the case of participation, only 1 of the 20 correlations was significant ($p < .05$), and one approached significance. Because this is approximately what is expected by chance, we concluded that there was no important relationship between participation and outcome. In the case of group-based work, we found only two significant correlations. This is little beyond what is expected by chance. In the case of self-based work, there were three significant correlations and three approached significance. All indicated a positive relationship between work and outcome. They included the Family of Origin, $r(47) = .34$, $p < .05$, and the Parental, $r(36) = .48$, $p < .01$, subscales of the Social Adjustment Scale interview of Weissman, Paykel, and Siegal (1972); the therapist's global rating of overall usefulness, $r(56) = .27$, $p < .05$; the Autonomy subscale of the Hirschfeld et al. (1977) Interpersonal Dependency Inventory, $r(48) = .26$, $p < .09$; the independent assessor's rating of target objective severity, $r(47) = .25$, $p < .09$; and the patient's global rating of overall usefulness, $r(53) = .23$, $p < .09$. Thus, there was evidence beyond what is expected by chance for a direct relationship between self-based work and favorable outcome.

Although the strongest results were found for self-based work, we realize that the results need to be replicated before they can be accepted as valid. There is presently only a suggestion of a direct relationship between self-based work and favorable outcome. There are several likely reasons why the correlations were not higher. First, there was a strong, positive treatment effect in the study, and the sample of patients who provided substantial session material for PWORS analyses were completers of treatment. Thus, outcome was limited to the good-to-excellent range for most of the sample. This likely served to restrict the possibilities of obtaining high correlations. Second, the PWORS is limited to assessing overt verbal signs of psychodynamic work during the sessions. Psychodynamic work that occurred silently during the sessions or that occurred outside the sessions was not assessed. Third, as the current book indicates, many other variables, either by themselves or in combination, are capable of influencing treatment outcome. Bloch and Crouch (1985) previously identified three large sets of such variables (i.e., conditions for change, therapist technique, and therapeutic factors). Because of the complexity, it is unrealistic to expect strong direct relationships between single therapeutic factors such as psychodynamic work and outcome.

McCallum, Piper, and Morin (1993) subsequently investigated another set of process variables that focused on the degree to which patients experienced and expressed affect in the groups. They were particularly interested in knowing whether the combination of work and affective experience would provide a stronger predictive model of treatment outcome. The results differed depending on the type of affects being investigated. In the case of positive affect (e.g., feeling positive, excited, close to someone, pleased, and accepted), direct relationships between their experience or expression and favorable outcome were found. In the case of negative affect (e.g., feeling afraid, sad, angry, guilty, and frustrated), the strongest predictors of favorable outcome involved the interaction of work and affect. Hence, this complexity of interacting variables is further complicated by the possibility that subtypes of variables interact differently to influence outcome.

Fourth, as Stiles (1988) noted, patients may require different amounts of therapeutic factors to achieve similar goals. The challenge in this case is to identify which patients require which amounts. That challenge, plus the consideration of more complex, interactive models, will preoccupy investigators for a long time.

APPLICATION OF THE SYSTEM OF ANALYSIS TO GROUP A, SESSION 3

The PWORS was applied to all of Session 3 of Group A, the therapy group available for common analysis with the systems of the current book. Therapist activity (presented as percentages) for STGP and for Group A are summarized in Table 10.1. For Group A, the PWORS analysis indicated that the cotherapists spoke 18% of the time, whereas the average speaking time for the STGP therapists was 14%. Thus, the percentage of therapist activity was similar in the two groups. In contrast, the percentage of therapist speaking time rated as self-based work (i.e., interpretative) in Group A (47%) was considerably lower than in the STGP groups (84%).

The distribution of types of dynamic components within the Group A cotherapists' interpretations was wishes (35%), anxiety (0%), defenses (4%), and expressions (61%). Thus, there was much less reference made to anxiety and defenses than in the STGP groups. The distribution of internal objects within interpretations was patient (88%), subgroup (0%), group as a whole (4%), therapist as a transference figure (4%), and therapist as a person (4%). There was considerably more focus on individual patients and less focus on the group as a whole than in the STGP groups. There was also less focus on the therapist as a transference figure and some personal disclosure on the therapist's part.

Differences in the percentages between the two types of therapists may reflect different theoretical orientations. In STGP, the strong emphasis

TABLE 10.1
Therapist Activity for STGP and Group A

Therapist Activity	STGP %	Group A %
Participation	14	18
Self-based work	84	47
Wishes	22	35
Anxiety	20	0
Defenses	34	4
Dynamic expressions	24	61
Object focus		
Patient	47	88
Subgroup	4	0
Group as a whole	39	4
Transference figure	10	4
Therapist as a person	0	4

Note. STGP = short-term psychodynamically oriented group psychotherapy.

on interpretation (84%) is consistent with a psychoanalytic orientation. The emphasis on interpreting defenses and anxiety is also consistent with the psychoanalytic orientation. In contrast, the therapists of Group A did not interpret the entire impulse-defense triad. Rather, they focused on the consequences of behaviors, affects, and cognitions (61%). That emphasis is consistent with several theoretical orientations, including the client-centered, cognitive, gestalt, and interpersonal schools.

Concerning the object focus of the two types of therapists, the differences may again reflect different theoretical approaches. The STGP therapists place emphasis on both individual patients and the group as a whole. This emphasis is consistent with the theories of Bion (1959) and Whitaker and Lieberman (1964). Specifically, group-dynamic therapists believe that it is important to interpret group dynamics. The group is the patient as much as its individual members. The fact that the STGP therapists interpreted transference 10% of the time was initially surprising. We had expected a stronger focus. The finding suggests that transference interpretations were judiciously offered, perhaps because of the associated anxiety. In some other work with short-term individual therapy, there is evidence that high levels of transference interpretations may be detrimental and that maintaining the dosage at about 10% is probably beneficial (Piper, Azim, Joyce, & McCallum, 1991).

Conversely, the therapists of Group A have an individual focus. Their approach does not emphasize the importance of communicating to the group members that their behavior reflects group dynamics. Their approach is consistent with client-centered, gestalt, cognitive, or interpersonal approaches to conducting group therapy.

Given the differences between the STGP and Group A therapists, it is notable that the patients' behavior was so similar. Participation and self-based work were 17% and 54% for STGP, and 14% and 52% for Group A. This finding may imply that patients engage in similarly therapeutic behavior regardless of the theoretical orientation of their therapists. Approximately half the time, patients engage in the kind of activity we consider work. The other half, patients may be engaging in behavior that we consider nonwork but that is nevertheless necessary for any therapeutic process. As previously mentioned, the challenge for investigators is to identify the different therapeutic factors that are operating and to consider the complex interactions of those factors that evolve in beneficial therapy sessions.

Results of the PWORS analyses for all of Session 3 for each of the 6 patients who attended are presented in Table 10.2. A fact evident from the table and confirmed in the STGP groups is the independence of participation and self-based work. In Session 3 the most active patients (Diane and Joe) were by no means the most work-oriented patients (Brad and Pat).

TABLE 10.2
PWORS Variable Percentages for Group A, Session 3 Patients

Patient	Participation %	Self-Based Work %	Group-Based Work %
Diane	38	50	36
Martha	19	75	27
Joe	24	27	12
Brad	6	94	11
Greg	10	43	9
Pat	3	83	5

Note. PWORS = Psychodynamic Work and Object Rating System.

Analysis of Session 3 also provided an opportunity to examine those parts of the session representing a shift from Phase II to Phase III, as identified by Beck (1974) in her theory of group development. According to the theory, Phase II is characterized by work on major organizational issues such as the completion of leadership selection and establishment of important norms, whereas Phase III is characterized by a cooperative work process involving personal disclosures. In our examination, Phase II was represented by Units 64–66, a defensive mode by Unit 69, the transition from Phase II to Phase III by Units 71–73, and Phase III by Units 82–84. The PWORS self-based work variable was used to represent work. In Phase II there was a greater amount of work (62%) than nonwork (38%) statements. In the defensive mode, this was reversed with work (34%) and nonwork (66%). In the transition, there were almost equivalent amounts of work (47%) and nonwork (53%) statements. In Phase III, there was a lesser amount of work (18%) than nonwork (82%) statements. Thus, the percentages of work decreased across the four periods from 62% in Phase II to 18% in Phase III. When the proportions of work and nonwork in Phases II and III were statistically compared, they were significantly different, $\chi^2(1, N = 48) = 7.64$, $p < .01$.

Regarding object focus, there were some nonsignificant differences between Phase II and Phase III. The most salient difference concerned whether a patient, when speaking, focused on himself or herself or another group member. In Phase II, the focus was on the speaker 28% of the time and on other members 58% of the time. In Phase III, the focus was on the speaker 44% of the time and on other members 53% of the time. In addition, in Phase II there was a focus on the group 8% of the time, whereas in Phase III there was no focus on the group. Thus, in Phase III there was a greater focus on the self and lesser focus on the group. The defensive mode was similar to Phase II regarding object focus. The transition was notable by its focus on the group (26%).

These differences appear to be consistent with the clinical material. Phase II was characterized by an exploration of several difficult issues that had been raised in the preceding session, particularly the behavior of Joe and the others' reactions to him. Attention was repeatedly directed to the impact that members had had on one another (e.g., "Maybe I was talking too much and irritating you"). To a lesser extent, references were made to intrapsychic processes (e.g., "You were holding something back"). These examples qualified as work because they dealt with the impact of part of a unit of the group on part of another unit of the group. In contrast, the defensive mode mainly consisted of scapegoating Joe rather than attempting to understand the events in the group.

During the transition, the focal patient, Joe, was ignored. The focus centered around two of the women. There was mix of exploring intrapsychic impact (e.g., "There are a lot of things I would like to tell about me in the group, [but] I don't have the nerve") exploring interpersonal impact (e.g., "I'm afraid it will bore them"), and storytelling (e.g., Martha describing an incident in a different group). Few references were made to the group.

In Phase III several lengthy statements were made by individuals (Martha, Diane, and Greg) about their relationships with their mothers. Much of the disclosures were informational, but parts were affect laden. However, there was little in the way of identifying dynamic impact in the context of conflict. There were some exceptions (e.g., Diane saying, "One thing that helped me is that I recognized that I really love my mother"). For the most part, though, the statements conveyed aspects of the individual's personal history. Thus, the focus on self was high and work was low.

ASSESSMENT AND FUTURE DIRECTIONS

In this chapter we have presented the Psychodynamic Work and Object Rating System and have considered some of its initial applications. Our orientation to group therapy stems from psychoanalytic theory. The definition and measure of work that we have chosen for the PWORS and that we have labeled *psychodynamic work* can be directly linked to the structural and dynamic points of view of psychoanalytic theory (i.e., the attempt to understand patient difficulties in terms of conflict among dynamic components such as wishes, fears, and defenses). In addition, the system's emphasis on objects provides a more precise statement of the nature of conflict and reflects current interest in object relations in psychoanalytic theory. It is clear that we have opted for specific rather than general definitions for the basic constructs of the system. We believe that the level of reliability and predictive validity that we have achieved thus far with the definition of psychodynamic work is a consequence of its level of specificity. There are, of course, limitations associated with such an approach. Although the PWORS monitors when work occurs, it does not infer the intent of work and nonwork behavior. In addition, only a limited domain of behavior is measured, and the utility of the system may prove to be restricted to only particular forms of group therapy. Time and usage will determine whether that is the case.

The primary application of the PWORS has been in a clinical-trial investigation of short-term therapy for patients who have experienced the loss of someone important. This application has revealed several things. First, the system can be used reliably. Second, it can be used to verify the nature of the treatment that has been provided including differentiation from other forms of treatment. Third, psychodynamic work is significantly related to pretherapy measurements of PM. Fourth, the evidence suggests that psychodynamic work may be directly related to certain kinds of favorable treatment outcome. These findings are in need of replication. In the future we hope to provide some of that work as we explore predictor–process–outcome relationships in group psychotherapy using the PWORS.

REFERENCES

Beck, A. P. (1974). Phases in the development of structure in therapy and encounter groups. In D. Wexler & L. N. Rice (Eds.), *Innovations in client-centered therapy* (pp. 421–463). New York: Wiley.

Bienvenu, J. P., Piper, W. E., Debbane, E. G., & de Carufel, F. L. (1986). On the concept of psychoanalytic work. *American Journal of Psychotherapy, 40,* 277–289.

Bion, W. R. (1959). *Experiences in groups.* New York: Basic Books.

Bloch, S., & Crouch, E. (1985). *Therapeutic factors in group psychotherapy.* Oxford, England: Oxford University Press.

Ezriel, H. (1973). Psychoanalytic group therapy. In L. R. Wolberg & E. K. Schwartz (Eds.), *Group therapy: 1973 an overview* (pp. 183–210). New York: Intercontinental Medical Book Corporation.

Fenichel, O. (1945). *The psychoanalytic theory of neurosis.* New York: Norton.

Greenberg, J. R., & Mitchell, S. A. (1983). *Object relations in psychoanalytic theory.* Cambridge, MA: Harvard University Press.

Hill, W. F. (1965). *Hill Interaction Matrix.* Los Angeles: University of California, Youth Study Center.

Malan, D. H. (1976a). *Toward the validation of dynamic psychotherapy.* New York: Plenum.

Malan, D. H. (1976b). *The frontier of brief psychotherapy.* New York: Plenum.

Marziali, E. A., & Sullivan, J. M. (1980). Methodological issues in the content analysis of brief psychotherapy. *British Journal of Medical Psychology, 53,* 19–27.

McCallum, M., & Piper, W. E. (1990a). A controlled study of effectiveness and patient suitability for short-term group psychotherapy. *International Journal of Group Psychotherapy, 40,* 431–452.

McCallum, M., & Piper, W. E. (1990b). The psychological mindedness assessment procedure. *Psychological Assessment: A Journal of Consulting and Clinical Psychology, 2,* 412–418.

McCallum, M., Piper, W. E., & Morin, H. (1993). Affect and outcome in short-term group therapy for loss. *International Journal of Group Psychotherapy, 43,* 303–319.

Piper, W. E., Azim, H. F. A., Joyce, A. S., & McCallum, M. (1991). Transference interpretations, therapeutic alliance and outcome in short-term individual psychotherapy. *Archives of General Psychiatry, 48,* 946–953.

Piper, W. E., Debbane, E. G., Bienvenu, J. P., de Carufel, F. L., & Garant, J. (1986). Relationships between the object focus of therapist interpretations and outcome in short-term individual psychotherapy. *British Journal of Medical Psychology, 59,* 1–11.

Piper, W. E., Debbane, E. G., Bienvenu, J. P., & Garant, J. (1982). A study of group pretraining for group psychotherapy. *International Journal of Group Psychotherapy, 32,* 309–325.

Piper, W. E., Debbane, E. G., de Carufel, F. L., & Bienvenu, J. P. (1987). A system for differentiating therapist interpretations from other interventions. *Bulletin of the Menninger Clinic, 51,* 532–550.

Piper, W. E., & McCallum, M. (1988). *Psychodynamic Work and Object Rating System (PWORS) manual.* Unpublished manuscript.

Piper, W. E., McCallum, M., & Azim, H. F. A. (1992). *Adaptation to loss through short-term group psychotherapy.* New York: Guilford Press.

Piper, W. E., Montvila, R. M., & McGihon, A. H. (1979). Process analysis in therapy groups: A behavioral sampling technique with many uses. In D. Upper & S. M. Ross (Eds.), *Behavioral group therapy: An annual review* (pp. 55–69). Champaign, IL: Research Press.

Stiles, W. B. (1988). Psychotherapy process–outcome correlations may be misleading. *Psychotherapy, 25,* 27–35.

Stock, D., & Thelen, H. A. (1958). *Emotional dynamics and group culture.* New York: New York University Press.

Thelen, H. A., Stock, D., Hill, W. F., Ben-Zeev, S., & Heintz, I. (1954). *Methods for studying work and emotionality in group operation.* Chicago: University of Chicago, Human Dynamics Laboratory.

Weissman, M. M., Paykel, E. S., & Siegal, R. (1972). *Social Adjustment Scale: Rationale, reliability, validity and scoring.* Unpublished manuscript.

Whitaker, D. S., & Lieberman, M. A. (1964). *Psychotherapy through the group process.* Chicago: Aldine.

11

THE INDIVIDUAL GROUP MEMBER INTERPERSONAL PROCESS SCALE

MICHAEL SEAN DAVIS, SIMON H. BUDMAN, AND STEPHEN SOLDZ

In this chapter we describe the development of the Individual Group Member Interpersonal Process Scale (IGIPS), a group therapy process measure based on an interpersonal, interactionally oriented approach to group psychotherapy. We delineate the nature of the group theory underlying the IGIPS as well as the entire developmental history of the instrument. The rationale for the creation of the measure and three successive revisions is then presented. In total, the development of the IGIPS represents the culmination of nearly a decade of research in the area of group psychotherapy. In addition, the structure and properties of the latest version of the system are described and research findings using the instrument outlined. Finally, we summarize and discuss the application of the IGIPS to Group A process data.

HISTORY AND THEORY OF THE SYSTEM

The IGIPS was designed to test the assumptions underlying an interpersonal, interactionally oriented approach to group psychotherapy. This approach, described in detail by Yalom (1985) and adapted to a time-limited format by Budman and Gurman (1988), presumes that group therapy has curative possibilities that are indigenous to the group treatment mode. According to this theory, the group becomes a "social microcosm" of the outside world in which maladaptive interpersonal patterns are replayed, recognized, and acknowledged. As group members reenact their interpersonal difficulties in the group, they are likely to receive disconfirming evidence about the beliefs that are causally related to maladaptive interactions. This provides individual group members with a unique opportunity to become aware of problematic interpersonal behaviors and to experiment with new, more effective ones.

In this model, therapists assume an active, structuring stance that primarily involves exploring and commenting on "here-and-now" group processes and their associative evolution. In addition, therapists take responsibility for galvanizing the group as a whole, drawing particular group members into interactions, setting limits on destructive behaviors, and tying themes back to central foci. When adapted to a brief, time-limited format, the model also incorporates the importance of a predetermined thematic focus, a sense of explicit time consciousness intended to mobilize change through the acknowledgment of existential limits, and an overt recognition of the group as part of a larger constellation of "therapeutic" experiences extending over the group members' life span.

The most influential factor in whether group members successfully use the opportunities inherent in the group therapy mode is group cohesiveness (Budman & Gurman, 1988). *Cohesion* is defined as the connectedness of the group, demonstrated by working together toward a common therapeutic goal, constructive engagement around common themes, and an open, trusting attitude that allows members to share personal material. A cohesive group atmosphere induces a sense of individual safety in group members, enabling them to acknowledge interpersonal weaknesses and to initiate and sustain the difficult process of change. Cohesion also keeps individual members coming to the group in the face of strong or frightening emotionality, such as confrontation or hostility, or during periods without direct rewards.

The initial attempt of the Harvard Community Health Plan–Mental Health Research Program (HCHP–MHRP) to study group behavior at the individual level resulted in the development of the "main actor" concept. The *main actor* is defined as the group member whose issues were most focused on in a given 30-min segment. Raters viewing videotapes of therapy sessions could identify main actors with high reliability. These early studies examined the relation of main actor process to pretherapy patient distress and therapeutic outcome. It was found that the number of times a patient was the main actor positively predicted outcome (Soldz, Budman, Demby, & Feldstein, 1990).

Main actor process was further examined using an adaptation of the Vanderbilt Psychotherapy Process Scale (VPPS). The VPPS was selected because the results of many studies have suggested a connection between VPPS dimensions and outcome within individual therapy (Gomes-Schwartz & Schwartz, 1978; O'Malley, Suh, & Strupp, 1983; Rounsaville et al., 1987; Suh, Strupp, & O'Malley, 1986; Windholz & Silberschatz, 1988). As many of the VPPS dimensions have potential relevance to group therapy, the scale was slightly modified and applied to individual patient behavior in the group setting. In one HCHP–MHRP study that used the modified VPPS suggested the existence of an interaction predictive of outcome between specific patient behaviors and the number of times a patient was the main actor within the group (Soldz, Budman, & Demby, 1992). Results of another study indicated that the number of times a patient was the main actor was predicted by pretherapy disturbance level, but it did not predict patient outcome (Soldz et al., 1990).

Despite these findings, it became clear that there were many limitations to the use of the VPPS as a measure of group process. For example, the VPPS was unable to take into account the various modes of focus an individual patient can adopt within the group setting. A patient in group therapy can choose to discuss personal issues or those of other group members (OGMs). No comparable choice confronts the individual therapy patient. Therefore, the VPPS was insensitive to this distinction. Researchers who have used the VPPS were forced to disregard the other-focused patient behaviors that occurred within the group and to examine only self-focused patient behaviors (main actors). This meant that many of the subtleties and complexities of the group process remained inaccessible to measurement and analysis.

Before embarking on the development of the IGIPS, the HCHP–MHRP also explored the possibility of using process measures other than the VPPS. Both an early version of the Therapeutic Work Scale (Connelly, Piper, & Braha, 1981) and the Experiencing Scale (Klein, Mathieu, Gendlin, & Kiesler, 1969; Klein, Mathieu-Coughlan, & Kiesler, 1986) were considered. These scales did not meet the specific needs of the intended research. As with the VPPS, the Experiencing Scale was designed for individual therapy and therefore was inherently limited in its application to the group format. Although more suited to group research, the sentence-by-sentence unit of analysis used by the Therapeutic Work Scale was too time-consuming. Moreover, our research team was unable to obtain acceptable reliability in our initial attempt at learning the scale. Most importantly, however, we decided against the other process measures because they were derived from different theoretical perspectives. By developing the IGIPS, the HCHP–MHRP was able to devise an individual-level instrument that was sensitive to both the group format and to our particular theoretical interests.

The IGIPS has undergone numerous revisions. Initially, IGIPS ratings were made on 30-minute segments of therapy groups. Each rater would follow 2 or 3 patients over a 30-minute period and would perform ratings on each patient at the completion of the segment. This methodology was adapted to be as cost-effective and time-effective as possible. Preliminary work with this method suggested, however, that raters had difficulty remembering and averaging the behaviors over such a long period of time. As a result, the reliability of these global ratings was extremely low. To correct this problem, the scale was restructured in a manner that resembles its present form, where ratings are performed on each "statement" made by a group member.

Since this fundamental shift in the unit of observation and rating, there have been three revisions of the scale: the IGIPS–I, IGIPS–II, and IGIPS–III.[1] Unless otherwise indicated, in this chapter we focus on the most recent version of the scale, the IGIPS–III. The primary goal of each revision was to make the rating protocol more practical and time-effective and ultimately to increase reliability. The revisions have also increased the scope of the phenomena that can be measured by the scale. For example, in revising the IGIPS–I, it was decided that the therapist should be rated as well as the group members and that the sequence of statements should be recorded. These modifications have made it theoretically possible to perform sequential analyses of group interactions and to explore the relationship between interventions and responses. As a result, the IGIPS has become a multifaceted, flexible group therapy process instrument.

CORRESPONDENCE BETWEEN THE THEORY AND THE SYSTEM

For the 5 years before its focus on individual group member behavior, the HCHP–MHRP had been engaged in an ongoing research program. The research program was a reaction to the lack of empirical research on the validity of the "curative factors" putatively associated with group therapy (Kaul & Bednar, 1986). Initially, the program analyzed behavior at the group level. It explored whether the concept of group cohesiveness was as theoretically and clinically useful as the concept of "therapeutic alliance" was in individual therapy. This goal was pursued in a series of studies of time-limited (15-session) outpatient therapy groups (Budman et al., 1987, 1988, 1989) that showed that group cohesiveness was related to outcome measures, such as improved self-esteem and reduced symptoma-

---

[1]Although more improvements and refinements could be made, because of the disbandment of the Harvard Community Health Plan–Mental Health Research Program research team, there are presently no plans to develop future iterations of the scale.

tology. These and other findings supported the clinical consensus that viewed cohesiveness as an important component of a successful group experience.

In these studies, cohesion was measured using the Harvard Community Health Plan Group Cohesiveness Scale (GCS). The scale consists of five subscales and a global scale. The five subscales are (a) Withdrawal and Self-Absorption vs. Interest and Involvement, (b) Mistrust vs. Trust, (c) Disruption vs. Cooperation, (d) Abusiveness vs. Expressed Caring, and (e) Unfocused vs. Focused. The global scale is Global Fragmentation vs. Global Cohesiveness. Raters view 30-minute segments of group therapy process and apply each scale to the group as a whole along a 10-point continuum. The GCS is presented more extensively in Budman and Gurman (1988).

After establishing a consistent link between cohesiveness and outcome at the group level, the HCHP–MHRP studied the microevents and individual group member behaviors that could affect cohesiveness and in turn differentiate between positive and negative outcome for groups and individuals. The IGIPS was created for this purpose. The guiding principle in the construction of the IGIPS was to select items derived from the concept of cohesiveness that could also be used and rated reliably at the microevent level. This presented several interesting challenges. The new format required raters to make ratings on brief statements that were sometimes only three words long. Making subtle or complex judgments about such short statements is intrinsically difficult and inevitably resulted in poor reliability. Consequently, items representing constructs from the GCS were often reworded to constrain the use of clinical inference or the reliance on implicit averaging across the poles of a dimension.

For example, the bipolar construct Abusiveness vs. Expressed Caring —which was rated reliably on the group global level but presented difficulties on the individual statement level—was broken into two unipolar dimensions, Expresses Negative Sentiment and Expresses Positive Sentiment, which had ratings that indicated the degree to which each characteristic was present in each statement. By subtracting the sum of Expresses Positive Sentiment from the sum of Expresses Negative Sentiment and then dividing the result by the total number of statements within a given unit of time, it was possible to obtain a reliable score that was conceptually similar to the original GCS item. Note, however, that not all the original GCS constructs were able to be translated in this manner. The research team was unable to adapt the construct Focused vs. Unfocused, a construct reflecting the degree to which the group retained a thematic coherence, to the statement format.

DESCRIPTION OF THE SYSTEM

Rating and Categories

IGIPS ratings are performed on each statement made by a group member. A *statement* is defined as a burst of speech of more than two words by a single person without a pause of more than 10 seconds. A typical statement is bounded by a statement made by other group members. Occasionally, a statement is bounded by a substantial (10-second) pause in an individual's burst of speech. Each rating indicates to whom the statement is referring (i.e., self, therapist, group as a whole, or other group member), the locational focus of the statement (i.e., life outside the group vs. inside the group), and whether the statement was self-initiated or elicited.

In addition to this and other fundamental information, derivative items from the GCS were adapted to the individual statement format. Examples of the adapted items include "Discloses Personal Material" and "Feels Connected to Others." IGIPS ratings obtained for each statement can be aggregated and combined to form a multitude of possible variables, including ones reflecting the sequential relationships of group interactions. Therefore, the IGIPS is an all-purpose instrument that has the potential to measure a wide range of group phenomena.

IGIPS ratings are made with reference to videotapes and transcripts of the therapy sessions. The videotapes help the raters ascertain the emotional tone of a statement, and the transcripts help them remember its content. After each statement, raters typically pause the videotape to determine whether it contained behavior that should be rated on any of the items. IGIPS–III consists of 23 items that raters need to consider. Some items are rated on a categorical basis, reflecting the presence or absence of a specific behavior. Other items are rated on a 0–9 Likert scale, reflecting the significance of the behavior. *Significance* is the intensity or judged psychological importance of a behavior. Given the theoretical orientation of the research team, significance ratings are explicitly associated with the degree to which the behavior reflects a heightened awareness of immediately present feelings and interpersonal processes combined with an increased understanding of the factors responsible for their existence. Although this principle is embedded in all the significance rating protocols, the actual guidelines for making the ratings emphasize different elements of the principle depending on relevance to each item. The section on strengths and limitations contains an example of significance ratings.

Many of the items also contain locational and object designations that indicate the locational focus (i.e., inside group or outside group) to which the behavior is referring or to whom the behavior is directed. For example, when using the item "Expresses Negative Sentiment," the rater is required to record the object toward which this sentiment was directed. The options include the group, the therapist, the self, the ID number of another group member, someone outside the group, or inanimate factors. Once the designations have been determined, the significance level of the sentiment is rated for each of the separate designations on a 1–9 scale. The item "Demonstrates Self-Awareness," however, uses a different set of designations. For this item, the options include awareness related to either group process or to life outside the group. Again, separate significance level ratings (using the 1–9 scale) are performed for each of the two designations. Each of the 23 items has a unique set of appropriate designations ranging from 0–7 (see Table 11.1 for definitions, types of ratings, and examples).

Limitations and Strengths

The degree of inference that is needed to perform ratings varies for each item. No inference is necessary for some items, such as "Length of Statement." It is required for other items, such as "Enhances OGM Awareness." As previous experience with scale development has demonstrated, greater inference usually means lower reliability. Therefore, a concerted effort was made to control the degree of inference. The challenge was to limit the inference without reducing the clinical relevance of the items. The solution to this dilemma involved the incorporation of rigid, theoretically meaningful guidelines into the significance rating procedures whenever possible.

This technique is best exemplified in the items that measure the degree of psychological mindedness, such as "Demonstrates Self-Awareness." Ratings for this item are made in a two-step process. First, the numerical range within which the rater can operate is established. Ratings are limited to the lower range (1–4) of the 9-point scale if the target patient demonstrates awareness of a feeling or interpersonal enactment without suggesting the cause of these occurrences. The midrange (3–7) is used when an ongoing pattern of behavior is acknowledged or when a coexisting cause of a feeling or interpersonal enactment is identified. Finally, the high rate (6–9) is used when a historical cause for a feeling, interpersonal enactment, or pattern of behavior is identified. For example, the statement "I've been depressed lately" would be limited to a lower range rating, yet the statement "The incident with my wife has made me depressed lately" would receive a midrange rating. On the other hand, the statement "I've been depressed lately. I usually get depressed when I am angry. My family never let anybody get angry, so I don't know what else to do" would receive a rating in the high range.

Once the range is determined, the final rating is adjusted based on examination of other criteria. These include the amount of total awareness

TABLE 11.1
Individual Group Member Interpersonal Process Scale Categories

Statement Categories	Type of Ratings	Examples
Item 1: Statement Number	The sequential number of each statement	The 3rd statement would receive a rating of 3, and the 450th statement would receive a rating of 450.
Item 2: Target Patient ID	The ID number of the patient making the statement	A statement made by a patient with an ID number of 6 would receive a rating of 6.
Item 3: Statement Length	Each 5-s interval represents 1 length unit	3-, 8-, and 45-s statements would receive a rating of 1, 2, and 9, respectively.
Item 4: Discusses Self	Frequency	"I was upset about what happened."
Item 5: Discusses OGM	Frequency	"You [OGM] seemed upset by what happened."
Item 6: Discusses Therapist	Frequency	"I think you [therapist] should make sure these things don't happen in here."
Item 7: Discusses Impersonal Issues	Frequency	"Society needs to provide more resources for children."
Item 8: Uses Humor	Frequency	A statement that elicits laughter in at least one OGM.
Item 9: Self-Initiated Statement Rated when statement was not made in response to a direct inquiry or comment.	Frequency	Therapist: "Who would like to start today?" Group member: "I have something to discuss."
Item 10: Discloses Personal Material Information an "average" person would usually not reveal to strangers in commonplace social situations.	Significance with inside- and outside-group designations	Outside-group designation: "I am uncomfortable in most social situations." Inside-group designation: "I feel inferior to the people in this group."
Item 11: Expresses Affect Statements delivered in a manner that could be appropriately characterized by an adjective connoting a specific emotion.	Significance	Statement delivered with a specific emotional tone, such as sad, happy, angry. Ratings reflect nonverbal behavior.

Item 12: Resistance to Affect Statements delivered in a manner that could be characterized as stiff, flat, detached, monotonic, or withdrawn.	Significance	Statement delivered with a specific tone that is unable to be described with an adjective connoting an emotion. Ratings reflect nonverbal behavior.
Item 13: Expresses Negative Sentiment Overt expressions of negative thoughts or feelings.	Significance with group, therapist, self, OGM, POG, and IF designations	OGM designation: "I didn't think you [an OGM] were helpful last week." IF designation: "Life sucks. There is no denying it."
Item 14: Expresses Positive Sentiment Overt expressions of positive thoughts or feelings.	Significance with group, therapist, self, OGM, POG, and IF designations	Self-designation: "Despite what everyone said, I think I did a good job." POG designation: "My sister has always been helpful to me."
Item 15: Feels Connected to Others Overt acknowledgment of similarity, shared experiences, or feelings of intimacy with others.	Significance with group, therapist, OGM, and POG designations	Group designation: "Everyone in the group has had problems with relationships."
Item 16: Feels Disconnected From Others Overt acknowledgment of feeling dissimilar, alienated, or detached from others. Also includes feelings of loneliness.	Significance with group, therapist, OGM, and POG designations	POG designation: "I never fit in with anyone in high school."
Item 17: Demonstrates Self-Awareness Overt acknowledgment of a feeling, pattern of behavior, or interpersonal enactment. Significance ratings are scored higher for identification of causes.	Significance with inside- and outside-group designations	Outside-group designation: "I like to keep things of a superficial level until I know someone well." Inside-group designation: "I am angry because you interrupted me."
Item 18: Exhibits Unawareness, Uncertainty, or Confusion Rated when unawareness, uncertainty, or confusion are exhibited in regard to identity, goals, or causes of a feeling, interpersonal enactment, or pattern of behavior.	Significance with inside- and outside-group designations	Outside-group designation: "I don't know why I was so mean to him back then." Inside-group designation: "I'm not sure how I feel about the group."
Item 19: Interpersonal Sensitivity A communication directed toward an OGM delivered in a warm, tolerant, or sensitive manner.	Significance	"I image that was difficult for you [an OGM]. It sounds like you did the best anyone could."

Table continues

TABLE 11.1 (Continued)

Statement Categories	Type of Ratings	Examples
Item 20: Interpersonal Insensitivity A communication directed toward an OGM delivered in a cold, intolerant, or insensitive manner.	Significance	"It doesn't sound like you [an OGM] were very effective in the situation. Couldn't you do any better."
Item 21: Asks Questions Any communication in question form directed to an OGM, the therapist, or the group as a whole.	Significance with inside- and outside-group designations	Outside-group designation: "How is your wife doing?" Inside-group designation: "What did you think about last week?"
Item 22: Enhances OGM Awareness A communication that highlights the existence of a feeling, pattern of behavior, or interpersonal enactment of an OGM. Significance ratings are scored higher for suggestion of causes.	Significance with inside- and outside-group designations	Outside-group designation: "It seems like you go through cycles of high and low energy." Inside-group designation: "You look sad today."
Item 23: Gives Advice A directive or suggestion intended to encourage an OGM to think, feel, or behave a particular way.	Significance with inside- and outside-group designations	Outside-group designation: "Tell your husband you can't handle that right now." Inside-group designation: "If you are angry with someone in here, then you should tell them."

Note. OGM = outside group member; POG = people outside group; IF = inanimate factors. In addition to statement number, patient ID, and length ratings, three other categories of ratings are possible for each statement: frequency, significance, and locational-object designations. Frequency ratings are binary ratings indicating the presence or absence of a behavior. Significance ratings are continuous ratings indicating the intensity or judged psychological importance of the behavior. The definitions and guidelines for making significance ratings adhere to a common principle but are implemented differently for each item. Location-object designations indicate the object to which a feeling is directed or the context in which a behavior occurs. The possible object designations include the group as a whole (group), therapist, self, OGMs, POG, and IFs; the context designations include outside the group and inside the group. Different designations are used for different items depending on appropriateness.

demonstrated within the statement, as well as the degree to which the awareness is differentiated and focused on the immediate present and interpersonal issues. Finally, the raters clinical inference about the importance of the insight can also influence the final rating.

Thus, ratings for the above item are constrained by specific theoretical assumptions. The most important of these are that (a) therapeutic growth is related to an elaborated understanding of the relationship between life experience and present behaviors and (b) in the group setting, this elaborated understanding is most effective when applied to interpersonal behaviors occurring within the immediate present. Similar constraints and techniques are used when making significance ratings for other items.

METHODOLOGY FOR ANALYSIS

Although the IGIPS–III contains only 23 items, the numerous designations associated with the items create thousands of formats for aggregating data. To organize this data into manageable units, it is necessary to create reduced items that combine these possible formats. Different researchers may use different reduced items depending on the unit of analysis and the requirements of their research. The criteria should be that their distributions are normal, their interrater reliabilities sufficient, and they measure discrete dimensions that overlap only minimally with other reduced items. Table 11.2 contains an experimental set of reduced items at the individual level, their available reliability coefficients, and formulas indicating how each item was created.[2]

Most scores for the reduced items are calculated by summing the relevant ratings at the statement level across an entire session and then dividing that sum by an appropriate denominator. Some reduced items use the total number of statements made by the patient as the denominator, whereas others use either the total number of self-focused or OGM-focused statements as the denominator. For example, the reduced item "Feels Connected to Group" is derived by subtracting the sum of "Feels Disconnected From Others" (with in-group designations) from the sum of "Feel Connected to Others" (with in-group designations) and dividing the result by the total number of statements made by the patient. Other reduced items, such as "Demonstrates Insight Into Own Life," are obtained by summing the ratings of the item "Demonstrates Self-Awareness" (with an out-group designation) and dividing by the total number of statements in which the patient discussed his or her own issues. Still other items use a different

---

[2]The items listed in Table 11.2 represent the most recent reduced items constructed by the Harvard Community Health Plan–Mental Health Research Program. This set of items was created to measure behaviors the research team considers to be theoretically important. Beyond their face validity, the validity of this set of items has not been established.

TABLE 11.2
IGIPS–III Reduced Items with Interrater Reliabilities

Reduced Items	ICC
Amount Spoken	
(ΣItem 3)	.96
Focuses on Self	
(ΣItem 4/TS)	.97
Focuses on OGMs	
(ΣItem 5/TS)	.88
Focuses on Impersonal or Abstract Issues	
(ΣItem 7/TS)	.81
Focuses on Group Process	
(Σany item with any inside-group designation/TS)	.92
Uses Humor	
(ΣItem 8/TS)	.91
Initiates Comments	
(ΣItem 9/TS)	.92
Discloses Personal Material About Own Life	
(ΣItem 10 with Designation OG/TS)	.56
Discloses Personal Material About Group	
(ΣItem 10 with Designation IG/TS)	.90
Expresses Affect	
[(ΣItem 11–ΣItem 12)/TS]	.79
Quality of Sentiment Expressed Toward Group	
[(ΣItem 14 with Designations G, T, OGM–ΣItem 13 with Designations G, T, OGM)/TS)]	.82
Quality of Sentiment Expressed About Life Outside Group	
[(ΣItem 14 with Designations IF and POG–ΣItem 13 with Designations IF and POG)/TS)]	.71
Feels Connected to Group	
[(ΣItem 15 with Designations G, T, OGM–ΣItem 16 with Designations G, T, OGM)/TS)]	.54
Feels Connected to People Outside Group	
[(ΣItem 15 with Designations POG–ΣItem 16 with Designations POG)/TS)]	.67
Demonstrates Insight Into Own Life Issues	
(ΣItem 17 with Designation OG/ΣItem 4)	.87
Demonstrates Insight Into Own Group Issues	
(ΣItem 17 with Designation IG/ΣItem 4)	.88
Demonstrates Insight Into OGM Life Issues	
[(ΣItem 21 with Designation OG + Item 22 with Designation OG)/ΣItem 5]	.65
Demonstrates Insight Into OGM Group Issues	
[(ΣItem 21 with Designation IG + Item 22 with Designation IG)/ΣItem 5]	.77
Amount of Input Received From Group	
(Σfrequency ratings from Item 14 through Item 16 + Item 21 through Item 23 received from group)	.98
Psychological Mindedness of Input Received From Group	
(Mean significance ratings from Item 21 + Item 22 + Item 23 received from group)	.83
Affective Quality of Sentiment Received From Group	
[(ΣItem 14 received from group–ΣItem 13 received from group)/Σinput received from group]	.82

Note. $N = 23$. The unit of analysis was individual group member behavior across a whole session. Two raters were used to rate eight group members in three different sessions (one member missed one session). ICC = intraclass correlation; Item = item numbers in Table 11.1; Σ = sum of indicated ratings for each individual group member across a whole session; TS = total statements made by a group member within a session; G = group; T = therapist; OGM = other group member; POG = people outside group; IF = inanimate factors; OG = outside group; IG = inside group.

method of calculation altogether. For example, the reduced item "Amount of Input Received From Group" is calculated simply by summing the number of times feedback is directed at a given patient.

Once the reduced items have been selected, the final step in the data reduction process involves conducting a principal-components analysis (PCA). The factors that emerge from the PCA should be used to analyze the data. The results of a PCA that was performed on reduced items from IGIPS–I are discussed later.

Reliability

The interrater reliabilities of the IGIPS–III reduced items listed in Table 11.3 appear to be good to excellent. Individual rater interclass correlation reliability was calculated from the ratings of two raters who viewed three sessions of an eight-member group. The unit of analysis used in these calculations was the individual group member behavior per session ($N = 23$; one member missed one session). The reliability ranged from .54 to .98, with a mean reliability of .82 and a median of .83.

Reliabilities for these 23 items were also calculated at the statement level. All 1,400 statements of two sessions were rated by different raters and then examined to ensure the correspondence between the sequence of ratings. At this level, reliability was notably lower but still acceptable. The intraclass correlations ranged from .33 to .86, with a mean of .65 and median of .69.

Reliabilities for earlier versions of the scale were also acceptable, although they were somewhat lower than for the IGIPS–III. Thirty-five 30-minute segments were rated by three different raters using the IGIPS–I. Reliability for the five factors derived from 12 reduced items ranged from .53 to .95, with a mean reliability of .70 (Soldz, Budman, Davis, & Demby, 1993). Reliability for the IGIPS–II, which more closely resembles the IGIPS–III, has also been calculated. Two raters rated 15 different 30-minute segments. When aggregated at the group level, the mean intraclass correlation of the nine reduced items used in a study exploring the component parts of cohesiveness was .80, the median was .85, and the range was .46–.94. Because each version of the IGIPS was revised with the goal of increasing reliability, it is not surprising that reliability tends to be higher for each new iteration of the scale.

PREVIOUS RESEARCH WITH THE SYSTEM

The three versions of the IGIPS have been used in a variety of studies with varying degrees of validity. The IGIPS–I was applied to the videotapes of the first 4 sessions of seven 15-session interpersonally oriented outpatient

TABLE 11.3
IGIPS Scores From the First Half of Session 3 of Group A

Reduced items	Main actor	Facilitators					Therapists		Group as a whole
	Joe	Greg	Diane	Brad	Martha	Pat	Helen	Alice	
Amount spoken	212	38	140	47	99	38	64	122	775
Discusses abstract issues	0.29	0.24	0.00	0.00	0.22	0.00	0.03	0.05	0.12
Discusses group process	0.57	0.42	0.87	0.45	0.38	0.91	0.60	0.74	0.61
Discloses personal material	1.3	1.2	1.1	0.30	1.3	1.2	0.20	0.60	1.1
Expresses affect	1.5	2.8	3.6	1.2	3.3	2.4	2.6	2.7	2.7
Feels connected to group	-0.36	0.12	-0.24	0.09	0.14	0.33	-0.08	0.12	-0.04
Insight into own issues	2.2	0.80	2.2	0.00	1.5	2.5	0.10	0.70	1.7
Insight into OGM issues	1.8	2.5	2.4	2.8	1.6	4.0	2.2	2.2	2.2

Note. Approximate cohesiveness rating: midlevel. IGIPS = Individual Group Member Interpersonal Process Scale; OGM = other group member.

therapy groups that contained a total of 52 patients. Twelve reduced items were used in the analysis. A PCA was performed on these reduced items. The literature suggests that a two-dimensional circumplex structure of Dominance and Affiliation underlies interpersonal behavior (Wiggins, 1979, 1982). Therefore, two factors were initially extracted and then subjected to a varimax rotation. The two circumplex dimensions were clearly visible. The first factor, which was theoretically consistent with the Dominance circumplex dimension, had positive loadings from "Expresses Affect," "Amount of Speech," and "Discloses Personal Material." The second factor, consistent with the Affiliation dimension, received loadings from "Connections With Others," "Responsiveness to Input," and "Positive Sentiment Toward Others."

These two factors, however, accounted for only 39% of the variance. Thus, standard procedures for determining the best factor structure were used, resulting in five factors that accounted for 74% of the variance. After varimax rotation, these five factors were as follows: Activity, Interpersonal Sensitivity, Comfort With Self, Self-Focus, and Psychological Mindedness. (see Appendix 11.A for a list of the reduced items that loaded on these five factors). Interestingly, this more comprehensive five-factor structure resembles the Big Five personality factors consistently found in factor analyses of personality descriptions (John, 1990; McCrae, 1989; McCrae & Costa, 1990). The Big Five has also been related to personality pathology in clinical samples (Costa & McCrae, 1990; Lyons, Ozer, Young, Merla, & Hyler, 1991; Soldz, Budman, Demby, & Merry, 1993; Wiggins & Pincus, 1989). The parallels between Activity and Extraversion, Interpersonal Sensitivity and Agreeableness, and Comfort With Self and the Big Five Neuroticism or Emotional Stability are clear. It also seems reasonable to associate Psychological Mindedness with Openness. Finally, it is possible to argue that the group behavior most representative of the Big Five Conscientiousness factor is the amount of talk directed at other people. This is because conscientious group members are likely to make an effort to further the group task by responding and reaching out to other group members. Because the remaining factor, Self-Focus, is the opposite of discussing others, it seems reasonable to identify this with the Big Five Conscientiousness dimension. This form of convergent validity both with the interpersonal circumplex model and the Big Five factors suggests that the IGIPS is capable of representing relevant and important dimensions of interpersonal behavior.[3]

Other findings from this study also support the validity of the IGIPS. Scores from the Self-Focus factor were positively correlated with the self-report measures of pretherapy symptomatic distress. The Comfort With Self

---

[3]For a more detailed discussion of the first Individual Group Member Interpersonal Process Scale I factor structure and its correspondence with the interpersonal circumplex and Big Five models, see Soldz, Budman, Davis, and Demby (1993).

factor scores were correlated with the therapist's global assessment of patient functioning. Finally, women scored higher than men on the Interpersonal Sensitivity factor score. This replicates other findings that show that women are more concerned with relationships and are more sensitive of the feelings of others (Gilligan, 1982; Lewis, 1976; Spence & Helmreich, 1978).

The IGIPS–II was also used in a study (Budman, Soldz, Demby, Davis, & Merry, 1993) designed to explore the component parts of group cohesiveness. In this study, 39 half-hour segments from 12 time-limited psychotherapy groups were measured on both the GCS and the IGIPS–II. Correlations between cohesiveness scores and the IGIPS–II reduced items aggregated across all group members suggested that particular group member behaviors are related to cohesion according to the phase of the group therapy. For example, outside-group-focused statements were positively correlated with cohesiveness in the beginning of the group but negatively correlated with cohesiveness at the end of the group. The reverse was true for inside-group-focused statements. These data are consistent with many of the stage-related theories of group development (Beck, Dugo, Eng, & Lewis, 1986; Budman & Gurman, 1988; MacKenzie, 1990).

Finally, there is preliminary, unpublished work with the IGIPS–III. In a long-term group for patients with personality disorders, the IGIPS–III was able to differentiate the early group process of patients diagnosed with avoidant personality disorders from the group process of patients without these diagnoses. These differences were theoretically consistent with the fourth edition of the *Diagnostic and Statistical Manual of Mental Disorders* (*DSM–IV*; American Psychiatric Association, 1994). Compared with the nonavoidant patients, the 2 avoidant patients scored markedly lower on most of the expected dimensions, such as level of verbal activity, initiative, expressed affect, and connectedness.

Similarly, IGIPS–III scores were able to differentiate the group process of histrionic patients. IGIPS–III ratings were performed on three early sessions of 14 patients distributed across five different time-limited psychotherapy groups. Seven patients received elevated scores on the Histrionic scale of the Millon Clinical Multiaxial Inventory II (Millon, 1987), and 7 patients received low scores on this same dimension. Each of the 7 histrionic patients were matched with a same-sex nonhistrionic patient in the same group. As with the avoidant patients, the group process of the histrionic patients differed from the nonhistrionic patients in ways consistent with the *DSM–IV*. Histrionic patients, for example, expressed more affect, initiated more statements, and expressed more feelings of being different from others.

Although the IGIPS has not yet been used in this type of work, it clearly has the potential for analyzing the sequence of interactions among group members in interesting ways. Unlike most work examining sequential interactions in psychotherapy (Bakeman, 1990; Gottman & Bakeman, 1986; Gottman & Roy, 1990), the IGIPS–III has quantitative, rather than simply categorical, capacities. This makes it possible to use correlational techniques rather than traditional methods (Gottman & Bakeman, 1986; Gottman & Roy, 1990). An interesting use of the scale, for example, might be to examine the correlations between the type of input received from other group members or the therapist and the emergence of demonstrated self-awareness.

APPLICATION OF THE SYSTEM OF ANALYSIS TO GROUP A, SESSION 3

An analysis of Group A provides an excellent opportunity to illustrate some of the potential applications of the IGIPS–III. Although there are a variety of possible uses for the scale, this illustration focuses on the most elemental ones. The methodological protocol and programming for the more intricate and exciting applications—such as sequential analyses—have not yet been developed.

In keeping with earlier HCHP–MHRP research endeavors, the purpose of the methodology that is presented here is to understand the development of cohesiveness at the group level. As referenced earlier, previous work with the IGIPS suggests a relationship between IGIPS scores and the cohesiveness level of the group as a whole. As an extension of this work, the HCHP–MHRP was interested in analyzing the behavior of the individual group members who assume the different roles indigenous to group therapy. These roles consist of the main actor, facilitator, and therapist. Main actors are the individuals whose issues are being explored by the group, and facilitators are those who help the main actor with this exploration.[4] In particular, we believe that the main actors may play an especially influential role in setting the tone for the group. Therefore, there may be some main actor behaviors that are more conducive than others to the development of group cohesiveness. This analysis is designed to illustrate how this methodology might work and how the IGIPS–III could contribute to this type of inquiry. It also provides an opportunity to explore whether clinical impressions of the session are accurately represented in the process.

Clinically, members of the HCHP–MHRP felt that one of the notable elements of the third session from Group A was the difference be-

---

[4]To be considered a main actor, it is necessary that the group focus on the individual's issue for a somewhat sustained period. Previous work with the concept suggests that main factor ratings can be made with extremely high reliability (Soldz, Budman, Demby, & Feldstein, 1990).

tween the first and second half.[5] The second half of the session appeared to be especially constructive. Many of the group members worked toward an understanding of their families of origin and explored how these family dynamics may have influenced their present difficulties. Most importantly, these efforts were cooperative. Most of the group members shared their experiences and related them to the overall theme of the discussion. The discussion appeared to be affectively stimulating to most group members. On the GCS, the second half of the session would receive a high cohesiveness rating.

The early part of the session would be characterized differently. The discussion was focused primarily on the concerns of Joe. Because he was interested in addressing events related to the group, the topic was necessarily relevant to the other group members. However, the other group members were unable to engage themselves in the discussion with the same amount of energy that was exhibited later. In addition, the focus of the discussion was often tenuous and unclear. Confusion and miscommunication resulted. Although the first half of the session may have been important for Joe, the majority of the group members were unable to engage in significant therapeutic work. On the GCS, the early part of the session would receive a midrange rating.

To illustrate these general differences between the early and later part of the session, we present the scores for eight basic IGIPS–III reduced items in Tables 11.3 and 11.4. The individual group member scores for both parts of the session are divided into three categories according to role: main actor, facilitator, and therapist. The aggregated IGIPS–III scores and approximate cohesiveness levels for both session halves are also presented.

The IGIPS–III scores accurately represented general clinical impressions. According to the aggregated group IGIPS scores, for example, many of the behaviors commonly associated with productive psychotherapy, such as the disclosure of personal material, the expression of affect, the achievement of insight, and the experience of connectedness, were all higher at the group level in the second half of the session than in the first.

In addition, individual member scores represented the different styles of presentation that characterized the main actors. Joe, the only group member who would qualify as a main actor in the first half of the session, discussed his problems in a highly abstract and general manner. This earned him high scores on the reduced IGIPS item "Discusses Abstract Issues." In addition, by simply attributing the conflict he was addressing to "personality differences," Joe made it difficult for OGMs or the therapists to relate

---

[5]The 13th statement from page 98 of the provided transcript was used as the dividing line between the first and second half of Session 3. This particular statement was selected because it is almost exactly in the middle of the session and it is where Diane began the transition to main actor. Also note that the last one-and-a-half pages of the transcript could not be rated because they were not on the audiotape.

TABLE 11.4
IGIPS Scores From the Second Half of Session 3 of Group A

Reduced items	Main actors			Facilitators			Therapists		Group as a whole
	Diane	Greg	Martha	Brad	Joe	Pat	Helen	Alice	
Amount spoken	234	84	120	14	55	0	13	69	589
Discusses abstract issues	0.07	0.19	0.06	0.00	0.26	—	0.00	0.02	0.09
Discusses group process	0.18	0.19	0.13	0.80	0.20	—	0.33	0.26	0.21
Discloses personal material	2.8	2.7	2.9	1.0	3.8	—	0.00	0.00	2.8
Expresses affect	3.8	3.9	3.5	2.4	3.0	—	2.4	2.6	3.4
Feels connected to group	0.13	−0.03	0.11	0.00	0.02	—	0.00	0.00	0.08
Insight into own issues	2.9	3.0	3.2	1.0	2.7	—	0.00	0.00	2.9
Insight into OGM issues	1.2	2.7	1.7	7.3	3.5	—	3.5	3.5	2.9

Note. Approximate group cohesiveness rating: high level. Dashes indicate no data. IGIPS = Individual Group Member Interpersonal Process Scale; OGM = other group member.

or respond to the issues he was raising. This was reflected in the relatively low facilitator and therapist scores on the reduced item "Insight Into OGM Issues." Moreover, Joe's presentation was characterized by a variety of other qualities that appeared to hinder group cohesiveness. As illustrated by his low score on the item "Expresses Affect," Joe discussed his issues in a flat monotonic voice. Also, although Joe was the main actor for a sustained period of time, the kind of personal information that he disclosed was not highly revealing for someone in the role. This became evident when comparing his score on the reduced item "Discloses Personal Material" with the main actor scores from the second half of the session. The content of Joe's presentation may have also influenced cohesiveness. One of the main themes that Joe addressed as a main actor was his perception of being different from the rest of the group. This was observed in his negative score on the item "Feels Connected to the Group." Such expressions of disconnectedness can be understood as an obstacle to positive group bonding, especially early in the group, because they are likely to make group members feel their experiences are irrelevant to one another.

In the second half of the session, Diane clearly functioned as the catalyst in establishing a new tone. Initially, Diane alluded to her personal issues in the abstract and general manner that was congruent with the presentation style established earlier in the session. With encouragement from other group members, however, Diane ultimately transcended this mode of expression. She was able to delve into a revealing and detailed discussion of painful childhood experiences and their impact on her life. Moreover, unlike Joe, Diane related her story in a spontaneous and affective manner. The difference between Diane and Joe is clearly visible in their main actor scores. As a main actor, Diane scored notably higher than Joe on "Discloses Personal Material," "Expresses Affect," "Feels Connected to Group," and "Insight Into Own Issues," whereas she scored much lower on "Discusses Abstract Issues."

The role Diane played in transforming the group atmosphere was implicated in the subsequent main actor episodes of the other group members. Both Greg and Martha were notably responsive to Diane's presentation and used it as a vehicle to compare and contrast their own personal histories. In addition, both of them appeared to emulate her style of presentation on several important dimensions, including topic, degree of affective expression, level of disclosed personal material, and depth of insight. The similarity in their presentation style was reflected in their main actor scores.

Interestingly, Joe also appeared to adopt the new presentation style initiated by Diane and sustained by Greg and Martha. Although too briefly and sporadically to qualify as main actor, Joe did discuss his own issues during the second half of the session. As illustrated by his IGIPS scores, Joe's behavior during these episodes was markedly different from his presentation in the beginning. Respectively, his scores on "Discloses Personal Material," "Expresses Affect," "Feels Connected to Group," "Insight Into Own Issues," and "Insight Into OGM Issues" were 1.3, 1.5, −0.36, 2.2, and 1.8, respectively, in the first half, compared with 3.8, 3.0, 0.02, 2.7, and 3.5 in the second half. Joe appeared to adopt the others' presentation style and, as a result, he became notably more vulnerable, emotional, connected, and insightful.

The differences between the two halves of the session can also be understood in terms of stage-related theories of group development that the HCHP–MHRP was interested in exploring. According to these theories, there are stages during group development in which it is most effective to engage the group members around specific tasks. Process-oriented interventions or discussions, for example, are theorized to be more useful late in the group, whereas a focus on personal history and life circumstances are thought to more useful in the beginning of the group. The usefulness of process behavior in understanding personal problems is difficult to discern without sufficient knowledge of personal history. Thus, groups that focus on process issues too early, without first becoming sufficiently familiar with background information, increase the risk of shallow and irrelevant feedback. This idea was illustrated by the early Group A session analyzed here. The process-focused discussion in the first half of the session, which received a .61 score on the aggregated reduced item "Discusses Group Process," was clearly less effective in engaging the group members than the historically focused discussion of the second half, which received a .21 score on the same item. Moreover, as these discussions were both initiated by the principal main actors—Joe and Diane—it provides an additional example of how main actors can influence the group experience.

ASSESSMENT AND FUTURE DIRECTIONS

The IGIPS is a scale that can be used in a variety of ways. The scale has the potential to address research questions at the group, individual, and statement levels. The scale is also sensitive to the roles associated with most forms of group therapy, such as main actor, facilitator, and therapist.

In addition, as the scale records the sequence of each statement and the individual to whom it is directed, research inquiries concerning interactive group processes becomes possible. Given this potential arsenal of information, there are many important group research endeavors to which the IGIPS can contribute. These include the relationship between interventions and responses, between individual level and group level behavior, between personality and group process, or between group process and outcome. Finally, although the IGIPS was derived from a particular theoretical orientation, many of the items are general enough to be used by research teams with different theoretical perspectives, thereby making it potentially useful at other research sites.

REFERENCES

American Psychiatric Association. (1994). *Diagnostic and statistical manual of mental disorders* (4th ed.). Washington, DC: Author.

Bakeman, R. (1990). *Sequential analysis and psychotherapy research.* Unpublished manuscript, Georgia State University.

Beck, A. P., Dugo, J. M., Eng, A. M., & Lewis, C. M. (1986). Analysis of group development. In L. S. Greenberg & W. M. Pinsof (Eds.), *The psychotherapeutic process: A research handbook* (pp. 615–705). New York: Guilford Press.

Budman, S. H., Demby, A., Feldstein, M., Redondo, J., Scherz, B., Bennett, M. J., Koppenaal, G., Sabin Daley, B., Hunter, M., & Ellis, J. (1987). Preliminary findings on a new instrument to measure cohesion in group psychotherapy. *International Journal of Group Psychotherapy, 37,* 75–94.

Budman, S. H., Demby, A., Redondo, J. P., Hannan, M., Feldstein, M., Ring, J., & Springer, T. (1988). Comparative outcome in time-limited individual and group psychotherapy. *International Journal of Group Psychotherapy, 38,* 63–86.

Budman, S. H., & Gurman, A. S. (1988). *Theory and practice of brief therapy.* New York: Guilford Press.

Budman, S. H., Soldz, S., Demby, A., Davis, M. S., & Merry, J. (1993). What is cohesiveness? An empirical examination. *Small Group Research, 24,* 199–216.

Budman, S. H., Soldz, S., Demby, A., Feldstein, M., Springer, T., & Davis, M. S. (1989). Cohesion, alliance and outcome in group psychotherapy. *Psychiatry, 52,* 339–350.

Connelly, J. L., Piper, W. E., & Braha, R. (1981). *The Therapeutic Work Rating System (TWS) manual.* Unpublished manuscript, McGill University, Montreal, Quebec, Canada.

Costa, P. T., & McCrae, R. R. (1990). Personality disorders and the five-factor model of personality. *Journal of Personality Disorder, 4,* 362–371.

Gilligan, C. (1982). *In a different voice.* Cambridge, MA: Harvard University Press.

Gomes-Schwartz, B., & Schwartz, J. M. (1978). Psychotherapy process variables distinguishing the "inherently helpful" person from the professional psychotherapist. *Journal of Consulting and Clinical Psychology, 46,* 196–197.

Gottman, J. M., & Bakeman, R. (1986). *Observing interaction: An introduction to sequential analysis.* New York: Cambridge University Press.

Gottman, J. M., & Roy, A. K. (1990). *Sequential analysis: A guide for behavioral researchers.* New York: Cambridge University Press.

John, O. P. (1990). The "Big Five" factor taxonomy: Dimensions of personality in the natural language and in questionnaires. In L. A. Pervin (Ed.), *Handbook of personality: Theory and research* (pp. 66–100). New York: Guilford Press.

Kaul, T., & Bednar, R. (1986). Research on group and related therapies. In S. Garfield & A. Bergin (Eds.), *Handbook of psychotherapy and behavior change* (pp. 671–714). New York: Wiley.

Klein, M. H., Mathieu, P. L., Gendlin, E. T., & Kiesler, D. J. (1969). *The Experiencing Scale: A research and training manual* (Vol. 1). Madison: University of Wisconsin, Extension Bureau of Audiovisual Instruction.

Klein, M. H., Mathieu-Coughlan, P., & Kiesler, D. J. (1986). The Experiencing Scale. In L. S. Greenberg & W. M. Pinsof (Eds.), *The psychotherapeutic process: A research handbook* (pp. 21–71). New York: Guilford Press.

Lewis, H. B. (1976). *Psychic war in men and women*. New York: New York University Press.

Lyons, M. J., Ozer, D. J., Young, L., Merla, M. E., & Hyler, S. E. (1991). *Relationship of the five factor model of personality to DSM–III personality disorders*. Unpublished manuscript, Boston University.

MacKenzie, K. R. (1990). *Introduction to time-limited group psychotherapy*. Washington, DC: American Psychiatric Press.

McCrae, R. R. (1989). Why I advocate the first-factor model: Joint analyses of the NEO-PI and other instruments. In D. M. Buss & N. Cantor (Eds.), *Personality psychology: Recent trends and emerging directions* (pp. 237–245). New York: Springer-Verlag.

McCrae, R. R., & Costa, P. T. (1990). *Personality in adulthood*. New York: Guilford Press.

Millon, T. (1987). *Manual for MCMI-II*. Minneapolis, MN: National Computer Systems.

O'Malley, S. S., Suh, C. S., & Strupp, H. H. (1983). The Vanderbilt Process Scale: A report on the scale development and a process–outcome study. *Journal of Consulting and Clinical Psychology, 51*, 581–586.

Rounsaville, B. J., Chevron, E. S., Prusoff, B. A., Elkin, I., Imber, S., Sotsky, S., & Watkins, J. (1987). The relation between specific and general dimensions of the psychotherapy process in interpersonal psychotherapy of depression. *Journal of Consulting and Clinical Psychology, 55*, 379–384.

Soldz, S., Budman, S. H., Davis, M. S., & Demby, A. (1993). Beyond the interpersonal circumplex in group psychotherapy: The structure and relationship to outcome of the Individual Group Member Interpersonal Process Scale. *Journal of Clinical Psychology, 49*, 551–563.

Soldz, S., Budman, S. H., & Demby, A. (1992). The relationship between main actors behaviors and treatment outcome in group psychotherapy. *Psychotherapy Research, 2*, 52–62.

Soldz, S., Budman, S. H., Demby, A., & Feldstein, M. (1990). Patient activity and outcome in group psychotherapy: New findings. *International Journal of Group Psychotherapy, 40*, 53–62.

Soldz, S., Budman, S. H., Demby, A., & Merry, J. (1993). Diagnostic agreement between the personality disorder examination and MCMI-II. *Journal of Personality Assessment, 60*(3), 486–499.

Spence, J. T., & Helmreich, R. L. (1978). *Masculinity and femininity: Their psychological dimensions, correlates, and antecedents*. Austin: University of Texas Press.

Suh, C. S., Strupp, H. H., & O'Malley, S. S. (1986). The Vanderbilt process measures: The Psychotherapy Process Scale (VPPS) and the Negative Indicators Scale (VNIS). In L. S. Greenberg & W. M. Pinsof (Eds.), *The psychotherapeutic process: A research handbook* (pp. 285–323). New York: Guilford Press.

Wiggins, J. S. (1979). A psychological taxonomy of trait-descriptive terms: The interpersonal domain. *Journal of Personality and Social Psychology, 37*, 395–412.

Wiggins, J. S. (1982). Circumplex models of interpersonal behavior in clinical psychology. In P. C. Kendall & J. N. Butcher (Eds.), *Handbook of research methods in clinical psychology* (pp. 183–221). New York: Wiley.

Wiggins, J. S., & Pincus, A. L. (1989). Conceptions of personality disorders and dimensions of personality. *Psychological Assessment, 1*, 305–316.

Windholz, M. J., & Silberschatz, G. (1988). Vanderbilt Psychotherapy Process Scale: A replication with adult outpatients. *Journal of Consulting and Clinical Psychology, 56*, 56–60.

Yalom, I. D. (1985). *The theory and practice of group psychotherapy* (3rd ed.). New York: Basic Books.

APPENDIX 11.A
PRINCIPAL-COMPONENTS FIVE-FACTOR STRUCTURE OF 12 REDUCED IGIPS–I ITEMS

First Factor: Activity
  How Often Spoke
  Discloses Personal Material
  Expresses Affect
Second Factor: Interpersonal Sensitivity
  Makes Connections With Other Group Members
  Sensitivity When Addressing Other Group Members
  Positive–Negative Sentiment
Third Factor: Comfort With Self
  Responsiveness to Input
  Self-Esteem
  Input Received When Self-Focused
Fourth Factor: Self-Focus
  Discusses Own Issues
Fifth Factor: Psychologically Minded
  Psychologically Minded When Self-Focused
  Psychologically Minded When Addressing Other Group Members

Note. Component loadings were subjected to varimax rotation. IGIPS–I = Individual Group Member Interpersonal Process Scale I.

APPENDIX 11.B
METHOD OF CALCULATING REDUCED ITEMS PRESENTED IN TABLES 11.3 AND 11.4

1. Amount Spoken

    Calculated by summing all the scores on the "Length of Statement" item. Each 5 s of speaking represents a rating of 1.

2. Discusses Abstract Issues

    Represents the percentage of overall statements containing reference to impersonal or abstract issues.

3. Discusses Group Process

    Represents the percentage of overall statements that contain an in-group designation rating on any item.

4. Discloses Personal Material

    Calculated by summing the significance ratings on the item "Discloses Personal Material," and then dividing that sum by the sum of frequency ratings on "Discusses Self." For purposes of this presentation, the outside-group and inside-group designations were ignored.

5. Expresses Affect

    Calculated by subtracting the summed significance ratings of "Resistance to Affect" from the summed significance ratings of "Expresses Affect" and dividing the result by the overall number of statements.

6. Feels Connected to Group

    Calculated by subtracting the summed significance ratings of "Feels Disconnected From Others" with inside-group designations from the summed ratings of "Feels Connected to Others" with inside-group designations and dividing the result by the overall number of statements.

7. Insight Into Own Issues

    Calculated by summing the significance ratings on "Demonstrates Self-Awareness" and dividing by the sum of frequency ratings on "Discusses Self." Outside-group designations and inside-group designations were ignored.

8. Insight Into OGM Issues

    Calculated by summing the significance ratings on "Asks Questions," "Enhances OGM Awareness," and "Gives Advice" and dividing by the sum of frequency ratings on "Discusses OGMs." Outside-group designations and inside-group designations were ignored.

Note. OGM = other group member.

V

SYSTEMS DEVELOPED FOR OTHER CONTEXTS AND NOW BEING APPLIED TO GROUP PSYCHOTHERAPY

12

THREE COMPLEMENTARY SYSTEMS FOR CODING THE PROCESS OF THERAPEUTIC DIALOGUE

ADRIENNE S. CHAMBON, A. KA TAT TSANG, AND ELSA MARZIALI

In this chapter we describe three systems for analyzing the therapeutic process. They share a central principle that successful therapeutic process is attributable to the transformation of meaning that takes place in the psychotherapeutic interaction. Clients and therapists work conjointly at reformulating statements about self and other and, in doing so, reveal identifiable strategies. The process of transformation is traceable to changes in client and therapist statements. The three systems provide complementary analyses of critical dimensions for understanding interpersonal engagement between clients and therapists, and therapeutic progress. They aim to render detailed and multilevel moment-to-moment accounts of interactions (Fuhriman & Barlow, 1994) by tracing the formulations and reformulations of group members as they engage with one another and with the therapists. Each of the three systems is applied to both client and therapist statements. They assess group patterns as a whole, interactional patterns among group members, and therapist and individual group members' contributions.

Although each process coding system was developed independently, they overlap conceptually and methodologically and have been tested within a research program that focuses on individual, group, couple, and family therapy. Preliminary application of the three systems to the transcripts of a psychotherapy group for borderline personality disorder (BPD; Munroe-Blum, 1995) showed complementarity in assessing therapeutic progress associated with successful clinical interventions. The refinement, modification, and extension of the three systems continue.

The systems combine theory-based constructs and discovery-oriented approaches. The Psychological Space Coding System (PSCS), developed by Marziali (1995), is the most clinical and theory based of the systems. Conceptually, the PSCS is an extension of Marziali's work on the therapeutic alliance. It evolved from the development of a group intervention modality for working with clients with BPD (Marziali & Munroe-Blum, 1994) that addresses the high reactivity of these clients to minute changes in interactions and to nuances in the wording of therapeutic interpretations. The PSCS builds on the concept of interpersonal "psychological space" and the management of that space in therapy. It provides a measure for assisting clients to reformulate and "open up" that space, moving away from polarized cognitions to experiencing alternative meanings and options.

The Negotiation of Therapy Agenda (NOTA) system, developed by Tsang (1995a), emphasizes the interactive aspect of engagement toward collaborative therapeutic work. It complements the PSCS by focusing on how meaning is negotiated between participants in the process of engagement. The NOTA system sequentially assesses the continuities and discontinuities in the formulations between speakers. By examining the transformations that occur between speaker-initiated turns of speech, NOTA tracks different degrees of engagement, ranging from collaboration, adaptation, and influencing to noncollaboration or disruption.

The Strategies of Telling and Talking (STT) approach, developed by Chambon (1993b, 1994), is a microanalytic, discourse-based approach. It attempts to capture the complexity of language variation in its subjective use. It tracks the structuration and transformation of meaning in the finer features of speech and narrative, and derives its analytical tools from literary theories and linguistics. Applied to clinical interactions, the STT begins with the assumption that meaning structures and patterns of relations are anchored in the ways that individuals use language to express themselves and to address one another. Discursive actions are used strategically in interpersonal situations. Speakers make selective and patterned use of language to indicate not only topic but subjective stance. Transformations in patterned stance are accompanied by changes in language use.

The PSCS and NOTA jointly focus on engagement, whereas the STT and NOTA share the concepts of negotiation and strategies of interaction.

All three systems examine the formulations and reformulations about self and other. They all track the speaker and the persons-about-whom statements are made, referred to as "person focus" or "character centering." The systems have overlapping foci on content and wording. The PSCS emphasizes wording about self and other within large topical units. The NOTA system looks at topic, character, and wording features in self–other statements and includes reference to process. The STT includes a dual focus on narrative features of character, narrator, and spatiotemporal setting as well as on microlevel speech features in wording and grammatical structure.

Although all three systems provide interactive, speaker-based analyses applied to both client and therapist statements, each targets a different level of analysis. The PSCS codes units defined by total speech turns (i.e., client and therapist). Speech markers differentiate between opening and closing statements as well as intention of each speech turn. The STT tracks finer reformulations and differentiation at the word and clause levels within speech turns and at the narrative level across larger segments. The NOTA coding system focuses on the interface between turns of speech for assessing continuity and discontinuity in content, speech feature, and procedural direction.

The systems apply different but complementary methods of analysis. The PSCS and NOTA are categorical coding systems that rely on the quantitative analysis of the coded material, whereas the STT is a descriptive qualitative discourse analysis approach that documents the actual wording. Psychotherapy process research tends to be split between paradigmatic and narrative approaches (Bruner, 1986; Rennie & Toukmanian, 1992). The paradigmatic approach is logicoscientific, seeking to develop and test hypotheses about causal relationships among phenomena. In contrast, the narrative approach is inductive and interpretative. This approach emphasizes the representation of experience by the individual. Reality is seen as constructed, involving complicated processes of meaning generation and transformation. It has been suggested that these modes are complementary and that the strengths of the two types of approaches should be maximized by incorporating both types of inquiry at different stages of study or to address different aspects of a research question (Rennie & Toukmanian, 1992). Our team research represents a collaborative attempt to develop a multimethod approach to the analyses of the therapeutic process by combining analytical systems derived from these two perspectives of inquiry. Our application of the three systems to the same process data has demonstrated their complementarity and has shown how their combined use can enhance the richness and complexity of the analysis.

In this chapter, we present each of the systems separately to highlight their respective contribution, progressing from larger to finer units of analysis. This is followed by a discussion of their overlapping findings and the integration of the systems.

THE NOTA CODING SYSTEM

History and Theory of the System

The NOTA coding system represents an attempt to study the complex process of client–therapist interaction in psychotherapy. Taking client–therapist interaction as the central process through which therapeutic aims are realized, the NOTA tracks the relative participation of both clients and therapists in the co-construction of clinical narratives. The codes and systematic notes generated by the system provide access to some of the major processes involved when clients and therapists work together. Such processes are often conceptualized and studied as therapeutic alliance, working alliance, or collaboration. Being less theory driven but more discovery oriented, the development of the NOTA system has elucidated significant processes and patterns that are immediately relevant to clinical practice. These include how clients and therapists negotiate control over the content of clinical narratives and the timing and sequence of their introduction.

The NOTA system was first developed by Tsang (1995a) to study the interactional process between client and therapist during individual psychotherapy to identify patterns associated with dropout and successful engagement. Research on psychotherapy dropout has been dominated by a correlational strategy that attempts to predict dropout on the basis of baseline client variables, therapist variables, and treatment variables. This strategy has limited success in explaining and predicting dropout. Reviewers of the literature suggest that researchers should abandon the search for demographic predictors and focus on more complex psychological variables such as clients' intentions and expectations and client–therapist interactions (Baekeland & Lundwall, 1975; Wierzbicki & Pekarik, 1993).

The NOTA system builds on Tracey's (1986) Topic Determination (TD) System, which assesses the change of topic between client and therapist speech turns. Whereas the TD system studies topic change in terms of a topic following–initiation dichotomy, the NOTA system assesses levels of abruptness of topic shifts. The NOTA system also separates between process and narrative dimensions that are undifferentiated in the TD system.

Working within the framework of the therapeutic alliance, Tracey (1986) focused on topic determination and found that the proportion of new topics initiated by one participant that were subsequently followed by the other participant was a good predictor of dropout status. Therapy transcripts from a sample of clients attending a university counseling center were used to test the coding system. The speech turn was used as the basic unit of analysis, and each speech turn was coded either as topic following or topic initiation. Topic initiation was coded when the first topic in a speech turn differed from the last topic in the previous speech turn in (a) content, (b) person as subject, (c) time reference, (d) level of specificity, or (e) if it constituted an interruption. If none of the criteria was met, the turn was coded as topic following. *Topic determination* (TD) was defined as the proportion of topic initiations that were subsequently followed by the other participant: *client TD* (i.e., the proportion of client-initiated topics followed by therapist) and *therapist TD* (i.e., the proportion of therapist-initiated topics followed by client). A third index of *dyad TD* measuring the extent that initiations were followed regardless of who did the initiating and following was used to assess the communicational harmony. Using these indexes, Tracey (1986) found that continuing dyads showed higher levels of both dyad TD and therapist TD than did dropout dyads. Client TD was not found to be strongly associated with continuance because client topic initiations occurred much less frequently than did therapist topic initiations.

Correspondence Between the Theory and the System

The TD system represents a definite advancement in understanding the clinical processes associated with dropout in that it is focused on the actual client–therapist interactive process instead of isolated client or therapist variables as in most other studies. The system has, however, failed to differentiate changes that are related to narrative aspects of the previous turn (i.e., content, subject, time, specificity) from changes that are related to process (i.e., interruption). Chambon (1994) argued that the psychotherapeutic process should be understood both in terms of narrative and speech dimensions. Whereas these two planes can be assessed and analyzed separately, it is believed that these two aspects of communication occur simultaneously and influence one another. In assessing the wide variety of shifts between speech turns, it has been found that the lumping of these dimensions together by the TD system misses much of the complexity and subtlety involved.

In developing the NOTA system, Tsang (1995a) modified Tracey's (1986) TD system. Instead of using the concept of "topic determination," which implies a more content-based strategy, Tsang introduced "negotiation of the therapy agenda" to better reflect the interactional nature of the process. Whereas determination can be an individual or collective action, negotiation is clearly an interactional process. "Therapy agenda" is also a broader concept than the idea of "topic" and can refer to both content and process dimensions. Whereas a participant's agenda may consist of specific topics to be discussed, it can also include process objectives such as maintaining control, containing anger, trying to please, competing, challenging, punishing, or frustrating. Examining the negotiation of the therapy agenda assumes that both client and therapist start with their individual agenda. In the course of psychotherapy, each individual attempts to advance her or his own agenda using a variety of narrative strategies. The agenda that is ultimately actualized in therapy is the outcome of the negotiation process between the client and the therapist. It involves changes and drifts in narrative dimensions, including topic, the character centered, interrupting the other participant's speech, and so on.

The five criteria used by Tracey (1986) to define topic change between speech turns were used as a reference in a discovery-oriented reading of therapy transcripts to determine whether alternative conceptualizations were possible. Repeat analyses showed that whereas interruption is a separate process strategy in securing air time and influencing the flow of the conversation, shifts in narrative content occur in terms of the thematic topic and the character centered between speech turns. A speech turn may extend or elaborate on the preceding turn, selectively focus on some aspect of it, or shift on to new topics and stage a new set of characters. These shifts also appear in different levels of abruptness or connectedness relative to the preceding turn. Some of these shifts may abruptly change the course of the conversation without regard to the preceding turn; other shifts may be more moderate in that some connection with the preceding turn is maintained. Specification of these differences resulted in the operational definition of categories of a coding system for the NOTA. Content codes are organized into three main categories, each with subcategories. Interruption is coded separately as a process marker. Initially, 10 subcategories were identified on the basis of individual psychotherapy sessions. Later work with group psychotherapy led to the inclusion of two more categories (resuming and zooming out) under the nonshift category.

Description of the System

Categories

The first category, the *nonshift* (NS) code, is given when a new turn follows the preceding turn, both in terms of topic and character centered. There are four subcategories of NS turns: (a) *Following* (NS:F), a turn follows the same topics of the preceding turn and centers the same characters; (b) *resuming* (NS:RS) is a speech turn that brings the conversation back to the original topic after it has been interrupted procedurally (e.g., a phone call, members coming in late or leaving early in group therapy; (c) *zooming out* (NS:ZO), which shifts away from specific events or character or both and refers to a generalized description or a general principle;

and (d) *selective focusing* (NS:SF), which focuses on one of the multiple topics or centers one or more of the characters covered in the preceding turn.

The second category, the *mediated shift* (MS) code, is given to turns that include content that is different from that of the preceding turn but the shift is not abrupt. The shift is mediated in the sense that there is specific reference to the preceding turn. There are four types of mediated shifts: (a) *Follow and turn* (MS:FT) is given to a speech turn that starts by following the preceding turn but changes the topic or character centered in the middle; (b) *causal link* (MS:CL) is given when a shift in either content or the character centered is connected to the preceding turn by way of an alleged causal relationship; (c) *backtracking* (MS:BT) is given when a speaker makes explicit reference to an earlier statement made by another participant; and (d) *procedural link* (MS:PL) is given when direct reference is made to the sequence and order of material to be worked on, such as "We will come back to this later, why don't you tell me more about. . . . "

The third category, the *abrupt shift* (AS) code, is given when speech turns clearly depart from the preceding turns either in terms of thematic content or the character centered. There are four types of abrupt shifts: (a) *Procedure* (AS:P) is given to speech turns such as the opening of a session after casual chat or small talk and those announcing the end of a session; (b) *character* (AS:C) is given when the character centered is changed abruptly without changing the topic; (c) *topic* (AS:T) is given when there is abrupt shift in thematic content but the same character is centered; and (d) *character and topic* (AS: C + T) is given to represent an abrupt content shift both in terms of thematic content and character centered.

Interruption (INT) occurs when a participant tries to initiate a turn before the other participant's turn has come to a natural stop. This coding is based on the audiotape recording and is given separately from the content codes (see Table 12.1 for a summary of NOTA codes).

Reliability

The NOTA codes were first developed through careful examination of audio recordings and transcripts of six psychotherapy sessions. After the codes had been specified and a coding manual had been written, the system was tested for interrater agreement on three psychotherapy sessions (more than 500 speech turns). With the first-level coding, which involves INT and the three categories of NS, MS, and AS, which are assessed separately, kappa values were above the .85 level. With the refined 12-category coding, kappa sometimes could not be computed because of the infrequent occurrence of some categories. This led to unequal numbers of columns and

TABLE 12.1
Negotiation of Therapy Agenda Coding System

Level 1		Level 2	
Nonshift	(NS)	Following	(F)
		Resuming	(RS)
		Zooming out	(ZO)
		Selective focusing	(SF)
Mediated shift	(MS)	Follow and turn	(FT)
		Causal link	(CL)
		Backtracking	(BT)
		Procedural link	(PL)
Abrupt shifts	(AS)	Procedure	(P)
		Character	(C)
		Topic	(T)
		Character and topic	(C+T)

Interruption (INT): This process code is given separately from the content codes.

rows. Kendall's tau-b was computed to provide some indication of the extent of the correlation between coders, and a tau-b of .86 was obtained. The same level of interrater agreement was maintained in the subsequent applications of the NOTA to individual and group psychotherapy studies (Tsang, 1995a, 1995b).

Validity

The NOTA system was also tested for its ability to differentiate dropout from continuer cases. Following the rationale of optimum-seeking sampling (Howard, Krause, & Orlinsky, 1986), the coding system was applied to four cases using a 2×2 design: dropout–continuer and a client with BPD, neurotic problem. Specific interactional patterns related to dropout were identified. These included the different levels of control over topic shifts, clients' accommodation of shifts made by therapists, and the use of disruptive strategies by therapists. Similar work with group psychotherapy has been planned, and a preliminary application of the NOTA coding system to group session was performed (Tsang, 1995b).

Qualitative Information

When the NOTA system is used to code clinical transcripts, a turn-by-turn descriptive record is kept of the narrative themes covered and the characters referred to. This information complements the coding of interactive patterns with the content of clinical narratives. It strengthens the anchoring of coded data to the clinical process and provides additional opportunity for further qualitative analysis.

Methodology for Analysis

The frequencies in the coded categories can be compared across sessions (e.g., early, middle, and late) or across groups (e.g., treatment vs. control) using nonparametric procedures such as the chi-square statistic. Analysis can be performed on aggregate group data as well as on individual data. Sequential patterns can also be analyzed with Dual Scaling (Nishisato, 1994), a statistical procedure developed specifically for categorical data. The procedure determines whether sequential patterns can be identified and whether differences in sequential patterns across sessions are attributable to chance.

Apart from providing a systematic procedure for coding how the therapy agenda is negotiated, the NOTA coding tracks the thematic content and the characters centered on a turn-by-turn basis. The themes and characters are recorded separately and can be analyzed qualitatively by focusing on their narrative content, especially their sequential patterns. Given the restricted space in the present chapter, however, the application of the NOTA system is focused primarily on the coding aspect with only limited interpretative illustration.

Application of the System to Group A, Session 3

Applying the NOTA coding system to the session chosen for this book demonstrates the potential utility of the system in group psychotherapy research. Table 12.2 shows the codes given to each participant in the entire session. Before even looking at the specific codes, the total number of turns (713) taken in the session shows that it is a very active one packed with verbal input. It also reflects the brevity of the turns with an average time of 7.6 seconds per turn. This may be an indication of the intensity or depth of processing of clinical material.

The number of speech turns taken by each participant provides an overall picture of their different levels of activity and participation. We found that Alice was the more active cotherapist. She took almost three times as many (160) speech turns as her partner Helen (58). Among the clients, Diane (155 turns) and Martha (132 turns) were the most active, followed by Greg (87 turns) and Joe (82 turns), whereas Pat (20 turns) and Brad (19 turns) were much less active by comparison. Note that the level of participation of individual therapists and clients does change across sessions. Their respective patterns can be traced readily if NOTA coding is performed on more sessions.

Compared with other group sessions analyzed with the NOTA system, the chosen session showed a low level of discontinuity as indicated by the infrequent abrupt shifts. This can be interpreted as a sign of positive engagement. When most participants feel that the group is working together

TABLE 12.2
Summary of Negotiation of Therapy Agenda Codes for Individual Participants

Participant	F	ZO	RS	SF	FT	CL	BT	PL	P	C	T	C+T	Total	INT	INT %
Helen	56	1	1	7	1				2			1	58	13	22
Alice	148	1	1	7	1				1			1	160	47	29
Therapists	204					0	0		3	0		1	218	60	
Martha	124		1	4			1		1	1			132	22	17
Greg	83	1			1				1	1			87	14	16
Pat	17			1									19	1	5
Brad	18		1	1								1	20	1	5
Joe	76	1	1	2		1	1						82	10	12
Diane	147	3	1			1	2		1			1	155	35	23
Members	465	5	4	8	1	1	4		3	2		2	495	83	
Total	669	6	5	15	2	1	4		6	2		3	713	143	

Note. Helen and Alice are the therapists in this group; the rest are group members. The NOTA codes are as follows: Nonshifts: F = following; ZO = zooming out; RS = resuming; SF = selective focusing. Mediated shifts: FT = follow and turn; CL = causal link; BT = backtracking; PL = procedural link. Abrupt shifts: P = procedure; C = character; T = topic; C+T = character and topic. INT = interruption; INT % = percentage of speech turns coded as INT.

and they can relate to the dominant discourse, there is little need for attempts to advance personal agenda through disruptive strategies. The result is a relatively smooth flow in which the introduction of themes and characters are achieved through NS or MS strategies.

We also observed that the clients in this session maintained high control over the agenda. Themes were usually introduced by clients, and major shifts in agenda were mainly made by them. The therapists and clients do not have distinctly different patterns of NOTA codes, as in other groups in which the therapists are accountable for proportionally more of the topic shifts. This reflects that *therapist functions* are, to a large extent, shared among the participants. Such patterns indicate an extremely non-directive therapy style and are consistent with the client-centered orientation of the therapists. This allows room for the clients to shape the therapy agenda and narrative that may contribute to positive engagement.

A sign of good engagement in group therapy is self-disclosure around the current theme. For example, when Diane was talking about her parents and childhood experiences, Greg joined in after a comment by the co-therapist Alice: "I—I wonder, maybe we'd get, I wonder if we'd get something out of it if I compared compared her parents and my parents now. Um, my mother was was was the one in the family that the kids all. . . ." Later on, another client, Joe, joined in with disclosures about his family. All these turns are coded as NS:F. In a poorly engaged group, there is either lack of joining in through self-disclosure, or there are clients advancing their own agenda by abruptly changing the topic. Such turns will be coded AS according to the NOTA.

Another sign of positive engagement is the active involvement of participants, their attention to what others are saying, and readiness to relate the issues raised earlier by others to the current discussion. This is captured by both the NS:RS and the MS:BT codes of the NOTA system. For example, in the early part of the session, after the group had started talking about Joe's performance in the last meeting, the therapists made a procedural shift (AS:P code) to explain the questionnaire that clients had to fill out. After this procedural interruption, Joe made an NS:RS move by saying "Well, let's get back to the last meeting." The group then focused on Joe, but the conversation later became generalized to overall observations and principles, which was marked by an NS:ZO code. Diane, however, refocused on Joe's original report of turmoil and upset about the last meeting by an MS:BT move: "Joe, (slight sigh) I was interested when you started out by saying that you had left here in a turmoil. Um, you know, and that you were upset for a couple of days. . . ." Such use of NS strategies has the effect of keeping the continuity of the discussions as well as ensuring that significant issues are not avoided or lost. The fact that all but one of these resuming and backtracking moves were made by clients instead of the therapists (see Table 12.2) is another sign of active involvement of the clients and their taking charge of the therapy agenda.

The reliance on MS strategies to change the topic is consistent with this pattern. For example, in the beginning of the session when members were coming in, they referred to the physical aspects of the environment. Greg brought in the issue of his own psychological confusion by an FT move that is an MS, and started the group discussion on psychological issues:

Alice: No and it seemed like the consensus was, stuffed. (laugh) Too full.

Martha: You too? [coded NS:F]

Alice: Yeah [laugh] [Nonturn]

Martha: Oh Lord, I can hardly breathe. [continuation of her own turn above]

Greg: Oh, I'm not stuffed, just confused (laugh). [coded MS:FT]

Whereas the content shift codes provide a clear picture of a well-engaged and working group, the INT codes have to be interpreted more carefully. The generally high frequency of INT can be interpreted as active competition for air time and in some cases can be seen as a strategy of resistance by clients to counteract therapist domination (Tsang, 1995a). With the present session, we can argue that this high frequency was a sign of active involvement. This argument is based on a qualitative review of the INT codes with reference to the notes on thematic content and characters centered. We found that the competing voices in this session were usually on the same topic instead of a different agenda. There were also instances of sentence completion and echoing. These were not coded as INT even when they physically overlapped with the preceding turn. In both sentence completion and echoing, the seemingly interrupting participant was not trying to take the speech turn away from the speaking participant but trying to assume the other's voice. These strategies were interpreted as signs of active involvement and shared understanding among members. For example,

Alice: To you it meant that he [Joe] had just closed the door.

Diane: Yes, it meant here, you know, yeah, I'm—I'm . . ..

Alice: He wasn't . . . [coded INT].

Diane: behind this door and if you don't know the, if you can't come in at my door, or something (slight laugh) . . . [continuation of her own speech turn].

Alice: I'm waiting; if you can't come in on my terms or in my way then you can't come in. [Alice is taking on the "voice" of Diane and completing the sentence for her; not coded INT].

Diane: And you can't come in [echoing, saying exactly the same thing that the other participant (Alice) is saying]. And of course that says to me, well now, somehow I can't come in. Yeah that's, and that's what's unfinished about it. . . .

Individual participants, however, had different ratios of INT to speech turn (see Table 12.2), and these could be interpreted as markers of individual communication style in the group. Both therapists, for example, had a high ratio (> 20%) of interrupting turns, which was more than four times that of the less active clients (5%). This interruption ratio may be used as one of the indexes of relative domination in the group process and can be traced across sessions by using the NOTA.

Apart from overall frequencies, NOTA codes can also be analyzed sequentially. In this session, all the AS interventions by the two therapists took place in the first third of the session, as did most AS turns made by the clients. The group then moved on smoothly without any abrupt turn until the last couple of minutes of the session, when Pat raised the issue of parents and love after the group had started to wind down. Finally, Diane brought the discussion to a close by making an AS:P. Another important observation is that all the AS turns in the session were followed by NS turns, another indication of a smoothly working process without any strong competition among participants to advance their own agenda.

Assessment and Future Directions

The NOTA system was first developed through careful study of therapy recordings and transcripts to identify patterns of shifts between speech turns. Preliminary applications to individual and group psychotherapy situations have demonstrated its potential both in global assessment of therapy sessions as well as tracking the relative participation, influence, and control over the agenda by individual participants in psychotherapy. It can provide specific information on the strategies used by participants to control, shape, or influence the therapy agenda. Sequential analysis of coding within and across sessions can both be performed. A manual specifying coding principles and illustrated by actual clinical examples has been developed. Apart from continual application in individual and group psychotherapy research, we expect that the system may be adopted for studies in couple and family therapy in the future.

There are two major challenges for the future development of the NOTA system. The coded components of the system aim at entire sessions and patterns of negotiation within it. As such, the system's sensitivity to narrative elements and their changes within smaller units of analysis is relatively limited. We hope that the qualitative notes on narrative themes can be organized more systemically and used more consistently in parallel with the codes. Another limitation of the NOTA at its present stage of development is the absence of extensive testing on a larger sample of participants. We anticipate that more extensive application of the NOTA coding system will strengthen confidence in its reliability and predictive capabilities.

THE PSCS CODING SYSTEM

History and Theory of the System

The PSCS was developed to assess the nature and function of "psychological space" within the context of group psychotherapeutic process. The coding system provides a systematic procedure for categorizing client–therapist dialogue on the dimensions of "opening psychological space" versus "closing psychological space." These dimensions were operationalized to capture the participants' capacities for cognitively processing ambiguity and uncertainty.

The psychological space construct was embedded in the design of an experimental model group psychotherapy tested in a treatment comparison trial with BPD (Marziali & Munroe-Blum, 1994). The model of group treatment tested (Interpersonal Group Psychotherapy [IGP]) was developed to address personality traits typical of BPD. Specifically, both the content and language mode of therapist responses were formulated to communicate tentativeness, ambiguity, and uncertainty. The aim was to alter the BPD client's propensity for polarizing meanings, which often results in the interruption of interpersonal transactions.

According to psychoanalytical perspectives about the psychological organization of clients with BPD, the polarization of meanings functions as a defense (splitting) against anxiety and impulse (rage). From this point of view, the aim of intervention (interpretation) is to alter the defense and open up the possibility of experiencing the meanings of both the anxiety and the impulse. IGP methods share similar aims, but the therapeutic response modes differ; classic interpretations (i.e., making explicit the associations among defense, affect, impulse, and the object) are avoided. Within the context of IGP, we hypothesized that although interpretations are intended to provide new meanings, there is the risk of reinforcing the client's defensive structure because of the form in which interpretations are delivered: definitive formulations of the client's life narratives. In contrast, IGP emphasizes a therapist response mode that affirms the client's worldview and that is formulated tentatively such that the choice of response, if any, is left to the client. The aim is to engage the client in a process that supports the experiencing of ambiguity without resorting to polarization. We hypothesized that within this state of ambiguity and uncertainty, the client is better able to access and process new meanings. For new meanings to be accessed and processed, the availability of psychological space is essential; that is, it is necessary for there to be a mental space in which the road map is unknown, or only partially known, and where the outcome cannot be predicted.

The notion of psychological space within the psychotherapeutic process is not new. It has been defined from varying perspectives. Winnicott's (1958, 1971) conceptualization of transitional objects and transitional phenomena in early development identified an "intermediate area of experience" between inner and outer reality. Hubner's (1984) analysis of the function of Winnicott's notion of potential space suggests that the acts, thoughts, and symbols of the potential space are "acts of meaning" that are ultimately object related. The primary growth-enhancing activity of potential space is the development of the capacity for symbolization. In a similar vein, Socor (1989) suggested that "therapeutic truth" is created in a transitional space. She defined the space between the client and therapist as "an intermediate area between personal truths, an encounter of subjectivities in which each provides substance for illusion" (p. 114).

Correspondence Between Theory and System

Challenges in Constructing Operational Definitions

Psychological space in the context of the psychotherapeutic process is defined as a partial suspension of what is known (cognition and memory) and experienced (perception and emotion). The function of psychological space is to accommodate the transformation of meanings (e.g., observations, facts, and emotions). Psychological space exists within interpersonal contexts, and its sustainability depends on the nature of the dialogue between self and other. The sustainability of not knowing, or partial knowing, requires tolerance of anxiety and ambiguity.

Indexes of Group Process, Development, or Change

Within the structure and function of group psychotherapy, we hypothesized that the therapist is expected to recognize the ways in which each client contributes to or inhibits the therapeutic process. Within the definition of the function of psychological space, this means that the therapist is particularly alert to actions, his or her own or those of the group members that constrict psychological space. Similarly, the therapist has the responsibility to respond in a manner that supports members' opening of psychological space and tolerating the accompanying anxiety. To achieve this, the therapist affirms the group members' views of the world (including their defensive views) and pursues the exploration of meanings through the use of statements that are presented in tentative, uncertain terms. The purpose is to avoid challenging group members' restricted views of their current or past life situations; to challenge the client is to risk reinforcing the client's constriction of psychological space. The goal is to introduce ambiguity, doubt, and confusion in an interpersonal group context. Furthermore, the therapist models the experiencing and containment of anxiety, thus opening psychological space needed for the acknowledgment, accommodation, and transformation of new meanings.

If it is necessary to suspend in part what is known to mentally process new and possibly disturbing meanings, then, technically, how might a therapist aid in this process? The options for therapeutic response are many; however, the PSCS system has selected for emphasis the "intention" of therapist responses and how the therapist frames each response (i.e., the mode). In the development of the PSCS, we hypothesized that if therapists were able to communicate to clients that they did not have specific answers to group member dilemmas, then group members would eventually forgo their demands for specific answers. They would also learn to model the therapists' more tentative, uncertain stance in which many "answers" are possible. Thus, the PSCS categories reflect attempts to capture the intention and mode of the dialogue between therapists and group members that distinguish two global types of statements: (a) those that convey uncertainty and confusion, as well as communicate openness to new information, and (b) those that convey specific opinion and directives as well as communicate avoidance of new information. The first type of coding categories are subcategorized as *Opening* statements; that is, they are viewed as opening psychological space within the therapist–group member dialogue, a condition that is necessary for the processing of new meanings. In contrast, the second type of coding categories are subcategorized as *Closing* statements and are viewed as reinforcing the restriction of psychological space and thus limiting the processing of new information.

In summary, the PSCS method for analyzing the therapeutic dialogue is applied to both therapist and client statements with the aim of discovering whether the parameters of the dialogue exist as hypothesized, whether therapists and clients differ in their proportional use of the Opening versus Closing statements, and whether there is a shift in their proportional use across the therapeutic process. Although not measured specifically, it is assumed that when clients shift from the primary use of Closing statements to a more frequent use of Opening statements, information is processed in new and expanding ways. Ultimately, this is reflected in the final outcome of the therapeutic endeavor.

Description of the System

Rating

The rating task involves a five-tiered process:

1. A coding unit is defined as a complete speech turn delivered by one of the group participants (therapists or clients); identification of the speaker is recorded. Each speech turn is coded in its sequence of occurrence.
2. A decision is then made about whether the speech turn is primarily Opening or Closing, and within each of these global categories (whichever has been chosen) one of four options about "intention" of the statement is selected.
3. If the speech turn does not qualify for any of the Opening or Closing categories, a decision is then made about whether two alternate codes can be applied: Provision of Information or Affirmation (operational definitions of these two additional codes are given below).
4. For those statements that qualify for the Opening or Closing designations, a decision is made about whether the statement has been framed in a Tentative or Definitive format. The Tentative format refers to the use of qualifiers such as "maybe," "possibly," or "I wonder." The Definitive format reflects certainty.
5. Finally, the person focus of the Opening or Closing statement is recorded.

The decision hierarchy is relatively simple to follow. The most challenging decision occurs at the second step, deciding whether the statement qualifies for the Opening versus Closing designation.

Categories

The coding system consists of 10 categories. Eight categories define different speech intentions according to each of the two global categories, Opening versus Closing. Four categories define *Opening Psychological Space*: O1, Open-ended questions; O2, Exploratory statements; O3, Doubtful explanatory statements; and O4, statements reflecting lack of resolution of conflict. Four categories define *Closing Psychological Space*: C1, Close-ended questions; C2, Confrontational statements; C3, Explanatory statements delivered with certainty; and C4, Directive statements. The two final codes include *Affirmation*, which captures responses that agree with or support the input of the previous speaker, and *Provision of Information*, which notes dialogue that is concrete and factual. Addendum codes for the eight Open versus Closed categories focus on (a) the speech mode, *Tentative* versus

TABLE 12.3
Psychological Space Coding System

Open (O)		Closed (C)	
O1	Questions, multiple responses possible	C1	Questions, specific responses required
O2	Exploratory statements, requests for extension of narrative	C2	Confrontational statements, argumentative
O3	Explanatory statements, Tentative format	C3	Explanatory statements, definitive format
O4	Statements reflecting lack of resolution of conflicts; dilemmas, hesitation, doubt	C4	Directive statements as to how to feel, think, behave

Alternate codes: Provision of Information (PI), Affirmation (AFF) providing agreement, support, and so on

Person focus: Self, Self–Other, Other, Other–Other

Definitive and (b) the person focus (*Self, Self–Other, Other,* or *Other–Other*; see Table 12.3).

Statements from Group A, Session 3 were selected to provide examples of operational definitions used to capture the clinical and theoretical meanings of the PSCS.

Opening Psychological Space

O1   Open question

> Martha: Was it that one of you didn't understand what he was getting at, at all, or was it the way he said it or. . . .

O2   Exploratory requests for extension of narrative

> Joe: . . . you said when you are dealing with groups there's irritation or you say there isn't harmony. I was wondering, uh, what is it that, you say were entertaining or you were with a group and there was friction or, uh, you didn't get along. I was wonderin' what, uh, (Mm hm) what the details of that were.

O3   Explanatory statements: Tentative format

> Brad: I kinda get the impression that you were here to express yourself and what you were trying to express was that you wanted peace . . . and maybe I was picking up here that what he was trying to get across was a sort of, his own needs for peace for,

uh, not being disturbed for trying to work things out this way and this led to more disturbance or criticism.

O4 Statements reflecting lack of resolution of conflict

Martha: Yeah. What might I have to offer. And it seems to me that we're not all quite sure just how, you know, we're gonna jump in and bare our secrets. . . .

Closing Psychological Space

C1 Closed question

Pat: . . . the specific question I had in mind was, Were you irritated with me?

C2 Statements that are confrontational, argumentative, or both

Alice: . . . it seems to me Joe's made it quite clear that he's spent quite a few days stewing about all of this, he didn't just cap it like that.

C3 Explanatory statements presented in a definitive format

Diane: . . . because you drifted into racial prejudice. Uh, then when you talked about, um, about this incident of the friend who played this rotten deal on you, um, you fringed on your internals, but you really stayed with the externals. That is what I mean, by . . .

C4 Statements or directives as to how to feel, think, or behave

Joe: I think that you just have to learn to tolerate it, get along with it; no fault of the person. It's just something that they're born with. You can't twist them.

Limitations and Strengths

As is obvious from these illustrations, the PSCS is confined to defining, parsimoniously, only limited meanings of therapist–group member dialogue. Clearly, much more is being communicated than the Open versus Closed intention of the coded statements. Similarly, other ways of capturing statement mode (Tentative vs. Definitive) are operative and may convey equally significant dimensions of speech mode. The PSCS was not designed to capture all that goes on in group therapist–member interactions. Rather, its strengths result from the selective theoretical assumptions about the ingredients necessary for effectively processing new information. Thus, the operational definitions of the PSCS are attuned to clinical observation; that is, if therapists reflect doubt and uncertainty, are clients eventually able to shift from polarizing meanings to reflecting on multiple options, no longer compelled to make choices from a restricted worldview of self and other?

Reliability

The coding system was initially tested on one completed group treatment selected from the experimental trial. We found that the PSCS could be applied to all speech turns regardless of speaker (group members or therapists). On the basis of considerable experience in applying the coding system to nonstudy transcripts, between- and within-judges agreement was high (75%–85%) for all of the categories, including the supplemental codes.

Validity

Although preliminary applications of the process coding system to transcripts of several psychotherapy groups are promising, the validity of the PSCS is easily challenged. The operational definition of "psychological space" and the hypothesis that this factor is operative and essential to the advancement of group psychotherapeutic process requires further validation, both theoretically and empirically. The face validity of the PSCS appears to have clinical relevance. The challenge is in demonstrating that therapist interventions do effect an "opening" of psychological space, such that alternate ways of perceiving self and other can be processed by clients in the context group member interactions. A further test of the validity of the PSCS would be to assess changes in client "experiencing" (Klein, Mathieu, Gendlin, & Kiesler, 1969) that would be expected to parallel shifts in clients statements from more closed categories to more open categories.

Learning the Rating Method

Because of the limited range of options for applying the PSCS system, the coding procedure is readily learned and adequate interrater reliability can be achieved in approximately 20 hours of training. As indicated earlier, the primary learning task involves distinguishing between statements that qualify for the Opening versus Closing designation.

Methodology for Analysis

At this stage in the development of the PSCS, the analysis of its application on transcripts of group sessions consists of summarizing frequencies of certain combinations of code categories. The possible combinations of codes per unit are many (8 intention × 2 mode × 3 person focus + 2 alternate = 50 possible permutations and combinations). Given the limited data set and the infrequency of occurrence of some of the code combinations, the remaining option for summarizing the data consists of separate frequency counts for (a) the two global categories (Opening vs. Closing); (b) the two alternate codes (Affirmation and Provision of Information); (c) the mode (Tentative vs. Definitive); and (d) the person focus (Self, Self–Other, and Other). Despite these limitations in analyzing the data, it is possible to track shifts in all the summary codes for each therapist and group member within and across sessions. Also, with sufficient frequencies by category, chi-square analyses can be conducted to examine shifts in frequency as, for example, in an early versus late group session.

Previous Research with the System

The PSCS was tested on data collected from a treatment comparison trial for clients with BPD in which one of the treatments consisted of an experimental model of group psychotherapy designed specifically to respond to the personality characteristics of the study cohort. (For theory regarding experimental treatment and study methods and results, see Marziali & Munroe-Blum, 1994). Five groups were treated during the study. The group intervention was time limited, consisting of 30 sessions. For testing the PSCS, Sessions 6 and 28 were chosen from the last group treated during the trial. The intention was to explore differences in the type and frequencies of PSCS codes for therapists (cotherapists) and members between an early and late group session. We hypothesized that the therapists would use statements that adhered to the experimental treatment model of group treatment (i.e., Opening, Tentative, and focused on Other) and would show a consistency of responses across the two sessions. In contrast, we expected that the group members would initially use more Closing and Definitive statements with focus on Self, but that by the 28th session there would be a shift to more Opening, Tentative, and statements focused on Self–Other.

Two clinical social workers were trained to use the PSCS system. Rater agreement on separate code categories ranged from 84% to 86%. For combined codes (intent, mode, and person focus), the agreement was 74%. Frequencies were generated for separate code categories for each therapist and for each of five group members for each coded session. Proportions of Opening-to-Closing units and Tentative-to-Definitive units were calculated and compared between Sessions 6 and 28. The frequencies for focus on Self, Self–Other, Other, and Other–Other and for Affirmation and Provision of Information were also generated. The shifts in the proportional use of Opening versus Closing statements and in the proportional use of Tentative versus Definitive statements were in the direction predicted for the group members. The group proportion mean of Opening over Closing statements for Session 6 was .27, and by Session 28 it had almost tripled to .78. A similar drift was observed for the group proportion of Tentative over Definitive statements: .17 for Session 6 and .50 for Session 28.

As predicted, the therapists' statements showed less shift and were consistently more Opening and Tentative. There was a significant shift in the use of Affirmation statements by the group members from Sessions 6 to 28. There were no notable differences between Sessions 6 and 28 in the person focus or Provision of Information statements. The results of this preliminary test of the PSCS showed that the coding system could be applied reliably and that the findings were consistent with both the theoretical and clinical predictions about the meaning and potential function of psychological space in the group therapeutic process (Marziali & Munroe-Blum, 1996).

Application of the System to Group A, Session 3

After training to reliability, two judges coded Group A, Session 3 transcripts (pp. 85–115). The same level of between-judges agreement, as reported earlier, was maintained. For the group as a whole, the proportion of each code category relative to total speech turns was calculated for Unit 69, pages 90–97 (Segment 2), and was compared with the calculated proportions for pages 112–115 (Units 82–84, Segment 4). The purpose was to examine the patterns of occurrence of the various codes as well as compare the shifts, if any, between the earlier and later segments of the same group session.

In Segment 2, more than half the response modes for all participants were Closing statements: "explanatory definitive" (38%) and "confrontational" definitive (17%). For the Opening categories, "explanatory tentative" (14%) and "casting doubt" tentative (11%) were the most frequently used. Twelve percent of all statements made were Affirming, and only one speech turn qualified for the Provision of Information code. The person focus for the therapists was primarily on Other (a client in the group) and on Other–Other (two or more clients, or client and Other outside of the group). The person focus for client statements was primarily Self–Other (22%), Self (14%), and Other–Other (10%). In terms of the language mode used overall, far more statements were delivered in a Definitive format (62%) than the Tentative format (22%).

In Segment 4, the frequency of Closing statements remained the same for the "explanatory definitive" (38%) category; however, the number of "confrontational" definitive statements decreased significantly (4%). Similarly, the frequency of Opening categories remained the same for "explanatory tentative" (13%), but there was a decrease in the "casting doubt" category (2%). The frequency of the Affirming statements almost doubled (21%) when compared with the frequency of use in Segment 2. The use of Provision of Information category remained low (6%). The pattern of person focus for the therapists remained the same as for Segment 2. However, the person focus for the clients shifted to more frequent references to Self–Other (42%) and fewer Self (6%) and Other–Other (2%) references. The balance in language mode remained relatively unchanged in this segment: Definitive, 46%; Tentative, 13%.

The therapists did not differ from each other or from the group members in terms of the type of statements (primarily Closing statements delivered in a Definitive format). In Segment 2, Alice made more affirming statements (4 of 5) than in Segment 4; the balance of Opening to Closing statements also shifted for Alice from Segment 2 (4 in Opening and 7 in Closing) to Segment 4 (4 in Opening and 4 in Closing). The balance between Tentative and Definitive format statements shifted similarly. Helen made fewer interventions overall, and most were Closing statements delivered in a Definitive format.

Clinical Interpretation

Through the analyses of these two segments of the group process, it was possible to illustrate the patterns and shifts that occurred in the frequency of use of the PSCS code categories. Overall, this was a group in which a considerable amount of the interaction was concerned with providing explanations about each other, to each other. In addition to providing explanation in Segment 2, the group was more confrontational and less affirming than in its Segment 4 responses. Also, in Segment 2, the clients' focused more on the self and less on self–other than in the later segment. We postulated that the shifts in categories of the PSCS from Segment 2 to Segment 4 may reflect an increasing willingness by the participants to accept new perceptions (a decrease in confrontational statements) and more support for others' viewpoints (Affirmation statements). Similarly, the clients' increased focus on Self and Other rather than focus on Self may also support our hypothesis of increased openness for engagement with others in the group. The clients' statements may mirror the therapists' approach to the group; that is, the therapists' frequent use of an explanatory Definitive format may have served to induct the clients into the process and function of group psychotherapy.

Relationship Between Research and Theory

Despite the encouraging findings from several applications of the PSCS, it cannot be said with certainty that the theoretical notion of Opening versus Closing psychological space is captured in the operational definitions of the system's categories. Nor is there any direct evidence to show that the use of these statements results in increased capacity for information processing as postulated. In the original study on which the PSCS was tested (reported earlier), the clients whose responses were found to shift from more Closing to more Opening statements between Sessions 6 and 28 did make important improvements. However, the associations between these shifts and posttreatment improvement are unknown. Despite the problems in supporting the validity of the PSCS, it appears to reflect something important about both the intent and mode of therapeutic dialogue. It is applicable to both therapist and client dialogue, such that differences among participants, and shifts across time, can be detected and compared.

Assessment and Future Directions

The PSCS continues to be tested for its application to individual and couples therapies. Some refinements to the codes are being considered. Furthermore, a statistical method, Dual Scaling (Nishisato, 1994), is being used to determine whether patterned sequences can be detected. The aim is to demonstrate that patterned sequences do exist and that shifts in the sequences across a therapy session or across sessions are not chance occurrences. As stated earlier, the validity of the PSCS needs to be established beyond its clinical relevance. Because the coding system was developed in the context of a clinical trial for clients with BPD, the congruence between code categories and the design of the experimental group treatment can be faulted for a circularity of definitions and meanings. Thus, only by meeting the challenge of testing the system on a wide range of treatment models and formats will it be possible to demonstrate that the construct of psychological space exists and that it is an important factor in determining an effective therapeutic process.

THE STT, A DISCOURSE ANALYSIS SYSTEM

The STT is a fine-grained method of analysis that documents how speakers use language in interactions and the recurrent patterns and transformation of their statements. Applied to psychotherapy exchanges, the STT examines (a) the ways in which clients formulate and reformulate meanings about self and other during psychotherapy; (b) how their statements come to be altered in the process of psychotherapeutic movement;

(c) conversely, how they persist in entrenched patterns; (d) how clients and therapists interactively share and diverge in their formulations about self and other; and (e) the contribution of participants to meaning transformation.

History and Theory of the System

Discourse Analysis and Psychotherapy

Discourse analysis is a broad umbrella approach to language behavior that analyzes how language is used in interaction (Potter & Wetherell, 1987; Schiffrin, 1994). The relevance of a discursive approach to psychology and psychotherapy (Edwards & Potter, 1992) rests on the assumption that the language patterns adopted by a speaker correspond to a specific cognitive organization. In a constructionist perspective, how people say things about themselves and others constitutes their representation of these relations, which in turn guides their interpersonal actions. A positive outcome of psychotherapy can be found in the redefinition of self–other relations and can be traced to the client's modified statements. In group exchanges, discourse analysis documents the individual, group, and interactive dimensions of language behavior, tracking convergent and divergent formulations between speakers.

Principles of Discourse Analysis

Unlike content analysis, which categorizes statements into discrete content categories, discourse methods examine how speakers concretely use words to shape topics and themes, and document these wordings. Methods of analysis are primarily descriptive and qualitative. Analysis rests on a number of presuppositions: the recurrence and variation of language patterns and their contextual use. A systematic discourse methodology tracks nuances of meaning in the context of the clause, the sentence, the speech turn, and the speaker's statements overall. The same word, used in different contexts, can have multiple uses and meanings.

Origins of the STT

In psychotherapy, most researchers have either examined ways of speaking through words, clauses, and speech turns (Essig & Russel, 1990; Labov & Fanshel, 1977; Laffal, 1987; Patton & Meara, 1987; Sherman & Skinner, 1988) or have analyzed statements with a "narrative lens" (Angus, Hardtke, & Levitt, 1992; Luborsky, Barber, & Diguer, 1992; Russel & van den Broek, 1992; Schafer, 1992; Sluzki, 1992; White & Epston, 1990). By contrast, the STT treats statements of self and other at two levels: (a) the story level conceived as the macrostructure of statements and (b) the speech level of words and clauses or microstructure of statements (Chambon, 1993b, 1994, 1995). The narrative level tracks meaning by reference to events, characters, and relationships, whereas word- and clause-based analyses capture small variations of meaning. This distinction is not relevant to the speakers themselves; in actual behavior, people tell stories through words. It is used conceptually for analytical purposes. The two levels require different units of analyses and rely on distinct sets of tools. This two-tiered type of analysis has been recommended by discourse analysts themselves. van Dijk (1985) argued that "the relation between narrative schemata and speech properties . . . remains to be made explicit" (p. 4). Similarly, Bruner (1990) combined narrative features with syntactical speech markers of subjectivity to indicate the speaker's attitude about an event.

Furthermore, most of the researchers of psychotherapy have tended to develop categories and to report aggregate frequencies of decontextualized statement types. STT analyses stay close to the actual formulations of the speakers and identify "how" and under what conditions (of language and interactional contexts) these formulations take place.

The systematic approach in the STT comes from the selection of analytical tools of relevance to the task at hand that have been drawn from (a) literary theories of narrative that include features of the story and the activity of telling (classified as narrative pragmatics; Genette, 1983; Prince, 1987, 1991; Rimmon-Kenan, 1983), (b) linguistic approaches in interaction (rather than language rules; Culioli, 1990; Eggins, 1995; Halliday, 1985; Langacker, 1987–1991; Talmy, 1988), and (c) speech-turn feature derived from conversational analysis. The selected tools are compatible in pragmatics terms and are complementary. Although the principles of analysis remain constant, the specific concepts used will vary across studies on the basis of the type of utterance or text that is being examined. Often, a developmental phase is needed to select, adjust, or even develop those tools and to make them explicit, conceptually and operationally. In the current analysis we track how formulations of self and other come to be modified in the group and the discursive means of transformation.

Description of the System

Categories

Narrative Features. The macrostory level articulates three features: character, narrator, and spatiotemporal scenes. Speakers tell stories about characters, distinguishable as Self and Other. The term *character centering* refers to the set of characters placed in main or focal narrative positions. The "narrator" is the commentator of the story who reflects on the events and adopts a perspective. The narrator may be the same as or different from the character in the story. "Spatiotemporal scenes" cover the life spaces in which characters and narrators are located. They can be classified into (a) *here-and-now*, which are in-session events between clients and therapists; (b) *here-and-then* references to previous session events; (c) *there-and-now*, which are out-of-session contemporaneous events involving clients and others in their life; and (d) *there-and-then* extraneous past events, future-situated, and hypothetical events. Therapeutic narratives often involve a story genre called the "family romance" that links childhood scenes, here-and-now in-session dynamics, and general atemporal comments on the actions of characters (Eggins, 1995).

Speech Features. The STT is not confined to listing the terms used by speakers, but instead performs a mapping of meaning. To do so, the STT examines the semantic deployment of terms and tracks the recurrence, variation, and expansion of word patterns for each speaker. Speech features include (a) the speech in turn that identifies the speaker, (b) lexical expressions (i.e., individual words, phrases, and word groupings used preferentially by speakers), and (c) grammatical features that provide information about the meaning of self–other.

Specification and expansion of meaning are tracked initially by identifying patterns of "lexical recurrence," "lexical elaboration," and "lexical-semantic connotation"—mechanisms used commonly in everyday speech. *Lexical recurrence* (or "reiteration") stands for the repetition of a key phrase or part of a phrase. *Lexical elaboration* takes place when a speaker clarifies an initial wording by adding an equivalent expression, as in the following two-part statement:

(1) he closed the door for me, . . . I can't come in.

The term *lexical-semantic connotation* refers to the deployment of an associated meaning triggered by the key phrase. In most cases, this occurs through a different wording, as in

(2) set me free . . . didn't care for me.

At this stage of development of the STT, the repeated phrases and variants are identifiable in a straightforward manner. The mapping of associative connotative terms needs further development to achieve greater validation and will be worked on in the future.

Meaning attributed to Self and Other is further elucidated in the grammatical (syntactic) features of statements. This is consistent with conceptualizations in psychology that emphasize locating Self ("I") statements and the structure of Self–Other statements (Patton & Meara, 1987; Schafer, 1992; Sluzki, 1992). The Structural Analysis of Social Behavior system (Benjamin, Foster, Roberto, & Estroff, 1986) and the Experiencing Scale (Klein, Mathieu-Coughlan, & Kiesler, 1986) examine the position of the "I" in narratives. A common clinical conclusion has been that greater use of an agentive Self, a Self that is situated at the center of the narrative and, as the source of action and relation, is associated with therapeutic progress.

The STT tracks which person (Self or Other) occupies the grammatical subject position in a subject + verb statement, differentiating between statements in which Other is the subject (3a) and statements in which Self is the subject (3b):

(3a) he closed the door   (3b) I'm behind the door.

In statements in which subject and object are both present, Self and Other may occupy the position of agent or of recipient. Two patterns are differentiated: Other-agent/Self-recipient (4a) and Self-agent/Other-recipient (4b), as in the following:

(4a) she set me free   (4b) I set her free.

A category of verbs, "epistemic predicates," such as "I think, believe, wish," indicate a perspective or point of view of the speaker (in psychology, see Bruner, 1990; Essig & Russel, 1990). These verbs position the subject as observer and commentator. They tend to be placed in the first clause of a clause complex, followed by dependent (projected) clauses. The subject of the two clauses are the same in self-reflective statements, such as

(5a) I think I want to tell inner things.

They are distinct when Self is observer/commentator and You/Other are the agents of actions:

(5b) I thought you/he wanted to . . .

Self can also be missing from a clause complex, as in

(6) she is asking you to open up.

Additional information about the Self can be traced to expressions of "modality," broadly conceived (Chambon & Simeoni, 1998; Halliday, 1985). These are verbs and adverbial expressions that further specify the meaning of a word. According to Culioli (1990), speech forms can be classified into Closed and Open forms (see also Chambon & Simeoni, 1998). Open expressions indicate variation and possibility, whereas Closed expressions indicate constraint or obligation (cf. Talmy, 1988). The following examples differentiate between open modalized expressions (a column) and closed modalized expressions (b column).

(a)	somewhat closed	(b)	totally closed
	very free		always free
	could be free		have to be free

Validity

The STT is a descriptive approach. The aim is not to reach a closed system of analysis, because, given the creativity in language use, we cannot predict the specific statements that a speaker will make. The validity of the system is based on the conceptual understanding of how discourse operates. Reliability is found in agreement on the surface trace of a phenomenon. Theoretical preparation and training are necessary to develop the ability to conduct a close reading of the text and to trace variations. Several principles of validation are helpful (Potter & Wetherell, 1987): (a) the assumption of coherence of speech by each speaker, (b) participant orientation (i.e., how a speaker responds to another speaker is indicative of meaning), and (c) the fruitfulness of the analysis (i.e., the extent to which it generates new meaning). It is and will remain a time-consuming type of analysis.

Initial attempts at joint analysis have shown high agreement on some features. Difficulties remain with expressions of vagueness and ambiguity that convey multiple meanings. We need to continuously clarify the concepts and document our analyses.

Previous Research With the System

The organizing principles and core concepts of the two-tiered (telling and talking) analysis were first developed in analyzing an individual session (Chambon, 1993a). The STT analysis identified change points or "shifts" in the client's statements and transformations in the versions of her story. It also showed the negotiated nature of the exchange between client and therapist as well as illuminated several strategies used by the therapist to shape the client's version and encourage cognitive reorganization (Chambon, 1994).

The system was then applied to the Gloria tapes (Shostrom, 1966) by conducting a comparative analysis of the three sessions held between this one client and the three therapists. This set of analyses led to identifying strategies of positioning self and other in the client's story and highlighted the relevance of spatiotemporal scenes (Chambon, 1993b). It also identified patterns of "modalization" as needing further development. The system was then applied to the beginning, middle, and end sessions of a successful group with clients with BPD using data from the IGP treatment program (Marziali & Munroe-Blum, 1994) mentioned earlier. This analysis operationalized the distinction between fixed and more fluid language, relying on the linguistic concepts of Closed versus Open modalizers (Chambon, 1995; Chambon & Simeoni, 1998). The therapists were found to model to the clients the more open style of speech. The more successful clients adopted this cognitive style and modified their speech, expanding their representation of interpersonal relations.

Findings, at this stage of development of the system, indicate that with successful therapy, clients make greater use of (a) "I," self-centered statements, (b) interactional (transitive) Self–Other statements, and (c) self-reflective statements. For the STT, the quantitative increase in certain types of statements is not as important as the detail of how those changes come about.

Application of the STT to Group A, Session 3

Discourse analysis, as a language-based approach, suspends inferences about the clinical implications of statements during the first round of analysis. Clinical interpretations of the findings constitutes a separate stage of analysis that requires expert validation. In the present study, Chambon is a clinician, and the analysis was further submitted to Tsang and Marziali for validation.

Narrative and speech patterns were analyzed in the early, middle, and late segments of the group session. Given the space limitations, we summarize the narrative patterns, and analyze the speech features from the early and the later segment in greater detail. For the latter, we began by identifying sequences in the session in which a key word or phrase was used more than once and explored by more than one speaker. These were seen as moments in which the group members were working minimally together. The two analyzed segments corresponded, respectively, to the end of Phase II and the transition to Phase III and to Phase IV, as discussed with the PSCS.

Narrative Transformation

Narrative shifts occurred in spatiotemporal scenes and in character centering. Group members tended to work around a focal scene, but the type of scene changed during the session. The early and middle segments of the transcript (Units 64–74) located the story primarily in current and recent past sessions of the group (the here-and-now and here-and-then), with secondary reference to contemporaneous scenes from other group or work situations (there-and-now). As the session progressed (Unit 75 onward), group members shifted to exploring childhood scenes (there-and-then), which they expanded through reflective, atemporal commentaries. In Unit 75, a group member, Joe, elicited family romance stories by inviting another participant, Diane, to talk about her childhood. Other group members then make comparisons to their own childhood narratives.

In terms of character centering, early narratives centered on a focal group member, Joe (Units 61–69), with the remaining group members focalized on the Other, away from the Self. In the middle segment (Units 70–74), group members struggled to change that pattern and to position their Self as focal character. Diane alternated between talking about Joe and herself: "Maybe you want something, but so do I." Martha says, "I thought about the things I might bring up."

A similar progression was repeated when evoking childhood scenes.

At first, participants encouraged the central speakers to expand on their stories "for that very reason *you* maintained sort of a mild, non-putting forth yourself toward him." Gradually, a multiple-narrator structure emerged in which group members related separate childhood stories and located their Self as the focal character. The shift was initiated when a group member (Greg) suggested comparing family stories: "I wonder if we'd get something out of it if I compared her parents and my parents, now, my mother. . . . " Yet, initially, speakers placed other family members at the center of their story and located their Self as an observer who evaluated the actions of Others: "My father was an authoritarian and an alcoholic, and my mother was the strong center and core of the family around which the children rotated." Progressively, they positioned their Self as the main character engaged in interactions.

Speech Pattern Transformation, Unit 69

The Unit 69 segment analyzed was organized around the phrase "closed door," which was repeated by several speakers. The sequence began as follows:

Diane: There's something about what he said that closed the door for me.

Table 12.4 illustrates the progression achieved between the initiating client (Diane) and one of the therapists (Alice). The client gradually reformulated her statement in more explicit relational terms. She situated herself in a clear, agentive position, making "I" statements, and expanded her reflective comments (see Table 12.4).

The client's initial statement is fuzzy and lacks an explicit agentive subject:

Diane: There's something about what he said that closed the door for me.

Diane placed her Self ("for me") in an ambiguous position either as a recipient of action or as a reflective commentator. The therapist disambiguated the statement and placed the client in an observer-reflective position, with the Other in an agent position:

Therapist: *To you* it meant *he* had just closed the door.

In response, Diane reformulated her statement into an action clause in which "I" was the distinct subject, moving from a state-agentive to a personalized object to an action-agentive wording:

(1) I'm behind this door   (2) my door   (3) I can't come in.

Diane then claimed Self as subject but had not yet located Self in a transitive, relational structure. She did so next, as she switched from meta-

TABLE 12.4
STT Analysis of Partial Reformation of "Closed Door" (Unit 69)

Speaker	Core Phrase and Variations	Reflective Comments	Elaboration
C	something		
		about what he said that	
	closed the door for me		
T		to you it meant	
	he had just closed the door		
C		yes it meant, here you know	
	I am behind this door		
			if you don't know the . . .
			if you can't come in
	at my door		
T			if you can't come in on my own terms, on my way, then you can't come in
C		somehow that says to me	
			and you can't come in
			I can't come in
		that is what is un-finished about it	
			we would function su-perficially, I would never know

Note. Dyadic exchange between C (client—Diane) and T (therapist—Alice). This table visually il-lustrates the transformative process, with statements presented sequentially. The three columns dis-tinguish between (a) the core phase and its variations, (b) reflective comments, and (c) elaboration of the meaning of the phrase and introduction of alternative terminology. Increasing prominence is given to the reflective and elaborative statements based on the core phase itself modified. STT = Strategies of Telling and Talking.

phorically concrete object referents ("closed door") to interpersonal state-ments about "knowing," with the related wording of "surface" versus "depth":

(1) closed door/come in   (2) knowing/superficially.

Other group members picked up on the relational wording, through mixed terminology.

Martha: Accept me as this kind of person that I close this door here.

Diane concluded with a fully stated relational statement:

Martha: *You* can only know *me* with my door closed.

Various phrasings illustrate the type of meaning work that participants were conducting. Thus, Martha produced a "closed" modalized statement about "knowing" which the therapist (Helen) reformulated into an "open" version:

Martha: You can't know me.

Helen: You can only know me so much.

The reflective dimension also underwent change and was modeled by the therapist. Helen accentuated the differential perspective of each speaker with contrastive statements:

Helen: I really don't understand this expression what it means . . . It means a lot *to you*, and *for me* it doesn't mean anything.

Following her cue, Diane responded by contrasting her understanding with that of Joe's, concluding,

Diane: This is how *I* hear it, now *he* may not be saying that . . .

This therapist introduces alternative Self–Other statements, as in

Helen: *I* get disturbed about *your* way *as you* get disturbed about *mine*.

This statement, which has the agent and recipient in the reverse positions, indicate that the positions were not fixed but that they could be flexibly arranged and could contain various degrees of difference and mutuality. Diane subsequently expressed a new understanding: "I guess there is an element of judgement in here or evaluation on my part." Further acknowledging the impact of the therapist's statement, she added, "I think Helen really hit it right on the head when she said to me, . . . you're absolutely right, I'm not willing to accept him on his terms."

The group interaction was not always smooth or successful. Ineffectiveness and difficulties can be traced discursively as well. When Alice reformulated "my door" as "on your terms," she introduced the phrase "can't accept." It was not picked up by the others at the time but resurfaced later on in Diane's concluding statement, "I don't accept him on his own terms." This delayed recurrence illustrates the role of timing for introducing new terms. Words introduced too early, or those that were not "in synch," were not integrated right away into the group's repertoire. This does not mean that they had not been heard because they could resurface at a later point.

In one statement, Alice used a dual focalization, centering initially on the Self of the client and later on Other:

Alice: And yet Diane, it seemed like *you* understood him very clearly to be saying that what *he* wanted is *to be* accepted as *he* was.

The client refused to follow the prompt and chose instead to focus the statement on herself:

> Diane: *I* didn't understand *him* saying that, and *I* guess what *I'm* saying now . . . it wasn't finished for me.

Late Segment (Units 83–84)

This segment occurred in the latter part of the session with the shift to childhood narratives. It was characterized by multiple narratives made by several clients about Self and Other. Group members examined complex sets of meanings regarding their relation to a close family member, parent, or sibling using the notion of "freedom." Three clients and one therapist used the same core term across 11 speech turns. This is a good illustration of shared but differentiated meanings.

The initial phrase—"leave me free"—is a complex expression that instantiates the notion of freedom but places the Self in the recipient position. This example illustrates that it is not the isolated term that is crucial but the actual phrasing with its complex meanings (see Table 12.5).

The first two client speakers modalized the word contrastively:

Martha:	very free	so free		
Diane:	always free	absolutely free	almost too free	utter freedom

Martha used Open modalizers of possibility ("very/so free,"), whereas Diane used Closed modalizers of constraint of increasing intensity ("always, absolutely, almost too, utter.") Each variant was expanded in self-agentive statements ("being free," column 3) and associated phrases (column 4).

Martha's freedom was dependent on Other's (her sister's) wishes: "She gives me freedom" and "she wants me to be free" (column 3). Martha was not fully agent. Furthermore, she associated freedom with her struggle for independence (column 4). By contrast, Diane positioned herself as agent ("being free," column 3). The phrase held for her the negative connotation of not receiving love of Other (mother). She was set free because she was not cared for. Her recipient Self was alternatively worded in the collective "we" of the sibling unit. Diane's ambivalence is indicated in the two-sided associations she made with the notion of freedom, where she alternated between the positions of agent and recipient—between "left home" and "got kicked out."

In conclusion (Unit 84), the therapist brought into a single statement the diverse expressions of group members: "You were free and you were not free, in that sense you had to." She tied together the apparently contradictory sets of meanings of the term *freedom* (i.e., positive and negative, openness/caring and constraint). The therapist provided a resolution to Diane's previous conflicted statements, who concurred by saying, "In that

344   CHAMBON, TSANG, AND MARZIALI

TABLE 12.5
STT Analysis of Lexical Variation and Expansion of Meaning through Connotation (Units 83–84)

Unit	Speaker	Lexical Variation		Connotation
		leave free (lf) *give freedom (gf)* *set free (sf)*	*being free/not free* (=f, ≠f)	*care/love* vs. *force* (others)
113/2b, 4	Martha	OT > lf (very) > I OT > lf (so) > I = f .	OT > want > (I > f)	*Positive polarity* (sister) kindly influence, the only one in my life, not hanging on to me; I had to acquire independence sense of identity
113/5 to 114/3	Diane	OT > lf (always) > I (we) OT > lf (absolutely) > I OT > lf (almost too) > I OT > gf (utter) > I OT > sf (always) > I	I (we) = f (always)	*Negative polarity* because (mother) she didn't love me be- cause . . . she didn't care about us, we left home we got kicked out.
115/12	Helen	YOU = f, YOU ≠ f		you had to
115/13	Diane	I (we) ≠ f		we had to we had no choice except when we rebelled

Note. Lexical variation maintains a core term. Connotation expands on the significance of the core. The agency-recipiency structure is based on the pronoun position of I, YOU, and OT (= Other) and direction of the relation: (>). OT > I = other/agent + self/recipient; I > OT = self/agent + other/recipient. STT = Strategies of Telling and Talking.

sense we were not free, we had to." In summary, a common theme was elaborated on between group members (clients and therapist), with variations and associations resulting in discursive movement.

Therapists' Strategies

The discursive strategies used by therapists were found in centering clients as the focal character in their narrative, eliciting from them Self-agentive statements and Self–Other relational statements, introducing reciprocal relational statements, and inviting explicit versus implicit statements of perspective. To these we can add rewording (lexical) strategies consisting of inviting reformulation and elaboration; attempting to modify the metaphoric language of clients into psychological, relational language, and juxtaposing disparate meanings into single statements to achieve integration and differentiation.

Disruptive statements made by therapists were traced to (a) the replacement of client language by their own and introducing alternative word groupings; (b) pacing seemed to be crucial, such that the development of associative meaning was best followed when preceded by reformulation; and (c) switching the focal agent from client-Self to Other (group member) led to a reclaiming by the client of his or her agentive position.

Summary

The group worked together on joint themes sharing common narrative features of character and scene. The group progressed from a single narrative to multiple narratives as participants struggled to develop their individual story. Group members shifted into childhood narratives and the meanings these relational patterns held for them in the present. The group progressed to complex and differentiated meanings. Group members expanded their self-reflections and shifted to making self-agentive statements within structures of self–other relations.

Clinical Interpretation

Group process changes were observed in this session. The group progressed from focusing on a single group member (scapegoating) to engaging in individualized transformative work. Clients explored difficult material and expanded the meanings of relationships and sense of self. Their exploration of childhood-based patterns of relation and the exploration of self–other agentive structure were the most noted features of discursive transformation.

The group process was led alternatively by therapists and by other group members who facilitated each other's exploration. The contribution of therapists involved exploring the multifaceted nature of experiences and complex meanings; integrating disruptive and contradictory feelings; encouraging assertive agentive and reflective statements; and, overall, introducing alternative statements to expand group members' understanding.

Assessment and Future Directions

The application of the STT illuminated meaning transformation in psychotherapeutic group process. Tracking detailed speech and narrative features represents a highly complex task. The two levels of analysis of the STT, narrative and speech, were found to be complementary. Character centering, in narrative terms, could be examined in greater detail through the agentive structure of statements. However, speech units do not neatly coincide with the narrative units of spatiotemporal scenes. Further examination of this two-tiered analysis needs to be refined.

Speech segments were selected on the basis of repeated and shared wording. This purposive sampling procedure helped define units of analysis. However, multiple key phrases can be found in a single session, and speech units are often embedded in a complex structure of statements. Examining such complex structures remains a task to be further clarified. Furthermore, the concepts of lexical expansion (reiteration through elaboration and association) helped document and assess the meaning work. Yet, whereas repetitions are easily identified at the surface level of statements, the nuances of transformations require further conceptualization. There are instances in which a phrase falls somewhere between an elaboration and a connotation. Additional empirically grounded analyses will help refine this understanding.

Overall, the strength of the system lies in the actual deployment of the many ways in which language is used. This is also its limitation: The work-intensive nature of the analysis precludes the detailed examination of all statements in a session. Any selection requires clarification of the criteria used. Referring to conceptual categories may suggest that a quantitative analysis based on broad categories will yield useful "hard" data. We believe that although quantitative analyses, derived from the STT, can provide a global indication of therapeutic process, they simplify the subtleties of actual language behavior and leave out the detailed lessons researchers can learn about how therapeutic movement is achieved.

INTEGRATION OF THE THREE SYSTEMS AS APPLIED TO GROUP A

Convergent Analyses

One segment from a latter part of the session is assessed sequentially with the NOTA, PSCS, and STT analytical systems to illustrate their complementarity. Each speech turn is indicated separately and followed by the analyses of the three systems.

Helen: Seems different, it's even more difficult with your sister because she's so good.

> NOTA: Coded NS:F. Helen connects with Martha's earlier statement regarding her difficulty in establishing her separate identity from her sister and gaining her own independence.
>
> PSCS: Coded C3, D, Z, corresponding to a Closed explanatory statement (C); Definitive format (D); person focus is on client and Other.
>
> STT: The segment is on family narratives, with distinct narratives from group members. This statement, made by the therapist Helen, is said in the reflective ("seems"), atemporal mode. The clause structure is nontransitive; statement is centered on Other.

Martha: And leaves me so free

> NOTA: Coded: NS:F. Martha continues from her previous turn; stays on the same topic.
>
> PSCS: Martha's statement, interrupted by Helen, is coded as one turn; Helen's interruption is not coded.
>
> STT: Martha introduces the key word of "freedom," with Open modalization "so free." Transitive statement with Other/subject (agent), Self object (recipient); this grammatical structure combined with the lexical term = freedom is determined by Other-than-Self.

Helen: and wants [interruption] . . . .

> NOTA: Coded: NS:F. Helen again tries to connect with Martha using a "sentence completion" strategy, but she is interrupted by Martha.
>
> PSCS and STT: They do not assess this as a unit, unlike the NOTA.

Martha: and wants me to be free. Yeah, if she was trying to hang on to me like my mother did, then I'd have somebody to, hm hm, to fight with, but she—she wasn't.

> NOTA: Coded: NS:F and INT. Martha has interrupted Helen to continue her own speech turn. The topic is maintained. Martha uses the same words "and wants" to start her speech turn.
>
> PSCS: Coded AFF = affirmation, agreement, supportive.
>
> STT: Martha makes a temporal narrative link to the past (family romance). The key phrase "free" is not modalized (modalization of 0). Clause structure is maintained: Other/subject–Self/object; however, projected clause ("wants/[that I] be free,") is somewhat more agentive.

348   CHAMBON, TSANG, AND MARZIALI

Diane: You know, I was just thinking as you were talking that when when you mentioned—mentioned about the difference that, from what you have said, the big difference between, apparently between my mother and your mother, and this might have some bearing to what you were saying Greg, a different bearing but I'll get to that, um, is that Mother—Mother always left us free . . .

> NOTA: Coded: NS:F. Diane connects her experience with those of Martha's and Greg's while staying on the same topic of mother and the theme of freedom.
>
> PSCS: Coded: C3, D, Y1. A closed explanatory statement (C3); Definitive format (D); person focus is on Self–Other (Y1).
>
> STT: Narrative link through contrast; continues past temporal setting. Closed modalization "always." Other/subject–Self/object, still not agentive.

Martha: Huh?!

> NOTA: Coded NS:F. Response indicating attention and interest, but not interrupting.
>
> PSCS and STT: They do not rate this.

Diane: . . . absolutely free from the time I can remember . . . [interrupted].

> NOTA: Diane continues with her own narrative.
>
> PSCS: Continuation of Diane's unfinished speech turn above; no separate code.
>
> STT: Narrative refers to continuous past since early childhood. Closed modalization "absolutely free."

Martha: You're saying what she said; you're saying the feeling that you got from her?

> NOTA: Coded NS:F and INT. Martha, following from her previous "Huh," interrupts Diane, but focuses on Diane's experience.
>
> PSCS: Question formulated in an Open format (O1); person focus is on Self–Other (Y1).
>
> STT: Reflective mode ("You're saying the feeling you got"). Martha centers the statement on Diane "you" and her relation with Other ("from her"). Martha's questioning is interpreted as arising from the divergence of meanings she and Diane associate with "freedom."

Diane: Almost too free. She didn't really a—and we, I got the feeling as a child that she didn't love me because because she gave us such utter freedom, in fact, I uh, all of us kids, the four of us at the time each of us reached 16 we left home. I mean we were, we just got kicked out of the nest (laugh) you know, "Get out, get out and make your own way," that sort of thing. But even prior to that she was she was setting us free even down in grade school because, I don't know, I'd have to really think how she did it except I was aware it was happening, that she was setting us free, always; in fact, maybe we were always free because she didn't care about us (laugh).

    NOTA: Coded: NS:F. Diane continues to elaborate on her experience, taking into account the points raised by other people in the group.

    SPCS: Open explanatory statement (O3); expressed in a Tentative format (T); person focus is on Self–Other (Y1).

    STT: Childhood narrative. For the first time, an explicitly negative statement about freedom, although tentatively worded ("almost too free"), followed by closed or absolute with negative inflection ("utter freedom") and closed modalization ("setting us free, always"). Transitive relation, Other/subject–Self/object ("she gave us/was setting us free[dom]"). Diane is not agentive. Associated meaning is negative ("she didn't love me because she . . . freedom"; "free because she didn't care about us"). The phrases—"we left home . . . we just got kicked out"— structurally reflect conflict in terms of agency.

The three systems capture the continuity of theme across speakers and concur on the person focus. According to the NOTA content coding, this is a smooth-running sequence with no abrupt change in topic or character center. The group stays focused on a common theme, with different members participating without changing the topic or competing to advance personal agenda. The process coding shows two incidents of interruptions, but the important point is that these interruptions occur in a context of joining and working together instead of competing voices and agendas. This highlights the important point that the clinical significance of a code has to be interpreted with reference to different discursive contexts.

The PSCS coding is complementary. According to PSCS, in this particular sequence, group members engage in a supportive exploration of meaning in their interactions. They use tentative wording that invites new formulations, such as an Opening question, and provide encouragement of each other's process through Affirmative statements. They explore their own personal meanings through Opening statements and a person focus on Self–Other.

The STT confirms the PSCS coding and complements that analysis around the Self–Other statements, showing the reformulation of personal meanings through increasingly explicit statements in which they rely on modalized rephrasings and expand on associated meanings. The STT adds information about the directionality of the Self–Other statements that are mainly Other-directed, with group members placing themselves in a recipient position. In a more advanced stage of therapy, one would expect a greater occurrence of self-agentive statements. In narrative terms, the STT complements the information about theme and character present in the other systems by indicating how group members link the past with the present in working through their individual narratives of family romance.

GENERAL DISCUSSION

The application of the three systems to group therapeutic interaction clearly demonstrates the contribution of each as well as their complementarity in adding depth and breadth to the analysis of therapeutic process. For example, the central finding of the NOTA analysis showed high continuity across speakers and flexibility of group members in accommodating to changing topics and procedural action. Clients initiated topics and were able to adopt collaborative strategies beyond strictly following one another using means the NOTA identified as strategies of continuation of speaker's content, direct linkages, and backtracking. The STT analysis highlights how group members contributed to narrative features of character and setting and how the group achieved thematic commonality by using shared lexical phrases. Also, the STT system shows how group members actively contributed to the process of transformation through narrative shifts and lexical elaboration. The PSCS system identified an overall group member shift toward psychological openness and parallel readiness for cognitive reorganization. The PSCS tracked a decrease in defensive confrontational statements, an increase in affirmation, exploration of uncertainty and alternative meaning, and accommodation to new information.

In terms of integration of the three systems at the global level, both the STT and the PSCS demonstrated enhanced differentiation of meanings among the group participants. The participants moved away from a single narrative focused on a single group member to multiple, differentiated narratives meeting each member's agenda. They explored increasingly multifaceted meanings of self–other relations and expanded their meaning systems, as assessed through lexical expansion, grammatical transformations, and the use of more tentative and open statements.

The person-focus analysis showed that, in the PSCS system, clients moved away from scapegoating and explaining each other's processes to greater openness for engagement with others as evident through the increased use of statements about self and other. Concurrently, the STT analysis indicated how group members moved away from making statements about others and increasingly positioned themselves at the center of their narrative, making increasingly transitive (Self–Other) statements, and shifted from recipient to self-agentive statements. Group members also became better able to differentiate between action and reflection. The STT and PSCS systems converge in the finding that disclosure and taking risks are associated with exploration of meaning and differentiation. The opening of new meanings was associated with a modified expression of self in relation to others.

According to the NOTA, abrupt shifts were avoided, whereas helpful mutative strategies such as *non-shift* and *mediated shift* were used. Similarly, the PSCS documented the importance of making affirming statements and open, tentative statements about self and other. At the more detailed level of words and phrases, the STT showed the usefulness of inviting clients to elaborate on their meanings through lexical expansion, open modalizers of variation and possibility, and grammatical strategies that encourage explicit relational statements about self and other. STT also indicated the useful strategy of promoting reflective statements about individual perspectives.

Assessment and Future Directions

The three systems illustrate common features of a speaker-based approach with a content-related person focus. The combination of two categorical systems with a discourse-analytic approach provides an integrated means of analyzing *what* and *how* therapeutic change occurs.

The NOTA points to the significance of flexible accommodation among participants that ensures engagement, collaboration, and enhanced disclosure within the group process. The STT shows how a group progresses through elaboration and differentiation, highlighting the interplay between shared group process and individual member process as reflected in the patterns of discourse. The PSCS shows how the opening of psychological space by the group participants is associated with alternative ways of perceiving self and self–other. Confirming Russel's (1987) suggestion, these findings indicate the possibility of a language-based assessment of therapeutic progress in terms of discursive differentiation and integration. The overall findings generated by the three systems identify support, mutuality, disclosure, and the balance between individuation and group cohesion as crucial features of psychotherapeutic progress. These analyses are consistent with previous research and provide group process markers on different levels of analysis.

The three systems can be usefully combined to perform multilevel–multimethod analyses. The overlap between systems will be further investigated in the future by exploring links among selected categories of the NOTA and PSCS and narrative and speech strategies of the STT. Similarly, the associations between each system and corresponding measures of group process such as group cohesion (Cohesiveness Scale; Budman, Soldz, Demby, Davis, & Merry, 1993), group phase (Group Phase Scale; Beck,

Dugo, Eng, & Lewis, 1986), and depth of psychological processing (Experiencing Scale; Klein et al., 1986) will be examined.

For each system, the current study provides new methods of inquiry. The NOTA makes the distinction between disengaged versus engaged interruptions and provides the link between interruption mode and content continuity. Although the STT also assesses shifts in the narrative, the next phase of development of the system will be to discriminate between more helpful and less helpful shifts. Strategies for examining the effects of progress and outcome of each of the systems, and in combination, will need to be developed. For example, in the NOTA, which factors contribute to the effective negotiation of the therapeutic agenda and ultimately to outcome? Is it possible to demonstrate that shifts from closed to open psychological space, as tracked by the PSCS, lead to more favorable outcomes? Similarly, which components of the narrative and speech-analytic strategies identified by the STT correspond to change? To answer these questions, researchers need to develop methods of analysis of interaction within and across the three systems. As was shown in the joint analyses of one sequence, apart from quantitative analysis, the findings of the PSCS and NOTA lend themselves to the qualitative data analysis of their analytical categories. Conversely, the complexity of STT findings can be collapsed into summary categories that would lend themselves to quantification.

In further exploration of the integrated contribution of the three systems, it will be important to connect their respective analyses to an integrated theoretical model for explaining the change processes in the group. We hope that the combined analyses can help clarify the relationship between change processes and outcomes and contribute to knowledge that is relevant to clinical practitioners.

REFERENCES

Angus, L., Hardtke, K., & Levitt, H. (1992). A rating manual for the Narrative Processing Coding System. Unpublished manuscript, York University, Toronto, Ontario, Canada.

Baekeland, F., & Lundwell, L. (1975). Dropping out of treatment: A critical review. Psychological Bulletin, 82, 738–783.

Beck, A. P., Dugo, J. M., Eng, A. M., & Lewis, C. M. (1986). The search for phases in group development: Designing process analysis measures of group interaction. In L. S. Greenberg & W. M. Pinsof (Eds.), The psychotherapeutic process: A research handbook (pp. 615–705). New York: Guilford Press.

Benjamin, L. S., Foster, S. W., Roberto, L. G., & Estroff, S. E. (1986). Breaking the family code: Analysis of videotapes of family interactions by Structural Analysis of Social Behavior (SASB). In L. S. Greenberg & W. M. Pinsof

(Eds.), *The psychotherapeutic process: A research handbook* (pp. 391–438). New York: Guilford Press.

Bruner, J. S. (1986). *Actual minds, possible worlds.* Cambridge, MA: Harvard University Press.

Bruner, J. (1990). *Acts of meaning.* Cambridge, MA: Harvard University Press.

Budman, S. H., Soldz, S., Demby, A., Davis, M., & Merry, J. (1993). What is cohesiveness? An empirical examination. *Small Group Research, 24,* 199–215.

Chambon, A. (1993a, June). *Dialogical strategies of therapeutic interventions: A comparative analysis of narrative focus and shifts in the Gloria tapes.* Paper presented at the meeting of the Society for Psychotherapy Research, Pittsburgh, PA.

Chambon, A. (1993b). Stratégies narratives du récit et de la parole: Comment progresse et s'échafaude une méthode d'analyse. *Sociologies et Sociétés, XXV,* 125–135.

Chambon, A. (1994). The dialogical analysis of case materials. In E. Sherman & W. Reid (Eds.), *Qualitative research in social work* (pp. 205–215). New York: Columbia University Press.

Chambon, A. (1995, June). *Tracking client and therapist interpersonal process of verbal moralization in group psychotherapy.* Paper presented at the meeting of the Society for Psychotherapy Research, Vancouver, British Columbia, Canada.

Chambon, A., & Simeoni, D. (1998). Modality in the therapeutic discourse. In A. Sanchez-Macarro & R. Carter (Eds.), *Linguistic choice across genres: Variations in spoken and written English* (pp. 239–264). Amsterdam: John Benjamins.

Culioli, A. (1990). *Pour une linguistique de l'énonciation.* Paris: Ophrys.

Edwards, D., & Potter, J. (1992). *Discursive psychology.* London: Sage.

Eggins, S. (1995). *An introduction to functional linguistics.* London: Pinter.

Essig, T. S., & Russel, R. L. (1990). Analyzing subjectivity in therapeutic discourse: Rogers, Perls, Ellis, and Gloria revisited. *Psychotherapy, 27,* 271–281.

Fuhriman, A., & Barlow, S. H. (1994). Interaction analysis: Instrumentation and issues. In A. Fuhriman & G. M. Burlingame (Eds.), *Handbook of group psychotherapy: An empirical and clinical synthesis* (pp. 191–222). New York: Wiley.

Genette, G. (1983). *Nouveau discours du récit.* Paris: Seuil.

Halliday, M. A. K. (1985). *An introduction to functional grammar.* London: Edward Arnold.

Howard, K. I., Krause, M. S., & Orlinksy, D. E. (1986). The attrition dilemma: Toward a new strategy for psychotherapy research. *Journal of Consulting and Clinical Psychology, 54,* 106–110.

Hubner, M. K. (1984). Pain and potential space: Toward a clinical theory of meaning. *Bulletin of the Menninger Clinic, 48,* 443–454.

Klein, M. H., Mathieu, P. L., Gendlin, E. T., & Kiesler, D. J. (1969). *The Experiencing Scale: A research and training manual* (Vols. 1 and 2). Madison: Wisconsin Psychiatric Institute.

Klein, M. H., Mathieu-Coughlan, P., & Kiesler, D. J. (1986). The Experiencing

Scales. In L. S. Greenberg & W. M. Pinsof (Eds.), *The psychotherapeutic process: A research handbook* (pp. 21–71). New York: Guilford Press.

Labov, W., & Fanshel, D. (1977). *Therapeutic discourse: Psychotherapy as conversation*. New York: Academic Press.

Laffal, J. (1987). Concept analysis of language in psychotherapy. In R. L. Russell (Ed.), *Language in psychotherapy: Strategies of discovery* (pp. 71–106). New York: Plenum.

Langacker, R. (1987–1991). *Foundations of cognitive grammar* (Vols. 1 and 2). Stanford, CA: Stanford University Press.

Luborsky, L., Barber, J. P., & Diguer, L. (1992). The meanings of narratives told during psychotherapy: The fruits of a new observational unit. *Psychotherapy Research, 2,* 277–290.

Marziali, E. (1995). *The psychological space coding system*. Toronto: Unpublished manuscript.

Marziali, E., & Munroe-Blum, H. (1994). *Interpersonal group psychotherapy for borderline personality disorder*. New York: Basic Books.

Marziali, E., & Munroe-Blum, H. (1996, November). *Psychological Space Coding System (PSCS): Development and preliminary testing*. Paper presented at the annual meeting of American Group Psychotherapy Association, San Francisco.

Munroe-Blum, H. (1995, June). The application of innovative process coding methods to therapeutic processes within individual, group, and couples psychotherapy. Symposium conducted at the Society for Psychotherapy Research Conference, Vancouver, British Columbia, Canada.

Nishisato, S. (1994). *Elements of dual scaling: An introduction to practical data analysis*. Hillsdale, NJ: Erlbaum.

Patton, M. J., & Meara, N. M. (1987). The analysis of natural language in psychological treatment. In R. L. Russell (Ed.), *Language in psychotherapy: Strategies of discovery* (pp. 273–301). New York: Plenum.

Potter, J., & Wetherell, M. (1987). *Discourse and social psychology*. London: Sage.

Prince, G. (1987). *A dictionary of narratology*. Lincoln: University of Nebraska Press.

Prince, G. (1991). Narratology, narrative, and meaning. *Poetics Today, 12,* 544–552.

Rennie, D. L., & Toukmanian, S. G. (1992). Explanation in psychotherapy process research. In S. G. Toukmanian & D. L. Rennie (Eds.), *Psychotherapy process research: Paradigmatic and narrative approaches* (pp. 234–251). Newbury Park, CA: Sage.

Rimmon-Kenan, S. (1983). *Narrative fiction: Contemporary poetics*. London: Routledge.

Russel, R. L. (1987). Therapeutic discourse: Future directions and the critical pluralist attitude. In R. L. Russel (Ed.), *Language in psychotherapy: Strategies of discovery* (pp. 341–351). New York: Plenum.

Russel, R. L., & van den Broek, P. (1992). Changing narrative schemas in psychotherapy. *Psychotherapy, 29,* 344–354.

Schafer, R. (1992). *Retelling a life: Narration and dialogue in psychoanalysis.* New York: Basic Books.

Schiffrin, D. (1994). *Approaches to discourse.* Oxford, England: Blackwell.

Sherman, E., & Skinner, K. W. (1988). Client-language and clinical process: A cognitive–semantic analysis. *Clinical Social Work Journal, 16*(4), 391–405.

Shostrom, E. L. (Producer) (1966). *Three approaches to psychotherapy* [Film]. Santa Ana, CA: Psychological Films.

Sluzki, C. E. (1992). Transformations: A blueprint for narrative changes in therapy. *Family Process, 31,* 217–230.

Socor, B. (1989). Listening for historical truth: A relative discussion. *Clinical Social Work Journal, 17,* 103–115.

Talmy, L. (1988). The relation of grammar to cognition. In B. Rudzka-Ostyn (Ed.), *Topics in cognitive linguistics* (pp. 165–205). Amsterdam: John Benjamins.

Tracey, T. J. (1986). Interactional correlates of premature termination. *Journal of Consulting and Clinical Psychology, 54,* 784–788.

Tsang, A. K. T. (1995a). *Negotiation of Therapy Agenda: Development of a process coding system.* Unpublished doctoral dissertation, University of Toronto, Toronto, Ontario, Canada.

Tsang, A. K. T. (1995b, June). *Negotiation of the therapy agenda in individual and group psychotherapy.* Paper presented at the annual international meeting of the Society for Psychotherapy Research, Vancouver, British Columbia, Canada.

van Dijk, T. (1985). Introduction: Levels and dimensions of discourse analysis. In T. van Dijk (Ed.), *Handbook of discourse analysis* (Vol. 2, pp. 1–11). London: Academic Press.

White, M., & Epston, D. (1990). *Narrative means to therapeutic ends.* New York: Norton.

Wierzbicki, M., & Pekarik, G. (1993). A meta-analysis of psychotherapy dropout. *Professional Psychology: Research and Practice, 24,* 190–195.

Winnicott, D. W. (1958). Transitional objects and transitional phenomena. *International Journal of Psychoanalysis, 34,* 89–97.

13

THE SYSTEM FOR ANALYZING VERBAL INTERACTION

ANITA SIMON AND YVONNE AGAZARIAN

HISTORY AND THEORY OF THE SYSTEM

SAVI (pronounced "savvy") is the acronym for the System for Analyzing Verbal Interaction whose development started in 1964. It is an observation system that defines and codes nine classes of verbal behavior by the theoretical criteria of approaching or avoiding the problems inherent in communicating and by the focus of the communication: person or topic. The nine classes are as follows: Fight, Flight, Compete, Personal Information, Factual Information, Influence, Empathize, Data Processing, and Integrate.

SAVI was designed to (a) focus on communication as a system output rather than as a characteristic of an individual; (b) define a group in terms of the potential communication resources of the group as a whole and its subgroups as well as in terms of a collection of discrete individuals; and (c) monitor the probability that content, contained in verbal behaviors used to transfer that content, is actually transferred from speaker to listener.

A core SAVI postulate is that certain verbal behaviors and sequences of behaviors being used to communicate information are themselves likely

357

to increase or decrease the problems inherent in the process of communication. This assumption is based on the work of three sets of theorists: Shannon and Weaver, Lewin, and Howard and Scott. Shannon and Weaver (1964) studied the process of information transfer and postulated that there is an inverse relationship between noise in the communication and the probability that information will be transferred. Lewin (1951), in his field theory, postulated that to the extent that restraining forces are reduced, the driving forces (inherently related to the goal) will be increased. Howard and Scott (1965), in their theory of stress, postulated that all human behavior can be explained as either approaching or avoiding the problems impeding the achievement of the goal.

A second postulate of the SAVI theory is that coding SAVI categories into a frequency grid results in consistent and recognizable patterns of communication that can be used to predict the probability that change will or will not occur for the system generating them. This allows one to test the hypothesis that, by reducing the restraining force of noise in the communications between, among, and within human systems, the strength of the vector toward the inherent goals of survival, development, and transformation will be increased and desired change will occur. This hypothesis is based on the following assumption: (a) Group-as-a-whole dynamics are a function of subgroup interactions; (b) subgroup interactions are a function of group member interactions; (c) the primary developmental task of a group is to develop a problem-solving communication pattern; and (d) until that is done, the potential for information transfer and resolution of problems is so low that, no matter what the content is, the group will remain fixated in the predominant communication modes of fight, flight, and unproductive pairing (Bion, 1959) or "as if" work (Agazarian, 1997). SAVI originated as a method for testing Agazarian's definition that the degree of "groupness" existing at any one time is a function of the interdependence of its parts (where "parts" is defined in terms of communication resources).

The SAVI codes of the dialogue of any group can be used to analyze the communication patterns of the group as a whole, subgroup, or of any set of individuals in the group, including or excluding the group leader. Furthermore, changes in communication patterns can be charted at any system level within, between, and among the systems of members, subgroups, or group as a whole. The advantage of developing a system of analysis that observes process at the group-as-a-whole, subgroup, and individual member levels is that it can be applied to groups that are based on different theories. The theory underlying this isomorphic potential in the analysis of SAVI data is general systems theory, which defines a hierarchy of isomorphic systems that are similar in structure and function (von Bertalanffy, 1969), and Agazarian's (1997) theory of living human systems, which defines the hierarchy of isomorphic systems as the systems of member, subgroup, and group as a whole that are energy organizing, self-correcting, and goal directed.

The coding methodology of SAVI has its roots in classroom observation systems, "anthologized" in 17 volumes by Simon and Boyer in 1971, especially the methodologies developed by Flanders (1965) and Bales (1950). From Flanders's observation system, SAVI adopted the units of coding and methods of data analysis described more fully in the body of this chapter. From the Bales system, SAVI adopted the core concept of collecting and analyzing the same data from group leaders as from group members, allowing for the determination of group leaders', not just members', input into generating the communication climate of a group.

SAVI's *acts of verbal behavior* are similar to the terms introduced in more recent work in the field. For example, Greenberg (1986) used the term *speech acts* instead of *verbal behavioral acts*, and Hill (1986) used *verbal response mode* to describe communication styles or patterns. Russel and Stiles (1979) developed a scale assessing the required degree of inference by coders, which they applied to observation systems. SAVI falls closer to the inference-free end of this scale; although SAVI coding does require inference from voice tone and grammar, it does not rely on inferential judgments of psychological processes or inferences about speaker motivation or intention.

CORRESPONDENCE BETWEEN THE THEORY AND THE SYSTEM

Challenges in Constructing Operational Definitions

In their information theory, Shannon and Weaver (1964) postulated an inverse relationship between noise in the communication channel and the probability that the information in the communication will be transferred. Shannon and Weaver (1964) defined *noise* as "things added to the signal which were not intended by the information source" (p. 7). In SAVI, *noisy behaviors* are those that introduce ambiguity or contradiction into the communication. These behaviors decrease the probability that the information will be transferred across a boundary, such as from sender to receiver.

SAVI codings of *approach behaviors* are the reciprocal of avoidance; they require a demonstration that information has crossed a boundary. Shannon and Weaver (1964) pointed out that "If Mr. X is suspected not to understand what Mr. Y says, then it is theoretically not possible, by having Mr. Y do nothing but talk further with Mr. X, to completely clarify this situation in any finite time" (p. 5). SAVI builds on this by defining approach behaviors as requiring a demonstration that information has transferred across an interpersonal (or intrapersonal) boundary. For example, the Square 8 approach behavior, Paraphrase, must reflect a statement made by another person; likewise, the Square 9 behaviors Building On, Valuing, or Agreeing with someone else's idea can happen only if the other person's idea was received and processed.

SAVI was created to generate categories of behavior that met the criteria of reducing or increasing the potential for transferring information. In identifying *avoidance behaviors*, we search the literature and identified authors studying defensive and nondefensive communication, such as Gibb (1961) and Ruesch and Bateson (1951), and our own criteria of the ambiguity, contradictions, or both between affect and content (Agazarian, 1969). We also used Gibb's discriminations between description and opinion. The criterion for approach behaviors was a demonstrated congruence between the affective and content components in the verbal behavior or evidence that an information transfer has taken place, such as someone answering a question asked by another person.

From these criteria, the operational definitions for the nine classes of behavior were derived. Categories were identified that operationalized the definition for each class. Each category defined a specific, discrete act of verbal behavior that was rated, not by its content but by its definition (see Figure 13.1). Some degree of inference (i.e., extrapolation from the grammar of the content and from voice tone) was required.

Indexes of Group Process, Development, or Change

The SAVI grid can be used to discriminate between different patterns of communications that are generated by differences in group process. Bion's (1959) basic assumptions of flight/fight, pairing, and work is an example. In Ahlin, Sandahl, Herlitz, and Brimberg's study (1996), use of the SAVI revealed similarities and differences between short-term group-analytic groups and behavioral therapy groups. The SAVI grid can also be used to depict the phases of group development, such as those defined by Bennis and Shepard (1956), Beck (1974, 1981a, 1981b), Agazarian and Peters (1981), and Agazarian (1994, 1997, 1999). Furthermore, the SAVI grid can be used to assess the changes in the probability of the transfer of information as the communication patterns change. As such, SAVI can be used as a diagnostic of the potential for therapeutic change, as a measure of therapeutic change, and as a map to increase the probability for therapeutic change.

Further Developments

Plans for the further development of the system include continuing the organized use of the system as a training tool to provide diagnostic and feedback information for clinicians (Simon, 1993) in marital, family, in-

	Person	**Data**	**Orientation**
A v o i d a n c e	**1** **Fight** Verbal acts that "put down" or abuse either oneself or others. The "put down" can be either through content or voice tone. Statements in which there are contradictions between or within components of the message—when the words do not match the music. • Attack 1-a • Self-Defense 1-sd • Complaint 1-c • Sarcasm 1-s	**2** **Flight** Statements spoken in factual language that are ambiguous in topic, content, or source. The speaker presents his or her mental map of the world "as if" it is the truth. This position contains gossip, jokes, anecdotes, and other "fictional facts," ruminations, vagueness, mind-reading and jargon—the verbal shorthand that cannot be understood unless one is "in the know." • Mind-Reading 2-mr • Gossip 2-g • Joking Around 2-ja • Jargon 2-j • Partial Phrases 2-p	**3** **Compete** Verbal behavior that orients information toward the speaker's own opinion "as if" it is unquestionably correct with implicit contradiction of all other opinions. These are competitive, "hidden-agenda," or "hidden fight" behaviors. • Yes-But 3-yb • Leading Question 3-lq • Oughtitudes 3-o • Interrupts 3-i • Contradicts 3-c

C o n t i n g e n t	**4** **Personal Information**
	Verbal behaviors that descriptively convey personal information accessed through the senses or through spontaneous knowledge of likes or dislikes based on feeling that can be verified only by the self, as well as opinions, rationalizations about the self, or explanations or interpretations of one's own behaviors in the present or past.
	
	• Information About Me: 4-in
	  Now
	• Information About Me: 4-p
	  Past
	• Opinions about me 4-o
		5 **Factual Information**
		Verbal behaviors that descriptively convey or solicit facts about the world or the self that can be verified by direct or private observation, by experimentation, or by reference to public data.
		
		• Facts and Figure 5-f
		• General Information 5-gi
		• Reports There and 5-r
		  Then
		• Narrow Question 5-ng
		• Broad Questions 5-bq
			6 **Influence**
			Verbal acts that convey the speaker's opinions and orientation to the world, people, events, ideas, and decisions.
			
			• Opinion 6-o
			• Proposal 6-p
			• Command 6-c
			• Impersonal 6-+
			  Reinforcement

A p p r o a c h	**7** **Empathize**
	Verbal acts that convey messages that are emotionally meaningful and close to the heart of the speaker or the listener.
	
	• Feeling Question 7-fq
	• Feeling Answer 7-a
	• Feeling Information 7-fi
	• Mirrors Other's Feeling 7-m
	  (empathy)
	• Nonhostile 7-sa
	  (self-assertion)
	• Affectionate Joke 7-aj
		8 **Data Processing**
		Verbal behaviors that demonstrate that information has been transferred from one speaker to another, either by congruently answering a preceding question or by accurately reflecting another's ideas.
		
		• Answer to a Question 8-a
		• Clarify Own Answer 8-c
		• Summarize 8-s
		• Paraphrase 8-p
		• Corrective Feedback 8-cf
			9 **Integrate**
			Cooperative acts that integrate and build on a communication between two or more people. Ideas are built on, supported, and expanded without competing, coopting, or preempting.
			
			• Agreements/Positive 9-+
			• Building on Others'
			  Ideas 9-b
			• Work Joke 9-wj

Figure 13.1. The System for Analyzing Verbal Interaction grid.

dividual, or group psychotherapy as well as for leaders in other disciplines, including teachers, managers, and trainers. Current research plans include supporting researchers conducting validity studies, using SAVI in research and doctoral dissertations, and using SAVI to further develop and research the application of systems-centered therapy to short-term therapy (Agazarian, 1996). Regarding the measure itself, a reorganization of the defined categories of verbal behavior into a grid to define the past–present–future dimension is planned (Lewin, 1951). This is the model that defines psychological time boundaries in a theory of living human systems.

DESCRIPTION OF THE SYSTEM

Rating

SAVI uses the coding methodology of Flanders's (1965) System of Verbal Interaction, in which an observer identifies and records ("codes") a category every 3 seconds or every change in category or speaker. Only verbal communication is coded. Visual cues are not used, although "nonverbal" cues, such as tone of voice, are so important for some categories that data are best collected with an audio component.

Like Bales's (1950) methodology, SAVI uses the same categories for coding the behaviors of members and leaders of the group being observed. Also like the Bales system, SAVI can generate a matrix of who spoke to whom by linking the identity of the speaker to each behavior code. These data can then be used to generate the communication patterns of each individual, which in turn can be compared with the pattern of the group as a whole. This analysis can also generate the patterns that are related to identifiable group roles by examining the patterns that are generated by the individuals who have taken roles such as leader, scapegoat, or identified patient. These role patterns can also be matched to the particular "group communication environment" in which they are generated. Therefore, although SAVI data are collected identically from every member of a group (including the leaders), the data can be analyzed to make comparisons between various subgroups (i.e., leader and members, scapegoat, and group) or between various specified individual members and subgroups or the group as a whole.

Categories and Classes

SAVI defines the structure of communication as a series of verbal behavioral acts that fall into nine discrete classes of behavior. The SAVI grid, as illustrated in Figure 13.1, consists of three rows and three columns, forming a grid of nine squares. Each of the nine squares represents a class of behavior. Each of these nine classes is operationalized by a discrete set of categories listed within the square.

As the verbal behaviors in a communication are coded, their frequencies are recorded in squares and a pattern of heavy, medium, or light use of various squares emerges. This pattern provides an instant snapshot of the communication. The categories are defined, with examples, in the coding manual (Simon & Agazarian, 1994). Their large number precludes their presentation in this chapter.

Both the classes (squares) and the categories and subcategories of behavior that define each class are determined by two sets of criteria. The first set of criteria sorts the behaviors into those that contain predominantly personal, factual, or orienting information and define the columns in the SAVI grid. The second set of criteria defines the rows by the probability that the information conveyed by the verbal behaviors in that row will be transferred in the communication act.

As displayed in the SAVI grid in Figure 13.1, the Person column defines categories of verbal behavior that approach or avoid communicating personal facts and feelings. The Data column defines categories of verbal behavior that approach or avoid communicating objective factual information. The Orienting column defines categories of verbal behavior that serve as either restraining or driving forces to the direction of the communication.

The rows of the SAVI grid indicate the potential inherent in the verbal act for transferring the information it contains. Behaviors in the avoidance row are relatively high in "noise" (i.e., the ambiguity or contradiction or both between the personal and factual component of information in the communication act). In contrast, behaviors in the Approach row contain evidence of a transfer of information across an intrapersonal or interpersonal boundary. The Contingent row behaviors contain unsolicited, neutrally toned, personal, factual, or orienting information. Whether information entered through the Contingent row in the SAVI grid is used for problem solving depends on (is contingent on) the overall communication pattern.

An illustration of how a short segment of dialogue is coded in the SAVI system is provided below. The first column identifies the speaker, the middle column depicts what was said, and the third column codes the initial of the speaker and the SAVI category of verbal behavior (see Figure 13.1). The SAVI code column provides the raw data used to generate a SAVI grid.

Speaker	Statement	SAVI code
George:	You're always complaining! (George, Square, 1, attack)	G 1-a

Speaker	Statement	SAVI code
Pauline:	I'm sorry. I know I complain a lot. And I try so hard! But I seem to keep doing it over and over.	P 1-sd
George:	(Angrily) You're doing it right now—you drive everyone around you crazy.	G 1-a
Margaret:	George—you talk like you think there's never anything wrong with you at all. You're very unfair to Pauline.	M 1-a
George:	I didn't mean to say that there's nothing wrong with me.	G-1-sd
	It's just that she's such a martyr, she makes me go wild!	G 1-a
Therapist:	It sounds to me like there are two sub-groups here—a group that is attacking themselves and a group attacking some-one else.	T 6-o
	What do you think about this?	T 5-bq

A SAVI coder's judgments are confined to what SAVI behaviors are being used, such as questions, opinion, or "yes-buts." Coders do not code by content, but tone of voice is taken into account. For example, the coder needs to be able to discriminate between hostile and affectionate tone of voice, neutral and blameful-complaining tone of voice, and the relative balance between the factual and personal components in the message as specified in the coding manual. The data coming from tone of voice are lost when only a written transcript is used.

In the process of coding, the verbal behavioral act that precedes the act to be coded helps to determine the code. For example, an answer can be coded only when it follows a question. Behaviors are not coded by inferences about either the speaker's motivation, announced intention, or the effect of the words on the listener, nor are global inferences made about roles, such as client or therapist, gatekeeper, task leader, emotional leader, defiant leader, or scapegoat. In the SAVI, roles are defined in terms of clusters of behaviors and identified by the patterns that are generated by the codes recorded in a SAVI grid.

Limitations and Strengths

SAVI deals only with verbal behaviors (including tone of voice and inflection), does not code nonverbal behaviors or activities, and does not code the content of the communication or its context. Other limitations are those inherent in all micro-observation systems: the length of time that it takes to train coders to an acceptable standard of reliability and, even with the aid of computers, the relatively cumbersome process of data analysis.

However, SAVI does fill the need for a tool that focuses on the process of communication. The SAVI also serves as a measure of group process, when *process* is defined as a sequence of behaviors that affect the potential for further information transfer. In addition, SAVI makes it possible to define groups in terms of the groups' potential communication resources. For example, rather than defining a group as a discrete collection of individuals whose sum of communications define it, SAVI enables the group to be defined and analyzed as a system. Using SAVI, data can be collected and organized isomorphically at many system levels: individual, subgroup, and group as a whole. Finally, SAVI allows the input and output transactions within and between the system hierarchy to be analyzed.

Reliability

Two types of coding reliability are reported in SAVI research: intracoder and intercoder. The most common measure of reliability used is the percentage of coder agreement. The SAVI has been used in dissertation studies by Agazarian (1969), Browne (1977), Cox (1976), Harvey (1976), Holst (1990), MacKinnon (1984), Smith (1970), Sturdevant (1991), Weir (1978), and Zimmerman (1970). The range for intracoder reliability is 80%–95%, and the range for intercoder reliability is 80%–91%. Smith (1970) used Scott's (1955) pi coefficient for her four raters (the range of coefficients was 60%–81%), and Zimmerman (1970) used Scott's pi coefficient with intracoder reliability of .87 and intercoder reliability of .85. MacKinnon also used an unusual additional test for reliability by comparing the codings of raters in different cities who had not trained together. This reliability figure was 79%. These figures ranged from acceptable to high levels of reliability for this type of scale.

Validity

The research base for SAVI validity is relatively undeveloped. We know of no large-scale, well-controlled studies of the validity of the constructs of the SAVI theory as operationalized in the SAVI grid. However, SAVI has been used in pilot studies that contribute to the development of the validity of SAVI. One test used to determine face validity asks people untrained in SAVI to think of the "worst" and "best" communicators they know. In informal research as part of our teaching, when given a set of SAVI categories, people untrained in SAVI consistently linked avoidance behaviors (i.e., attacks, self-defense, sarcasm, complaints, mind-reading, jargon, yes-butting, discounting, asking leading questions, interrupting) to the "worst communicator they know." Approach behaviors (e.g., paraphrasing, summarizing, answering questions directly, building on others' ideas, sharing feelings, asking others about their feelings, mirroring others' feelings) were linked to their "best." In a pilot study contributing data about SAVI's construct validity, Sturdevant (1991) found a relationship between the Experiencing Scale (Klein, Mathieu, Gendlin, & Kiesler, 1969), which she used to measure intrapersonal process as indicated by awareness of a bodily-felt referent and SAVI. She reported that " . . . rating on the EXP [Experiencing] Scale and SAVI tended to rise or fall together. In other words, changes in intrapersonal experiencing and interpersonal verbal behavior occurred almost simultaneously, and in the same direction (Sturdevant, 1991, p. 25). Further contributing to the development of SAVI's construct validity, Weir (1978) found that hospital "staff's perception of patient co-operation was significantly related to the patient's verbal behavior. . . . Avoidance was inversely correlated with co-operation" (p. 61).

Ahlin et al. (1996) found that SAVI and another observation system, the Matrix Representational Grid (MRG), resulted in the same overall judgments of the groups assessed, which was reported in the study as convergent validity. In their study, which analyzed short-term behavioral therapy and group-analytic group treatments of alcohol-dependent clients, SAVI and MRG showed that both types of groups frequently used contingent behaviors. SAVI showed that the short-term group-analytic groups (which showed significantly more alcohol-free days by clients even after 19 months) used significantly more Square 7 Approach-to-Person behavior than did the short-term behavioral therapy groups.

Norms

Data from the SAVI pilot projects, dissertations, and the group used throughout this book suggest that cross-purpose talk is the predominant pattern among professionals, paraprofessionals, and people in general who are untrained in communicating in a way that transfers information needed to solve problems (Agazarian, 1969; Ahlin et al., 1996; Browne, 1977; Cox, 1976; MacKinnon, 1980). The predominant behaviors of the cross-purpose talk pattern are unsolicited contingent behaviors (opinions, facts, questions), often punctuated by Square 3 behaviors of yes but, leading questions, and interruptions. As MacKinnon (1980) concluded from her findings, it seems that "conversations perhaps proceed as monologues disguised as dialogues" (p. 95).

Learning the Rating Method

It takes 30–40 hours of training to learn to code in SAVI. Typically, the primary researcher and coder-trainees practice together listening to a tape and marking codes on a transcript. Disputes are settled by turning to the SAVI definitions in the coding manual. Practice is continued until an acceptable level of reliability is reached. Usually, researchers practice coding on tapes of the actual (or similar) groups that will be the subject of research, but the practice is done on sections that will not be used to generate research data. To date, we know of no standardized "practice tapes" that have been developed.

METHODOLOGY FOR ANALYSIS

Classes and categories of verbal behavior are both summarizing units for SAVI analysis. Once data are generated, they are summed into frequency counts, either by category or by class. These data can then be arranged in the SAVI grid, which provides a visual representation of the pattern of communication generated by the group being observed. For example, defensive communication is manifested in a heavy buildup of frequencies of behaviors in the Avoidance row.

When the *identity* or *role* of the speaker is important, separate grids can be built containing the frequencies of codings of the behaviors of specific individuals or subgroups. This grid can be compared with other grids containing the frequencies of codings of other subgroups or the group as a whole.

When the communication *climate* of the group is of interest, row frequencies can be computed and ratios designed to establish the balance of approach and avoidance behaviors. These are discussed in detail later in this chapter.

When the *sequence* of communication behaviors is important, the data can be arranged in a format that resembles a musical score, with Categories 1–9 listed vertically and each behavior (linked to a speaker ID code) listed horizontally. Reading across the page, one can track a discussion behavior by behavior. This method illustrates how a dialogue unfolds over time. It tracks how a conversation remains within one dimension or flows in and out of the approach, contingent, and avoidance dimensions.

SAVI data can also be summarized into a matrix of "sequence pairs." The coding unit of a sequential matrix consists of a pair of verbal behaviors rather than a single category. The first of each pair serves as the stimulus and the second as the response. SAVI data were originally presented using this highly labor-intensive method of coding, and a detailed description of the methodology has been provided by Simon and Agazarian (1967). With computers, the power of displaying data as a "sequential matrix" becomes more available to researchers.

When SAVI is used in a research setting, the frequencies of behaviors or classes, or proportions (percentages), are the primary ways of quantifying these data. When comparing data from different segments of dialogue, researchers have often been required to convert frequencies to percentages or proportions to control for unequal numbers of codings generated from each segment.

Basic statistical methods for testing the differences between the frequencies of proportions applied to SAVI data are the z ratio and the analysis of variance to test for the presence of differences (MacKinnon, 1984; Smith, 1970; Weir, 1978; Zimmerman, 1970). In the next section, we summarize some of these analyses.

PREVIOUS RESEARCH WITH THE SYSTEM

SAVI has been used in dissertation studies in medical, educational, organizational, counseling, and self-help group settings, among others. The findings from these pilot studies tend to validate the use of SAVI as describing important aspects of interpersonal communication. SAVI has also been used in a comparative study of group-analytic groups and behavioral therapy groups (Ahlin et al., 1996).

Zimmerman (1970) used an analysis of variance method to test whether there would be differences in certain frequency counts and SAVI grid areas among teachers in two groups who scored high and low on other variables. Zimmerman found a relationship between SAVI behaviors and self-actualizing scores as measured on the Personal Orientation Inventory (Shostrum, 1964).

Weir (1978) found that medical staff's perceptions of patient cooperation with treatment "was significantly related to the patient's verbal behavior" (p. 61). Weir computed an index called the "quality of verbal interaction" (QVI). In this formula, total behaviors equal the sum of all avoidance, contingent, and approach behaviors used in the segment being observed.

$$QVI = \frac{\text{approach behavior} - \text{avoidance behavior}}{\text{total behaviors}}$$

Weir (1978) noted that "this formula yields a score which ranges from $+1$ to -1, with the positive scores reflective of problem solving (approach) of the task of communicating; negative scores reflective of avoidance of the task and zero scores reflective of no obvious direction in the communication task" (p. 39). Weir used Pearson product–moment correlations to estimate the relationship between a patient's QVI index and measures such as patient total satisfaction with hospitalization and their perception of health (p. 233).

MacKinnon (1980), in studying professionals' and paraprofessionals' interactions with the parents of children with disabilities, found that neither professionals nor paraprofessionals use a greater proportion of approach behaviors than the parents. She reported that "cross-purpose pattern of communication predominated over problem solving . . . for all groups." She summarized that "in cross purpose talk, information is given but not utilized" (p. 94), and goes on to say that "89% of the paraprofessionals' exchanges with parents involved their giving opinions and asking questions" (p. 98). MacKinnon used a z test to compare the proportion of avoidance behaviors used by professionals (psychologists, physical therapists, etc.) with that of parents of children with chronic disabilities to determine whether verbal behaviors were connected with the role of the participants in the study. She also used Pearson product–moment correlations to correlate variables such as age and experience with the percentage of approach behavior used by physicians, other helping professionals, and parents of children with disabilities being treated by these professionals (MacKinnon, 1980, p. 74). She reported that the implications of the cross-purpose talk pattern included a lowered potential for cooperation with treatment plans, in this case the clients (parents) not asking questions and the staff not finding out what was bothering their clients. Using SAVI, she was able to behaviorally specify steps for improving professionals' communications with clients. Cox's (1976) and Browne's (1977) research using SAVI showed similar findings on a cross-purpose talk pattern.

Sturdevant's (1991) study, as discussed in the section on validity, showed that at both the individual and group levels there was a relationship between intrapersonal processing, as measured by the Experiencing Scale, and interpersonal behavior, as measured by SAVI.

Ahlin et al.'s (1996) study used SAVI and the MRG to observe group psychotherapy methods for alcohol-dependent patients in Sweden. Ahlin et al. found that both the short-term behavioral therapy and group-analytic approaches had similarly frequent uses of contingent behaviors. The number of alcohol-free days was found to be significantly better after 19 months for the group-analytic group than for the behavioral therapy group. Six percent of the group-analytic group's behaviors were in the Approach Square 7, compared with about one half of 1% of the behavioral therapy group's. This was a major SAVI finding.

In an informal study, Agazarian and Peters (1981) examined the behaviors that made up different roles, using "role" as the bridge construct between group and individual dynamics. The first clusters analyzed were those that characterized the autocratic, democratic, and laissez-faire leadership behaviors described in the three styles of leadership in Lewin, Lippit, and White's (1939) research. The authors coded several role plays of the three styles with different sets of students and obtained consistent and different student communication patterns under the conditions of the three different leadership styles. This enabled the concept of "role" to be operationalized by defining it as a cluster of SAVI verbal behaviors. This approach was repeated with Blake and Mouton's (1965) "managerial grid," resulting in different patterns from people role playing four different roles: high task/low person, high person/low task, low task/low person, and high task/high person.

The main areas of the authors' interests include clinical observations of the relationships between SAVI verbal behaviors and both phases of group development and defense modification in Systems Centered (Agazarian, 1997) therapy and training groups. The authors have a strong interest in comparing the effectiveness of group therapists trained and untrained in SAVI, as well as the impact of SAVI training to clients themselves as part of their treatment. Another area of research interest is exploring the physiological consequences of experiencing and generating chronic avoidance versus approach behaviors in individual, group, marital, and family therapeutic, education, and work settings.

APPLICATION OF THE SYSTEM OF ANALYSIS TO GROUP A, SESSION 3

To illustrate SAVI data analysis, we have used SAVI to analyze segments of the taped psychotherapy group, called Group A, which has been the common database throughout this book. This SAVI analysis is being presented in an illustrative manner. Only parts of the segments chosen by the editors have been rated. The SAVI analysis was conducted from a group-as-a-whole perspective.

We and two trained SAVI coders coded the verbal behaviors from selected segments of Group A, Session 3: parts of Unit 69 (2 of 7 pages of transcript); Units 72 and 73; and Units 82 and 83. The editors characterized Unit 69 as being part of a scapegoating pattern in Phase II and Units 72–73 as part of a phase shift and Units 82–83 as part of Phase III. The SAVI analysis reveals information about how a group approached and avoided transferring information through its use of defensive or nondefensive behaviors.

A data-to-opinion ratio (D-O) was computed for each of the sample segments rated (see Table 13.1). The D-O ratio compares the here-and-now, reality-based data in a group's interaction with the group's speculations and opinions about current and past events inside and outside the group. The ratio is computed by subtracting the sum of the Opinion plus There-and-Then SAVI categories from the sum of the Data plus Here-and-Now SAVI categories. The result is divided by the sum of both sets of categories, generating a number ranging from +1 to −1, with 0 representing a balance. The Data plus Here-and-Now categories consist of Square 5 behaviors (i.e., Facts, General Information, and Questions),

TABLE 13.1
Data-To-Opinion Ratio and Weir's (1978) Quality of Verbal Interaction
(QVI) Ratio of Selected Segments in Group A

	Prephase Shift		Phase Shift		Postphase Shift	
Ratio	Unit 69A	Unit 69B	Unit 72	Unit 73	Unit 82	Unit 83
D-O	−.64	−.69	−.74	−1.00	−.65	−.69
QVI	−.18	−.11	−.18	−.14	−.17	−.02

Note. Range = 1 − 1 to + 1.

Square 4 behaviors (i.e., Information About Me-Now), and Square 8 behaviors (i.e., Answers to Questions, Clarifying Own Answers With Data, Corrective Feedback, Paraphrasing, and Summarizing). The Opinions plus There-and-Then categories consist of Square 6 behavior (i.e., Opinions), Square 5 behavior (i.e., Reports There-and-Then), and Square 4 behaviors (Opinions About Me and Information about Me-Past). A D-O ratio that is positive shows a preponderance of Data and talk about what is happening in the group here and now, contrasted with Opinions and discussions about the past or speculations about the future by group members. We consider a D-O ratio on the positive side of the range (i.e., one showing higher group use of Data and Here-and-Now behaviors) to be more optimal for transferring reality-based data necessary for problem solving. A sample rating of a group demonstration of group-as-a-whole leadership, with conference volunteer members conducted in New York, had D-O ratios of .07 and .1. Table 13.1 shows that the D-O ratios ranged from −1 to −.5 for the rated segments of Group A. A strong predominance of Opinions and There-and-Then behaviors was evident in Group A.

Weir's (1978) QVI ratio was also computed for the sample-rated segments (see Table 13.1). As discussed earlier, this ratio compares verbal behaviors that maximize and minimize the potential for information transfer. The QVI ratios for all rated segments in Group A, both pre- and postphase shift, showed more avoidance than approach behaviors (see Table 13.1) considered to reflect the lower information-transferring potential of Group A. The QVI ratios for the coded New York group show more approach than avoidance (.32 and .40) considered to reflect the groups' higher information-transferring potential.

The results of QVI ratios and D-O balance ratios generate research and clinical questions about the transfer of information in the analyzed communication. For example, for Group A, the question might be, What is the group not talking about in the here and now? Also, what interventions would be needed to change the group's opinions about personal and group reality into hypotheses that could be tested in group reality?

It was of particular interest to determine what similarities would appear between the SAVI categories of verbal behavior and the descriptions of the units selected. For example, would the "scapegoating" unit give us a pattern that resembled a SAVI fight pattern? Would Group A's postphase shift work pattern resemble a SAVI work pattern? In fact, the SAVI patterns from both the pre- and postphase shift units basically resembled SAVI "as if" work patterns: low in the approach categories that SAVI associates with work.

Our next step was to analyze the SAVI patterns that emerged for each of the units rated, beginning with Unit 69, the unit described by the editors as occurring before the phase shift, which was marked by a shift from critical or hostile responses to supportive responses toward the scapegoat leader.

"Talking about" dissatisfactions with another person uses a different set of communication behaviors than a direct attack on the person. The frequencies of behaviors used in each of the 9 squares in the two parts (A and B) of Unit 69 that were rated are displayed in Figure 13.2. We found that the group did not use either the direct (Square 1) or the indirect (Square 3) behaviors that are characteristic of SAVI scapegoating: There were no instances of SAVI Square 1 behaviors of Attack, Blame, or Sarcasm. It was of interest to determine how this group used Square 3 (Compete) behaviors to transfer their scapegoating content. For the 175 behaviors categorized in Unit 69, 21% (37 behaviors) fell in Square 3, but relatively few of these behaviors fell in the categories that corresponded to indirect scapegoating: discounts (0), yes-buts (3), contradictions (2), and leading questions (1). Thirty-one of the 37 Square 3 behaviors fell into a single category: interruptions.

On closer examination of Unit 69A, we discovered that interruptions were divided almost equally between the group interrupting the leader (8 times) and the leader interrupting the group (7 times). From this, we hypothesized that the interactions between the leader and member subgroups

	Person	Data	Orientation
Avoidance	1 Fight 0	2 Flight 3	3 Compete 21
Contingent	4 Personal Information 13	5 Fact Information 4	6 Influence 49
Approach	7 Empathize 1	8 Data Processing 4	9 Integrate 5

Figure 13.2. The System for Analyzing Verbal Interaction grid pattern: frequencies as the percentage of total ratings for Group A, Unit 69A and 69B, prephase shift.

maintain the group equilibrium at the implicit goal level (i.e., the goal implied by the way the group behaves) rather than at the explicit goal of work.

We next looked at the content discussed during these competitive interchanges. We found examples of the communication stalemate underlying apparent group compliance with the leader. For example:

Member: Now if you can't know me on these terms . . .

Leader: (interrupts) . . . I wanna get to know you . . .

Member: (finishes sentence) . . . then you can't know me! (laughter).

Returning to the content of Unit 69 (theoretically "listening for the voice of the group"), the group talked about not being able to reach Joe (the designated scapegoat):

There's something about what he said, that closed the door for me. If you can't come in at my door . . .
. . . as far as you and I are concerned we would function superficially . . .
. . . you can only know me with my door closed.

Theoretically, the group's voice indicated that the group's contending, superficial communication pattern kept the door closed to intimacy and sharing. This communication pattern defeated the leader's many attempts to interpret what was said.

Why did this happen? We hypothesized that the group as a whole (including both members and leaders) had little freedom of expression within this SAVI contending communication pattern of opinions, interruptions, and avoidance behaviors. The underlying frustation was verbally expressed by blaming "Joe" for keeping the door closed and behaviorally expressed in the contending communication pattern between the leaders and the group.

We now turn to the postphase shift patterns, derived from the content of Units 82 and 83. The SAVI grid for Unit 82 is represented in Figure 13.3. Unit 83 is represented in Figure 13.4. On inspection, it appears that there were aspects of the postphase shift patterns that made it unlikely that the information would be available in a form that was useful for work. For example, the Fact square (Square 5) was relatively unused. When facts were used, they tended to contain information about the past rather than the present. Personal information (Square 4) focused more than twice as much on giving opinions about the self than with giving factual information about the self. Also, in Square 6, the Influence square, the predominant category was Opinion. These patterns typify as-if work, in which opinions are unconnected to the facts needed to solve either interpersonal or work problems.

The next analysis was of the phase shift units (Unit 73). The SAVI

	Person	Data	Orientation
Avoidance	1 Fight 1	2 Flight 11	3 Compete 11
Contingent	4 Personal Information 35	5 Fact Information 7	6 Influence 30
Approach	7 Empathize 0	8 Data Processing 1	9 Integrate 5

Figure 13.3. The System for Analyzing Verbal Interaction grid pattern: frequencies as the percentage of total ratings for Group A, Unit 82, postphase shift.

pattern for Unit 73 was especially interesting and is presented in Figure 13.5. Segment 73 showed the first concentrated use of the Approach to Person data square (17% in Square 7). Thus, the SAVI grid of the phase shift did show a pattern different from the as-if work patterns of the pre- and postphase shift. Here the group introduced personal communication into the pattern.

We conducted a microexamination of Unit 73, allowing us to examine the conversation behavior by behavior (similar to following a musical score of the flow among Approach, Contingent, and Avoidance). Unit 73 was the least typical segment of those analyzed in that it showed a relatively high use of both Square 7 (Approach to Person) and Square 2 (Avoidance of Data) behaviors. This pattern appears to indicate both a potential for, and a flight from, the intimacy which the group had been seeking.

	Person	Data	Orientation
Avoidance	1 Fight 0	2 Flight 2	3 Compete 5
Contingent	4 Personal Information 51	5 Fact Information 0	6 Influence 37
Approach	7 Empathize 0	8 Data Processing 0	9 Integrate 5

Figure 13.4. The System for Analyzing Verbal Interaction grid pattern: frequencies as the percentage of total ratings for Group A, Unit 83, postphase shift.

	Person	Data	Orientation
Avoidance	1 Fight 0	2 Flight 24	3 Compete 7
Contingent	4 Personal Information 10	5 Fact Information 12	6 Influence 31
Approach	7 Empathize 17	8 Data Processing 0	9 Integrate 0

Figure 13.5. The System for Analyzing Verbal Interaction grid pattern: frequencies as the percentage of total ratings for Group A, Unit 73, phase shift.

Group A: Unit 73

Brad: I thought you wanted to keep the waters rough and rumpled up. (Opinion, 6)
Laughter

Martha: Aha! (Joking Around, 2).
General Laughter

Greg: She was ready for a fight. (Opinion, 6)
General Laughter

Joe: Yeah, she wanted. . . . (Partial Thought, 2)

Greg: I am, too, as a matter of fact. (Feeling Information, 7)
Laughter and unclear voices throughout

Martha: Do you have . . . are you feeling this way, too? (Feeling Question, 7)
(Alice laughs throughout)

Greg: Oh, I'm, . . . I've been ready for a fight all week, and that I'm—I sort of feel like I . . . a . . . clam . . . (Feeling Answer, 7) . . . in a shell, or maybe a hermit crab. (Joking Around, 2)
Laughter

Martha: All right! Who's gonna start it!? (Feeling Question, 7)

Greg: I just went back in. (Joking Around, 2)
Loud laughter

Greg: Why don't we pick on somebody to attack, somebody else. (Proposal, 6)

According to the editors, Unit 73 met their criteria for a part of the phase shift. The SAVI pattern for this segment demonstrated an increase in the potential for interpersonal work. The microanalysis showed that laughter and group interruptions did not divert the information flow as they did in the earlier patterns. For example, although feeling information was interrupted, it was immediately reinforced by a feeling question, which was then answered. In spite of this change, the feeling dimension was immediately followed by "joking around," and the empathic work potential was pulled up and away into flight. It gave the impression of a soft and vulnerable group that peeped out of its shell, saw an impending fight, took flight into laughter, and then went back into the shell.

RELATIONSHIP BETWEEN RESEARCH AND THEORY

There is a fundamental relationship between research and theory in the development and use of SAVI. SAVI was originally developed as an operational definition of Agazarian's early theoretical formulation: The degree of groupness existing at any one time is a function of the interdependence of its parts. "Parts" is defined in terms of communication resources, in which communication resources are defined in terms of Shannon and Weaver's (1964) relationship between noise in the communication channel and the probability of information transfer. As soon as it became clear that the discriminations could be made between a high and low probability of information transfer from SAVI grids, Agazarian used SAVI to explore the communication patterns of other common group variables, such as Bion's (1959) flight–fight basic assumption cultures and the Lewin et al. (1939) democratic and autocratic leadership styles.

We also analyzed the SAVI grids that represented coexisting individual, subgroup, and group-as-a-whole communications (Agazarian, 1985). Analyzing the patterns of these different levels, as well as the input and output communications between them, Agazarian operationalized the general systems theory construct of isomorphy (von Bertalanffy, 1969). This in turn led to the final formulation of a theory of living human systems (Agazarian, 1997).

We have used the SAVI as a guide to developing clinical descriptions of leadership behavior in groups. Clinical observations using SAVI matrix definitions has significantly influenced concept development of Agazarian's (1997) theory of the dynamics of the developmental phases in groups, the recognition of the clusters of verbal behaviors that characterize them, and the leadership communications that contribute to modifying defensive communication that would otherwise fixate the group in a phase.

We have also found the SAVI to be valuable for making discriminations within similar communication contexts, such as between the group-as-a-whole communication patterns to deviants that result in creating an identified patient as different from those that create a scapegoat role (Agazarian, 1992). Finally, it has been useful in discriminating between different types of group therapies and between different therapists' adherence to the behavioral protocol for their particular therapeutic orientation as specified by training manuals; see, for example, the Ahlin et al. (1996) work on therapists' behaviors and leadership philosophy of behavioral therapy groups compared with group-analytic groups for alcohol-dependent clients.

ASSESSMENT AND FUTURE DIRECTIONS

The unique value of the SAVI system is that it encourages one to think isomorphically about the different system levels in groups. It enables the input and output communications between systems to be observed while also making it possible to identify the communication pattern that is specific to each system involved. For example, one informal study showed that, whereas the overall pattern of cross-purpose talk remained constant throughout a group psychotherapy session (i.e., the group-as-a-whole system), the individual (i.e., members system) communication patterns changed significantly from one 10-minute section to another. The changing outputs from these patterns, however, "corrected" any deviation from the overall pattern of the group as a whole. In one instance, when the group members all demonstrated a work pattern, it was the therapists' input that maintained the system in cross-purpose talk (Agazarian, 1985).

We are committed to bringing the process of research into clinical practice. Therefore, we have introduced the SAVI to our clients in a variety of ways and in various settings. For example, the SAVI-generated communication grid is a map on which clients can trace their relationships with themselves and others as they move from "red light" avoidance behaviors to "green light" approach behaviors. Clients and professionals have reported applying the SAVI method to themselves as couples, families, and individuals in therapy, at home, at work, and in other settings such as decision-making meetings or in organizations requiring strategies for change.

We have found that people seem to know intuitively which categories are problematic for them. We have also found that, in general, people do not know which categories to use to get them out of trouble. Therefore, training clients in the underlying theory of nonnoisy communication allows them to take charge of modifying their own defensive communication. We are currently using the SAVI not only as a research tool but also as a tool for trainers, group leaders, teachers, therapists, and managers and their clients and staff in vivo (Simon, 1993, 1996).

REFERENCES

Agazarian, Y. M. (1969). A theory of verbal behavior and information transfer. *Classroom Interaction Newsletter, 4,* 22–33.

Agazarian, Y. M. (1985, February). Patterns of verbal interaction in individual and group-as-a-whole systems. In A. Beck (Chair), *Multiple views of an episode in a long term group*. Symposium conducted at American Group Psychotherapy Association Annual Convention, New York.

Agazarian, Y. M. (1992). A systems approach to the group-as-a-whole. *International Journal of Group Psychotherapy, 42*, 177–205.

Agazarian, Y. M. (1994). The phases of group development and the systems-centered group. In V. Schermer & M. Pines (Eds.), *Ring of fire: Primitive affects and object relations in group psychotherapy* (pp. 36–85). New York: Routledge.

Agazarian, Y. M. (1996). An up-to-date guide to the theory, constructs and hypotheses of a theory of living human systems and its systems-centered practice. *The SCT Journal: Systems-Centered Theory and Practice, 1*, 3–12.

Agazarian, Y. M. (1997). *Systems-centered therapy for groups*. New York: Guilford Press.

Agazarian, Y. M. (1999). Phases of development and the systems-centered group. *Small Group Research, 30*(1), 82–107.

Agazarian, Y. M., & Peters, R. (1981). *The visible and invisible group, two perspectives on group psychotherapy and process*. London: Routlege & Kegan Paul.

Ahlin, G., Sandahl, C., Herlitz, K., & Brimberg, I. (1996). Developing the Matrix Representation Grid (MRG): A method of observing group processes. Findings from time-limited group psychotherapy for alcohol dependent patients. *Group, 20*, 145–173.

Bales, R. F. (1950). *Interaction Process Analysis*. Cambridge, MA: Addison-Wesley.

Beck, A. P. (1974). Phases in the development of structure in therapy and encounter groups. In D. Wexler & L. N. Rice (Eds.), *Innovations in client-centered therapy* (pp. 421–463). New York: Wiley Interscience.

Beck, A. P. (1981a). Developmental characteristics of the system forming process. In J. Durkin (Ed.), *Living groups: Group psychotherapy and general system theory* (pp. 316–332). New York: Brunner/Mazel.

Beck, A. P. (1981b). The study of group phase development and emergent leadership. *Group, 5*, 48–54.

Bennis, W. G., & Shepard, H. A. (1956). A theory of group development. *Human Relations, 9*, 415–437.

Bion, W. R. (1959). *Experiences in groups*. London: Tavistock.

Blake, R. R., & Mouton, J. (1965). *Managerial grid*. Houston, TX: Gulf Publishing.

Browne, R. M. (1977). *Patient and professional interaction and its relationship to patients' health status and frequent use of health services*. Unpublished doctoral dissertation, University of Toronto, Toronto, Ontario, Canada.

Cox, B. A. (1976). *Communication systems in psychotherapy: An empirical investigation into the treatment ideologies of patients and therapist*. Unpublished doctoral dissertation, Simon Frazer University, Burnaby, British Columbia, Canada.

Flanders, N. A. (1965). *Teacher influence, pupil attitudes, and achievement* (Research

Monograph No. 12, OE-25040). Washington, DC: U.S. Office of Education Cooperative.

Gibb, J. R. (1961). Defensive communication. *Journal of Communication, 11,* 141–148.

Greenberg, L. S. (1986). Change process research. *Journal of Consulting and Clinical Psychology, 54,* 4–9.

Harvey, R. B. (1976). *A study of communication change in group process seminars using the Sequential Analysis of Verbal Interaction.* Unpublished doctoral dissertation, Bryn Mawr College, Bryn Mawr, PA.

Hill, C. E. (1986). An overview of the Hill counselor and client verbal response modes category systems. L. S. Greenberg & W. M. Pinsof (Eds.), *The psychotherapeutic process: A research handbook* (pp. 139–151). New York: Guilford Press.

Holst, P. (1990). *Male and female communication patterns before and after personal narratives in a long-term support self help group.* Unpublished doctoral dissertation. Temple University, Philadelphia.

Howard, A., & Scott, R. A. (1965). A proposed framework for the analysis of stress in the human organism. *Journal of Applied Behavioral Science, 10,* 141–160.

Klein, M. H., Mathieu, P. L., Gendlin, E. T., & Kiesler, D. J. (1969). *The Experiencing Scale: A research and training manual* (Vol. 1). Madison: Wisconsin Psychiatric Institute.

Lewin, K. (1951). *Frontier in group dynamics.* New York: Harper & Row.

Lewin, K., Lippit, R., & White, R. (1939). Patterns of aggressive behavior in experimentally created "social climate." *Journal of Social Psychology, 10,* 271–299.

MacKinnon, J. R. (1980). *An empirical investigation of dyadic verbal interaction in the chronic paediatric health care delivery system.* Unpublished doctoral dissertation, University of British Columbia, Vancouver, British Columbia, Canada.

MacKinnon, J. R. (1984). Health professionals' patterns of communication: Cross-purpose or problem solving? *Journal of Allied Health, 4,* 3–12.

Ruesch, J., & Bateson, G. (1951). *Communication: The social matrix of psychiatry.* New York: Norton.

Russel, R. L., & Stiles, W. B. (1979). Categories for classifying language in psychotherapy. *Psychological Bulletin, 86,* 404–419.

Scott, W. A. (1955). Reliability of content analysis: The case of nominal coding. *Public Opinion Quarterly, 19,* 321–325.

Shannon, C. E., & Weaver, W. (1964). *The mathematical theory of communication.* Urbana: University of Illinois Press.

Shostrum, E. L. (1964). An inventory for the measurement of self-actualization. *Educational and Psychological Measurement, 24,* 207–217.

Simon, A. (1993). Using SAVI for couples' therapy. *Journal of Family Psychotherapy, 4,* 39–62.

Simon, A. (1996). SAVI and individual SCT therapy. *The SCT Journal: Systems-Centered Theory and Practice, 1*, 65–71.

Simon, A., & Agazarian, Y. M. (1967). *SAVI: Sequential Analysis of Verbal Interaction.* Philadelphia: Research for Better Schools.

Simon, A., & Agazarian, Y. M. (1994). *SAVI coding manual.* Philadelphia: Systems-Centered Press.

Simon, A., & Boyer, E. G. (1971). *Mirrors for behaviors: An anthology of classroom observation instruments* (Vols. 1–17). Philadelphia: Research for Better Schools.

Smith, J. A. (1970). *The effects of modeling behavior on the communications of clients in counseling situations.* Unpublished doctoral dissertation, University of Missouri, Kansas City.

Sturdevant, K. S. (1991). *A pilot study of intrapersonal and interpersonal process as measured on the Experiencing Scale and the Sequential Analysis of Verbal Interaction (SAVI).* Unpublished master's thesis, University of Iowa, Ames.

von Bertalanffy, L. (1969). *General systems theory: Foundations, development, applications* (Rev. ed.). New York: Braziller.

Weir, R. (1978). *Treatment and outcome as a function of staff-patient interaction.* Unpublished doctoral dissertation, University of Toronto, Toronto, Ontario, Canada.

Zimmerman, K. W. (1970). *Verbal classroom interaction and characteristics including self-actualization of home economics teachers.* Unpublished doctoral dissertation, Iowa State University, Ames.

14

USE OF STRUCTURAL ANALYSIS OF SOCIAL BEHAVIOR FOR INTERPERSONAL DIAGNOSIS AND TREATMENT IN GROUP THERAPY

LORNA SMITH BENJAMIN

The Structural Analysis of Social Behavior (SASB) is a lens that dissects interpersonal and intrapsychic behavior into three dimensions: (a) attentional focus, (b) love versus hate, and (c) dominance–submission versus emancipation–separation. This SASB helps sharpen clinician perception of therapy process and of the content of patient narratives. It also facilitates the clinician's ability to make links between current maladaptive patterns and early social learning. A developmental social learning interpretation of psychopathology proposes that attachment to early important individuals sets internal patterns and rules that are reflected directly in adult behavior. The connections are manifest through one or more of three copy processes: be like him or her, act as if he or she is still there and in charge, and treat yourself as he or she did. This developmental perspective suggests that patient behavior in group therapy will be organized by rules and patterns learned in the patient's early years. Use of the "SASB lens" makes the connection to the past apparent and provides an objective measure of patterns and links. The treatment implication is that early attachments driving problem patterns should be addressed and let go. Then, new behaviors can more easily be learned and maintained. In this chapter I apply the SASB lens and the developmental social learning perspective to the maladaptive behaviors of Joe and Diane in Group A. Alternative, possibly more effective treatment suggestions that stem from this system of analysis are then discussed.

The SASB can bring interactions from a wide variety of contexts into sharp focus. It dissects interpersonal and intrapsychic interactions into three dimensions: (a) focus (other; self; other turned inward); (b) love versus hate; and (c) enmeshment (dominate–submit) versus differentiation (emancipate vs. separate). The model, questionnaires, coding system, and software have been used to study both process and content in a variety of settings including individual, family, couples, recreational, and group therapies. It has contributed to the assessment and understanding of origins, manifestations, and changes in psychopathology. Training of executives, psychotherapists, and parents is another ongoing application of the SASB. Its methods and predictive principles can be used to describe relevant interpersonal and intrapsychic processes regardless of the perspective of the therapist or the therapy. Some of the more unusual but clinically useful applications have included patient ratings of their relationships with their hallucinations, their drug of abuse (e.g., heroin, cocaine, alcohol), their sexual abuser, their sexual victim or prey, or their mentor.

The purpose of this chapter is to illustrate some uses of SASB-based methods and concepts relative to group therapy. This is part of an overall attempt to operationalize case formulation and treatment theory in a way that can help therapists select an optimal intervention for a given moment from any school or mode of therapy.

HISTORY OF THE SASB SYSTEM

Harry Stack Sullivan (1953) was influential in translating psychoanalytic theory (i.e., the war between the id and the superego, mediated by the ego) into more explicit interpersonal terms. Murray (1938) offered a list of needs that he said reflected Sullivan's interpersonal view. Leary (1957) arranged some of Murray's needs in a circle based on two underlying axes: love versus hate and control versus submission. That model is known as the Interpersonal Circumplex (IPC), and it is accompanied by a widely used trait checklist called the Interpersonal Adjective Scale (see Wiggins, 1982). My own method for assessing "object relations" is based on the SASB (Benjamin, 1974, 1984, 1995). The SASB model integrates the IPC and a model of parenting behavior offered by Schaefer (1965). The SASB model incorporates and integrates many aspects of its predecessors and resolves some contradictions. It adds a method for directly connecting social perceptions and self-concept. A recent comparison of the SASB and the IPC can be found in Benjamin (1996c).

Theory of the System: The Application of the SASB to Group Therapy

There are many approaches to group therapy, including a Yalom-like (client-centered) emphasis on human experience, a cognitive–behavioral therapy-like focus on solving a specific set of problems, and a combination of these two (e.g., see McKay & Paleg, 1992).

As with individual therapy, there is a need for solid research evidence demonstrating more exactly what comprises and enhances effectiveness in group therapy. Lacking clear evidence in support of a guiding theory, practitioners and administrators can become confused. The various approaches are associated with different "rules" that prescribe divergent ways of composing, conducting, and assessing group therapy. It is difficult for the clinician to know what to do or what not to do. The ideal answer to these dilemmas would be to develop a testable theory of group therapy that is supported by convincing evidence. Such a theory could guide intervention and assess outcome. It could document that certain interventions in specific contexts are indeed effective.

It is not easy to construct such a theory. Among other things, the theory must be accompanied by reliable and valid measures that will assess the theoretical concepts invoked in the therapy. Ideally, the tested theory would link therapy events directly to the psychopathology that is being treated and to good outcome.

Without a tested theory to guide the choices, the problem of how to know what is and is not a good intervention can seem overwhelming. Practitioners continue to do what they believe in as they attempt to deal with large numbers of difficult patients. They do what they know, do the best they can, and typically find research to be of little help (Soldz & McCullough, 2000). The dilemma of how to know what works and why is a subject of increasing interest (Goldfried & Wolfe, 1996; Stricker & Trierweiler, 1995). A keystone to a better structure would be successful operationalization of theories and methods that can explain and guide clinical concepts and practices. Once the problems, the interventions, and the results are well defined, more meaningful study of what is effective in group and other therapies could proceed.

The SASB (Benjamin, 1974, 1984), which is nearing the end of its third decade of development, has been attempting to address these issues. SASB development has been focused on operationalizing interpersonal and intrapsychic events in a way that provides good reliability and clinical validity to definitions of psychopathology, therapy process, and outcome.

A book that applies SASB-based procedures to the problem of diagnosis and treatment of individuals with personality disorders is available (Benjamin, 1996b). In a monograph in preparation, I attempt to show how the clinician can develop a case formulation and effectively use that to select techniques from different schools and types of therapy for a given person in a given context at a given moment (Benjamin, in press). Recognition that the SASB has the potential to contribute to the goals of more effectively operationalizing important clinical concepts has come from others (Carson, 1994; Henry, 1996).

The SASB model is only a lens. Effective use of it requires an accompanying theory of psychopathology linked to a theory of intervention. It can be useful to clinicians and researchers of different theoretical orientations. This chapter is confined to my own preferred version of psychopathology and psychotherapy, one that draws heavily on the idea that what children learn greatly affects how they behave in adulthood. Several lines of thought are used in the present perspective. They include interpersonal psychoanalysis, attachment theory, operant conditioning, and studies of imitative learning. Sullivan (1953) is credited with translating psychoanalytic theory into interpersonal terms. Fairbairn (1952), Sandler (1981), and Bowlby (1969, 1977) wrote in different but equally compelling ways about the role of early attachment in psychopathology (Bartholomew & Horowitz, 1991; Florsheim, Henry, & Benjamin, 1996; Hazen & Shaver, 1994). Studies from a variety of disciplines have empirically established that poor attachment leads to a broad range of problems in adulthood (Baumeister & Leary, 1995). Coming from an altogether different perspective, B. F. Skinner (1939) made the profound observation that what works, we do again. This is the main theme of his model for operant conditioning. Typically, what works was originally defined in terms of satisfying "basic" drives such as food or sexuality or avoidance of pain. The present approach combines Skinner's observations about the effects of consequences and the recognition that attachment is a primary driver of human activities. What "works" or what is "reinforcing" is defined, essentially, as what brings hope of better attachment. Another part of the present theory of development of psychopathology is the recognition of the importance of imitation (Asendorpf & Baudonniere, 1993), or copying.

Important People and their Internalized Representations Are the Target of the Treatment

The present perspective gathers most heavily from Bowlby's (1969, 1977) description of "internal working models" that guide the person's expectations and responses. Bowlby marked both in clinical and research terms, the overwhelming importance of the relationship with the "attachment object" in human development. The SASB model, which describes adult interpersonal and intraphysic patterns, can be used to "operational-ize" early relationships and their associated internal working models. The SASB-coded adult patterns and the SASB-coded descriptions of internal working models are linked through three simple copy processes: (a) be like (or be the opposite of) an important other, usually the parent or parent equivalent (*identification*); (b) act as if the parent or parent equivalent is still there (*recapitulation*); and (c) treat yourself as the parent (*introjection*) did. I have called the internalizations (internal working models) that reflect these copy processes *important persons and their internalized representations* (IPIRs; Benjamin, 1994, 1996a). With the SASB lens, one can operation-alize current patterns, the IPIRs, and see connections that may not be otherwise apparent.

Why do humans have such a strong tendency to copy and to maintain the copied patterns even when they are clearly maladaptive? The mecha-nism may be biochemical. Results of recent studies (Kraemer, 1992) suggest that early attachment experiences affect the neurochemistry in primates. It appears that attention and hugs from the parenting figure are enormously calming and important. The effects are likely mediated by changes in neu-rochemistry. It is a small step to generalize from literal hugging between toddler and parent to psychological hugging between a person and his or her internalized representation of a parent. In short, the "reinforcers" of the copy process probably are the unconscious belief that behaving ac-cording to the early rules will bring the desired approval and warmth (psy-chological hugs) from the IPIRs. Every psychopathology is a gift of love (Benjamin, 1993, 1996a, 1996b). These attachments are so powerful that they cause the individual to have distorted views of others and to give what seem to be inappropriate responses. Because devotion to IPIRs or-ganizes and maintains the psychopathology, it is the central target of the treatment approach.

CORRESPONDENCE BETWEEN THE THEORY AND THE SYSTEM

Indexes of Process, Development, or Change

The clinical meaning of this analysis of psychopathology is that the patient's therapy task will be to (a) recognize that he or she is behaving according to old expectations and rules, (b) decide to give up those wishes and to grieve all the losses that entails, and (c) make a commitment to learn new and better ways of being. Therapists should help the patient successfully negotiate these tasks. The SASB model can help the clinician recognize and clearly reflect the patterns and connections for the patient or client.

The model can also help the clinician help the patient and the group clearly envision new and more attractive alternatives. Ideal goals are specified by the SASB model: Normality at its best is characterized by good attachment, by moderate levels of differentiation and enmeshment (defined later), and by flexibility that permits contextually appropriate response. In other words, the therapy goal is to help individual members be more likely to be friendly in their interactions, to be able to show moderate amounts of power and submission, and to show moderate amounts of independent self-definition. These baseline positions can be exhibited with contextually appropriate flexibility. In addition, the normal individual can become hostile, totally withdrawn, powerful, or deferential if the context requires it. Extremes of hostility or power or distancing would be contextually appropriate and normal, for example, in acute, life-threatening situations.

The normal and pathological mechanisms that shape personality are identical. The difference is only in quality. Normal people have copied figures that model good attachment processes, whereas people with maladaptive patterns are devoted to IPIRs who did not. Maladaptive IPIRs demonstrate patterns that are hostile and that are over- or undersaturated with power or that are over- or underrepresented by differentiation. People who are attached to IPIRs that regularly implement these abnormal behaviors become addicted to the accompanying behaviors (i.e., be like him or her; act as if he or she is still there; treat oneself as he or she did). SASB-based measurement methods, illustrated later in this chapter, can help clinicians and researchers identify and track these characteristics and the links among them.

SASB and Group Therapy

The group therapy approach based on these assumptions about developmental learning is called "SASB-based reconstructive interpersonal group therapy" (SASB–RIGT). It parallels in most respects MacKenzie's (1990) group therapy. Based on considerable experience, MacKenzie's discussion of the evolution of group process is clinically compelling. He found that the use of the SASB during an individual orienting session before group therapy facilitates the therapy. Group members complete the SASB Intrex (Benjamin, 1988) questionnaires assessing their relationships with important current and past figures. In the orienting individual session, he reviews the computer-generated results from individuals so that they begin the group process aware of their interactive patterns and of any connections to early figures. MacKenzie modified the standard SASB Intrex in a way that increases its usefulness in therapy. Rather than asking for ratings of a standard series of relationships (e.g., lover, mother, father, their marital relationship), he first conducts a survey to identify key figures and then has them rated. This obviously is a superior application because it identifies nonparental IPIRs, such as older siblings, important teachers, or peers. Because nonparental figures are often internalized, MacKenzie's method of using the Intrex questionnaires has a better chance of demonstrating SASB-RIGT connections between important early figures and current problems.

In the SASB–RIGT, there is a consistent focus on the (SASB-coded) connections between current patterns and unconscious wishes. This emphasis was recently demonstrated in a brief group with sophisticated graduate students who were fully aware of my beliefs about the importance of early experience with parents. I was finishing a class in group therapy, and the students asked to have a brief therapy session for themselves. Using only one class time, I narrowed the problem definition to "how you feel about your professional career." The students felt that there was little or no connection between this topic and their early childhood. Everyone made a personal statement about his or her career. Several shared the sentiment that the trail toward licensing seemed very long and they were very tired, even "burned out." Moreover, they felt somewhat defeated in that they believed that they probably would be overworked with emotionally taxing caseloads and not be paid very well once they were licensed. I was saddened to hear how disenchanted they seemed about their profession. The realities of the marketplace are indeed increasingly harsh. The students recognized that the work is important, and so they resolutely continued their studies. However, they were relieved to learn that so many others shared their weariness. Nobody thought this situation had much to do with his or her own personal histories. Noting that life is always challenging and full of disappointments, I decided to pursue the possibility that their natural and understandable reactions to the current professional scene were intensified by their own "issues." I suggested that volunteers keep their tired feeling in mind and try to remember back in time when they had felt the same or were reminded of something similar. In brief conversations with four of the five volunteers, we found direct connections between these current feelings about career and conflicted relations with a parent.

For example, one student said he was pursuing this therapy career to "make a living," but his first love was music for its own sake. He was sad that he rarely had time to make music any more. Previously, he had "dropped out" for several years just to play different instruments. He had not used his musical skills to make a living. He just made music. His free association was to his beloved grandfather, a musician who refused to make a living and support his family. The student had many fond memories of the times he spent with his grandfather. His father had been furious with his grandfather for dereliction of duty and was himself a great provider. The student said he was "blown away" to realize that his career conflicts (i.e., make music vs. make a living by working hard) directly mirrored the fight between his father and his grandfather. He was trying to "work it out" with each of them, and the task was impossible. His ongoing conflict about music versus a career as a therapist was a derivative of his attachment to these IPIRs.

A Generic Definition of Psychosocial Treatment That Applies to Group and Other Therapies

If we had been an ongoing group, the student in the group therapy class would be encouraged to share his feelings and views about that family fight and his own relation to it. He need not continue the internalized fight between his father and grandfather. Eventually, he would separate himself psychologically from the agendas of those two important parent figures (differentiate) and be free to decide what he truly wanted to do himself. The group could help him develop the will and the courage to do this. That plan would reflect the following view of psychosocial treatment, whether it is administered in the individual, group, family, couples, or other format.

Psychosocial treatment, whatever the forum, essentially involves learning about one's patterns, where they came from, and what they are for; deciding to give up the wishes and fears that support those patterns; and learning better patterns. Case formulation therefore involves clearly recognizing current problem patterns, seeing their connections to wishes and fears in relation to early figures, and planning interventions that will help the patient or client give up those old fantasies and begin work on learning new patterns that are more adaptive in adult life.

When a person's patterns of interaction with self and others change, so does psychiatric symptomatology (Benjamin, 1996b). For example, depression often accompanies perceived abandonment (and felt loss), feelings of being overwhelmed (and helpless), or both. When these patterns of perception and reaction are changed for the better, depression can lift.

These descriptions of psychopathology and psychosocial treatment provide guidelines for determining and assessing therapy interventions. The rule is that interventions must conform to one or more of five correct therapy tasks (Benjamin 1996a, 1996b): (a) collaborate against the problem patterns; (b) learn about present patterns and their connections to IPIRs; (c) block maladaptive patterns; (d) enable the will to change (give up old wishes in relation to IPIRs; and (e) learn new, more adaptive patterns. Any intervention in any mode, including spontaneous life events, is correct if it contributes to one of the five therapy tasks.

Group therapy clearly is a medium that is able to contribute to the five therapy tasks. For example, if a group helps a member who is unaware or unwilling to recognize and work with problem patterns, the group can enhance collaboration against the problem (Step 1). It is easy for group therapy to enhance learning about current patterns (Step 2). Experiential groups with a developmental emphasis can contribute to learning about origins of problem patterns, although they also are at high risk for enabling them. For example, suppose a group member has identified with an indignant, judgmental, and blaming parent. A group that encourages blaming of parents simply will be enabling old ways of relating for this member. On the other hand, a group that has a norm against externalizing and that facilitates responsible personal choice will be less likely to enable blaming. Groups such as Alcoholics Anonymous or Narcotics Anonymous can be helpful in blocking maladaptive patterns such as alcohol and drug abuse (Step 3). Groups can inspire new attachments that are associated with more adaptive norms. By inspiring new loyalties and ideals, groups can help enable the will to change. The therapy group, especially if it goes on for some time, has extraordinary power to become a new internalization, a collective IPIR (Step 4). Finally, group therapy can help people learn and practice new ways of interacting (Step 5).

An intervention can be assessed for effectiveness primarily by looking at the group member's response to it. If the intervention helped the member realize one of the five steps, it was effective. The effect of the intervention matters more than therapist intention. Of course, this does not mean therapists are responsible for patient or client decisions and responses. It merely means that effectiveness is measured in terms of what contributes optimally to the five steps from the patient or client's perspective. Therapists cannot expect to be "perfect" and achieve one of the steps with every intervention. The best one can do is maximize the likelihood of effectiveness. Interventions that conform to the five steps should relate strongly to good outcome. Outcome must be assessed in terms of changes in the internalized representations and the current interpersonal and intrapsychic patterns. Although there are studies in the literature that support aspects of this formulation, a review is not possible here. The formulations are testable but have not yet been tested in a research study, to my knowledge.

Implications of These Definitions for Outcome Measures

Psychopathology is defined in terms of internalization of relationships with figures that reflect poor attachment. Psychotherapy must change those internalizations so that current relationships are free to develop "on their own." Outcome must measure psychopathology, normality, therapy process, and internalizations in a metric that connects them all. Henry (1996) described this as the PTO (pathology, treatment, and outcome) challenge. The SASB methods provide a promising beginning at solving this PTO problem. Further details on how the SASB can do this are given later in this chapter.

Because the SASB model is accompanied by parallel models for affect and cognition (Benjamin, 1996b), it also is possible to track symptoms such as depression, affect, or thought disorders and relate them to the therapy process. For example, suppose a patient or client assumes that when others do not pay attention to him or her, it is because he or she is judging him or her unfavorably and there is nothing he or she can do about it. This is likely to dispose the patient or client to depression because he or she feels abandoned and criticized when others are not focused on him or her. These two perceptions are associated via the parallel models with hopelessness (object loss) and helplessness, two major facets of depression that have been well documented empirically. Similar parallels can be drawn for other Axis I (American Psychiatric Association, 1994) symptoms. Outcome measures in terms of traditional symptomatology can therefore be closely woven into SASB-based research and clinical outcome protocols.

DESCRIPTION OF THE SYSTEM

The SASB model, shown in Figure 14.1, divides interpersonal space into three domains, each built on orthogonal axes that range from hate to

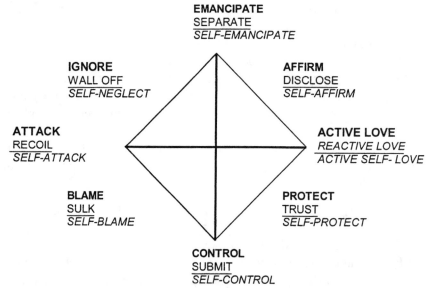

Figure 14.1. The simplified Structural Analysis of Social Behavior cluster model. Labels in boldface type describe initiating focus directed toward another person (parentlike behaviors). The underlined labels describe reactive focus on the self (childlike behaviors). Adjacent boldface and underlined labels mark complementary pairings. For example **AFFIRM** complements DISCLOSE. [One draws for, enhances the other.] Labels in italics show what happens when other focus is turned inward toward the self (introjection). For example, if someone is **AFFIRM**ed by an important other, he or she is more likely to show behaviors described as *SELF-AFFIRM*. From Benjamin, 1996a, p. 55. Reprinted with permission.

love on the horizontal and from enmeshment to differentiation on the vertical dimension. The three domains are (a) initiating focus on another person (parentlike behaviors; e.g., hostile control), (b) reactive focus on the self (childlike; e.g., resentful submission), and other focus turned inward toward the self (introjection; e.g., guilt or hostile control of self). The three types of focus are shown in Figure 14.1 by different typefaces.

For example, if you deliberately ignore someone, your focus is on other and the behavior will be described by the section of the model marked in uppercase boldface typeface. Your ignoring behavior is hostile and will be plotted on the left-hand, hostile side of the model. Finally, your behavior gives the other person separate space, and so it is plotted in the upper half of the model. The three decisions locate the point **IGNORE** in the boldface space, upper left-hand quadrant of Figure 14.1. In other words, when you ignore someone, you are focused on them, you are hostile, and you give them separate space. The behavior of ignoring someone has been dissected into the three underlying dimensions of the SASB model: focus, love versus hate, and enmeshment versus differentiation.

Although most individuals easily understand the connotations of love and hate, specification of the dimension that extends from enmeshment and differentiation is more elusive. On the vertical dimension, enmeshment is defined by the lowermost point. Note that **CONTROL**, located at 6 o'clock and shown in boldface, is opposite the uppermost point, **EMANCIPATE**. A parent who engages in **CONTROL** while the child SUBMITS is enmeshed. A parent who can **EMANCIPATE** the child is permitting differentiation. If the parent does not permit differentiation in a Western culture, the child must SEPARATE on his or her own. For example, toward the end of Session 3, Martha discussed healthy differentiation: "I think the toughest thing for me was to separate myself emotionally. . . . I choose to go my different direction [SEPARATE] and I am right in doing this [SELF-AFFIRM]. I can make my own kind of life. I am not bound to being the kind of person I've been [SELF-EMANCIPATE]."

Classifications are affected by context. For example, suppose you pass by someone on the street and do not speak. If you do not know the person, this is a neutral action, and you **EMANCIPATE** the person or SEPARATE from his or her, depending on your focus. On the other hand, if the person is a friend and you do not speak, you are being hostile. That component changes the description of your behavior from **EMANCIPATE** to **IGNORE**. In Group A, Diane continually described Joe in this way. She saw his focus on her as hostile and distant. Toward the end of Session 3, it became clear that she felt the same way about her mother.

That is basically all there is to describing therapy interactions in terms of the SASB model. Interpersonal and intrapsychic events are coded as they are reported in therapy narratives (content) or acted out between group members or between members and the therapist. Descriptions always reduce to the three dimensions: focus, love–hate, and enmeshment–differentiation. The copy processes are observable simply in terms of whether the same dimensions describe early and current relationships. Therapy process is described in terms of who focuses on whom, whether participants are friendly or hostile, and whether they are enmeshed or differentiated. Higher resolution is obtained when one attends to the degree of love or hate and to the degree of enmeshment or differentiation. The version of the SASB model that appears in Figure 14.1 defines only points on the poles of the axes and points located halfway (i.e., at 45-degree angles) between the respective axes.

In addition to describing interpersonal and intrapsychic events in terms of love versus hate and enmeshment versus differentiation, the SASB model offers predictive principles. Events that are shown in boldface and underlined type at the same location on the model (e.g., 6 o'clock) are closedly related by the principle of complementarity. These behaviors are likely to appear together. For example, the parent, spouse, boss, or friend who shows **CONTROL** draws for the child, spouse, employee, or friend to SUBMIT. The person who SUBMITs, encourages others to **CONTROL**.

The principle of introjection ties self-concept to interpersonal experience with important others. Parents exhibiting behaviors shown in boldface are facilitating self-concepts shown by the adjacent points in italic type. For example, a parent who favors **CONTROL** encourages a child to implement *SELF-CONTROL*. A group that is genuinely **AFFIRM**ing encourages a member to *SELF-AFFIRM* (e.g., "if they think I am OK, maybe I am not so bad after all"). On the other hand, a group that engages in one upsmanship (**BLAME**/SULK) facilitates guilt and shame (*SELF-BLAME*). Session 3 for Group A was remarkable in its ability at the end of the session to produce healthy behaviors that would be described as *SELF-EMANCIPATE* and *SELF-AFFIRM*.

Opposites are shown geometrically at 180-degree angles. The opposite of **CONTROL** is **EMANCIPATE**. The opposite of SUBMIT is SEPARATE. During adolescence, the child is likely to show the antithesis of the desired reaction to parental **CONTROL**, namely SEPARATE, shown on the model at 12 o'clock. An antithesis is the opposite of the complement. Joe, for example, showed the antithesis of his childhood position. As a child, he had to SUBMIT to his father's unreasoned and unpredictable demands. As an adult, he made a big point of letting others do and be whatever they wanted (**EMANCIPATE**).

The names *parentlike* and *childlike* are prototypical. The therapist typically shows parentlike behaviors, meaning only that he or she focuses on others, namely the patients or clients. In individual therapy, the patient typically focuses on self (childlike), not the therapist. However, the focus is defined by the dimensionality of behavior, not by gender, age, role, or other such variables. It is not unusual, especially with individuals with personality disorders, to see that the child **CONTROL**led the parent, the patient controls the therapist, and the employee controls the boss rather than vice versa. In Group A, for example, Diane exerted substantial control. Group therapy, which offers a wide variety of interactive opportunities, is especially adapted to helping individuals learn to be flexible and balanced in their focus. Some people need to learn to focus more on others, whereas other people need to learn to focus more on themselves.

Rating

The SASB Intrex questionnaires can be used to assess perceptions of self and others (Benjamin, 1984, 1994a). Important relationships are rated by the client or by an observer on a scale ranging from 0 (never, not at all applicable) to 100 (always, perfectly applicable). The SASB short-form series is relatively brief and can give a good sketch of patterns with significant others and early figures. The standard assessment is of introject at best and worst states; relationship with a significant other person at best and worst states; and recalled relationships with mother, with father, and of their marital interactions. MacKenzie (1990) added assessments of other important relationships throughout the developmental cycle. As mentioned earlier, he meets individually with each prospective group member and reviews results of the SASB questionnaire assessments. This allows each group member to have an idea of their patterns and of the more overt connections (similarities, opposites, complements, introjections) to early figures.

Objective observer coding manuals have been provided by Benjamin, Giat, and Estroff (1981), Grawe-Gerber and Benjamin (1989), and Humphrey and Benjamin (1989). The coding system requires the observer to identify speech or thought units and interactants in that unit and then to dissect both the process and the content in terms of the underlying dimensions: focus, love versus hate, and enmeshment versus differentiation (See Figure 14.1). Rating of process, content, or both during therapy sessions is more difficult and time intensive than is administering the questionnaires.

The transcript is broken into thought units. A thought unit is a complete thought within a single speech. There can be more than one thought unit to a speech. Videotapes (or audio tapes if video is not available) are viewed to provide nonverbal information about the messages being transmitted. After defining thought units, the interpersonal or intrapsychic referents, labeled X (e.g., Diane) and Y (e.g., Joe), are identified. Each thought unit is coded for process or content or both, depending on investigator choice. The term *process* refers to the transaction in the moment. Content captures the story within the narrative. For example, in Group A, Session

3, Diane said to Joe, "When you talked about the, uh, the Negro, somehow for me you were staying again almost with the externals because, your fringed on your internals, but you emphasized your externals." Diane's process (X = Diane to Joe, Y) was to focus on Joe in a way that was mildly hostile and controlling. Her criticism is best described by the model point of **BLAME**. The content of Diane's thought unit was about Joe's focus on himself within the group. Her language was unusual, but its structure suggests that she viewed Joe as separate and hostile. The closest model point is WALL-OFF. Diane was complaining that Joe did not disclose enough. The SASB categories that summarize this event are as follows: Diane's process to Joe, **BLAME**; Diane's content, Joe to Diane, WALL-OFF.

Although many SASB research users report only therapy process, I believe that the most effective usage considers the interface between process and content. For example, as I illustrate later, the content about Joe in Diane's speeches portrays him as WALLed OFF. However, the process codes of Joe in the group do not confirm that. In fact, he engaged in quite a bit of DISCLOSEure, a fact confirmed by the content of Brad's description of Joe. When one also considers the content of Diane's description of herself in relation to her father as WALLed OFF, as well as her observation that she needed to do that to be safe, one can then interpret her inappropriate description of Joe as a projection of her own defense with her father. This kind of analysis represents nothing new. It reflects clinical wisdom that has been successfully practiced by many dynamically oriented clinicians for years. What is different is the simplicity and clarity with which the SASB coding system can capture that somewhat elusive clinical wisdom.

Figure 14.1 is a simple version of the SASB model. Its points are described in more detail in the SASB full model (Benjamin, 1984), a version that is recommended for coders. For example, the full model includes four points in the region of hostile control (**BLAME**, in Figure 14.1): put down, act superior; accuse, blame; delude, divert, mislead; and punish, take revenge. The SASB long-form questionnaire items provide more detail for these full-model points: Put down, act superior is "S puts O down, tells O his or her ways are wrong and S's ways are better." Blame is "S accuses and blames O, tries to get O to believe and say O is wrong." Delude, divert, mislead is "S misleads O, disguises things, tries to throw O off track." Punish, take revenge is "S harshly punishes and tortures O, takes revenge." These richer descriptions of that part of interpersonal space provide the coder more guidelines than, say, the short-form questionnaire items that accompany the point **BLAME** in Figure 14.1: S puts O down, blames him or her, and punishes him or her.

Messages from one person to another are often complex. They contain more than one message at a time, and sometimes these inextricable strands are contradictory. It is vital for the clinician and the researcher to be able to describe and study such complicated transmissions. For example, the therapists and Diane struggled with what she meant when she said Joe said, "You can only know me with my door closed." This is a puzzling statement. The SASB dissection of it is that she felt that Joe commanded her to know him (**CONTROL**) even though he hid (WALL OFF) behind the "door" of meaningless rambling. The summary of this complex code is **CONTROL** + WALL OFF. This type of control usually is seen in highly coercive settings in which abject submission is required and the well-being and views of the recipient do not matter. It is predicted that more exact narratives from Diane about her relationship with her father would show that this behavior involved exactly this type of transaction. The idea would be that her experience of her father was that he was arbitrarily controlling and he never let much of his own self show. The SASB dissection of the message, and the user's recognition of other contexts in which that particular complex code has been associated with relentless control, can help the clinician quickly understand the member at a deep level. Of course, all inferences have to be checked with the member. Any reflection or linking that does not make sense to the member is treated as invalid, at least until more data help develop a consensus.

The SASB software is designed to dissect exchanges by speaker, subdivided according to whom the speech is directed and, if the user desires, by who answers that speech. Content analyses also separate tallies according to who is being discussed. Note that the coding of process goes beyond who is speaking directly to whom. For example, Person D might speak to Therapist A about Person J in a way that blames him. The exchange from Person D to Therapist A is recorded as DISCLOSE, and a process code of **BLAME** is entered for Person D to Person J. This capacity to describe process in context is vital to accurately capture group process, and it has been used successfully in family research (Humes & Humphrey, 1994).

Limitations and Strengths

The biggest limitation of the SASB system is its comparative complexity and that learning and implementing coding is a time-intensive process. A recent conversion of the DOS software to Windows 95 has made it considerably easier to use, but it still requires understanding of basic software operations such as editing and copying and saving files.

The strength of the SASB system is its ability to strip relatively complex ideas about psychopathology, psychotherapy, and outcome into testable chunks. The categories have strong clinical validity that can be understood by patients or clients as well as by clinicians. The links between research and practice are strong and direct. In short, the SASB operationalizes interpersonal and intrapsychic interactions in terms that are useful from a variety of clinical perspectives. The power of the developmental learning application of the SASB method that is described here is best appreciated by seeing videotapes of the process. Ultimately, it will need to be tested in formal therapy outcome studies.

Reliability

The reliability of the questionnaire measures, defined in terms of internal consistency, is typically .90 or more. Test–retest reliability is also high in normal samples but less so in patient samples (Benjamin, 1988). Reliability of the coding system is usually greater than .80 if the measure is a correlation of the summary profiles (percentage in each SASB category) between independent observers. If the test is a weighted kappa applied on a moment-to-moment basis, reliability drops considerably. It is still within the acceptable range for kappa, usually reaching levels of .60 or more (Grawe-Gerber & Benjamin, 1989; Humphrey & Benjamin, 1989).

Validity

A more complete discussion of the content, predictive, and concurrent and construct validities of the SASB technology appears in Benjamin (1996a). Methods of testing validity include factor analysis, dimensional ratings analysis, circumplex analysis, clinical contrast groups, and more. Data from a wide range of contexts usually support the validity of the model and of the predictive principles. The IPC theorists are critical of the fact that, although the SASB clusters typically emerge in the correct order when self-ratings are factor analyzed, clusters are not equally distributed at uniform angles around the circumplex (e.g., Pincus, 1998; Pincus, Newes, Dickinson, & Ruiz, 1998). My response to that criticism is that factor analysis of self-ratings depends on the attributes of the raters. There are culturally supported associations that have nothing to do with underlying structure. For example, in American culture, submission is seen as friendly. The correlation between friendliness and submission means that the SASB submission cluster is skewed in the friendly direction. Similarly, control is seen as hostile. The association between control and hostility causes the control SASB cluster to be skewed in the hostile direction.

This failure in angular placement is greatly reduced when the tests of validity involve rater judgments about the dimensionality of the SASB items, as distinct from the applicability of the items to themselves. Under the dimensional ratings procedure, the ordering of clusters is correct, as it is under factor analysis of self-ratings. With this procedure, however, clusters are also placed almost equidistant from one another. Angular placement of the clusters in models reconstructed on the basis of dimensional ratings of items (rather than people) is good.

The least "successful" tests of the validity of the SASB model are tests of concurrent validity. For example, a comparison of data based on the IPC and on the SASB in an inpatient population (Benjamin, 1994) shows relatively little overlap. Rather than suggesting a problem with the SASB model, however, that finding demonstrates that these two interpersonal circles are measuring different attributes. For example, the SASB easily describes various forms of social withdrawal so characteristic of depressed individuals, whereas the IPC does not. Descriptions of depressed inpatients on these two instruments are therefore not much alike.

Norms

Normal respondents do rate themselves in terms of predicted normal space (Benjamin, 1988). They self-describe in terms of the SASB clusters that depict friendliness (**ACTIVE LOVE**/REACTIVE LOVE), moderate degrees of enmeshment (**PROTECT**/TRUST), and moderate degrees of differentiation (**AFFIRM**/DISCLOSE). By defining normality in terms of these particular qualities in relationship, the SASB system differs dramatically from the IPC system, which defines normality in terms of moderate (not extreme) intensity rather than quality.

According to the SASB-based definition of normality, a good outcome for group therapy would be for members to learn to occupy baseline positions of friendliness in relation to self and others. This friendliness would be characterized by the propensity to show moderate degrees of independence and moderate degrees of interdependence or enmeshment.

Learning the Rating Method

Learning to use the SASB questionnaires is relatively simple. Learning to code videotapes of sessions for research use is much harder. Similarly, learning SASB coding to use "on-line" in therapy sessions takes a bit of time and practice. An experienced clinician can get the idea in a one-day workshop. However, that broad understanding needs to be sharpened by many hours of practice. On the other hand, an undergraduate student without clinical experience might need as many as 1,000 hours of training followed by still more practice. However, many believe that such training dramatically increases the student's clinical skills. Methods for learning SASB coding include apprenticeship, classes, manuals, and group discussions, all followed by practice with feedback. Critchfield and Henry are currently working on a CD-ROM that could provide efficient interactive learning directed by a computer.

PREVIOUS RESEARCH WITH THE SASB SYSTEM

A recent overview of the SASB models and of the various parameters that are provided by the software appears in Benjamin (1996a). A survey of SASB-based research appears in the introduction to a series of articles on the SASB that appeared in the *Journal of Consulting and Clinical Psychology* (Benjamin, 1996d). Applications specific to group therapy can be found in MacKenzie (1990) and Hartkamp and Heydtmann (1994). Use of the SASB in family therapy is illustrated by Humes and Humphrey (1994), Laird and Vande Kemp (1987), and Grigg, Friesen, and Sheppy (1989). Highlights of therapy applications in individual work come from a variety of theoretical perspectives. For example, client-centered work has been described by Coady (1991a, 1991b) and Quintana and Meara (1990). SASB application in a gestaltlike (emotional experiencing) therapy can be found in Greenberg, Ford, Alden, and Johnson (1993). Interpersonal therapies have been studied by Henry, Schacht, and Strupp (1986, 1990), Johnson, Popp, Schacht, Mellon, and Strupp (1989), and Rudy, McLemore, and Gorsuch (1985). Psychoanalytic therapies have been studied using the SASB by Hartley (1991) and Tress (1993). Brief therapies were assessed using the SASB by Svartberg and Stiles (1992). A powerful version of cognitive–behavioral therapy has been tracked using the SASB by Shearin and Linehan (1992).

APPLICATION OF THE SASB SYSTEM TO GROUP A, SESSION 3

Brief Description of Group A, Session 3

The group was trying to form and decide on the level of discourse and, implicitly, its purpose. Joe had talked a lot about some incidents that bothered him, but Diane said his dialogue was not really "personal." She summarized his message as follows: You can only know me with my door closed. Diane was persistent with her accusation that he talked a lot without saying anything. At times, she became aggressive. For example, she accused him of racial prejudice when his story implied the opposite. Meanwhile, Pat tried to ask whether Joe was made at her during the last session. However, Joe and Alice (a therapist) reframed Pat's inquiry so that she admitted she was irritated with Joe for monopolizing the conversation while saying things were not really to the point. Martha observed that when the group focused on Joe, members did not have to speak up themselves. She told a story about a time that she spoke up in a group and felt humiliated by the response. Brad noted that Joe was the only one who had risked disclosure, and yet he was being attacked for nondisclosure. Brad suggested that Diane loved to fight and was bothered by Joe's peaceful autonomy. Greg joined in, saying he, too, would love a fight but suggested that it was time for the group to pick on somebody new. Martha and Helen (another therapist) objected to the idea of having to fight at all. Joe responded with a nurturant inquiry toward Diane, who confessed that she, too, feared rebuke if she "expressed her values."

Martha made a definitive intervention as she asked whether Diane could provide an example of being rebuked for her values. Martha facilitated this line of inquiry by offering a description of her own comparable experience with parents. Diane responded with disclosure about disappointment with her parents, and the two explored the theme of strengths and weaknesses of parents. Other members joined in. Diane's father was alcoholic and abusive. She had identified with him in that she threw plates, which she noted was a milder version of her father's violence. Several other group members described their fathers as intimidating when inebriated. They described their mothers as exercising strong control, albeit indirectly. They concurred that their mothers' endurance of suffering garnered loyalty that caused distancing from fathers. Some members were angry with their mothers and wished they had a chance to know their fathers better. Martha said she was perplexed about her deep love of parents, given their offenses toward her. However, she invoked the model of her sister, who found a way to "let go" of her parents (differentiate). Martha and Diane compared and contrasted childhood experiences, exploring the dialectic between parental control that seemed excessive versus freedom giving that could seem like neglect. Joe deepened this by wondering whether he had been too permissive with his own son in his effort to avoid recapitulating the abusive control of his childhood. The session ended with an exploration of how to define and find "perfect love." Members were disclosing freely and possibly working together at existential "problem solving."

Examples of Psychopathology in Group A

Illustrations in this and other sections of this chapter center on Diane and Joe because they were the key figures in the scapegoating process prominent in Session 3. Diane, the lead accuser, identified with her father's rages in that she felt fine about "throwing plates" (be like him, copy process). Her anger at Joe for his "control" of the session through incessant talking, plus his failure to disclose anything "meaningful," was a direct recapitulation of her relationship with her father (act as if he is still there, copy process). She learned it was safer to hide. She said, "Of course we learned very young to stay out of his way and in fact we had no communication with him at all. I think it wasn't until my teens that I even tried to communicate with him and then I was scared to even say, 'It's a beautiful day,' cuz I never knew when he would bat me." Greg made the following link: "For that very reason you maintained sort of a mild, no putting forth yourself toward him most of the time I take it," Diane responded: " . . . I wouldn't dare be anything else." Therefore, Diane hid herself in relation to the group. She also projected the attribute of nondisclosure onto Joe and became indignant about it. Finally, Diane's weak self-esteem can be seen as an internalization of the scorn associated with her father (copy process 3, treat yourself as did he and they—the small town that disapproved of his drinking and their family).

Frequently, the wish for love persists in the form of fear of the IPIR. For example, Joe made a point of being separate and letting others be free to do and be whatever they wish. He realized in this session that he might be doing the opposite of what his father did. Doing the opposite would represent a fear of being like his father. As he did this, he would show his love for his sons and his anger at his father. It likely also would represent a wish that his father would have been the kind of parent Joe was. The rigidity and passion with which Joe held to this position suggested that he was still attached to his father. Joe still gave his father the power to direct his way of being, albeit in mirror image. The connection between Joe's litany about letting others be was still a testimonial of attachment to his father. To be completely free, or differentiated, Joe needed to be able to do and be anyway at all, whether it was like or the opposite or totally unrelated to his father's ways.

Therapy Step 1: Collaborating Against Problem Patterns

Therapists often have to support problem patterns, such as Diane's blaming, to develop a working contract. Externalizing patients simply will not accept a therapy relationship if confronted about every problem inter-action. However, it is important to know when to leave the "supportive" (potentially enabling) stance with the problem member and begin to con-front it so that collaboration against the problem patterns can begin in earnest. Diane did not show evidence of beginning such a collaboration in Session 3. By contrast, Joe collaborated to work against his problem pat-terns when he wondered whether he was overreacting to his father's abusive control because he had trouble setting limits with his own children. This difference would suggest that Joe should show more constructive change on interpersonal outcome measures than Diane.

Therapy Step 2: Learning About Patterns, Where They Came From, and What They Are for

Diane needed to see that she had misread Joe because of her learning with her father. She needed to see that her lashing out at him was being like her father. In this behavior, she said in effect, "I show my loyalty to and affection for my father by re-creating interpersonal situations that re-semble my relationship with him. I also act like him." Then she needed to reflect on whether she truly wished to maintain such a direct connection to her father.

Therapy Step 3: Blocking Maladaptive Patterns

Diane remained comfortable with her indictment of Joe for failing to share anything meaningful with the group. She did this despite the therapists' efforts to help Diane focus on her own feelings rather than on Joe's perceived shortcomings. Finally, Brad, a group member, directly confronted Diane with the irony of her complaining about Joe's alleged failure to disclose. Brad said, "Joe has . . . probably talked the most and said the most, uh, revealed I think the most. . . . He's the only one in a way who has sort of begun to, you know, open up at all." The therapists supported this perspective and from there, the group moved more constructively.

Therapy Step 4: Enabling the Will to Change

Toward the end of Session 3, several members talked about their disappointment in relation to their parents and the need to let go of the hope of having their needs met by their parents. Groups that effectively can encourage members to let go of ancient wishes have a greater impact on personality. This process need not be explicit or conscious. Groups and current relationships can sometimes override the old IPIRs. The variables that enhance this process are not known, but they will be important to identify.

Therapy Step 5: Learning New Patterns

Benevolent processes were modeled by some group members. Good examples were offered by Brad, who was nurturing, and Martha, who was inspired by the importance of "letting go." Martha said, "I think the toughest thing for me was to separate myself emotionally and not in any day-to-day relationship because I have no relationship with them, to say . . . their way of life is wrong and the way I've been living is wrong, and I choose to go in my different direction and I am right in doing this, and, um, I can make my own kind of life. I am not bound to being the kind of person I've been. . . ." The therapists supported the idea of finding one's own path.

The SASB model can help the clinician optimally implement the five therapy steps by sharpening the definition of therapy content and process. For example, if Diane were engaged in hostile control of Joe (therapy process) and the therapists recognized she was identifying with a parent who did the same (from coding the content of her narratives), they would, at the least, try to resist enabling continuation of the blaming pattern. Under the cathartic model, they might to the opposite: encourage expression of her anger. Models make a big difference. According to the SASB–RLGT model, Diane would need to recognize her process and its early roots before she would have a chance to decide whether she really wanted to continue to be like her father.

Application of SASB Coding to Group A

The SASB (content) codes of Diane's view of Joe during Segment 2 of Session 3 are shown by the dark bars of Figure 14.2. This segment was

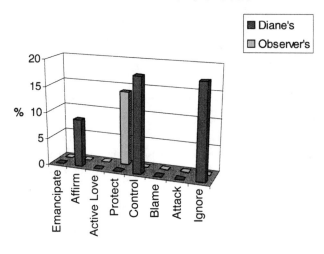

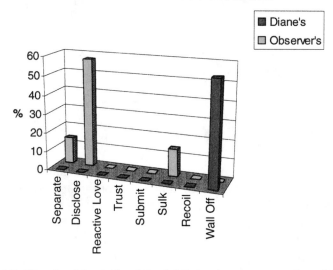

Figure 14.2. Structural Analysis of Social Behavior content codes of Diane's view of Joe during Segment 2 of Session 3 are compared with the objective observer's codes of actual process from Joe to Diane. The discrepancy between these perceptions was measured with a Spearman rank correlation coefficient. The correspondence between Diane's description of Joe with her and the objective ratings was −.327.

defined by the editors, and the data are represented in terms of the percentage of codes generated in all thought units in this segment. It is clear that Diane saw Joe as controlling and as ignoring when he was focused on her (upper part of the figure). To a lesser extent, she saw Joe as affirming. When reacting to her (lower part of the figure), Diane saw Joe as walled off.

The objective observer's process codes of Joe in relation to Diane for that same period of time are shown by the hatched bars in Figure 14.2. The observer described Joe mostly as protective of and disclosing to Diane. There were also instances of his sulking in relation to her and of clearly separating himself from her. The Spearman rank correlation coefficient between Diane's description of Joe with her and the objective ratings was −.327. The discrepancy between Diane's experience of Joe and the objective observer ratings was large. Eventually, Brad pointed this out to Diane.

Figure 14.3 shows that the therapist, Alice, accurately reflected Diane's view of Joe during the scapegoating in Session 3. The Spearman rank correlation coefficient between Diane's view of Joe and the content of Alice's speeches to Diane about Joe relating to Diane was .755 ($p <$ .05). Combined with the fact that Alice's process in relation to Diane was primarily **AFFIRM**ing, Figure 14.3 shows how SASB coding can be used to define empathy that is accurate. The therapist was **AFFIRM**ing in process, and the content of the therapist's speeches matched the content of the member's corresponding speeches. The corresponding speeches involved the same referents. In this instance, the analysis was of all references of the type: Joe to Diane subdivided by whether Alice or Diane was the speaker.

Figure 14.4 (upper graph) shows the correspondence between Diane's view of Joe, expressed during Segment 2, and her description of her parents, revealed in Segment 4. It is clear that she saw both as controlling and ignoring her. Joe was seen as being walled off and mildly affirming. Her parents were described as emancipating. The correspondence as measured by Spearman correlation was .477 ($p <$ .05). If one accepts the SASB theory that adjacent categories are correlated (a fact that has been strongly supported in the validity studies), then the Spearman correlation, which treats each category as independent, underestimates the similarity. For example, Joe's walling off (see Figure 14.4, lower graph) and the parent's emancipation were closely related psychologically. Each represented a high degree of differentiation. If her parent's codes called emancipate had been classified as walled off, the correlation would have been .882. Nonetheless, leaving the profiles exactly as recorded by objective observation and shown in Figure 14.4, there was a significant association between Diane's view of Joe and her experience of her parents as she described them during Segment 4, Session 3. Figures 14.2–14.4 show that Diane's view of Joe, em-

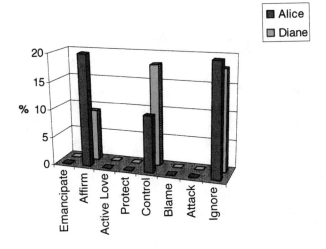

Alice reflects Diane's view of Joe's focus

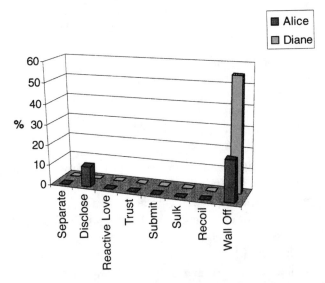

Alice reflects Diane's view of Joe's reaction

Figure 14.3. Structural Analysis of Social Behavior content codes of the empathic reflections to Diane about Joe from the therapist, Alice, during Segment 2 of Session 3. The Spearman rank correlation between Diane's view of Joe and the content of therapist's responses to Diane when Joe was a referent was .755 ($p < .05$).

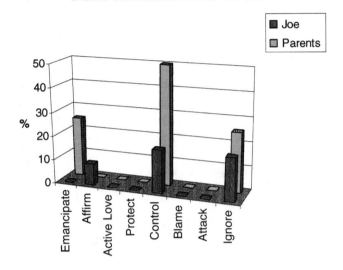

Diane describes focus on her

Diane describes reaction to her

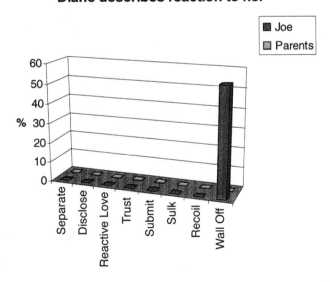

Figure 14.4. Structural Analysis of Social Behavior content codes of Diane's view of Joe in Segment 2 and her view of her parents, revealed in Segment 4. The correspondence as measured by a Spearman rank correlation was .477 ($p < .05$). Figures 14.2–14.4 show that Diane's view of Joe, empathically reflected by the therapist, was much different from that of an objective observer but highly similar to her view of her parents.

pathically reflected by Alice, was much different from that of an objective observer but was similar to her view of her parents.

The data in Figures 14.2–14.4 represent the entire universe of codes for the individuals mentioned in the segments analyzed. These formal analyses can be interpreted as accurate characterizations of those relationships at that point in time. The trends identified were not based on arbitrarily selected speeches. Rather, they emerged from a comprehensive and objective analysis of a total (and independently defined) segment. The figures therefore represent a fair sampling of the patterns. They illustrate how the SASB-based method can operationalize the idea that early attachments drive current problem patterns. The example concentrated on Diane's psychopathology, which was manifested as distorted perception and inappropriate behaviors stemming directly from experience with an early attachment object. The formal analysis also showed that the therapist was highly empathic with Diane. The proposed theory of psychopathology and psychotherapy would suggest that, contrary to folk wisdom and usual and customary practice, empathy in this case was at risk for enabling rather than blocking Diane's problem pattern. Further research on that particular conclusion (empathy is not always "good") is under way in a different therapy study. The point here, though, is that the SASB-based methodology can provide ways of asking and testing important questions about what is and is not helpful in therapy.

The SASB coding process favors microscopic analysis at the dyadic level. However, it is possible to assign referents to larger entities such as the "group." This would be useful when a member might speak about an issue, such as what it was like to have an alcoholic parent, to no one in particular. Particular coalitions could be assigned their own referent, too. That assignment would depend on the theoretical preference of the user. My own preference is to tailor the group experience to the individual learning needs as defined by the interface between the case formulation (their copy processes) and the five steps.

CLINICAL INTERPRETATION

As noted earlier, the data showed that Diane's view of Joe was wildly discrepant from that of the objective observer (and Brad). Her view of him was strongly associated with her experience of her parents. This supports the view of psychopathology as distorted views and responses that relate directly to early attachment objects. The SASB method has operationalized what Sullivan (1953) called "parataxic distortion." A learning theorist might call it (interpersonal) "generalization."

The clinician using the SASB-based formulation of psychopathology would note that Diane's descriptions of Joe were not based in reality (measured by consensus from "reasonable" observers) and that they did match her early learning. The task then becomes to use the group to help her realize that she distorted in this way, that when she responded to her perception with blame, she was identifying with her early painful attachment object. She was recapitulating the pattern of painful hostile enmeshment from her childhood. Once she recognized this (Step 2), she might be motivated to learn new self-talk that would help her inhibit the urge to **BLAME** (Step 3) and work on grieving the loss of the relationship with her father that never was (Step 4), so that she may learn new and better (more friendly, less controlling) ways of being (Step 5).

Descriptions of patterns in terms of the SASB dimensions make congruence among psychopathology, therapy process, and outcome possible. For a relatively simple example, a problem pattern for Diane was her proclivity for **BLAMING** (hostile control). The IPIR theory and the content toward the end of Session 3 suggest that this problem behavior represents identification with her father. The treatment implication is that therapy process should attend to that link and help her separate from him and his ways of being. The outcome measure would look for a reduction in **BLAMING** and an enhancement of its opposite, **AFFIRM**ation of others. The parallel affect model would suggest that Diane is likely to feel depressed if she is not in control and when she is self-critical. If she becomes more attached to others, and less controlling, she would move into the region of more positive affect. Similarly, her cognitive style would be less constricted and sharply focused on details that offend her and would be more broad and open.

The analyses here represent only a fragment of what could be done with Session 3 of Group A. The data analysis concentrated on Diane's view of Joe as seen from her perspective, the observers, Alice's reflections, and Diane's views of her parents. Other individuals had much different experiences and would have much different codes. Each would be analyzed and treated in terms of his or her own copy processes and attachments. In group therapy, dyadic experience is expanded by the phenomenology of "the group." Evidence in support of an experience of "the group" is that outside of therapy, people's self-talk can become, "The group won't like this" or "I've got to tell the group about this. Let's see now, what would the group do? Oh yes; I'll do that." This sort of self-talk reflects internalization of the group as an IPIR. The fact that it often is so subjectively compelling is, I believe, the reason that a group therapy can be so potent. Unfortunately, that power works both ways. I am convinced that some groups create "contagion." Groups can develop destructive norms involving escalating symptomatology. Lacking framing in terms of the five steps, or some other constraining model, group members in these situations can go out and find new disasters with which to regale or be accepted by the group.

Perhaps the most important point from the present analysis is that there must be an organizing (testable and refutable) theory to guide the practitioner, whether the therapy is individual or group or otherwise. For example, Figure 14.3 shows Alice functioning as a superb client-centered therapist. Accurate empathy presumably correlates with good outcome. From my perspective, however, empathy shown for parataxic distortions, such as Diane's, might only enable problem patterns. This possibility that empathy can be destructive, depending on its intersection with the case formulation, therapy content, and process is the focus of a dissertation study (Pugh, 1999).

ASSESSMENT AND FUTURE DIRECTIONS

The SASB lens was created to reflect what people talk most about in therapy: themselves and their relations with others. The questionnaires are written in simple language that patients or clients understand easily. Internal consistency is high (Benjamin, 1974, 1984). The coding system operationalizes both therapy content and process at acceptable to good levels of reliability (Benjamin, 1995). It is capable of describing simple interpersonal and intrapsychic interaction and more elusive and complicated processes such as complex communications (Humphrey & Benjamin, 1989), distortions and defenses (Benjamin, 1994), and underlying wishes (Moore, 1998; Paddock, in press). Combined with explicit interpersonal and intrapsychic theory of psychopathology, an SASB-based description of therapy can guide clinician interventions drawn from a variety of different "schools" and modes such as individual, group, couples, or family therapy. Assessments of problems, treatment procedures, and outcome can use the same rationale and the same metric. Correspondences among theory, practice, and research are direct.

The SASB lens has been applied to *Diagnostic and Statistical Manual of Mental Disorders* descriptions of personality disorders (Benjamin, 1996b) and has yielded useful predictions about developmental history and effective interventions. Some of those have recently been independently confirmed empirically (Isaac & Henry, 1996). Presently, I am preparing a monograph that will provide substantial detail on the interface between case formulation and therapy interventions (Benjamin, in press). In addition, there is an upcoming book on the SASB models and technology and the variety of research uses (Pincus & Benjamin, in press). There have been many studies published using SASB methods to test different perspectives on psychopathology and therapy. I know of no formal research study that has tested the specific claims made here about the role of IPIRs in psychopathology. In addition, there have been relatively few researchers who have used SASB methods to study group theory or therapy.

REFERENCES

American Psychiatric Association. (1994). *Diagnostic and statistical manual of mental disorders* (4th ed.). Washington, DC: Author.

Asendorpf, J. B., & Baudonniere, P.-M. (1993). Self-awareness and other-awareness: Mirror self-recognition and synchronic imitation among unfamiliar peers. *Developmental Psychology, 29,* 88–95.

Bartholomew, K., & Horowitz, L. M. (1991). Attachment styles among young adults: A test of a four-category model. *Journal of Personality and Social Psychology, 61,* 226–244.

Baumeister, R. F., & Leary, M. R. (1995). The need to belong: A desired for interpersonal attachment as a fundamental human motivation. *Psychological Bulletin, 117,* 497–529.

Benjamin, L. S. (1974). Structural Analysis of Social Behavior. *Psychological Review, 81,* 392–425.

Benjamin, L. S. (1984). Principles of prediction using Structural Analysis of Social Behavior. In R. A. Zucker, J. Aronoff, & A. J. Rabin (Eds.), *Personality and the prediction of behavior* (pp. 121–173). New York: Academic Press.

Benjamin, L. S. (1988). *Short form Intrex user's manual.* Madison, WI: Intrex Interpersonal Institute.

Benjamin, L. S. (1993). Every psychopathology is a gift of love. *Psychotherapy Research, 3,* 1–24.

Benjamin, L. S. (1994). SASB: A bridge between personality theory and clinical psychology. *Psychological Inquiry, 5,* 273–316.

Benjamin, L. S. (1995). Good defenses make good neighbors. In H. R. Conte & R. Plutchik (Eds.), *Ego defenses: Theory and measurement* (pp. 53–78). New York: Wiley.

Benjamin, L. S. (1996a). An interpersonal theory of personality disorders. In J. F. Clarkin (Ed.), *Major theories of personality disorder* (pp. 141–220). New York: Guilford Press.

Benjamin, L. S. (1996b). *Interpersonal diagnosis and treatment of personality disorders* (2nd ed.). New York: Guilford Press.

Benjamin, L. S. (1996c). A clinician-friendly version of the interpersonal circumplex: Structural Analysis of Social Behavior (SASB), *Journal of Personality Assessment, 66,* 248–266.

Benjamin, L. S. (1996d). Introduction to the special section on Structural Analysis of Social Behavior (SASB). *Journal of Consulting and Clinical Psychology, 64,* 1203–1212.

Benjamin, L. S. (in press). *Reconstructive learning therapy: Methods for treating the untreatable.* New York: Guilford.

Benjamin, L. S., Giat, L., & Estroff, S. E. (1981). *Manual for coding social interaction in terms of Structural Analysis of Social Behavior.* Unpublished manuscript.

Bowlby, J. (1969). *Attachment and loss: Vol. 1. Attachment.* London: Tavistock Institute of Human Relations.

Bowlby, J. (1977). The making and breaking of affectional bonds. *British Journal of Psychiatry, 130*, 201–210, 421–431.

Carson, R. C. (1994). Reflections on SASB and the assessment enterprise. *Psychological Inquiry, 5*, 317–335.

Coady, N. J. (1991a). The association between client and therapist interpersonal processes and outcomes in psychodynamic psychotherapy. *Research on Social Work Practice, 1*, 122–138.

Coady, N. J. (1991b). The association between complex types of therapist interventions and outcomes in psychodynamic psychotherapy. *Research on Social Work Practice, 1*, 257–277.

Fairbairn, W. R. D. (1952). *An object relations theory of the personality.* New York: Basic Books.

Florsheim, P., Henry, W., & Benjamin, L. S. (1996). Integrating individual and interpersonal approaches to diagnosis: The structural analysis of social behavior and attachment theory. In F. Kaslow (Ed.), *Handbook of relational diagnosis* (pp. 81–101). New York: Wiley.

Goldfried, M. R., & Wolfe, B. E. (1996). Psychotherapy practice and research: Repairing a strained alliance. *American Psychologist, 51*, 1007–1016.

Grawe-Gerber, M., & Benjamin, L. S. (1989). *Structural Analysis of Social Behavior (SASB): Coding manual for psychotherapy research.* Bern, Switzerland: Research report from the Psychologischen Institut der Universitat Bern.

Greenberg, L. S., Ford, C. L., Alden, L., & Johnson, S. M. (1993). In-session change in emotionally focused therapy. *Journal of Consulting and Clinical Psychology, 61*, 78–84.

Grigg, D., Friesen, J. D., & Sheppy, M. I. (1989). Family patterns associated with anorexia nervosa. *Journal of Marital and Family Therapy, 15*, 29–42.

Hartkamp, N., & Heydtmann, M. (1994). The influence of "history taking" peer groups on the relation of medical students towards patients. *Gruppenpsychotherapie und Gruppendynamik, 30*, 276–296.

Hartley, D. (1991). Assessing interpersonal behavior patterns using Structural Analysis of Behavior (SASB). In M. Horowitz (Ed.), *Person schemas and maladaptive interpersonal patterns* (pp. 221–260). Chicago: University of Chicago Press.

Hazen, C., & Shaver, P. R. (1994). Attachment as an organizational framework for research on close relationships. *Psychological Inquiry, 5*, 1–22.

Henry, W. P. (1996). Structural Analysis of Social Behavior as a common metric for programmatic psychopathology and psychotherapy research. *Journal of Consulting and Clinical Psychology, 64*, 1263–1275.

Henry, W. P., Schacht, T., & Strupp, H. H. (1986). Structural Analysis of Social Behavior: Application to a study of interpersonal process in differential psychotherapeutic outcome. *Journal of Consulting and Clinical Psychology, 54*, 27–31.

Henry, W. P., Schacht, T. E., & Strupp, H. H. (1990). Patient and therapist introject, interpersonal process, and differential therapy outcome. *Journal of Consulting and Clinical Psychology, 58,* 768–774.

Humes, D., & Humphrey, L. L. (1994). A multimethod analysis of families with a poly-drug dependent or normal adolescent daughter. *Journal of Abnormal Psychology, 103,* 676–685.

Humphrey, L. L., & Benjamin, L. S. (1989). *An observational coding system for use with Structural Analysis of Social Behavior: The training manual.* Unpublished manuscript, Northwestern University Medical School, Evanston, IL.

Isaac, M., & Henry, W. P. (1996, June). *Assessing key maladaptive interpersonal dynamics in adult intimate relationships: The Attitudes About Significant Relationships Questionnaire.* Paper presented at the Society for Psychotherapy Research, Amelia Island, GA.

Johnson, M. E., Popp, C., Schacht, T. E., Mellon, J., & Strupp, H. H. (1989). Converging evidence for identification of recurrent relationship themes: Comparison of two methods. *Psychiatry, 52,* 275–288.

Kraemer, G. W. (1992). A psychobiological theory of attachment. *Behavioral and Brain Science, 14,* 1–28.

Laird, H., & Vande Kemp, H. (1987). Complementarity as a function of stage in therapy: An analysis of Minuchin's structural family therapy. *Journal of Marital and Family Therapy, 13,* 127–137.

Leary, T. (1957). *Interpersonal diagnosis of personality: A functional theory and methodology for personality evaluation.* New York: Ronald Press.

MacKenzie, K. R. (1990). *Introduction to time-limited group psychotherapy.* Washington, DC: American Psychiatric Press.

McKay, M., & Paleg, K. (1992). *Focal group therapy.* Oakland, CA: New Harbringer.

Moore, A. M. (1998). *Structural analysis of what alcoholics hope for when starting to drink.*

Murray, H. A. (1938). *Explorations in personality.* New York: Oxford University Press.

Paddock, J. (in press). *Structural analysis of fantasied mentors.*

Pincus, A. L. (1998). Structural Analysis of Social Behavior (SASB) circumplex analyses and structural relations with the interpersonal circle and the five-factor model of personality. *Journal of Personality and Social Psychology, 74,* 1629–1645.

Pincus, A. L., & Benjamin, L. S. (in press). *Structural Analysis of Social Behavior: A scientific method for studying psychopathology and psychotherapy.*

Pincus, A. L., Newes, S. L., Dickinson, K. A., & Ruiz, M. A. (1998). A comparison of three indexes to assess the dimensions of Structural Analysis of Social Behavior. *Journal of Personality Assessment, 70,* 145–170.

Pugh, C. (1999). *Effects of therapist affirmation depend on context.* Unpublished doctoral dissertation, University of Utah, Salt Lake City.

Quintana, S. M., & Meara, N. M. (1990). Internalization of therapeutic relationships in short-term psychotherapy. *Journal of Counseling Psychology, 37,* 123–130.

Rudy, J., McLemore, C. W., & Gorsuch, R. L. (1985). Interpersonal behavior and therapeutic process: Therapists and clients rate themselves and each other. *Psychiatry: Journal for the Study of Interpersonal Processes, 48,* 264–281.

Sandler, J. (1981). Unconscious wishes in human relationships. *Contemporary Psychoanalysis, 17,* 180–196.

Schaefer, E. S. (1965). Configurational analysis of children's reports of parent behavior. *Journal of Consulting Psychology, 29,* 552–557.

Shearin, E., & Linehan, M. M. (1992). Patient therapist ratings and relationship to progress in dialectical behavior therapy for borderline personality disorder. *Behavior Therapy, 23,* 730–741.

Skinner, B. F. (1939). *The behavior of organisms.* New York: Appleton-Century-Crofts.

Soldz, S., & McCullough, L. (Eds.). (2000). *Reconciling empirical knowledge and clinical experience: The art and science of psychotherapy.* Washington, DC: American Psychological Association.

Stricker, G., & Trierweiler, S. J. (1995). The local clinical scientist: A bridge between science and practice. *American Psychologist, 50,* 995–1002.

Sullivan, H. S. (1953). *The interpersonal theory of psychiatry.* New York: Norton.

Svartberg, M., & Stiles, T. C. (1992). Predicting patient change from therapist competence and patient-therapists complementarity in short-term anxiety-provoking psychotherapy: A pilot study. *Journal of Consulting and Clinical Psychology, 60,* 304–307.

Tress, W. (Ed.). (1993). *SASB: Die Strukturale Analyse Sozial Verhaltens—Ein Arbeitsbuch fur Forschung, Praxis und Weiterbildung in der Psychotherapie* [SASB: Structural Analysis of Social Behavior—A workbook for research, practice, and training in psychotherapy]. Heidelberg, Germany: Roland Asanger Verlag.

Wiggins, J. S. (1982). Circumplex models of interpersonal behavior in clinical psychology. In P. C. Kendall & J. N. Butcher (Eds.), *Handbook of research methods in clinical psychology* (pp. 183–221). New York: Wiley.

VI

AN OVERVIEW OF
THE SYSTEMS

15

COMPARISON OF THE SYSTEMS OF ANALYSIS: CONCEPTS AND THEORY

ARIADNE P. BECK AND CAROL M. LEWIS

The nine systems of analysis featured in this book have emerged from a rich set of theoretical and research efforts that have taken place over the past 80 years. In this chapter, we highlight the basic concepts used by these systems to investigate the group therapy process and their theoretical roots. A list of the systems, their acronyms, and the authors is provided here to assist readers in following this chapter.

Chapter 6. The Group Emotionality Rating System (GERS), by S. W. Karterud

Chapter 7. Hill Interaction Matrix (HIM), by A. Fuhriman and G. M. Burlingame

Chapter 8. The Member–Leader Scoring System (MLSS or Mann), by S. Cytrynbaum

Chapter 9. The Group Development Process Analysis Measures (GDM), by C. M. Lewis, A. P. Beck, J. M. Dugo, and A. M. Eng

Chapter 10. The Psychodynamic Work and Object Rating System (PWORS), by W. E. Piper and M. McCallum

Chapter 11. The Individual Group Member Interpersonal Pro-

cess Scale (IGIPS), by M. S. Davis, S. H. Budman, and S. Soldz

Chapter 12. Three Complementary Systems for Coding the
Process of Therapeutic Dialogue, by A. S. Chambon, A. K. T. Tsang, and E. Marziali

Chapter 13. The System for Analyzing Verbal Interaction
(SAVI), by A. Simon and Y. Agazarian

Chapter 14. The Structural Analysis of Social Behavior
(SASB), by L. S. Benjamin.

THEORETICAL BASES OF THE SYSTEMS OF ANALYSIS

The nine systems of measurement objectively investigate many theoretical concepts regarding group process. The GERS and the MLSS investigate how the group process evokes affects and defensive processes. The HIM and the PWORS assess whether therapeutic work is taking place during the interaction studied. The IGIPS, the SAVI, the Negotiation of Therapy Agenda (NOTA), the Psychological Space Coding System (PSCS), and the Strategies of Telling and Talking (STT) are designed to assess aspects of the group interaction, communication, and thought processing that are believed to be conditions necessary for therapeutic work to take place. The GDM assess the development of structure in the group and how it affects the tasks involved in therapeutic work. The SASB examines members' perceptions of themselves and others, formulates specific therapeutic tasks for each individual, and assesses therapeutic change. As a whole, the systems allow for an examination of the interdependence of individual psychological processes with group-as-a-whole processes, group development, and change.

The theoretical bases from which these systems have emerged were developed by several contributors to group theory as well as by many of the pioneers in the psychology of individual dynamics and individual psychotherapy. Figure 15.1 shows the connections among the systems in this book and their theoretical sources, displayed in a historical time frame. As might be expected, Freud (1921/1951) had a broad influence on the development of the thinking about group process in therapeutic contexts, in spite of the fact that psychoanalysis, for many years, did not recognize groups as a legitimate method for the treatment of emotional problems. Beyond Freud, Harry Stack Sullivan (1953), Melanie Klein (1948/1952), and Otto Rank (1936) introduced their own enriching ideas to the development of the emerging fields of psychoanalysis and psychotherapy, which then influenced many theories of group therapy. Sullivan in particular translated important Freudian concepts into interpersonal terms. A new set of influences entered the scene through Skinner's (1939) focus on be-

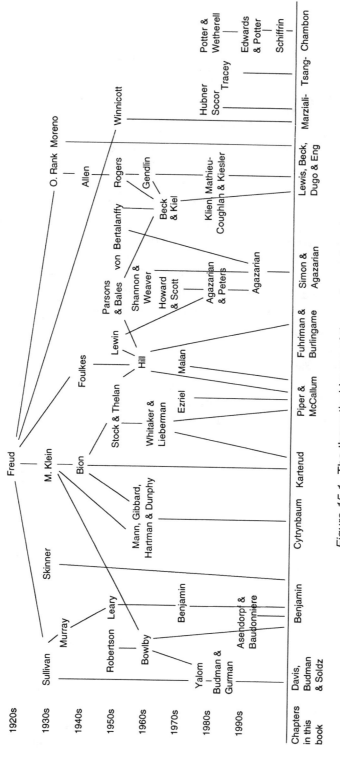

Figure 15.1. The theoretical bases of the systems of analysis.

haviorism, which eventually led to cognitive–behavioral therapy and an alternative to psychoanalysis and its focus on the unconscious. Moreno (1934, 1950), with his interest in social action and the social milieu, developed psychodrama, which highlights the social and familial contexts for the emergence of patient problems. His work also highlighted the way groups can be crucibles for healing by allowing corrective experiences to emerge. Murray (1938) helped introduce a focus on normal adult needs and behaviors that broadened the scope of issues and concerns in psychology. Because these theorists wrote during the early years of the emergence of psychology and psychoanalysis, they naturally influenced a wide range of subsequent theories.

These early theories emphasize the influence of the social context and primary relationships in the psychological development of each individual. Each in its own unique way focuses on some aspects of the early developmental forces influencing the individual. The examination of group processes allows a closer study of the interactive behavior of individuals and how this affects individual psychodynamics. It is possible to view the influences from primary developmental relationships as well as interpersonal processes in and from a wider social sphere.

Psychological injuries to individuals, or psychological impediments to development, have formed the impetus to examining and understanding psychopathology as well as what is needed for normal development. Isomorphic with that, the potential for destructive behavior on the largest scale, that of war, has been part of the impetus for broadening the understanding of human psychology in the social context and behavior in the face-to-face, here-and-now group.

World War II created an impetus to the further development of group approaches to psychotherapy. For one reason, large numbers of men, women, and children needed psychological attention because of the war and its atrocities. Furthermore, the horror of this war led to many intelligent efforts to prevent war in the future, including an attempt to understand group behavior and to develop methods for resolving conflicts without the use of wars.

As major breakthroughs occurred in mathematics, physics, and biology, and many new fields emerged during the 20th century, a much wider set of influences began affecting the study of psychotherapy generally and of groups in particular. The effect was one of a widening circle of study, examining psychological aspects of social processes and integrating this study with further study of the individual. As Figure 15.1 indicates, this growth continues to this day. Some of the newer sources of theoretical influence include the following: biology or systems theory (von Bertalanffy, 1950), sociology (Parsons, Bales, & Shils, 1953), group dynamics (Foulkes,

1948; Gibbard, Hartman, & Mann, 1974; Lewin, 1951; Mann, Gibbard, & Hartman, 1967; Stock & Thelan, 1958), child guidance and treatment (Allen, 1942; Robertson, 1952, 1953; Winnicott, 1958), the development of client-centered therapy in a research-oriented university context (Gendlin, 1962; Klein, Mathieu-Coughlan, & Kiesler, 1986; Rogers, 1951), attachment theory (Bowlby, 1969), information theory (Shannon & Weaver, 1964), the study of stress (Howard & Scott, 1965), and the study of narratives and discourse analysis (Edwards & Potter, 1992; Potter & Wetherell, 1987; Shiffrin, 1994). This rich set of resources has blended into a number of approaches that address a variety of aspects and levels of process in the therapeutic group.

SUMMARIES OF THE SYSTEMS: THEORETICAL BASES AND CONCEPTS

In this chapter we summarize the basic concepts used by the authors of the nine systems of analysis presented in this book. Figure 15.1 is a diagram of the theoretical roots of, and influences on, each system of analysis. Table 15.1 provides brief summaries of the dimensions addressed by the systems. The systems are presented in the same order in which they appear in this book. In this summary we also indicate which parts of the group system are addressed by the measures. Looking at the group as a system (Miller, 1978), it can be described as follows:

Suprasystem 1: Community and general culture in which the group is conducted
Suprasystem 2: Context in which the group is conducted
System: The group as a whole
  Subsystem 1: Subgroups
  Subsystem 2: Dyads
    a. Client–client
    b. Client–therapist
    c. Therapist–therapist
  Subsystem 3: Individual members.

In the set of measures in this book, aspects of the subsystems and system are addressed but not the two aspects of the suprasystem. Within each aspect of the group system, mentioned earlier, there are different dimensions of process that can be tracked (see Table 15.1). Each measure can be summarized in different ways to track different aspects of the group system. We briefly note what the authors have done in the summaries that follow. However, readers should keep in mind that many of the measures can be summarized in other ways as well.

TABLE 15.1
Dimensions Addressed by the System of Analysis

System and Chapter Author	Results are Reported About			Affect	Information	Defensive/Open	Focus	Level of Activity	Roles	Power
	Ind.	Interp.	Grp.							
GERS Karterud	x		x	Affective states		All codes are defenses: fight–flight, pairing, dependency, or neutral		ID speaker no. of statements; no. of defensive codes		
HIM Fuhriman & Burlingame	x	x	x		Content styles Nonmember Topic Group Member centered Personal Relationship	Work styles Prework Conventional Assertive Work Speculative Confrontive	ID person focused on	ID speaker, role, and no. of statements	Client Therapist	
MLSS Cytrynbaum		x	x	Impulse area: Hostility/Affection		Ego-state area: Anxiety/Depression/Guilt/Self-Esteem	Levels of inference regarding member-leader relation	ID no. of acts ID speaker	Describes specialist roles	Power-relations area: Dependency/Independence/Counterdependence
GDM Lewis, Beck, Dugo, & Eng	x	x	x	Change in emotional tone: Hostility/Support	Topic-Oriented Group Focus Unitizing Procedure	Experiencing level of self-exploration or in response to other member	Group-level normative or organizational vs. personal; ID spoken to	ID speaker; Word and pronoun counts	ID client and therapist; ID emergent leader roles	
PWORS Piper & McCallum	x	x	x		Object Linking	Nonwork: Externalizing description	Object focus	ID speaker; no. of statements and length		

420   *BECK AND LEWIS*

System	Ind.	Interp.			Work: ID single dynamic component, ID two or more dynamic components				
IGIPS Davis, Budman, & Soldz	x	x	Emotional tone; Positive–negative statements	Topic	Awareness of self and others; interpersonal sensitivity	ID spoken about; ID spoken to	ID speaker; no. of statements and length	Main actor, facilitator, therapist	Connectedness
NOTA Tsang	x			Control of and timing of introduction or shift of topic		Character	Speech turn; sequence		Collaboration vs. Disruption
PSCS Marziali	x		Affirmation	Provision of information	Opening/Closing psychological space	ID person focused on	ID speaker		
STT Chambon	x			Words, phrases, and word groupings used preferentially	Closed vs. Open modal expressions	Character, narrator, spatiotemporal scene	Speech turn		
SAVI Simon & Agazarian	x	x	Congruence between affect and content	Potential to transfer information regarding Person/Data/Orientation	Approach/Contingent–Avoidance; combinations of codes define D-O	ID spoken to	ID speaker; ID sequence	Roles based on clusters of codes	Influence on level/style of discourse; control of information
SASB Benjamin	x		Hate–love	Content coded with same categories	Enmeshment/differentiation	ID of self/other/ other turned inward; ID spoken to	ID speaker		

Note. Ind. = individual; Interp. = interpersonal: dyadic or subgroup; Grp. = group as a whole; D-O = Data-Opinion ratio.

The GERS

In the GERS, Karterud builds on the concepts of Bion (1961) regarding the psychodynamic theory of defensive processes as they are manifested in small-group interaction. He also builds on the work of Stock and Thelan (1958) in operationalizing these ideas. Bion theorized that task activities are threatened by collective, regressive, and usually unconscious forces within the group. Expression of the affects present in members results in the occurrence of several types of emotionality in groups, called "basic assumption (BA) emotionality."

Bion's (1948, 1959, 1961; Klein, 1946) theory emerged from a Kleinian perspective. Klein believed that the ability of the therapist and the group as a whole to "contain" and interpret disturbing emotions such as envy, greed, and hatred would enable group members to work together from the "depressive" position. The awareness of such issues facilitates an improved capacity for integration, self-understanding, perception, and the capacity for love and gratitude.

The GERS relates psychological processes as these are shaped in early development, with individual perceptions and behavior in the group setting. Thus, the GERS explores the nature of defensive processes in the individual and how these influence and limit behavior in the group setting.

The GERS rates emotionality present in the group through statement-by-statement ratings of emotion. Karterud (1990) considered the ratings of statements as "microunits" of speech. Taken together and summed across larger, more natural segments such as sessions, these microunits may accurately indicate the BA emotionality and defensive processes present in the group as a whole. BA emotionality can also be summarized at the individual level and related to other measures of the individual. For example, the concept of valence has received some support from GERS analysis of behavior in groups. Seven to 20% of the differences in BA emotionality among group members was explained by diagnosis. The rating categories include fight, flight, dependency, and pairing, consistent with the BA emotions theorized by Bion (1961). There is also a category of neutral, or no rateable, emotion. In Bion's theory, BA emotionality is an impediment to work. However, work is not directly measured in the GERS.

Qualitative analysis with another tool derived from psychodynamic theory, group focal conflict analysis (Whitaker & Lieberman, 1962), helps confirm that the GERS distinguishes between groups. Group focal conflict theory analyzes group process as the group negotiates solutions to psychodynamic conflicts at the group-as-a-whole level. Some solutions are considered "enabling," whereas others are "restrictive" of the group's ability to work and therefore of the individual's ability to change. Data from research studies with the GERS has enabled some norms to take shape regarding the types and levels of emotionality present in the group as a whole when various BAs are operative.

The HIM

The HIM (Hill, 1965a, 1965b, 1973) builds on the work of Bion (1948, 1959, 1961), Lewin (1951), Stock and Thelan (1958), Bales (1953, 1958), and Bales and Strodtbeck (1951). These theoretical influences were the background to Hill's larger goal: the construction of a measure that would help develop a theory of group process for therapy groups. Hill's intention was to build a pantheoretical scale that would not depend on any particular theory. The HIM describes and categorizes therapeutic interaction and then weights the categories according to values for accomplishing the tasks of treatment. Hill believed that interaction leading to therapeutic growth must be member centered, that the group member must experience interpersonal threat, and that a group member must clearly take the role of patient while another group member or members take the role of therapist. Although the GERS focuses on the effects of defenses on group-as-a-whole process, the HIM explores the way confrontation of defenses affects therapeutic work.

Each unit, a statement, is described on two dimensions: content style, which describes the subject addressed, and work style, which describes the manner in which the content is addressed. The categories that make up the matrix reflect the emphasis of the HIM on the study of therapeutic work and the way change takes place in group psychotherapy. The columns of the matrix define the content style of the group talk, which is coded Topic, Group, Personal, or Relationship. The rows define the work style used in the interaction and are coded Conventional, Assertive, Speculative, and Confrontive. Although work style is coded, the HIM does not directly define therapeutic work or directly assess its accomplishment. Its goal is to enable empirical study of these processes. The scale is ordinal, with weights assigned according to the therapeutic value placed on the kind of interaction expected to help facilitate therapeutic work and change. The value of each cell in the matrix is weighted according to Hill's concept of what types of behavior are of greatest therapeutic value for the facilitation of individual change. Speculative and confrontative work style, and personal and relationship content, make up the fourth, most heavily weighted quadrant of the HIM. The interpersonal interaction considered most closely related to therapeutic growth and change is behavior coded Confrontive in work style and coded Relationship in content style. Hill encouraged others to make changes or adjustments in the weights according to the theory or treatment used, but the HIM is usually used with the weights developed by Hill.

The HIM has been used in many research studies and the data summarized in various ways. In this book the authors have summarized ratings for the group as a whole and for two subgroups, namely all of the clients and both of the therapists, within specific segments of interaction in Session 3.

The MLSS

The MLSS was originated and revised by Mann (Mann et al., 1967; Mann et al., 1970). Like the GERS, it is derived from Bion's (1961) theory of group dynamics, ego psychology, and Kleinian object relations traditions (Klein, 1946, 1948/1952). The system assumes that authority issues are central in each group member's experience and that these concerns are evoked as primary processes. These issues must be addressed in the group setting in the relative absence of the structure and restraints of traditional role expectations. The MLSS views each individual's behavior as overdetermined by predisposition and previous personal experience and by interpersonal pressures in the group.

During group-as-a-whole development, which has been studied with the MLSS, role specialists emerge who then enact roles that represent important elements in the inner, often unconscious, fantasies of group members. The enactment of roles by members allows the group to confront and resolve basic emotional needs and accomplish therapeutic work. The roles facilitate the expression and resolution of conflict over authority issues. The group members also develop a collective fantasy. The group fantasy and the enacted roles represent the externalization of inner conflict related to coping with primary processes in the uncertain atmosphere of the group. Phases of group development have been identified: (a) Initial Complaining, (b) Premature Enactment, (c) Confrontation, (d) Internalization, and (e) Separation and Terminal Review. In this theoretical approach, the resolution of internal group conflict is considered the force that propels group development.

The system has been applied to training and work groups and to classrooms. Cytrynbaum and Conran (1979) found six phases in their study of classroom groups.

The MLSS system blends quantitative and qualitative methods of analysis. Rating units are relatively small and are called "acts." They vary from a single word or a sigh to a long monologue, and they must contain a uniform expressed feeling. Expressed feelings are interpreted with respect to how they reflect a member's feelings toward the designated leader and are therefore data about the dyad subsystem of client and therapist.

The system emphasizes the role of displacement and symbolization in understanding the expression of feeling in group members. The system assumes that a member might express feelings symbolically, directly, or indirectly. It also assumes that in the process of expressing feelings a member may form inner "symbolic equivalents" or displacements for herself or himself or for the object of the feelings.

Levels of inference are also coded, describing degrees of displacement and symbolization of the speaker's feelings judged to be present in the speech act (Hallberg, 1995). For instance, the speaker might refer to the leader directly and express feeling as his or her own, or refer to others inside or outside the group and express personal feelings; in each case, however, this system judges the behavior as to what it means about the member's feeling toward the leader. The 18 rating categories of the system are grouped into three main areas of the phenomena rated, including the Impulse area (hostility/affection; affect expressed toward the leader); the Power-Relations areas (dependency, independence, or counterdependence; reaction to authority); and feelings in the self or about the self in relation to the leader or the Ego-State area (anxiety, depression, guilt, or self-esteem).

The GDM

The GDM were originally designed to track the characteristics of shifts between phases of group-as-a whole development. Other objectives were added as the work progressed, including measures to assess processes within phases and measures of leadership emergence and of the informal leaders' characteristic behaviors throughout a group's life. The work is based on Beck's (1974, 1981a, 1981b) theory of group development. The process measures address individual, dyads, subgroup, and group-as-a-whole aspects of the group system. A separate test has been developed to identify emergent leaders (Brusa, Stone, Beck, Dugo, & Peters, 1994).

Drawing on developmental psychology, social psychology, social anthropology, an early awareness of systems theory (von Bertalanffy, 1950), and training in client-centered therapy (Rogers, 1951), Beck wrote a theory of group development with her first collaborator, Kiel (Beck & Kiel, 1967). Since then, she has elaborated the theory in greater detail (Beck, 1974, 1981a, 1981b) with the collaboration and contributions of Brusa, Dugo, Eng, Lewis, and Peters.

The theory identifies nine potential phases that describe the evolving structure-creating process of a group and four emergent leaders (i.e., Task, Emotional, Scapegoat, and Defiant). They participate in a dialectical process in which group-as-a-whole conditions are created, which then facilitate or hinder individual and relationship change processes in a therapy group.

Some phase-relevant tasks are crucial to the progress of a group in developing and enabling an environment for change. Knowledge of these tasks allows the leader to enable the group to address the tasks within an appropriate time frame. Each phase creates opportunities to address a range of intrapsychic, interpersonal, and group-as-a-whole issues that can stimulate work on members' personal developmental impasses. An individual's self-work combines with his or her observation and facilitation of the work of others to stimulate a higher level of awareness about the process of therapeutic change.

The GDM are designed to study the evolving structure in the group, the common and unique characteristics of phases of group development and, as part of this overall task, to identify the boundaries of phases or the points of transition from one phase to another. In addition, the roles of the emerging leaders in facilitating or hindering this process are observed. The measures build on the work of Bales (1953, 1958), who found that groups move back and forth between structural issues and task issues. He identified two of the four leaders named in this work (Bales & Strodbeck, 1951).

The Topic-Oriented Group Focus Unitizing Procedure is used to unitize group interaction, which is then rated with the Normative Organizational/Personal Exploration Scale. This scale enables study of the dynamic nature of the group's focus on building structure and accomplishing therapeutic tasks (Dugo & Beck, 1983). This scale is focused on group-as-a-whole interaction and identifies the initiation and completion or interruption of discussion of particular topics.

The Hostility/Support Scale identifies the presence of hostility, criticism, or support in members' responses to each other. This scale measures change in affect and helps identify the transition between Phase II, in which conflict and negative emotion are part of the group's developmental work, and Phase III, in which the group begins to work more cooperatively (Beck, 1983). This scale can be used to assess subgroup affective responses toward one member, or dyadic behavior by connecting the ratings to speaker/spoken-to identification.

The Experiencing Scale assesses an individual member's self-exploration and a therapist's or fellow member's response to that exploration (Klein et al., 1986). Here, the scales have been applied to the study of group development, in which the scale has been found to be helpful in identifying fluctuating levels in the member's awareness, understanding, and articulation of group-level issues both individually and collectively (Lewis, 1985).

The speech behavior measures show the participants' levels of activity in the group, which is one source of data about the leadership roles; the use of pronouns by members, subgroups, or the whole group; and the identification of speaker/spoken to (Beck, Eng, & Brusa, 1989; Eng & Beck, 1982). The Sociometric Test of Leadership Emergence has been designed for the identification of the four leadership roles in the group (Brusa et al., 1994). The whole set of measures produces data about intrapsychic work, interpersonal issues and work, and group-as-a-whole behavior related to both personal and group structural changes.

The PWORS

The PWORS is based on psychoanalytic theory (Ezriel, 1973; Freud, 1921/1951; Malan, 1976a, 1976b), including object relations theory (Bion, 1959). It is also based on the work of Stock and Thelan (1958) and Hill (1965a). The PWORS is designed to assess basic constructs related to these theories: the presence and complexity of psychodynamic work, the reference to objects or persons (Object Focus), and whether object linking takes place during the group interaction. The term *Object Linking* refers to the identification of a shared interpersonal process between a unit of the group and two other objects. The PWORS builds on Hill's work with the HIM and seeks to focus more directly on the measurement of therapeutic work in the group. In contrast to the HIM, the PWORS defines work on the basis of psychodynamic and object relations theory (Piper & McCallum, 1988; Piper, McCallum, & Azim, 1992). Change is hypothesized to be directly related to the accomplishment of psychodynamic work, especially the identification of two or more dynamic components that are in conflict.

The PWORS defines four categories that describe statements according to the level of work present. It also notes whether the objects addressed in the statement are internal or external to the group. The categories of work and nonwork are defined according to the principles of psychodynamic theory regarding the types of understanding that facilitate therapeutic growth. For instance, the presence and complexity of dynamic components such as wishes, anxieties, and defenses are factors in determining the category definitions.

Work here is defined as an attempt by a group member to understand the problems of one or more members of the group or of the group as a whole in terms of conflict among dynamic components. Dynamic components are internal forces such as wishes, reactive anxiety, defensive processes, and dynamic expressions that affect one or more members or the whole group. The conflict may take place within one member, between two or more members, or the group as a whole. The proportion of an individual's participation that is rated as work with PWORS measurement (self-based work) has been found to correlate with positive outcome measures of psychotherapy and with psychological mindedness. In the analysis of Group A, data summarized for the group as a whole was used to compare the different parts of the session.

The IGIPS

The IGIPS is designed to test assumptions underlying an interpersonal and interaction-oriented approach to group therapy. The system reflects principles in the work of Yalom (1985) and Budman and Gurman (1988). These theories contend that group cohesiveness is the most influential factor in whether the therapeutic potential of the group is realized. *Cohesiveness* is defined as "the connectedness of the group" manifested in working together toward a common therapeutic goal; constructive engagement around a common theme; and an open, trusting attitude that allows members to share personal material. The IGIPS measures components of group cohesiveness. Individual change occurs in a group through the replay, recognition, and acknowledgment of the individual's issues and problems. Originally conceived of as a global scale used in earlier research studies, the IGIPS' creators established a link between cohesiveness and outcome at the group level. Group cohesion is comparable to the therapeutic alliance in individual psychotherapy.

The team then turned its attention to a process measure that would rate each statement. The IGIPS is an attempt to operationalize cohesiveness at the behavioral level of individual acts in order to relate it to outcome for both individuals and groups. There are many behavior categories measuring the components of interaction. When analyzed together, they can demonstrate the presence or absence of cohesion. The categories cover emotional tone; positive–negative statements; topic; awareness of self and others; interpersonal sensitivity; the concept of connectedness; and the identification of the roles of main actor, facilitator, and therapist. A method of reducing items creates a smaller number of categories. This also allows more flexibility in generating categories for different studies. The system identifies the main actors in any segment rated, the level of cohesiveness present, and the components of cohesive behavior. The data can be summarized at any of the layers of the group system or subsystems.

Three Complementary Systems for Coding the Process of Therapeutic Dialogue

The NOTA, PSCS, and STT are a set of measures that focus on different aspects of the transformation of meaning and its impact on the psychotherapeutic process.

The NOTA

Building on earlier work by Tracey (1986), Tsang developed the NOTA to track shifts in the therapy agenda or topic. The NOTA measures behaviors related to theoretical concepts widely regarded as basic aspects of the therapeutic process: group cohesiveness and the therapeutic alliance. This discovery-oriented measure tracks the client's and therapist's control over the content of clinical narratives, their timing, and the sequence of introduction of new content.

The goal is to identify certain characteristics of the manner in which clients and therapists work together. At each speech turn, the NOTA identifies whether the turn continues the topic and characters from the previous turn (nonshift), or whether it is a mediated or abrupt shift. In a mediated shift, a reference is made to the content of the previous turn, whereas an abrupt shift is a clear departure from the preceding turns. Interruptions are also coded. The NOTA reports on different degrees of engagement ranging from collaboration, adaptation, and influencing to noncollaboration or disruption. Significance is placed on the therapeutic alliance and the patterns of negotiation that appear to be associated with dropout or successful engagement in therapy.

Data measurements can be reported about individual member's level of activity (number of speech turns) and communication style (ratio of interruptions to speech turns). Group-as-a-whole levels of continuity or discontinuity and positive engagement are assessed by aggregating the types of shifts. Control of the agenda is assessed by comparing the number of therapist and client theme introductions.

The PSCS

The PSCS was designed to assess the management of interpersonal space in therapy. The PSCS evolved from clinical experience with the therapeutic dynamics involved when working with individuals with borderline personality disorder. The concept of psychological space is based on Winnicott's (1958) theory of the role of transitional objects and transitional phenomena in early developmental experience. The PSCS focuses on the potential for openness to meanings and the potential to sustain a state of uncertainty, possibility, and questioning, which requires the tolerance of anxiety. The importance of expressing possibility in verbal communication is a primary focus here and is thought to strongly influence the therapeutic alliance and depth of exploration by the patient.

Speech turns are defined as either Opening or Closing, with several subcategories rated within each. Speech turns are also designated as Tentative or Definitive in format. The goal of the PSCS is to identify the presence or absence of conditions necessary for the openness to and processing of new information. Measures are generated for tracking each group participant on the proportions of Opening to Closing statements and Tentative to Definitive statements. Data summarized for the group as a whole allow comparison of whole sessions early and late in the group process. In Group A, Phase II to Phase III segments of Session 3 were compared.

The STT

The STT examines the way in which clients formulate and reformulate meanings (i.e., meaning structure and patterns of relations) during the psychotherapy process. The research identifies key words or phrases that appear to be linked to changing perceptions and concepts, and tracks how the change takes place. This is a discovery-oriented process that looks at the macrostory level, speech features, and closed–open forms of modal expression. Closed represents the expression of constraint or obligation, whereas open represents the indication of variation or possibility.

Building on recent work in discourse analysis applied to the field of psychology (Edwards & Potter, 1992; Potter & Wetherell, 1987; Shiffrin, 1994), Chambon (1993) focused initially on individual psychotherapy and is now expanding into family and group therapy. The STT assumes that meaning structure and patterns of relations are anchored in the ways that individuals use language to express themselves and to address one another. Transformations in meaning structure and patterns of relations are accompanied by changes in language use. This gives a microanalysis of individual speech patterns and their evolution in the context of interaction.

This method is not based on any particular theory about change. However, the method documents the generation of meaning and movement, corresponding in psychological terms to "process." The STT tracks the recurrence, elaboration, and expansion of word patterns.

The method is currently focused on lexical elaboration and tracks the following features:

> *Narrative, on the macrostory level:*
>> Character
>> Narrator
>> Spatiotemporal scenes
> *Speech:*
>> Speech turn
>> Individual words, phrases, and word groupings used preferentially
> *Closed versus Open forms of modal expressions:*
>> Grammatical subject position
>> Source of action or relation.

Future plans include the development of lexical semantic connotation.

The SAVI

The SAVI was designed to assess the potential for transferring information through verbal and nonverbal (i.e, voice, pace, affect, and timing) means. It also assesses the problem-solving potential in groups. The SAVI is based on several important theories, including Lewin's (1951) idea that to the extent that restraining forces are reduced, the driving forces inherently related to the goal will be increased. Howard and Scott's (1965) theory that all behavior can be viewed as either approaching or avoiding problems that lie on the path toward a goal influenced the category system structurally. The SAVI assesses communication as a product of a system (von Bertalanffy, 1968) rather than as a characteristic of an individual. The aim of the system is to assess the potential for communication, or whether "information transfer" has been achieved. The assumption is that this would allow problem solving to take place and facilitate the accomplishment of a group's tasks.

The author's expectations are that data from the SAVI ratings, when organized into the SAVI grid, will result in consistent and recognizable patterns of communication that can be used to predict the probability of change. For example, ambiguity or contradiction are considered noise (Shannon & Weaver, 1964) and prevent the transfer of information. Approach behaviors must actually cross a boundary and be received by the listener.

In therapy contexts, the task of the group is to develop a problem-solving communication pattern to facilitate individual change. Nine classes of behavior form the SAVI matrix. In each of the nine classes of behavior, various categories for rating are defined. The three rows of the grid are broadly defined as the following: avoiding exchange of information; approaching a meaningful exchange or communication; and contingent, in which the behavior is neither approach nor avoidance, and its usefulness must be determined by other components of the interaction. The three columns of the grid classify the content of information shared: Person, Data, and Orientation. Measurements can be produced for group-as-a-whole, subgroup, dyad, or individual aspects of the group system.

The SAVI was originally designed to study educational group processes, but it has since been applied to medical, psychiatric, and other work settings. More recently, the analysis has been adapted to use within the group, family, and individual treatment contexts to help clients increase their awareness of their communication patterns and the consequences of those patterns in their relationships.

The SASB

The SASB is based on a well-developed line of thinking from Sullivan's (1953) translation of psychoanalytic theory into an interpersonal perspective. Murray's (1938) list of needs, related to Sullivan's view, was then translated into the Interpersonal Circumplex by Leary (1957). Benjamin's (1974, 1984, 1994) own integrative theoretical work, which also draws on Bowlby's (1969) and Asendorpf and Baudonniere's (1993), is the basis for the system, which she developed and which has received wide application in research on individual therapy. The system has recently been applied clinically (MacKenzie, 1990) to selecting patients for group therapy.

The SASB codes all interpersonal behaviors on a circumplex of possible behaviors based on several underlying dimensions. Several descriptive categories for behavior are arranged according to the anchoring underlying concepts that define the central axes. The circumplex is defined by two axes with polarized definitions: love versus hate and enmeshment versus differentiation. The number of categories allows for clear distinctions and provides concreteness to the operational definition of the axes. In addition, the thought or speech units are rated according to whether the speaker is directing action toward another, reacting to another, or acting or reacting to the self. Both individual behavior and the perception of others are viewed as being based on psychodynamics learned in early family relationships. The SASB model can clarify an individual's learned set of expectations and how these distort his or her perceptions of others. The model accomplishes this through a comparison of group members' views with each other or with a rater's more objective assessment of the dialogue.

This complex system can be used to define the problems, goals, and steps in achieving goals for an individual client. It can also be used to identify interpersonal dynamics in dyadic, familial, or group contexts. The categories are defined in interpersonally oriented terms.

Currently, the system is being used to operationalize the steps of therapeutic change identified by Benjamin (1996a, 1996b).

1. Collaborating against problem patterns.
2. Learning about patterns, where they come from, and what they are for.
3. Blocking maladaptive patterns.
4. Enabling the will to change.
5. Learning new patterns.

SUMMARY OF CONCEPTS USED IN THE NINE SYSTEMS

Table 15.1 shows the main dimensions that are addressed by the nine systems of analysis: Affect, Information, Defensive/Open, Focus, Level of Activity, Roles, and Power.

The Affect column is predominantly focused on the positive–negative dimension of affect, which has appeared in studies of relationships in many contexts. It is generally considered a crucial dimension, influencing the quality of relationships, cohesion, group development, leadership selection, and outcome of task behavior. Most of the systems have codes for affect for statements made from any group member to any other person in the group. The MLSS looks at this dimension, with a particular focus on the designated leader–member relationship.

The Information column addresses the idea that for change to take place in the individual, some form of data or information must be exchanged between the speaker and the others in the group. Whether the issue being addressed is intrapsychic, interpersonal (the relationship addressed being in the group or elsewhere), or at the group-as-a-whole level, or whether the issue is historic or here and now, the work is done through engagement with others and through a shared focus on the topic by the whole group. None of the systems would consider long-monologue, individual therapy in the group context to be highly desirable.

All the systems have included either intrapsychic or interpersonal concepts in the Defensive/Open column. This reflects the way group processes and the potential for change stir strong responses such as anxiety or depression in group members. The response to these experiences then depends on the capacity of each individual and the group to do therapeutic work. This in turn depends on the willingness of individuals to participate in a change process and the capacity of group members and leaders to facilitate relevant work processes in others. There are measures in this set of systems that reflect all of these aspects of group process. The conceptualization of defensive/open behavior, of course, has a long history in theories of pathology and treatment methods. The earlier systems leaned heavily on formulations based in a psychodynamic orientation, and this continues in the present. Other recently designed systems have incorporated a more social psychological or linguistic influence. Newer systems have also become more behaviorally focused, requiring less interpretation of inference on the rater's part. There are some powerful tools here that, used together, might deepen the understanding of the work of therapy and the processes through which change takes place in group contexts.

The Focus column shows that many systems identify the person about whom the speaker is communicating as well as the person being addressed. With the MLSS, Cytrynbaum also rates levels of inference in a speaker's statement regarding his or her relation to the leader. Dugo, who is part of the GDM group, identifies the focus of the entire group on group-level normative-organizational issues versus personal exploration issues. Chambon adds an identification of the spatiotemporal scene to character and narrator coding.

The Level of Activity column shows that all systems have some way of coding the speaker. Some also have measures of time, number of words, or number of statements to assess the percentage of group time that is used by each participant.

The Roles column does not have entries for all systems. Those systems that do identify roles primarily distinguish between client and therapist (i.e., the formal roles in the group system that are relevant to the task of therapy). Several systems also recognize that group clients may serve facilitating, interviewing, or confronting functions in relation to each other and that some individuals may have more consistent informal roles. The MLSS describes specialist roles, whereas the GDM identifies emerging informal leadership roles with a sociometric measure. The GDM system then relates these roles to behavioral measures. The SAVI analysis uses clusters of codes to identify roles unique to any particular group interaction. The HIM recognizes that clients may take the therapist role and IGIPS identifies a main actor role.

Several dimensions of the concept of power are found in four of the systems. They include dependence and counterdependence versus independence (the MLSS); connectedness, which is relevant to cohesion (the IGIPS); collaboration versus disruption (the NOTA); and influence on the level or style of discourse and control of information (the SAVI).

The dimensions in Table 15.1 address important group structural and emotional issues. The nine systems of analysis cover several dimensions describing intrapsychic and interpersonal behavior. If we add to this the variety of ways in which the data collected can be summarized (i.e., by individual, dyad, subgroup, or group as a whole) and the variety of other measures to which these process measures can be related, researchers have rich resources for furthering the study of group psychotherapy process and of the group system and its subsystems.

FUTURE DIRECTIONS

Mahoney's (1991) integrative book on human change highlights the importance of studying the complex realm of interpersonal interaction and how it effects individual growth and change:

> The impact of humans upon humans is, epistomologically, one of the most fascinating and frightening facts of the social and behavioral sciences. That impact is fundamentally related to at least three things: human emotionality, self-reflection, and the use of symbols. . . . Studies have taught us that the human mind is unmistakably interpersonal. (p. 263)

The collection of concepts and measures in this book presents an opportunity to assess these kinds of dimensions in processes at a number of levels of the system that is a psychotherapy group. The further study of events, micro- and macroprocess changes, substantive content, and interpersonal communication characteristics looked at over time in the group may be facilitated by a theoretical framework such as systems theory. A systems theory approach to generating a framework for the study of such a complex entity as a psychotherapy group facilitates the investigation of what is known, what needs clearer development or measurement, and how the levels within the system might interact. As outlined in detail by Miller (1978), and summarized by Miller and Miller (1992), a systems approach must address several critical dimensions, including structure, process, and levels. An earlier attempt was made to bring a systems theory focus to group psychotherapy (Durkin, 1981). It influenced a number of people in their practice of group therapy. This has been represented most recently by Agazarian's (1997) systems-centered group psychotherapy. With the currently available measures, however, a more detailed and comprehensive research approach to the complexity of group process could be made within a systems framework.

This effort could be enhanced by drawing on a variety of new developments in related fields. Some examples are as follows: Organizational psychology could offer its new models, which define more than one level of analysis and help address issues such as the effects of context on the individual (Rousseau, 1985) and isomorphic relationships and discontinuities between levels (House, Rousseau, & Thomas-Hunt, 1995). Dynamical systems theory, applied to psychotherapy, tracks synergetic effects with time series analyses. In this analysis, patterns are identified that at first may have appeared to be unpredictable, chaotic processes (Tschacher & Scheier, 1997).

In addition, new theoretical work exists on change processes, and new concepts and methods are emerging from research on individual psychotherapy. First, researchers must restate their primary focus. Drawing again on Mahoney (1991), the critical core issue that those who study group psychotherapy need to address is the same as the one all psychotherapy theory must address:

> "Society" . . . emphasizes our essential connectedness to one another and, simultaneously, the ultimate recursiveness (reflexivity) of our understanding and activities. When supplemented with the insights derived from studies of human psychological development . . . , two clear statements emerge: emotionally charged human relationships constitute the most powerful contexts in which significant psychological change is facilitated, neglected, or hampered; and relationships with the self—which are forged and revised in interpersonal relationships —are central to the quality of an individual's life experience. Together, these assertions reflect the complex and generative reciprocity of self and social system. Out of respect for that complexity and reciprocity, professional services must consistently honor both the individual in the system and the system in the individual. (pp. 263–264)

In group psychotherapy, researchers have direct access to the individual, the relationship to a therapist, and to a microcosm of the social system in the form of peers sharing a task and a process. Research on group therapy should also "consistently honor both the individual in the system and the system in the individual" (Mahoney, 1991, p. 264). This would be accomplished if future studies focus on an analysis of aspects of the group system, and their interaction and impact on the individual, mirroring Mahoney's plea.

Working from a systems perspective to organize future research would have the additional benefit of facilitating a more integrative theory-building process. Some of that kind of benefit can be observed in recent work on personality, pathology, and individual psychotherapy. Some examples of this are Kiesler's (1996) integration of "Sullivan's interpersonal therapy and its contemporary interpersonal theory derivatives, interactional psychiatry, and research in nonverbal communication" (p. xi); Safran and Segal's (1990) integration of interpersonal process perspectives and cognitive therapy; and Benjamin's (1986, 1993) work, as seen in this book and other publications, which brings together ideas and methods from psychodynamic, cognitive, and interpersonal theoretical sources. In concert with this work is the effort to integrate concepts from chaos and complexity theories with theory of psychological processes. Masterpasqua and Perna (1997) bring together the thinking of a group of writers on this subject who represent a range of interests in psychology: developmental psychology, psychopathology, and individual and group psychotherapies. These approaches build on multiple sources of theory to provide a more meaningful and detailed tracking of the interpersonal communication process.

Beyond the psychotherapy field, there are additional areas in which new theory and research may contribute concepts and measures on the various aspects of the system that are now missing in psychotherapy research. One example of this has to do with the peer affiliative process. There has been so much focus in psychology and psychotherapy on the parent–child bond that the significant sibling and peer experiences have been neglected. Many psychotherapy clients have had damaging experiences in the sibling and peer contexts that interfered with healthy development. For others, sibling and peer relationships may have been a significant support in coping with difficulties in early family relationships. Group therapy is a context where corrective new experiences with peers can have a powerful impact on clients.

Directly relevant to this impact is work on the effect of interpersonal feedback in group contexts. Feedback has been found to relate to changes in group behavior, to changes in insight into the self, and to changes in behavior outside the therapy group. The relative effects of positive, negative, or combined positive–negative feedback (Morran, Robinson, & Stockton, 1985) have been examined, and the results support a combination of both positive and negative feedback for the recipient. This is a line of investigation that could clearly be combined with measures in this book to further illuminate and differentiate the impact that therapists or fellow group members have on clients in group therapy.

Cognitive–behavioral studies of behavioral rehearsal and its significance in the change process can contribute new insights into the processes that occur in a therapy group, which is a rare context for receiving feedback and support to integrate new behaviors and experiences into a client's emerging self-image.

This is not an exhaustive overview of the creative new developments but an illustration given to highlight the fact that the integration of multiple approaches and sources of information are taking place in the social sciences generally, and in the field of psychotherapy research and theory building, and that would be equally generative if applied to group psychotherapy.

REFERENCES

Agazarian, Y. M. (1997). *Systems-centered therapy for groups.* New York: Guilford Press.

Agazarian, Y. M., & Peters, R. (1981). *The visible and invisible group: Two perspectives on group psychotherapy and process.* London: Routlege & Kegan Paul.

Allen, F. H. (1942). *Psychotherapy with children.* New York: Norton.

Asendorpf, J. B., & Baudonniere, P. M. (1993). Self-awareness and other awareness: Mirror self-recognition and synchronic imitation among unfamiliar peers. *Developmental Psychology, 29,* 88–95.

Bales, R. F. (1953). The equilibrium problem in small groups. In T. Parsons, R. F. Bales, & E. A. Shils (Eds.), *Working papers in the theory of action* (pp. 111–161). New York: Free Press.

Bales, R. F. (1958). Task roles and social roles in problem-solving groups. In E. E. Maccoby, T. M. Newcomb, & L. Hartley (Eds.), *Readings in social psychology* (pp. 437–447). New York: Holt, Rinehart & Winston.

Bales, R. F., & Strodtbeck, F. L. (1951). Phases in group problem-solving. *Journal of Abnormal and Social Psychology, 46,* 485–495.

Beck, A. P. (1974). Phases in the development of structure in therapy and encounter groups. In D. Wexler & L. N. Rice (Eds.), *Innovations in client-centered therapy* (pp. 421–463). New York: Wiley Interscience.

Beck, A. P. (1981a). Developmental characteristics of the system forming process. In J. Durkin (Ed.), *Living groups: Group psychotherapy and general system theory* (pp. 316–332). New York: Brunner/Mazel.

Beck, A. P. (1981b). The study of group phase development and emergent leadership. *Group, 5,* 48–54.

Beck, A. P. (1983). A process analysis of group development. *Group, 7,* 19–26.

Beck, A. P., Eng, A. M., & Brusa, J. B. (1989). The evolution of leadership during group development. *Group, 13,* 155–164.

Beck, A. P., & Keil, A. V. (1967). Observations on the development of client-centered, time-limited, therapy groups. *Counseling center discussion papers, 13.* Chicago: University of Chicago Library.

Benjamin, L. S. (1974). Structural Analysis of Social Behavior. *Psychological Review, 81,* 392–425.

Benjamin, L. S. (1984). Principles of prediction using Structural Analysis of Social

Behavior. In R. A. Zucker, J. Aronoff, & A. J. Rabin (Eds.), *Personality and the prediction of behavior* (pp. 121–173). New York: Academic Press.

Benjamin, L. S. (1986). Using SASB to add social parameters to Axis I of DSM-III. In T. Millon & G. L. Klerman (Eds.), *Contemporary issues in psychopathology: Toward the DSM-IV* (pp. 599–638). New York: Guilford Press.

Benjamin, L. S. (1993). *Diagnosis and treatment of personality disorders: A structural approach.* New York: Guilford Press.

Benjamin, L. S. (1994). SASB: A bridge between personality theory and clinical psychology. *Psychological Inquiry, 5,* 273–316.

Benjamin, L. S. (1996a). An interpersonal theory of personality disorders. In J. F. Clarkin (Ed.), *Major theories of personality disorder* (pp. 141–220). New York, Guilford.

Benjamin, L. S. (1996b). *Interpersonal diagnosis and treatment of personality disorders* (2nd ed.). New York: Guilford.

Bion, W. R. (1948). Experiences in groups: I. *Human Relations, 1,* 314–320.

Bion, W. R. (1959). *Experiences in groups.* New York: Basic Books.

Bion, W. R. (1961). *Experiences in groups.* London: Tavistock.

Bowlby, J. (1969). *Attachment and loss: Vol. 1. Attachment.* London: Tavistock Institute of Human Relations.

Brusa, J. A., Stone, M. H., Beck, A. P., Dugo, J. M., & Peters, L. N. (1994). A sociometric test to identify emergent leader and member roles: Phase 1. *International Journal of Group Psychotherapy, 44,* 79–100.

Budman, S. H., & Gurman, A. S. (1988). *Theory and practice of brief therapy.* New York: Guilford Press.

Chambon, A. (1993, June). *Dialogical strategies of therapeutic interventions: A comparative analysis of narrative focus and shifts in the Gloria tapes.* Paper presented at the meeting of the Society for Psychotherapy Research, Pittsburgh, PA.

Cytrynbaum, S., & Conran, P. (1979). Impediments to the process of learning. *Illinois School Research and Development, 15*(2), 49–65.

Dugo, J. M., & Beck, A. P. (1983). Tracking a group's focus on normative-organizational or personal-exploration issues. *Group, 7,* 17–26.

Durkin, J. (Ed.). (1981). *Living groups: Group psychotherapy and general system theory.* New York: Brunner/Mazel.

Edwards, D., & Potter, J. (1992). *Discursive psychology.* Newberry Park, CA: Sage.

Eng, A. M., & Beck, A. P. (1982). Speech behavior measures of group psychotherapy process. *Group, 6,* 37–48.

Ezriel, H. (1973). Psychoanalytic group therapy. In L. R.. Wolberg & E. K. Schwartz (Eds.), *Group therapy: 1973—An overview* (pp. 183–210). New York: Intercontinental Medical Book Corporation.

Foulkes, S. H. (1948). *Introduction to group-analytic psychotherapy.* London: Heinemann.

Freud, S. (1951). Group psychology and the analysis of the ego. In J. Strachey

(Ed. and Trans.), *The standard edition of the complete psychological works of Sigmund Freud* (Vol. 18, pp. 69–143). London: Hogarth Press. (Original work published 1921)

Gendlin, E. T. (1962). *Experiencing and the creation of meaning: A philosophical and psychological approach to the subjective.* New York: Free Press of Glencoe.

Gibbard, G. S., Hartman, J., & Mann, R. D. (Eds.). (1974). *Analysis of groups.* San Francisco: Jossey-Bass.

Hallberg, M. (1995). The impact of gender and authority: Differential responses of males versus females in the context of three group relations conferences held in the Tavistock tradition (Doctoral dissertation, Northwestern University, 1995). *Dissertation Abstracts International, 56*(07), 4061B.

Hill, W. F. (1965a). *Hill Interaction Matrix.* Los Angeles: University of Southern California, Youth Study Center.

Hill, W. F. (1965b). *Hill Interaction Matrix scoring manual.* Los Angeles: University of Southern California, Youth Study Center.

Hill, W. F. (1973). *Hill Interaction Matrix (HIM): Conceptual framework for undertaking groups.* New York: University Associates.

House, R., Rousseau, D. M., & Thomas-Hunt, M. (1995). The meso paradigm: A framework for the integration of micro and macro organizational behavior. *Research in Organizational Behavior, 17,* 71–114.

Howard, A., & Scott, R. A. (1965). A proposed framework for the analysis of stress in the human organism. *Journal of Applied Behavioral Science, 10,* 141–160.

Karterud, S. (1990). *Group Emotionality Rating System manual.* Oslo, Norway: Ulleval University Hospital.

Kiesler, D. J. (1996). *Contemporary interpersonal theory and research: Personality, psychopathology and psychotherapy.* New York: Wiley.

Klein, M. (1946). Notes on some schizoid mechanisms. In M. M. R. Khan (Ed.), *Envy and gratitude and other works 1946–1963* (pp. 1–24). London: Hogarth Press.

Klein, M. (1952). *Contributions to psycho-analysis 1921–1945.* New York: Anglobooks. (Original work published 1948)

Klein, M. H., Mathieu-Coughlan, P., & Kiesler, D. J. (1986). The experiencing scales. In L. S. Greenberg & W. Pinsof (Eds.), *The psychotherapeutic process: A research handbook* (pp. 21–71). New York: Guilford Press.

Leary, T. (1957). *Interpersonal diagnosis of personality: A functional theory and methodology for personality evaluation.* New York: Ronald Press.

Lewin, K. (1951). *Field theory in social psychology.* New York: Harper.

Lewis, C. M. (1985). Symbolization of experience in the process of group development. *Group, 9,* 29–34.

MacKenzie, K. R. (1990). *Introduction to time-limited group psychotherapy.* Washington, DC: American Psychiatric Press.

Mahoney, M. J. (1991). *Human change processes: The scientific foundations of psychotherapy*. New York: Basic Books.

Malan, D. H. (1976a). *The frontier of brief psychotherapy*. New York: Plenum.

Malan, D. H. (1976b). *Toward the validation of dynamic psychotherapy*. New York: Plenum.

Mann, R., Arnold, S., Binder, J., Cytrynbaum, S., Newman, B., Ringwald, B., Ringwald, J., & Rosenwein, R. (1970). *The college classroom: Conflict, change, and learning*. New York, Wiley.

Mann, R., Gibbard, G., & Hartman, J. (1967). *Interpersonal styles and group development: An analysis of the member–leader relationship*. New York: Wiley.

Masterpasqua, F., & Perna, P. A. (1997). *The psychological meaning of chaos*. Washington, DC: American Psychological Association.

Miller, J. G. (1978). *Living systems*. New York: McGraw-Hill.

Miller, J. G., & Miller, J. L. (1992). Cybernetics, general systems theory, and living systems theory. In R. L. Levine & H. E. Fitzgerald (Eds.), *Analysis of dynamic psychological systems* (Vol. 1, pp. 9–34). New York: Plenum.

Moreno, J. L. (1934). *Who shall survive? A new approach to the problem of human relationships*. Boston: Beacon Press.

Moreno, J. L. (1950). Sociometric theory of leadership and isolation. *Sociometry, 13*, 382–383.

Morran, D. K., Robinson, F. F., & Stockton, R. A. (1985). Feedback exchange in counseling groups: An analysis of message content and receiver acceptance as a function of leader versus member delivery, session, and valence. *Journal of Counseling Psychology, 32*, 57–67.

Murray, H. A. (1938). *Explorations in personality*. New York: Oxford Press.

Parsons, T., Bales, R. F., & Shils, E. A. (Eds.). (1953). *Working papers in the theory of action*. New York: Free Press.

Piper, W. E., & McCallum, M. (1988). *Psychodynamic Work and Object Rating System (PWORS) manual*. Unpublished manuscript.

Piper, W. E., McCallum, M., & Azim, H. F. A. (1992). *Adaptation to loss through short-term group psychotherapy*. New York: Guilford Press.

Potter, J., & Wetherell, M. (1987). *Discourse and social psychology: Beyond attitudes and behavior*. London: Sage.

Rank, O. (1936). *Will therapy*. New York: Knopf.

Robertson, J. (1952). *A two-year old goes to hospital* [Film], (Available from New York University Film Library, New York, NY)

Robertson, J. (1953). Some responses of young children to loss of maternal care. *Nursing Times, 49*, 382–386.

Rogers, C. R. (1951). *Client-centered therapy: Its current practices, implications, and theory*. Boston: Houghton Mifflin.

Rousseau, D. M. (1985). Issues of level in organizational research: Multi-level and cross level perspectives. *Research in Organizational Behavior, 7*, 1–37.

Safran, J. D., & Segal, Z. V. (1990). *Interpersonal process in cognitive therapy*. New York: Basic Books.

Shannon, C. E., & Weaver, W. (1964). *The mathematical theory of communication*. Urbana: University of Illinois Press.

Shiffrin, D. (1994). *Approaches to discourse*. Cambridge, MA: Blackwell.

Skinner, B. F. (1939). *The behavior of organisms*. New York: Appleton-Century-Crofts.

Socor, B. (1989). Listening for historical truth: A relative discussion. *Clinical Social Work Journal, 17*, 103–115.

Stock, D., & Thelen, H. (1958). *Emotional dynamics and group culture*. Washington, DC: National Training Laboratories.

Sullivan, H. S. (1953). *The interpersonal theory of psychiatry*. New York: Norton.

Tracey, T. J. (1986). Interactional correlates of premature termination. *Journal of Consulting and Clinical Psychology, 54*, 784–788.

Tschacher, W., & Scheier, C. (1997). Complex psychological systems: Synergetics and chaos. In F. Masterpasqua & P. A. Perna (Eds.), *The psychological meaning of chaos* (pp. 273–298). Washington, DC: American Psychological Association.

von Bertalanffy, L. (1950). The theory of open systems in physics and biology. *Science, 3*, 23–29.

von Bertalanffy, L. (1968). *General system theory: Foundation, development, applications*. New York: Braziller.

Whitaker, D. S., & Lieberman, M. A. (1962). Methodological issues in the assessment of total-group phenomena in group therapy. *International Journal of Group Psychotherapy, 12*, 312–325.

Winnicott, D. W. (1958). Transitional objects and transitional phenomena. In *Collected Papers: Through Paediatrics to Psycho-Analysis*. London: Tavistock.

Yalom, I. D. (1985). *The theory and practice of group psychotherapy* (3rd ed.). New York: Basic Books.

16

A SUMMARY OF THE APPLICATION OF THE SYSTEMS OF ANALYSIS TO GROUP A, SESSION 3

CAROL M. LEWIS AND ARIADNE P. BECK

In this chapter we summarize the results of the application of the nine systems of analysis to one group psychotherapy session, Session 3 of Group A. The session provided a common database from which examples could be chosen to illustrate some of the variables and category definitions used by the systems. We compare the analyses made by each of the systems to highlight the value of examining data from multiple perspectives. To accomplish this, we present results within the sections of Session 3 identified as part of Phase II, the transition or phase shift, and Phase III as well as across the entire session. The authors report data for the group as a whole and about individual members of the group as well as their role and function in the group process. Group A was a 15-session, time-limited outpatient group. Session 3 was chosen because it illustrates a phase shift, from Phase II to Phase III, and portions of the session from the two different phases contain interaction that might differ in some ways.

In the second phase of group development, a group must establish the structure that will allow the members to address their work effectively. This includes goal setting, the development of basic norms, and the emergence of informal leaders. These processes generally stimulate anxiety about differences among members, especially with regard to their mode of self-expression, and about how these differences will affect the group's ability to work together. Issues of competition, hostility, and power become manifest in reaction to the perception of differences, and one individual, called the *Scapegoat Leader* in Beck's (1983) theory, is often criticized or blamed for the stress felt during this period. For the group to work effectively, members must find a way to manage conflict and differences by means other than aggression and power. They must also recognize the importance of anxiety about self-disclosure and the question of acceptance by the group as factors in the group's dilemma at this time. In Phase III, the members begin to work together more cooperatively, taking up the challenge of self-disclosure, and assisting one another with interest, inquiry, and more careful listening.

Session 3, as well as Sessions 1, 2, 4, and 5, are described in chapter 5. The description in chapter 5 provides readers with a context both before and after the target session used for the comparison. Chapter 5 describes Session 3 in terms of the flow of topics discussed and includes some transcript material to provide readers with a sense of the way the members expressed their concerns.

Although the entire session was available for the authors' use, four smaller segments were chosen within the session for those who wanted to rate a smaller set of material. Following are brief descriptions of the segments:

- Segment 1 is from Phase II (also known as Units 64–66 in the transcript). It is considered part of the members' efforts to begin to understand their participation in scapegoating a member named Joe.
- Segment 2 is from Phase II (also known as Unit 69). Is a reassertion of the anger toward and criticism of Joe.
- Segment 3 is from the transition section between Phases II and III (also known as Units 71–73). The group members resolve their issues with Joe and acknowledge their fears of self-disclosure.
- Segment 4 is from Phase III (also known as Units 82–84). It is an example of the type of data sharing about self and personal history in which the members engaged during the early part of Phase III.

The first two segments were taken from Phase II. As the session began, the group members were working to resolve the issues and tasks of the second phase of group development. The group members began by expressing concern about the events of the previous session and the need to process them.

In the first segment, members were examining how they had been acting and were exploring their feelings and reactions. They were actively inquiring of one another, especially of the scapegoated member, Joe, in examining what had been happening and trying to understand it. The group members discussed individual perceptions and reactions to Joe, but they seemed to be intensifying and clarifying their awareness of feelings about what had happened and how they understood it rather than putting additional pressure on Joe.

In Segment 2, one group member, Diane, continued to voice her irritation with, criticism of, and inability to accept Joe. Diane expressed many opinions about Joe and her reactions to him, and others focused on trying to help her see these as opinions and reactions and to compare them with those of other members. They tried to examine her persistence in focusing on her reaction to Joe and tried to help her gain a perspective on her own behavior.

Finally, a focus emerged that the group members found it hard to jump in and talk about some things because of anxiety rather than because of Joe. Segment 3 was part of the phase shift itself. Martha stated, "We're not all quite sure how, you know, we're gonna jump in and bare our secrets" (Beck, 1970, p. 96; Beck et al., 1986, p. 690). The group members identified wishing to self-disclose, thinking ahead about it, and holding back with thoughts such as, "That'll be boring." They explored anxieties about rejection and related previous experiences of it. They directly associated "looking for a fight" with anxious avoidance of self-disclosure and then proceeded to face the task.

Segment 4 was a sample from Phase III illustrating the initial efforts of members to reveal their backgrounds. This small segment involved members listening as Martha was telling about her early family experience, and Diane worked with her, comparing experiences.

The contrast in the content of the two halves of the session is clear. In the first half of the session, still in Phase II, the group members focused on and examined part of their own interaction and the experience they had created together so far. Members stated their positions in idiosyncratic detail, comparing, challenging, and attempting to influence one another. At the phase shift, they achieved a consensus of perception and an expression of feelings of anxiety that facilitated focus on the task of self-disclosure. In the second half of the session, as Phase III began, members listened, cooperated more easily, and facilitated one another's task of sharing some personal information. There was still a significant degree of anxiety present as each one attempted self-disclosure of his or her own historical background information.

To find evidence of a transition from Phase II to Phase III of group development, Beck (1983) defined three dimensions of change in the group process. The three dimensions were chosen on the basis of a review of the literature and represent differences between the two phases that have been agreed on by theorists. The same dimensions are used to aid the summary discussion of what each of the systems of measurement found in Session 3:

1. Change from an atmosphere of tension, anger, criticism, or discomfort to one of more positive feeling and support.
2. Change from relatively defensive behavior to more open and mutually exploratory behavior.
3. Change from concern, apprehension, and struggle regarding organizational and normative issues to a focus on individual members and their personal concerns.

In the following discussion we summarize what each system of analysis showed about Session 3. Readers are referred to the chapters on each of the individual systems of analysis for further details. Because each of the systems is referred to at various times throughout this discussion, the names of the systems and the chapters where further information can be found are listed here:

- The Group Emotionality Rating System (GERS), chapter 6
- The Hill Interaction Matrix (HIM), chapter 7
- The Member–Leader Scoring System (MLSS), chapter 8
- The Group Development Process Analysis Measures (GDM), chapter 9
- The Psychodynamic Work and Object Rating System (PWORS), chapter 10
- The Individual Group Member Interpersonal Process Scale (IGIPS), chapter 11
- Three Complementary Systems for Coding the Process of Therapeutic Dialogue (STT, NOTA, and PSCS), chapter 12
- The System for Analyzing Verbal Interaction (SAVI), chapter 13
- The Structural Analysis of Social Behavior (SASB), chapter 14.

Among the systems, some are designed to use large blocks of interaction for analysis, whole sessions, or groups of sessions. Many are constructed for use with different-sized data samples, and they can be used to describe smaller portions of interaction. The authors applied their system to the transcript or audiorecording or both of the session just as they would in their use of the system in research. They unitized and rated, or coded the data as they might normally do. For some systems of measurement, the authors have provided a description of the session as a whole and have identified some aspects of process that characterize the entire session. Other systems describe differences in process dimensions between the Phase II and Phase III portions of Session 3 or differences among the sample segments.

The discussion is arranged in parts according to the period of interaction described. Tables 16.1–16.4 show the findings of each system according to periods of time during Session 3. Table 16.1 shows findings from the first half of the session, which occurred in Phase II. Table 16.2 shows findings from the phase shift or transition, and Table 16.3 shows findings for the second half of the session, which occurred in Phase III. Table 16.4 shows findings based on the ratings of the entire session. Table 16.5 shows findings from individual members.

SUMMARY OF FINDINGS FOR PHASE II

Dimension 1: A Period of Tension, Anger, Criticism, and Discomfort

To look for evidence of a transition from anger, criticism, and discomfort in Phase II to a more positive feeling and mutual support in Phase III, the GDM used the Hostility/Support Scale ratings of group members statements to the identified Scapegoat Leader. In this group, the expression of criticism and anger toward the Scapegoat Leader, Joe, occurred frequently during Phase II. During the first half of Session 3, the period during which Phase II ended in this group, some critical and angry statements to the Scapegoat Leader continued to occur. During the first sample segment, when members were reflecting on their behavior toward Joe in the last session, most statements toward him were supportive ones. During the second sample segment, one group member, Diane, expressed her frustration and ambivalence about accepting Joe, and some critical and angry statements continued to occur.

The focus of the group on Joe was identified and described by the IGIPS, and the Strategies of Telling and Talking (STT). The IGIPS identifies one main actor, Joe, in the Phase II portion of Session 3. *Main actors* are individual members whose issues are being explored by the group. The IGIPS described Joe as discussing personal issues in a general and abstract manner, and expressing little affect, qualities for which other group members criticized him and with which they felt uncomfortable. The STT described the interaction in this portion of the session as one central narrative, focused on Joe, so that most of the group members' contributions during this time period were "other focused."

Ratings of Diane and Joe with the SASB indicated that the perceptions Diane expressed about Joe were different from a neutral observer's ratings of his behavior toward her. Diane saw Joe as controlling and ignoring, and his behavior to her was rated as protective and disclosing. The STT's analysis of Diane's language during this period suggests that she strug-

TABLE 16.1
Summary of Findings from Phase II

System	Finding
IGIPS	• A middle range of cohesiveness was found. • There was one main actor, Joe, who discussed issues in a general and abstract manner with little affect.
STT	• Samples of interaction selected by the researcher showed one central narrative, focused on Joe. Most members' parts in the narrative were here-and-then focused and "other focused." • The spatiotemporal scenes were the current and recent group sessions.
HIM	• Data occurred fairly equally in each of the four content areas defined by the HIM: Topic, Group, Person, and Relationship. • Some Confrontive work was present, but the work style was mostly Speculative (47%). • Forty-one percent of the interaction fell in Quadrant IV.
GDM	• Hostility/Support Scale ratings of statements addressed to the Scapegoat Leader, Joe, indicated the expression of criticism or negative comments. • The NO/PE Scale indicated that the focus of the group was on normative and organizational issues. • In Segment 1, Experiencing Scale ratings between 2.0 and 3.0 were consistent with members describing their views of events and articulating feelings about them as they tried to understand recent aspects of the group interaction. • In Segment 2, Experiencing Scale ratings remained near Level 2.0 as members compared perspectives, challenged each other, and tried to influence one another but did not articulate feelings from an inner stance.
PSCS	• In ratings of Segment 2, 55% of the statements were rated Closing, including 38% rated in the Explanatory Definitive category and 17% rated in the Confrontive Definitive category. • Most statements were made in a Definitive format (62%) than in a Tentative format (22%). • Twelve percent of statements were rated Affirming.
SAVI	• Segments selected by the researcher showed more "opinions about the past" than "data," or facts, stated about the present. Data-opinion ratios were below 1.0. • More avoidance than approach was indicated by the ratings. Quality of verbal interaction ratios indicated a low probability of "information transfer." • The largest proportion of behaviors were those rated Influence (49%) and Compete (21%).
PWORS	• Segment 1 contained more statements rated work (62%) than nonwork (38%). • Segment 2 contained more statements rated nonwork (66%) than work (34%).
GERS	• The basic assumption of fight–flight predominated.
SASB	• Ratings of Segment 2 showed that Diane's views of Joe were discrepant from his actual behavior. Diane saw Joe as controlling and ignoring her. She saw him as walled off. The objective coding of Joe's behavior in relation to Diane described Joe as being protective of and disclosing to Diane.

Note. IGIPS = Individual Group Member Interpersonal Process Scale; STT = Strategies of Telling and Talking; HIM = Hill Interaction Matrix; GDM = Group Development Process Analysis Measures; PSCS = Psychological Space Coding System; SAVI = System for Analyzing Verbal Interaction; PWORS = Psychodynamic Work and Object Rating System; GERS = Group Emotionality Rating System; SASB = Structural Analysis of Social Behavior; NO/PE = Normative Organizational/ Personal Exploration Scale. The information reported was based on ratings of part or all of the Phase II portion of Session 3.

TABLE 16.2
Summary of Findings from the Phase Shift

System	Finding
HIM	▪ All interaction occurred in Quadrants III and IV of the HIM; 83% of the interaction was coded in the cells of Quadrant IV. ▪ The work style was Speculative, and the content included personal and relationship themes.
PWORS	▪ Forty-seven percent of the statements were rated as psychodynamic work.
GDM	▪ A higher proportion of statements were addressed to the "whole group." ▪ Experiencing Scale ratings of Level 3.0 and above indicated that the group members maintained an awareness of specific feelings. The quality of feelings were the main focus, with a description of events playing a lesser role. ▪ The group members ceased to focus on or criticize Joe. ▪ The focus of the group was in a period of transition from discussing normative to personal issues. Members acknowledged their involvement in placing Joe in the center of their action and attention to avoid their own self-disclosure.
MLSS	▪ Interaction during this period facilitated greater involvement, enactment, and expression of affect than earlier in the session.
STT	▪ Members struggled to position the self as well as the other as the focal characters in the narrative process.
SAVI	▪ The largest proportions of behaviors were rated Influence (31%), Empathize (17%), and Flight (24%).

Note. HIM = Hill Interaction Matrix; PWORS = Psychodynamic Work and Object Rating System; GDM = Group Development Process Analysis Measures; MLSS = Member–Leader Scoring System; STT = Strategies of Telling and Talking; SAVI = System for Analyzing Verbal Interaction. The information reported was based on ratings of part or all of the phase shift or transition portion of Session 3.

gled to move from the position of a recipient of actions, and commentator, to that of a subject.

The GERS identified fight–flight as the predominant basic assumption (BA) emotionality present during Session 3. One period of heightened fight–flight emotionality occurred during the Phase II part of the session. Karterud (chapter 6) notes that the BA fight–flight is one that can evoke a fear that the group will fall apart and that this may especially be so at this early time in the group's life.

The MLSS indicated that the group members were struggling with dependent and counterdependent longings, anxiety, and hostility toward the group leaders. Cytrynbaum (chapter 8) sees the hostile feelings toward the scapegoat leader as displaced hostility, aroused in relation to issues of authority evoked by the group structure and the formal leaders. Data from all of these measures add evidence that the first half of Session 3 in Group A was a period of tension, anger, criticism, and discomfort and that Joe and the therapists were the focus of that feeling.

TABLE 16.3
Findings from Phase III

System	Finding
GDM	▪ The focus of the group was on personal issues. ▪ The Scapegoat Leader, Joe, was not the focus of the interaction and was not criticized. ▪ Experiencing Scale ratings showed a modest level of self-exploration, as members tentatively began disclosing personal history.
STT	▪ The spatiotemporal scene focused on childhood stories. The narrative began with one member focusing on self, and others facilitating, and moved to a multiple narrative structure with several members narrating from the position of self, with stories mingling.
IGIPS	▪ A high range of cohesiveness was found. ▪ Disclosure of personal material, expression of affect, achievement of insight, and experience of connectedness were found more frequently than in the first half of the session. ▪ Three main actors were present: Diane, Greg, and Martha. They disclosed personal material and expressed affect and insight regarding personal issues.
HIM	▪ Most content was personal (65%). ▪ The work style was Speculative (58%). ▪ Fifty percent of the interaction fell in Quadrant IV. ▪ In Segment 4, 95% of the content was personal, 58% of the work was Speculative, and 27% of the interaction was coded as Confrontive work style with personal content.
PWORS	▪ Eighteen percent of the statements were rated as psychodynamic work.
PSCS	▪ In Segment 4 fewer closing statements were made than in Segment 2. The decrease occurred in the Confrontive Definitive category (4%). Thirty-eight percent of statements were still rated Explanatory Definitive. ▪ Affirming statements were more frequent than in Segment 2 (22%). ▪ The language mode retained the same proportions as that in Segment 2: Definitive statements 46% and Tentative statements 13%.
SAVI	▪ Ratings of Units 83 and 84 showed a predominance of Personal Information (35% and 51%) and Influence (30% and 37%) codes.
SASB	▪ Ratings of Segment 4 indicated that Diane's views of Joe, as expressed in Segment 2, corresponded to her description of her parents in this segment of interaction.
MLSS	▪ Members worked to differentiate their mothers and their fathers.
GERS	▪ The basic assumption of "pairing" occurred close to the end of the session and might have been a response to anxiety about whether the group would survive or "disintegrate."

Note. GDM = Group Development Process Analysis Measures; STT = Strategies of Telling and Talking; IGIPS = Individual Group Member Interpersonal Process Scale; HIM = Hill Interaction Matrix; PWORS = Psychodynamic Work and Object Rating System; PSCS = Psychological Space Coding System; SAVI = System for Analyzing Verbal Interaction; SASB = Structural Analysis of Social Behavior; MLSS = Member–Leader Scoring System; GERS = Group Emotionality Rating System. The information reported was based on ratings of part or all of the Phase III portion of Session 3.

TABLE 16.4

Summary of Findings for the Whole of Session 3, Group A

System	Finding
GERS	▪ A high level of basic assumption emotionality was present compared with other groups (31% of the statements). ▪ The dominant basic assumption was fight–flight. ▪ The therapist, Alice, was very active, contributing as many statements as other active members (189 statements). ▪ Joe's behavior showed the highest level of emotionality rated (49%). ▪ Diane, Martha, Alice, and Joe were the "protagonists" in expressing fight–flight and pairing emotionality.
MLSS	▪ There was a predominance of dependency and anxiety in group members (both expressed and denied affect) as well as some hostility. ▪ Diane, Martha, and Joe were the most active group members. ▪ The group struggled with dependent and counterdependent longings largely displaced from the relation to the leaders.
HIM	▪ Forty-seven percent of the group interaction occurred in the most therapeutic quadrant of the HIM, but in the cell of the quadrant requiring the least interpersonal risk. ▪ The work style of the group was Speculative (53%), and the content style was Personal (47%). ▪ The session contained 647 statements rateable with the HIM. Clients made 452 of the statements, and therapists made 195 of the statements. ▪ The primary therapist, Alice, contributed 22% of the total talk, more than would be expected if each person contributed equally (12%).
NOTA	▪ A low level of discontinuity was indicated in the session; few abrupt shifts in topic or person focus were present. Members introduced themes and characters mediated shift speech turns. ▪ Clients maintained control of the agenda, introducing themes and making shifts. ▪ Members were involved and ready to relate to what others said. This was indicated by the "resuming" form of nonshift and the "backtracking" form of mediated shift. ▪ The session was an active one packed with verbal input. There were 716 speech turns observed (Alice, 160; Helen, 58; Diane, 155; Martha, 132; Greg, 87; Joe, 82; Pat, 20; and Brad, 19).
PWORS	▪ The rate of therapist activity was similar to that of psychodynamically oriented therapists studied, but the proportion of the activity rated as psychodynamic work was different. ▪ Forty-seven percent of the statements of the Group A therapists were rated as psychodynamic work. Eighty-four percent of the statements made by therapists in the study of short-term psychodynamically oriented group therapy were rated as work. ▪ Members' behavior was similar to patients in other groups studied with this measure. In the session as a whole, members engaged in activity rated as psychodynamic work about half the time.

Note. GERS = Group Emotionality Rating System; MLSS = Member–Leader Scoring System; HIM = Hill Interaction Matrix; NOTA = Negotiation of Therapy Agenda; PWORS = Psychodynamic Work and Object Rating System. The information reported was based on ratings of the entire session.

System	Therapist			
	Alice	Helen	Greg	Joe
GDM: Sociometric test: Informal role	Emergent Task Leader		Emergent Emotional Leader	Emergent Scapegoat Leader
GDM: Speech behavior measure (% Words spoken)				
Segment 1	21.6	2.5	0.0	32.7
Segment 2	17.7	8.5	0.5	10.6
Segment 3	8.9	0.0	7.6	1.5
Segment 4	10.6	2.6	3.3	0.0
PWORS				Most active
GERS	Very active			Behavior more regressed than others: high in emotionality (E = 49%)
	Protagonist in fight–flight and pairing emotionality			Protagonist in fight–flight and pairing emotionality
MLSS	Most active of coleaders; high in showing dominance; some pseudoequality and counterdominance	High in showing dominance; some pseudoequality and counterdominance	Moderate level of activity; effective work leader; very sensitive to impulse and affect life of group	Very active in Phase II; fades in Phase III; moves back and forth between dependence and counterdependence
HIM	22% total talk, predominantly Speculative	9% of total talk		
NOTA	Most active therapist: 160 speech turns	58 speech turns	87 speech turns	82 speech turns
IGIPS			Also a main actor in Phase III	Phase II main actor; expressed affect; high on discusses abstract issues; low on feels connected
SASB				Joe was protective of Diane and disclosed to her

Note. GDM = Group Development Process Analysis Measures; PWORS = Psychodynamic Work and Object Interaction Matrix; NOTA = Negotiation of Therapy Agenda; IGIPS = Individual Group Member Interpersonal

16.5
Individual Members

| | Client | | |
Martha	Diane	Brad	Pat
Emergent Defiant Leader	Reactivated attack on Joe in Phase II; led in sharing histories in Phase III		Originally led attack on Joe
5.9	0.0	11.4	25.9
6.5	44.6	10.9	0.7
38.0	27.8	16.2	0.0
53.2	30.3	0.0	0.0
	Most active	Most work oriented	Most work oriented
Protagonist in fight–flight and pairing emotionality	Protagonist in fight–flight and pairing emotionality		
Most active; work on longing for care and approval from parents in Phase III; competing with Diane and coleaders	Most active; heroic work leader during transition; work on longing for care and approval from parents in Phase III	Relatively inactive; speaks at points of strong affect or impulse expression in group; on periphery of group	Relatively inactive; vulnerable and compliant
133 speech turns	Most active client: 155 speech turns	19 speech turns	20 speech turns
Also a main actor in Phase III	First main actor in Phase III; shifts from abstract manner to expresses affect; feels connected, discloses personal material and insight into own issues		
	Diane saw Joe as controlling and ignoring her, as walled off to himself and others		

Rating System; GERS = Group Emotionality Rating System; MLSS = Member–Leader Scoring System; HIM = Hill Process Scale; SASB: Structural Analysis of Social Behavior.

Dimension 2: A Period of Defensive Behavior

The Psychological Space Coding System (PSCS) found that more than half of the statements in Segment 2, which took place during the Phase II portion of the session, were rated as Closing statements. More statements were made in a Definitive format (62%) than in a Tentative format (22%). Many of the Definitive statements were Explanatory, but some were Confrontive. Therefore, group members talked during this segment in a way that asserted meaning.

Ratings of selected portions within the sample segments with the SAVI categorized the largest proportions of behaviors as Influence (49%) and Compete (21%). The quality of verbal interaction ratios computed from the SAVI ratings of these selections from Phase II, as well as selections from other parts of the session, showed more avoidance than approach. The data-opinion ratio used with the SAVI described members as exchanging more opinions about the past than facts about the present.

Ratings with the HIM described the work style of the group in Phase II as Speculative and Conventional. Even though 41% of the interaction in this period fell in Quadrant IV of the HIM, the portion of the matrix describing behaviors most likely to facilitate therapeutic change, the Speculative and Conventional manner of the group, indicated an uncertain and tentative stance toward work.

The PWORS and the Experiencing Scale (part of the GDM) described some differences in work between the two sample segments that took place in Phase II. PWORS' ratings of Segment 1 contained more statements rated as psychodynamic work (62%) than nonwork (38%), and the Experiencing Scale ratings indicated that members described perceptions of events and articulated feelings about them. In the second segment, there were more statements rated nonwork than psychodynamic work (34%), with the PWORS and Experiencing Scale ratings indicating that members compared perspectives but did not articulate feelings.

The IGIPS reported a midrange of cohesiveness in Phase II. Davis et al. described the focus of the discussion as tenuous, with some confusion present.

The data reflect both the efforts of the group members to work together and the presence of defensive behavior that limited the quality of work that was possible.

Dimension 3: A Period of Concern and Apprehension About Organizational Issues and Norms

The Normative Organizational/Personal Exploration (NO/PE) Scale, developed as part of the GDM to assess the overall focus of the group as a whole, described that focus as being on normative and organizational issues during this portion of the session. The concern of the group about normative issues was reflected in the varied content ratings of the HIM. Group interactions in this period were evenly divided in amount across all four of the content categories of the HIM: Topic, Group, Personal, and Relationship. Fuhriman and Burlingame (chapter 7) note that this indicated uncertainty and ambiguity among the members about how to proceed and about what would be the focus of the group. The overall focus of the group on organizational and normative issues was also indicated by the STT's description of the macrolevel processes in Phase II. This analysis described the spatiotemporal scenes of the dialogue. During this period the spatiotemporal scenes located the story in the Here-and-Now and Here-and-Then of current and recent group sessions (i.e., the focus is on the group's process).

These three measures added data that the focus of the group in Phase II was on its own process as an entity and on the rules for participation in it. Forays into personal and relationship issues occurred but were not sustained.

SUMMARY OF DATA ON THE PHASE SHIFT, OR TRANSITION

The transition from Phase II to Phase III took place during a short period of interaction about halfway through Session 3. The Hostility/Support Scale (the GDM) identified this as the point at which members ceased to focus on or criticize the Scapegoat Leader, Joe. The Speech Behavior Coding System (the GDM) identified a higher proportion of statements during this period that were addressed to the "whole group." The Experiencing Scale (the GDM) ratings of this period indicated that group members maintained an awareness of specific feelings and that awareness of feelings was the main focus, with description of events playing a lesser role. Members articulated the insight that, by focusing on Scapegoat Leader Joe, they had avoided self-disclosure. The NOPE Scale (the GDM) indicated that the focus of the group was in a period of transition from discussing normative issues to discussing personal issues. The data from these measures of the GDM taken together were used as evidence for the phase shift from Phase II to Phase III in this session (Beck, Dugo, Eng, & Lewis, 1986). During the phase shift, the STT also described the group members as beginning to focus more on self as well as on others in the narrative process.

Forty-seven percent of the statements made during this transition period were rated as psychodynamic work by the PWORS, which was about the same proportion as for the whole session. All of the interaction occurred in Quadrants III and IV of the HIM, with 83% of the interaction taking place in Quadrant IV. HIM ratings indicated that the work style continued to be Speculative. With the SAVI, the largest proportions of behavior were coded Influence (31%), Flight (24%), and Empathize (17%). The MLSS interpreted interaction during this period as facilitative of greater involvement, enactment, and expression of affect than earlier in the session. Although the members' defenses were still present, some insight had developed, and the characteristics of interaction in this brief period indicated a potential for therapeutic work and change.

SUMMARY OF DATA DURING PHASE III

Dimension 1: A Period of Relatively Positive Feeling and Mutual Support

With the transition to Phase III, a change was expected from the expression of criticism, conflict, and tension to the expression of mutual support and more positive feelings. During Phase II, the Scapegoat Leader was a focus of negative feelings and discomfort, and this was expected to change in Phase III. The Hostility/Support Scale (the GDM) data indicated that criticism of Scapegoat Leader Joe did not take place during the second half of Session 3 once Phase III had begun. The speech behavior measures (the GDM) identified a shift of attention away from the Scapegoat Leader. In Segment 4 from Session 3, which took place during Phase III, the Scapegoat Leader was not addressed at all by other members.

The GERS data indicated that fight–flight remained the predominant BA emotionality throughout Session 3. After the transition, this defense was still present, but the fight–flight emotionality was contained by the group members' focus on criticisms of parental figures. Karterud (chapter 6) interprets that both the focus on Joe in the first half of the session and on parents in the second half expressed the frustration and anxiety felt by the members about the therapists. Near the end of the session, a period of BA pairing emotionality occurred, which Karterud interprets as an expression of continued underlying anxiety about whether the group would survive.

The MLSS also assumed the continued presence of underlying issues and affect relevant to the member–leader relationship. Cytrynbaum (chapter 8) notes that, after the transition, a period of work differentiating members' experiences with their parents occurred but that the members' anxiety about whether they could depend on the leaders was not overtly articulated. Cytrynbaum sees the work on issues with parents as being evoked by and displaced from longings in relation to the group leaders.

Data from the IGIPS indicated a higher range of cohesiveness in the second half of the session than in the first half. Components of the process that were found more frequently in Phase III than earlier in the session included the disclosure of personal material, the expression of affect, the achievement of insight, and the experience of connectedness. The Scape-goat Leader had been identified as the only main actor in the Phase II portion of Session 3, but three main actors were present in the second half of the session after Phase III began. Each of the three main actors, Diane, Greg, and Martha, disclosed personal material, expressed affect, and showed insight about personal issues (the IGIPS). Although anxieties remained, an accommodation was achieved that allowed the members to give one another more support and to focus on sharing personal historical issues relevant to the therapeutic work they went to the group to do.

Dimension 2: A Period of More Open and Mutual Exploration

The STT described the narrative in the Phase III portion of the session. It began with one member's focus on herself and became a multiple narrative in which several members participated from a position of self-focus. These members were the three main actors identified by the IGIPS: Diane, Greg, and Martha. The stories mingled as the members worked on similar issues related to childhood experiences with their parents. The MLSS noted that the members worked to differentiate their fathers and mothers during this period. During the beginning of Phase III, the MLSS identified Diane's performance in the interaction as being similar to that of a "heroic work leader." Her exploration of painful aspects of her relationships with her parents, and her anger, facilitated greater independence of the members from the group leaders for a time. Her work led to more involvement and expression of affect among other group members.

Ratings of Segment 4 with the PSCS identified two changes in comparison with Segment 2. Statements described as Confrontive Definitive were found less often in Segment 4. Statements described as Affirming occurred more frequently.

Data from the HIM, the PWORS, and the Experiencing Scale (the GDM) all indicated a moderate degree of therapeutic work consistent with the tentative beginning of work on individual issues that was taking place. The Experiencing Scale indicated a modest level of self-exploration, as might be expected of a group first attempting to approach therapeutic work. Eighteen percent of statements in Segment 4 were identified as psychodynamic work by the PWORS, which was less than that found in the three other sample segments, indicating relatively less frequent identification of the components of psychodynamic conflict. The HIM indicated that the work style remained Speculative in the Phase III portion of the session. Fifty percent of the interaction in Phase III fell in Quadrant IV of the HIM and the content during that time was predominantly personal. Although the overall work style remained Speculative, thus moderating the level of interpersonal confrontation present, some work did take place in the Confrontive work style, with personal content. Members worked together in a supportive manner on similar issues but at a moderate level of therapeutic work.

Dimension 3: A Period of Focus on Individual Members and Their Personal Work

The NO/PE Scale (the GDM) indicated that the focus of the group in the Phase III portion of the session was on personal issues. HIM ratings of this half of the session identified 65% of the content as personal, an increase from about 25% in the Phase II portion of the session. SAVI ratings of Units 83 and 84 (part of Segment 4) indicated that the largest proportion of ratings occurred in the category of providing personal information.

The macroanalysis of the STT described the spatiotemporal scenes in Phase III as being focused on childhood stories. In Phase III, one narrator, Diane, spoke from the position of self, and other members assisted the narrator in expanding the story. As the interaction continued, several members spoke from the position of the self, all focusing on childhood stories, and their narratives intermingled. The microanalysis of the STT described a movement in the narrative of members from a position as the recipient of actions to being both the subject and the agent of actions in the narrative.

These measures indicated a shift of attention to personal, historical material. The group members appeared to be moving cautiously toward work but not yet ready to be vulnerable.

Overall, the data from this set of measures supported the three dimensions of change between Phases II and III that were identified by the earlier review of literature (Beck, 1983). The level of therapeutic work throughout the session remained moderate, indicating a continued high level of anxiety and lack of readiness to plunge into more threatening work. We may conjecture that the stresses involved in the Phase II processes could not be easily put to rest.

FINDINGS SUMMARIZED ACROSS THE SESSION

Several systems summarized ratings of the entire session, in keeping with the usual procedures for data analysis with those measures. These findings provide a description of the session as a whole (see Table 16.4).

A high level of BA emotionality was present compared with other groups, and the predominant BA found was fight–flight (the GERS). Joe's behavior had the highest proportion of BA emotionality rated among the members.

Diane, Martha, Joe, and Alice were the most active in expressing fight–flight and pairing emotionality (the GERS). Diane, Martha, and Joe were the most active group members (the MLSS, Negotiation of Therapy Agenda [NOTA], HIM, and PWORS). Alice was a very active therapist, contributing as much to the verbal interaction as the more active members (the GERS, HIM, and NOTA).

The MLSS indicated a predominance of dependency and anxiety within the group members, both denied and expressed. The theory underlying the MLSS associates the affect present in the group process with emotion and expectations experienced by the members in regard to the leaders and interprets the affects in terms of basic group-level processes. Feelings of dependency, anxiety, and hostility were present, and the group struggled with dependent and counterdependent longings displaced from the leader (the MLSS).

The work style of the group was cautious. Forty-seven percent of the interaction was rated in the most therapeutic quadrant of the HIM, but in a Speculative manner, avoiding some personal risk. The Speculative work style allowed the group members to approach one another and offer feedback, but with a tentative quality that reduced the level of "interpersonal threat." Some interaction also occurred that was rated as a Confrontive work style with Relationship content. These types of interaction are weighted most heavily by the HIM because of the importance attributed to these behaviors in the therapeutic process.

Almost half the statements of both patients and therapists were rated as "psychodynamic work" by the PWORS. The PWORS measures the presence or absence of psychodynamic work. The proportion of statements made by members that were rated as psychodynamic work was similar to that for members of short-term psychodynamic groups previously studied with the PWORS.

The NOTA tracks the contribution of members and therapists to the development of the clinical narrative within the session by identifying whether each new turn continues the topic and person focus of the previous turn (nonshift) or whether it makes a change (i.e., a mediated shift or an abrupt shift). The data from the NOTA showed a low level of discontinuity in Session 3, with few abrupt shifts found. This indicated a good level of engagement among group members, who related easily to the dominant aspect of the discourse and made changes or introduced new themes using nonshift or mediated shift speech turns. Session 3 contained 716 speech turns, indicating an active session with many relatively brief turns.

Themes to be discussed were usually introduced by the clients, and major shifts were mainly made by them (the NOTA). The involvement of members and attention to what others said, as well as readiness to relate to issues raised by others, were indicated by the "resuming" form of nonshift and the "backtracking" form of mediated shift. When interruptions were made, competing voices wanted to speak about the same topic. At times the interruptions simply echoed or completed the thought and content of the preceding turn and were indications of shared understanding and involvement. The NOTA found that the group members maintained control of the agenda and were involved and willing to relate to what others discussed. Little discontinuity occurred during the session; members introduced themes and changes of focus in a manner that linked new topics to old.

The data summarized on the basis of ratings of the entire session describe some qualities of the group interaction that remained about the same throughout the session. The GERS and the MLSS ordinarily analyzed data summarized across long lengths of interaction, usually blocks of several sessions or more. The GERS and the MLSS indicated the presence of anxiety-laden emotion in the members. These underlying dimensions of affect remained the same throughout Session 3. The NOTA system summarizes data for each session as a whole. The NOTA indicated consistent engagement among the members, with little discontinuity in the discourse. The PWORS and the HIM are used with data samples of various sizes. Summarizing data for the whole session, the PWORS and the HIM showed that therapeutic work took place at about the same rate about half of the time.

Although the group is clearly cautious, there are also several indications of their potential for productive work. What the members accomplish in this session is a sharing of data and feedback on which they may build in later sessions.

FINDINGS ABOUT INDIVIDUAL MEMBERS

Table 16.5 shows the results reported about the individual members of Group A in Session 3.

The Therapists

Alice was a very active leader, more active than her coleader, Helen who was in training (the NOTA, HIM, MLSS, and GERS). The HIM found her talk to be predominantly speculative, and the MLSS found both formal leaders to be high in showing dominance and pseudoequality with some counterdominant behaviors. Alice was considered one of four members who were the protagonists in fight–flight and pairing emotionality (the GERS). The others were Joe, Martha, and Diane. The GDM's sociometric identified Alice as the emergent Task Leader, whereas Helen was not identified as an Emergent Leader.

The theoretical orientation of the therapists in Group A was principally client centered, and their behavior differed in expected ways from psychodynamically oriented group therapists previously studied with the PWORS. Although the rate of participation, or activity, of the therapists of Group A was similar to that of the psychodynamically oriented therapists studied, the percentage of their responses rated as work (i.e., interpretation) was less. In a study of short-term psychodynamic group therapy, 84% of the therapists' responses were rated as work, and in Session 3 of Group A, 47% of the therapists' responses were rated as work. The Group A therapists focused primarily on individual members and less on the group as a whole, made some personal disclosures, and focused on the consequences of behavior and the feelings and thoughts of the members, but not frequently on anxiety and defenses. The HIM data show that client members focused more on group and relationship subjects than did the therapists in the Phase II portion of the session. The therapists can be said to have contributed to the mode of speculative, cautious talk in this group.

The Members

Joe, the emergent Scapegoat Leader (the GDM), was identified as the main actor in the first half of the session by the IGIPS. Joe was most active during the first half of the session and less active in the second half. Joe was the only main actor in this portion of the session, which occurred while the group was still in Phase II. IGIPS ratings determined that he discussed personal issues in an abstract and general manner (i.e., a high score on Discusses Abstract Issues) and that his voice expressed little affect (i.e., a low score on Expresses Affect). He also expressed his perception that he was different from the rest of the group (i.e., a low score on Feels Connected to the Group). Other members and the therapists tried with difficulty to respond to the issues Joe raised.

Using MLSS data, Cytrynbaum (chapter 8) describes Joe as moving back and forth between dependence and counterdependence. In regard to GERS data, 49% of the statements made by Joe were rated as containing BA emotionality, a higher percentage than for any other group member.

Diane was an active member throughout Session 3. The IGIPS identified her as the first of three main actors in the Phase III half of the session, with Greg and Martha being the other two. Diane's participation as the first main actor in Phase III was part of the behavior described as being like that of a "heroic work leader" from the viewpoint of an MLSS rater. Although she began to focus on her personal issues in a general and abstract manner consistent with Joe's presentation earlier, she was able to change from that mode with the encouragement of the other members. She then revealed painful childhood experiences with spontaneity and feeling. Her IGIPS scores contrasted with those of Joe in Phase II. Her scores were higher on Discloses Personal Material, Expresses Affect, Feels Connected to Group, and Insight Into Own Issues, and she had lower scores on Discusses Abstract Issues.

Diane's presentation facilitated those of Greg and Martha, who then explored their own personal issues in a similar manner. Diane and Martha were both described as working on longing for care and approval from their parents during Phase III (the MLSS). Martha was identified as the emergent Defiant Leader by the GDM's sociometric test. She was active in Segments 3 and 4 and was described by MLSS data as being competitive with Diane and the coleaders. Greg was identified as the emerging Emotional Leader (the GDM sociometric) and as an "effective work leader" who was sensitive to the impulse and affective life of the group (the MLSS). Diane, Martha, and Greg, the three main actors identified in Phase III by the IGIPS, were the three members described by the STT as developing a multiple narrative, during which each worked from a position of focus on the self but whose stories and turns at participating mingled.

IGIPS data of Joe's participation in the second half of the session indicated that his style of participation changed with that of others in Phase III. Joe's scores on Discloses Personal Material, Expresses Affect, Feels Connected to Group, and Insight Into Other Group Members' Issues were all higher in Phase III. Although Joe adopted the new style in discussing his own issues, his self-focused presentation was too short to be considered that of a main actor in the Phase III portion of the session.

Brad and Pat were relatively inactive compared with the others, although Pat was active in leading a critical attack of Joe during Segment 1 in Phase II (the GDM). The PWORS, however, showed Brad and Pat to be the most work-oriented members of the group. Although they were less active than others overall, a higher proportion of the statements each of them did make were rated as psychodynamic work.

DISCUSSION AND CONCLUSION

The variables of behavior that were rated by the measures combined to form a more complex and detailed objective description of the group interaction than any one measure could provide. Differences were noted between Phases II and III in the content of the discussion, including the main group members focused on (the IGIPS and STT), and the themes that formed the topics (the HIM, SAVI, NO/PE Scale, STT, and IGIPS). Changes in the communication processes relevant to forming conditions conducive to therapeutic work were found between Phase II and Phase III (the PSCS, IGIPS, HIM, STT, Hostility/Support, NO/PE Scale). More involvement and expression of affect were facilitated for a portion of the session during and after the phase shift (the MLSS, IGIPS, and HIM).

The NOTA described a consistency during the entire session in the way group members had a common focus on a topic or person and were ready to share thoughts and reactions to the topic at hand. The group members controlled the agenda and made changes in topics or individuals taking center stage in a manner that retained continuity with the previous discussion.

The affective dimensions measured, like the level of BA emotionality across the session (the GERS), and the type of underlying affects expressed (the MLSS), also formed part of the characteristics of the process of the group as a whole that were stable during the session. The overt content through which these unconscious emotions were expressed differed in the Phase II and Phase III parts of the session. During Phase III, the externalization of conflict enabled the group members to begin to form a work environment that provided mutual support and acceptance.

The HIM, PWORS, and the Experiencing Scale all described consistencies in the amount or level of work that occurred across the entire session as well as differences between portions of the session. The differences found between periods of work within the session were relatively small in degree, but they were qualitatively significant. The overall level of work in the session was a modest or moderate one, as might be expected of a group meeting for just the third time. The consistencies were characteristic of an early period of therapy in which therapeutic work was just beginning. The differences were consistent with tasks inherent in the process of development of the group as a whole.

Differences among the individual members of the group were also described. Several of the systems noted the rates of participation among the members. The MLSS, the GDM, the IGIPS, and the STT interpreted the function and the effect of the behavior of the most active members. The GDM and the MLSS described informal leadership roles among the members and how these facilitated the developmental process.

The measures were able to differentiate the behavior of individual group members related to the variables rated. Different interpretations of group members' behavior illustrated the manner in which behavior was influenced by many forces, including individual psychodynamics and group dynamics. Researchers may begin to understand the interrelation of these processes with the use of a theoretical framework such as general systems theory, which postulates that the processes of interaction at multiple levels of a system are isomorphic and reflect qualities of the whole system.

For example, Diane's behavior was described at the level of individual psychodynamic processes by the SASB and in terms of its function at the group-as-a-whole level by the MLSS. The SASB data illustrate how perceptions and reactions among the group members provide the material and opportunities for individual work.

The SASB ratings of Diane and Joe in Session 3 showed that Diane's perceptions of Joe were similar to her perceptions of experiences she described with her parents and different from a neutral observer's rating of Joe's behavior in the group and toward Diane. Her perceptions of Joe were, of course, influenced by her own past personal experiences and her own psychodynamic processes. This kind of information can be used in the formulation of treatment goals and in assessing whether an individual group member has benefited from the therapy process.

Diane's work in confronting her own personal feelings and reactions facilitated the group by bringing the focus of their attention closer to basic personal relationships and issues. The MLSS system interpreted the quality of the affect present in the session as being determined by aspects of the relationship with the group leaders, but it also saw Diane's work as she described her relationship with her parents as facilitating the group's ability to address these issues more productively by associating them with emotions in other important relationships and in a context allowing for further work. The SASB ratings defined individual therapeutic goals for Diane, and the MLSS data provided a context for interpreting the affective and dynamic dimensions of the session in terms of the group members' relationships to the leaders.

Diane's personal work was facilitated by a lengthy period of interaction during which the group members and leaders questioned her feelings and reactions toward Joe and by the combined work among members to understand their feelings and behavior in the group. From the point of view of group development theory and group-as-a-whole processes, Diane's feelings and reactions toward Joe were determined in part by the tasks of group development, including the need for the group members to form norms for coping with difficult feelings and for how they would approach their task of self-disclosure and personal work. Her personal work at the beginning of Phase III was facilitated by the preceding awareness among all the members of anxiety about the risks of self-disclosure and involvement.

The change in Joe's behavior noted by the IGIPS was another example of the interaction of individual behavior and group-as-a-whole processes. In Phase II, his talking about personal matters in a general and abstract manner, with little expression of affect, seemed to evoke a critical response from others in the group. In Phase III, Joe's behavior showed qualities of participation shared by other members after the phase shift, including disclosing personal material, expressing affect, and sharing insight into other members' issues. This change paralleled the change in the entire group from more to less defensive behavior. In both halves of the session, Joe's scores were similar to those of other members. How the individual dynamics of Joe's behavior interacted with other subsystems and with the group as a whole, how Joe influenced the group, and how the group process influenced Joe would require further analysis, but the data indicate that these influences were present.

The data from Session 3 of Group A provide an example of how the systems of measurement assess group-level processes and provide information about the work and process dimensions of individual members. The categories of many of the systems are relevant to personal work style as well as group-level characteristics. Because the measures assess the interaction through the moment-by-moment behavior of the individual members, the data can then be aggregated for the group-as-a-whole or subgroup observations as well as for individual members. The diversity of focus among the systems allows the possibility of an objective, measured description of the group interaction and dynamics and a detailed and complex picture of the group process.

At present, systematic description and observation are the primary activities in the study of group psychotherapy. During this process, it is of value to have various researchers working with a variety of theories and systems of measurement. The diversity of systems and breadth of conceptual foundation will assist the discovery of the most productive distinctions in interactive process and the choice of variables that warrant further study. Diversity will also help create a base for the integration of theory.

The development and implementation of measuring techniques is an important task of process research. The development of techniques that are adequate to pursue the investigation of theoretical concepts contributes to the definition and refinement of the theoretical concepts while the method of observation is being constructed and again in reexamination after data have been collected. The demands of formulating an operational definition require a shift from a more general or abstract level of theoretical statement to a more concrete level of observable and measurable behavior and further the focus on understanding change processes at the behavioral level.

The idea of being able to make a valid link between specific behavioral aspects of the data of verbal interaction, and broader theoretical concepts, is integral to the study of group psychotherapy processes. Any specific act of speech or behavior can represent only a part or component of a more complex concept. The researcher attempts to operationally define the concept or process studied by identifying behaviors that represent specific parts of the process. By recognizing and verifying the presence of the behaviors expected, a process, or theoretical concept about how groups work, can be studied empirically.

Orlinsky and Howard (1978) observed that in the study of psychotherapy, a single, common theoretical paradigm had not yet been shaped. A diverse set of psychotherapy processes and descriptive languages of them are the subject of study. The work of forming descriptions and explanations of processes of interest will lead to an ability to discuss them and to form a more complete and coherent theoretical framework of psychotherapeutic change and growth. Our suggestion regarding general systems theory is that it can provide an organizing structure within which the study of multiple aspects of the therapeutic process can be more easily discussed.

Greenberg and Pinsof (1986) noted the potential importance of multiple levels of observation and description on process research. They suggested that various different units of observation, such as the speech act and the episode (e.g., in the study of group process an episode could be a Topic-Oriented Group Focus [TOGF] unit [the GDM] or a group session), can facilitate forming a coherent explanation of the whole. In group psychotherapy research, multiple levels of observation and the use of rating units and summarizing units appropriate to the levels can facilitate investigating the various processes studied.

The definition of variables and of rating categories are essential components of the study of theoretical concepts through process analysis. Each of the systems in this book has emphasized the development of categories that can be reliably rated and that adequately represent certain theoretical variables. The set of categories chosen must make sufficient distinctions within the behavior studied to enable accurate and reliable measurement of variables. The variables themselves must be clearly related to theoretical concepts. When these standards are met, process analysis is a tool enabling the refinement of theory.

A combination of carefully constructed instruments, continued work in the operational representation of constructs with categories and variables, the application of the instruments to data in various studies that can contribute to construct validity, and the use of simple statistical designs will provide the means to further the study of therapeutic and group dynamic processes. Simple and clear statistical designs that allow analysis and interpretation of the data with little manipulation are often the most desirable. Many process studies aim to produce a representation of the process visible across time in behavior and interaction. Although the labor-intensive nature of the work makes the accumulation of data slow, the variety of instruments now available provides the means, if used creatively and in concert with each other, to produce an improved understanding of therapeutic group processes.

REFERENCES

Beck, A. P. (1970). *Transcript of fifteen sessions of Group A.* Unpublished manuscript, Chicago.

Beck, A. P. (1983). A process analysis of group development and emergent leadership. *Group, 5*(4), 48–54.

Beck, A. P., Dugo, J. M., Eng, A. M., & Lewis, C. M. (1986). The search for phases in group development: Designing process analysis measures of group interaction. In L. S. Greenberg & W. M. Pinsof (Eds.), *The psychotherapeutic process: A research handbook* (pp. 615–705). New York: Guilford Press.

Greenberg, L. S., & Pinsof, W. M. (Eds.). (1986). *The psychotherapeutic process: A research handbook.* New York: Guilford Press.

Orlinsky, D. E., & Howard, K. I. (1978). The relation of process to outcome in psychotherapy. In S. Garfield & A. Bergin (Eds.), *Handbook of psychotherapy and behavior change* (pp. 283–329). New York: Wiley.

AUTHOR INDEX

Numbers in italics refer to listings in the reference sections.

Ackerman, N., 67, *79*
Acomb, D. B., 55, *62*
Advani, M., 53, *61*
Agazarian, Y. M., 31, *41*, 358, 360, 362, 363, 365, 366, 367, 369, 370, 376, 377, *377*, 378, 380, 417, 435, *437*
Ahlin, G., 30, *41*, 360, 366, 368, 369, *377*, *378*
Alden, L., 6, *18*, 74, *81*, 398, *410*
Aldridge, J., *18*
Alexander, J. F., 70, 72, 73, 78, 79, *79*, 80, 82, 83, *84*
Allen, F. H., 417, 419, *438*
Allen, G., 77, *82*
American Psychiatric Association, 125, *131*, 298, 304, 390, *409*
Amir, L., 116, *132*
Anderson, A. R., 155, *170*
Anderson, C., 25, 33, 39, *43*
Anderson, E., 5, *18*, 25, *42*
Anderson, H., 68, *81*
Anderson, L. R., 53, *61*
Angus, L., 335, *353*
Argote, L., 56, *63*
Aries, E., 53, *61*
Armelius, B. A., 116, *132*
Armelius, K., 116, *132*
Arnold, S., *216*, *440*
Ascher, E., 137, *171*
Asendorpf, J. B., 384, *409*, 417, 431, *437*
Azim, H. F. A., 33, *45*, 272, 277, 281, 427, *440*

Babad, E. Y., 116, *132*
Baekeland, F., 314, *353*
Baetge, M. M., 55, *62*
Bagarozzi, D. A., 77, *83*
Bagdonoff, M., *217*
Bair, J., 215, *215*
Bak, P., 7, *17*
Bakeman, R., 299, *304*
Bales, R. F., 9, *18*, 28, *41*, 49, 51, 52, 53, 54, *61*, 64, 122, *132*, 222, 259,

260, 359, 362, *378*, 417, 418, 423, 426, *437*, *440*
Balfour, F. H. G., 115, *133*
Bank, L., 76, *84*
Barber, J. P., 25, *45*, 335, *355*
Barke, K. H., 77, *82*
Barlow, S. H., 6, *18*, 28, 29, 30, *43*, 150, 153, 156, 157, 167, 168, 169, *170*, *171*, 311, *354*
Barnum, K. R., 168, *170*
Barr, M. A., 155, *172*
Barrett, J., *280*
Bartholomew, K., 384, *409*
Barton, C., 70, 80, *84*
Bateson, G., 76, 80, 360, *379*
Battersby, C. P., 155, *170*
Baudonniere, P. M., 384, *409*, 417, 431, *437*
Baumeister, R. F., 384, *409*
Beaton, A. E., 244, 247, 248, *259*
Beavin, J. H., 75, 76, *84*
Beck, A. P., 4, 10, 16, *18*, 28, 35, 36, *41*, 42, 87, *87–1*, 88, 95, 100, 108, 110, 128, *132*, 222, 223, 224, 225, 228, 229, 230, 231, 232, 233, 234, 235, 236, 237, 238, 240, 241, 242, 2434, 244, 245, 247, 248, 249, 253, 256, 257, *259*, 260, *261*, 278, 280, 298, 304, 352, *353*, 360, 378, 417, 425, 426, *437*, *438*, 444, 445, 455, *466*
Bednar, R. L., 24, 25, 32, 38, *41*, 42, 44, 155, *170*, *172*, 174, 286, *305*
Benjamin, L. S., 70, 74, 80, 337, *353*, 382, 383, 384, 385, 386, 388, 389, 390, 393, 394, 396, 397, 398, 408, *409*, *410*, 411, 417, 431, 432, 436, *437*, *438*
Bennett, M. J., *304*
Bennis, W. G., 222, 260, 360, *378*
Bentley, J., 153, 157, *171*
Ben-Zeev, S., *133*, 265, *281*
Bergin, A. E., 8, *18*, 32, *42*
Beutler, L., 32, *42*, *44*
Beyebach, M., 67–1, *80*

Bienvenu, J. P., 265, 266, 280, 281
Bigelow, G. S., 156, 157, 170
Binder, J., 216, 440
Bion, W. R., 113, 114, 115, 116, 118, 122, 125, 126, 131, 132, 264, 265, 277, 280, 358, 360, 376, 378, 417, 422, 423, 424, 427, 438
Blaauw, E., 33, 42
Blake, R. R., 370, 378
Blanchard, P. N., 53, 61
Bloch, S., 28, 42, 275, 280
Blocher, D. H., 155, 171
Booraem, C., 32, 43
Borgatta, E. F., 53, 61
Boscolo, L., 68, 83
Bowen, M. B., 68, 80
Bowlby, J., 384, 410, 417, 419, 431, 438
Boyd, R. C., 155, 174
Boyd, R. E., 155, 170
Boyer, E. G., 359, 380
Braaten, L., 32, 42
Braha, R., 285, 304
Brandt, L., 214, 215, 215
Brimberg, I., 30, 41, 360, 378
Brown, D., 217
Brown-Standridge, M. D., 78, 80
Browne, R. M., 365, 366, 369, 378
Bruner, J. S., 313, 336, 338, 354
Brusa, J. A., 35, 36, 42, 224, 229, 248, 249, 260, 425, 426, 437, 438
Budman, S. H., 30, 32, 33, 39, 42, 46, 284, 285, 286, 287, 295, 297, 297–3, 298, 299–4, 304, 305, 352, 354, 417, 428, 438
Burgoon, J., 33, 42
Burlingame, G. M., 5, 18, 25, 28, 32, 33, 36, 42, 43, 46, 148, 168, 170, 171
Burton, M., 215, 215
Butler, R. R., 53, 61

Campbell, L., 32, 45
Carli, L. L., 53, 61
Carson, R. C., 384, 410
Carter, C. E., 155, 173
Cassotta, L., 57, 61
Castore, G. F., 137, 138, 139, 140, 170
Catina, A., 29, 36, 37, 39, 42
Cecchin, G., 68, 83
Chamberlain, P., 75, 76, 80, 83

Chambon, A., 312, 315, 335, 338, 339, 354, 430, 438
Chapple, E. D., 57, 58, 62
Chen, K., 7, 17
Chevron, E. S., 305
Chodoff, P., 280
Cline, R. A., 73, 80
Cline, V. B., 73, 80
Coady, N. J., 398, 410
Cobb, L,. 58, 62
Cockayne, T., 153, 157, 171
Cohen, S. P., 54, 61
Coles, J., 73, 80
Connelly, J. L., 285, 304
Connolly, M. B., 18
Conran, P., 176, 179, 181, 183, 185, 187, 188, 189, 194, 197, 215, 424, 438
Constantine, J. A., 70, 84
Conyne, R. K., 155, 157, 158, 170
Cooney, N., 30, 43
Corbishley, A., 32, 44
Corsini, R., 141, 144, 170
Costa, P. T., 297, 304, 305
Coulehan, R., 79, 80
Cox, B. A., 365, 366, 369, 378
Crews, C. Y., 156, 157, 170
Crits-Christoph, P., 6, 18, 25, 45
Crouch, E. C., 28, 42, 275, 280
Culioli, A., 336, 338, 354
Curran, V., 176, 194, 197, 199, 200, 214, 215, 215
Cutler, C., 77, 81
Cytrynbaum, S., 176, 179, 181, 183, 185, 187, 188, 189, 194, 197, 199, 200, 201, 213, 214, 215, 215, 216, 424, 438, 440

Dabbs, J. M., 57, 62, 64
Davidson, C., 18
Davis, J. P., 80
Davis, M. S. , 30, 42, 46, 295, 297–3, 304, 305, 352, 354
Debbane, E. G., 265, 266, 280, 281
de Carufel, F. L., 266, 280, 281
DeJulio, S. S., 152, 153, 156, 157, 171, 172
Demby, A., 30, 33, 42, 46, 284, 285, 295, 297, 297–3, 298, 299–4, 304, 305, 352, 354
de Shazer, S., 68, 80

Deutsch, M., 54, *65*
Diamond, G., 79, *80*
Dickenson, K. A., 396, *411*
Dies, R., 29, 37, *46*
Diguer, L., 335, *355*
Donald, G., Jr., 58, *62*
Dossick, S., 155, *172*
Dowd, E. T., 155, *171*
Drescher, S., 28, 32, *42, 43*
Drummond, R. J., 154, 155, *173*
Dugo, J. M., *18*, 28, 35, *41, 42*, 87, 88, 110, 128, *132*, 224, 228, 229, 238, 242, 247, 257, 259, 260, 261, 298, *304*, 353, *353*, 425, 426, *438*, 455, *466*
Duncan, T., 76, *84*
Dunphy, D. C., 177, *216*
Durkin, H., 6, *18*
Durkin, J., xvii, *xviii*, 435, *438*
Dye, C. A., 155, *171*

Edwards, D., 335, *354*, 417, 419, 430, *438*
Edwards, K. J., 155, *173*
Eggins, S., 336, 337, *354*
Elkin, I., *18*, *305*
Elliot, R., 25, 33, 39, *43*
Ellis, J., *304*
Ellis, M. V., 78, *81, 83*
Elmore, M. A., 222, *260*
Eng, A. M., *18*, 28, *41*, 87, 88, *110*, 128, *132*, 228, 243, 247, 259, 260, 298, *304*, 353, *353*, 426, 437, *438*, 455, *466*
Enke, H., 33, *46*
Epston, D., 68, *84*, 335, *356*
Ericson, P. M., 72, 76, *81*
Escudero Carranza, V., 67–1, 77, 80, *81*
Essig, T. S., 335, 338, *354*
Estroff, S. E., 70, *80*, 337, *353*, 393, *410*
Ettin, M., 25, *43*
Evans, M. S., 57, *62*
Ezriel, H., 115, *132*, 265, 266, *280*, 417, 427, *438*

Fairbairn, W. R. D., 384, *410*
Fanshel, D., 335, *355*
Farace, R. V., 76, *83*
Feldstein, M., 284, 299–4, *304, 305*

Feldstein, S., 57, *61, 63*
Fenichel, O., 265, *280*
Finley, R., 150, 157, *170*
Fisher, B. A., 156, 157, *171*
Flanders, N. A., 359, 362, *379*
Flohr, D., 35, *44*
Florsheim, P., 384, *410*
Flowers, J., 32, 33, *43*
Ford, C. L., *18*, 74, *81*, 398, *410*
Forgatch, M. S., 76, *80, 83*
Foss, T., 28, *44*, 116, 117, 118, 121, *133*
Foster, S. W., 70, *80*, 337, *353*
Foulkes, S. H., 31, *43*, 115, 123, *132*, 137, *171*, 417, 418, *438*
Foushee, H. C., 55, 56, *62, 63*
Francis, A., 35, *44*
Frank, J. D., 9, *18*, 26, 27, 28, 30, *45*, 137, *171*
Freud, S., 113, 114, *132*, 416, 417, 427, *438*
Frey, J., *80*
Friedlander, M. L., 67, 71, 74, 75, 77, 78, 79, *80, 81*, 82, 83, 84
Friesen, J. D., 398, *410*
Frost, A. G., 51, *63*
Fuhriman, A., 5, 6, *18*, 25, 28, 29, 30, 32, 36, *42, 43*, 148, 150, 157, 167, 168, *170, 171*, 311, *354*
Futoran, G. C., 50, 54, *62*

Ganzarain, R., 115, *132*
Garant, J., 265, 266, *281*
Garfield, S., 25, 32, *43*
Gaul, R., 77, *81*
Gazda, G. M., 35, *43*, 155, *174*
Gendlin, E. T., 237, *260*, 285, *305*, 330, *354*, 366, *379*, 417, 419, *439*
Genette, G., 336, *354*
Getter, H., 30, *43*
Giat, L., 393, *410*
Gibb, J. R., 72, *81*, 360, *379*
Gibbard, G. S., 28, *44*, 115, *132*, 176, 180, 190, 194, 213, *216*, 417, 419, *439, 440*
Gibson, D. L., 155, *170*
Gilligan, C., 298, *304*
Gilstein, K. W., 157, 158, *171*
Glass, G. V., 5, 19, 23, *46*
Goldfried, M. R., 383, *410*
Gomes-Schwartz, B., 285, *304*
Goolishian, H. A., 68, *81*

Gorlow, L., 137, *171*
Gorsuch, R. L., 398, *412*
Gottman, J. M., 299, *304*
Gough, H. G., 280
Gradolph, J., *133*
Granda, K. L., 176, *216*
Grawe-Gerber, M., 393, 396, *410*
Greenberg, J. R., 266, 280
Greenberg, L. S., xii, *xiii*, xvii, *xviii*, 6, 7,
        8, *18*, 25, 26, *43*, 68, 74, 78, 79,
        81, 82, 359, *379*, 398, *410*, 466,
        467
Greene, L., 214, 215, *216*
Greene, L. R., 35, 36, *44*, 115, *132*, 214,
        215, *216*
Grigg, D., 398, *410*
Gruenfeld, L., 30, *45*
Gruner, L., 149, 151, *172*
Gurman, A. S., 284, 287, 298, *304*, 417,
        428, *438*
Gutierrez, E., 77, *81*

Haaser, B., 29, *46*
Hackman, J. R., 50, 51, 53, 54, 60, *62*
Haines, S. C., 49, *64*
Haire, M., 58, *63*
Haley, J., 68, *82*
Hallberg, M., 176, 193, 194, 197, 198,
        199, 201, 213, 214, 215, *216*,
        425, *439*
Halliday, M. A. K., 336, 338, *354*
Hamblin, D., 32, *44*
Hammonds, T. M., 156, 157, *171*
Hannan, M., *304*
Hansen, W. D., 150, 157, *170*
Hardcastle, D. R., 155, *171*
Hardtke, K., 335, *353*
Hardy, G. E., 6, *18*
Hare, A. P., 53, 54, 55, 62, *64*, 222, *260*
Harper, H., 39, *46*
Hartkamp, N., 398, *410*
Hartley, D., 398, *410*
Hartman, J., 28, *44*, 115, *132*, 176, 180,
        190, 194, 199, 213, *216*, 417,
        419, *439*, 440
Hartson, D. J., 157, 158, *171*
Harvey, R. B., 365, *379*
Haughey, J., 32, *46*
Hayes, D. P., 58, *62*
Hazen, C., 384, *410*

Heatherington, L., 67, 74, 75, 77, 78, 79,
        80, *81*, 82, 83, 84
Heffinger, R., 33, *46*
Heinicke, C., 222, *260*
Heintz, I., 265, *281*
Heller, T., 58, *64*
Helmreich, R. L., 298, *306*
Henry, W. P., 384, 389, 398, 408, *410*,
        411
Herlitz, K., 30, *41*, 360, *378*
Heydtmann, M., 398, *410*
Highlen, P. S., 71, *81*
Hill, C. E., 25, *44*, 359, *379*
Hill, I. S., 138, 140, *171*
Hill, P. S., 151, 156, 157, *171*, *174*
Hill, W. F., *133*, 136, 137, 138, 139, 140,
        142, 144, 146, 147, 149, 150,
        151, 152, 153, 154, 161, *170*,
        171, *172*, *173*, 222, 258, *260*,
        265, 280, *281*, 417, 423, 427,
        439
Hillman, L., *217*
Hines, P., 32, *44*
Hinshelwood, R. D., 115, *132*
Hirokawa, R. Y., 52, 55, *62*
Hirschfeld, R. M. A., 275, 280
Hoch, E. L., 137, *171*
Hogg, M. A., 49, *64*
Holahan, W., 34, *45*
Hollingshead, A. B., 60, 62, *64*
Holst, P., 365, *379*
Hood, V. G., 115, *133*
Hopper, C. H., 57, *64*
Horowitz, L. M., 384, *409*
Horwitz, L., 115, *132*
House, R., 435, *439*
Houts, P. S., 156, 157, 158, *172*, *174*
Howard, A., 358, *379*, 417, 419, 430,
        439
Howard, K. I. , 40, *45*, 318, *354*, 465,
        467
Hubner, M. K., 325, *354*, 417, *439*
Humes, D., 395, 398, *411*
Hummel, T. J., 155, *170*
Humphrey, L. L., 74, 83, 393, 395, 396,
        398, 408, *411*
Hunter, M., *304*
Hyler, S. E., 297, *305*

Imber, S., *305*
Isaac, M., 408, *411*

Isbell, S., 32, 36, *44*
Isohanni, M., 33, *44*

Jackson, D. D., 75, *84*
Jacobson, N. S., 68, *82*
Jaffe, J., 57, 61, *63*
Jaffee, C. L., 53, *61*
Janke, G., 29, *46*
Jensen, M., 222, *261*
John, O. P., 297, *304*
Johnson, B., 79, *81*
Johnson, M. E., 398, *411*
Johnson, S., 68, *82*
Johnson, S. M., 6, *18*, 74, *81*, *82*, 398, *410*
Joyce, A. S., 33, *45*, 277, *281*

Kadden, R., 30, *43*
Kagan, N., 158, *172*
Kanas, N., 37, *44*, 155, *172*
Kanki, B. G., 56, *63*
Kaplan, M. F., 55, 56, *63*
Kaplan, S., 54, *65*
Kapur, R., 32, *44*
Karau, S. J., 54, *63*
Karterud, S., 28, *44*, 115, 116, 117, 118, 121, 123, 124, 126, 131, *132*, *133*, 422, *439*
Kashy, D., 34, *45*
Katzell, R. A., 53, *63*
Kauffman, S. A., 7, *18*
Kaul, M. A., 155, *172*
Kaul, T. J., 24, 25, 32, 38, 41, 42, *44*, 155, *172*, 286, *305*
Kavanagh, K., 76, *80*
Keith, D., 68, *84*
Kelly, J. R., 50, 53, 54, 62, *63*
Kennard, D., 32, *44*
Kerlinger, F. N., 119, *133*
Kernberg, O., 115, *133*
Ketrow, S. M., 52, *63*
Kibel, H. D., 115, *133*
Kiel, A. V., 417, 425, *437*
Kiesler, D. J., xii, *xiii*, 7, 8, *18*, 233, 237, 260, 285, *305*, 330, 337, *354*, 366, 379, 417, 419, 436, *439*
Kiesler, S., 60, *63*
Kilstrom, D. R., 157, 158, *173*
Kircher, J. C., 25, *42*

Kirscht, J. P., 58, *63*
Kivlighan, D., 32, 33, 35, *44*, *47*
Klein, M. H., 113, 114, *133*, 232, 233, 237, 238, *260*, *261*, 285, *305*, 330, 337, 353, 354, 366, 379, 416, 417, 419, 422, 424, 426, *439*
Klein, N., 73, *80*
Klerman, G. L., *280*
Knox, P., 36, *45*
Koenig, G. R., 155, *174*
Kohut, H., 131, *133*
Kolden, G., 40, *45*
Koller, P., 37, *44*
Koppenaal, G., *304*
Korchin, S. J., *280*
Kraemer, G. W., 385, *411*
Krathwohl, D. R., 158, *172*
Krause, M. S., 318, *354*
Krupnick, J., *18*
Kunce, J. T., 157, 158, *171*
Kurash, C., *217*

Labov, W., 335, *355*
Lacoursiere, R. B., 117, *133*, 222, *260*
Laffal, J., 335, *355*
Laird, H., 74, *82*, 398, *411*
Lake, R. A., 137, 138, *170*
Lambert, M. J., 8, *18*, 152, 155, *172*
Landesberger, H. A., 53, *63*
Landy, E. E., 155, *172*
Langacker, R., 336, *355*
Lassiter, W. L., 71, *81*
Lauber, J. K., 55, *62*
Lawler, M., 32, *44*
Leary, M. R., 384, *409*
Leary, T., 74, *82*, 382, *411*, 417, 431, *439*
Lee, F., 155, *172*
Leik, R. K., 53, *63*
Leith, W. R., 155, *173*
Levitt, H., 335, *353*
Lewin, K., 136, *173*, 358, 362, 369, 376, 379, 417, 419, 423, 430, *439*
Lewis, C. M., *18*, 28, 41, 88, *110*, 128, *132*, 228, 232, 233, 244, 247, 256, 257, 259, *260*, *261*, 298, *304*, 353, 353, 426, *439*, 455, 466
Lewis, H. B., 298, *305*
Lewis, J., 155, *173*
Liang, D. W., 56, *63*

Lichtenberg, J. W., 36, 45, 77, 82
Liddle, H. A., 79, 80
Lieberman, M. A., 9, 18, 26, 27, 33, 45,
    119, 123, 124, 134, 265, 266,
    277, 281, 417, 422, 441
Lindberg, F. H., 157, 158, 173
Linehan, M. M., 398, 412
Lion, C., 30, 45
Lippit, R., 369, 379
Litt, M., 30, 43
Littlepage, G. E., 51, 63
Lodahl, T. M., 58, 63
Lolas, F., 33, 46
Lovelock, J., 7, 18
Luborsky, L., 25, 45, 335, 355
Lundwall, L., 314, 353
Lyons, J. S., 74, 83
Lyons, M. J., 297, 305

McCallum, M., 33, 45, 272, 273, 275,
    277, 281, 427, 440
McCrae, R. R., 297, 304, 305
McCullough, L., 383, 412
McDaniel, S. H., 72, 83
McGihon, A. H., 265, 281
McGrath, J. E., 50, 53, 54, 60, 62, 63, 64
McIntire, W. G., 155, 173
McKay, M., 383, 411
MacKenzie, K. R., 29, 37, 45, 46, 298,
    305, 386, 393, 398, 411, 431,
    440
MacKinnon, J. R., 365, 366, 368, 369,
    379
McLemore, C. W., 398, 412
Mahoney, M. J., 434, 435, 440
Malajak, N., 33, 46
Malan, D. H., 115, 133, 266, 267, 268,
    280, 417, 427, 440
Manderscheid, R. W. 155, 157, 158, 174
Mann, R., 176, 177, 179, 181, 189, 190,
    191, 192, 194, 199, 200, 213,
    216, 417, 419, 424, 440
Mann, R. D., 53, 65, 115, 132, 176, 180,
    213, 216, 222, 261, 419, 439
Manning, N., 115, 132
Marcus, D., 34, 45
Mark, R. A., 76, 82
Marmar, C., 25, 37, 44, 45
Marrs, A., 79, 81
Martin, E. A. 149, 173

Marziali, E. A., 266, 280, 312, 324, 331,
    332, 339, 355
Masterpasqua, F., 436, 440
Matarazzo, J. D., 57, 63
Mathieu, P. L., 237, 260, 285, 305, 330,
    354, 366, 379
Mathieu-Coughlan, P., 232, 233, 260,
    261, 285, 305, 337, 354, 417,
    419, 439
Mayes, S., 215, 216
Meara, N. M., 335, 337, 355, 398, 412
Mejia, J., 73, 80
Mellon, J., 398, 411
Melnick, J., 156, 157, 170
Merla, M. E., 297, 305
Merry, J., 30, 42, 297, 298, 304, 305,
    352, 354
Mider, P. A. 155, 173
Miles, M. B., 9, 18, 26, 45
Milford, D., 71, 81
Miller, C. E., 53, 55, 56, 63
Miller, J. G., 6, 18, 419, 434, 440
Miller, J. L., 434, 440
Miller, R., 158, 172
Miller, T. I., 5, 18, 23, 46
Millon, T., 298, 305
Minuchin, S., 68, 69, 82
Mishler, E. C., 122, 134
Mitchell, S. A., 266, 280
Mobley, J., 35, 43
Montvila, R. M., 265, 281
Moon, S. M., 79, 84
Moore, A. M., 408, 411
Moreland, R. L., 49, 56, 63, 64
Moreno, J. L., 417, 418, 440
Morin, H., 275, 281
Morran, D. K., 32, 33, 44, 46, 436, 440
Morrill, R. S. ,157, 158, 173
Morris, C. G., 53, 64
Morris, C. J., 50, 51, 53, 54, 60, 62
Morrison, T., 214, 216
Moses, R., 57, 61
Mouton, J., 370, 378
Mullison, D., 35, 44
Munroe-Blum, H., 312, 324, 331, 332,
    339, 355
Muro, J. J., 154, 173
Murray, H. A., 74, 82, 382, 411, 417,
    418, 431, 440
Muth, D. Y., 15, 132

Nehis, N., 32, 45

Nelson, V., 257, *261*
Newberry, A. M., 72, 73, *82*
Newell, G. L., 156, 157, *174*
Newell, R. M., 78, 80, *83*
Newes, S. L., 396, *411*
Newman, B., *216, 440*
Newman, F. L., 24, 25, 43, *46*
Nicolis, G., 7, *18*
Niemiren, P., 33, *44*
Nishisato, S., 319, 334, *355*
Norton, R., 53, *64*

O'Conner, K. M., 60, 62
O'Malley, S. S., 285, *305, 306*
Orlinsky, D. E., 40, *45,* 318, *354,* 465, *467*
Ozer, D. J., 297, *305*

Packard, T., 29, *43*
Paddock, J., 408, *411*
Page, R., 32, *45*
Paleg, K., 383, *411*
Parsons, B. V., 70, *80*
Parsons, T., 53, *64,* 417, 418, *440*
Patrick, R., 214, 215, *216*
Patterson, G. R., 68, 75, 76, 80, 83, *84*
Pattison, E. M., 136, *173*
Patton, M.J., 335, 337, *355*
Paykel, E. S., 275, *281*
Peak, T., 156, 157, *174*
Pekarik, G., 314, *356*
Perna, P. A., 436, *440*
Peters, L., 35, *42*
Peters, L. N., 224, 229, 247, 248, 259, 260, 261, 425, *438*
Peters, R., 360, 369, 378, 417, *437*
Peterson, J. P., 157, 158, *173*
Piercy, F. P., 78, *80*
Pincus, A. L., 297, *306,* 396, 408, *411*
Pines, M., 115, *133*
Pinsof, W. M., xii, *xiii,* xvii, *xviii,* 7, 8, *18,* 67–2, *70,* 71, 72, 78, 83, *84,* 466, *467*
Piper, W. E., 33, 41, *45,* 265, 266, 272, 273, 275, 277, 280, 281, 285, 304, 427, *440*
Polley, R. B., 54, 55, *64*
Pollio, H. R., 157, 158, *173*
Popp, C., 398, *411*

Potter, J., 335, 339, *354, 355,* 417, 419, 430, *438, 440*
Powdermaker, F. B., 9, *18,* 26, 27, 28, 30, *45*
Powell, E. R., 153, *173*
Prata, G., 68, *83*
Prigogine, I., 7, *18*
Prince, G., 336, *355*
Proudman, S., 35, *44*
Prusoff, B. A., *305*
Pugh, C., 408, *412*
Putnam, L. L., 52, *64*

Quigley, S., 32, 35, *44*
Quintana, S. M., 398, *412*

Rand, K. H., 156, 157, *174*
Rank, O., 416, 417, *440*
Rapin, L. S., 155, 157, 158, *170*
Ratti, L. A., 74, *83*
Ray, J., *80*
Raymond, L., 71, 78, 81, *83*
Redondo, J. P., *304*
Reed, B., 215, *217*
Reid, J., 76, *80*
Reilly, S., *18*
Rennie, D. L., 313, *355*
Rhodes, N., 53, *65*
Rice, K., 118, *133*
Rimmon-Kenan, S., 336, *355*
Ring, J., *304*
Ringwald, B., *216, 440*
Ringwald, J., *216, 440*
Ringwald, J. W., 176, 199, *217*
Robbins, M. S., 78, 80, *83*
Roberto, L. G., 70, 80, 337, *353*
Roberts, J., 32, *44*
Robertson, J., 417, 419, *440*
Robinson, F. F., 436, *440*
Robinson, M. B., 155, *173*
Robison, F., 33, *46*
Roe, J. E., 155, *173*
Rogers, C. R., 417, 419, 425, *440*
Rogers, E., 77, *81*
Rogers, L. E., 72, 76, 77, 81, *83*
Rohde, R., 32, *46*
Roller, B., 257, *261*
Rosenberg, B., 141, 144, *170*
Rosenkrantz, J., 115, *132*

Rosenthal, R., 58, 65
Rosenwein, R. E., 176, 199, *216, 217,*
    440
Rosie, J., 33, *45*
Rossiter, C. M., 156, 157, *174*
Rothschild, A., *80*
Rotter, N. G., 53, 63
Rounsaville, B. J., 285, *305*
Rousseau, D. M., 435, *439, 440*
Rowe, C., *18*
Roy, A. K., 299, *304*
Ruback, R. B., 57, 58, 62, *64*
Rudy, J., 398, *412*
Ruesch, J., 360, *379*
Ruiz, M. A., 396, *411*
Russel, R., 352, *355*
Russel, R. L., 335, 338, *354, 356, 359,*
    379
Russell, R., 40, *45*

Sabin Daley, B., *304*
Safran, J. D., 436, *441*
Sandahl, C., 30, *41,* 360, *378*
Sandler, J., 384, *412*
Sargent, J., 78, *83*
Sartre, J. P., 119, *133*
Satir, V., 68, *83*
Satterfield, J., 25, *46*
Schacht, T., 398, *410*
Schacht, T. E., 398, *411*
Schaefer, E. S., 382, *412*
Schafer, R., 335, 337, *356*
Schectman, Z., 33, *46*
Scheier, C., 435, *441*
Scherz, B., *304*
Schiavo, R. S., 70, *80*
Schiffrin, D., 335, *356*
Schmidt, G. W., 51, *63*
Schoenfeld, F., 37, *44*
Schwartz, J. M., 285, *304*
Scogin, F., 32, *44*
Scott, R. A., 358, *379,* 417, 419, 430,
    439
Scott, W. A., 365, *379*
Segal, Z. V., 436, *441*
Seligman, M., 23, *46,* 155, *174*
Selvini Palazzoli, M., 68, *83*
Sexton, H., 34, 35, *46*
Shannon, C. E., 358, 359, 376, *379,* 417,
    419, 431, *441*
Shapiro, D. A., *18,* 39, *46*

Shappell, S., *18*
Shaver, P. R., 384, *410*
Shearin, E., 398, *412*
Shepard, H. A., 222, 260, 360, *378*
Sheppy, M. I., 398, *410*
Sherman, E., 335, *356*
Shields, C. G., 70, 72, 83, *84*
Shiffrin, D., 417, 419, 430, *441*
Shils, E. A., 418, *440*
Shoham-Salomon, V., 25, *46*
Shooter, A. M., 115, *133*
Shostrom, E. L., 339, *356*
Shostrum, E. L., 368, *380*
Siegal, R., 275, *281*
Siegel, S. M., 71, 77, *81, 84*
Silbergeld, S., 155, 157, 158, *174*
Silberschatz, G., 285, *306*
Simeoni, D., 338, 339, *354*
Simon, A., 359, 360, 363, 367, 377, *380*
Simon, L., 77, *81*
Sisson, C. J., 155, *174*
Sisson, P. J., 155, *174*
Skinner, B. F., 384, *412,* 416, 417, *441*
Skinner, K. W., 335, *356*
Skjervheim, H., 119, *133*
Sklar, A. D., 156, 157, *174*
Skowron, E. A., 67, 79, *81*
Slater, P. E., 49, 52, 53, 61, *64*
Slavin, R., 32, *46*
Sluzki, C. E., 68, 76, *84,* 335, 337, *356*
Smith, A. J., 155, *172*
Smith, J. A., 365, 368, *380*
Smith, M. L., 5, *18,* 23, *46*
Socor, B., 325, *356,* 417, *441*
Soldz, S., 30, 33, 42, *46,* 284, 285, 295,
    297, 297–3, 298, 299–4, *304,*
    305, 352, *354,* 383, *412*
Sotsky, S., *18,* *305*
Spain, J., *217*
Speer, D. C., 24, *46*
Spence, J. T., 298, *306*
Sprenkle, D. H., 70, 79, *84*
Springer, T., *304*
Sproull, L., 60, *63*
Stava, L. J., 155, *174*
Stein, R. T., 58, *64*
Sterne, D. M., 155, *174*
Stiles, T. C., 398, *412*
Stiles, W. B., 39, *46,* 275, *281,* 359, *379*
Stinchfield, R., 32, 33, *46*
Stock, D., 116, *133,* 265, *281,* 417, 419,
    422, 423, 427, *441*

Stockton, R. A., 32, 33, *44*, *46*, *436*, *440*
Stogdill, R. M., 58, *64*
Stone, D. R., 157, 158, *171*
Stone, M., 35, *42*
Stone, M. H., 224, 229, 244, 257, 260, 261, *425*, *438*
Stone, P. J., 55, *64*
Stoolmiller, M., 76, 78, *84*
Strauss, S. G., 60, *64*
Strickler, G., 383, *412*
Strodtbeck, F. L., 53, *61*, *65*, 222, 259, 423, *426*, *437*
Strupp, H. H., 285, *305*, *306*, 398, *410*, *411*
Sturdevant, K. S., 365, 366, 369, *380*
Suh, C. S., 285, *305*, *306*
Sullivan, H. S., 74, *84*, 382, 384, 406, *412*, *416*, *417*, *431*, *441*
Sullivan, J. M., 266, *280*
Svartberg, M., 398, *412*

Talmy, L., 336, 338, *356*
Taylor, S., 25, *42*, 215, *217*
Telschow, E. F., 137, *171*
Thacher, B., *217*
Thelen, H. A., 116, 117, 118, *133*, 265, *281*, *417*, *419*, 422, 423, 427, *441*
Thomas-Hunt, M., 435, *439*
Thorne, A., 32, *44*
Thorne, J. W., 156, 157, *170*
Thune, E. S., 157, 158, *174*
Tickle-Degnen, L., 58, *65*
Tischler, N. G., 214, 215, *216*, *217*
Toseland, R. W., 156, 157, *174*
Toukmanian, S. G., 313, *355*
Tracey, T. J., 314, 315, 316, *356*, *417*, 428, *441*
Tress, W., Hrsg., 398, *412*
Trierweiler, 383, *412*
Trombley, J., *80*
Trujillo, N., 50, *65*
Tsang, A. K. T., 312, 314, 315, 318, 322, *356*
Tschacher, W., 435, *441*
Tschuschke, V., 29, 33, 36, 37, 39, *42*, *45*, *46*
Tucker, S. J., 71, *84*
Tuckman, B. W., 222, *261*
Tukey, J. W., 244, 247, 248, *259*
Turner, C. W., 70, 72, 78, 80, 82, 83, *84*

Uhlemann, M. R., 155, *173*, *174*

Vande Kemp, H., 74, *82*, 398, *411*
van den Broek, P., 335, *356*
van Dijk, T., 336, *356*
Venet, T. G., 53, *63*
Voigt, H., 32, 33, *47*
von Bertalanffy, L., 6, *18*, 358, 376, 380, *417*, *418*, *425*, *431*, *441*
Vurembrand, N., 33, *46*

Waldron, H. B., 70, 72, 73, *84*
Waldrop, M. M., 7, *18*
Walsh, K. G., 78, *84*
Wanlass, J., 28, *42*
Warner, R. M., 58, *65*
Watkins, J., *305*
Watzlawick, P., 75, *84*
Waxler, N. E., 122, *134*
Weaver, W., 358, 359, 376, 379, *417*, 419, 431, *441*
Weigel, R. G., 155, *174*
Weininger, R., 32, 33, *47*
Weins, A. N., 57, *63*
Weinstein, L., *217*
Weir, R., 365, 366, 368, 371, *380*
Weiss, D., 37, *44*
Weissman, M. M., 274, *281*
Werbel, W. S., 156, 157, *171*
Wetherell, M., 335, 339, *355*, *417*, 419, 430, *440*
Wheeler, J., 33, *47*
Whisler, E. W., 51, *63*
Whitaker, C., 68, *84*
Whitaker, D. S., 119, 123, 124, *134*, 257, 261, 265, 266, 277, *281*, *417*, 422, *441*
White, K. R., 156, 157, *174*
White, M., 68, *84*, 335, *356*
White, R., 369, *379*
Wierzbicki, M., 314, *356*
Wiggins, J. S., 297, *306*, 382, *412*
Wilder, D., 32, *45*
Wildman, J., 67, 77, *81*
Williamson, S. A., 54, *61*
Windholz, M. J., 285, *306*
Winnicott, D. W., 325, *356*, *417*, 419, 429, *441*
Winter, D., 32, 35, 36, *44*, *47*

Wish, M., 54, 65
Wittner, W. K., 157, 158, *172*
Wolfe, B. E., 383, *410*
Wood, J. T., 52, 65
Wood, W., 53, 65
Worthington, E. L., 156, 157, *171*
Wright, E. W., 157, 158, *171*

Yalom, I. D., 9, *18*, 26, 40, 45, *47*, 156,
    157, *174*, 284, 306, 417, 428,
    441
Young, L., 297, *305*

Zarle, T. H., 155, *174*
Zelditch, M., Jr., 53, 65
Zim, A., 156, 157, *174*
Zimmerman, K. W., 365, 368, *380*

SUBJECT INDEX

Activity-focused systems, 57–59
  definition, 50
  strengths and weaknesses, 59
  and task-performing groups, 57–59
Activity level, 33
Acts
  Interaction Process Analysis System, 52
  Member-Leader Scoring System, 176, 190–193
  System for Analyzing Verbal Interaction, 359
Adjective Checklist, 54
Affect, 420–421, 432
Affiliation
  Individual Group Member Interpersonal Process Scale factor, 297
  Interpersonal Circumplex model, 297
Agentive self, 337, 341, 346
Airplane cockpit crew member study, 55–56
Alcoholism, 31
Altruism construct, 144
Anxiety
  case study (Group A, Session 3), 208–211, 276
  gender effects, 200–201
  Member-Leader Scoring System, 194, 196, 198, 200–201, 208–211
  Psychodynamic Work and Object Rating system, 267, 269–270, 273, 276
  short-term psychodynamic therapy study, 273, 276
Approach behaviors
  case study (Group A, Session 3), 370–375
  definition, 359–360
  face validity of category, 365–366
System for Analyzing Verbal Interaction, 358–360, 365–376, 430–431
"As if" group behavior, 114
Assertive work, 146–148
Attachment experiences

case study (Group A, Session 3), 399–408
in group therapy, 389
neurochemistry, 385
outcome implications, 389–390
and psychopathology development, 384–385
and Structural Analysis of Social Behavior, 384–385, 399–408
Attrition rate, 25
Authority relations
  case study (Group A, Session 3), 201–212
  gender effects, 200–201, 213–215
  Member-Leader Scoring system, 176, 189, 200–215, 424
Autocratic leadership style, 369–370
Automatic Vocal Transaction Analyzer, 57
Avoidance behavior
  case study (Group A, Session 3), 370–375
  definition, 360
  face validity of category, 365–366
  System for Analyzing Verbal Interaction, 360, 365–376, 430–431
Avoidant personality disorder, 298

"Basic assumption emotionality"
  Bion's theory, 113–116, 264, 422
  case study (Group A, Session 3), 126–131
  Group Emotionality Rating System differences, 117
  therapeutic community groups study, 124–126
Behavioral Rating System, 116
Big Five personality factors, 297
Bion, W.R., 113–116, 264–265, 422
Blackfoot scale, 138–140
Blacks. See Interracial factors
Blaming behavior
  case study (Group A, Session 3), 407
  coding of, 394–395

Blaming behavior (*continued*)
   Structural Analysis of Social Behavior
      model, 392–395, 407
Borderline personality disorder
   Interpersonal Group Psychotherapy,
      324–325, 339
   Negotiation of Therapy Agenda cod-
      ing, 318
   psychoanalytic perspective, 324
   valence pattern, 125–126

Case example. *See* Group A, Session 3
      case example
Chaos theory
   and complex systems, 7
   group interaction application, 36
Character centering, 336, 340
Circumplex model. *See* Interpersonal Cir-
      cumplex model
Clause-based analysis, 336–338
Client-centered groups, 156
The Client Experiencing Scale, 232–238
   case study (Group A, Session 3), 250–
      255
   description, 232–238
Closed expressions
   case study (Group A, Session 3), 343–
      344
   Strategies of Telling and Talking ap-
      proach, 338–339, 343, 430
Closing statements, 326–334
   case study (Group A, Session 3), 332–
      334
   Psychological Space Coding System,
      326–334, 429
Cognitive Constructions Coding System,
   79
Cohesiveness. *See* Group cohesion
Coleadership, 257
Collaboration
   Negotiation of Therapy Agenda cod-
      ing, 314
   and Structural Analysis of Social Be-
      havior, 388–389, 400
   as therapy task, 388–389, 400
Collective unconscious forces, 114–115,
   177, 424
Communication patterns
   categories and classes, 362–364
   coding methodology, 362
   methodology for analysis, 367–368
   System for Analyzing Verbal Interac-
      tion, 357–380

Complementary interaction
   family therapy studies, 74–75
   Structural Analysis of Social Behavior
      model, 392
Computer-mediated decision-making
   groups, 60
Conflict behavior, 75–78
Confrontive work, 146–148, 265, 423,
   459
Construct validity, 39
Content style dimension
   case study (Group A, Session 3), 159–
      166
   in Hill Interaction Matrix, 144–147
   therapeutic value weightings, 144–147
Controlling behavior
   family therapy coding systems, 75–78
   Structural Analysis of Social Behavior
      model, 392–393, 396
Conventional work style, 146–149
Convergent validity, 39
Conversational patterns, 57–59
Cooperative behavior, 75–76
Couples therapy, 74–75

Data collection, 38–39
Data-to-opinion ratio, 370–371
Decision-making groups, coding system,
   55
Defensive behavior, 420–421, 433
   case study (Group A, Session 3), 276,
      454
   Experiencing Scale measure, 228
   family therapy coding system, 72–73
   and group development changes, 228
   Psychodynamic Work and Object Rat-
      ing System, 267–269, 273, 276
   short-term psychodynamic therapy
      study, 273, 276
Defensive and Supportive Communica-
      tion Interaction Coding System,
      72–73
Defiant Leader role
   definition, 225
   and group development phases, 227
Democratic leadership style, 369–370
Dependency
   Bion's theory, 114, 264
   case study (Group A, Session 3), 126–
      128, 208–212

Group Emotionality Rating System, 117, 120, 124–128
and group regression, 114
Member-Leader Scoring System, 194, 196, 198, 208–212
personality disorders valence pattern, 125–126
therapeutic community groups, 124–126
Depression
Member-Leader Scoring System, 194, 196–198
and perceived abandonment, 388, 390
valence pattern, 125–126
Directive leadership style, 158
Discourse analysis
case study (Group A, Session 3), 340–351
principles of, 335–336
and psychotherapy, 335
Strategies of Telling and Talking approach, 334–353, 429–430
Discriminant validity, 38
Displacement
case study (Group A, Session 3), 211–212
Member-Leader Scoring System, 176, 190–193, 211–212, 424–425
scoring of, 191–193
Dominance
family therapy coding system, 75–78
Individual Group Member Interpersonal Process Scale factor, 297
Interpersonal Circumplex factor, 297
Dropout prediction, 314–315
"Drug metaphor," 33
Dual Scaling, 334
Dynamic expressions
Psychodynamic Work and Object Rating System, 267–268, 273, 276
resultant expressions comparison, 267
short-term psychodynamic therapy study, 273, 276
Dynamical systems theory, 435

Efficacy research, 24
Ego psychology, 189
Ego-State category
case study (Group A, Session 3), 203–207

Member-Leader Scoring System, 193–197, 203–207, 425
Electronically-mediated communication, 60
Emotion-focused therapy
change events, 79
Structural Analysis of Social Behavior coding, 74–75
Emotional Leader role, 224–227, 425
definition, 224–225
and group development phases, 225–227
Emotionality
case study (Group A, Session 3), 126–128, 458–459
Group Emotionality Rating System, 113–134, 422–423
Hostility Support Scale, 228
Enabling behavior, 389
Encounter groups, 27
Enmeshment-differentiation dimension
case study (Group A, Session 3), 407
classification of, 391
coding of, 393
Structural Analysis of Social Behavior clusters, 391–393, 397, 407, 432
"Epistemic predicates," 338
Equilibrium hypothesis, 51
Experiencing Scale
case study (Group A, Session 3), 250–255
description of, 232–236
exploratory study of, 244–248
group development phases, 228–230, 232–236, 245–248, 426
group research limitations, 285
reliability, 237
and System for Analyzing Verbal Interaction, 366, 369
Experiential therapy
Family Therapist Coding System, 71
quantitative study, 27
Explicit interaction, 28
Exploratory behavior
Experiencing Scale, 228, 241–242
and group development phases, 228, 457–458
Externalizing statements
as nonwork category, 268–269
rating of, 271

Facilitative statements, 233, 237
Facilitators, 299–302
"Family romance," 337, 340
Family Relational Control Communication Coding System, 76–78
   structural versus systemic family therapy, 77–78
   validity, 77
Family Therapist Coding System, 70–71
Family therapy process, 67–84
   Family Therapist Coding System, 70–71
   group therapy process differences, 69
   interaction-based coding systems, 72–75
   observational coding, 67–84
   theoretical approach effects, 71–75
Fantasy, 177, 424
Feedback
   group context relevance, 436
   SYMLOG system measure, 30
Female therapists. See Gender effects
Field theory, 358
Fight-flight dimension
   Bion's theory, 114, 264
   case study (Group A, Session 3), 126–131, 449, 458–459
   in group regression, 114
   personality disorders valence pattern, 125–126
   therapeutic community groups study, 124–126
Fish-bowl experience, 156
Freud, Sigmund, 416–417
Function-Oriented Interaction Coding System, 55

Gender effects
   and authority reactions, 200–201, 213–215
   contextual and methodological considerations, 214–215
   family therapist interactions, 72–73
   Interpersonal Sensitivity factor scores, 298
   leader behavior, 53
   Member-Leader Scoring System, 200–201, 213–215
General systems theory

overview, 6–7
   and System for Analyzing Verbal Interaction, 358, 376
Generalizability question, 24
Grammatical analysis, 337–338
Group A, Session 3 case example, 87–110, 443–467
   Group Development Process Analysis Measures, 249–255, 446–466
   Group Emotionality Rating System, 126–131, 446–466
   Hill Interaction Matrix, 159–166, 446–466
   Individual Group Member Interpersonal Process Scale, 299–303, 446–466
   Member-Leader Scoring System, 201–212, 446–466
   Negotiation of Therapy Agenda System, 319–323, 347–351, 446–466
   Psychodynamic Work and Object Rating System, 276–279, 446–466
   Psychological Space Coding System, 332–334, 347–351, 446–466
   Strategies of Telling and Talking approach, 340–351, 446–466
   Structural Analysis of Social Behavior, 398–408, 446–466
   System for Analyzing Verbal Interaction, 370–376, 446–466
Group-as-a-whole processes
   case study (Group A, Session 3), 464–465
   Group Development Process Analysis Measures, 228, 245–249, 425–426
   and group focal conflict analysis, 422
   Member-Leader Scoring System, 424
   Normative Organizational/Personal Exploration Scale, 228, 238–242, 246, 429
   Psychodynamic Work and Object Rating System, 266–267
   System for Analyzing Verbal Interaction, 358, 370–376
   Topic-Oriented Group Focus Unitizing Procedure, 242
Group cohesion
   assessment, 287

case study (Group A, Session 3), 299–303
data collection weaknesses, 39
definition, 284, 428
five-factor model, 32
Individual Group Member Interpersonal Process Scale correlations, 298–303, 428
as moderator variable, 27
and outcome, 286–287
research review, 31–32
theoretical and clinical usefulness, 286–287
Group Cohesiveness Scale, 287, 298
Group development
clinical insights, 256–257
and group cohesion, 32
Group Development Process Analysis Measures, 221–261
leadership roles interaction, 224–227
Member-Leader Scoring System, 177, 179–181, 186–187
phases of, 222–258
and Structural Analysis of Social Behavior, 385–386
and System for Analyzing Verbal Interaction, 360
Group Development Process Analysis Measures, 221–261, 425–427
case study (Group A, Session 3), 249–255, 446–466
description of, 230–244, 420
dimensions, 420
exploratory study of, 244–249
history, 221–227
leadership roles in, 224–226
methodology for analysis, 244
theoretical basis, 221–227, 416–421
Group dynamics. See also Psychodynamically-oriented therapy
Bion's theory, 113–116
and Hill Interaction Matrix, 136–137, 149–150
Group Emotionality Rating System, 113–134, 422–423
case study (Group A, Session 3), 126–131, 446–466
dimensions, 420
history, 113–116
limitations and strengths, 119

methodology for analysis, 123
rating categories and rules, 120–121
reliability, 121–122
theoretical basis, 113–116, 416–421
therapeutic community groups study, 124–126
Group focal conflict analysis, 123, 130–131, 422
Group matrix, 123
Group problem solving
interaction process analysis, 51–53
phases, 51
in System for Analyzing Verbal Interaction, 358, 368
Group Sessions Rating Scale, 30–31
Group structure effects, 156
Guilt
group focal conflict analysis, 130–131
Member-Leader Scoring System, 194, 197–198

Harvard Community Health Plan Group Cohesiveness Scale, 287, 298
Hermeneutics, 119
Hill and Hill Interaction Matrix, 138, 140–141
Hill Interaction Matrix, 135–174, 423–424
case study (Group A, Session 3), 159–166, 446–466
clinical implications, 168
content style dimension, 144–147, 423
dimensions, 144–149, 420
group dynamics theory influence, 136–137, 149–150
HIM-G, HIM-A, and HIM-B, 153–155
HIM-SS-1965 revision, 141, 150–153, 155–159
history, 136–139
reliability, validity and normative data, 150–153
research findings, 154–159
theoretical basis, 136–139, 416–421, 423
therapeutic values in, 142–148, 167–168
training, 168
work style dimension, 147–149, 423
Hill, W. F., 136–139

Histrionic patients, 298
Hostility
  case study (Group A, Session 3), 203–211
  Member-Leader Scoring System, 193–195, 203–211
Hostility/Support Scale
  case study (Group A, Session 3), 250–253
  categories, 231
  description of, 230–232, 426
  emotional tone measure, 228
  exploratory study of, 244–248
  and group development phases, 229–232, 244–248, 258
  reliability, 232
Humor effects, 158

"I" statements, 337–339
  case study (Group A, Session 3), 341
  as outcome predictor, 339
Identification, 385
Imitation
  and internal working models, 384–385, 399
  and psychopathology development, 384
Implicit interaction, 28
Impulse category, 193–194, 425
Impulse-defense triad, 267
Individual Group Member Interpersonal Process Scale, 283–306, 427–428
  and Big Five personality factors, 297
  case study (Group A, Session 3), 296, 299–303, 446–466
  critique, 30–31
  description, 288–293, 421
  dimensions, 421
  history, 283–286
  limitations and strengths, 289, 293
  methodology for analysis, 293–295
  personality disorders differentiation, 298
  ratings and categories, 288–293
  reliability, 294–295
  research findings, 295–299
  revisions, 286
  theoretical basis, 283–286, 416–421
Individual psychotherapy
  group process research comparison, 38

microprocesses, 6
process research controversies, 25
Inferences
  Individual Group Member Interpersonal Process Scale, 289
  Member Leader Scoring System, 176, 192–193, 424
  Psychodynamic Work and Object Rating System, 270–271
Information transfer, 359, 363, 431
Insight-oriented therapy, 71
Interaction chronograph, 57–58
Interaction process analysis, 49–65
  activity-focused approach, 57–59
  conceptual developments, 60
  difficulty of, 50
  in task-performing groups, 49–65
  technology effects on, 60
Interaction Process Analysis, 51–55
  critique, 28, 53–55
  reliability, 122
Internal working models
  case study (Group A, Session 3), 399–408
  group therapy application, 388–389
  outcome implications, 389–390
  and Structural Analysis of Social Behavior, 384–385, 388–389, 399–408
  as treatment target, 384–385, 388–389
Interpersonal Adjective Scale, 382
Interpersonal Circumplex model
  and Individual Group Member Interpersonal Process Scale, 297
  and Structural Analysis of Social Behavior, 74, 382–383, 396–397, 431–432
Interpersonal Dependency Inventory, 275
Interpersonal Group Psychotherapy, 324–325, 339
Interpersonal Process Recall, 158
Interpersonal processes
  Group Development Process Analysis Measures, 228
  Individual Group Member Interpersonal Process Scale, 30–31, 283–286
  Structural Analysis of Social Behavior, 381–412

Interpersonal styles
    cluster analysis, 181, 184–185
    Member-Leader Scoring System, 179–
        189
Interpersonal support, 27
Interpersonal threat
    definition, 142
    in Hill Interaction Matrix, 142–144
    protected versus vulnerable work
        model, 149
Interpretation
    and Interpersonal Group Psychother-
        apy, 324–325
    in psychoanalytic work, 266, 276–277
Interracial factors
    and interpersonal style, 188–189
    Member-Leader Scoring System, 181,
        188–189
Interrater reliability. See Reliability
Interruption
    case study (Group A, Session 3), 322–
        323, 350
    Negotiation of Therapy Agenda sys-
        tem, 315–318, 322–323, 350
Intrex questionnaire, 387–388, 393
Introjection
    assessment, 393
    and Structural Analysis of Social Be-
        havior, 385, 391–393
Isomorphic group levels, 14, 358–359,
    376–377

Klein, Melanie, 416–417, 422

Laissez-faire leadership style. 369–370
Language-based approach. See Discourse
    analysis
Latent feelings, 176
Leader behavior/roles
    activity-focused research, 58
    case study (Group A, Session 3), 201–
        212
    classification schemes, 33
    group development interaction, 224–
        227, 231
    Group Development Process Analysis
        Measures, 224–226
    Hill Interaction Matrix research, 156
    Member-Leader Scoring System, 175–
        215
    research review, 32–33

sociometric test, 248–249
    System for Analyzing Verbal Interac-
        tion, 369–370
Leader-directed groups, 158
Level of an act
    in Member-Leader Scoring System,
        176, 192–193
    scoring of, 192–193
Lexical patterns, 337, 344–345
Love-hate dimension
    coding of, 393
    Structural Analysis of Social Behavior
        clusters, 390–393, 397, 432

"Main actor" concept
    assessment, 285
    case study (Group A, Session 3), 299–
        303, 447
    definition, 284, 299
    Individual Group Member Interper-
        sonal Process Scale, 284–285,
        299–303
    outcome link, 284–285
    ratings reliability, 299n4
Male therapists. See Gender effects
The Mann system. See Member-Leader
        Scoring System
Marital Therapy Interaction Scale, 78
Mathematical modeling, 7
Matrix Representation Grid
    critique, 30–31
    SYMLOG system comparison, 31
    and System for Analyzing Verbal Inter-
        action, 366, 369
Meaning structure. See Discourse analysis
Member-Leader Scoring System, 175–
        217, 424–425
    applications, 177–189
    case study (Group A, Session 3), 201–
        212, 446–466
    categories, 193–194, 420
    dimensions, 420
    gender effect studies, 200–201, 213–
        214
    and group development, 179–180
    history, 175–177
    interracial studies, 181, 188–189
    levels of inference, 176, 192–193, 424
    methodology for analysis, 198–200

Member-Leader Scoring System
(*continued*)
nonrational roles, 177–179
reliability, 194–198
scoring rationale, 191–192
theoretical basis, 175–177, 416–421,
424
Meta-analyses, 24–25
Mock jury deliberations study, 55–56
Models, theoretical, 40
Moderator variables, 27
Moreno, J. L., 417–418
Multidimensional scaling
description of, 35
process research applications, 35–36
Murray, H. A., 417–418

Narratives
case study (Group A, Session 3), 340–
351
Negotiation of Therapy Agenda system, 314–318
paradigmatic approach comparison, 313
Strategies of Telling and Talking system, 335–338, 340–351, 430
National Training Laboratory Institute,
116
Negotiating, 123
Negotiation of Therapy Agenda system,
312–313, 347–353, 428–429
case study (Group A, Session 3), 319–
323, 347–351, 446–466
categories, 316–317, 420
description of, 316–318
dimensions, 420
history and theory, 314–316
methodology for analysis, 319
in multimethod, multilevel analysis,
312–313, 347–353, 428–429
qualitative analysis, 318
reliability, 317–318
sequential analysis, 319, 347–351
theoretical basis, 314–316, 416–421
validity, 318
Noise
categories, 363
definition, 359
information transfer relationship, 359,
363, 431
System for Analyzing Verbal Interaction, 359, 363, 376, 431

Noncomplementary interactions, 74–
75
Nondirective leadership style, 158
Nonrational roles, 177–179
Normative Organizational/Personal Exploration Scale
case study (Group A, Session 3), 238–
242
description of, 238
group-as-a-whole measure, 228
and group development phases, 229,
238–242, 244–248
reliability, 238
strengths and limitations, 243
Novice-expert therapist discrimination,
70–71

Object focus, 268, 270–271
case study (Group A, Session 3), 276–
277
Psychodynamic Work and Object Rating System, 268, 270–271, 276–
278
rating of, 270–271
Object linking, 268, 270–271, 427
Object relations
and Member-Leader Scoring System,
189
Psychodynamic Work and Object Rating System, 266, 268, 270–271,
273–279
psychopathology development link,
384–386
and Structural Analysis of Social Behavior, 382–386
Open expressions
case study (Group A, Session 3), 343–
344
Strategies of Telling and Talking approach, 338–339, 343–344,
430
Opening statements, 326–334
case study (Group A, Session 3), 332–
334
Psychological Space Coding System,
326–334, 429
Operant conditioning, 384
Organizational psychology, 435
Outcome research, 24–26

Pairing
    Bion's theory, 114
    case study (Group A, Session 3), 126–131
    Group Emotionality Rating System, 117, 120, 126–131
    and group regression, 114
Paradigmatic approach, 313
"Parataxic distortion," 406, 408
Parent training, 76
Participation rate, 271–272, 274–275
    case study (Group A, Session 3), 276–278, 319–323
    and leaders, 58
    Negotiation of Therapy Agenda coding, 314–316, 319–323
    and outcome, 274–275
    Psychodynamic Work and Object Rating System, 271–272, 274–278
    self-based work independence, 277–278
Peer-led groups, 156
Peer relationships, 436
Personal Orientation Inventory, 368
Personality disorders
    Individual Group Member Interpersonal Process Scale ratings, 298
    Structural Analysis of Social Behavior application, 384, 408
    valence pattern, 125–126
Phrase-based analysis, 337–338, 430
Positivist method, 119
Power issues, 420–421, 434
    case study (Group A, Session 3), 203–211
    in family therapy coding systems, 75–78
    Member-Leader Scoring System, 193–194, 196, 203, 425
Problem solving. See Group problem solving
Process Analysis Scoring System, 190
Projective identification
    Bion's group dynamics theory, 114
    case study (Group A, Session 3), 130–131
    in Group Emotionality rating System, 118, 130–131
    Member-Leader Scoring System, 177
Psychodynamic Work and Object Rating System, 263–281, 427

    case study (Group A, Session 3), 276–279, 446–466
    components, 267–268
    description of, 268–272
    history, 264–266
    inference in, 270–272
    nonwork and work categories, 268–270
    rating system, 270–271
    reliability, 272
    short-term group psychotherapy study, 272–276
    strengths and limitations, 271–272
    theoretical basis, 264–266, 416–421
    work construct in, 264–266
Psychodynamically-oriented therapy
    Bion's contributions, 113–116
    Family Therapist Coding System, 71
    Group Emotionality Rating System, 113–134, 422
    Hill Interaction Matrix, 135–174
    Member-Leader Scoring System, 175–217
    in process-outcome studies, 26–27
    SYMLOG studies, 29–30
Psychological mindedness, 273–274
    assessment, 273–274, 289
    Individual Group Member Interpersonal Process Scale, 289, 297
    Psychodynamic Work and Object Rating System, 273–274
Psychological Space Coding System, 312–313, 324–334, 429
    case study (Group A, Session 3), 332–334, 347–351, 446–466
    categories, 327–329, 421
    coding, 328
    description of, 327–328
    dimensions, 421
    history, 324–326
    limitations and strengths, 329–330
    methodology for analysis, 331
    in multimethod, multilevel analysis, 312–313, 347–353, 429
    preliminary study of, 331–332
    rating process, 327
    reliability, 330
    sequential analysis, 334, 347–351
    theoretical basis, 324–326, 416–421
    validity, 330
Psychometrics, and process research, 38–39

Qualitative information, 318
"Quality of verbal interaction" index,
    368, 371
Quantitative studies, 29–37

Racial factors. *See* Interracial factors
Rank, Otto, 416–417
Reaction to Group Situation Test, 116
Reactive anxiety, 267, 269–270
Reality-oriented groups, 156
Recapitulation, 385
Regression, 114–116
Reliability
    Experiencing Scale, 237
    Group Emotionality Rating System,
        121–122
    Hill Interaction Matrix, 150–152
    Hostility/Support Scale, 232
    Individual Group Member Interper-
        sonal Process Scale, 294–295
    Interaction Process Analysis system,
        122
    Member-Leader Scoring System, 194–
        198
    Negotiation of Therapy Agenda sys-
        tem, 317–318
    Psychodynamic Work and Object Rat-
        ing System, 272
    Psychological Space Coding System,
        330
    Structural Analysis of Social Behavior,
        396
    System for Analyzing Verbal Interac-
        tion, 365
Repertory grid technique
    interpersonal dynamics changes, 36
    process research application, 35–36
Resiliency, 105
Resistance, 75–76
Responsive work style, 146–148
Resultant expressions
    dynamic expressions comparison, 267
    rating, 271
"Role" construct, 369–370

SASB intrex questionnaire, 387–388,
    393
SAVI system. *See* System for Analyzing
    Verbal Interaction

Scapegoat Leader role, 225–227, 425
    definition, 225
    exploratory study, 245–249
    and group development phases, 225–
        227, 231–232, 245–249, 444,
        447
Scapegoating
    and group development phases, 231
    internal working models link, 399–
        400, 403
    System for Analyzing Verbal Interac-
        tion, 372–373
Self-disclosure
    case study (Group A, Session 3), 321,
        445
    and group development phases, 226–
        227, 231, 245–247
    Negotiation of Therapy Agenda sys-
        tem, 321
    SYMLOG system measure, 30
Self-esteem, 194, 197–198
Self-exploratory statements, 233, 235–
    236, 245–247, 457
Self-Other statements, 337–339, 343–
    346
Self psychology, 131
Semantic differential
    interpersonal dynamics changes, 36
    process research application, 35–36
Sequential analysis
    Dual Scaling, 334
    Individual Group Member Interper-
        sonal Process Scale, 298–299
    Negotiation of Therapy Agenda sys-
        tem, 319
    Psychological Space Coding System,
        334
    Strategies of Telling and Talking ap-
        proach, 347–351
    System for Analyzing Verbal Interac-
        tions, 367–368
"Sequential matrix," 367
Sex differences. *See* Gender effects
Short-term psychodynamic psychotherapy,
    272
Sibling relationships, 436
Significance ratings, 288–289, 293
Situation analysis, 26–27
Skinner, B. F., 416–418
Social Adjustment Scale, 274–275

Social perception, 35
Social relations model, 34
Socioeconomic status, and family therapy, 73
Socioemotional leaders
    gender role distinctions, 53
    in task-oriented groups, 52–53
Sociometry
    emergent leadership identification, 248–249
    leadership roles differentiation, 36, 229
    process research application, 35
Sound-silence patterns, 57
"Spatiotemporal scenes," 336–337, 340
Speculative work, 146–148, 265, 423, 457, 459
Speech Behavior Coding System, 228–229, 426
    case study (Group A, Session 3), 250–254
    description, 243–244
    exploratory study of, 247–248
    group development phases, 229
Speech patterns
    case study (Group A, Session 3), 340–351
    Strategies of Telling and Talking approach, 337–338, 340–351
Speech turns, 315–316
    case study (Group A, Session 3), 319–323
    categories, 316–317
    Negotiation of Therapy Agenda system, 315–323
    Strategies of Telling and Talking approach, 336
Splitting, 130–131
    borderline personality disorder, 324
    group focal conflict analysis, 130–131
Statement analysis
    Individual Group Member Interpersonal Process Scale, 288
    Psychodynamic Work and Object Rating System, 270–271
Strategic therapy, 71
Strategies of Telling and Talking approach, 312–313, 334–353, 429–430
    case study (Group A, Session 3), 340–351, 446–466

categories, 336–338, 421
description, 336–339
dimensions, 421
history, 335
in multimethod, multilevel analysis, 312–313, 347–353, 429–430
research findings, 339–340
sequential analysis, 347–351
theoretical basis, 335, 416–421
validity, 338–339
Stress theory, 358
Structural Analysis of Social Behavior, 381–412, 431–432
    case study (Group A, Session 3), 398–408
    cluster model, 390
    dimensions, 421
    family therapy studies, 74–75
    group therapy application, 383–390
    history, 383–383
    and "internal working models," 384–386
    and Interpersonal Circumplex, 382–383, 396–397, 431–432
    limitations and strengths, 395–396
    norms, 397
    object relations theory link, 382–386
    and personality disorders, 384, 408
    rating system, 393–395
    reliability, 396
    research findings, 397–398
    theoretical basis, 383–390, 416–421
    training, 397
    validity, 396–397
Structural-strategic therapy, 72, 77–78
Submissive behavior
    family therapy coding system, 75–78
    Structural Analysis of Social Behavior model, 392, 396
Sullivan, Harry Stack, 416–417
Supportive communications, 72–73
Symbolization
    case study (Group A, Session 3), 211–212
    Member-Leader Scoring System, 176, 190–193, 211–212, 424–425
    scoring of, 191–195
Syntactic analysis, 337–338

System for Analyzing Verbal Interaction, 357–380, 430–431
    case study (Group A, Session 3), 370–376, 446–466
    categories and classes, 362–364, 421
    coding methodology, 362
    description of, 362–367
    dimensions, 421
    and Experiencing Scale, construct validity, 366
    as group development index, 360
    history, 357–362
    limitations and strengths, 364–365
    and Matrix Representational Grid, 366
    methodology for analysis, 367–368
    norms, 366
    reliability, 365
    research findings, 368–370
    sequence of communication analysis, 367
    theoretical basis, 357–362, 416–421
    training, 366–367
    validity, 365–366
System for the Multiple Level Observation of Groups (SYMLOG)
    critique, 28–30, 54–55
    description of, 54
    Matrix Representation Grid comparison, 31
    methodological strengths, 30
Systemic family therapy, 77–78
Systems theory
    group framework trends, 434–435
    mathematical modeling, 7
    overview, 6–7
    and System for Analyzing Verbal Interaction, 358, 376

T-groups, 156
Task Leader role, 224–226, 425, 460
    definition, 224
    and group development phases, 225–226
Task leaders, gender effects, 52–53
Task performing groups, 49–65
    activity-focused approach, 57–59
    and gender roles, 53
    interaction process analysis, 49–65
    leadership roles in, 52
    process-focused approach, 50–55, 59
    setting-focused approach, 55–56, 59

Teacher-As Typology system, 181–183, 186, 188–189
TEMPO system, 54
Temporal factors
    and activity-focused research, 57–58
    in change process analysis, 34–35
Therapeutic alliance, 314, 429
Therapeutic community studies, 124–126
"Therapeutic factors"
    methodological drawbacks, 40–41
    research review, 28
Therapeutic Interaction Coding System, 72
Therapeutic relationship, 33
Therapeutic values
    case study (Group A, Session 3), 157–166
    and group content style, 144–147
    and group work style, 146–148
    Hill Interaction Matrix framework 142–144
Therapeutic Work Scale, 285
Therapist Experiencing Scale, 232–236
    case study (Group A, Session 3), 250–255
    description, 232–236
Therapy Process Coding System, 75–76
Time series analysis, 34–35
"Time-talking" measures, 58
Topic Determination System, 314–315
Topic-Oriented Group Focus Unitizing Procedure, 242–243, 426
    description, 242
    strengths and limitations, 243
Transference phenomena
    case study (Group A, Session 3), 276–277
    Psychodynamic Work and Object Rating System, 271, 273, 276–277
    short-term psychodynamic therapy study, 273

Unconscious forces
    Bion's theory, 114–116
    Member-Leader Scoring System, 177, 191, 201, 424–425
    scoring, 191
    Structural Analysis of Social Behavior focus, 387

Valence theory
    in Bion's "basic assumption groups,"
        114
    personality disorders pattern, 125–126
    validity, 125–126
Validity
    Family Relational Control Communi-
        cation Coding System, 77
    Hill Interaction Matrix, 150–154
    Negotiation of Therapy Agenda sys-
        tem, 318
    in process measures, 38–39
    Psychological Space Coding System,
        330
    Strategies of Telling and Talking ap-
        proach, 338–339
    Structural Analysis of Social Behavior,
        396–397
    System for Analyzing Verbal Interac-
        tion, 365–366
Values. *See* Therapeutic values
Vanderbilt Psychotherapy Process Scale,
    285
Verbal behavior
    coding methodology and categories,
        362–364
    methodology for analysis, 367–368
    System for Analyzing Verbal Interac-
        tion, 357–380
Vocalization patterns, 57–58

We group, 243–244, 248

Wishes
    case study (Group A, Session 3), 276
    Psychodynamic Work and Object Rat-
        ing System, 267, 273, 276
    short-term psychodynamic therapy
        study, 273, 276
Women. *See* Gender effects
Word-based analysis, 336–338, 430
Work construct, 147–149
    affect interaction, 275
    "basic assumption groups" relationship,
        264–265
    Bion's theory, 114–116, 264–265
    case study (Group A, Session 3), 159–
        166, 276–279, 459
    definition, 264–267, 427
    functions, 270
    in Hill Interaction Matrix, 141, 147–
        149, 423
    history, 264–265
    levels of, 269–270
    and object relations, 266
    in Psychodynamic Work and Object
        Rating System, 264–280, 427
    categories, 268–270
    rating of, 270–271
    reliability, 272
    short-term psychodynamic therapy
        study, 272–276
    therapeutic value weightings, 147–149

ABOUT THE EDITORS

Ariadne P. Beck, MA, is a licensed clinical psychologist in private practice in Oak Brook, Illinois. She has coordinated the Chicago Group Development Research Team for 24 Years and is also a management consultant with SAGE: Consultants in Organizational Change. She received her master of arts degree from the University of Chicago where she did further graduate studies, was on the staff of and directed group therapy training at the Counseling and Psychotherapy Research Center, and conducted many training programs for employment service personnel at both local and national levels. Later, she was director of the counseling center at the Illinois Institute of Technology. As former chair of the research committee at the American Group Psychotherapy Association, she initiated this book. Her major areas of research interest have been the creation of a theory, and design of a methodology to assess the theory, on the phases of group development and emergent leadership in psychotherapy and work groups, and on the phases of development of the coleadership relationship based on a systems–developmental approach. She has published articles and chapters on these topics in a variety of publications. She is active in a number of professional organizations and currently serves on the board of Division 49 (Group Psychology and Group Psychotherapy) of the American Psychological Association and on the editorial board of *Group Dynamics: Theory, Research, and Practice.*

Carol M. Lewis, MS, is a staff member at the Mental Health Center of Mercy Hospital and Medical Center in Chicago, Illinois. In her clinical work, she provides psychotherapeutic services for patients of diverse ethnic backgrounds. With colleagues on the Group Development Research Team, she has studied the processes of group development and how they affect the psychotherapy process. Her work has included the study of the formation of shared perceptions among group members and their role in group level processes, and the study of development of facilitative behavior among group members. Her published works have appeared in various books and journals. She is active in the International Society for Psychotherapy Research and the American Group Psychotherapy Association, as well as Division 49 (Group Psychology and Group Psychotherapy) of the American Psychological Association.